THE LEGENDS OF
THE JEWS

THE LEGENDS OF
THE JEWS

BY

LOUIS GINZBERG

VI

NOTES TO VOLUMES III AND IV
FROM MOSES IN THE WILDERNESS TO ESTHER

PHILADELPHIA
THE JEWISH PUBLICATION SOCIETY OF AMERICA
5729—1968

PRINTED IN
THE UNITED STATES OF AMERICA

TO THE MEMORY OF MY DEAR FRIEND
AND COLLEAGUE

ISRAEL FRIEDLAENDER

לקדושים אשר בארץ המה ואדירי כל חפצי בם

CONTENTS

MOSES IN THE WILDERNESS

Vol. III

[1] Tosefta Sota 4.8; PK 10, 85b; Mekilta Beshallah (פתיחתא)
24a; Shir 1.7. Comp. vol. II, pp. 181–182. ShR 18.10 reads: Moses
was occupied with taking care of Joseph's body and with procuring
the material Jacob had prepared for the tabernacle; comp. vol. III,
p. 164.
[2] An unknown Midrash quoted by Sabba, Beshallah 74b; BHM VI,
112; Aggadat Shir II, 3; comp. also Schechter on the last-named passage.
Concerning the fragrance that emanates from the live as well as the
dead bodies of the pious, see note 92 on vol. I, p. 334 and vol. II, p. 19.
Comp. also Berakot 43b where it is said that in the time to come the
young men of Israel will give forth a fragrance like Lebanon. As
to the fragrance of the dead bodies of the pious in Christian legend,
see *The Passing of Maria*, second version, 10, and Smith, ZDMG 66, 167.
[3] ShR 20.19; PK 10, 86a–86b. On the extension of Egypt see
Pesahim 94a and vol. II, pp. 364, 374. The magic dogs are a reminiscence of Serapis who was represented as being of dog-like form; see
Tertullian, *Ad Nationes*, 11.8. Later sources speak of several kinds of
magic animals such as dogs, lions, and bulls. As soon as a fugitive
slave met any of these animals, they would bark, roar and bellow until
the fugitive was captured; but at the time of the exodus from Egypt
none of the animals raised its voice; see Yalkut David, Exod. 11.7.
For further details on the finding of Joseph's coffin, see note 723; vol.
II, pp. 181–182, and vol. III, pp. 66, 122, and note 156.
[4] Mekilta Mishpatim 20, 98a; ShR 31.9; Targ. Yer. Exod. 22.
30.
[5] Perek Shirah (end); Yalkut I, 187.
[6] Mekilta Beshallah (פתיחתא) 23b. Before the children of Israel
left Egypt it had never happened that a slave escaped from that
country, which was closed on all sides; Mekilta Yitro 1, 58b; Mekilta
RS 88. Comp. note 3.—Moses kept the coffin containing Joseph's
body in his tent during the time that Israel journeyed through the
wilderness; Pesahim 67a; comp. note 422 on vol. II, p. 183.
[7] Zohar II, 45a–45b; comp. note 230 on vol. II, p. 371.

1

⁸ Mekilta Beshallah (פתיחתא) 23b; Mekilta RS 38; ShR 20.11–
17 (here many more reasons are given for Israel's long wanderings
through the wilderness). See also Sifra 18.3, where it is said: The
Canaanites honored Abraham, and as a reward for this a respite of
forty years was granted to them. Comp. note 413 on vol. II, p. 151.
That the journey through the wilderness was an exercise in discipline
and an encouragement to study is also mentioned in *Recognitiones*,
1.35. Comp. Josephus, *Antiqui.*, II, 15.3, and vol. III, p. 285.

⁹ ShR 20.16. According to *Hadar*, Exod. 13.17, the Philistines
were kinsmen of the Egyptians, and on account of this kinship God
did not wish that Israel should march through the land of the Philistines.

¹⁰ Mekilta Beshallah (פתיחתא) 23b–24a and Shirah 9, 42b–43a;
Mekilta RS 37–38; Sanhedrin 92b; ShR 20.11; PK 10, 85a–85b; PRE
48; Wa-Yosha' 54; Yerushalmi Targumim Exod. 13.17; Targum Ps.
78. 9; Targum I Chron. 7.21–22; see also Yelammedenu in Yalkut
II on Ps. 78, and Tehillim 81, 368. The chief of the Ephraimites is
called גנון ינון, and גוון in PRE—the correct reading is not certain;
ינון seems to be most likely; comp. Ps. 77. 17, and Sanhedrin 98b,
where ינון is one of the names of the Messiah—whereas according to
the text of the Yerushalmi Targumim given in Mahzor Vitry 167,
Ganon was the name of the king of the Philistines who attacked and
destroyed the Ephraimites led by Jair. This legend very likely
represents a kind of reminiscence of a historical event, the wars between Egypt and Canaan which are frequently mentioned in the Tel-
Amarna Letters. See Levy, *Monatsschrift*, 55, 285, and Ginzberg,
Unbekannte Sekte 339–340. In the latter passage it is suggested that
there is a connection between the legend about the premature exodus
of the Ephraimites and the belief in the advent of the Messiah, the son of
Ephraim, who will precede the Messiah, the son of David. As to the
war between Egypt and Canaan in pre-Israelitish times, see, also Jub. 46.
9–11, where it is said that Amram participated in the war of Egypt
against Canaan and died in the Promised Land. The obscure reference
in Shir 2.7, to the premature attempt of the exodus in the time of Amram
is to be explained in accordance with Jub., *loc. cit.*, and the Midrashim
quoted above, which record the failure of the Ephraimites. Comp.
note 12 on vol. II, p. 251, and vol. IV, p. 332. Joseph, who rose to
power and dignity in Egypt, gave himself up to the enjoyments of life to
such an extent that he forgot his father who was mourning his son's death
and did not inform him that he was still alive (comp. vol. II, p. 44,
and note 370 on vol. II, p. 137). As a punishment for this sin, two

2

hundred thousand descendants of Joseph—the Ephraimites—perished
at the hands of the Philistines; see Hasidim 231 and 232. This supposition is very likely due to the phrase רבים ימים ויתאבל used in I Chron.
7.22, in connection with the death of the Ephraimites, and in Gen.
37, 34, when the tidings of Joseph's death were brought to Jacob.
Josephus, *Antiqui.*, II, 15.3, likewise speaks of earlier wars that took
place between the Philistines and the Hebrews.

11 Yashar Shemot 137a–137b; PRE 58; Mekilta Beshallah
(פתיחתא) 24a; comp. vol. II, p. 246.

12 Mekilta Beshallah 1, 25a–26a and Shir 1.13; Mekilta RS
42–43. Dibre ha-Yamim 11 relates that the mixed multitude (ערב
אספסוף=רב; comp. note 462) attempted to force Israel to return to
Egypt; but in the ensuing battle between the Hebrews and the Egyptians the latter were almost entirely annihilated, so that only few of
them reached Egypt to inform Pharaoh of Israel's flight. Comp. also
Yashar Shemot, 145b–146a.

13 Mekilta Beshallah 1, 25b–26a; Mekilta RS 41; Targum Yerushalmi Exod. 14.2; comp. vol. II, p. 367. See vol. III, p. 13, where
it is narrated that the Egyptians were furthermore misled by the fe-
licitous course of their preparations for the war against Israel.

14 An unknown Midrash quoted in Sifte Kohen, Exod. 14.2;
this is a combination of Mekilta Beshallah 1, 26a and Mekilta RS
41 with Pesahim 119b. On the treasures of Joseph and the Egyptians
see Abkir in Yalkut I, 230; vol. I, 125, and vol. III, pp. 27, 286.

15 Mekilta Beshallah 1, 26b–27a; Mekilta RS 43–44. A sentence
not found in our text of the Mekilta but quoted in *Hadar*, and *Imre
No'am*, Deut. 25.18, reads: Amalek said: Pharaoh will attack Israel
in the front and I in the rear. Comp. note 139. The magicians
are mentioned only in Zohar II, 46b, whereas the Mekiltas have agents
(this is how אקטורין, in Mekilta RS קטורין, is to be translated)and messengers of Pharaoh. See vol. III, p. 10. As to Pharaoh the "cosmocrator", see Abkir in Yalkut I, 241, and Mekilta Shirah 6. At
the exodus the power of Egypt sank; Hallel 95; comp. note 738.

16 Zohar II, 51a–51b.

17 Mekilta Beshallah 1–2, 27a–27b; Mekilta RS 44–45; Tan.
Shofetim 13. The last named source adds that Pharaoh presented
the chieftains of the army with pearls and precious stones, to win them
over to his plans. As to the fact that pagans attribute great importance
to omens, see vol. IV, p. 301. On the chariots of war see Yerushalmi
Kil'ayim 7,31c.

[18] Mekilta Beshallah 1, 26a; Mekilta RS 41. That Dathan and Abiram, the implacable enemies of Moses (comp. note 75 on vol. II, p. 282), remained in Egypt is found only in Targum Yerushalmi, Exod. 14.3; this is probably based upon the midrashic source quoted in *Sekel*, Exod., *loc. cit.*; see also *Haggadat Teman* 22.

[19] Mekilta Beshallah 2,27b; Mekilta RS 45; ShR 15.15; comp. vol. II, pp. 358, 367, vol. III, p. 10.

[20] Mekilta RS 41.

[21] ShR 21.5 and 15.15. Comp. also Tan. Shofetim 13–14; Mekilta Beshallah 1, 26a and 28b; Mekilta RS 41–42. On the guardian angel of Egypt, see note 41. The midrashic basis for the legend about the angel of Egypt is the use of the singular (נסע) in Exod. 14.10. According to another interpretation this verse speaks of Mizraim, son of Ham (Gen. 10.6), who came to the assistance of his descendants the Egyptians, the inhabitants of Egypt–Mizraim. See *Hadar*, Exod., *loc. cit.*; Zohar II, 19b.

[22] Mekilta Beshallah 2, 28a–28b; Mekilta RS 46. The sinners in Israel said: God cannot deliver Israel from the hands of their masters, and He therefore commanded them to flee from the Egyptians. To show mankind His power, God caused Pharaoh to follow the Israelites that He might perform His miracles at the Red Sea; see ER 7.44. As to the power Moses exerted over his people, comp. vol. III, p. 107.

[23] Mekilta Beshallah 2, 29a; Mekilta RS 47; Yerushalmi Ta'anit 2, 65d; Targum Yerushalmi Exod. 14.13 and 2 Targum Yerushalmi Exod. 14.3; PRK (Grünhut's edition) 43; Wa-Yosha' 51–52. The last two sources speak of the three divisions of the tribes. This is in agreement with ps.-Philo 11B who states that the tribes of Reuben, Issachar, Zebulun, and Simeon formed the first division; Gad, Asher, and Dan the Second; Levi, Judah, the Joseph tribes, and Benjamin the third. Yashar Shemot, 146a, divides the tribes as follows: Reuben, Simeon, and Issachar formed the first party; Zebulun, Benjamin, and Naphtali the second; Judah, Dan (read ודן instead of ובן), and the Joseph tribes the third; Levi, Gad, and Asher the fourth. The task of the last-named was to intimidate the enemy by noise. The midrashic statement about the divided counsel of the tribes is derived from Ps. 68.28 (comp. the references given in notes 36 and 388),and not from Judges 5.15–16, as maintained by James on ps.-Philo, *loc. cit.* See also Philo, *Moses*, 2 (3).33, who remarks that the Israelites were ready to throw themselves into the waters of the sea. Josephus,

Antiqui., II. 15, 4, says: The people threw stones at Moses (see Num.
14.10); but he, self-reliant and fearless, calmed the people with his
words, and made them stop the weeping and clamoring of the women
and children. Reference to the weeping of the women and children
is also found in Wa-Yosha', which, like Josephus, made use of Num.
14.1.

²⁴ Abkir in Yalkut I, 233; comp. vol. III, p. 14, and ps.-Philo 11B.

²⁵ Josephus, *Antiqui.*, II. 16, 1; the prayer in Yashar Shemot,
146b, reads differently.

²⁶ Mekilta Beshallah 3, 29–30a; Mekilta RS 47–48. The Derashot in these sources are based on the conception that just as the physical
order of the world is maintained by fixed laws of nature, so the moral
order cannot exist without Israel. Now inasmuch as the existence
of the physical world depends upon the existence of moral man (see
note 8 on vol. I, p. 50), it is manifest that Israel is indispensable to the
world. The other point brought out by these Derashot is that the
Israelites on account of their trust in God and because of the merit
of their fathers, are entitled to expect that divine help would come to
them; comp. Targum Yerushalmi Exod. 14.15.

²⁷ ShR 21.7; Zohar II, 33a, 34a, and 181b, as well as III, 101b
and 218a; PRK 33a. Comp. also note 34 on vol. II, p. 240, and Index,
s. v. "Job". A statement similar to that of the Midrash is found in
Jub. 48.15–18, which remarks that God kept Mastemah bound from
the fourteenth of Nisan to the eighteenth thereof, that he might not
accuse Israel. See also the comment of Mekilta Beshallah 4, 30
and Mekilta RS 47, on the use of the name האלהים in Exod. 14.19.

²⁸ Abkir in Yalkut I, 241, and Wa-Yosha' 39. A somewhat
different version of this legend is found in *Hadar*, Exod. 14.10. Comp.
note 110 on vol. I, p. 235, and vol. II, p. 318.

²⁹ ShR 21.1 and 6, which in the main follows Mekilta Beshallah
2, 29b–30a.

³⁰ Wa-Yosha' 38–39; ShR 21.6; Mekilta RS 49–50. The sea
did not want to divide its waters before the Israelites because they
rebelled against God; Tehillim 114, 475. Conflicting with this view
there is the statement that Israel saw no other way to be delivered
from the Egyptians than by passing through the Red Sea; for that
day being Sabbath, they were unable to try their fortune in war;
See BHM VI, 37. Comp. the following note, and vol. IV, p. 11.

³¹ Targum Yerushalmi Exod. 14.21. As to the rod of Moses,
see PK 14, 140a; Tehillim 114, 475; DR 3.8; vol. II, pp. 291 and 293.

[32] Mekilta RS 50; this is very likely a late source and is identical with that made use of in Sekel 182; ShR 21.6; DR 3.8; Hallel 95–97; Wa-Yosha' 51; Tehillim 114, 475; PRE 42; PR 19, 140; *Haggadat Teman* 55. In all these passages stress is laid upon the fact that it was God's will, not the rod of Moses, that performed the miracles. BHM VI, 37, finds it even necessary to interpret הרם (Exod. 14.16) in the sense of removing: God told Moses to lay the rod aside before dividing the sea. *Hadar* and *Imre No'am* on Exod., *loc. cit.*, quote, from Tehillim, a lengthy passage bearing upon the controversy between Moses and the Red Sea. A poetical rendering of this dialogue is given in 2 Targum Yerushalmi Exodus 14.29, and in a somewhat different version by the Targum fragment in *Kaufmann-Gedenkbuch*, 235.

[33] Mekilta Beshallah 4, 31a; Mekilta RS 50; Tehillim 18, 147; ShR 21.6.

[34] Abkir in Yalkut I, 234; Makiri Ps. 136, 258; *Hadar* and *Da'at* on Exod. 14.21; *Eshkol* 2, 105; Al-Barceloni 11; Or Zarua' II, 136b, No. 314; the last-named source gives an essentially different version. Comp. also Shu'aib, Beshallah 30b and Aggadat Bereshit 17.35. An old stratum of this version is found in Mekilta Beshallah 5, 31b and 6, 33a, as well as in Mekilta RS 51 and 54.

[35] Mekilta Beshallah 4, 30b–31a; Mekilta RS 49–50. Concerning the darkness, see vol. II, p. 359. According to PRE 42, it was the angel Michael who made himself "a wall of fire" between Israel and the Egyptians. Philo, in a similar manner, identifies the pillar of fire with an angel; see *Moses*, 1.29.

[36] Mekilta Beshallah 5, 31a–31b; Mekilta RS 50–51; Sotah 37a; Tan. B. I, 208; Aggadat Bereshit 74, 145; PRE 42; Aggadat Shir 2, 29; Tehillim 68, 320; 76, 341; 114, 474; Hallel 95; Tosefta Berakot 4.18; Yerushalmi Targumim Exod. 14.16; Targum Ps. 68. 26; Wa-Yosha' 52. As to those who first entered the sea, comp. Josephus, *Antiqui.*, II, 16.2, who maintains that Moses was the first to jump into the sea. See note 23; vol. II, p. 14; vol. III, p. 195.—On the ten miracles (this number is mentioned Abot 5, 4) see also Mekilta Shirah 6, 40a; Mekilta RS 64; Tan. Beshallah 10; PRE 42; Tehillim 114, 473; Hallel 96; ARN 33, 96 (second version 36, 94, and 38, 99); Wa-Yosha' 51; Midrash Shir, 38b; Midrash Temurah 111, quotation from Tan. in Makiri Ps. 136, 258. Several features of this legend are found in Wisdom 19.7–10 (the sea was changed into a pleasure-ground, as in Tehillim, *loc. cit.*), in Philo, *Moses*, 1.32, and 2 (3).34 (the sea was changed into a highway, as in 2 ARN,

99), and in Josephus, *Antiqui.*, II, 16.2. Comp. also Theodoretus, Exod. 14.16.—In Mekilta Beshallah 6, 33b, Mekilta RS 55, ShR 23.9, and Passover Haggadah three different opinions are given as to the number of the plagues inflicted upon the Egyptians at the Red Sea. Fifty, two hundred, and two hundred and fifty, respectively are the numbers represented in these opinions. The conflicting views are based on the assumption that at the Red Sea the plagues were five times as many as in Egypt ("the hand of the Lord" was seen at the Red Sea, whereas in Egypt His "finger" only was visible; compare Exod. 8.15 with 14.31). On this point they all agree, but they differ with respect to the exact nature of the plagues in Egypt, which, according to all views, were composite.

³⁷ ShR 21.10; Wa-Yosha' 51; 2 ARN 38, 10; Yelammedenu in Yalkut I, 764

³⁸ Targum Yerushalmi Exod. 14.22; Wa-Yosha' 51. Comp. vol. IV, p. 5. This is the reply of the legend to the rationalists who maintain that the passage through the Red Sea took place during the low tide. Artapanus, 436b, is the oldest exponent of this rationalistic view.

³⁹ Br 92.2; Midrash Shir 22b, where, however, the presence of these prominent persons is spoken of in connection with the redemption from Egypt; comp. also ShR 18.10 with regard to Jacob's presence. Zohar II, 53a (this is the source of Shu'aib, 30a) further adds the presence of the twelve tribes, *i. e.*, the sons of Jacob. "The six mothers" *i. e.*, Sarah, Rebekah, and Jacob's four wives, are mentioned in this connection, it seems, only in this source and in the piyyut כך נזרו for the Great Sabbath, in the Italian Mahzor. See Index,s. v. "Mothers". Rashi on Ta'anit 5b, catchword אף הוא, Hasidim 34, Sekel, 190 read in BR, *loc. cit.*, ישראל סבא (on this expression see vol. V, p. 276, top). According to these authorities, Exod, 14.31 (and Israel saw) is to be explained as "and Jacob saw". The contrast to ישראל סבא is מצרים סבא in the source quoted in note 21.

⁴⁰ Wa-Yosha' 39–40, which is based on Abkir in Yalkut I, 241. For another version of this legend see vol. III, pp. 17–18. Concerning Pharaoh's blasphemous language see vol. II, p. 333; on the Hebrew child used as mortar see vol. III, p. 372. *Hadar*, Exod. 24.10, combined two sources for this legend, the version on p. 28b being taken from Wa-Yosha', whereas in 40a an unknown Midrash is reproduced. Abkir in Yalkut I, 243, has a third version of this legend.

⁴¹ Abkir (perhaps Wa-Yosha'), according to *Hadar*, Exod.

14.10; ShR 21.5. That God first executed judgment on the angel of Egypt and then on the Egyptians is an old Haggadah; see Mekilta Shirah 2, 36b and Mekilta RS 58. The Mekiltas also know of the general rule that God's wrath is first visited upon the guardian angels before the nations entrusted to their care are punished. This view is found in many passages of the Talmud and Midrash; see ShR, *loc. cit.*, Shemuel 18, 98 (on the text comp. *Abkat Rokel*, 1.2); DR 1.22; Shir 8.14; Tan. Beshallah 13; Tan. B. II, 53, and V. 32; Sukkah 29a, according to Rashi's interpretation of this passage, which, however, is hardly correct, as the Talmud evidently refers to the idea that idols which are worshipped are punished; comp. vol. II, pp. 250 and 348. See also Wa-Yosha' 45; Midrash Temurah 110; PK 4, 41a; Zohar II, 52b and 54b; *Batte Midrashot* I, 27. The last-named source is the only one which refers to the guardian angel of every individual as well as to that of every nation. Comp. vol. III, pp. 277, 340, and 369, and vol. IV, pp. 93 and 301. As to the burning of idols in Gehenna on the Day of Judgment, see EZ 21, 34; comp. also BR 28 (beginning), and Vol. V, p. 418, note 118 towards end of page.

⁴² Wa-Yosha' 46–47. As to the older view concerning Rahab, see vol. I, p. 18, and comp. Sekel 182. In the latter legend Rahab is the "prince of Egypt" and at the same time Uzza is the "prince of the sea". See the quotation from Wa-Yosha' (not in our text) in *Hadar*, Exod. 14.16. Abkir in Yalkut I, 234, makes Sammael the guardian angel of Egypt, and gives the following dialogue between God and him. Sammael said: The Israelites worshipped idols in Egypt, and yet Thou wishest to perform miracles for their sake. When the prince of the sea heard these words he became exceedingly wrathful against Israel, and wanted to drown them. Whereupon God replied to Sammael: "O thou fool, did Israel worship idols voluntarily? Was it not due to their servitude which deprived them of their senses?" These words of God turned away the anger of the prince of the sea from Israel to the Egyptians. Zohar II, 270, made use of Abkir, but, in accordance with the above-mentioned sources, changed Sammael to Rahab. Comp. also Mekilta Beshallah 6, 33a.

⁴³ ShR 22; Mekilta Beshallah 6, 32b, and Mekilta RS 53-54; Tehillim 18, 147. Josephus, *Antiqui.*, II, 15.3, states that six hundred chariots of war, fifty thousand horsemen, and two hundred thousand footmen of the Egyptians were drowned in the Red Sea, whereas Jub. 48.14 gives a million and one thousand as the number of those that were drowned. *Shalshelet* 96 is based on Josephus and not on rab-

binic sources which are by far more liberal with numbers, maintaining that the Egyptian army consisted of nine thousand myriads. Comp. Mekilta Beshallah 1, 27a–27b and *Pa'aneah* Exod. 14.7.

⁴⁴ Mekilta RS 51–52, taken verbatim from Aggadat Shir 1, 16–17; *Kaufmann-Gedenkbuch* p. 3 (Hebrew); comp. also Tan. Shofetim 14; Midrash Shir 11b; Mekilta Beshallah 6, 33a, and Shirah 4, 37b; Mekilta RS 54; Shir 1.9; Tehillim 18, 142–144; ARN 27, 183. The legend about the "heavenly mare", mentioned in the sources quoted above, is very likely connected with the idea that the cherub has the form of a mare. Comp. note 94 on vol. I, p. 81 and note 47.

⁴⁵ Tehillim 18, 14b; PR 21, 104a; Wa-Yosha' 45; BaR 8.3; ARN 27.83. Accompanied by nine thousand myriads of angels (on this number see note 43), God appeared at the Red Sea. The angels said unto Him: "Permit us to execute Thy will upon the Egyptians..." God, however, refused their request, saying: "I shall not be content until I Myself have inflicted punishment upon the enemies of Israel." See Mekilta RS 52–53, and in abridged form *Pa'aneah*, Exod. 14.7. This legend in its original form wished to narrate the execution of the last of the plagues, not the drowning of the Egyptians; see note 213 on vol. II, p. 366, and the following notes.

⁴⁶ Mekilta Beshallah 2, 28b; Mekilta RS 46–47; Yerushalmi Sotah 7, 22b; Tehillim 18, 143; Midrash Shir 11b–12a. Most of the sources add that Moses showed the Israelites the multitudes of the angels that came to their assistance; comp. preceding note. Josephus, *Antiqui.*, II, 16.3, also speaks of the thunder and lightning at the destruction of the Egyptians. Ps. 18.13, *seq.*, was taken by Josephus, as by the Rabbis (comp. Tehillim, *ad loc.*) to refer to the miracles which were performed at the Red Sea.

⁴⁷ Aggadat Shir 1, 17; this is the source of Mekilta RS 52. Wa-Yosha' 52 proves quite clearly that this legend is a modification of the one concerning the "heavenly mare" = cherub; see note 44.

⁴⁸ Mekilta Beshallah 5, 32a; Mekilta RS 52; somewhat differently Aggadat Shir 1.7. The idea concerning the provenance of the treasures from the river Pishon is found only in Targum Yerushalmi Exod. 14.9, and Num. 38.8. Comp. vol. II, p. 371, and vol. III, p. 11.

⁴⁹ Mekilta Beshallah 5, 32a; Mekilta RS 52; Tehillim 18, 143.

⁵⁰ Mekilta Beshallah 6, 33a; Mekilta RS 54. In these sources ft is presupposed that the Egyptians suffered great agony before they perished, see note 55. Concerning the angels see note 45.

⁵¹ Wa-Yosha' 52, which is a combination of Mekilta Shirah

5, 38b and 7, 41, Mekilta RS 62 and 65. The two parties among the Egyptians spoken of by Philo, *Moses*, 30, correspond to the first and third, respectively, of the Midrash. The Haggadah found in Exod. 18.11 is support for the view that the drowning of the Egyptians was the punishment for the drowning of the Hebrew male children; see Tosefta Sotah 3.13; Mekilta Shirah 6, 40a; Jub. 48.14.

52 Mekilta Beshallah 6, 33a, and Shirah 2, 36a–36b; Mekilta RS 54, 58. The Great Sea emptied itself into the Red Sea, and the enormous quantities of water tossed the Egyptians about hither and thither; Mekilta Shirah 5, 38b, and Mekilta RS 62. Furthermore, the abyss ascended and united itself with the waters above in the heaven, so that the Egyptians met their death while engulfed in gloomy darkness; Mekilta, *loc. cit.*; Tehillim 18, 137. The interpretation of נערמו מים (Exod. 15.8) as "and the water acted with cunning", given in Mekilta, *loc. cit.*, Onkelos, and Ephraem (I, 216D), *ad loc.*, is the midrashic support for the legend concerning the different punishments which the water inflicted on the Egyptians, according to the grades of wickedness.

53 Abkir in Yalkut I, 235; Wa-Yosha' 52; Yerahmeel, 159 (the Hebrew text is given by Schechter, *Zadokite Fragments*, LIX–LX); *Hakam ha-Razim* in Yalkut Reubeni Exod. 15.7. In the last-named source it is the "prince of the Face" (the angel of His presence, Is. 63.9) who executes punishment upon the magicians. This agrees with Yerahmeel who makes Metatron the executioner. The identity of these two angels is presupposed in numerous places in the mystic literature; see Index, s. v. "Metatron". Comp. also *Hadar* and *Imre No'am* on Exod. 15.10. Concerning the seizure of the hair-locks, see note 276 on vol. I p 394

54 Wa-Yosha' 52–53 *Dibre ha-Yamim* 11; Midrash Aggada, Exod. 14b; Sekel, 186, *Hadar*, Exod. 14.28; PRE 43; BHM V, 51; Tosefta of Targum Jonah 3.6; Yerahmeel, 128. Comp. vol. II, p. 150, and vol. III, p. 467, where Pharaoh is said to keep guard at the portals of hell. In the old sources different opinions are expressed as to the fate of Pharaoh: he was drowned simultaneously with his army; he was the last Egyptian to be drowned after having witnessed the struggle of his people and their destruction; he was the only Egyptian who escaped death, in order that he might see the power and might of God. Mekilta Beshallah 6, 33a; Mekilta RS 54; Midrash Tehillim 106, 455. Pharaoh, the inhabitants of the sinful cities, the builders of the tower of Babel, Sennacherib, and Nebuchadnezzar

committed the following eight sins which brought destruction upon them: Neglect of justice, idolatry, incest, bloodshed, blasphemy, arrogance, slander, and obscenity; ER 15.74 and 31.158.   Comp. Index, s. v. "Noachian Laws".   Comp. vol. VI, p. 364, note 60.

⁵⁵ Mekilta Beshallah 5, 32a-32b and 6, 33a-33b; Mekilta RS 53-54; Tehillim 22, 180 (on the text see Yalkut I, 240); Philo, *Moses*, 2 (3).34; Wisdom 10.20; Josephus *Antiqui.*, II, 16.6. Somewhat differently in ER 1, 12, where it is stated that the garments of the Egyptians did not sink with the bodies, but were washed ashore and appropriated by the Israelites.   This source maintains that "as a rule", God punishes the wicked while they are naked; Comp. vol. IV, p. 375.

⁵⁶ Mekilta Shirah 9, 42a; Mekilta RS 67-68; PRE 42; Wa-Yosha' 53; Targum Yerushalmi Exod. 15.12; Tehillim 22, 188-189; Ekah 1, 73-74. Comp. note 413 on vol. II, p. 151; vol. I, p. 80; vol. IV, p. 37.

⁵⁷ Mekilta Beshallah 6, 33b; Mekilta RS 55; Tan. Beshallah 4. The advance of Pharaoh with his mighty army caused a change of heart among the Israelites. They repented of their sins, and, trusting in God, they invoked His help which did not fail them in their hour of distress; PRE 42 and ShR 25.5; comp. however, the conflicting view in vol. III, pp. 36-37, and the following note.

⁵⁸ Tehillim 18, 137; Shemuel 29, 134-135; Shir 4.3.   Comp. also 'Arakin 11a and Yerushalmi Pesahim 4, 30c with reference to the atoning power of the song of the Levites in the Temple   The Midrashim quoted above speak at great length of the sin which Israel had committed; comp. the preceding note.   An unknown Midrash, quoted by Shu'aib, Beshallah, 30a-30b, maintains that the reason why the Israelites sang the song (Exod. 15) was to be found in the Halakah, Berakot 54b, according to which a man returning from a sea-voyage, in order to thank God for having escaped death, must recite the benediction (ברכת הגומל): "Blessed art Thou, O Lord our God, King of the universe, who bestowest benefits upon the undeserving (literally, *the guilty*), and hast also bestowed all good upon me."

⁵⁹ Mekilta Shirah 1, 34a-34b, and Mekilta RS 56-57. The "ten songs" are often referred to in the haggadic literature; but opinions differ as to the songs which are to be included in this group; see Targum Song of Songs 1.1; Aggadat Shir 1.10 and 2.29 on the Song of Abraham; Makiri Is. 5.37 and Ps. 96, 111; *Responsen der Geonim* (ed. Harkavy, No. 66) and the interesting essay on these songs by Epstein, *Mi-Mizrah u-mi-Ma'arab* I. 85-89. Concerning the song of the night of redemp-

tion, see vol. II, pp. 368, 373. According to the Haggadah, Solomon composed Psalm 30, and the superscription of that Psalm is explained to mean: "A Song of the dedication of the house of David", i.e., the Temple.

⁶⁰ Tan. B. II, 60–61; Tehillim 106, 454; ShR 23.7; Ekah (פתיחתא)
24. According to another legend, God silenced the song of the angels with the words: "The work of My hands is drowning in the sea, and ye wish to chant songs!" See Megillah 10b; Sanhedrin 39b ("God does not rejoice at the punishment of the sinners"); PK 29, 189ª; Yalkut II, 940 (from an unknown source; the word מדרש is not found in the editio princeps, and its insertion in later editions is unjustifiable, as this Haggadah does not occur in Midrash Mishle which is designated by Yalkut as מדרש in the part of that work belonging to Prov.; it is perhaps borrowed from Yelammedenu); R. Solomon ben ha-Yatom, 120, based on an unknown Midrash (comp. Chajes, XXX); Zohar I, 57b, 61b, and II, 170b; see also Mekilta Shirah 5, 34b. PK, *loc. cit.*, is the source for the statement made by many codifiers (see, e.g., *Bet Yosef, Orah Hayyim* 490) that the entire Hallel is recited only on the first day of Passover because on the seventh day the Egyptians were drowned. Concerning the song of the angels which follows that of Israel, see Midrash Tannaim, 71; Yerushalmi Sukkah 5, 55b; vol. I, p. 17, and II, p. 373. An unknown Midrash quoted by *Hadar*, Exod. 15.8, speaks of the song chanted by the water at the drowning of the Egyptians. This statement is very likely based upon a misunderstanding of Onkelos, *ad loc.*; see Mekilta Shirah 6, 40a. See Index, s.v. "Angels, Song of"; "Water, the Song of". The very angels who counselled God against the creation of man (see vol. I, p. 53) descended from heaven to listen to the song chanted by Israel, and then returned to their place to sing their song of praise to God; Tosefta Sotah 6.5. Comp. vol. VI, 397, note 32.

⁶¹ Wa-Yosha' 40–41, which, in the main, follows older sources (comp. references cited in note 25 on vol. II, pp. 257–258, and add PK, 47, 189a–189b; BHM VI, 38; *Haggadat Teman* 35, which reads: The clean animals suckled the male children of the Hebrews); PRE 42; Targum Yerushalmi Exod. 15.2; ShR 23.18.

⁶² Mekilta Shirah 1, 34a; Mekilta RS 56; Shir 1.15 and 4.1; Yalkut I, 241, giving Mekilta as source, but this passage is not found in our texts of this Midrash; ShR 23.9. Comp. the following note.

⁶³ Mekilta Shirah 1, 35a, Mekilta RS 57 (better text); Sotah, Mishnah 5.4; Tosefta 6.3; Yerushalmi 5,20c; Babli 30b. The manner

of reciting the Hallel is, according to the sources quoted above, the same as the song at the Red Sea; comp. Elbogen *Studien z. Gesch. d. jüd. Gottesdienstes* 57. According to Yelammedenu in Yalkut II, 527, on Hosea 11, and ShR 22.8, Moses composed the song and the people sang it; comp. vol. III, pp. 338–339. ShR differs from the old source (comp. note 59) also in this respect that it declares the song at the Red Sea to have been the first ever sung in God's honor.

⁶⁴ Mekilta Shirah 1, 35a; Sotah, Tosefta 6.4; Yerushalmi 6, 29c; Babli 30b; Tehillim 8, 77; Zohar II, 60a. Comp. vol. III, p. 90.

⁶⁵ Mekilta Shirah 3, 37a; Shir 2.14, 3.7, and 4.3; Zohar II, 60a. Comp. vol. III, p. 106.

⁶⁶ Targum Yerushalmi Exod. 15.18. According to this authority verse 18 concludes the song, whereas others consider verse 19 as the end. See Mekilta RS 70–71, where the nineteen verses of the song are said to correspond to the nineteen benedictions of the 'Amidah (according to Babylonian ritual); Lekah Exod., *loc. cit.*, and 20.11.

⁶⁷ Wa-Yosha‘ 55.

⁶⁸ Kohelet 1.9. Comp. vol. II, p. 302.

⁶⁹ Abkir in Yalkut I, 241.

⁷⁰ Mekilta Shirah 10, 44a; Mekilta RS 71; PRE 42. According to Philo, *Moses*, 2 (3).34, the song was chanted by mixed choirs composed of men and women, whereas the Rabbis strongly disapprove of mixed choirs; see *e. g.*, Sotah 48a. Comp. also Philo, *De Vita Contemplativa*, 11, concerning the mixed choirs among the Essenes.

⁷¹ Targum Yerushalmi Exod. 15.21.

⁷² ShR 24.2; Mekilta Wa-Yassa‘ 1, 44a; Mekilta RS 71–72. It is stated in the Haggadah that the Israelites brought along with them from Egypt an idol which they worshipped (or kept?) for a long time; see Mekilta Beshallah 3, 29b; PK 11, 99a; Sanhedrin 103b, where this idol is declared to be identical with that made by Micah; Pesahim 117a (on עומד בבכי see *Responsen der Geonim*, No. 119, pp. 86–88, and it is to be corrected as suggested by Lebrecht, *Kritische Lese*, 23–35); Yerushalmi Sukkah 4, 54c; ARN 34; Sifre N., 84; Tan. B. IV, 79, and V, 25; Shir 1.4; ShR 41.1; Tehillim 101, 427. Comp. note 127 on vol. IV, p. 49; Comp. vol. VI, p. 375 and Index, s.v. "Baalbek".

⁷³ Abot 5.4. On the ten temptations see note 708.

⁷⁴ Tan. B. II, 63; this very likely is the source of Sekel 205; comp. note 55.

⁷⁵ Mekilta Wa-Yassa‘ 1, 44b where the text is to be corrected in accordance with Mekilta RS 72; ShR 24.4.

⁷⁶ Tan. B. II, 63–64. This legend is related to the one forming the basis for the Apocryphal work "Daniel and the Dragon"; see note 112 on vol. IV, p. 338.

⁷⁷ Mekilta Wa-Yassa' 1, 44b; Tan. B. II, 63; Shir 1.4. Comp. vol. II, p. 375.

⁷⁸ ShR 24.4; Wa-Yosha' 46, which reads: The snakes stretched themselves out in order to allow Israel to pass over them as over a bridge. See reference given in note 241 on vol. II, pp. 374–375.

⁷⁹ Mekilta Wa-Yassa' 1, 45a; Mekilta RS 72. Concerning the sweet waters of the Red Sea see vol. III, p. 22.

⁸⁰ Philo, *Moses*, 1.33. Josephus, *Antiqui.*, III, 1.2, likewise attempts to excuse the behavior of the people.

⁸¹ Mekilta Wa-Yassa' 1, 45b; Mekilta RS 72–73; Targum Yerushalmi 16.22. Comp. the following note.

⁸² Mekilta Wa-Yassa' 1, 45b, and Mekilta RS 72–73; in abridged form, Tan. B. II, 64–65, 124, and Tan. Beshallah 23–24. On the conception that God employs the same means in inflicting pain and in curing it, see also Aggadat Bereshit 66, 132. The Mekiltas and the sources depending on them contain different opinions as to the kind of tree which made the waters of Marah sweet, and it seems as if the Tannaim attempted to explain away the miracle, maintaining that the change in the taste of the waters brought about by the tree was due to natural causes. A rationalistic view similar to this is expressed by Josephus, *Antiqui.*, III, 1.2, whereas Philo, *Moses*, 1.33, is not quite sure whether the tree caused the cure in a natural way, or whether "it was then created for that special purpose". The Mekiltas offer also an allegorical explanation of the tree. According to this interpretation, the word "tree" represents the Torah which is "the tree of life". This allegory presupposes the legend that this tree was identical with the tree of life, or, to be more accurate, a branch of that tree, It is true that our texts of the Mekilta have no trace of that legend, but Makiri, Prov. 3, 4b, quotes it from the Mekilta. Ps.-Philo 13A likewise writes: And He—God—showed him the tree of life, whereof he cut a piece, which he took and put into Marah, and the water of Marah became sweet. Closely connected with this legend is the one found in *Zohar Hadash* Beshallah, according to which Moses threw his rod, called here also עץ, tree or wood. This rod is said in other sources to have been taken from the tree of life; see ARN 157, ed. Schechter. Comp. also *Kaufmann-Gedenkbuch* 6 (Hebrew). An entirely different explanation of the events of Marah is found

in Zohar III, 124b, where it is stated that the bitter waters of Marah served the purpose to establish which of the women were chaste and which were not (comp. Num. 5.18, *seq.*), and therefore Moses wrote God's Name on the tree (this is taken from Targum Yerushalmi, Exod. 15.25) in accordance with the law concerning a woman suspected of adultery (see Sotah 2.3). Ps.-Philo, *loc. cit.*, and 21A asserts that the waters of Marah "followed them in the desert for forty years, going up with them into the hills and coming down with them to the plains." In another passage, 12C, ps.-Philo, in agreement with rabbinic and other sources, makes the same statement concerning "the well" (of Miriam), and the suggestion may be hazarded that the first passage contains an interpolation by a copyist who confused "the well", which is very frequently spoken of in Hebrew sources as באר ש מרים (the well of Miriam; comp. vol. III, pp. 50, *seq.*), with באר ש מרה (the well of Marah). Comp. note 126.

⁸³ Mekilta Wa-Yassa' 1, 46a; Mekilta RS 73–74; Targum Yerushalmi Exod. 15.25–26; Sanhedrin 56b; Seder 'Olam 5. Comp. also DR 2.18 and Tan. B. II, 65.

⁸⁴ Mekilta Wa-Yassa' 1, 45a; Mekilta RS 72; Baba Kamma 82a; Targum Yerushalmi Exod. 15.22. As to the reading from the Torah, see vol. IV, p. 356. Comp. also the allegory concerning the tree quoted in note 82.

⁸⁵ Josephus, *Antiqui.*, III, 1.3; Mekilta Wa-Yassa' 1, 46b where מקולקל or מקולל is to be read instead of מהולל, in accordance with Mekilta RS 74 and MHG II, 170.

⁸⁶ Mekilta Wa-Yassa' 1, 46b; Mekilta RS 74; MHG II, 170-171. Josephus maintains that the quails episode took place at Elim (Exod. 19.12, *seq.*), where the people murmured on account of the dearth of water. His attempt to "improve" upon the legend, known to us from rabbinic sources, concerning the scant supply of water at Elim is rather a failure, as quails are a poor substitute for water. Philo, *Moses*, 1.34, against Josephus and the Midrashim, maintains that Elim was a place distinguished for its abundance of water and wealth of vegetation.

⁸⁷ Philo, *Moses*, 1.34; comp. the following note, where references to rabbinic and patristic sources containing the same allegory are cited. Concerning the symbolic significance of the palm-tree, see BR 40.6 and the parallel passages given by Theodor.

⁸⁸ Mekilta Wa-Yassa' 1, 46; Mekilta RS 74; MHG II, 171; Targum Yerushalmi Exod. 15.26 and Num. 33.9; Tertullian, *C.*

Marc., 4.24. The tragedian Ezekiel, 446 describes the appearance of a wonderful bird at Elim. The text is quite obscure, and it seems that the poet wanted to describe how it came about that the Israelites discovered the twelve wells at Elim. They followed the wonderful bird (phenix?), which, accompanied by many other birds—"for birds of every kind hovered in fear behind this stately form"—flew over the wells. In legends birds are frequently spoken of as guides to water.

⁸⁹ Philo, *Moses*, 1.35; Josephus, *Antiqui.*, III, 1.3–5. The Haggadah very frequently refers to the miracle in connection with the cakes they had taken along with them out of Egypt. See *e.g.*, Seder 'Olam 5; Mekilta Wa-Yassa' 1, 46b; Mekilta RS 74; Kiddushin 38a (the cakes tasted like manna); ShR 25.4; Mekilta Bo 14, 15a; Tan. Bo 9; Shir 1.8. Since ordinarily one partakes of two meals a day, the sources quoted above speak of the sixty-one meals which the cakes provided from the evening meal of the day of the exodus, *i. e.*, the fifteenth day of Nisan, till the fifteenth day of Iyar. Josephus, *Antiqui.*, III, 1.3, remarks that the provision they took along with them out of Egypt became exhausted after thirty days, whereas the rabbinic sources emphasize the fact that they took food of one meal that lasted them for a month.

⁹⁰ Mekilta Wa-Yassa' 1, 47a, the text of which is to be corrected in accordance with Mekilta RS 74. The Mekiltas quote an opinion according to which the Israelites spoke the truth when they declared that they enjoyed plenty of food in Egypt. As slaves of the royal household, they were supplied with food in plenty free of charge. For the status of Israel in Egypt see note 164 on vol. II, p. 334. On the three days of darkness see vol. II, p. 345, and vol. III, p. 390.

⁹¹ Philo, *Moses* 1.36.

⁹² ShR 25.4–5. That the manna, the well, and the other heavenly gifts which Israel received in the wilderness were rewards for Abraham's kindness and piety is very frequently mentioned in the Haggadah; see Tosefta Sotah 4.2–6; Baba Mezia 86b; BR 48.10; Mekilta Beshallah (פתיחתא), 25a; WR 24.8; PR 14, 57a; BaR 14.2; Kohelet 11.1; Tan. B. I, 87; ER 12.68.

⁹³ Mekilta Wa-Yassa' 2, 47a–47b; Mekilta RS 75; Sifre N., 89; Abkir in Yalkut I, 258; Yoma 76a; Sifre Z., 198; comp. also Philo, *Leg. Allegor.*, 56.

⁹⁴ PRE 3; Yerahmeel 1.3. The prevalent opinion, however, is that the manna was created in the twilight between the sixth day and the Sabbath; see Abot 5.6; Sifre D., 355; and the numerous references

cited in note 99 on vol. I, p. 83. Luria's suggestion, PRE, *ad loc.*, to read בין השמשות instead of ביום השני is not acceptable. It is obvious that the view of this Midrash is that the "bread of the angels" was created on the very same day on which the angels themselves were created (see vol. I, p. 16). Comp. also Targum Yerushalmi Exod. 16.15, and the following note.

⁹⁵ Tan. B. II, 67; this is the source of Makiri Ps. 78. 26. The idea that the manna is the bread of the angels is based on Ps. 78.25; see Septuagint, *ad loc.*; Wisdom 16.20; Yoma 75a, where this interpretation of לחם אבירים is maintained by R. Akiba. The colleague of the latter, R. Ishmael, however, strongly objects to the view that angels partake of food (comp. note 143 on vol. I, p. 243), and hence the change of "bread of the angels" to "bread prepared by angels" or "bread prepared in the place inhabited by angels", *i. e.*, in heaven. Comp. Targum Ps., *loc. cit.* See also vol. II, p. 173; vol. III, p. 117; Sibyl., proem 87, which reads: They will partake of the sweet bread coming from the starry heaven.

⁹⁶ Hagigah 12b.

⁹⁷ Mekilta Wa-Yassa' 4, 50b; Mekilta RS 78. In view of the statement in PK 5, 49b, and BR 48.10, one is inclined to assume that in the Mekiltas the expression לעולם הבא is used inaccurately instead of לעתיד לבוא, *i.e.*, the messianic times; see reference to Sibyl. at the end of note 95.

⁹⁸ Tehillim 78, 345; Tan. B. II, 67. In these sources the two interpretations of אבירים (Ps. 78.25) "the mighty", *i.e.*, angels, and אֵבָרִים "remaining in the body"—are blended together; comp. Yoma 75b; note 95; vol. III, pp. 246 and 278.

⁹⁹ Tan. B. II, 14 and 61 (text is corrupt); ShR 25.3; Yoma 75a; Sifre N., 89; Sifre Z., 197–198; Tosefta Sotah 4.3; Wisdom 16.21; Ephraem I, 218. See also Josephus, *Antiqui.*, III, 1.6; *Recognitiones*, 1, 35; ER 12.60; BHM VI.39; vol. III, p. 65.

¹⁰⁰ Mekilta Wa-Yassa' 3, 48b–49a; Mekilta RS 76; Tehillim 76, 346. The grains of the manna looked like pearls, and the ground upon which it fell was like a golden table; Yoma 75a.

¹⁰¹ Sifre N., 89; Sifre Z., 198; Mekilta Wa-Yassa' 3, 48b–49a; Mekilta RS 76. As to the meaning of אופסים in Mekilta, *loc. cit.*, see Löw in *Hoffmann-Festschrift*. 119–120, who takes it to be a corrupt form of אסקופים "threshold". The Bodleian MS. of the Mekilta has אספים, and a Genizah fragment of that Midrash in the same library reads אספיים.

¹⁰² Tan. B. II, 67; Sifre N., 89, and Sifre, Z., 197. A somewhat different view is found in Mekilta Wa-Yassa' 47b; Mekilta RS 75. Yoma 75a reads: For the pious the manna fell at the door of their tents; ordinary men had to go to the field and gather it; the wicked found it only after a laborious search.

¹⁰³ Midrash Tannaim, 191; Tan. B. II, 66–67; TargumYerushalmi Exod. 16.21 (read perhaps בני עממיא instead of ב׳ ישראל); Abkir in Yalkut I, 258, whose text of Mekilta Wa-Yassa' 2 (beginning) reads אין ראוי אלא לכם, which is in agreement with the Bodleian MS. of that Midrash, and Mekilta RS 75. See also Lekah, Exod. 16.21, according to which Targum Yerushalmi, *loc. cit.*, is to be emended to ומדין לאלהא דבני ישראל. Zohar II, 191b asserts that even the mixed multitude could not partake of the manna.

¹⁰⁴ Yoma 76a; Tehillim 23, 201; Tan. B. II, 66–67; Mekilta Wa-Yassa' 3, 49a–49b; Mekilta RS 77.

¹⁰⁵ Tan. B. II, 66; Yelammedenu No. 51 = BHM VI 87–88; Abkir in Yalkut I, 258; Tosefta Sota 4.3.

¹⁰⁶ Mekilta Wa-Yassa' 3, 49b; Mekilta RS 77; Yoma 76a. Comp. vol. III, p. 73.

¹⁰⁷ Yoma 75a, based very likely on Mekilta Wa-Yassa' 5, 51a, the correct text of which is found only in Mekilta RS 79. For the text of the Babli passage see Rabbinovicz, *ad loc.*, and R. Bahya on Exod. 16.31, who seems to have had the reading given by Rabbinovicz. Lekah and *Hadar*, on the other hand, have the same text as our editions. See also Zohar II, 63a

¹⁰⁸ Mekilta Wa-Yassa' 2, 47b, and 4–5, 50–51a; Mekilta RS 75 and 78–79; Tan. B. 67–68. Tosafot on 'Erubin 38b, caption ואין, maintain that according to some Midrashim one would have to assume that the manna did descend on the holy days; but the Tosafists, it seems, failed to establish their view.—As to the phrase "the new world", see the Apocalypse of Baruch 32.6. Concerning the manna as the food of the pious in the world to come, see vol. III, p. 44.

¹⁰⁹ Shabbat 118b. It is presupposed here that the commandment concerning the observance of the Sabbath was revealed at Alush, the place where the manna descended for the first time. This view is explicitly stated in Yerushalmi Yom Tob 2, 61a, and DR 3.1, whereas according to another opinion, the commandment concerning the Sabbath was given at Marah; see vol. III, p. 39; Seder 'Olam 5; Yerushalmi, *loc. cit.*, and references cited in note 83. The statement, Sifre Z., 66, that the Israelites observed one Sabbath only, very likely refers

18

to the first Sabbath they had observed at Marah before they arrived at Alush; comp. also Tehillim 92, 402. A Haggadah, which seems to be another version of the one given in the text, reads: If the Israelites would but observe one Sabbath, they would forthwith be redeemed from exile; see Shabbat, *loc. cit.*; Yerushalmi Ta'anit 1, 64a; Tehillim 95, 420; ShR 25.12; WR 3.1. See also the very interesting collection, of midrashic sayings (among them quotations from unknown sources) on the observance of the Sabbath as leading to redemption, in Shibbale Ha-Leket 96–97. That some Israelites desecrated the very first Sabbath was partly the fault of Moses who failed to communicate the law of Sabbath in proper time; Tan. B. II, 67. Comp. the following note.

110 Tan. B. II, 67; Tan. Tezawweh 11; Mekilta RS 78; ShR 25. 10. In the last-named source, as well as in WR 13.1, it is stated that Moses forgot to communicate in due time the laws of Sabbath to the people (see Exod. 16.23). This negligence on his part was due to his indignation and excitement on account of the wicked action of Dathan and Abiram. On other occasions, too, anger had a bad effect on Moses (comp. vol. III, pp. 192 and 413); this should serve as a warning to all to avoid anger, since even "the wisest of the wise" neglected his duty in time of anger. Comp. note 862.—As to the worms which betrayed the sinners, comp. Targum Yerushalmi and Midrash Aggada, on Deut. 21.8. A rather confused account of this legend is also found in the Koran 2.67.

111 Mekilta Wa-Yassa' 6, 51b, and Mekilta RS 80. Comp. vol. III, p. 7.

112 Mekilta Wa-Yassa' 5, 51b; Mekilta RS 80; Shekalim 6,49c. For further details concerning "the concealed objects", see vol. III, p. 161; vol. IV, pp. 24, 234, 282, 320, *seq.*, and 350. The oldest form of this legend knows only of three concealed objects which Elijah will restore; these are: three jugs, one filled with manna, another with water from the well of Miriam (this is how מים, Mekilta, *loc. cit.*, is to be understood; מי נדה of our editions is a later emendation; comp. PRK 32 a), and the third with the sacred oil. The τρισσὰ σήματα in Sibyl. 2.188 correspond literally to the שלשה סימנים of the Midrashim quoted above. Comp. vol. III, p. 303.

113 Mekilta Wa-Yassa' 5, 51b; Sifre D., 304; Seder 'Olam 9 and 10; Tosefta Sotah 11.10; Ta'anit 9a; Tan. B. IV, 2–3; Tan. Bemidbar 2; Mishle 14, 74; BaR 1.2 and 14.20 (towards the end); Shir 4.5; Hashkem 19b; Yelammedenu in Yalkut II, 15, 554, and 578, as well as

'*Aruk*, s.v. אפרכוס; PRK, 34b. Slight traces of this legend are to be found also in Philo's remark (*Moses*, 1.36) that God caused the manna to descend in order to honor the leader (Moses), etc. Ps.-Philo 21A writes: "And afterwards, when Moses was dead, the manna ceased to come down...And these are three things which God gave His people for the sake of three persons: the well of the water of Marah, for Miriam's sake (see note 82); the pillar of cloud, for Aaron's sake; the manna, for Moses' sake. And when these three came to an end, these three gifts were taken away." The agreement of ps.-Philo with the sources quoted above is to be noticed even in the phraseology.

114 Sode Raza in Yalkut Reubeni Exod. 16.14; comp. Zohar II, 191b.

115 Midrash Shir 36a. Comp. vol. III, p. 53.

116 Mekilta Wa-Yassa' 2–3, 47b–48b; Mekilta RS 76; Sifre N., 97; Yoma 75b, where the different kinds of quails are described. The Mekiltas are of the opinion that Exod. 16 13, *seq.*, and Num. 11.31, *seq.*, refer to the same event (see Friedman on Mekilta Wa-Yassa' 3, note 5), whereas ER 12.60 maintains that, as a reward for Abraham's hospitality (see vol. III, p. 43), God caused the quails to come down twice to the camp of Israel, once before the revelation at Sinai (see Exod., *loc. cit.*), and a second time after the revelation (see Num., *loc. cit.*). Philo, *Moses*, 1.37, presupposes that the quails came down regularly during Israel's wanderings through the wilderness. See also Sekel 212, and vol. III, pp. 245, 253, *seq.*

117 Yoma 75a–75b.

118 Berakot 48b. The prayer given in the text is the first bene-diction of Grace after Meals according to the Ashkenazic ritual. See also Hasidim 399, which reads: Before they ate the manna they pronounced the benediction: "Blessed art Thou, O Lord our God, King of the universe, who giveth bread from heaven." This is a slightly modified form of the benediction on bread, substituting 'heaven' for 'earth'.

119 Mekilta Beshallah (פתיחתא), 23a; comp. vol. III, pp. 7 and 48.

120 Mekilta Wa-Yassa' 6, 52a; Mekilta RS 80–81; Tan. Be-shallah 22; ShR 26.2; Targum Yerushalmi Exod. 17.1.

121 Tan. Beshallah 22. See Mekilta Bo (פתיחתא), 2a, and vol. III, pp. 125, 283.

122 Mekilta Wa-Yassa' 6, 51a-52b. Tan. Beshallah 21; ShR 26.2; Mekilta RS 81. In this connection the Midrashim just quoted remark, with reference to Exod. 17.6, that God indicated to Moses

the place where he should look for the presence of the Shekinah, namely, where the rock shows the imprint of a human foot. This strange statement is very likely the oldest reference to the religious significance of the dolmens, whose form is described here as being similar to that of the human foot (toes?). Is סֻלָּם ("ladder") perhaps to be read instead of אָדָם? Comp. note 27.

¹²³ ShR 26.2. Comp. vol. III, p. 311 (end of paragraph).

¹²⁴ Mekilta Wa-Yassa' 6, 52b; Tan. Beshallah 22; ShR 26.2. See Index, s.v. "Moses, Rod of".

¹²⁵ Seder 'Olam 5; Tan. B. IV, 127; comp. also references given in note 113.

¹²⁶ Mekilta Wa-Yassa' 5, 51b, and parallel passages given in note 311. The name "Miriam's well" is not found in tannaitic sources, but is of frequent occurrence in later literature; comp., *e.g.*, Shabbat 35a; WR 22.4; BaR 18.22; Tehillim 24, 206. Comp. also note 84.

¹²⁷ PRE 3; comp. note 94; vol. I, pp. 324 and 349, as well as vol. II, p. 291.

¹²⁸ Yalkut I, 764, on Num. 21.18, excerpted, perhaps, from Yelammedenu; see *Likkutim* (ed. Grünhut), IV, 58, and vol. I, p. 324.

¹²⁹ Tosefta Sukkah 3.11–13, and a somewhat different version in the unknown Midrash cited in Yalkut I, 426; BaR 1.2 and 19.26; Tan. B. IV, 3 and 127–128; Tan. Bemidbar 2 and Hukkat 21. Onkelos and Targum Yerushalmi Num. 21.16, *seq.*; Berakot 54b; Zohar II, 191b (the source of the last-named, if not Yalkut, *loc. cit.*, is the Midrash itself cited there); vol. III, pp. 338–339. I Cor. 10.4 has an allegory of this legend, wehereas ps.-Philo in 12C speaks of the well of water following them in the wilderness for forty years, and in 13A he refers to the well that followed them in the wilderness for forty years, going up with them into the hills and coming down into the plains. Comp. note 84. Ephraem 1, 263 is either based on ps.-Philo or on Jewish tradition communicated to him orally. Comp. Grünhut, *Likkutim*, II, 10a–10b, and IV, 58b; Meleket ha-Mishkan 97–98.

¹³⁰ Tan. B. IV, 127–128; Tan. Hukkat 21; BaR 19.26; Midrash in Yalkut I, 426; Yelammedenu in '*Aruk*, s.v. דכסמי. Comp. preceding note and Grünhut, *Likkutim*, IV, 49b.

¹³¹ Tan. B. III, 74–75, which has the additional statement that the Israelites will enjoy this gift in messianic times, and if not for their sins, they would have continued to enjoy it after they entered the Holy Land.

¹³² Tehillim 23, 200; Midrash Shir 36b, as quoted in Yalkut

II, 588, on Song of Songs 5; Yelammedenu in 'Aruk, s. v. אוף (comp.
Grünhut, Likkutim, IV, 44b); Shir 4.11; PK 10, 93b. In Shir 4.14
and in the sources cited in note 115 it is the manna which is said to
have served as a perfume. On other rival claims between the manna
and Miriam's well, see vol. III, p. 65, l. 13; concerning the tastes of
these heavenly gifts, see note 113 and vol. III, p. 44. Ephraem I,
287 A, follows the Haggadah which favors the well.
    133 Midrash Shir 37a. Sifre N., 95, asserts that the well contained
"fat fish."
    134 Shabbat 35a; Yerushalmi Kil'ayim 9, 32c (bottom); WR 22.4;
Kohelet 5.8; Tehillim 24, 206; Tan. B. IV, 128; Tan. Hukkat 21; BaR
19.26. In all these sources it is presupposed that the well like the
manna (see vol. III, p 44) will return in the time to come, and in PRE
51 we have a detailed description of the various services which the well
will render at that time. This, in the main, follows the Haggadah
recorded in vol. III, p. 53. Yelammedenu in Yalkut II, 15, on
Josh. 5, as well as II, 378, on Zechariah 9, is closely related to PRE.
See also Tosefta Sukkah 3.3–10; Sanhedrin 100a; Tan. Pinehas 14;
the statement, in Tan. and in Sanhedrin, concerning the potion of
healing in the time to come refers to the water of Miriam's well, as is
explicitly asserted in Tosefta, loc. cit. See further Kaftor wa-Ferah, 139.
    135 BaR 18.22; WR 22.4; Kohelet 5.8. A legend, mentioned by
many medieval authors, maintains that at the termination of the
Sabbath Miriam's well moves about from river to river from well to
well. It is therefore recommended to draw water at this time when
one might be fortunate to get the "healing water" of the miraculous
well. See Toratan shel Rishonim I, 59; Ha-Orah 230; Orehot Hayyim
Shabbat 69a. We very likely have here a legend in which different
elements are blended together. The drawing or drinking of water
at the termination of the Sabbath is undoubtedly connected with the
view that it is dangerous to drink water immediately before the termination of the Sabbath. The reason for the latter is because at that time the
souls of the departed take their last sip before returning to Gehenna
(comp. vol. V, p. 143, note 36), when the respite granted to them during
the Sabbath is at an end; see Tehillim 11, 102, and references given by
Buber. The story (John 5.4) about the pool and its heavenly power
is very likely connected with our legend about Miriam's well. See
also Tertullian De Anima 50.
    136 PK 2, 21a–21b; PR 12, 52a, and 13, 55a–55b; Tan. B. I, 41,
and II, 70–71; Tan. Beshallah 25 and Ki-Teze 9; Shabbat 118a (con-

cerning Amalek's attack on Israel as a punishment for the desecration of the Sabbath, see note 109); Mekilta RS 81–82; PRE 43; ShR 26.2; Sanhedrin 106a; Berakot 5,6; Mekilta Amalek 1, 53a–53b. Comp. also Yalkut I, 938 (end). Concerning the seven clouds, see vol. II, p. 374.

¹³⁷ PK 3, 26b; Tan. B. II, 71, and V, 40. The second etymology of the name is also found in Philo, *Leg. Allegor.*, 2.66, and in *De Cong. Quaer. Erud. Causa*, 11.

¹³⁸ Midrash quoted in *Da'at*, Exod. 17.18; a somewhat different version is given in *Hadar*: Esau made his son Eliphaz take an oath that he would kill Jacob and thus regain the birthright which Jacob had acquired through guile. Timna, the wife of Eliphaz, however, dissuaded him from attempting to take Jacob's life, pointing out to him the danger involved in measuring his strength against that of a hero like Jacob. Eliphaz followed his wife's advice, and had to content himself with taking away Jacob's possessions (see vol. I, pp. 345–347) without attempting his life. Esau, disappointed in his son, adjured his grandson Amalek to kill Jacob, but he, too, was persuaded by his mother Timna to let Jacob alone, pointing out to him that the descendants of Abraham were destined to serve the Egyptians, and the killing of Jacob would transfer the servitude upon Esau's children. As long as Israel was in Egypt, Amalek held his peace. But no sooner had the Israelites completed their term of servitude and left Egypt than they were attacked by Amalek. Sabba, Exod., *loc. cit.* 77a, on the other hand, quotes a Midrash according to which it was Timna who incited her son Amalek to attack Israel. See also vol. I, pp. 379 and 422–423; vol. III, pp. 272, 331, and 411; ER 24, 125–126, where it is stated that Eliphaz is to be blamed for having neglected the education of his son Amalek, who, unrestrained by his father, became wicked. Lekah Gen. 27.45 and Exod. 17.8 reads: Eliphaz, a pious and righteous man, refused to obey his father's command concerning Jacob. See also DR 2.29; Shu'aib, Zakor, 37c; Sekel 321; note 318 on vol. I, p. 421.

¹³⁹ Mekilta Shirah 11, 43a; Tan. Ki-Teze 9; comp. vol. III, p. 11.

¹⁴⁰ Mekilta Amalek 1, 53a; Mekilta RS 81–82; Midrash Tannaim 170; Tan. B. V, 40–41; Tan. Ki-Teze 9; PK 3, 26b; Josephus, *Antiqui.*, III, 12.1; Targum Yerushalmi Exod. 16.8, where sixteen miles are given as the distance between Amalek's place of settlement and the encampment of the Israelites. The army of Amalek consisted of four hundred thousand warriors (Gorion III, 27; Yashar Shemot, 147a, and *Dibre ha-Yamim* 11, give different numbers), each of whom re-

ceived great payment (Aggadat Shir 5, 46; text is corrupt). The war took place in the month of Iyar; Aggadat Esther 29; comp. vol. III, 272, and IV, p. 407. The ingratitude of Amalek is to be explained in accordance with the legend given in vol. I, p. 421.

¹⁴¹ PK 3, 27a–27b; PR 12, 52a-52b; Tan. B. V, 41–42 (read ‫נישול‬ ‫היה‬ ‫נינוח‬); Tan. Ki-Teze 9–10; Sifre D., 296; Midrash Tannaim 170; PRE 44; Targum Yerushalmi Exod. 17.8 and Num. 11.1, as well as Deut. 25.19. On the registers of the Jews kept in the Egyptian archives, see Mekilta Beshallah 1, 27; on the sinful Danites, see vol. III, pp. 171, 223, 232, 233, 244, 303, and vol. IV, p. 112; Sekel 321. Comp. also note 72, and Index, s. v. "Dan, Tribe of". The Christian legend accordingly declares the anti-Christ to be of the tribe of Dan. See Bousset, *Antichrist*, Index, s. v. "Dan". Even the early tannaitic sources use Amalek as a designation for Rome (see note 147), and in the legend Amalek's sneering at the Abrahamic covenant characterizes the attitude of the Romans (especially during the Hadrian persecutions) towards this very important ceremony; see notes 19 and 25 on vol. I, p. 315. In later literature Amalek, *i. e.*, Rome, stands for Christianity; see Zunz, *Synagogale Poesie*, 439, and *Literaturgeschichte*, 620. In the Kabbalah Amalek = Sammael = evil inclination; comp. Zohar III, 289b. It is highly interesting to observe that Justin, *Dialogue* 131, is acquainted with this use of the name Amalek. As to the refusal of the clouds to protect the sinners and those that were levitically impure, see Sifre N., 83; Targum on Song of Songs 2.5; vol. I, p. 242; vol. II, p. 375.

¹⁴² PR 12, 49a–50a, 53a, and 13, 54a–54b; PK 3, 28a–28b; Tan. B. 5, 43; Tan. Ki-Teze 10; Mekilta RS 87; Aggadat Esther 65, which reads: Only when the descendants of Rachel participated in war were the Israelites victorious. Comp. vol. I, p. 369; vol. IV, pp. 240–241. As to the contest between Joseph and Esau, see BR 99.2 and ShR 26.3.

¹⁴³ Mekilta Amalek 1, 53b; Mekilta RS 82; ShR 26.3; Targum Yerushalmi Exod. 17.9.

¹⁴⁴ Midrash quoted by R. Bahya on Exod. 16.9 and *Menot ha-Levi*, 69a. Comp. the similar legend in Yerushalmi Rosh ha-Shanah 3, 59a, to the effect that Amalek, who was a great magician, selected, for the attack on Israel, those of his warriors whose birthday was on the day of the battle. The reason for this was because "one is not easily slain on his birthday." Moses, however, confounded the course of the heavenly bodies (‫מזלות‬), and thus frustrated Amalek's device.

24

The last statement refers to Moses' causing the sun to stand still (see reference in note 146), so that Amalek's warriors were not certain as to the actual time of their birthday. See also We-Hizhir Exod. 34a; Yashar Shemot 147a; *Dibre ha-Yamim* 11.

145 Mekilta Amalek 1, 54a–54b; Mekilta RS 82–83; Targum Yerushalmi Exod. 17.10–13; PRE 44. Moses' hesitation is recorded in Exod. 17.9, where it is said that he waited a day before he undertook to attack Amalek. The haggadic explanation of the raising and the lowering of the hands (found also in Mishnah Rosh ha-Shanah 3.8) would seem to be directed against the Christian view, according to which it was a symbolic representation of the cross (see Barnabas 12.2; Justin, *Dialogue*, 90 and 91), but Philo, *Moses*, 1.39, offers an explanation which is similar to that of the Rabbis. Philo's other statement that Moses, before going to war, was sprinkled with the waters of purification is based on the correct assumption that in ancient Israel warriors had to be purified before going to war; see 1 Sam. 21.6 and comp. also the legends, vol. III, p. 57, line 17, note 849 and Index, s. v. "Purification"; Sifre D., 258. The statement of Bahir (quoted as Midrash by Nahmanides and Shu'aib on Exod. 17.11) that Moses lowered his hands because one should not pray with raised hands longer than three hours is perhaps intended to discourage this form of prayer which is so much in favor among Christians. On Joshua's war against Amalek, see vol. IV, pp. 3–4; concerning Hur see vol. III, p. 121; vol. IV, p. 158.

146 ER 2, 10; Tehillim 19, 167; Tan. Tezawweh 9; Sifre D., 306, reads The sun stood still as soon as Moses said: "Give ear, ye heavens." Comp. also note 947 and note 43 in vol. IV, p. 11. Concerning the different occasions when Moses caused the sun to stand still, see below note 245

147 Tan. B. V, 41 and 45; Tan. Ki-Teze 9 and 11; PK 3, 27a; PR 12, 52a; Mekilta Amalek 2, 55a, and 56a–56b; Mekilta RS 84–85; Tehillim 9, 86; Haserot in *Batte Midrashot* I, 32a. Comp. also the quotation from the Yerushalmi (not in our editions) in *Bet Yosef, Orah Hayyim* 137. In all these sources Amalek represents Rome; hence the reference to the destruction of the Temple by him; but comp. vol. III, p. 332 on the destruction of the first Temple by Amalek.

148 Mekilta Amalek 2, 56b; Mekilta RS 84; Tan. B. V, 44; Tan. Ki-Teze 11; PK 3, 28b; PR 12, 51a.

149 ER 24, 126. Comp. note 138.

150 Mekilta Amalek 2, 56a, the text of which is to be corrected in accordance with the reading in Mekilta RS 84 and Bodleian MS.

The conception "that God joins Himself unto His people when it suffers and when it rejoices" (vol. II, p. 88) is of frequent occurence; see Mekilta Bo 14, 16a; Mekilta RS 27; Sifre N., 84 and 161; Megillah 29a; Ta'anit 16a; Yerushalmi Sukkah 4, 54c; Ta'anit 1, 64a; Sanhedrin 4 (end); ShR 15.12 and 23.5; WR 9.3; BaR 2.2 and 7 (towards the end); DR 4.1; Ekah 1, 92 and 2, 110–111; ER 17, 89; Shemuel 4, 55; Tehillim 9, 89; 27, 223; 91, 401; Tan. B. III, 68 and 61, as well as IV, 9; Tan. Ahare 12; Aggadat Bereshit 71, 140; PK 5, 47a; Shir 4.7 and 5.2; BHM VI, 37. Comp. also vol. II, pp. 118, 187, 303, 374; vol. IV, p. 312. In practically all these passages two originally different conceptions are blended together: the primitive conception that the suffering of a people indicates the impotence of its god, and the mystic-religious one that the essence of God manifests itself in the history of mankind, and especially in the history of Israel. Accordingly God participates in the sorrows and joys of Israel. In Mekilta Bo, *loc. cit.*, and Sanhedrin 6.5, the second conception is expressed in an individualistic manner, and it is accordingly stated that the suffering of an individual, even of a sinner who suffers for his sins, causes God to grieve; comp. note 60. Later mystics frequently speak of the "exile of the Shekinah" (*Galut ha-Shekinah*) which each and every Jew ought to bewail more than any national calamity or his own misfortune.

[151] ShR 27.5; PK 3, 21a and 22a; Tan. B. II, 70; Shemuel 12, 81. It is said: Jethro was in Amalek's army, and after the defeat of the latter, he came to Moses. See also Mekilta Yitro 1, 56b–57a; Zebahim 116a; Yerushalmi Megillah 72b (bottom); ER 5, 30, where three different views are given concerning the time of Jethro's arrival: 1) he came immediately after the Red Sea had been crossed; 2) after the defeat of Amalek; 3) after the revelation at Sinai. Concerning Jethro's position at Pharaoh's court, see vol. II, pp. 254, 296; vol. III, pp. 11 and 74. See more details concerning Jethro vol. II, pp. 287–291.

[152] Mekilta Yitro 1, 58a; Mekilta RS 87.

[153] Tan. B. II, 73; Targum Yerushalmi and Midrash Aggada Exod. 18.6–7; Mekilta RS 87. Concerning the clouds which enveloped the camp, see vol. II, p. 375; vol. III, p. 57.

[154] Mekilta Yitro 1, 58a–58b; Mekilta RS 87; ER 5, 30; Targum Yerushalmi Exod. 18.6; Tan. Yitro 6. See also Zohar II, 69b (Jethro brought his sons with him to make them proselytes to Judaism); Lekah Exod. 18.5, whose text of the Mekilta seems to have been

different from ours. On the idea of attracting proselytes by kindness, see the remarks of Tan. B. I, 63–64; DZ 1 (= Yalkut I, 213); *Batte Midrashot* I, 45a. The Midrash quoted by R. Jacob of Coucy, SMG, positive precept 10, and negative precept 116, is identical with Tan., *loc. cit.*

¹⁵⁵ Mekilta Yitro 1, 58b; Mekilta RS 87 (the sentence about the importance of peace is taken from Perek ha-Shalom; comp. *Reshit Hokmah* end, who quotes it from that source), BHM III, 129.

¹⁵⁶ Mekilta Yitro 1, 58b–59a; Mekilta RS 87–88; Sanhedrin 94a; Tan. B. II, 71–72; Tan. Yitro 7; Targum Yerushalmi Exod. 18.8–11; Zohar II, 5a. Concerning the manna, the well, and the six gifts promised to Israel, see vol. III, pp. 44, 47, and note 132. Philo, *De Ebriet.*, 11, seems likewise to assert that Jethro did not become a proselyte to Judaism prior to his visit to Moses. Comp. the different view found in DR 2.26, and vol. III, p. 289, according to which Jethro had abandoned idolatry even before Moses came to Midian. Mekilta and Sanhedrin 94a seem to assume that Jethro's visit to Moses took place immediately after the Exodus, even before the crossing of the Red Sea; see note 151. As to the impossibility of escaping from Egypt, see note 3; Zohar III, 212a (the magic of Balaam made it impossible for anyone to escape); Shu'aib Wa-Era, 26d.

¹⁵⁷ Josephus, *Antiqui.*, III, 3.1.

¹⁵⁸ Mekilta Yitro 2, 59a; Mekilta RS 88; Sifre D., 38; Midrash Tannaim 30; Kiddushin 32b.

¹⁵⁹ Josephus, *Antiqui.*, III, 3.1.

¹⁶⁰ Lekah, Exod. 18.13; comp. also Pa'aneah *ad loc.*

¹⁶¹ Lekah Exod. 18.17.

¹⁶² Mekilta Yitro 2, 59b–60a; Mekilta RS 89–90. Concerning the seven qualifications of a judge, see Maimonides, *Yad, Sanhedrin*, 2.7, who very likely made use of an old source. Comp. Midrash Tannaim 95.

¹⁶³ Sifre D., 11–13; Midrash Tannaim 6–8. Comp. vol. III, 248, *seq.*, where the appointment of the seventy elders is described by the Haggadah in accordance with the rules governing the appointment of judges.—The appellative "son of Amram" is a derogatory one; see vol. III, pp. 109, 110, 118, 176, 177, 178, 273, 297, 310, 312, 349, 384, 432, 464, 476, 479; vol. IV, pp. 305, 306, 309. Tehillim 11, 45, and BaR 18.17 cite the scripture passages where David is called "son of Jesse", and remark that those who spoke of him in this manner

27

intended to slight him.   See also I Maccabees 16.15.—On the blessing of Moses see vol. III, pp. 187 and 454.

¹⁶⁴ Sifre D., 13–17; Midrash Tannaim 7–10.   As to the number of the judges and officers, see Sanhedrin, Mishnah 1 (end); Babli 17b–18a; vol. III, p. 383, and vol. IV, p. 95.   The number one hundred and twenty in Acts 1.15 is to be explained in accordance with Sanhedrin, *loc. cit.*   Josephus, *Antiqui.*, III, 4.1, in contrast to the view of the Rabbis, maintains that the people had to ratify the appointment made by Moses; but the Rabbis are of opinion that the people acted only in the capacity of advisers.   Comp. also Philo, *Moses*, I, 29; vol. III, p. 155.   In the tannaitic sources quoted above (as well as in 'Erubin 100b; Alphabet R. Akiba 19; ShR 30.10; DR 1.10; Midrash Tannaim 95) it is stated that Moses did not succeed in finding men for office who combined all these qualifications (on the nature of these qualifications, see above note 162 and Hashkem 7–10) of the ideal judge as described by Jethro.   On the respect due to a judge, see vol. III, p. 220.

¹⁶⁵ Mekilta RS 90–91, which is very likely taken from a version of Perek ha-Shalom different from ours; see Perek ha-Shalom in *Reshit Hokmah*, end (= BHM III, 125).   See also Midrash Tannaim 97; Hashkem 5a–5b.

¹⁶⁶ Mekilta Yitro 2, 60a, the text of which is to be corrected in accordance with Mekilta RS 91.

¹⁶⁷ Josephus, *Antiqui.*, III, 4.2.

¹⁶⁸ Sifre N., 78 and 80.   See a similar remark with regard to the daughters of Zelaphehad in vol. III, p. 394.

¹⁶⁹ Tehillim 78, 345–346; comp. vol. III, pp. 45–46.   Concerning Jethro's love for the Torah, see Sifre N., 78; Tan. Yitro 4; Sifre Z., 74; Mekilta RS 91.

¹⁷⁰ Sifre N., 78–80; Sifre Z., 76–78; Mekilta Yitro 2, 60a; Mekilta RS 91; Targum Yerushalmi Exod. 18.27.   Moses is described as king (of Israel) not only in the Midrashim quoted above, but also in many other passages; comp. vol. III, pp. 142, 153, 187, 188, 251, 286, 288, 296, 298, 384, 455.   See also Midrash Tannaim 213; Tan. Beshallah 2; Tehillim 1,3, where Deut. 33.5 is referred to Moses, who is thus described as "king in Jeshurun."   The Hellenistic writers Demetrius and Philo, as well as Justus of Tiberias, call Moses the king of the Jews; see Schürer, *Geschichte* (third edition) IV, 449.   Comp. also Ibn Ezra on Gen. 35.31.—Tosefta Bikkurim 1.2 and Yerushalmi 1, 64a, maintain

that the descendants of Jethro enjoyed the legal status of pure blooded Israelites and not of proselytes. Comp. note 783.

[171] Sifre N., 81, and D., 52; Sifre Z., 70; ARN 35, 105; Targum Yerushalmi Num. 10.32; Midrash Tannaim 5; Mekilta Deut. 5. In the text (vol. III, p. 73, end of second paragraph) Benjamin is to be read instead of Judah.

[172] Sifre Z., 76–77; Sifre N., 78, and D., 352; Mekilta Yitro 2 60a; Mekilta RS 91–92 (the descendants of Jethro abandoned their lucrative enterprises, and devoted themselves to the study of the Torah, supporting themselves by making pottery; comp. ARN 35, 105); Temurah 16a. Comp. vol. IV, p. 29.

[173] Mekilta Yitro 2, 60b; Mekilta RS 91–92; Sifre N., 78; Sifre Z., 77; Tan. Wa-Yakhel 8; PR 40, 167b. In Mekilta RS 85 Jonadab the Rechabite is censured for his friendship with Jehu (see 2 Kings 10.15, seq.) but the text is very likely corrupt. The parrallel passage in ARN 9,42 (second version 17,36) proves that it is Jonadab the nephew of David (see 2 Sam. 13.3) who is described in the Mekilta as wise but wicked. For further details concerning the descendants of Jethro see vol. III, p. 380.—The Holy Land, the Temple, and the Davidic kingdom were given to the Israelites conditionally, and they lost them as soon as they sinned; but the Torah, the priesthood, and the distinction of being called the Children of God were conferred upon the Israelites unconditionally. Israel therefore retained the latter gifts for ever. See Midrash Tannaim 39–40 and Ozar Midrashim I, 38–39 (read קריאת); but Mekilta Yitro 2, 60b, and Tehillim 132, 516, do not know of the last-named gift.

[174] Tan. B. II, 74–75; PK 12, 103b and 106a; see also Midrash Aggada Exod. 18.27. A conflicting view maintains that Jethro's visit to Moses took place before the revelation on Sinai; see note 151.

[175] PK 12, 106a; Tan. B. II, 75. Medieval authorities quote the following legend from an unknown Midrash. While the Israelites were still in Egypt it was announced to them that fifty days after the exodus from Egypt the Torah would be revealed unto them. As soon as they were redeemed from bondage, they were so eager for the arrival of the promised day that they began to count the days, saying each day: "Now we have one day less to wait for the revelation of the Torah." To commemorate this counting, the Torah has prescribed to count the days from Passover to the Feast of Weeks (comp. Lev. 13.15–16), the so-called "Counting of the 'Omer". See Shibbale ha-Leket 210, 236; Orehot Hayyim 84a, 5; Abudrahim, Sefirat ha-

'Omer; Shu'aib I, Pesah, 51c; Sabba, Emor 104c; comp. also R. Bahya Exod. 3.12.

¹⁷⁶ PK 12, 104a and 106a–107a; Tan. B. II, 75–76; Shir 2.5; BHM 6.45; comp. vol. II, p. 374, and vol. III, p. 213, The Torah is personified in the legend, which accordingly narrates that the Torah rejoiced in the fact that it would be given to Israel. See vol. III, p. 188.

¹⁷⁷ Mekilta Rs 97; Mekilta Bahodesh 3, 64a (on the number of Israelites necessary in order that the Shekinah might dwell in their midst, to which reference is made in the Mekilta, see also Sifre N., 84; Yebamot 64a; Ketubot 17a; Baba Kamma 83a); Tan. Yitro 9; Tehillim 119, 490; Semahot 7; DR 7.8; WR 13.2; BR 70. 9; PR, 198a–198b; ER 23, 124–24, 125; Zohar II, 78b, and III, 22b. Just as the "recipients of the Torah" and the place of its revelation were predestined and selected for various reasons, even so was the time of the revelation. The Torah was to remain in heaven for a thousand generations after the creation (see Ps. 105.8), and in view of the fact that "nine hundred and seventy-four generations" had elapsed before Adam was created (see note 5 on vol. I, p. 4), the time of Moses, the twenty-sixth generation after Adam, was the proper time for the revelation. See Zebahim 116a; Shabbat 88a; Tan., *loc. cit.;* Tehillim 105, 449; Aggadat Bereshit 49, 100; BR 28.4 and the numerous parallel passages cited by Theodor on "the thousand generations". Concerning the generation of the revelation, see also vol. III, pp. 109 and 313.—The time that elapsed from the creation till the revelation was the "time of Grace", since mankind without the Torah as a guide could only be sustained by the grace of God. See Pesahim 118a; Tehillim 136,519.

¹⁷⁸ PR 12, 106b, Tan. B. II, 74; BHM VI, 40; Ekah (פתיחתא) 20; Mekilta Bahodesh 1, 62a; Mekilta RS 94; Targum Yerushalmi 19.2; WR 9.9; PRE 41.

¹⁷⁹ PK 12, 105a–105b (אותיותיה משולשות "the number of the letters of the Hebrew alphabet are divisible by three", since it amounts to twenty-seven); Tan. B. II, 73; Tan. Yitro 10; Midrash 'Aseret ha-Dibrot 41–42.

¹⁸⁰ Shabbat 89a–89b; BHM VI, 90; Lekah, Exod. 19.18; Tan. IV, 7; Shir 4.4. Comp vol. II, p. 302.

¹⁸¹ Sifre D., 343, 142b; Midrash Tannaim 210; Mekilta Bahodesh 5, 67a, and 1, 62a; Mekilta RS 93; 'Abodah Zarah 2b; ER 24, 122; EZ 11, 192; Hashkem 2b; WR 13.2; PK 5, 43b and 32, 199b–200a; PR 33, 142a; 'Aseret ha-Dibrot 68; Tan. B. III, 28, and V, 54–55;

Tan. Berakah 4; Sifre D., 311; Baba Kamma 38a; Ekah 3.123; BHM VI 39; Zohar II, 91b, and 191a–192b; 4 Ezra 7.20–210; Apocalypse of Baruch 48, 40; ps.-Jerome, *Quaestiones in Jud.* 5.4–5. The idea underlying this widespread legend is that the heathen nations showed their unfitness to take upon themselves the yoke of the Torah by their immoral and lawless conduct, which knew no restraint, not even the seven restrictions imposed upon the children of Noah (see Index, s. v. "Noachian Laws"), which are the minimum of laws necessary for the maintenance of civilization. The people of the Torah is at the same time the boldest among the nations (as the dog is the boldest among the animals and the cock among the birds), ready to repel all attacks upon its teachings and doctrines; see Yom Tob 25b. Rashi, *ad loc.*, takes this talmudic passage to mean that Israel was given the Torah, in order that, by its discipline, it might soften the "hardness" of the people that is the "hardest" among the nations. This idea, though somewhat common in the rabbinic sources and in the New Testament (see *e. g.* Gal. 3.24), cannot be read into the passage of Yom Tob, *loc. cit.*—The six hundred and thirteen precepts of the Torah are frequently mentioned in the Talmudim and Midrashim, but are not found in tannaitic sources. Sifre D., 76 (נ׳מצות) refers to the three verses of Deut. 12.23–25 which contains the prohibition against the use of blood, and is not to be emended to תרי״ג מצות, as is done by Friedmann, *ad loc.*, while in the parallel passage (Midrash Tannaim 53) the word מאות after נ׳ is to be stricken out. In Mekilta Beshallah 5, 57a, בתרי״ג is a later addition, as may be seen from the parallel passage in Sifre D., 343. MHG I, 226, has תרי״ג מצות in the dictum of the Tanna R. Eliezer the son of R. Jose ha-Galili.—Concerning the refusal of the nations to accept the Torah, see also vol. III, pp. 205, 341, 454, and vol. IV, p. 307.

    [182] Abkir in Yalkut I, 276; BHM VI, 40–41; ER 6,35, where Adam and Noah, too, are cited as examples of piety. On Joseph, see vol. II, p. 183, and vol. III, p. 201.

    [183] Targum and Tosefta Targum Jud. 5.5; Targum Ps. 68.16–17; BR 99.1; Tehillim 68, 318; PR 7, 27a; Mekilta Bahodesh 5, 66b; Yelammedenu in Yalkut II, 47, and in Makiri Prov. 29, 85b; ʿAseret ha-Dibrot 66. On the reward of "the modest Sinai", see also vol. III, p. 304.

    [184] Tehillim 68, 318; comp. vol. IV, p. 197. In the time to come God will cause the heavenly Jerusalem to descend upon these four mountains: Tabor, Hermon, Carmel and Sinai; see the quotation from an unknown Midrash (Yelammedenu?) in Makiri Is. 52, 195,

31

and a similar statement in Yelammedenu in Yalkut II, 319, on Isa. 2 (here, probably owing to a printer's error, Hermon is missing, and the heavenly Jerusalem is substituted, as is often the case, by the Temple; see Vol. V, 292, note 141), as well as *Zerubbabel* (ed. Wertheimer, 12a) according to which a fifth mountain, Lebanon, is to share this glory. Comp. also Tehillim, *loc. cit.*

185 BR 99.1; comp. vol. II, p. 303 on the "cleanliness" of the thorn bush. The revelation of the Torah did not take place in the land of Israel, but in the wilderness. By this God showed that the Torah was not given exclusively to Israel, but to all the inhabitants of the earth. For the same reason the Torah was not revealed secretly, but openly, in the presence of all mankind (comp. vol. III, p. 91); see Mekilta Beshallah 1, 62a (פנגוס = φέναξ, "swindler", *i.e.*, acting in a stealthy manner), and 5, 67a; Midrash Tannaim 209. Comp. also Tan. B. IV, 7; Tan. Bemidbar 6; BaR 1.7. According to Philo, *De Decalogo*, 1, the wilderness was selected as the place for the revelation because the cities are defiled by the impious and iniquitous conduct of men towards God and their fellows. For a similar view on the cities see note 181 on vol. II, p. 351.

186 Tehillim 68, 318, and reference given in note 184. The explanation of the word Moriah as the place whence the teaching of God went forth (see BR 55.7, and the numerous parallel passages cited by Theodor, as well as note 253 on vol. I, p. 285) presupposes, perhaps, the legend that originally Sinai formed part of Moriah; see Tosafot and R. Isaiah di-Trani on Ta'anit 16a.

187 'Aseret ha-Dibrot 66 (read נדולים...במשפחה); *Batte Midrashot* IV, 34; Mekilta Bahodesh 9, 72a; Sotah 5a; Yelammedenu in Yalkut II, 960, on Prov. 22. Different opinions are expressed as to whether Moses acted rightly or not in covering his face at the appearance of God in Horeb (see Exod. 3.6). According to one view this was an act of humility for whicn he was rewarded, while according to another he was punished for his reluctance to accept the distinction conferred upon him. See Berakot 7a; ShR 3.2 (and the parallel passages given on the margin). Comp. also Ecclesiasticus 50.11; vol. III, pp. 137, 209, as well as vol. II, p. 305.

188 Mekilta RS 94; Sifra 1.1; MHG II, 203; Mekilta Bahodesh 2, 62a; Shabbat 86b–88a (different opinions are given here as to whether the revelation took place on Friday, the sixth of Sivan or on the Sabbath, the seventh of that month; but all agree that בחדש, Exod. 19.1, means "the new moon" and not "the month"; comp. Seder 'Olam 5,

and the references given by Ratner); Targum Yerushalmi Exod.
19.2–3. Jub. 1.1, in opposition to this view, maintains that the Torah
was revealed on the fifteenth of Sivan.—Concerning the distinction
of the third month as compared with all the other months of the year'
see vol. III, pp. 78–79, and the sources quoted in note 179, to which
the following should be added: BHM VI, 40; PR 20, 95a–96a; Tan. B.
II, 76; PK 12, 107a. These read: The Torah was given in the month
of Sivan when Gemini are in the Zodiac, to indicate that it does not
belong to Israel alone, but also to his twin brother Esau (that is, the
Gentiles). Comp. notes 181 and 185.

¹⁸⁹ Mekilta RS 94 (read אמהות instead of בנים): Moses received
this distinction for the sake of the fathers and the mothers; see Index,s.v. "Mothers, Merits of"; ShR 25.2; 1 and 2 Targum Yerushalmi
Exod. 19.3. Comp. also Shabbat 87a; Sifre N., 99; Mekilta Bahodesh 2, 62b. The statement in Mekilta RS, *loc.cit.*, that "everything"
was done for the sake of Jacob is also found in Yalkut I, 276. See
note 35 on vol. I, p. 317; Index s.v. "Jacob, the Merits of."

¹⁹⁰ ShR 25.2; PRE 41. These sources remark: Because men
do that which women wish them to do. See also Philo, *De Ebriet.*
13: Women adhere to customs.

¹⁹¹ Mekilta Beshallah 2–3, 62b–64b, and 9, 72a (concerning the
employment of the Hebrew language by Moses, referred to in this
passage, see also Sifre N., 39, and the parallel passages cited by Friedmann,as well as Mekilta D. 4, where the meaningless ובסתרים is to be emended to ובסדרים "in proper order", as in Mekilta, *loc. cit.*); Mekilta RS
94–96; Targum Yerushalmi Exod. 19.4–7. Comp. note 242. Concerning the honor due to the elders, see vol. II, pp. 330 and 363–364. As to
the view that God's messengers return to Him and make their report as
soon as they have carried out His command, comp. Mekilta Bo (פתיחתא)
2a and Midrash Tannaim 210. Philo, *Moses*, 1.27, explains the
designation of Israel as a kingdom of priests to mean that Israel works
for the salvation of all mankind. A similar remark is found in Alphabet of R. Akiba 28 ('ז): The righteous among the Gentiles act as the
priests of God. The proverb that "hearing is not like seeing" is found
also in Philo. *De Special. Leg., De Judice* 2, and *De Confusione Ling.*
27. Comp. also *Vita Mosis* I, 49; Herodotus, I, 8. As to the application of this proverb to the revelation of the Torah, see PR 41, 174a;
Shir 1.2. Moses went beyond that which he was commanded by
God: he was asked to tell the people to observe "two days of preparation, prior to the revelation of the Torah, but he added a third

day. God, however, submits to the words of the pious, and the state-ment of Moses was not altered.   See BHM VI, 41, which, in the main, follows Shabbat 87a.   Comp. note 239.

¹⁹² Mekilta RS 96–97 (is this the source of Meiri, *Magen Abot*, 61?); Keritot 9a; Gerim 2; Mekilta Bahodesh 3, 63b–64a.   The ab-lution before the revelation is also referred to by Philo, *De Decalogo*, 11; Yebamot 46a; Yerushalmi Shabbat 9, 12a.

¹⁹³ Lekah Exod. 24.5; ER 9, 52.   These read: The innocent youth, though not of priestly descent are worthy to offer sacrifices upon the altar.   Comp. vol. III, p. 93 and note 205, for the dissenting view as to who "were the priests" on that day.

¹⁹⁴ Mekilta Bahodesh 3, 63b; Mekilta RS 96–97 (this source does not know of the view found in the Mekilta that twelve pillars were erected, one for each of the twelve tribes); Targum Yerushalmi Exod. 24.4.   As for the exact nature of these sacrifices, see Hagigah 6a; Midrash Tannaim 57; Sifre N., 143.

¹⁹⁵ Midrash Tannaim 56–57; WR 6.5, which contains the addi-tional remarks that the angel assumed the form of Moses (probably a reminiscence of the legend, given in vol. II, p. 282, that Michael assumed the form of Moses), and that one half of the blood became black, while the other remained red; Haserot 41 in Leket Midrashim 11. *Hadar*, Exod. 24.6, has Gabriel instead of Michael.   Comp. In-dex under the names of these two angels.   WR explicitly states that one half of the blood was sprinkled upon the people; but the tannaitic sources (Midrash Tannaim 57 and Mekilta Bahodesh 3, 63b), as well as the Tar-gumim on Exod., *loc. cit.*, maintain that the blood was sprinkled upon the altar "to atone for the people."   It seems that the older sources at-tempted to combat the Christological doctrine of the atoning power of blood, derived in Hebrews 9.19–22 from the sprinkling of the blood upon the entire people and the book.   The last part of the statement is entirely unknown in rabbinic sources.   The remark that "there is no atonement without blood", made in *Hadar* in this connection, is a sacrificial law often referred to in the Halakah; see *e.g.*, Sifra 1.4 and Yoma 5a.—Opinions differ greatly as to the nature of the book of the covenant which Moses read to the people on this occasion; see Midrash Tannaim 56 and Mekilta, *loc. cit.*   As to the view that this book was the Torah (in its entirety), see 1 Macabees 1.57, where the Book of the Covenant is used as a synonym for the Torah.   Concern-ing the covenant, see further Mekilta Mishpatim 20. 102a; Sifre D., 104; Midrash Tannaim 75; but Tan. Nizzabim (beginning) and Tan.

B. V, 49, offer a somewhat different version of the Haggadah about the covenant. See also, on the covenant, Tosefta Sotah 8.10; Babli 37b; Yerushalmi 6, 21c; Hagigah 6a–6b; Mekilta Mishpatim 20, 102a; Lekah Deut 2.99. In Nedarim 25a it is pointed out that Moses told the people that no mental reservation would avail them, since their oath of allegiance to God would have to be taken in conformity with the meaning which He Himself assigns to it.

¹⁹⁶ Shir 1.4; Tehillim 8, 76–77; 'Aseret ha-Dibrot 68 (according to this source, Abraham's sin consists in having loved Ishmael); BHM VI, 42; Mekilta RS 100; Mishle 6,53 (here Israel offers the heavens, the earth, and the mountains as guarantors; but God rejects them because they are to perish in the time to come; see vol. III, pp. 431–432); an unknown Midrash quoted by Shu'aib, Wayyigash, 21a. On the sins of Abraham and Jacob, see vol. I, pp. 235, 411; vol. V, pp. 228, 316; on the children in their mothers' wombs see vol. III, p. 34. Concerning the death of infants as a punishment or atonement for the sins of their parents, see Shabbat 32b; Midrash Shir 13a; Hashkem 3a–5a. Until the revelation of the Torah God visited the sins of the generation upon all alike, without discriminating between the righteous and the wicked—many a "Noah" died in the deluge, and many an innocent child perished with the builders of the tower—but after the revelation of the Torah punishment and reward are meted out to each and every individual according to his merits; see Tan. Re'eh 3.

¹⁹⁷ Mekilta RS 94; ARN (beginning); ShR 28.2; Yerushalmi Targumim Exod. 19.13 (*Hadar*, Exod. 34b, top, is based upon 2 Targum Yerushalmi). Concerning the heavenly punishment by fire, see also Targum Yerushalmi Num. 1.51, 3.10 and 38. In contrast to the Yerushalmi Targumim, Mekilta Bahodesh 3, 64 understands Exod. 19.12–13 to refer to punishment by the hand of man.

¹⁹⁸ Mekilta RS 85 and 99 (on the sounds see below, note 213); Mekilta Yitro 1, 57a, and Bahodesh 3-4, 64b–65a, as well as 5, 67a–67b; Zebahim 116a; Mishle 21,90; PR 20,95a; PRE 41; Nispahim 55; Josephus, *Antiqui.*, III, 5, 2–3 (the address of Moses to the people presupposes that the book of the covenant mentioned in Exod. 24.7 is identical with the part of the Pentateuch from Gen. 1.1 to Exod. 19; comp. the references cited in note 195); 4 Ezra 3.18–19. In the last-named source it is stated that the "four gates of heaven" opened on that occasion; see a similar remark in BHM VI, 41-42, but in this passage קולות ד' is very likely to be read; comp. Mekilta Bahodesh 3, 64b (bottom). Lengthy descriptions of the violent motions of the

entire universe at the time of the revelation of the Torah are given by ps.-Philo 11.5; 15.6; 23.10; 32.7–8. Obviously Jud. 5.4–5 and Hab. 3.3, *seq.*, served as models for these descriptions as well as for those found in rabbinic sources. Comp. also vol. III, 95–96.

¹⁹⁹ PR 21, 99b–100a, where it is also remarked that the earth feared lest the revelation of the Torah should increase the sinfulness of man and thus cause the destruction of the world. Comp. vol. I, p. 55.

²⁰⁰ PRE 41; Shir 1.12 and 5.3. Concerning the description of God as the "bridegroom of Jacob's daughter" (*i.e.*, Israel), see DR 3.12 and Aggadat Bereshit 41, 126 (נסם, Exod. 20.10, is here derived from נסא = נשא "to marry"), which is the source of Mahzor Vitry 311. Some rabbinic sources speak of Israel as the bridegroom and of the Torah as the bride, at whose wedding God (and Moses) acted as best man; see *Orehot Hayyim* II, 67; ShR 41.6; Epstein, *R. Moses ha-Darschan* 42–43.

²⁰¹ Mekilta Bo (פתיחתא) 2a and Bahodesh 4, 65b; Mekilta RS 101; Sifre N., 116 (comp. Friedmann, note 22); Yerushalmi Targumim Exod. 21.19; Berakot 45a. Concerning Moses' powerful voice, which could be heard throughout the entire camp, see Aggadat Shir 32 and note 228 on vol. II, p. 370; note 521. The later authorities (Jewish as well as mohammedan; comp. Goldziher, *La Notion de la Sekina*, 12) employ the expression "The Shekinah spoke through Moses' mouth", which is very likely nothing more than a striking paraphrase of this statement of the Mekilta. Philo, *Quis......Haeres Sit*, 5, seems to have shared this view. The Targumim mentioned above speak of "the heavenly music" heard on this occasion, and in all likelihood this is the meaning of ps.-Philo 11.3, who refers to the "music of the instruments sounding aloud" at the revelation on Sinai.

²⁰² Mekilta RS 100; Mekilta Bahodesh 3, 65a (top); Shabbat 88a and 129b; 'Abodah Zarah 2b; Midrash Shir, 44a; Shir 8.5; Tehillim 75, 337, and 76, 342; Tan. Noah 3. It is stated: "Israel was willing to accept the written Torah, but not the unwritten, and God was therefore obliged to use force (this Midrash is the source of *Or Zarua'* 1, 7a; *Hadar* and *Da'at*, Exod. 19.17); PRE 41. Concerning the idea that the existence of the world is conditioned upon the acceptance of the Torah, see also Shir 1.90; PR 21, 99b–100a; Midrash Aggadah Lev. 25.1. Note 26 and note 8 on vol. I, p. 50.

²⁰³ Shabbat 88a (this passage speaks of two crowns instead of the crown and the girdle of the other sources); PR 10, 37a; 21, 103b,

28, 154a; PRE 27 (equipped with these gifts they became like angels);
Tehillim 91, 397, and 103, 435; ShR 45.2 and 51.8; Shir 1.3, 4.13,
and 8.5; Tan. Tezawweh 11 and Shelah 13; Tan. B. IV, 76, and II,
25, 99; BaR 16. 25; PK 16, 124b; EZ 4, 179; Ekah (פתיחתא) 24.24
and 2.117–118; 'Aseret ha-Dibrot 68; BHM VI, 46; Makiri Tehillim
50, 275. Yelammedenu in Recanati Ki-Tissa has a version of this
legend which differs essentially from that found in the other sources.
Sabba, Zaw, 95c, reads: They lost the second crown in Jeremiah's
time, when they refused to listen to the word of God, See also *Menorat
ha-Maor* III, 1.5, which quoted an unknown Midrash. Comp. vol.
III, p. 132.

²⁰⁴ PR 21, 101a and 102a; comp. *Hadar*, Exod. 33.7, and PRE
41 (end). As to the other explanations of Moses's shining face, see
vol. III, pp. 119, 137. 143, 438. The crowns as well as the other
heavenly gifts are said to have been the reward given to the Israelites
for their willingness to accept the Torah before they knew its contents.
This willingness they expressed in the words "All that the Lord hath
spoken will we do as soon as we have heard it" (see Exod. 24.7; ונשמע,
literally, we shall hear). This attitude is often referred to as the highest stage ever reached by Israel in the religious development; see,
e.g., Shabbat 88a; Gittin 7a; Tan. B. II, 11, and III, 94. There is
however, a dissenting view, according to which the Israelites, even
at the moment when they expressed their willingness to accept the
Torah, were employing nice words without intending to fulfil them;
see Mekilta Mishpatim 13, 89b–90a; Tosefta Baba Kamma 7.9;
Tan. B. I, 77; WR 6.1; DR 7.10; ShR 42.8.

²⁰⁵ PRE 41; ShR 28.3; Mekilta RS 102; Mekilta Bahodesh 4,
65b–66a; BaR 12.7; PR 5, 20b,. Concerning the first-born as priests,
see vol. I, pp. 320, 332, and comp. (on the other hand), Zebahim 115b,
and vol. III, p. 88 (bottom); note 139. The sources quoted at the beginning of this note, as well as Ephraem I, 222D, maintain that Nadab and
Abihu performed the priesly service not only on this occasion but also
previously.

²⁰⁶ PRE 41; Nispahim 55. The legend of the "ascent of Sinai"
is also found in Philo, *De Decalogo*, 11, and in several of the sources quoted in note 202. Concerning the ten revelations (literally, "descents")
of God, see BR 38.9 and parallel passages quoted by Theodor. The individual opinion of a Tanna who flourished about the middle of the second
century is quoted: The Shekinah never descended upon the earth,
nor did Moses and Elijah ever ascend to heaven; the heavenly voice

heard on Sinai made it seem as though the glory of God descended upon the mountain; comp. Mekilta Bahodesh 4, 65b, and Sukkah 5a, where instead of כבוד ("glory") שכינה ("Shekinah") is used. Comp. notes 296, 919, and note 32 on vol. IV, p. 200.

²⁰⁷ Aggadat Shir 1.14; PR 21, 202b–203a; ER 22, 119; PR 12, 107b; Tan. Zaw 12; Tan. B. II, 76–77; III, 20; IV, 13; ShR 29.8; BHM V, 68; Tehillim 68, 318–319; Targum Ps. 68.18.   On the crowns see vol. III, pp. 92–93, and on the piety of the Levites comp. vol. III, p. 130.   The slaves and bondwomen who were present at the revelation of the Torah on Sinai saw more of the Glory of God than the prophets Isaiah and Ezekiel; Mekilta Bahodesh 3, 64a; see a similar remark in Tehillim, *loc. cit.;* comp. also vol. III, pp. 94, 106, 227 and 230.

²⁰⁸ PR 21, 203b; PK 12, 108a.

²⁰⁹ PR 21, 105–106a, where numerous explanations of the "first word" *Anoki* are given; BHM VI, 42; ER 1, 22; Midrash 'Aseret ha-Dibrot 47.   Comp., however, vol. II, p. 300, where it is said that the Israelites spoke the Hebrew language in Egypt; see also note191. On the use of the word *Anoki* in God's revelations to the patriarchs, see PR 33, 153a, and note 140 on vol. I p. 352.

²¹⁰ 'Aseret ha-Dibrot 69–70, which is based on old sources; see Tosefta 'Arakin 1.10 (on the twelve miles, the extent of the camps, see 'Erubin 55a, as well as note 445 and Index, s. v. "Camps, Extent of"); Sifre D., 313; Mekilta Beshalah 2, 63b and 9, 71b; Shabbat 88b; Tehillim 31, 338 (God enabled the idols to worship Him, *i. e.,* the whole of nature recognized God's power); 68, 317–318; 119, 490–491; Midrash Shir 2b; BHM VI, 42; ER 22, 119–120; Shir 1.2 and 4.4; Targum Yerushalmi Exod. 20.2; Mahzor Vitry 320 (probably based on Midrash Shir 2a, or 'Aseret ha-Dibrot, *loc. cit.*); Shu'aib, Yitro, 33b (his source seems to be a text of Shir 2.4 different from ours; comp. his quotation, in Bemidbar, 73b, from "Midrash Hazita").   Ps.-Philo 23.10 and 32.7–8 is acquainted with several features of this legend; comp. above note 198.—Concerning the angels who accompanied God on mount Sinai, see vol. III, pp. 92 and 94.   Some sources, however, maintain that there were no angels on mount Sinai, since even these heavenly beings, had they been near there at that time, would have been burned by "the words"; PR 33, 156a–156b; comp. also note 248.—Each of the two hundred and forty-eight members of the body urge man, saying: "Fulfil God's commandment", and each of the three hundred and sixty-five days of the years likewise says: "Beware of the prohibition decreed

by God"; See PK 12, 101a; Tehillim 32, 244. On the six hundred and thirteen laws of the Torah see above, note 181. Concerning the dew which quickens the dead, see note 22 on vol. I, p. 10, and Index, s.v. "Dew". Shabbat 88b, Midrash Shir 7a, 38b, 44b, and Zohar II, 84b, speak of the heavenly fragrance that spread over Israel at the time of the revelation. The purpose of this fragrance was very likely to restore the breath of life to the dead bodies. Comp. ps.-Philo 32.8, which reads: Then—at the giving of the Torah—did paradise give forth the fragrance of its fruits.

211 Mekilta Bahodesh 2, 66b, and Shirah 4, 37b.

212 Mekilta RS 103–104; MHG II, 215; Mekilta Mishpatim 20, 102a. Comp. also ps.-Philo 11.2, which reads: For men might say: "We have not known Thee, and therefore have not served Thee." I will therefore take vengeance upon them, because they have known My laws. This is given by the author as a comment on the first commandment of the Decalogue.

213 ShR 29. 9, which has the additional remark that the voice heard on Sinai had no echo. With regard to this voice, the following statement of the Jewish philosophers is to be noted. "God", says Philo, *De Decalogo*, 9, "commanded that an inaudible voice be formed in the air." The very same view is expressed by Sa'adya Gaon (quoted by Judah b. Barzillai, 314) and R. Judah ha-Levi, *Al Khazari*, I, 89. A Christian parallel to this legend concerning the complete standstill of nature is the one given in *Protevangelium of James* 18, in connection with the birth of Jesus. The Jewish legend evidently wishes to emphasize the fact that the revelation came directly from God; comp. note 248, and vol. IV, p. 198.

214 ShR 5.9 and 28.6; Shabbat 88b; Tehillim 68, 317, and 92, 403; Tan. B. II, 13–14; Tan. Shemot 25; Midrash Shir 2b; BHM VI, 39 and 45; Yelammedenu in Yalkut II, 709 and 843 on Ps. 19 and 92, respectively. In all these sources "the seven voices" (*i.e.*, sounds or tones) which were heard on Sinai are referred to, whereas in Berakot 6b and BHM V, 33 mention is made of only five voices, and in BHM VI, 41 (read 'ד instead of 'ה; comp. Judah b. Barzillai, 130–131, and note 198) the number is still futrther reduced to four. The seven sounds of the trumpet at the resurrection referred to in BHM VI, 58, are modelled after the seven sounds on Sinai. The seventy tongues stand for all the languages of the world; see vol. I, p. 173 and note 72 pertaining thereto.

215 ShR 28.6; Tan. Yitro 11; PRE 41; Lekah V. 99, where it is

said that the same happened at the second covenant; concerning which see vol. III, p. 89. The idea underlying this legend is related to one of the legends given in vol. III, pp. 141–142.

²¹⁶ PK 12, 110a–110b; PR 21, 100b–102a, and 33, 155b; BHM VI, 39–40; Midrash Shir 39b; ShR 5.9 and 28.6; Tan. B. II, 13–13; Philo, *De Posterit. Caini*, 43. See also Mekilta Shirah 4, 37b; v. VI, 359–360. In the Decalogue the singular is used (*e.g.*, I am the Lord *thy* God, and not *your* God), in order that everyone should say: On my account the world was created, and on my account the Torah was given. One righteous man is more precious in the sight of God than the whole of mankind: see ER 25, 126–127 (whence Lekah V, 17–18) and similarly Philo *De Decalogo* 10. Comp. also Sanhedrin, Mishnah 4.5, and Babli 103b, as well as ARN 31, which read: The soul of one righteous man weighs as much as the whole world. See note 8 on vol. I, p. 50. For other explanations of the use of the singular in the Decalogue see note 306 and PR 21, 106b. At the time of the revelation complete harmony existed in Israel (see vol. III, p. 79), the entire nation having only one mind and therefore addressed by God as one person; Zohar III, 84.

²¹⁷ Mekilta 6, 67a–68b; Mekilta RS 105–106 (the Haggadot given in this passage concerning the five kingdoms are also found in BIIM VI, 44, and Midrash Aggada Exod. 20.5); Targum Yerushalmi, Ephraem, and Theodoretus on Exod. 20.3–6. See also ps.-Philo 11.6, which reads: I am the Lord thy God, a jealous God, visiting the sins of them that sleep upon the living children of the ungodly, if they walk in the ways of their fathers. Comp. note 251.

²¹⁸ Targum Yerushalmi Exod. 20.6. Theodoretus and Vulgate, *ad loc.*, agree with this view that the second commandment forbids not only a false oath, but also swearing in vain. Comp. Yerushalmi Shebu'ot 3, 34c for the halakic discussion of this point.

²¹⁹ Yalkut Reubeni Gen. 1.1,2b, quoting Sode Raza; Zohar II, 91b; Ma'asiyyot 111; Raziel 11a (beginning ועתה אשכילך); comp. vol. IV, p. 96. God said to the Israelites: "Swear not falsely, that your young children die not on account of this"; BHM VI, 44, which, in the main, follows Shabbat 32b; comp. note 196. Besides this punishment for swearing falsely, Shabbat, *loc. cit.*, mentions many other afflictions. Comp. also ps.-Philo 11.7, which reads: Thou shalt not take the name of the Lord thy God in vain, that My ways be not made vain. This is very likely a mistranslation of the Hebrew, which read: לא תשא את שם יי אלהיך לשוא אשר לא ישיא דרכי, "Thou

shalt not take the name of the Lord thy God in vain, that the roads of My land (literally, that My roads) become not desolate." See Shabbat 33a, which has: On account of swearing falsely or swearing in vain the roads become desolate. Perhaps the original read אשיא "I shall not make desolate."

²²⁰ Alphabet of R. Akiba 14 (אל"ף 7) and the second version 63 (ז"ן ש"ת), which has the additional remark that the joy of Sabbath is one-sixtieth of the world to come. The source for this statement is Berakot 57b.

²²¹ BR 11.8; PR 23, 117b. The view that "everything was created in pairs" is a favorite with the Gnostics, but is also found in pseudepigraphic, rabbinic, and patristic writings. See Clementine *Homilies* 19.12 and *Recognitiones* 3. 59, 8.53; Apocalypse of Baruch 69.3–4; Lactantius, *De Ira Dei*, 13; Tertullian *Adversus Omnes Haereses*, 4; The "Midrash Temurah", is, as the name indicates, entirely devoted to the explanation of the doctrine of syzygies. Comp. Joel, *Blicke*, I, 7, 161, and Ginzberg, *Jewish Encyclopedia*, II, 114, s. v. "Clementina, ".—The variants in Exod. 20.8 and Deut. 5.12 gave rise to many a haggadic interpretation; comp. Shebu'ot 20b, which reads: *Zakor* ("remember") and *Shamor* ("observe") were uttered as one word, a feat which cannot be achieved by the human voice; Mekilta Bahodesh 6, 69a; Midrash Tannaim 21. In the last named source the statement quoted from Shebu'ot is applied as a solution for many other contradictions occurring in Scripture, as, *e.g.*, the one discussed in Matthew 12.5. See also Bahir 57, which is the source of Zohar I, 48b; II, 92a; III, 92b, 224a; Nahmanides, *Emunah u-Bittahon*, 19. Medieval authorities quote the Midrash זכור בים ושמור ביבשה "*Remember* while thou art at sea, and *observe* while thou art on dry land" (on the sea it is often impossible to observe the Sabbath laws strictly); see SMG, positive precept 29; *Shibbale ha-Leket* 50, No. 65; Shu'aib, Ahare Mot, 62d; *Kimha Dabishuna* נר שבת. This Haggadah is found in PR 23, 116b, but most of the authorities just mentioned did not quote it directly, as may be clearly seen from the introductory phrase of SMG (שמעתי יש במדרש).

²²² PR 23, 121a–121b; Kiddushin 31a; BaR 8.4; Philo, *Quis Rer. Div. Haeres Sit*, 35. Comp. vol. I, p. 153.

²²³ 'Aseret ha-Dibrot 76. The commandment concerning the honor due to parents is the "severest" (*i.e.*, the most important) of all the commandments of the Torah; Yerushalmi Kiddushin 1,61b; DR 6.2. He who honors his parents commits no sins, but if one fails

to honor his parents, evil visitations come upon him; ER 16, 134.

²²⁴ Niddah 31a; Kiddushin 30b; Kohelet 5.10; Wehizhir II, 120; Yerushalmi Kil'ayim 8, 31c. These passages state: God, the father and the mother contribute three things each in the formation of a child, God giving the spirit, breath and soul. According to 4 Ezra 8.8, the human body consists of fire and water, whereas Philo, *De Mun. Opif.* 51, maintains that it is formed of four elements, fire, water, air, and earth. Comp. note 15 on vol. I, p. 55.

²²⁵ Kiddushin 31a; ER 26, 134.

²²⁶ Yerushalmi Peah 1, 15d, and Kiddushin 1, 61b; PR 23, 122b; comp. also Mekilta Bahodesh 8, 70a, which is at the same time the source of the well-known saying: God regards the honor shown to parents as though it were shown to Himself; and conversely He counts the neglect to honor parents as an insult to Himself; Mekilta RS 110; Sifra Kedoshim (beginning); Midrash Tannaim 23; Kiddushin 30b; Tan. B. V, 16–17; Tan. Ekah 2. See also Josephus, *Antiqui.*, IV, 8.2, and *Contra Apionem*, 2.27–28; Philo, *De Decalogo*, 22, and *Special. Leg.*, *De Col. Par*, 1; ps.-Phocylides, 5.8; Sibyl. 3, 594. The words of Philo, *Special. Leg.*, *loc. cit.*, "parents hold a middle position, between the divine and human kind", go back to a Stoic source (see Prächter, *Herakles der Stoiker*, 45, *seq.*); but the idea underlying this statement is genuinely Jewish.

²²⁷ 'Aseret ha-Dibrot 78; Yerushalmi Targumim Exod. 20.13; comp. Abot 5.8 (עָנוּי means "delaying", not "suppressing"); ARN 28.114 (second version 41, 114–115).

²²⁸ PR 24, 124b (here תִּרְצָח is taken to stand for תַּצְרַח "cause to cry aloud"; similarly Mekilta RS 110 reads: As long as the murderer lives, the blood of the victim cries, *i. e.*, seethes); DR 2.25; *Visio Pauli* 18; Enoch 22.7. He who sheds the blood of his fellow-man destroys the likeness of God; see Tosefta Yebamot 8(end); BR 34.14 (see the numerous parallel passages cited by Theodor). A similar statement is found in Philo, *De Decalogo*, 25.

²²⁹ 'Aseret ha-Dibrot 79; ER 34.14; DR 2.25. These passages read: All ascend from Hell (that is, they are not consigned to eternal damnation), except adulterers, those who put their fellow-men to shame, and those who give opprobrious names to their fellow-men; Baba Mezi'a 58b; comp., on the other hand, Rosh ha-Shanah 16b–17a. A very realistic description of the punishment of the murderer is given in BHM V, 144–146.

²³⁰ Targum Yerushalmi Exod. 20.13; BR 26.5; Yerushalmi Sotah
1, 17a; BaR 9.33; Tan. Bereshit 12.   A different view concerning the
punishment for adultery is found in Abot 5.7.   For "fourfold adultery"
(*i. e.*, lustful eyes, etc.), see Mekilta RS 3; BHM VI, 45; PR 24, 124b.
²³¹ Yerushalmi Targumim Exod. 22.13; comp. Abot 5.7.
²³² PR 24, 125b; WR 22.6; comp. vol. I, 153.
²³³ Yerushalmi Targumim Exod 20.13; PR 24, 125b; EZ 3,175;
comp. vol. I, pp. 160–161 and vol. IV, pp. 109–110.
²³⁴ Yerushalmi Targumim Exod. 20.14; comp. Abot 5.7.   The
division of the Decalogue as given in vol. III, 98, *seq.*, is the only one
known in rabbinic sources.   Sifre N., 112, 113, does not consider
Exod. 20.3–6 as forming part of the first commandment, but describes
idolatry as being at the same time an infringement of the first commandment, "since he who professes idolatry denies God".   Philo, *De Decalogo*,
passim, and Josephus, *Antiqui.*, III, 5.5, divide the Decalogue in a
manner different from that of the Rabbis; they count 20.2–3 as the first
commandment, 4–6 as the second, 7 as the third, 8–11 as the fourth,
12 as the fifth, 13 as the sixth, 14 as the seventh, 15 as the eighth, 16 as
the ninth, and 17 as the tenth.   Comp. *Jewish Encyclopedia*, IV, 495.
²³⁵ BaR 9.12; PR 16, 107a–107b.   For a different version of
the Haggadah about the sin which leads to the breaking of all the Ten
Commandments, see *Kad ha-Kemah* (חמדה) 86b; *Orehot Zaddikim*, 14.
Concerning covetousness as the source of all evil, see also Philo, *Special.
Leg., De Concup.* 2; *Milhamot Melek ha-Mashiah*, 117; Lactantius,
Div. Instit. 5.6; comp. *Ha-Hoker* I, 67.
²³⁶ Mekilta Bahodesh 8, 70b (obviously the sentence שע"ז שקולה
כנגד ניאוף stands for ז"ע כנגד שקולה שניאוף; comp. PR 21, 107b–108a);
BaR 9.12; Zohar II, 90a; see also Philo, *De Decalogo*, 12, and 12 Testaments, Reuben 4.6., which read: Fornication removes the soul from God,
and brings it near the idols.   See also Clemens Alexandrinus, *Stromata*,
6.17.
²³⁷ PR 21, 108a.   For a differnt version of the Haggadah concerning the Ten Commandments and the words of Creation, see Lekah
Deut. 5.6; BHM VI 46; Zohar II, 11b–12a.   Comp. vol I, p. 49.
²³⁸ Mekilta Bahodesh 9.71a–72b, and 3, 64a; Mekilta RS 113.
As to the awful vision on Mount Sinai which almost caused the people
to die, see vol. III, pp. 95–96, and Berakot 22a.   As to the visibility
of the audible and the audibility of the visible see also 4 Ezra 5.37,
which speaks of *imago vocis*; Philo, *Moses,* 2(3).97; *De Decalogo*, 11; *De
Migratione Abrahami*, 11.   The last-named passage, in which the author

43

allegorizes, is the source of Origen, *Con. Cel.*, 6.62. Comp., however, the quotation from Philo, *De Decalogo*, 9, given in note 213. Concerning the idea that the divine visions granted to the Israelites on Mount Sinai were greater than those seen by the prophets, see also DR 7.8; Zohar II, 82a, 94a, 146a. Comp. note 64 and vol. III, p. 34. According to one view the Israelites were granted power over the Angel of Death at the time of the revelation; see Mekilta, *loc. cit.*; note 262; vol. III, pp.120, 278.

²³⁹ Shabbat 87a; ARN 1 (second version 2, 9–11); Sifre N., 103; PRK 24a; ER 18.101, which reads: Moses warned the people three days before the revelation not only to keep themselves clean from ritual impurities, but also from sin and evil which contaminate the soul and heart of man; comp. vol. II, p. 316, and vol. III, p. 256. In the sources quoted above mention is made, in this connection, of "the fence which Moses made around the Law"; he was commanded to tell the people to observe two days of preparation, but he added a third day "as a fence". Comp. note 191.

²⁴⁰ Mekilta RS 114; Mekilta Bahodesh, 9, 72a, where the reading כנס הזה, found in Yalkut I, 301, and Lekah Exod. 20, 10 is supported by Mekilta RS. Israel received three gifts at Sinai: The feeling of shame (*i. e.*, modesty), the feeling of compassion, and the feeling of kindness; MHG II, 238; Nedarim 20a; Kallah 1, 4b; ER as quoted in Mahzor Vitry 317, but not in our texts. Comp. vol. IV, p. 110. As to the great influence of Moses upon the people, see Yelammedenu in Yalkut II, 447, on Is. 40; ER 22, 120, and 23, 122; vol. III, p. 14.

²⁴¹ Aggadat Shir, which is the source of Makiri Ps. 89.76. See also Mekilta Bahodesh 9, 72a; Mekilta RS 114; Yalkut I, 301, quoting an unknown midrashic source; DZ 4 = Yalkut I, 815; Shu'aib Wa-Yikra 44b. Concerning the souls of the pious see also Philo, *De Plant. Noë* 4, which reads: The pure souls are in the loftiest places.

²⁴² Mekilta RS 114; WR 1.14; Yebamot 44b; Tehillim 90, 387–388, where it is stated that Isaiah, and according to some also Elijah, retained his consciousness in his moments of prophecy; comp. DR 2.4, which reads: Moses and Isaiah, the greatest of the prophets. Sifre Z. 83 and 84 reads: The revelation granted to Moses came directly from God, and not through an angel; comp. note 248; Sifre N., 103; Sifra 9.7; Zohar III, 261b–262a; Nahmanides, *Emunah u-Bittahon*, 18; Philo, *De Plant. Noë*, 6. The last-named authority uses the same phrase as the Rabbis to describe the clearness of Moses' visions: Moses looked through a clear glass, the other prophets through a

dark glass; comp. I Corinth. 13.12 and 2 Corinth. 3.18; Tertullian, *Adversus Praxean* 14. The view is also expressed that Moses was the only original prophet, whereas all other prophets confirmed the prophecies uttered by Moses; ShR 42.8; vol. III, p. 97. All other prophets received the divine communications in the language of the Targum (*i. e.*, Aramaic), but Moses in the Hebrew language; Vital, *Likkute Torah* on Gen. 15.12; comp. vol. III, p. 87, and note 191. The angels, with the exception of Gabriel who is master of all the seventy tongues (Comp. vol. II, p. 72), are said not to understand Aramaic. The statement that God appeared in a pillar of cloud to three prophets only (comp Ps. 99, 6-7) is perhaps directed against Mark 9.7. Comp. vol. II, pp. 257-258, 356, and vol. IV, p. 69.

²⁴³ Shir 1.2; Yelammedenu in Yalkut II, 479 on Is. 14, and 317 on Jer. 31. In contrast to the view expressed in the sources quoted above, as well as in Makkot 24a (top), Tan. Wa-Yelek 2; PR, 12, 111a, and in many other passages in rabbinic literature, to the effect that the first two commandments only were heard by Israel directly from the mouth of God, there is another opinion which maintains that all the Ten Commandments were heard by Israel from the mouth of God; see Mekilta Bahodesh 4, 66a, and 9, 71b (bottom); Mekilta RS 114 (verse 19); Philo, *Moses*, 2 (3).27, and *De Decalogo*, 5; Josephus, *Antiqui.*, III, 5.4. Comp. also Horayyot 8a-8b; PRE 41; ShR 33.6; quotation from an unknown Midrash in *Shibbale ha-Leket* 7 (on the correspondence between the Ten Commandments and the Ten Words of Creation mentioned there, see vol. III, pp. 104-105). Rashi, on Makkot, *loc. cit.*, quotes from the Mekilta the midrashic support for the first view, as given in PRE; but nothing to this effect is found in our texts of the Midrash (Bahodesh 6, 69a refers to Ps 62, 12 in an entirely different connection), and it is very likely that מכילתא in Rashi stands for ספרי; see Sifre N., 42. Comp. *Geonica* II, 307, note 2.

²⁴⁴ PRE 41 (end); Tehillim 22, 200; comp. vol. III, p. 79, for further details concerning the great distinction of the generation of the revelation. In striking contrast to this view is the opinion of R. Akiba, according to whom this generation lost its share in the world to come; see Sanhedrin Mishnah 9. 3, Tosefta 13.10-11, Babli 110b, and Yerushalmi 9, 29c. It is true that, as may be seen from the passages just quoted, R. Akiba's view is entirely rejected by the other scholars. See also WR 32.2; Tehillim 130, 490; vol. II, p. 302.

²⁴⁵ PRE 41, where היום כפול is to be taken literally. The sun stood still for Moses on the day of the battle with Amalek (see note

146) and on the days of the battles against Sihon and Og (see vol. III, pp. 340 and 469), as well as at the time when Moses commanded heaven and earth to stand still and listen to him, saying: "Give ear, ye heavens, and I will speak and let the earth hear the words of my mouth." See Ta'anit 20a; 'Abodah Z. 25a; Tehillim 19, 167; PR 3, 13b; Sifre D., 306 (131a, in the middle of page); Lekah, Deut, 32.1 and 24.12; DR 10.2–3; DZ 30. A Midrash quoted in *Hadar*, Deut. 32.1, reads: Moses refused to submit to the Angel of Death, saying unto him: "I shall not die, but live, and declare the works of God." The angel of Death replied: "God has the sun and the moon to praise Him and to declare His glory." Whereupon Moses bade the sun and the moon stand still and he began to praise God. In Sibyl. 5, 256–259 it is said that Moses, the best of the Hebrews—Philo, *Moses*, 1 (beginning), and Midrash Tannaim 186 call him the greatest and most perfect man—made the sun and the moon stand still. Comp. note 947.

²⁴⁶ ARN, both versions at the beginning; Seder 'Olam 6; Yoma 4b; Yerushalmi Ta'anit 4, 68b. According to another view given in the sources just quoted, Moses ascended, without further preparations, in the morning immediately after the revelation on Sinai. See also Mekilta RS 96.

²⁴⁷ Ma'ayan ha-Hokmah 58–60; PR 20, 96a–98a; Yalkut Mishpatim (end). The fragment published in BMH V, 165–266 very likely forms part of Ma'ayan ha-Hokmah; comp. also Mahzor Vitry 323–325; Zohar I, 5a; II, 58a; III, 78b. The description of Sandalfon and Gallizur, quoted in *Ketab Tamim* 5, 9 from a Midrash which is no longer extant, agrees in the main with that of Ma'ayan.—As to how *M*oses found his way through the dark clouds, see Yoma 4b and Philo, *Quaestiones*, Exod. 2.48. On the angels guarding the gates of heaven, see Ascension of Isaiah 24, *seq.* Concerning the opposition of the angels to the creation of man, see vol. I, p. 53. On Sandalfon and the crown which he places on the head of the Lord, see Index, s. v. "Sandalfon." The description of a certain distance as "a journey of five hundred years" is of frequent occurrence in the legends; see vol. I, p. 11; vol. II, p. 307; comp. also Yerushalmi Berakot 9, 13a. The conception about the fire of Rigion is certainly of Persian origin, being identical with Hvareno of the Avesta, concerning which see Cumont, *Mysteries of Mithra*, index, s. v. That Moses saved himself by holding on to God's throne is a very old legend; see Shabbat 88a; vol. V, p. 417, bottom; comp. note 273; vol. III, pp. 124, 138 (top). When the angels attempted to expel Moses from heaven, he said to

them: "I am permitted to sit in the place where ye are not even allowed to stand." See quotation from Nahmanides in Neubauer's *The Fifty-third Chapter of Isaiah* I.76. As to the question whether Moses sat or stood in heaven, see Megillah 21a.

²⁴⁸ Ma'ayan ha-Hokmah 60–61 and PR 20, 98a, 25, 128a, which in the main follow old sources; see Shabbat 88b; ARN 2, 10; DR 7.9 and 8.2; Shir 8.11; Tehillim 8, 74–75. These sources read: When, owing to the worship of the golden calf, the first tables were broken, the angels rejoiced, thinking that Israel, because of his sins, lost the Torah. God, however, pointed out to the angels that they too, had transgressed the command of the Torah (comp. vol. V, p. 328, note 29) when, as Abraham's guests, they partook of forbidden food and ate meat with milk; PRE 46; Tan. B V, 51; Mekilta RS, 101–102 (not tannaitic); Zohar II, 3. When the angels were about to attack Moses, God changed his face, making him look like Abraham; He then said to the angels: "Are ye not ashamed to attack him in whose house ye ate and drank!" Turning to Moses God said: "It is on account of the merits of Abraham that thou hast come into possession of the Torah." On the "prince of the Torah" and his attitude toward Moses, see also BHM II, 116–117, and vol. III, p. 305. This legend, however, must not be taken to express the idea that the Torah was revealed by an angel; the function of Yefefiyyah is that of a teacher of the Torah and not that of one who reveals it. Concerning angels as teachers of a chosen few, see vol. V, p. 117, top. The old authorities very frequently emphasize the direct character of the revelation of the Torah; Sifre Z., 84; Mekilta Ki-Tissa 1, 103b (comp., however, Mekilta RS 160); Hagigah 3b; second version of ARN 1, 2. Philo, *Moses*, 2 (3).23, writes: The laws were partly revealed by God Himself, through the medium of divine prophecy (hence Philo, *Moses*, 1, and the Rabbis, Yerushalmi Sotah 6.1, describe Moses as the interpreter of the sacred laws) partly in the form of questions and answers, revealing the will of God (comp. *e. g.* Num. 9.8), and some of them were promulgated by Moses while in a state of ecstasy. Though this tripartite division of the Torah is quite unknown to the Rabbis (they condemn as a heresy the view which would admit even that one word of the Torah was written by Moses himself, and not received by him from heaven; see Sanhedrin 99a), they agree with Philo that the revelation was not through the medium of angels. The view of Paul, Galatians 3.17, is not Jewish, but rather anti-Jewish; comp. Ginzberg, *Unbekannte Sekte*, 246–249, where this passage of Galatians, as well as Josephus, *Antiqui.*, XV, 5.3, and Jub. 1.17, is fully

discussed.   See also, above, note 242, and vol. III, p. 97.   A rather advanced view is held by an unknown Jewish author of the middle ages according to whom, Moses, while inspired by the holy spirit, nevertheless made use of written and oral sources for the compilation of the history prior to his own times as recorded in the Book of Genesis. See Neubauer, *Medieval Jewish Chronicles* I, 163.

²⁴⁹ Shabbat 89a.   A different version of this legend is found in *Hadar*, Num. 14.7.   In Babylon it was considered bad manners for a pupil to greet his master before being greeted first, but in Palestine, on the other hand, a pupil was expected to greet his master first; see Berakot 27b and Yerushalmi 2, 4b; comp. Müller, *Hilluf Minhagim* 32, No. 33.

²⁵⁰ Menahot 29b.   For another version of this legend, see vol. II, pp. 325–326.   Comp. also PK 4, 29b, which reads: Things not revealed to Moses were known to R. Akiba.   See also the quotation from *Sefer Tagin* (not in our texts) in Yalkut Reubeni, Exod. 19.2. On the meaning of קוץ, Menahot, *loc. cit.*, see Derenbourg, *Journal Asiatique*, I, 247.

²⁵¹ Sanhedrin 111a–111b; Baba Kamma 50b; PK 16, 166b; Yerushalmi Ta'anit 2, 65b; comp. vol. II, p. 304, and vol. III, p. 135, 138, 280.   In one respect, however, it was Moses who made God to be more compassionate than He had intended to be.   God first revealed to Moses that He would visit the sins of the fathers upon their children. Moses objected to this, saying: "Many a wicked man bore a pious child; why should the latter suffer for the sin of the former?"God recognized the justice of this objection, and promulgated the law: The children shall not be put to death for their fathers; every man shall be put to death for his own sin (Deut. 24.16); see BaR 19.33.   Comp. also vol. III, p. 98, and note 217.

²⁵² Yerushalmi Peah 2, 17a; WR 22.1; ShR 47.1; Kohelet 1.10 and 5.8; comp. vol. III, pp. 97 and 119.

²⁵³ PK 4, 40; BaR 19.7; Tan. B. IV, 118; Tan. Hukkat 8.

²⁵⁴ Tehillim 19, 166–167; ShR 47.5 and 8.   God taught him by day, and during the night he repeated his lessons; Tan. Ki-Tissa 36; Tan. B II, 119; PRE 46; Targum Lamentations 2.19.   The night is the best time for serious study, and hence it was devoted by Moses to the study of the oral law; see 'Erubin 65a; WR 19.1; Shir 5.11; Shemuel 5, 57; Comp. note 83 on Vol. IV, p. 101 and Vol. III, p. 143, first paragraph.   There is an angel on whom a label is attached bearing the inscription *Hesed* ("Grace").   During the day the label is

attached to the angel's front, and by night to his back. By means
of this the angels know to distinguish between night and day. See Pa-
'aneah Raza, Exod. 13.21, and comp. Index, s. v. "Israel", Angel.
As to the sun and moon worshipping God before they begin their
task, see vol. I, p. 25. Concerning the grinding of the manna by angels,
see vol. III, p. 44.

²⁵⁵ PR 20, 98b; PK 1, 4b; BaR 12.8; Shir 3.11. The place where
Moses was during the forty days is described by ps.-Philo 12.1 as
the one "where is the light of the sun and the moon"; comp. note 260.

²⁵⁶ ShR 41.6; comp. vol. III, p. 114. According to Jub. 32.25,
Jacob likewise forgot the things cummunicated to him by an angel
from the heavenly tables. While ShR and many other passages describe the great efforts Moses made to acquire the knowledge of the Torah,
it is maintained by Yerushalmi Horayyot 3.48c that he became the
great master of the Torah without the slightest exertion. Comp. the
following note.

²⁵⁷ Shabbat 89a (comp. the Midrash quoted by Tosafot); Sanhedrin
26b; Kallah 8, 15a. Moses put his life in danger for the sake of the
Torah, Israel, and the maintenance of Justice (comp. Exod. 2.12);
as a reward for this, Scripture speaks of the "Torah of Moses", of
"Israel the people of Moses", and of the "justice of Moses"; see Mekilta
Shirah 1, 34b; Midrash Tannaim 96; Tan. B. V, 29; Tan. Ki-Tissa
35; PR 5, 14b (here the erection of the Sanctuary is substituted for
Israel); BaR 12.9; ShR 30.4; Tehillim 1, 15, and 30, 235–236. For
other explanations of the expression "The Torah of Moses" (Malachi
3.22), see vol. II, pp. 277, 278, 309; vol. III, pp. 117, 141, 429.

²⁵⁸ PRE 19 and 46; Abot 5.6 (the characters and the stylus, mentioned there as having been created during the twilight of the first
eve of Sabbath, very likely refer to the character and stylus used for
the tables; see, however, note 99, on vol. I, p. 83); Shabbat 104a (on
this passage, see *Hoffmann-Festschrift*, 113–114); Shekalim 6, 49b
where the following conflicting opinions are given: 1) five commandments were engraved on one table and five on the other; 2) all the Ten
Commandments were engraved on each of the two tables; 3) the Ten
Commandments were on both sides of each of the two tables; 4) the
Ten Commandments were on each of the four sides of each of the two
tables (read in *Responsen der Geonim*, ed. Harkavy 11, טטרגונא instead of
אצטרגא); Sifre D., 313; Sifre N., 101; Shir 5.14 (whence Lekah Exod. 31.18
states that the sapphire employed for the tables was taken from the
Throne of Glory; see, however, Zohar I, 131b, according to which

the tables were hewn out from the *Eben Shetiyyah*); ShR 47.6; Midrash Shir 40b; Zohar II, 84a–84b; Philo, *Quaestiones*, Exod. 2, 42. This legend about the nature of the tables is an attempt to express in popular form the view strongly emphasized by Philo (*De Decalogo*, 29, and *De Special. Leg. passim*) that the Ten Commandments contain the kernel of the entire Torah. The division of the six hundred and thirteen precepts of the Torah into ten classes, with the Ten Commandments as headings, is first found in the writings of Sa'adya Gaon, who perhaps followed Philo, whose book *De Special. Leg.* is the first attempt in this direction. It is worthy of notice that the talmudic-midrashic sources never speak of the Decalogue as containing the entire Torah, though this view is expressed with regard to the Shema'; see Yerushalmi Berakot 1, 3c. In this connection it may be mentioned that the section of Lev. 19, *seq.*, is said by the Rabbis to contain the Decalogue; see WR 24.5. Comp. notes 302 and 306.

[259] Shir 5.14.

[260] Tan. Ki-Tissa (end). God gave the Torah to Moses with His right hand; see EZ 11, 192; PK 32, 200a; Tehillim 1, 15; 16, 124; 18, 155; Mishle 6, 54; Tan. Berakah 3. God holds life and justice in His left hand, and grace and the Torah in His right, one who does justice and observes the Torah receives life from God as an act of His grace; see WR 4.1; DR 5.4; Koheleth 3.16 (end). On the radiance of Moses' face see the references given above, note 204, as well as PK 4, 37a; Tan. B IV, 114, and the parallel passages cited by Buber; notes 295 and 309. Zohar II, 58a, and Shu'aib Ki-Tissa (end) are based on Tan., *loc. cit.*, where an opinion is quoted to the effect that "the rays sent forth" from the countenance of Moses owed their existence to the sparks which emanated from the Shekinah at the time when Moses received instruction in the Torah from God. Zohar adds (on whose authority?) that after Israel worshipped the golden calf the radiance of Moses' face lost its lustre, retaining only a thousandth part of its original strength, so that the angels who formerly dreaded to come near him attempted to attack him. Comp. vol. II, p. 306. Ps.-Philo 12.1 explains the radiance of Moses' face in the following manner: He was covered with an invisible light, for he had gone to the place where is the light of the sun and moon (comp. note 255), and the light of his face overcame the brightness of the sun and moon. The place of the great light is, of course, the place of the Shekinah.

[261] PR 96b; PRE 41.

²⁶² EZ 4, 179–180. That originally the Torah was given to Israel as a weapon against the Angel of Death, is an old conception;
see Tan. B. II, 112, IV, 76, and the parallel passages cited by Buber
in his note on the latter place, as well as *Batte Midrashot* III, 14–15;
vol. III, p. 278; note 238.

²⁶³ Yerushalmi Ta'anit 4, 68c (top); Sanhedrin 102a; ShR 43.2;
Koheleth 9.11; Ekah 1.62.

²⁶⁴ Shabbat 89a; Tan. B. II, 112–113; Tan. Ki-Tissa 19 and Beha-
'aloteka 14; ShR 41.7; Targum Yerushalmi Exod. 32.1. The error
of the people consisted in including, in their calculation, the day of
the ascent, whereas Moses, in speaking of forty days, had "complete
ones" in mind, excluding the day of ascent, which he partly spent on
earth. See Rashi and Tosafot on Shabbat, *loc. cit.* Disappointed
in their expectation to see their leader return, they came to Aaron
with the request to appoint another leader (אלהים in Exod.32.1 means
judge, leader). See *Hadar, ad loc.*, 42d and 43a.

²⁶⁵ PRE 45; ShR 41.5; WR 10.3., 7.1, and 2.1 (the women of this
generation were pious); BaR 15.21 and 9.44; EZ 4, 180; Sanhedrin
7a; Tan. B. II, 113; Tan. Ki-Tissa 19; Targum Yerushalmi Exod.
32.3–5; Zohar II, 191a and 192a. The legend that Aaron was intimidated by the people, especially when he saw the violent death of Hur,
is also mentioned by Ephraem I, 224a. On Hur, see vol. III, pp. 60,
159. According to vol. III, p. 28, Jannes and Jambres met their death
at the Red Sea; see Index, s. v. "Jannes and Jambres". Concerning
another attempt to exculpate Aaron, see below, note 351. On the
piety of the women see vol. III, pp. 174, 393; on the New Moon as
a festive day, see *Menorat ha-Maor, Rosh Hodesh.*

²⁶⁶ Midrash Shir 13a–13b. This is very likely the source of
Hadassi, 45a (numbers 117–118) and 134d (numbers 362–363). For a
different version of this legend, see vol. II, p. 182, and note 493 referring
to it. Grünbaum *Neue Beiträge*, 151 gives the Arabic version. For
a third version see note 126 on vol. IV, pp. 49–50. There is some
relation between this legend and the one found in early Christian writings, according to which the Egyptians identified Joseph with Serapis;
see Tertullian, *Ad Nationes* 2.8, and *Specilegium Syriacum* 89; comp.
note 271. In PRE this legend is abridged in the following manner:
Aaron found a golden plate, upon which the Divine Name was engraved,
together with the form of a calf. When Aaron threw this piece of gold
into the fire, a bleating calf came forth, for Sammael had entered it,

and started to bleat to deceive the Israelites.   See vol. I, p. 155, where a similar part is ascribed to Sammael.

²⁶⁷ PK 9, 78a; WR 27.8; Tan. B. III, 94; Tan. Emor 11; ShR 42.6; Shir 1.9, which reads: The Egyptian magicians made the calf move about as if it were alive.   Comp. the preceding note; vol. III, pp. 120, 127, 211, 245.

²⁶⁸ Ginzberg, *Haggadot Ketu' ot* 53–54, 64–66 = *Haggoren* IX; BaR 15.21, and, on the other hand, comp. vol. III, p. 248.   As to "the redemption of God from Egypt", see note 150.

²⁶⁹ PRE 45.

²⁷⁰ Tehillim 3, 37; ShR 41.1; Yerushalmi Sanhedrin 10, 28b; WR 5.3.   *Yalkut David*, Exod. 32.1, quotes Midrash and Targum Shir 2.17 to the effect that the clouds of glory departed from the Israelites as soon as they worshipped the golden calf.   As far as can be ascertained, this legend is found neither in the Midrashim nor in the Targum (certainly not in the passage referred to).   Did the author of *Yalkut David* use manuscripts?   In vol. III, p. 374, it is said that the clouds of glory were not withdrawn from the Israelites when they worshipped the golden calf.   Comp. vol. III, p. 93, top.

²⁷¹ Ginzberg, as above, note 268; ShR 3.2, 42.5, and 43.8; Tan. Ki-Tissa 21.   This legend presupposes an old Haggadah, according to which, Ps. 106.20 refers to "the ox of the Merkabah" (Ezekiel 1.10); but as early as the time of R. Akiba great objections were raised to this view; see Mekilta 6.33 (the text is rather "doctored"); Mekilta RS 45; Shir 1.9; Tehillim 106, 455–456.   See also Lekah, Exod. 32.4, which reads: They noticed that the feet of angels were like those of calves (see Ezekiel 1.7), and therefore they made the golden calf.   The identification of the golden calf with the Apis of the Egyptians frequently mentioned by early Christian authors (comp. *e. g.*, *Apostolic Constitution*, 6.20; Lactantius, *Divinae Institutiones* 4.10) is unknown in the old rabbinic sources.   Ziyyoni, however, on Exod. 32.1 quoted from the "Book of the Magicians" a lengthy description of the Apis cult (introduced by a magician called Apis in the ninety-second year of Jacob), which is said to be identical with the worship of the golden calf.   Comp. also note 3.   Pa'aneah, Exod. 32.4, writes: They had noticed in the sand along the shore of the Red Sea that the imprints left by the feet of the angels were like those of the feet of calves, and therefore they adopted the form of a calf for their idol.   This is a slight modification of Lekah, *loc. cit.*   Comp. also note 122 on the imprints on rocks.   At the request of Ezekiel, God changed "the ox

of the Merkabah" into a Cherub (comp. Ezekiel 1.10 with 10.14), so that He might not be constantly reminded of Israel's sin. See Haggigah 13b.

²⁷² ShR 41.7 and 42.4; Tan. B. II, 113. Comp. the reference to Zohar cited in note 260.

²⁷³ See the sources given in previous note. On clinging to the throne, see vol. III, pp. 112 and 138.

²⁷⁴ PRE 45; ShR 41.7 and 44.8; DR 3.2; Tehillim 7, 65–66 (in this passage it is said: At first God did not consider the merits of the fathers, for even they were not free from sin. Comp. vol. III, pp. 89–90), and 18, 142; Koheleth 4.2; PR 10, 38b. According to another version of this legend, Af and Hemah (on these angels see vol. II, pp. 308 and 328) were buried alive opposite the grave of Moses; see Imre No'am (end); comp. also Sotah 14a and Tosafot, *ad loc.*; Targum Yerushalmi Deut. 9.19 and 34.6. The episode of the struggle of Moses and the destroying angels, as narrated in this legend, is said in PRE, *loc. cit.*, to have taken place after Moses had descended from Sinai. This is in agreement with many other sources which tell of Moses' intercession for Israel after his descent; see vol. III, pp. 131, *seq.*

²⁷⁵ Midrash Shir 14b–15b (on Ra'ah see note 196 on vol. II, p. 358); ShR 42.5 and 44.9 (God hinted to Moses that He waited only for the prayer of the latter to avert the execution of the threatened punishment; this is also found in 42, end; ER 4,17; Ephraem I, 225B; Tertullian, *Adversus Marc.* 2.26; Theodoretus, Exod. 32.10); PK 16, 128b. As to the idea that Moses owed his distinguished rank to Israel, see vol. II, pp. 51 and 283. On the three-legged bench (*i. e.*, the descendant of the three patriarchs), see vol. III, p. 279. *Kimha Dabishuna* Shekalim quotes a Midrash to the effect that God intended to choose the pious among the Gentiles for His people and place them in Paradise instead of the wicked Israelites. Comp. note, 540.

²⁷⁶ ShR 42–44; Tan. Ki-Tissa 21–24; DR 3.11–15; BaR 5.15. Concerning the rejection of the Torah by the sons of Esau, see vol. III, p. 81; on the readiness of Israel to trust in God and in Moses, see vol II, p. 364; on the guilt of the "mixed multitude" in making the golden calf, see Zohar I, 25a, 26a, and 28b; note 207. That God had revealed to Moses, even before the exodus from Egypt, the future defection of Israel, is also recorded in vol. II, p. 317. The Haggadah often discusses the question why God is "jealous of idols", though they are things of nought; see Mekilta Bahodesh 6, 68 (on the text see *Ma'asiyyot* ed. Gaster 33); Mekilta RS, 105; 'Abodah Zarah 54b–55a.

As to the idea that God submitted to the law of absolving vows, see quotation from an unknown Midrash in Yalkut Reubeni Num. 30. 14; against this idea comp. vol. III, p. 421.

²⁷⁷ Lekah, Exod. 32.19. On the devotion of Joshua to his master, see *Batte Midrashot* III, 26, and Index, s. v. "Joshua".

²⁷⁸ Koheleth 9.11; ShR 41.1; Yerushalmi Taanit 4, 68c (top); comp. also Philo, *Moses*, 2 (3).19. In Koheleth attention is called to the errors committed by Joshua on these two occasions when he attempted to impress his views on Moses; see Num. 11,28–29.

²⁷⁹ Yerushalmi Ta'anit 4.68c; ARN 2,11 (both versions); Shabbat 87a; ShR 19.3 and 46.3; Pesahim 87b; PRE 46; Targum Yerushalmi Exod. 32.19; Baba Batra 14b; Tan. Ki-Tissa 26 and 'Ekeb 11; ER 21, 117; EZ 4, 180; *Batte Midrashot* III, 13 (Yelammedenu?); PR 20, 96b. The Pesikta is the only source in which Joshua is said to have participated in the breaking of the tables; see also Ziyyoni, Deut. 5.6. In Shabbat, *loc. cit.*, three things are enumerated which Moses did on his own authority and which were later sanctioned by God; these are: He broke the tables, added a day of preparation for the revelation on Sinai, and gave up conjugal life. Concerning the two last-named points see vol. II, p. 316; vol. III, pp. 107 and 355–356; note 191. In opposition to all the sources just quoted, it is maintained in DR 3.14 that God reproached Moses for breaking the tables in his anger at the sinners, and told him that the world would not exist for a moment if He grew angry as easily on account of the sins of man; see vol. I, p. 304 and vol III, p. 116. The disappearance of the writing from the tables is also referred to by ps-Philo, 12.5, who says: And he looked upon the tables, and saw that they were not written, and he hastened and broke them. On the gigantic struggle of Moses, see vol. III, p. 141; concerning the weight of the tables, comp. also Targum Yerushalmi Exod. 31.18. It is noteworthy that the tables and the rod of Moses were not only of the same weight (sixty seah), but also of the same material, that is, sapphire; see vol. II, p. 293, and note 280 on vol. II, p. 292.

²⁸⁰ Zohar II, 113b; comp. the following note.

²⁸¹ Yoma 66b, which also gives the dissenting view that the three different forms of death (*i e.*, execution by the Levites, death caused by the water, and death from the plague) depended upon the manner of worshipping the calf; 'Abodah Zarah 44a; Yerushalmi Sotah 3, 19a; BaR 9.48; PR 10, 38a; Tan. Ki-Tissa 26; PRE 45; Targum Yerushalmi Exod. 32.30, which says: The lips of him who had devotedly worship-

ped the idol became tightly closed "like gold"; Tosefta 'Abodah Zarah 4.19. A different version of this legend is found in ps.-Philo 12.7: And it was so, if any man willed in his mind that the calf should be made, his tongue was cut off (by the drinking of the water); but if any one was constrained thereto by fear, his face shone. Ephraem I, 126 A-B gives this legend in agreement with the Rabbis. Ps-Jerome on 1 Samuel 7.6 maintains that Samuel preformed the same ordeal as Moses; comp. Ginzberg, *Haggada bei den Kirchenv.* I, 21–23. The Christian legend tells of a similar ordeal in later times; see The Gospel of ps.-Matthew 12. In opposition to the view that the execution of the idolaters was ordered by Moses on his own authority (ER 4, 17), there are some Rabbis who maintain that he did it at the command of God; see Mekilta Bo 12, 12b, according to the reading of Yalkut II, 43; Rashi and Lekah on Exod. 32.27. The Levites, who not only refrained from worshipping the calf, but, jealous for God, killed the idolaters (comp. Tehillim 1, 13, and vol. III, pp. 94, 170), received the reward for their piety, and became the servants of the Sanctuary; see Philo, *Moses*, 2(3) 20 and 37, as well as *Special. Leg.* (on Priests), 1.4, 322–24. Comp. Index, s. v. "Levites".

282 ER 4,17. The same number of Israelites lost their life by drinking the water; Shu'aib, Ki-Tissa, 40b.

283 Tan. Ki-Tissa 26; Berakot 32a. In the latter passage the intercession of Moses for Israel is very graphically described.

284 *Hadar*, Exod. 27.20; *Da'at* and R. Bahya, 22.23; Zohar III, 246a; comp. also *Pa'aneah* Exod. (end). From the section of Shemot in which the birth of Moses is recorded, to the end of the Pentateuch, the section of Tezawweh is the only one in which the name of Moses is not mentioned. Another explanation of "Thy book" (Exod. 32.32) is that it refers to the book of—eternal—life in which all the pious are entered; see Midrash Tannaim 211; Wehizhir I, 78; comp. also Berakot 32a and Sotah 14a, where this explanation is presupposed. As to the readiness of Moses to sacrifice himself for the sake of Israel, see PR 22, 111a; Zohar I, 67b; note 257. Moses, David, Habakkuk, and Jeremiah are four pious men, who, carried away by their prayers, addressed unbecoming words to God; see Tehillim 90.385. For further details concerning this prayer of Moses for Israel, see Berakot 7a–7b and DR 13.11. In most of the passages where this prayer is spoken of, his supplications on Sinai (Exod. 32.11) and those which he made after the descent therefrom are dealt with as one prayer. Comp. note 274.

²⁸⁵ ShR 45.1–2.   Zohar 1, 52b and 63b (on this occasion they lost their immaculate state; comp. vol. III, p. 108); Shu'aib, Ki-Tissa, 40b; Targum Yerushalmi Exod. 33.6–7 (this is the only passage in which occurs the statement that Moses hid the heavenly gifts in the tent in which he taught the Torah); PK 17, 129b; Tehillim 25, 212; Ekah 1.58; EZ 4, 180; Berakot 63b; DR 3.15; Tan. Ki-Tissa 26–27; Tan. B. II, 115–116. On the heavenly gifts, see also references in note 202.   In most of the sources it is stated that these gifts will be returned to Israel in the time to come.   See also vol. III, p. 463.

²⁸⁶ Seder 'Olam 6.   Moses ascended into heaven on Thursday, and descended therefrom on Monday; it is therefore customary to fast on these days; see Tan. B. I, 94 (on the text see *Ketab Tamim*, 88), and Midrash Wayekullu 18.   These fast-days are mentioned in Luke 18.12 and BR 76.3.   According to PRE 46, Moses spent only the first and last forty days in heaven, *i. e.*, from the seventh of Siwan to the seventeenth of Tammuz, and from the twenty-ninth of Ab to the tenth of Tishre, whereas the forty days intervening between these two periods he remained on earth praying to God to forgive the sin of Israel.   See Luria, *ad loc.*, and EZ 4, 180.

²⁸⁷ ShR 44.5–9; Midrash Shir 13b; DR 3.15 (in this passage it is stated that there were at that time in Israel, besides Moses, seventy-seven pious men: the seventy members of the Sanhedrin, Aaron and his four sons, Caleb and Phineas; comp. vol. III, p. 127;   Shir 1 (end); Aggadat Bereshit 5.13–14; Tan. B. II, 90–91.   As to the conception that the pious are considered as living even after their departure from this world, see Berakot 19a–19b; Midrash Tannaim 101; Mekilta RS, 127; MHG I, 527; Philo, *De Josepho*, 43; 4 Maccabees 7.20 and 16.25; Matthew 8.22 and 22.31–32; 1 Timothy 5.6–7.   Comp. also note 72 on vol. I, pp. 75–76.   For a poetical description of the "living death" of the wicked, see *Ben ha-Melek we-ha-Nazir* 20.

²⁸⁸ Berakot 7a, where one opinion is recorded to the effect that God granted Moses also his third wish, and revealed to him "His ways" whereby He ordains good and evil in His world; Tehillim 25, 211. The difference between the presence of the Shekinah and that of an angel is the same as that between the immediate and mediate working of God; see note 62 on vol. I, 16; note 115 on vol. II, p. 304 and note 20 on vol. IV, p. 7.

²⁸⁹ ShR 25.6; Tan. Ki-Tissa 27; B. II, 116; comp. also Berakot 34b; Tan. B. V, 9; vol. III, p. 420.

²⁹⁰ Shu'aib, Debarim (beginning), 98c; this is very likely the source

of *Kimha Dabishuma,* מי ימלל (Musaf for the Day of Atonement), and of the Judeo-German rendering of this legend, concerning which see Grünbaum, *Chrestomathie*, 215, *seq.* The Hebrew original remained unknown to this author, as well as to Krauss, *Ha-Goren*, 215, *seq., J. Q. R*, New Series, II, 349 *seq.*, and Friedländer, *ibid.* III, 179–180. Comp. also Gaster, *Exempla*, 432. On the German rendering of this legend, see Brockhaus in *ZDMG*, XIV, 706, who calls attention to the fact that the Persian poet Jâmî made use of this legend. From the Judeo-German writings this legend found its way into the hasidic literature. Modern writers, ignorant of the old sources in which this legend occurs, credit it to the Hasidim. A variant of this legend is No. 353 in Gaster *l. c.*, where however it is Solomon to whom God's justice is revealed.

²⁹¹ EZ 6, 182–183. As to the problem of the theodicy, see also Berakot 7a; 2 ARN 22, 46, which is the source for Midrash Aggada Exod. 20.12. Next to Moses it was Habakkuk who wished to find out "the ways of the Lord"; comp. Tehillim 7, 70-71; 87, 343; 90, 389; Tosefta of Targum Hab. 3.1; Mahzor Vitry 170. The legend about Habakkuk refusing to leave the circle, which he drew, before God had given him an answer to his question (see Ta'anit 23a) very likely refers to Habakkuk's question concerning "the ways of the Lord". For the view that God showed Moses all the generations, see also vol. III, p. 154; comp. further vol. I, p. 61.

²⁹² PRE 46; comp. vol. II, p. 326.

²⁹³ Berakot 7a; ShR 45.5; comp. note 187, and vol. II, p. 305.

²⁹⁴ Megillah 19b; comp. vol. IV, p. 200.

²⁹⁵ PR 10, 37b; Tan. Ki-Tissa 37; ShR 47.7. As to the radiance of Moses' countenance, see vol. III, pp. 93, 119, 143, and the notes appertaining to these passages.

²⁹⁶ PRE 46; PR 10, 37b; Sifra (end of Baraita de-Rabbi Ishmael). The phrase "born of woman" is a designation of contempt in the mouth of an angel; see vol. II, p. 313; vol. III, p. 113; vol. IV, pp. 335, 395. Neither the angels nor the Holy Creatures (*Hayyot ha-Kodesh*) see God or hear His voice; but the pious, after their death, see Him. See Sifre N., 103; Ta'anit, Babli (end). The same conception is also found in *Recognitiones*, 3.30, and Theophilus, *Ad Autol.* 7.—Concerning the attack of the angels on Moses, see vol. III, pp. 112, *seq.*, 129. On the appearance of God on earth, see note 206. According to Sifre D., 343, and Midrash Tannaim 211, there are only four appearances of God: 1) He appeared in Egypt to redeem Israel (comp. vol. II, p. 366);

2) on Sinai to reveal the Torah; 3)He will appear to take vengeance on Gog and Magog; 4)and finally He will appear in the Messianic age.

²⁹⁷ Rosh ha-Shanah 17b. As to the thirteen attributes of God, see the references given by Simonsen in *Lewy-Festschrift*, 271. This scholar also calls attention to 4 Ezra 7.132–139, which represents a Midrash on the Thirteen Attributes. Comp. also Ginzberg, *Compte Rendu* 23 (*R.E.J.* LXVII, 137–138); see also EZ 4, 183; Hasidim 123; *Kimha Dabishuna* אל מלך; Maimonides' *Responsa*, 87. The older talmudic-midrashic literature refers quite frequently to these attributes; comp. Rosh ha-Shanah, *loc. cit.*, as well as Tan. B. I, 91; *Nispahim* 42 (EZ, 23); PK 6, 57a; PR 5, 22a; 16, 79b–80a, and 194a; Tehillim 93, 416; Hashkem 3b. Tehillim only knows of the dissenting opinions which count ten or eleven attributes of God. Comp. note 15 on vol. I, p. 8.

²⁹⁸ Sanhedrin 111a (bottom); Tehillim 93, 416. The views cited in these passages differ as to which attribute appeared to Moses to be the most exalted; each of the following attributes is named for this distinction: Long-suffering, grace, compassion, and truth. See also quotation from Tan. (not found in our texts) in Makiri, Ps. 92, 98, and vol. III, pp. 115–116· 280.

²⁹⁹ PRE 46; ER 1, 3–4. Comp. vol. III, p. 148. Philo remarks, in reference to Exod 33.23, that the human intellect cannot conceive the essence of God, but only His activities; see *De Posteritat. Caini*, 48 (end); *De Profugis*, 29; *De Mut. Nom*, 2. Maimonides, *Guide of the Perplexed*, I, 21, gives an explanation of Exod., *loc. cit.*, which is in almost every detail identical with that of Philo. On the very curious statement (Berakot 7a) that Moses saw God's phylacteries (Tefillin), which is certainly not to be taken literally, see R. Hananel in *Responsa der Geonim*, Lyck edition, No. 115; Or Zarua' I, 21b–21c; REBN (ראב"ן) 42b. *Baruk she-Amar* 5d quotes, from Berakot *loc. cit.*, a statement concerning the form of these phylacteries. This statement, however, is found neither in Berakot nor elsewhere.

³⁰⁰ EZ 4, 180–181; ER 17, 86; Tan. Pekude (end); Tan. B. I, 94; Seder 'Olam 6; Ta'anit 30b; Baba Batra 12a. See also Yoma 20a, which reads: On the Day of Atonement Satan has no power to bring an accusation against Israel.

³⁰¹ PRE 46; comp. also the reference given in the preceding note. As to the everlasting continuation of the institution of the Day of Atonement (*i. e.*, its observance in the time to come), see Mishle 9, 61 and vol. VI, end.

³⁰² ShR 46.1.   For a conflicting view comp. vol. III, pp. 119, 197.

³⁰³ PRE 46; Mishle 23, 94, where השניים should be read instead of הראשונים.

³⁰⁴ PR 5, 21b; BaR 12.4; Tan. B. I, 193; Tan. Ki-Tissa 31 and Naso 17; *Batte Midrashot* III, 3 (Yelammedenu?). Comp. the dissenting view in an unknown Midrash quoted in Yalkut I, 854, according to which the second tables were given amid great ceremonies like the first. Lekah Deut. 10.3 agrees with this latter view. See the following note.

³⁰⁵ DR 3.17; Tosefta Baba Kamma 7.4.   A different version is found in an unknown Midrash in Yalkut I, 854: God disapproved of the act of Moses in breaking the tables (see above note 279), and therefore spoke to him as follows: "If thou hadst made these tables thyself, thou wouldst not have broken them; make thou now another pair of tables, that thou mayest appreciate their worth." God then showed him a sapphire quarry under the Throne of Glory (comp. note 258 and the following note), out of which Moses made an exact replica of the first tables.   See also ps-Philo 12 (end), who writes: Hew thee out therefore two tables of stone from the place where thou didst hew out the former, and write upon them again My judgments which were on the first.   In Exod. 34.1 it is plainly stated that God Himself wrote the words upon the second tables, and accordingly one is justified in assuming that the original Hebrew of ps-Philo had וכתבתי which, however, was misread as וכתבת by the translator.—If the first tables had not been broken, Israel would never have forgotten the Torah; 'Erubin 54a; comp. also vol. III, p. 108.

³⁰⁶ Nedarim 38a; ShR 46.2 and 47.3; WR 32.2; Koheleth 9.11 (God showed Moses the sapphire quarry in his own tent); PRE 46; Tan. Ki-Tissa 29, 31 and 'Ekeb 9 (in this passage, in agreement with the Midrash quoted in the preceding note, it is said that the sapphire quarry was under the Throne of Glory, in allusion to Exod. 24.10); BaR 9.48 (read סַפִּיר instead of סָפַר); Sifre Z., 82; ARN 9, 41; Midrash

Aggada Num. 12.2.   In Vol. III, p. 141 line 6, Sapphire is to be read instead of diamond.   On the fifty gates of wisdom, see vol. IV, p. 130, and the note appertaining to it.   Concerning the qualifications of the prophet, see Maimonides, *Shemonah Perakim* 8.   As to the idea that the Torah was originally intended only for Moses, see BaR, *loc. cit.*; DR 3.11; ShR 48.5 and 47.9; note 216; vol. III, p. 118.   See also

PR 21 106a, where the use of the singular in the Ten Commandments is commented upon in this connection. Comp. note 216.

³⁰⁷ ShR 46.2. Comp. vol. III, pp. 5–6.

³⁰⁸ ShR 47.1–4; Tan. Ki-Tissa 34 and Wa-Yera 5; Tan. B. I, 88 and 118; PR 5, 14b; Yerushalmi Peah 2, 17a; WR 22.1; BaR 14.10 (end); Koheleth 1.9; Megillah 19b. The anti-Christian tendency of the Haggadah is obvious. The Church has the Bible in Greek, and yet refutes the oral law. Concerning "the completeness" of the Torah revealed to Moses, see also vol. III, pp. 97 (where it is stated that all the souls were present at the revelation) and 197. As to Moses being a king, see note 170. On the idea that the existence of the world is conditioned upon Israel's acceptance of the Torah, see note 202. On the verbal difference between Exod. 20.2, *seq.*, and Deut. 5.6, *seq.*, see references cited in note 221, to which should be added Lekah Deut. 5.12. In this source attention is called to the fact that the *Decalogue* in Deut. contains all the letters of the Hebrew alphabet, whereas the letter ט is missing in the Exod. version. The explanation of this missing ט, as given in Baba Kamma 55a, is that the word טוב ("good") could not be applied to the first tables, since they were broken. Lekah, *loc. cit.*, though he had no variant reading of Baba Kamma, *loc. cit.*, assigns an entirely different meaning to the simple words of the Amoraim. For other explanations of the missing ט, see *Emunah u-Bittahon* 19 (this was borrowed by R. Bahya, notwithstanding his words מה שרמזו במדרש) and Recanati, Exod. 20.17. Later authorities have a good deal to say about the distribution of the six hundred and twenty letters—corresponding to the six hundred and thirteen precepts of the Torah and the seven Noachian precepts—over the tables, which, according to an old tradition (see Shekalim 15, 49b) measured one by three hand-breadths; see Ginzberg, *Geonica* II, 23 and 35–36; Al-Barceloni, 68–69; BaR 13.16 and 18.21; Tan. Korah 12; Lekah Exod. 20.14; Ginzberg, *Compte Rendu* 21 (=*R.E.J.* LXVII, 135); Ziyyoni, Deut. 5.6.

³⁰⁹ ShR 47.5 and 3.1; Tan. Ki-Tissa 36–37; Tan. B. II, 118–120; Makiri Prov. 30.3. Concerning the eating of the angels while guests of Abraham, see note 143 on vol. I, p. 243, and note 94. As to the idea that the radiance of the Shekinah sustains the angels, see Berakot 17a; Kallah 2,4a. The explanation of Exod. 14.11, found in the last-mentioned source, is identical with that given by Philo, who likewise declares that "seeing God" was unto Moses the same as food and drink to other mortals; see *Moses*, 2(3).2. The view that the rays coming

forth from Moses' face had their origin in the writing upon the tables is presupposed also in Corinthians 3.7. Comp. the following note, as well as notes 204, 260, 295. Hasidim 296 narrates that the radiance of glory was seen on a pious man at the time of his death, which phenomenon is explained in the following way: God, at the time of signing "the decrees of this man's death", caused a drop of ink to fall over him.—As to the manner in which Moses divided his study periods, see vol. III, p. 116, and Megillah 21a.

³¹⁰ Lekah Exod. 34.10. See also *op. cit.* 24, where a reason is assigned for the fact that this distinction was conferred upon Moses on the occasion of the giving of the second tables and not before. According to ER 4, 17–18, this was Moses' reward for his intercession for Israel after they had worshipped the golden calf. The earlier Midrashim, however, present a different view, and maintain that the radiance of the face of Moses preceded the giving of the second tables; see DR 23.11; PK 4, 37a; PR 14, 62b; Tan. B. IV. 114; comp. also references given in notes 204, 269, 295. Ps.-Philo, 12.1, is also of the opinion that Moses received this distinction when he ascended heaven for the first tables; see also Yalkut Reubeni Ki-Tissa (end). When Moses was commanded to write down the verse "And the man Moses was the meekest of all men" (Num. 12.3), he, on account of his humility, was very reluctant to obey and he therefore wrote a very small ו in the word ענו "meek", so that it might also be read as עני "poor". Not having used up the ink of his pen, he wiped it on the hair of his forehead, and from this the radiance of his face originated; see Onkeneira, *Ayyumah Kannidgalot*, 17a, who quotes an unknown Midrashic source. Comp. Sifre Z, 163, and note 490.

³¹¹ PK 5, 45a; PR 15, 69a; Shir 3.70; Shemuel 17, 97; BaR 11.3. Concerning fear as a consequence of sin, see vol. I, p. 76, and Berakot 60b.

³¹² 'Erubin 54b; Mekilta RS, 6; Mekilta Bo 3, 3b. As to the studying of a text four times, see Mekilta RS, 117; Tan. Yitro 15 and Wa-Yakhel 4; BR 4.5; ShR 40.1; Yosippon (?) in Mahzor Vitry 88; Zohar I, 5a.

³¹³ PR 10, 36b–37b; PK 2, 10b; Tan. Ki-Tissa 4. On the humiliation of Moses on account of Israel's sin, see vol. III, p. 125. The Midrashim just mentioned play on the double meaning of תשא ראש in Exod. 30.12, which signifies "count" and "hang". See also quotation, from an unknown Midrash, in *Hadar, ad loc.*

³¹⁴ PK 2, 17b–18b (the numerical value of the initial letters of

the names of the twelve tribes, if counted as thousands, corresponds to the number of people as given in Num. 1.46); PR 10, 40b; Tan. B. II, 197–108; Tan. Ki-Tissa 9. On the census at the time of the Exodus, see vol. III, p. 391; on the census during Saul's reign, see Yoma 22b and Targum on 1 Sam. 15.4 (based on Pesahim 64a); on the inauspicious census in David's time, see vol. IV, pp. 111–112. The counting of the number of Jews, whether of the entire people or of a section thereof, is forbidden by the Jewish law; see Berakot 62b, Josephus *Antiqui.*, 181.

³¹⁵ PK 2, 18b–20a; PR 10, 40a; Tan. B. II, 108–109; Tan. Ki-Tissa 9–11; Shekalim 1, 46b, and 2, 46d. God produced the coin from under His throne; see Shekalim and PK, *loc. cit.* But PRE 48 remarks in this connection: God used each finger of His right hand to bring about deeds of salvation and redemption; with the little finger He pointed out to Noah the way to the ark; with the finger next to it He slew the Egyptians; with the middle finger He wrote the Ten Commandments upon the tables; with the finger next to it He pointed out to Moses the half-Shekel to be given by every Israelite for his atonement. He will use His entire hand to destroy Esau and Ishmael. On the text of PRE see *Hadar* (the source is erroneously given as Pesikta) and *Da'at* on Exod. 30.21. In the latter source it is said that God pointed out to Moses the New Moon (see vol. II , p. 362) with His fourth finger. Comp. vol. II, p. 18, and vol. III, p. 50.

³¹⁶ ShR 51.4; Tan. B. II, 126–127; Tan. Pekude 2 and 6. Comp. also Yelammedenu in Yalkut I, 723 (read אין תורה אלא לשון סהדות; ER 30, 148. Comp. vol. III, pp. 138 and 151.

³¹⁷ Midrash Aggada, Exod. 27.1, which quotes an unknown midrashic source.

³¹⁸ Tan. B. IV, 35; Tan. Naso 11, which reads: I have, in heaven, a temple, a hall (היכל), and a throne; PK 2, 20a–20b; PR 16,84b; Tehillim 91, 395–396; BaR 12.3. Com. also *Likkutim*, II, 2a; 2 Enoch 45, 204; Ecclesiasticus 32.1–5. See vol. I, p. 3.

³¹⁹ PR 2, 18b (emphasis is laid upon the place where the Shekinah dwells, and not on sacrifices); Tan. Naso 22; BaR 12.6.

³²⁰ PR 5, 16a; Tan. Naso 19 and Terumah 9; Tan. B. II, 94; Shemuel 26. Comp. vol. III, p. 185.

³²¹ Tan. Pekude 2; Midrash Aggada, Exod. 38.21; Yelammedenu in Yalkut I, 719, and supplement No. 54 (= BHM VI 89); Shu'aib, Pekude 41c; comp. vol. I, pp. 51–52. The tabernacle is also explained to be, in its form, a symbolic representation of the human body, see

Shu'aib, Terumah 36b–36c, and *Shibbale ha-Leket* 3 (BR is given as the source in this passage); Tadshe 2 and 10. A third view finds in the tabernacle a symbol of heaven and of what it contains. See Tadshe 2; PK 1, 5a; *Likkutim* II, 3b– 4a, and vol. II, pp. 165–166. Comp. note 346.

³²² Tan. Terumah 5–8; Tan. B. II, 90–92; Shir 4.13; Zohar II, 148a. Yalkut I, 429 (= *Likkutim* II, 8b, which is the source for Yalkut Reubeni Deut. 1.1), counts only eleven materials, whereas Mahzor Vitry 314, which quotes Wehizhir (not found in our text of this work), has fifteen. See also Lekah and Midrash Aggada on Exod. 25.3.

³²³ Tan. Terumah 7 (during the reign of Ahasuerus the Mede the destruction of Israel was sought by Haman by means of money; see Esther 3.9; "Red Rome" is an allusion to the identification of Rome with Edom; see note 19 on vol. I, p. 314); Tan. B. II, 91–92; Hashkem 10a; Lekah Exod. 25.3; *Kad ha-Kemah*, *Lulab* I 140, and '*Osher* II, 28b; see vol. III, pp. 166–167.

³²⁴ ShR 40.2. Philo, *Moses*, 2(3).3, speaks of the incorporeal patterns, according to which Moses was to make the furniture of the tabernacles. The same idea is expressed in his *Quaestiones*, Exod. 2, 52 and 82–83. Comp. vol. III, p. 160. Concerning the Book of Adam, see vol. I, p. 61, vol. III, pp. 136 and 398.

³²⁵ ShR 48.3–4; Tan. B. II, 121–123; Tan. Wa-Yakhel 4–5. As to the statement that Miriam was Bezalel's great-grandmother, see vol. II, p. 253; concerning his father Hur, see vol. III, p. 121. Bezalel was thirteen years old at the time of the erection of the tabernacle, and his father was only eight years his senior. The "former generations" became mature, physically and mentally, at a very early age. See Sanhedrin 69b; Yerushalmi Yebamot 10, 11b (Caleb begot his son at the age of ten); Kiddushin 1, 59c. Comp. vol. II, p. 122, and vol. III, p. 283.

³²⁶ Berakot 55a; Koheleth 7.11; Aggadat Shir 5, 36–37, where an opinion is quoted, according to which Bezalel and his assistant Oholiab went up Mount Sinai, where the heavenly Sanctuary was shown to them; BR 1.14; Yerushalmi Peah 1, 15b. The etymological explanation of the name Bezalel as meaning "In the Shadow of God" is also given by Philo who finds in it an indication that Bezalel's conception of God was "shadow-like", whereas that of Moses was a substantial one; see *Leg. Alleg.*, 3.31, and *De Plant. Noë*, 6. As to the question whether the ark or the tabernacle was made first, see also vol. III, pp. 156–157, 160–161, and 176. It is very doubtful

whether the combination of letters spoken of in the Haggadah is identical with the Philonic ideas. Comp. Index, s. v. "Letters". On the assent of the people, comp. note 164.

³²⁷ ShR 40.4; Tan. Ki-Tissa 13; PR 6, 26a; 'Arakin 16a. Comp. also vol. III, p. 222. The names mentioned in 1 Chron. 4.1–2 are taken by the Haggadah to be those of Bezalel.

³²⁸ ShR 48.3; Tan. B. II, 122–123; Tan. Wa-Yakhel 5. Comp. also PRE 3. Concerning the spirit which God will shed over the animals in the time to come, see 2 ARN 43, 60.

³²⁹ ShR 50.1–2; Tan. Wa-Yakhel 5; Tan. B. II, 124. Comp. also vol. III, p. 155, where a different opinion is quoted, according to which the Sanctuary was first erected and subsequently the ark was fashioned. See also vol. III, pp. 160–161 and 176. God commanded Moses to make the entire nation participate in the work of the ark, in order that all might have a share in the Torah kept in the ark; ShR 34.2. Comp. Tan. Wa-Yakhel 7, which reads: Bezalel fashioned the ark with his own hands, whereas the rest of the work was done by others under his direction.

³³⁰ Tan. Wa-Yakhel 7; BaR 4.13 and 5.1; Yelammedenu in Yalkut I, 729; Tehillim 22, 185–186; Baba Batra 14b; Shir 1.2 and 3.5; DR 7.9; Yoma 21a, which states: The ark did not diminish the empty space of the Holy of Holies; see parallel passages cited on margin as well as Yerushalmi Baba Batra 6, 15c, and comp. note 65 on vol. IV, p. 156. Just as the ark, the receptacle of the Torah, was within and without of fine gold, even so must a scholar, the possessor of the Torah, take care that his inside is like his outside, that is, he must be sincere. See Yoma 72b, as well as Philo, De Ebriet. 21; Quaestiones, Exod. 2, 54. In 2 Clemens, 12, a saying attributed to Jesus, reads: The kingdom of God will not arrive before the inside of man will be like his outside. It is quite obvious that in this saying the rabbinic phrase תוכו כברו (comp. Yoma 72b; Tan., loc. cit.; Leket Midrashim, 6b and 7b) is made use of.—The identification of the ark with the promised angel (see Exod. 23.20) is first found in Lekah, Exod., loc. cit. This identification is very likely based on old sources. Comp. the reference in note 435. Of all the furniture and vessels of the Sanctuary the ark is the only one whose measure is given in fractions (see Exod. 25.10); this indicates that, like the ark, the human receptacle of the Torah ought to be humble of spirit and contrite (=broken) of heart; Kad ha-Kemah, Gaawah (end). See also the explanation of the four staves of the ark as given in Lekah, Exod. 25.12.

[331] Shekalim 6, 49b; Sotah, Tosefta 7.18 and Yerushalmi 8, 22b–22c; Baba Batra 14a–14b; Meleket ha-Mishkan 6; Sifre N., 82; Sifre Z., 191.   A different view is given in Yerushalmi Sotah, *loc. cit.*, according to which there was only one ark which served as a receptacle for the two sets of the two tables, for the scroll of the Torah, and for the presents offered by the Philistines (see 1 Sam. 6.8).

[332] Meleket ha-Mishkan 7; Shekalim, Mishnah 6.1–2; Tosefta 2.18; Talmud 7, 49b; Tosefta Sotah 13.1; Yoma 53b–54a; EZ 25, 129.   Comp. Friedmann's remarks on Meleket ha-Mishkan, *loc. cit.*; vol. III, pp. 48, 161.

[333] Tadshe 2; Sukkah 5b; ShR 41.6; DR 3.16.   The symbolic representation of the ark, as given by Philo, *Moses*, 2(3).8, and *Quaestiones*, Exod. 2, 62, offers many points of resemblance to that of the Midrashim.   With reference to the Cherubim, Josephus, *Antiqui.*, 6.5, writes: Cherubim are flying creatures, whose form is not like any creature, but which Moses saw near the throne of God.

[334] Sukkah 5a; Mekilta Bahodesh 4, 65; comp. also Yerushalmi Shabbat 1, 2d.

[335] Baba Batra 99a; a somewhat different version is given in Yoma 54a–54b.   Comp. also Onkelos and Targum Yerushalmi on Exod. 25.20.   The raising of the curtain during the festivals is also mentioned by Josephus, *Antiqui.*, III, 6. 4.

[336] Meleket ha-Mishkan 7; Yoma, Tosefta 2(3).7 and Babli 64a; comp. vol. III, p. 163.

[337] Meleket ha-Mishkan 8; Menahot Tosefta 11.9, and Babli 98b–99a; Shekalim 6, 50a–50b.   On the qualities of the south and the north, see vol. I, pp. 11–12, and the notes appertaining to them.   Philo, *Moses*, 2(3).10, writes: The table on which bread and salt are laid (salt is in agreement with Septuagint Lev. 24.7; whereas the Rabbis, Menahot 11, 5–8, and Josephus, *Antiqui.*, II, 6.6, know nothing of salt) was placed on the northern side, since of all the winds, the north wind is the most beneficial for the production of nourishment.   See also Yelammedenu 53=BHM VI, 88.

[338] BaR 15.9; Tan. B. I, 49–50; Tan. Beha'aloteka 6.   The pattern, fashioned of fire, for the ark, the table, and the candlestick came down from heaven to Moses, that he might be able to make these vessels of the sanctuary.   According to another view, it was Gabriel who taught Moses how to fashion the candlestick; see Menahot 29a.   Comp. also note 315, vol. III, p. 219, and note 202 on vol. II, p, 362.

[339] Tadshe 2; Meleket ha-Mishkan 10; Menahot, Tosefta 11.10,

and Babli 99a; Shekalim 6, 50a. Comp. vol. III, pp. 159–160, where
a similar statement concerning Solomon's tables is given. The symbolic explanation of the seven branches of the candlestick, as representing the seven planets, is given by Philo, *Vita Mosis*, 2(3).9; *Quis......
Haeres Sit*, 45; Josephus, *Antiqui.*, III, 6.7; as well as by the Midrashim,
Tadshe 11; Tan. Beha'aloteka 6; Yalkut I, 219. The last-quoted
source reminds one of Philo's words. Comp. also vol. III, p. 151.

³⁴⁰ Tadshe 11. As to the view that paradise is situated in the
north, see note 33 on vol. I, p. 11. The passage in Tadshe concerning
the south is not very clear, and it may be translated: There—in the
south—is only one light, that of the Shekinah. In Baba Batra 25b
the candlestick is explained to be a symbolic representation of the Torah
(comp. Ps. 119.105). A similar explanation is found in the Apocalypse
of Baruch 17.4 and 59.2.

³⁴¹ Tan. B. IV, 50; Tan. Beha'aloteka 6; BaR 15.9. Comp.
vol. III, pp. 48 and 158.

³⁴² Tan. Terumah 10–11. Concerning the heavenly beings,
some of which are made of fire and some of water, see the statements
in PK 1, 3a (numerous parallel passages are cited by Buber; comp. also
ARN, second version, 24, 48–49, note 63 on vol. I, p. 16) which refer to Michael and Gabriel, as well as to those angels who are made
partly of fire and partly of snow. On the sea of ice, see vol. I, p. 13.
As to the idea that the cedars used for the Temple blossomed and
bore fruit, see also Tan. B. IV, 32, which reads: Everything in the
Temple, even the gold, was fruitful and multiplied; BaR 11.3 and 12.4;
ShR 35.1; Shir 3.8; Yoma 21b and 39b; vol. I, p. 97 and vol. III, p. 159.
The belief in the generative power of precious stones was widespread
in the middle ages; see Kunz, *The Magic of Jewels and Charms.*

³⁴³ Tadshe 11. The view that the soul is sustained by fragrant
odors is widespread; see, *e. g.*, Berakot 43b, and the explanation given
by many medieval authorities concerning the custom of smelling spices
at the termination of the Sabbath; comp. Mahzor Vitry 117.

³⁴⁴ Tan. Terumah 9–10; Tan. B. II, 91 and 94–95; ShR18.10,
33.8, and 35.1; BR 15.1 (numerous parallel passages are cited by Theodor)
and 94.4. Concerning Tahash, see vol. I, p. 34; concerning the view
that Jacob prepared the necessary building material, see above, note
1, and vol. I, pp. 118–119. Shu'aib, Terumah 37b, quotes an unknown
Midrash to the effect that the Shittim-wood for the tabernacle came
from paradise, whence Adam took it with him when he was driven
out of that place. Subsequently it came into the possession of

Abraham, who bequeathed it to Isaac.   The latter, in his turn, bequeathed it to Jacob, who took it with him to Egypt.   At the Exodus, the Israelites took it with them to the desert.   According to Targum Yerushalmi Exod. 26.28, the middle bar was made of the wood taken from the tree which Abraham planted at Beer-sheba (comp. vol. II, p. 119). The angels felled this tree when the Israelites crossed the Red Sea, and threw it into the waters thereof, while an angel proclaimed: "This is the tree which Abraham planted in Beer-sheba."   The Israelites took the tree out of the water, and later made of it the middle bar, whose length was seventy cubits.   This bar became circular when the tabernacle stood erect, so that it held all the boards together; but as soon as the boards were removed the middle bar became as straight as a rod.

³⁴⁵ Yoma 72a (bottom); Rashi, *ad loc.*, who remarks that the boards were hidden and will be brought out again in the time to come. See vol. III, p. 194.

³⁴⁶ Midrash Aggada Exod. 26.7, based on an old source, since Abbahu, who flourished about the end of the third century, is quoted as the authority.   See also ShR 33.4 and 35.6; PK 1, 4b–5a; BaR 12.8; Shir 3.11.   The correspondence between the stars and the golden clasps, spoken of in the sources just quoted, is also referred to in Shabbat 99a and Yerushalmi Megillah 1, 72c–72d.   The most elaborate symbolic explanation of the tabernacle, found in rabbinic sources, is the one given by R. Shemaiah of Soisson in his treatise on the tabernacle published by Berliner in *Monatsschrift* XIII, 225–231 and 258–264.   A. Epstein, *Mikkadmoniyyot* (supplement), 2–4, calls attention to the close resemblance of the symbolic explanation, as given by R. Shemaiah, to that found in Tadshe and Bereshit Rabbete, all three attempting to show that man, the world, and the Sanctuary correspond to one another.   Shu'aib, Terumah 36b, drew upon a source closely related to the three mentioned above, whereas *Shibbale ha-Leket* 3 is a direct quotation from Bereshit Rabbete, and accordingly בבראשית רבתי is to be read instead of בבר' רבא as found in our texts.   Noteworthy is the following quotation from a Midrash given by R. Shemaiah (*op. cit.*, 226), which reads: God said unto Moses: "Behold the celestial sanctuary, and erect the terrestial sanctuary in like fashion."   Comp. vol. III, p. 53, last paragraph.   The symbolic explanation of the tabernacle as given by Philo, *Moses*, 2(3),3–10, and particularly *Quaestiones*, Exod. 2, 51–124, has many points of contact with that of the Rabbis. Clemens, *Stromata*, 4.6, is altogether based on Philo.

³⁴⁷ Tadshe 2; comp. Index, s. v. "Heavens".

³⁴⁸ Tadshe 10. The seventy names of God, of Israel, and of Jerusalem are enumerated in Aggadat Shir 1, 8–10. Comp. Schechter *ad loc.*

³⁴⁹ Tan.Terumah 10.

³⁵⁰ ShR 35.5; Pesahim 118b. The Haggadah frequently speaks of Esau (=Rome) priding himself of his descent from Abraham, and says that in the time to come he will attempt to save himself by claiming relationship with Jacob (=Israel); see Yerushalmi Nedarim 3, 38a, and Tan. B. III, 15. All these Haggadot are very likely to be taken as anti-Christian. As to the gifts offered by the Gentiles to the Messiah, see also Enoch 53.1 and 90.30. Concerning the four kingdoms and their symbolic representations, see vol. III, p. 153.

³⁵¹ ShR 37.1–4; Tan. Terumah 10; Shemuel 23, 112; Koheleth 7.1; Tehillim 101, 427–428, which read: The tribe of Reuben was rejected because of Reuben's sin in connection with Bilhah; the tribe of Simeon on account of their sins at Shittim (comp. vol. III, p. 382); the Joseph tribes because Joseph slandered his brethren. Comp. vol. II, pp. 5 and 6; ER 13, 63, and 31, 157, which read: Aaron strove to reconcile Israel to his God (see vol. III, p. 328), and he was therefore chosen to perform the work of reconciliation (*i. e.*, atonement) in the Sanctuary. Concerning Aaron's real motives in fashioning the golden calf, see vol. III, p. 121, as well as *Da'at* and *Hadar* on Exod. 3.2. As to Moses's aspiration to the priesthood, see vol. III, p. 316. Comp. vol. III, p. 182.

³⁵² Tan. B. II, 100–101; Tan. Terumah 10–13; ShR 38.1.

³⁵³ WR 10.6; Zebahim 88b; 'Arakin 16a; Yerushalmi Yoma 9, 44b–44c; Shir 34.1; Yelammedenu in Yalkut I, 513 (this passage agrees literally with WR). See also Yoma 7a–7b (in this passage atoning power is ascribed to the mitre only and that in a limited degree) and 72a–72b. A very elaborate symbolic interpretation of the priestly garments is given by Philo, *Moses*, 2(3).2–14, and *Special. Leg.* 15–6, of which Josephus, *Antiqui.*, III, 7.7, seems to have made use, but of which no trace is found in rabbinic literature. The tripartite division of the tabernacle, as a symbol of the tripartite division of the cosmos into water, dry land, and heaven, is given by Josephus and in Tadshe 2 (beginning).

³⁵⁴ ShR 33.8, with the additional remark that the Jews at that time were so rich, that any one of them would have been able to defray

the cost of the erection of the tabernacle. See also Yoma 95a; Zohar III, 23b; comp. vol. III, pp. 176, 193.

355 Maimonides' *Yad, Kele ha-Mikdash* 9.9 (he undoubtedly follows a tannaitic source); Sotah 36a, and Yerushalmi 7, 21d. See the thorough study of Epstein, *Mikkadmoniyyot*, 83-90, and comp. also *Responsen der Geonim*, Harkavy's edition, 3, as well as the following note.

356 Yoma 73b; Sotah 36b. Comp. also Epstein, *Mikkadmoniyyot* 83-90, as well as Aristeas 97, and Josephus, *Antiqui.*, III, 7.5. In order to have all the letters of the Hebrew alphabet engraved upon the stones, it was necessary to include the names of the three patriarchs, as well as the words "all these are, etc." (Comp. Gen. 49.28). Had some letters been missing, the oracular sentences would not have been possible. See vol. III, p. 172.

357 R. Bahya on Exod., 28.17, which is the source for Toledot Yizhak, *ad loc.*; *Talpiyyot*, s. v. האבנים סגולת, makes use of R. Bahya's description, but does not follow it in every detail. See also ShR 38.8-9; Lekah and Targum Yerushalmi on Exod. *loc. cit.*; Targum Yerushalmi Num. 2.2-25 (this passage differs from Targum on Exod.); Targum Song of Songs 2.12. The old rabbinic literature has no remarks about the peculiarities of the twelve stones, and there can be no doubt that R. Bahya, or rather the source which he followed, is based upon some medieval lapidarium. Steinschneider, *Semitic Studies in memory of Kohut* 64, *seq.*, gives a bibliography of lapidaria composed by Christian authors in the Middle Ages. Of course, the relation between the peculiarities of the stones and the history of the tribes is of Jewish origin. Comp. Index, under the names of the Twelve Tribes. See vol. III, pp. 233, 238; vol. IV, p. 24.

358 Yoma 73a-73b and Yerushalmi 7, 44c. The Urim and Thummim ceased to give oracular answers immediately after the death of the first prophets; Sotah 9.12. According to Tosefta 13.2 and Babli 48b, by the "first prophets" are meant those prophets who lived during the first commonwealth, so that the time when the Urim and Thummim ceased to function is identical with the time of the destruction of the first Temple. Yerushalmi 9, 24b, however, offers the opinion that the expression the "first prophets" refers to Samuel and David, and accordingly the Urim and Thummim did not function in the first Temple. Targum Yerushalmi, Exod. 28.30, maintains that the high priest gave the oracular answers by means of the "great and holy Name" which was engraved upon the Urim and Thummim as well as up-

on the *Eben Shetiyyah.* The sources quoted in notes 355 and 356 do not make the slightest allusion to the Name being engraved upon the stones of the breast-plate. Concerning the statement that the Name was engraved upon the *Eben Shetiyyah,* see Index, s. v. On the lustre of the stones, see vol. III, p. 455; vol. IV, p. 8. The view given in Lekah, Exod. 29.15, as that of יש אומרים is quite unintelligible to me.

³⁵⁹ Mekilta Shabbat 2, 104b; Mekilta RS 165. See also Sifra 19.3 and 4 Maccabees 2.10, with reference to the honor due to parents, which one is not to observe when it conflicts with the honor due to God.

³⁶⁰ Tan. as quoted in *Shibbale ha-Leket* 67–68; Abkir in Yalkut I, 408; *Rokeah* 53 (the source, though not given by the author, is very likely Abkir). Comp. also Megillah 4a; Lekah, Exod. 34.34 (end); Zohar II, 203. The last-named passage reads: Moses communicated the laws of Sabbath to the Israelites before they worshipped the golden calf. But many of the people, misled by the "mixed multitude" (see vol. III, pp. 122–123), did not observe them, and Moses therefore repeated them after the death of the "mixed multitude" (see vol. III, p. 130). This time he addressed himself exclusively to the Jews. The source of Zohar is Lekah, Exod. 35.4. The Sabbath as the day of study and religious instruction is of frequent occurrence in Jewish literature; see *e. g.,* Pesahim 68b; Yer. Shabbat 15, 15a; PR 23, 116a and 121a; Philo, *Special. Leg.* 2.6; *Vita Mosis,* 2(3).27 (in this passage it is regarded as an institution of Moses); ps-Philo 11.7.

³⁶¹ Shabbat 90a. Comp. Lekah, Exod. 34.34.

³⁶² Shekalim 1, 45d; Lekah, Exod. 35.22; ShR 41.2 (which remarks: All that was necessary for the building of the tabernacle was brought in the short space of "two morning hours"); BaR 12.37; Tehillim 101, 428; Tan. B. II, 90; Tan. Terumah 4(it is stated in this passage: God's blessing was on everything which the people brought, so that even little things were put to great use).

³⁶³ Shabbat 74b and 99a; Targum Yerushalmi Exod. 35.26. The goats came every day, with the exception of Sabbath and the New Moon, to the women, and offered their wool for the hangings of the Tabernacle; Shu'aib, Wa-Yakhel, 42b, On the New Moon as a festival of the women, see vol. III, pp. 121–122 and next note; on the animals participating in the erection of the Tabernacle, see vol. III, p. 156.

³⁶⁴ Aggadat Shir 4, 79 (the word שלמה in this passage probably means, not "cloak", but, as in Deut. 22.17, the garment used by the bride); BaR 9.14 (it says: They disposed of their mirrors as a proof

of their chastity); Tan. Pekude 9, reads: The women provided their husbands with food consisting of fish which came to them in a miraculous way as soon as they let their pitchers down into the well to draw water. See Sotah 11a, and comp. further PRK 15a on fish as a food conducive to fecundity. The statement with regard to the praise of the women in the passage cited by *Hadar*, Exod. 35.22, reads somewhat differently from that in the sources quoted above; it also adds that the women received the New Moon as a festival (see the preceding note), as a reward for their devotion to their nation by bearing and raising children under very trying circumstances. In the legends about the mirrors of the women, expression is given to the thought that it is the intention which counts more than the deed; comp. Mishnah Menahot (end), which reads: Whether one does much or little—does not matter—provided the intention is for the sake of heaven. The story told in WR 3.5 of the poor widow and the high priest, as an illustration of the importance of the intention, is very much akin to that of Mark 12.44; Philo, *Moses*, 2(3).15, seems to presuppose a Haggadah similar to that given by the Rabbis concerning the mirrors presented by the women.

³⁶⁵ Tan. B. IV, 40; Tan. Naso 27 (the text is corrupt); comp. vol. III, pp. 192–193. As to the provenance of these stones, see vol. III p. 169, as well as Targum Yerushalmi Exod. 35.27, where it is stated that the clouds fetched them from the river Pishon (see Gen. 2.12), and placed them in the wilderness (read מדברא instead of מדבחא), where the princes found them. Comp. vol. III, p. 27. A similar legend is given in the following verse of Targum, according to which the clouds brought the perfumes from paradise, and placed them in the wilderness for Israel. In Yoma 75a, the clouds which carried the precious stones are identical with those which brought the manna. It therefore seems reasonable to assume that Targum did not draw upon this passage.

³⁶⁶ Tan. B. II, 125; Tan. Wa-Yakhel 10; ShR 50.4–5. Comp. the different opinion concerning the order of the work, as given in vol. III, pp. 155, 156–157.

³⁶⁷ PR 24a–24b (on the text, see *Orehot Hayyim* I, 26d), which has the additional remark that the month of Kislev was later compensated with the feast of Hanukkah, in memory of the dedication of the Temple under the Maccabees; Tan. Pekude (end); ShR 52.2. On Isaac's birthday see note 203 on vol. I, p. 261; vol. IV, p. 155. On the derogatory expression "son of Amram", see note 163, and comp. the phrase

"son of Bath-sheba" in vol. VI, p. 155.   On the people finding fault with Moses, see vol. III, p. 69.

³⁶⁸ Tan. B. II, 129; Tan. Pekude 7, and Ki-Tissa 27; ShR 51.6; Kiddushin 33b; Yerushalmi Bikkurim 3, 65; Zohar II, 226 (which reads: A heavenly voice told the people of the use made of the supposedly missing item); Midrash Aggada Exod. 38.21; Hadassi, 132a. No. 358. Similarly *Manhig, Tefillah,* 39, knows the tale about the sudden appearance of the hooks which came to defend Moses against his accusers. See also Toledot Yizhak, Exod., *loc. cit.,* and *Ayyumah Kannidgalot,* 16a, where this legend is given in accordance with the *Manhig* version.

³⁶⁹ ShR 51.2; Tan. Pekude 5; Tan. B. II, 127; Midrash Esfah in Yalkut I, 737; Sifre Z., 62 and 110.   Comp. Hoffmann, *Wichtigste Instanzen gegen die Graf-Wellhausensche Hypothese,* 81.   To remove all suspicion, Moses took Ithamar to participate with him in drawing up the accounts of the treasury of the tabernacle; ShR, *loc. cit.*

³⁷⁰ Tan. Pekude 11; Tan. B. II, 132–133; ShR 52.2–3. As a reward to Moses for his great devotion to the work of erecting the tabernacle, Scripture speaks of the erection of the tabernacle "by Moses" (Num. 7.1) and not " by Israel". See Tan. Ki-Tissa 35; BaR 12.1. Com. note 257.

³⁷¹ Horayyot 11b and Keritot 5b; in both passages it is also stated that until Josiah hid the sacred oil (vol. III, p. 48) all the high priests and those kings who did not come to the throne by inheritance were anointed with the oil prepared by Moses. During the second commonwealth neither the high priests nor the kings were anointed with the "oil of ointment", though some of the kings were anointed with balsam. But according to PRK, 42a, Aaron and his sons and Zadok were the only "anointed priests"; among the kings, Saul, David, Joash, and Jehoash enjoyed this distinction.   Comp. Ginzberg, *Unbekannte Sekte* 319–320; WR 3.5 and 10.8; ARN 1, 1 and 34, 100; BaR 12.15, 14.13, and 18.9; PK 1, 7a; Sifre N., 92, Sifre Z., 53–54 (this passage gives a very detailed description of the ceremony of anointing) and 57; Shekalim 9, 49c–49d; Sifra 7.35 and 8.10; Tehillim 133, 517; Tan. Korah 6; Tan. B. IV, 90; Shir 1.10; Midrash Shir 34b (which reads: Through a miracle not a drop of the sacred oil was spilled;) Ekah 1,87; *Batte Midrashot* III, 16. The emphatic manner in which many of the passages just quoted state their view that neither Aaron nor the Messiah will be anointed in the time to come leads one to assume the probability that this opinion is directed against the Christian Messiah, literally

⁴the anointed one". Com. Ginzberg, *op. cit.*, note 4 on p. 348, and note 23 on vol. IV, p. 84.

³⁷² PK 4, 38a–38b (this passage quotes also the dissenting view, according to which Moses performed the services of high priest during the last forty years of his life; this opinion seems to have been shared by Philo, who describes Moses as a high priest; see *Quis....Haeres Sit*, 38); Zebahim 101b–102a; Ta'anit 11b; Yerushalmi Yoma 1, 38b; WR 11.6; BaR 9.44; ShR 37.1; Tehillim 91, 423–424; PR 14, 63b–64a; comp. note 121 on vol. II, p. 316.

³⁷³ Tan. B. III, 19.21; Tan. Zaw 10–12; WR 10.9; *Likkutim* II, 4b; BR 5.7 (numerous parallel passages are cited by Theodor); DR 4.11; PR 1, 2a (on the text see *Rokeah*, 221); PK 12, 108a–108b, and 20, 143a–143b; ARN 35, 106; Baba Batra 76b; Sifre D., 1. The question as to how, at the time of the resurrection, all the numberless multitudes will find place in Palestine engaged the attention of Sa'adya Gaon; see *Emunot we-Deot*, 7 (= BHM VI, 148–149). See vol. III, pp. 212, 311–312; vol. IV, p. 6. An allusion to the legend that all the Israelites were assembled in the Sanctuary is very likely to be found in Enoch 89.36. As to the date of the consecration of the priests, see Sifre D., 44; Seder 'Olam 7 and parallel passages given by Ratner.

³⁷⁴ Sifra 8.15 and 35; Seder 'Olam 7; Tosefta Menahot 7.6, *seq.*; PK 6, 6a–6b; PR 5, 15a; Yerushalmi Yoma I, 38b; BaR. 13.2.

³⁷⁵ Tan. B. II, 21–22; Tan. Shemini 1; BR 100.7; Yerushalmi Moed Katan 3, 82c; comp. also Tan. B. I, 222, and Tan. Wa-Yehi 17, as well as note 64 on vol. I, p. 142.

³⁷⁶ Seder 'Olam 7; Sifra 9.1; BR 3.9; Shabbat 86b; PR 7, 27b; BaR 13.6; Tadshe 10. Comp. also Sifre Num., 44, and Shekalim 1. 2a (beginning).

³⁷⁷ Tan. B. III, 24; Tan. Shemini 10; WR. 11.6; Comp. note 372; vol. II, p. 316 and vol. III, pp. 168–169.

³⁷⁸ Sifra 9.1.

³⁷⁹ Tan. B. III, 24; Tan. Shemini 3. Comp. vol. II, pp. 328–329.

³⁸⁰ Sifra 9.2–24. Concerning the atonement for the selling of Joseph, see ShR 30.7 and vol. II, p. 25. On the admonition of Moses to drive away the evil inclination, see Philo, *Moses*, 2(3).17, according to whom one of the sacrifices offered up on this occasion was intended to convey to the Israelites the thought that even the virtuous are not free from sin. On the fire of the altar, see 2 Maccabees 2.10; vol. III. pp. 161–162, 245; vol. IV, p. 353. Besides the fire of the altar, it was the smoke by which God's grace was indicated; see Tan. Tezawweh

15; Midrash Shir 28b; PK 27, 171b (by the smoke of the fire of the altar on the Day of Atonement one could judge whether the new year would be prosperous or not); PR 47, 190b; Tan. B. III, 60; WR 20.4; Yoma 21b; Baba Batra 147a. On the likeness of the fire of the altar to a lion, see Yoma, *loc. cit.*, and Zohar III, 32b–33a.

³⁸¹ PR 5, 15a–16a, 18b, 20b–22b; Tan. B. IV, 37–40; Tan. Naso 16–19, 23, and 25, as well as Pekude 11; BaR 12.4, 7. 12. Concerning the Shekinah's withdrawal to heaven, see vol. II, p, 260; Tehillim 8, 76–77. In the old sources the view prevails that the terrestrial sanctuary corresponds to the celestial one (comp. *e. g.*, Mekilta Shirah 10, 43b; BaR 45.7; Index, s. v. "Sanctuary Celestial"), whereas the later Haggadah reverses the relation between these two sanctuaries, maintaining that after the destruction of the terrestrial sanctuary the celestial one was erected to serve as a place of atonement for Israel; see BHM V, 63, where Michael, not Metatron, is the celestial high priest, in agreement with Hagigah 12b and Seder Rabba de-Bereshit 24. An attempt to harmonize these two conflicting views is given in the text, in accordance with the sources cited at the beginning of this note, maintaining that the two sanctuaries were established simultaneously. See also *Hadar*, Lev. 9.2, which reads: Michael was appointed high priest—of the celestial sanctuary—at the same time as Aaron. R. Bahya, Exod. 40.17, cites Hagigah, *loc. cit.*, as source for the harmonizing legend; but this is probably a slip of the pen, or his text of the Talmud contained this later addition. The Karaite writer Kirkisani, in his treatise on Jewish sects (still in manuscript), quotes a lengthy passage from the Talmud on Metatron's priestly functions and activities as teacher. Comp. vol. I p. 385; vol. III, p. 149; Zohar II, 241a, and III, 3b.—Concerning Moses' fiery (red) face, see PK 27 (end); on the change of the intercourse between God and man after the establishment of the tabernacle, see Shir 2.3 and parallel passages. Concerning demons, comp. Tehillim 17, 130–131, and 55, 292; Ekah 1.63; Baba Kamma 21a. As to the blessings of Moses on this occasion, see Sifra 9.18; Tosefta Menahot 7.8; Seder 'Olam 6; *Likkutim* II, 1b–2a; quotation from later (unknown) Midrashim by Shu'aib, Pekude(end); comp. also vol. III, pp. 69 (bottom) and 454.

³⁸² Seder 'Olam 7; Zebahim 102a; PK 27, 170a; Tehillim 75, 338; WR 20.2; Mishle 31, 112; Koheleth 2.2; Tan. B. III, 50–57; Tan. Ahare 1; Shir 3.6; Sifra 10.1–2; Sifre N., 44; Sanhedrin 52a; Tan. B. I, 50 (which asserts that their bodies were burned, but not their garments); Tan. Noah 15 and Shemini 12; Targum Yerushalmi

Lev. 10.2. The tannaitic Midrashim just quoted cite an opinion' according to which the angels pushed the two sons of Aaron out of the holy place before they were burned. On Moses' kingship see note 170. On the position of Phineas as "priest of war", see vol. III, p. 389.

³⁸³ Tan. B. III, 61–64 and 67–68; Tan. Ahare 6; WR 29. 4–12; BaR 2.23; PK 27, 172a–174b; Tehillim 78, 356; Shebi'it 6, 36c; 'Erubin 63a; Sifra 9.2; Sanhedrin 52a; Yelammedenu in 'Aruk, s. v. חה (2), and No. 46 = BHM VI, 86. Concerning the improper conduct of Aaron's sons in looking at the divine vision on Sinai, see vol. III, 248 and note 187. Philo, *De Profugis*, is of the opinion that Nadab and Abihu, in their "love and affection for God, were willing to die in body, that they might live before the Lord." A similar view is found in Sifra 10.1; comp. note 599.

³⁸⁴ PR 47, 189b. Moses, who was only a Levite and not a priest, was not permitted to enter the place of the tabernacle which was assigned to the priest; comp., however, note 372. As to the punishment of leprosy, see vol. III, p. 214, and note 30 on vol. IV, p. 262, as well as vol. I, p. 364.

³⁸⁵ Sifra 10.2–7 (this section does not belong to Sifra proper, but to a tannaitic Midrash of the school of R. Ishmael); Zebahim 115a (on the text see Al-Barceloni, 128 and *Shittah Mekubbezet, ad loc.*); Targum Yerushalmi Lev. 10.4–5. Concerning the conception that God is glorified by the death of the pious, see John 12.28. On Aaron, the lover of peace, see vol. III, p. 328; on the direct revelation received by him, see notes 387, 405. Opinions differ as to whether the bodies of Nadab and Abihu were injured by the heavenly fire, which brought about their death, or not; but all agree that their garments remained intact; Sifra 10.2; Sanhedrin 52a; Tan. B. I, 50; Tan. Noah 15. Comp. note 382.

³⁸⁶ Sifre D., 31; Rosh ha-Shanah 18b; Zohar III, 56b and 57b; on the atoning effect of the death of the pious, see further Yerushalmi Yoma 1, 38b; Tan. B. III, 64 and 66, and parallel passages cited by Buber.

³⁸⁷ Sifra 10,16, 19–20; WR 13.1; ARN 26 (second version 60), 111 (see Schechter, note 29); Yelammedenu in Yalkut II, 139, and 1 Sam. 27; Zebahim 101a–101b; Hashkem 7a–7b; Wehizhir II, 171; comp. notes 110, 406, 599, 862.

³⁸⁸ BaR 12.16–21, which is based on older sources; see PK 1, 7a–10a; PR 7, 26b and 28a (in this passage it is explicitly stated that the story about Nahshon is derived from the similarity of the name

נחשון to the word נחשול "billow"; hence this legend does not reflect
the self-sacrificing character of the patriarchal house during the second
century, as suggeted by Oppenheim in *Ha-Hoker*, I, 97–99); Sifre
Z., 54–56; ARN 11, 45–46; Tehillim 101, 428–429; Shir 6.4; Sifre N.,
45–47. Concerning the princes of the tribes, see vol. III, pp. 169
(the "notables" referred to stand for the princes), 175–176, and 249;
on Issachar, the wise and learned tribe, see Index, s. v. On the animals living forever, see Vol. V, pp. 422–423 and note 345. Concerning
David's error see vol. III, p. 395, and vol. IV, p. 96. On the courage
and self-sacrificing character of the tribe of Judah at the crossing of
the Red Sea, see vol. III, pp. 21 and 221, as well as the sources cited
in note 36, and BaR 13.4, 7. Comp. Tan. B. IV, 40, and Tan. Naso 27.

389 Sifre N., 47–51; Sifre Z., 56; BaR 13.2; Tan. Naso 20. Comp.
also WR 8.3, and vol. III, p. 201.

390 BaR 13.14–16. It is often stated in the Hagadah that
Jacob foretold the history of the future to his sons; see, *e. g.*, vol.
II, p. 141. On Solomon, the Cosmocrator, see vol. III, p. 355, and vol.
IV, p. 125. Concerning Judah's sin, see note 62 on vol. II, p. 25.
For other explanations of the sin-offering, see Sifre N., 51; Lekah Num.
7.16. Comp. Sifre N., 52; Sifre Z., 56; Targum Yerushalmi Num. 7.19.

391 BaR 13.17; Sifre D., 354. Comp. Index, s. v. "Zebulun".

392 BaR 13.18. On Reuben, the type of the repentant sinner,
see note 60 on vol. II, p. 24.

393 BaR 13.19. The faithless woman died immediately after
she tasted the dust on the floor of the tabernacle (see Num. 5.6, *seq.*);
hence the sanctuary is described as the "avenger of unchastity".

394 BaR 13.20. On Jochebed's age at the time of her death,
see note 817. Concerning the undiminished spirit of Moses, see vol.
III, p. 251. As to Israel's three virtues, see vol. II, p. 300. On
Israel's idolatry in Egypt, see vol. II, p. 341. Concerning the merits
of Jacob and Joseph, see vol. II, p. 7; vol. III, p. 16.

395 BaR 14.2 (end) and 5; Tan. B. IV, 42–44; comp. vol. II, pp.
94 and 183, as well as vol. III, p. 82. On the correspondence of the
incidents in Joseph's life with those of Jacob, see vol. II, p. 4 *seq.*

396 BaR 14,6–7; Tan. B. IV, 42 and 45; Tan. Naso 28 and 30.
Comp. vol. III, p. 183.

397 BaR 14.8. On Herod's atonement, see Baba Batra 3b–4a.

398 BaR 14.9. On Samson, see note 115 on vol. IV, p. 47.

399 BaR 14.10. Besides the seventy nations, the descendants

of Noah (comp. note 72 on vol. I, p. 173), there are sixty kingdoms, twelve Ishmaelitic and forty-eight Edomitic; hence there are altogether one hundred and thirty nations. As to the refusal of the Torah by the nations, see vol. III, pp. 81 and 355. On the three, or rather four crowns, see Abot 4.13; ARN 41, 130 (second version 48, 130–131). The last-named passage reads: Moses acquired the first crown, Aaron the second, David the third, but the fourth may be acquired by everyone. See also Yoma 72b; Sifre N., 119; ShR 34.2; Shemuel 23, 112; Koheleth 7.1.

⁴⁰⁰ BaR 14.11. On Naphtali's swiftness, see note 217 on vol. I, 371. Concerning Abraham's power over the evil inclination, see note 276 on vol. I, p. 292. As to Abraham's age at the time of the "covenant between the pieces", see vol. V, p. 230, note 115. The Hebrew word for "bowl" is מזרק, from the root זרק, the meaning of which is "to throw."

⁴⁰¹ BaR 14.12 and 18; Tadshe 10; Alphabet of R. Akiba 35 (לו); PRK Grünhut's edition, 89–90; comp. Excursus II, Naphtali. The vital parts of the human body are only slightly different from the "ten guides", as may be seen from Koheleth 7.19. It is therefore safe to assume that BaR and Tadshe have blended together the two different views concerning the anatomical division of the human body; but see vol. IV, p. 147. On the sons of Zerah comp. Seder 'Olam 21, and vol. II, p. 283.

⁴⁰² BaR 14.18; Tadshe 10.

⁴⁰³ Sifre Z., 57–58; Sifre N., 53–56; BaR 14.13. Symbolic explanations of the gifts of the princes are given, besides BaR 13–14 and Tadshe 10, also in Targum Yerushalmi Num. 7.84–88 and Yelammedenu in Yalkut I, 714.

⁴⁰⁴ Tan. B. III, 4–5; Tan. Wa-Yera 3. Comp. also WR 1.5 and Yelammedenu in Yalkut II, 940 on Prov. 8.

⁴⁰⁵ BaR 14.19–22, which is based on older sources; comp. Sifre Z., 48, 55, 58–59, and 108; Sifre N., 58; Sifra 1.1; Mekilta (beginning); ARN 2, 10. The view prevalent in tannaitic sources is that Aaron never received a direct revelation, and that the passages in the Pentateuch which apparently presuppose direct revelations to Aaron (see *e. g.*, Lev. 10.3) are intended to convey that God told Moses to communicate certain revelations to Aaron. For a dissenting view see vol. II, p. 341; vol. III, pp. 190, 216. On demons, or rather angels of destruction, see vol. II, p. 226; vol. III, p. 186. It is noteworthy that, according to the Haggadah, the ministering angels, left the holy of holies as soon

as the high priest entered it on the Day of Atonement; see PR 47, 190a, 191a; Yerushalmi Yoma 5, 42c. Philo, *Quis Rer. Div. Haeres Sit*, 5, remarks: God instructed him, not in brief sentences, but gave him an unbroken and continuous answer. These words seem to be directed against the view of the Rabbis that God always allowed a pause between the different laws which He imparted.

[406] Gittin 60a; Sifre Z., 55, speaks of fifteen revelations received by Moses on this memorable day.

[407] WR 26.6.

[408] Sifre 7.36; BaR 14.13.

[409] Tan. B. IV, 50–51; Tan. Beha'aloteka 8; BaR 15.12 and 1.12; Midrash Tannaim, 215; Sifre N., 67; comp. vol. II, pp. 259, 300–301, and 341; vol. III, pp. 94, 130, and 438. Yalkut II, 589, on Malachi 2.4, quotes a Midrash, according to which the prophet Malachi refers to the Abrahamic covenant as the "covenant of Levi" (see Malachi 2.8), because the tribe of Levi was the only one that held fast to the Abrahamic covenant during Israel's stay in Egypt.

[410] Midrash Aggada Num. 98.6–16; BaR 4.8, 12.7 and 15 (this passage reads: The Levites defiled themselves through the dead bodies of the worshippers of the golden calf—Exod. 32.26, *seq.*—and accordingly had to be purified). Comp vol. I, p. 320; vol. III, pp. 23 and 122. It was only through a miracle that the presence of *all* Israel at the consecration of the Levites was made possible. Comp. vol. III, p. 180.

[411] WR 26.9; Koheleth 12.7; Ekah (פתיחתא) 23.19. Comp. Aristeas 93.

[412] BaR 7.1, 4, 6; Mekilta Bahodesh 3, 64a, and 9, 71b; Sifre N., 1; WR 18.4; PR 7, 28a, and 15, 78b; Zohar II, 51b; *Toratan shel Rishonim* II, 26. Comp. vol. II, p. 374, vol. III, p. 78.

[413] BaR 7.4–5; Tan. Mezora' 4; Tan. B. III, 48–50; WR 17.3; Tosefta Nega'im 6.7; PRK 37a; Zohar III, 206a. Comp. vol. I, p. 112; vol. IV, p. 259; vol. III, p. 87.

[414] Sifre N., 68; Sifre Z., 66–67; Pesahim 6a; Midrash Aggada Num. 1.1. Comp. vol. III, pp. 107 and 356.

[415] WR 21.7; PR 47, 189b–191b; PK 27, 176a–176b; Tehillim 10, 96; Yerushalmi Yoma 1, 39; Yelammedenu 49 = BHM VI, 87, and in *'Aruk*, s. v. דריה (this passage reads: The high-priest is greater than Michael; the latter pleads for Israel only with words, while the former intercedes in their behalf with deeds); Tan., quoted by Makiri on Prov. 24.6; an unknown Midrash cited in *Imre No'am* on Exod. 38.32 reads: Satan seized the high priest by the throat to prevent him from

performing the service in the holy of holies. Comp. note 405; vol.
II, p. 226; vol. III, pp. 185, 210.

⁴¹⁶ WR 12.1 (end); but comp. note 405. It is, however, possible
that the word יחד in WR means: He revealed a law which referred
exclusively to Aaron and his sons. Comp. Sifre Z. 48 and 108.

⁴¹⁷ PK 4, 39a–39b, and 41b; PR 14, 46a–46b and 66a; Tan. B.
IV, 117 and 120; Tan. Hukkat 8; BaR 12.15, 13.15, and 19.6; *Batte
Midrashot* III, 8 (from Esfah?); Sifre N., 44; Niddah 9a (bottom);
Yoma 57a (top), which reads: God dwells with the Israelites even when
they are in a state of impurity (quoted as an answer given by a Rabbi
to a polemical argument of a מין, that is, a Judeo-Christian). See also
Aggadat Shir 4, 37 (this passage reads: In the time to come God will
remove the impurity of idolatry, unchastity, and bloodshed from Israel);
Tosefta Parah 3.5, which reads: When the Israelites were exiled to
Babylon, they took with them the ashes of the red heifer. The legend,
found in Pahlavi literature (comp. *R.E.J.*, 19, 51), that the Jews
took with them to Babylon water and dust from Jerusalem is an inaccurate representation of the statement of the Tosefta. Shu'aib,
Hukkat, 88c, quotes, from Mishnah Parah 3.5, the statement that
the Messiah will furnish the tenth red heifer. But our texts of the
Mishnah contain the remark that from Moses until the destruction
of the Second Temple nine red heifers were furnished, one by Moses,
etc. Nothing is, however, said about the red heifer in the time to come.

⁴¹⁸ BaR 15.5–7; Tan. B. IV, 47–48; Tan. Beha'aloteka 4–5;
comp. Shabbat 22b; ShR 35.23.

⁴¹⁹ Yelammedenu in Yalkut I, 719 (beginning of Beha'aloteka),
and *Orehot Hayyim* I, 4b. Comp. BHM I, 134–135, and the following
note, as well as vol. IV, pp. 36 and 6.

⁴²⁰ Midrash quoted in Or Zarua' I, 139, No. 321; Nahmanides
on Num. 8.2. The passage quoted from Yelammedenu in *Orehot
Hayyim* (comp. preceding note) very likely refers to the Hanukkah
lights, and not to the lights in the Temple. Comp. BHM I, 135,
and note 367.

⁴²¹ Tan. B. III, 28–29; Tan. Shemini 8. For another legend
concerning the candlestick, see vol. III, pp. 160–161. Comp. also vol.
II, p. 362 with reference to the legend about the three things which
God had to demonstrate to Moses. Sifre Z. 60–61, reads: God showed
Moses the pattern of the candlestick four times; 1) when He showed
him the patterns of all the sacred vessels; 2) when He made him watch
Michael beat out the golden plates of the pattern (this is how the word

ממתיח is to be understood; this word is used instead of מרקיע on account of the phrase מיכאל מותח which is often quoted; comp. BR 3.9 and parallel passages cited by Theodor, ממשיח of MHG and the first edition of the Yalkut is a worthless reading); 3) He showed him the candlestick in the process of making; 4) when the candlestick was completed. See also quotation from Mekilta (R. Simon?) by Hadassi, *Eshkol*, 30a, Nos. 82, 338.

⁴²² Rashi on Num. 1.1, based on an uknown midrashic source. Comp. BaR 1.10; Lekah Num. 2.1; vol. III, p. 146.

⁴²³ MHG Numbers I (in manuscript).

⁴²⁴ Midrash Aggada Num. 1.4–14 (the phrase נילוס נינוס "the small Nilus" is employed in contrast to "the great Euphrates;" comp. BR 16.3), and, in abridged form, *Pa'aneah* and *Imre No'am* on Num., *loc. cit.* As to Reuben's repentance, see vol. II, p. 24. On Judah's confession of sin, see vol. II, p. 36. On Nahshon, see vol. III, p. 195. On Issachar and Zebulun, see vol. II, p. 144. On the explanations of the names of Elishama, Ammihud, Gamaliel, and Pedahzur, see also Tan. B. IV, 43; Haserot 49, and parallel passages cited by Buber on Tan.   Concerning the meaning of the name Benjamin, see Midrash Aggada Num. 27.38; vol. I, p. 415.   On the beauty of the women of Asher, see vol. II, p. 145; vol. III, p. 461. Concerning the tribes of Gad, see vol. IV, pp. 16–17 (ישמעאלים is to be read instead of מצריים in Midrash Aggada). On the successful adversaries of Amalek, see vol. I, p. 369 and vol. III, pp. 57–58. On the sinful tribe of Dan, see vol. III, pp. 57 and 171. For other explanations of the names of the princes see *Hadar*, Num. 7.28, and Hasidim 438.

⁴²⁵ Lekah Num. 1.46. The taking of the census lasted only one day, the people and the leaders being equally anxious to carry out God's command without delay; Lekah Num. 1.17. See vol. IV, p.23.

⁴²⁶ *Pa'aneah* on Gen. 49.2; *Baal ha-Turim* and *Imre No'am* on Num. 1.46. Lekah Num., *loc. cit.*, on the contrary, maintains that this tribe consisted of males only.

⁴²⁷ BaR 1.12 and 3.7 which is very likely based on an old source, since Kalir in his piyyut איתן for Shekalim, and Rashi on Num. 1.49 (Tan. Bemidbar 15, end, is not Rashi's source, as Berliner erroneously maintains), neither of whom was acquainted with BaR, made use of a source in which the tribe of Levi was described, as in BaR, as the body-guard (לניון) of God.

⁴²⁸ PK 2, 20b; BaR 3.8; Tan. B. IV, 16–17; Tan. Bemidbar 16. Comp. vol. II, p. 122, and the note appertaining to it.

⁴²⁹ PK 2, 20b–21a; BaR 3.9 and 7.2; Tan. Bemidbar 16. Comp. vol. III, p. 145. Aaron, though belonging to the tribe of Levi, was not included in the census of the Levites; ARN 34, 109, and parallel passages cited by Schechter. This is given as an explanation of the dots upon ואהרן (Num. 3.39). Comp. Blau, *Masoretische Untersuchungen*, 9, seq.

⁴³⁰ PK 23, 154b–155a; WR 29.11; BaR 3.8; Tan. B. IV,17–18; Tan. Bemidbar 17; PRE 28 (in this passage we have instead of the seven worlds—see vol. I, p. 90—the seven parts of the world, and the Holy Land is counted as the seventh); Tehillim 9, 86–87. For the praise of the "seven", see also Philo, *De Mun. Opif.* 30, seq. Comp. Vol. V, p. 157, top; Index,s. v. "Seven".

⁴³¹ BaR 4.98. Comp. vol. I, p. 320; vol. III, p. 211.

⁴³² Sanhedrin 17a and Yerushalmi 19c; Tan. B. IV, 20–21; Tan. Bemidbar 21;BaR 4.9–10; PK 2, 21a. Comp. vol. III, pp. 94, 230, 249–250.

⁴³³ Sifre N., 63; Sifre Z., 62; Hullin 24a.

⁴³⁴ Ta'anit, Tosefta 4(3).2 and 2.1; Babli 27a; Yerushalmi 4, 67d–68a; Tehillim 1, 1; comp. also Sifre Z., 62.

⁴³⁵ BaR 5.1 and 8; *Batte Midrashot* IV, 35. Concerning the ark, see vol. III, pp. 157–158; Sifre Z., 192. In the latter passage the identity of the ark with the "angel of the Lord" seems to be presupposed, comp. note 330. As to walking backwards while carrying the ark, see Yoma 53a. On the Levites being barefooted, see vol. V, p. 420, note 122.

⁴³⁶ BaR 7.6 and 8.

⁴³⁷ Yerushalmi Shabbat 10, 12c; BaR 4 (end); *Batte Midrashot* IV, 34; BHM III, 122. In the last source Aaron is also praised for his modesty, because he did not consider it beneath his dignity to remove the ashes from the altar; the last sentence is quoted from the Agur, a Midrash which is no longer extant; see Brüll, *Jahrbücher*, V, 98, and Gaster, *Zeitschrift f. heb. Bibliographie* X, 92-94.

⁴³⁸ Yerushalmi Shabbat 12, 13c; BaR 7.3 and 11.

⁴³⁹ BaR 2.3 and 8; Tan. B. IV, 11; Tan. Bemidbar 12; Shir 2.4 (quoted by Shu'aib, Bemidbar with numerous variants) and 6.11. On the number of angels who accompanied God on Sinai, see vol. III, pp. 49 and 227. On the instructions given by Jacob concerning the standards, see vol. II, p. 148. Comp. also *Hadar*, Exod. 13.17, which reads: They made use of the standards at the exodus from Egypt.

⁴⁴⁰ BaR 2.10 (here no reason is given for the statement that Reuben corresponds to Michael; but the reason is found in Targum

Yerushalmi Num. 2.10); PR 46, 188a, here the text reads correctly
פתח מיכאל, and not פתח משה, as BaR has it; BHM II, 39 (Michael in
the front, Gabriel to the right), and VI, 49. In the last passage,
as well as in the unknown Midrash quoted in *Kimha Dabishuna* (on חיות,
Minhah service of the Day of Atonement) the four Hayyot take the
place of the four archangels. The identification of the Hayyot with
the four archangels, Michael, Gabriel, Raphael, and Uriel, was already
known to the Gnostics; see Origen, *Contra Celsum* 6.30. In PRE 4
the order is: Michael to the right, Gabriel to the left, Uriel in front,
and Raphael in the rear; comp. also Zohar III, 118b. An allegory of
the old legend is to be found in ARN 43, 121, which reads: The throne
of glory has four standards, righteousness, justice, grace, and truth.
Concerning the three, or rather seven heads of the heavenly hierarchy
see note 13 on vol. I, p. 54. The expression "Gabriel to the left" occurs
also in Enoch 24.1, whereas according to Ascension of Isaiah 8.7,
all "angels are to the left". On the identity of Uriel with Suriel,
see Ginzberg, *Unbekannte Sekte*, 35–37 and 245. Comp. Vol. V, p.
159, line 6 from bottom.

⁴⁴¹ BaR 2.10 and 3.12; Konen 38; PR 47, 188a–188b; BHM
VI, 47; Kaneh 31d–32a. On Issachar, see vol. II, p. 144. On Reuben, see
vol. II, p. 24. On Dan see vol. III, p. 57. As to the south being
the blessed region, see vol. III, p. 160. *Likkutim* II, 2b–3b, and DZ
19, consider that the division of the twelve tribes corresponds to the
twelve signs of the Zodiac.

⁴⁴² Targum Yerushalmi Num. 2.3–25. Comp. the following note.

⁴⁴³ Kaneh 32b–32c; Midrash Aggada Num. 2.2; Yerahmeel 53,
149; Ziyyoni, Bemidbar (fragmentary); *Imre No'am*, Num. 10.34;
Sabba, Bemidbar 110a–110b; Al-Barceloni 8. Epstein, *Mikkadmoniyyot*
87–90, justly remarks that the Haggadah concerning the standards
found in Targum Yerushalmi (see the preceding note) goes back to
a source made use of by these medieval authors. Comp. also vol. III,
pp. 237–238 and 243.

⁴⁴⁴ Sifre N., 84; Meleket ha-Mishkan 14, 83; Tan. B. IV, 12
(the short statements of the tannaitic sources are elaborated here);
Midrash in Yalkut at the end of Exodus = *Likkutim*, II,13b–15b. Comp.
also Yerushalmi 'Erubin 5, 22c; Yerahmeel 53, 151–152; vol III, p. 243.

⁴⁴⁵ Midrash in Yalkut I, 426 = *Likkutim*, II, 13b; Yerahmeel
53, 155–156. A different version of this legend is found in Yalkut
I, 427 = *Likkutim* II, 13b. Comp. Tan. B. IV, 12; Tan. Bemidbar
12; *Batte Midrashot* III, 18; vol. III, pp. 53 and 288. The description

of the camp as a square of twelve miles is already found in very old sources; see, *e. g.*, Mekilta Bahodesh 2, 62b; 9, 71b, and in many other passages. Comp. note 210.

⁴⁴⁶ PR 10, 92a–92b; DR 7.11; Shir 4.11; Tehillim 23, 199–200; comp. vol. III, p. 109. Justin, *Dialogue*, 131, is acquainted with the legend concerning the miraculous growth of the garments.

⁴⁴⁷ BaR 2.7; Tan. B. IV, 12; Midrash Aggada Num. 2.2 (Issachar's emblem was a donkey, that of Zebulun was a house); Yerahmeel 52, 153, where it is stated that Issachar's emblem was a donkey, as in Midrash Aggada; Ziyyoni, Num. 1.1; Shu'aib Bemidbar, 74a; *Imre No-'am* at the end of Bemidbar. The old form of this legend, as given in Targum Yerushalmi Num. 2.3, *seq.*, knows only of four insignia for the four main divisions of the camp, which are: Lion for Judah; manikin for Reuben (neither ברחילא of the editions, nor בראילא of the MS. is correct; read ברונא=ברולא, literally, "little son"); fish for Ephraim; serpent for Dan. These four images of animals are chosen in accordance with Gen. 48.16; 49.9, 17, where Judah is described as a lion, Dan as a serpent, Ephrain as a fish, while the manikin for Reuben owes its origin to the mandrakes found by Reuben, which looked like manikins; comp. Index, s. v. The later Haggadah could not resist the temptation of identifying the four insignia of the camp with the figures at the holy throne (comp. vol. III, p. 231, concerning the correspondence of the celestial divisions with the terrestial ones), and hence in Lekah Num. 2.2, *seq.*, the eagle replaces the serpent. Epstein, *Mikkadmoniyyot* 87, *seq.*, is to be corrected accordingly. Yerahmeel 53, 152–153, gives a lengthy exposition of the symbolic representations of the four elements by the four standards. Similar expositions in a somewhat abridged form are found in other writings of the Middle Ages; see Ziyyoni, *loc. cit.*, and Epstein, *loc. cit.* As to the correspondence between the colors of the flags and those of the stones in the high priests's breast-plate, to which the sources just quoted refer, see the description of these stones in vol. III, pp. 169–172.

⁴⁴⁸ Esfah in Yalkut I, 683. Comp. also BaR 13.8, where it is said: The tribes of Reuben, Simon and Levi preserved their family records, *i. e.*, did not intermarry with those who were not of pure Jewish blood, and therefore Scripture describes their family trees separately from those of other tribes (Exod. 6.14, *seq.*). Comp. note 6 on vol II, p. 189. The Gentiles said: "The Egyptians were the masters of the Hebrew men, how much more so of the Hebrew women!" God therefore commanded the angel who is appointed over pregnancy to make the Jewish child-

ren look like their fathers. No one doubted any longer the purity of the Jewish race; Shir 4.2; PK 10, 82b; BaR 9.154; comp. also BR 79 (end) and Kiddushin 70b. Comp. vol. V, p. 245, note 204.

449 WR 33.4–5; BaR 9.14; Tan B. III, 163; Tan. Emor 24; Targum Yerushalmi Lev. 29.10; comp. also BaR 3.6, which reads: Israel's redemption from Egypt was rewarded for the chastity of the women, see also Zohar II, 4a; Sifre 24.10.

450 Yashar, Shemot, 133b. Another version of this legend is given in vol. II, p. 279; see also PRE 48 (here the wronged husband is described as belonging to the tribe of Levi), and note 7 on vol. II, p. 191.

451 WR 33.3; Tan. B. III, 162–163; Tan. Emor 23–24; Sifra, Lekah (cursed Moses!), and Tan. Yerushalmi on Lev. 24.11; Sabba' (at the end of Emor). Zohar III, 106a, which is very likely based on a midrashic source (comp. *Hadar*, *Da'at* and *Pa'aneah* on Lev., *loc. cit.*), reads: The bastard attempted to cause the death of Moses by cursing him with the Name, and in this way to avenge his Egyptian father who had been killed by Moses in the same manner; see vol. II, p. 288. The secret of the bastard's descent was divulged in consequence of his quarrel with the Danites (comp. also Yelammedenu in Yalkut II, 961, on Prov. 25), for Moses himself did not care to reveal family secrets (see Toesfta 'Eduyyot, at the end), especially as bastards die young if their descent remains a secret; see Yerushalmi Yebamot 8, 9c–9d; WR 33.6–7; Wisdom 3.16 and 4.6. According to a later source (comp. Azulai, *Petah 'Enayim* on Yebamot 78a), the short-living of bastards dates only from the time of Ezra, who prayed to God to make the bastards die young, so that the purity of the Jewish people might be preserved. The mocking words of the bastard with reference to the law concerning the shewbread were without foundation. It is true that the loaves remained a whole week on the table; they were, however, as fresh at the end of the week as at the time they were taken from the oven; Menahot 29a. Comp. RITBA (ריטב״א) on Yoma 21a.

452 Sifre N., 105, 113, 114, 133; Sifre Z., 103–105; Sifra 24.12; Shabbat 96b; Baba Batra 119b. To exculpate—partly at least—the father of the pious virgins (comp. vol. III, pp. 391, *seq.*), it is said that Zelophehad was willing to sacrifice his life that the people might learn by his death that the desecration of the Sabbath is a very grievous sin; comp. Targum Yerushalmi Num. 15.32–35 and *Imre No'am*, at the end of Shelah who gives a Midrash, not Targum, as source for his statement. See also notes 813, 814. Philo, *Moses*, 2(3).27–28

(which reads: They found Moses in the house of study; this is in agreement with Sifra), and *Special. Leg., de Col. Par*, 8, describes the episode of the Sabbath breaker in a manner similar to that found in
rabbinic sources. According to Tosefta Yebamot 1.10, and parallel
passages in Babli and Yerushalmi, the high-priestly family of Caiafas
(קיפא, "ape") hailed from Bet Mekoshesh, "the house of the stick-
gatherer". In view of the legend—undoubtedly Jewish—found in
Koran 2.60, that Moses transformed the Sabbath breakers into apes,
one is inclined to trace some connection between the Caiafas ("apes")
and their place of origin, "the house of the stick-gatherer", the מקושש
being the typical case of the Sabbath breaker. See note 790.

453 ER 26, 132; this is very likely the source of Mahzor Vitry,
637; *Orehot Hayyim*, 58d; Lekah and *Imre No'am* on Num. 15.38.

454 Sifra 24.12; comp. also the references to Philo and tannaitic
Midrashim given in note 452.

455 Targum Yerushalmi Lev. 24.12; Num. 9.8, 15.34, and 27.5;
comp. also Philo, *Vita Mosis*, 2(3).24, and Sifre N., 68.

456 Yelammedenu in Yalkut I, 739; Wayekullu in *Likkutim*,
II, 17a–17b. On the ark, see vol. III, pp. 235 and 428.

457 Sifre N., 82; Sifre, Z., 191 (read קורסור "cursor" for קנסור);
Tan. Wa-Yakhel 7; Targum Yerushalmi Num. 10.33.

458 Sifre N., 85; Sifre Z., 79 and 193.

459 Rashi and Midrash Aggada on Num. 11.1, which is very likely
based on an older source. Concerning the "forced marches" see Sifre
N., 82, and Sifre D., 2; Sifre Z., 191. In Sifre D., 2, it is said that if
the Israelites had not sinned, they would have reached the Holy
Land in one day. Comp. note 456.

460 Sifre N., 85; Sifre Z., 79 and 193–194; PRE 35 (on the text
comp. *Batte Midrashot*, III, 30);Targum Yerushalmi Num. 11.1. Comp.
R. Bahya on Num. 11.1, who gives a different view to the effect that
they were afraid of Moses to utter their complaints in a loud voice.

461 An unknown Midrash quoted by R. Bahya on Lev. 9.24,
and in MHG Num. 11.1. Sifre Z., is not the source of this Haggadah,
as was erroneously assumed by Horovitz who incorporated it in his
edition of this tannaitic Midrash (pp. 79–80), for R. Bahya was not
acquainted with this tannaitic work. *Toledot Yizhak*, Lev., *loc. cit.*,
is directly based on R. Bahya, and is not to be regarded as an independent
source. See also PRK, 16a, and vol. I, p. 107.

462 Sifre N., 84 and 86, which also gives the opposite view that
the fire caused the death of the most prominent men; Sifre Z., 194;

Targum Yerushalmi Num. 11.1; Kiddushin 75b; Yerushalmi Gittin 1, 43d (top); BR 95.4; Tan. B. IV, 60; Tan. Beha'aloteka 16 (the members of the Synhedrion were consumed by the fire=Sifre Z., *loc. cit.*); BaR 15.24.

⁴⁶³ PRE 52; *Batte Midrashot*, III, 30; comp. vol. I, p. 16...

⁴⁶⁴ Sifre N., 86; Sifre Z., 194.

⁴⁶⁵ PRE 53; Sifre Z., 80 and 194 (according to the second passage the fire disappeared in the same place where it broke out; the first passage is therefore a literal quotation from PRE, and not of tannaitic origin like the second); Sifre N., 85–86. Concerning the fire of the altar, see vol. III, p. 184.

⁴⁶⁶ Tan. Wa-Yishlah 2; Yalkut I, 732 (in this place the sources from which the extracts were taken are not described; the quotation from Sifre 86 closes with במקומה; the extract which follows it, up till שקעה בארץ, is taken from PRE 53; the next passage is practically identical with Tan., *loc. cit.*; the closing remarks on the reason for the punishment by fire is found in Tan. B. IV, 60, though expressed in a somewhat different manner); Yelammedenu in Yalkut I, 813.

⁴⁶⁷ Sifre N., 86; Sifre Z., 194.

⁴⁶⁸ Sifre N., 86–89; Sifre Z., 194–198; BaR 7.4; ShR 25.3. Concerning the manna, see details given in vol. III, pp. 44, *seq.*, 334–335, and note 90. The rather obscure remarks of Tosefta Sotah 6.7 about the abundance of fish Israel enjoyed in Egypt are to be explained in accordance with the legend given in note 364. Comp. also DZ 19. A very interesting conversation between R. Meshullam (ben Kalonymos) and an Arabian prince about the ingratitude of the Israelites, who complained about the heavenly gift of manna, is recorded in Sabba', Beha-'aloteka, 116b.

⁴⁶⁹ Sifre N., 87 and 90; Sifre Z., 195 and 198–199; Shabbat 130a; Yoma 75a; Yerushalmi Ta'anit 4, 68d; BaR 15.24; Tan. B. IV, 61; Tan. Beha'aloteka 16; Targum Yerushalmi Num. 11.5 and 10. In Mekilta RS 26, חנם is taken in its literal sense: they did not wish to use their cattle for food, and desired to receive meat like bread—manna— for nothing.

⁴⁷⁰ Josephus, *Antiqui.*, III, 13.1. The tannaitic sources maintain that Num. 11.7 is to be taken as the protest of Scripture against the slanderous words of Israel in the preceding verse; see Sifre N., 88; Sifre Z., 195; Tosefta Sotah 9.2. Josephus makes one of the people utter the protest!

⁴⁷¹ Sifre N., 90; Sifre Z., 199; Targum Yerushalmi Num. 11.12–15.

⁴⁷² Tan. B. IV, 60–61; Tan. Beha'aloteka 16; BaR 15.24; quotation from an unknown Midrash in Yalkut I, 732 (on the source of Yalkut, see note 466). Comp.vol. III, pp. 123 and 188. According to BaR 13.20, the elders appointed by Moses were the same men who, braving all danger, accompanied him on his first visit to Pharaoh's court. For the opposite view see vol. II pp. 330–331. The explanation of Exod. 24.2 in Lekah agrees with the view of Ephraem I, 223A, according to which the elders received their prophetic gift not at Sinai, but later when Moses appointed them. Concerning the death of the elders by the fire from heaven at Tabera, see reference in note 462.

⁴⁷³ Tan. B. IV, 61; Tan. Beha'aloteka 16; 15.25.

⁴⁷⁴ Tan. B. IV, 58; Tan. Beha'aloteka 13; BaR 15.20; Targum Yerushalmi Num. 11.16; Sifre N., 92; Sifre Z., 200. Comp. vol. III, p. 193.

⁴⁷⁵ Sifre N., 92; Sifre Z., 200. Comp. vol. III, p. 340.

⁴⁷⁶ Midrashic fragment (Esfah?) published by Buber, from a Vatican MS., in the Hebrew periodical *Keneset Israel* (1885), 309, *seq.*, and thence by Chones, in his supplement to *Rab Pe'alim*, 149–150. Comp. Sifre N. 95; Sifre Z., 201–202; Sahnhedrin 17a and Yerushalmi 1, 19c; Tan. B. IV, 56–57; Tan. Beha'aloteka 12; BaR 15.19. Comp. vol. III, p. 227. The Vatican fragment made use of some, and perhaps of all, the sources just quoted.

⁴⁷⁷ Esfah in Yalkut I, 736, where two lists of names are given; a third list is found in the fragment quoted in the preceding note. But none of the lists has been carefully preserved, as quite a considerable number of names is corrupt. Despite the corrupt state of the texts, one easily recognizes the principle guiding the authors in the selection of the names. The elders of each tribe bear names which are found in Scripture to have been borne by persons belonging to that particular tribe; comp.,*e. g.*, the names of the six elders of the tribe of Simeon with Gen. 46.10 and Num. 25.14. In view of this fact, it is safe to assume that כניה is to be read instead of חנניה, since the former name is that of a Levite (see 1 Chron. 15.22), but not the latter. A fourth list of names of the elders is found in Mahzor Vitry 388, giving as his authority a responsum of R. Nissim (flourished in North Africa at the beginning of the eleventh century), which enumerates the names of the seventy-eight pious men (he counts six elders for each tribe, and adds Moses, Joshua, Caleb, Eliezer, Ithamar, and Phineas) who wrote the section of Haazinu (=Deut. 32.1–43) in Scripture. It is hard to say anything definitely as to the meaning of "the writing of Haazinu", but there

can be no doubt that seventy-two of these seventy-eight pious men are meant to stand for the seventy-two elders appointed by Moses. See also Aristeas 47–50, which gives a list of the seventy-two elders who translated the Scripture into Greek. In Esfah (both lists), among the elders of the tribe of Benjamin, there is one named סנאב or סניאב, for which סנואה or סנאה is to be read in accordance with Nehem. 11.9 and 1 Chron. 9.7. The tannaitic sources also call a Benjamite family "the sons of סנאה"; comp., *e. g.*, Ta'anit 4.5.

⁴⁷⁸ Esfah in Yalkut I, 737. As to this tent, see vol. III, p. 177, and note 369.

⁴⁷⁹ Sifre Z., 200–201 (it was one of the ten times that God descended upon earth; comp. notes 260 and 919); Sifre N., 93; Tan. B. IV, 57–58 and 61; Tan. Beha'aloteka 12 and 16; BaR 15.19, and 25, as well as 13.20; Targum Yerushalmi Num. 11.23. That the gift of prophecy conferred upon the elders remained with them until the end of their days, is asserted by Onkelos and Targum Yerushalmi Num. 11.25, whereas Sifre, *loc. cit.*, gives a different opinion. See vol. III, p. 252. The likening of Moses to a burning candle from which many others are kindled occurs not only in the Midrashim just quoted, but also in Philo *De Gigantibus* 6, from which Theodoretus, Num. 11.17, may have borrowed it. In the philosophic literature of the Middle Ages this figure of speech is of frequent occurrence with reference to the wise and their disciples; see, *e. g.*, *Tikkun Middot ha-Nefesh* 5.2, *Musare ha-Pilosofim* 3.2 and 6.9. Comp. also Sifre Z., 163, and Aphraates, 122.

⁴⁸⁰ Tan. B. IV, 51–54, which also gives the conflicting view that not even David made use of the trumpets, neither of those fashioned by Moses nor of any others; Tan. Beha'aloteka 9–10; BaR 15.15–16; Koheleth 8.8; Menahot 28b; BR 96.3; Sifre N. 75; Z., 70. A detailed description of these trumpets and the music produced by them is given in Sifre N., 72–74; Sifre Z., 70–73; Yerahmeel 53, 151–152.

⁴⁸¹ Tan. B. IV, 57; Tan. Beha'aloteka 12; BaR 15.19 (here Eldad and Medad are identified with Elidad and Samuel mentioned in Num. 34.20–21; but comp. vol. III, p. 253). See also Sifre N., 95; Sifre Z., 8 and 201–202; Sanhedrin 17a and Yerushalmi 1, 19c; note 476. As to the great piety of these two prophets, see vol. IV, p. 158. According to BaR 3.7, they survived Joshua.

⁴⁸² BaR 15.19; Tan.B. IV, 57; Tan. Beha'aloteka 12; Yerushalmi Targumim Num. 11.26 (with regard to the punishment of the people of Magog, it is said here that a fire from under the holy throne will

descend and consume their souls, leaving their bodies unimpaired. Comp. note 59 on vol. IV, p. 269, and Index, s. v. "Souls, Burning of"); Sifre N., 95; Sifre Z., 202; Sanhedrin 17a, and Yerushalmi 1, 19c. According to ps.-Philo 20.5, the prophecy of Eldad and Medad read: After that Moses resteth, the captaincy of Moses shall be given unto Joshua the son of Nun. This is in harmony with the tannaitic Midrashim quoted above, and Ephraem I, 257E, who know nothing of the prophecy referring to the time to come. Hermae Pastor, 2.3, quotes from the Book of Eldad and Medad who prophesied to the people in the wilderness as follows: "Nigh is the Lord to them that repent". Comp. Ps. 145.18. In the *Stichometry* of Nicephorus the writing of Eldad and Medad occupied four hundred stichoi. Comp. Schürer, *Gecshichte* (4th edition), III, 360–361. See also note 484.

⁴⁸³ BaR 15.19; Tan. B. IV, 57; Tan. Beha'aloteka 12; Sifre N., 96; Sifre Z., 202–203; Yerushalmi Targumim Num. 11.28, which read: Prevent the prophetic spirit from resting upon them (on the text see Shu'aib, *ad loc.*, who quotes from Targum Yerushalmi מנע מנהון רוח קדשא); Sanhedrin 17a (which reads: Appoint them to offices, and they will die a premature death). Comp. above, note 278, and note 57 on vol. IV, p. 17.

⁴⁸⁴ *Hadar, Da'at, Pa'aneah*, and Shu'aib on Num. 11.26; ps.-Jerome on 1 Chron. 4.17. A certain R. Hillel, who flourished at the end of the twelfth century, visited the Holy Land, where he found the following inscription on the tomb of these prophets: "Brothers of Aaron on the paternal side, but not on the maternal." See the rabbinic sources quoted at the beginning of this note. Targum Yerushalmi Num. 11.26, on the contrary, maintains that Eldad and Medad were the sons of Jochebed and Elizaphan the son of Parnach (Num. 34.25), whom she married after she had been divorced from Amram (see vol. II, p. 262), shortly before the birth of Moses. It is very strange that Targum makes Amram re-marry Jochebed after she had been married to someone else, which is explicitly forbidden by the law (see Deut. 24.4). Yahya, *Shalshelet*, 13a, quotes, from PRE and Rashi on Chron., the statement found in Targum Yerushalmi, that Jochebed was the mother of Eldad and Medad. It is hard to believe that Yahya's references are correctly cited, as it is unlikely that his texts of PRE and Rashi differed from ours. If it is not a slip of the pen, it is all the worse for that author, who purposely quotes wrong authorities to make a strange statement acceptable! R. Nissim, quoted in *Imre No'am*

Mass'e at the end, identifies Eldad with Elidad; comp. note 481, and Beer, *Monatsschrift* VI, 643–650.

485 Sifre N., 95; Sifre D., 31; Sifre Z., 201 (פטורת means "excuse", from פטר "to be free from doing a thing"); Tosefta Sotah 6.6. This legend is an attempt to exculpate Moses of the sin of doubting God's omnipotence, as expressed in his words in Num. 11.21. He never doubted that God was able to send down meat to "suffice" their bodily desires; but knowing the consequeces of their foolish desire, he argued with God that it would not be for the people's real benefit to have their desire gratified. See also Tehillim 23, 199, and R. Nissim quoted in *Imre No'am* on Num., *loc. cit.* Philo *Quis Rer. Div. Haeres Sit*, 5, likewise has some difficulty in explaining the audacious words of Moses as recorded in Num., *loc. cit.*, and similar passages of Scripture. See also Ephraem I, 257, and Theodoretus, Num., *loc. cit.*

486 Sifre N., 97–98; Sifre Z., 81 and 201; Tosefta Sotah 4.4; Mekilta Wa-Yassa' 3.48b; Mekita RS 76–77; comp. vol. III, pp. 49–50. *Pa'aneah* on Num. 11.33 quotes Tehillim (not found in our text) to the effect that those only were punished who asked for meat to satisfy their gluttony, but not the sick and weak who needed meat for their sustenance. See also Targum Yerushalmi Num. 11.31–33.

487 Targum Yerushalmi Num. 11.31; Yoma 75b.

488 Yelammedenu in Yalkut I, 738; Hashkem 17b; Sifre N., 99; Sifre Z., 81–82 and 203–204; ARN 9, 39; Tan. III, 46; Tan. Zaw 13. In all these passages and in many others (comp., *e. g.*, Mo'ed Katan 17b; Tehillim 9, 70 and 72; 2 Targum Yerushalmi Num. 12.1; 2 ARN 43, 122; see also Theodoretus on Num., *loc. cit.*) it is assumed that the "Cushite woman" spoken of in Num., *loc. cit.*, refers to Zipporah, "who was distinguished for her beauty and piety as the Cushite—Ethiopian—is distinguished for his dark color." But Targum Yerushalmi Num., *loc. cit.*, finds in this biblical verse an allusion to the "queen of the Ethiopians whom Moses was forced to marry while fleeing from Pharaoh." Comp. note 80 on vol. II, p. 289.

489 ARN 11, 39–40; Hashkem 18a; Sifre N., 100 (the dissenting view is given here that they only spoke evil of Moses among themselves, but never in his presence; see vol. II, p. 7, with regard to Joseph's attitude toward his brethren; comp. further vol. III, p. 262); Sifre Z., 82. See also the references given in the preceding note. On Moses' continence, see vol. II, p. 316; vol. III, pp. 107, 258, and 394–395. Comp. also ARN 2, 9–10.

490 Esfah in Yalkut I, 739; Sifre N., 101 (the dissenting view is

given here that the three patriarchs surpassed Moses in meekness; comp., however, Hullin 89a, and Philo, *De Ebrietate*, 23, who appraise Moses higher than the patriarchs, see also note 961); Sifre Z., 82–83; ARN 9, 41, and 12, 51–52. In the last passage the humility of the angels is described as the ideal type ; this is in agreement with the view given in the tannaitic Midrashim just quoted. See also Midrash Aggada Num. 12.3. The legend concerning Moses' meekness, quoted from *Ayyumah Kannidgalot* in note 310, is partly found in *Hadar*, Num. 12.3. This passage also states that on this occasion only did Moses forsake his great virtue, when he said to the multitude clamoring for water: "Are *we* to bring you forth water out of this rock?" (Num. 20.10). He spoke as though he and Aaron could make the water flow from the rock, whereas they only acted as God's messengers. Comp. note 613.

⁴⁹¹ Sifre N., 102; Sifre Z., 83; Tan. B. III, 46; Tan. Zaw 13; Yelammedenu in Yalkut I, 738 and Esfah (?), ibid, 739. Comp. vol. II, p. 328.

⁴⁹² Sifre Z., 83–84; Sifre N., 102; Esfah in Yalkut I, 739; Zohar III, 3a. Comp. vol. III, p. 108.

⁴⁹³ Sifre Z., 84; Sifre N., 103 (two views are given here with regard to the interpretation of Num. 12.7, whether "the house of God" includes or excludes the angels; comp. also Midrash Aggada, beginning, on Moses' superiority to the angels); Esfah in Yalkut I, 739 (א״ל = אמרו לו המלאכים). Comp. vol. III, p. 107, and note 489 (end). For the proverb concerning the thief and the receiver, see also Kiddushin 56b, which reads: Not the mouse is the thief, but the hole where the stolen thing is hidden.

⁴⁹⁴ Sifre N., 104–105; Sifre Z., 84–85; Shabbt 97a; Tan. B. III, 46; Tan. Zaw 13; ARN 9.39. Concerning leprosy as a punishment for slander, see vol. III, p. 214. Comp. also PRE 45 (on the text see *Batte Midrashot*, III, 32–33), which reads: There is no cure for him who slanders his fellow-man; how great then should be the punishment of him who slanders his brothers!

⁴⁹⁵ Sifre Z., 85 and 87; Sifre N., 105; ARN 39–40; Midrash Aggada Num. 12.10. The question why Aaron was not punished like his sister was raised by Irenaeus, *Fragmenta*, 32, and his answer is similar to that of of the Rabbis. The view that Aaron became leprous for a brief moment is not shared by all authorities; see the sources quoted in note 494, where it is asserted that Aaron was not punished at all. Comp. also PRE 45 (on the text see *Batte Midrashot* III, 32 and Sifre Z.. 85), which remarks: Aaron was not punished with leprosy,

for if he were he would not have been able to perform his priestly functions.

⁴⁹⁶ Sifre N., 105; Sifre Z., 85–86; ARN 9, 41; Targum Yerushalmi Num. 12.12, which is followed by Midrash Aggada, *ad loc.* (נפל=כמת). Concerning the idea that leprosy is equal to death, see vol. I, p. 364 and vol. III, p. 190.

⁴⁹⁷ ARN 9, 41 (on the drawing of the circle, see note 895); DR 6.13; Sifre N., 105–106; Sifre Z., 87; Berakot 32a and 34b; Zebahim 102a–102b; WR 15.8; Zohar I, 24b. See also Tosafot on Baba Batra 111a (catchword ק׳ין), and R. Bezalel Ashkenazi כללי התלמוד, Marx' edition, 188, where the quotation from Sifre (*loc. cit.*?) reads קל וחמר למלך וכהן נדול. The king and high priest is God, and not Moses, as the Tosafists maintain. Comp. Sanhedrin 39a, where God is described as priest.

⁴⁹⁸ Sifre N., 106; Sifre D., 275 (it is said here that they did not put down their tents until Miriam appeared); Sifre Z., 87 and 203; Sotah 1.9; Targum Yerushalmi Num. 1.15–16, and second version 13.1; Yelammedenu in Yalkut I, 742. Concerning the mode of procedure in breaking up the camp, see vol. III, p. 235.

⁴⁹⁹ Midrash Tannaim 157; Sifre N., 99; ARN 9, 40 (second version 42, 116). Comp. note 489.

⁵⁰⁰ BaR 16.6; Tan. B. IV., 64; Tan. Shelah 5; ARN 9, 39; *Likkutim*, IV, 28b–29a.

⁵⁰¹ Sifre D., 20; Midrash Tannaim 11. Comp. also ER 29, 144, and Sifre N., 136.

⁵⁰² Midrash Tannaim 11; Yelammedenu in Yalkut I, 743, as well as in '*Aruk*, s. v. טכני and כסל (comp. *Likkutim*, IV, 28a–28b); BaR 16.7; Tan. B. IV, 64–65; Tan. Shelah 5.

⁵⁰³ Sifre D., 20; Midrash Tannaim 11–12; ER 29, 144; BaR 16.8; Tan. B. IV, 65; Tan. Shelah 5. Philo, *Vita Mosis*, 1.40–41, likewise dwells upon the fact that the sending of the spies was due to the initiative of Moses, and was not by a command from God. The same view is shared by Josephus, *Antiqui.*, XII, 14.1, who gives the address delivered by Moses to the people, in which he explains to them his plan to send spies. The contradiction between Num. 13.2 and Deut 1.22–23 was noticed by the Rabbis, who reconciled these verses, whereas Philo and Josephus ignore the passage in Num. It is noteworthy that ps-Philo, 15.1, takes the trouble to state explicitly that "Moses sent spies to spy out the land, for so was it commanded him." Reference is frequently made to the piety, wisdom, and high position of the spies;

see Yelammedenu in Yalkut I, 743; BaR 16.5 (where it is stated that
the spies were selected by Moses and the people on account of their
piety, and God approved of the selection); Tan. B. IV, 64; Tan. Shelah
4; Philo, *Moses*, 1.41; Josephus, *Antiqui.*, III, 4.2; quotation from an
unknown Midrash in *Imre No'am* on Exod. 28.12.

⁵⁰⁴ Zohar III, 158a, which is the source for Yalkut Reubeni,
Num. 13.17 (the reference to Targum is very likely a printer's error);
comp. also BaR 16.1 (end), where היו רשעים means "they became wicked",
and not "they were wicked", as may be seen from the statement *ibid.*
16. 5, and in the other sources cited in the preceding note.

⁵⁰⁵ Midrash Aggada Num. 13.4; Tan. Haazinu 7. Comp. Sotah
34b; BaR 16.10; Tan. B. IV, 64–66. Concerning the name of Joshua,
see Ecclesiasticus 46.1, as well as Matthew 1.21; Justin, *Dialogue*,
113, and Tertullian, *Adversus Judaeos*, 9. The Christian writers apply
to Jesus (= Joshua) the son of Joseph what the Jewish Haggadah claims
for Joshua the son of Nun.

⁵⁰⁶ *Likkutim*, II, 20c; BR 46.1; ShR 6.1; WR 19.2; Shir 5.11;
Tan. Korah 12.

⁵⁰⁷ Tan. B. IV, 66; Tan. Shelah 6; BaR 16.12; ER 29, 144; Sotah
33b; Yelammedenu in *'Aruk*,s. v. חרם; Lekah and *Pa'aneah* on Num.
13.17; Sifre D., 22; Midrash Tannaim 12.

⁵⁰⁸ Baba Batra 15a–15b. Comp. the following note and Index,
s. v. "Job".

⁵⁰⁹ Sotah 35a. Wherever the spies came they met mourners, for
all the people mourned for Job. But not being acquainted with the
real reason of this general mourning, the spies exclaimed: "This is a
land that eateth up the inhabitants thereof" *ibid.*; comp. also vol.
III, p. 278. According to *Yalkut David* Num. 13.32, it was the custom
of the Amorites to delay the burial of a pious man a long time, and then
bury a number of other men with him in the same coffin, in order that
"the merits of the pious may protect the other men." When the
spies saw the numerous corpses buried at the same time (they were
all buried with Job), they thought that Palestine was a land that "eateth
up the inhabitants thereof". See also the midrashic fragment published
by Schechter in *Semitic Studies*, 494, and Lekah, Num., *loc. cit.*

⁵¹⁰ Seder 'Olam 8; Ta'anit 29a; Targum Yerushalmi Num.
13.21. Comp. Ratner on Seder 'Olam. Concerning the identity of
Paran with Kadesh, see Lekah, Num. 13.18; Sa'adya Gaon, *Emunot
we-De'ot* 3,92.

⁵¹¹ BaR 16.12–13; Tan. B. IV, 66–67; Tan. Shelah 6 and 8;

Sotah 34b; Sifre D., 37. On the plague which raged in Palestine during the visit of the spies, see note 509, and vol. III, p. 278.

512 Sotah 34b; BaR 16.11; Tan. B. IV, 66; Tan. Shelah 7; Midrash Aggada Num. 13.22. Concerning the giants, see vol. I, pp. 25 and 151; vol. III, pp. 269, 340. On the "throwing up of plots from the ground", see vol. II, p. 106.

513 Midrashic fragment published by Schechter in *Semitic Studies* 492; comp. *Hadar* and *Pa'aneah*, Num. 13.2 and 28 as well as Gaster, *Exempla*, 321. On the gigantic statures of the spies, see Sotah 10b.

514 ER 29, 144–145. Comp. vol. III, pp. 266, 273–274; vol. IV, pp. 9–10.

515 Zohar III, 160b; R. Bahya on Num. 13.7. The latter did not draw upon Zohar, but upon midrashic sources, as he explicitly states, and it is very likely that Zohar made use of the same source. Comp. also Rashi and Midrash Aggada, Num. 13.33. According to Mekilta Shirah 9, 43a, the spies remained undetected through a miracle: if anybody wanted to betray them, he was rendered as "still as a stone", that is, dumb. Ps.-Philo, 15.2, speaks of another miracle, which was performed for the spies. He writes: "For they (*i. e.*, the spies) saw how that as they went up, the lightning of the stars shone, and the thunders followed, sounding with them." Does this mean that the spies journeyed by night by the supernatural light of the stars which shone for them?

516 Sotah 35a. See the opposite view in vol. III, p. 274.

517 Sotah 34b; Zohar III, 158b–159a. Comp. vol. III, p. 264; Sotah 35a (top).

518 Yerushalmi Sotah 7, 21d; Babli 34a; PR 27, 132a; BaR 16.14 and 16; Tan. B. IV, 67–68; Tan. Shelah 8–9; Philo, *Vita Mosis*, 1.41–42. According to another view, none of the spies, with the exception of Caleb and Joshua, was able to carry the vine. See the passage quoted by R. Bahya from a Midrash, Num. 13.23 (from Yelammedenu? See *Likkutim*, IV, 29b); Zohar III, 160b.

519 Shir 4.13, which gives also the dissenting view, according to which the wine required for the libations came from the vines growing around Miriam's well. Comp. vol. III, p. 3. Targum Song of Songs 1.14 maintains that the wine for the libations came from En-Gedi. In tannaitic literature we meet with the view that the Israelites brought no sacrifices whatsoever during their journey through the wilderness; see Sifre N., 67; Sifre Z., 66, and the parallel passages given by Horovitz (the first edition of Yalkut I, 555, has ספרי correctly, and not ס' זוטא

as in later editions; Horovitz is to be corrected accordingly); Hagigah 6b. There is also a view that the Israelites in the wilderness were not permitted to partake of any meat except of a sacrifice; see Sifre D., 75; Hullin 16b–17d. As to the public sacrifices (קרבנות צבור), it is said in the tannaitic Midrashim just quoted that they were taken care of by the Levites, with the assistance of the few pious men of the other tribes.

⁵²⁰ BaR 16.16; Tan. B. IV, 68; Tan. Shelah 8. Concerning "the leaping of earth", or to be accurate, the contracting of the earth, see note 287 on vol. I, p. 294. The extent of the Holy Land is four hundred parasangs in length by four hundred parasangs in width; see, *e. g.*, Megillah 3b and Baba Kamma 82b.

⁵²¹ ER 29, 145. Concerning the measurement of the camp, see note 445, and vol. III, p. 473. Instead of the enormous size of the house of study, Aggadat Shir 2, 32, (read בבמד"ר = בית מדרשו בבית and comp. Schechter *ad loc.*) refers to the supernatural strength of Moses' voice which carried for twelve miles, from the house of study to the end of the camp. Concerning Moses' voice, see note 201 and note 228 on vol. II, p. 370.

⁵²² Sotah 35a; BaR 16.17; Tan. B. IV, 68; Tan. Shelah 8; Lekah Num. 13.25–27 (based, in the main, on Ketubot 111b); Yelammedenu in 'Aruk, s. v. פקד = *Likkutim*, IV, 29b.

⁵²³ Midrash Aggada Num. 13.28. For the opposite view see vol. III, pp. 268 and 273–274. Concerning Caleb's visit to Hebron, see vol. III, p. 270.

⁵²⁴ Midrash quoted by R. Bahya on Num. 13.22; Zohar III, 159a.

⁵²⁵ BaR 16.18; Tan. B. IV, 68; Tan. Shelah 89; Yelammedenu in 'Aruk, s. v. ספר 4; Zohar III, 162a. On Amalek, see Lekah Num. 13.29; vol. III, pp. 55–56.

⁵²⁶ Sotah 35 (ריש קטיעא) "headless" *i. e.*, a fool; comp. ShR 41.7, which has the expression קציעי צואריא; on Joshua's lack of intelligence, see Index, s. v.); BaR 16.19; Tan. B. IV, 68; Tan. Shelah 10. Joshua died childless (according to Megillah 14b however, he had daughters, but no sons) as a punishment for his audacity in giving advice to Moses, without having been asked for it (comp. vol. III, p. 253). According to others, he was punished for having kept the army in camp one night more than was necessary, thus preventing the men from joining their wives; comp. 'Erubin 63a–63b; Comp. note 847. On "son of Amram", see note 163.

⁵²⁷ Aggadat Shir 6, 41 and 88–89; a doublet of this legend is found in vol. III, p. 269. The text of Aggadat Shir is badly corrupted;

וטפח...אמר להם למה באתם בשביל···לא באנו אלא שאמרנו...אתם· :read
On Caleb's mighty voice, see vol. III, p. 440.

528 Sotah 35a; Tan. B. IV, 66; Tan. Shelah 7 and Mass'e 4; BaR 16.11; Yerushalmi Ta'anit 6, 68d. Comp. Geiger, *Kebuzzat Maamarim*, 47, and Ginzberg in supplement to Geiger, 383–384.

529 Tan. B. IV, 66; Tan. Shelah 7; BaR 16.11. For the opposite view see vol. III, p. 70.

530 Tan. Mass'e 4; BaR 23.6. Comp. also Yerushalmi Ma'aserot 1, 48d, and Ta'anit 4, 68d. The last passage reads: When the spies returned to the camp they found Moses and Aaron instructing the people in the laws of Hallah and Orlah. Whereupon they remarked to them mockingly: "Ye have not entered the promised land; why then do ye trouble yourselves about laws which are to be observed in the Holy Land only?" Comp. Hallah 2.1.

531 Tan. B. IV, 84; BaR 16.3; Sifre D., 24; Midrash Tannaim 12.

532 Yelammedenu in Yalkut I, 743 on Num. 14.1, as well as in 'Aruk, s. v. דבר 2 = *Likkutim*, IV, 29b–30b; midrashic fragment published by Schechter in *Semitic Studies*, 492. Comp. also Sifre D., 24. On the text of Yelammedenu, see Epstein in *Ha-Eshkol* VI, 209–210. It is, however, best to read: כודות ברזל לאמה של מים יכולה לבלום וכו' Comp. PR 20, 97, and accordingly כאודות בר'=כודות בר'. See also the legend about the giants at the time of the flood, vol. I, p. 159. On the "night of weeping", see Sotah 35a; Ta'anit 29a; Yerushalmi 4,68d; Tan. B. IV, 690; Tan. Shelah 12; BaR 16.20; ER 29, 145; Ekah 1.60–61; Targum Yerushalmi Num. 14.1; Jerome on Zech. 8.18–19. Comp. sources quoted note 510.

533 Tehillim 106, 455; comp. Index, s. v. "Dathan and Abiram."

534 Midrash Tannaim 1–2. Comp. also Alphabet of R. Akiba 47 (ר').

535 Lekah Num 14.2–9. On the fall of the guardian angel, see notes 41, 670.

536 BaR 16.21; Tan. B. IV, 69; Tan. Shelah 12.

537 Sifre D., 24–25; Midrash Tannaim 12.

538 BaR 16.21; Tan. B. IV, 69; Tan. Shelah 12; Yelammedenu in Yalkut I, 743 on Num. 14.1; Sotah 35a (where it is said that the cloud caught up the stones thrown at Moses and Aaron); ER 29, 144. The Talmud, and very likely also the Midrashim just quoted, presuppose that the Israelites, in their wrath against God, threw the stones towards the clouds.

539 Tan. B. IV, 75–78; Tan. Shelah 13; BaR 16.24; Makiri, Ps.

82, 56 (quoting Tan. B. *loc. cit.*) and 78, 26. On the loam of the Red
Sea, see ShR 24.1. See also the opposite view in vol. III, p. 22. On
the manna, see vol. III, pp. 44, and 246. On the plague raging in
Palestine during the visit of the spies, see vol. III, p. 267; comp.
Yerushalmi Ta'anit 4, 68a. Concerning the Torah as a weapon against
the Angel of Death, see vol. III, pp. 107 and 120. The explanation
of Ps. 82.6, as referring to the "generation of the wilderness" who
received the Torah, is found also in John 10.34–35. Comp. *Likkutim*
IV, 31a–31b.

⁵⁴⁰ DR 5.13; Yelammedenu in Yalkut I, 743 on Num. 13.1. The promise of a blessing by God, even if made conditionally, is always fulfilled;
Moses became the ancestor of a clan numbering six hundred thousand
men, corresponding to the number of Israel at the time of the exodus;
thus the promise made to Moses, "I will make of thee a great nation",
was fulfilled. See Berakot 7a; Targum Yerushalmi Exod. 24.10; BaR
16.25; Tan. B. IV, 79; comp. note 55 on vol, IV, p. 317.

⁵⁴¹ Lekah Num. 14.13–15. Comp. vol. III, p. 126. Moses'
prayer for Israel, which stayed the decree of annihilation from being
executed against them, in connection with the worship of the golden
calf, is made use of by the Haggadah for his intercession in connection
with the slander of the Holy Land by the spies.

⁵⁴² BaR 16.25; Tan. B. IV, 78; Berakot 32a. Concerning Lilith,
see vol. I, p. 65.

⁵⁴³ Yelammedenu in Yalkut I, 743, on Num. 14, and II, 507,
on Job 17; PK 16, 166a–167b; *Likkutim*, IV, 32b–33a. The special
virtues of the patriarchs and other persons of biblical times, distinguished
for their piety, are: Abraham was very zealous for the observance of
the Abrahamic covenant; Isaac excelled in prayer; Jacob was famed for
his truth; Joseph for his chastity (but perhaps חסידות in this passage
means "lovingkindness"; comp. note 3 on vol. II, p. 4 where Joseph is
designated as חסיד); Moses was distinguished for his modesty; Aaron
for his love of peace; Phineas for his zeal for God. Comp. also the
geonic (?) piyyut רחמנא אדכר in the Sefardic and cognate liturgies.

⁵⁴⁴ Tan. B. IV, 81; BaR 16.22 and 28; DR 5.13; PK 26, 166a–
167a; ER 29, 144. Comp. vol. III, pp. 115–116.

⁵⁴⁵ DR 5.13; BaR 26.25; Yelammedenu in *Likkutim*, IV, 33a
(bottom); Tan. B. IV, 70; Tan. Shelah 13; Berakot 32a.

⁵⁴⁶ BaR 16.23 and 3.7; Tan. B. IV, 70–71 (read at bottom of 70:
לא ניכנס); Tan. Shelah 13; Baba Batra 121b; Esfah (?) in *Batte Midrashot*
III, 8. According to the old Halakah, one becomes of age at twenty

years, see vol. III, p. 300, and note 69 on vol. I, p. 326, and this is the reason for the statement in Baba Batra, *loc. cit.* But the Midrashim do not accept this view of the old Halakah. This explains the difference between the Talmud and the Midrashim, quoted above, with regard to the punishment of the men below twenty. As to women being free from this punishment, see Tehillim 1, 13–14, and vol. III, p. 398.

547 Yerushalmi Ta'anit 4, 69c, and Babli 30b; Baba Batra 121a–121b; Ekah (פתיחתא) 23. 36–37; Shemuel (end); Tehillim 78, 348; Lekah Num. 14.23. With the exception of the two last-mentioned sources, the other passages give many other reasons for the origin of the festival of the fifteenth of Ab.—When God decreed the death of these sinners He at the same time also decreed that Israel should in the future be exiled into foreign lands, so that "all the earth be filled with the glory of the Lord." See Lekah Num. 14.22. Israel was severely punished for the slanderous report of the spies, in accordance with the gravity of the sin; for slander is the most abominable sin. See Midrash Tannaim 140; 'Arakin 15a; vol. III, pp. 261–262.

548 Yebamot 72a (it is said in this passage that the blowing of the north wind is a sign of God's grace, and hence it did not blow in the years of His displeasure, except at the moment of midnight, which is "the acceptable time"; comp. vol. I, p. 12); PK 5, 50b; Shir 2.13. Comp. vol. IV, p. 7. See also Sifra 1.1; Mekilta Bo (פתיחתא), 2a (bottom) and the references given in note 550.

549 Sifre Num. 67; Zebahim 115a–115b; Mo'ed Katan 15b. Comp. above note 519.

550 Mekilta Bo 1, 2a–2b; Sifra 1.1; Ta'anit 30b, and Yerushalmi 3, 66c. According to MHG I, 673, Moses spent these years of God's displeasure in mourning for Israel's severe chastisement. His dejected spirit was the cause of his not receiving divine revelations during this period, since the Shekinah dwells only on those whose spirit is joyful. Comp. vol. II, p. 116, and the note appertaining to it. A similar statement was very likely to be found in ER 29, 145, where the text after כל אותן...שנה is incomplete. As to the conception that Moses and all the other prophets owed their distinction to Israel, see vol. III, pp. 51 (end) and 125.

551 Sifre N., 135, and Sifre D., 29; Midrash Tannaim 17; Mekilta Amalek 2, 55a. Comp. vol. III, p. 317.

552 Sotah 35a (here also we have the dissenting view that they died of croup); Koheleth 9.12, which reads: They died because the members of their bodies fell apart. Comp. also Acts 12.23, where

it is said that Herod was eaten up by worms as a punishment for his blasphemy. The same death overtook the blasphemer Antiochus IV; see 2 Maccabees 9.9.

553 Baba Batra 117b; comp. Tan. B. IV, 65; BaR 16.9, which says: Joshua took the reward of the spies.

554 Yerushalmi Kiddushin 1, 59c. Comp. note 325.

555 Midrash Aggada Num. 14.25.

556 Tan. B. IV, 81–82; BaR 17.3; *Likkutim* IV, 35b–36b. According to some authorities, the Israelites were wounded, but not killed, by their enemies, so that the Name of God should not be desecrated. Comp. *Hadar* and *Da'at* on Deut. 1.44. Concerning Zelophehad, see vol. III, pp. 240 and 392.

557 ER 29, 146.

558 Koheleth 3.11. Comp., however, Sifre D., 38, and vol. III, p. 7, according to which the Canaanites, hearing of Israel's design on Palestine, destroyed the buildings, felled the trees, and burned the crops. Concerning this passive form of warfare, see Herodotus IV, 120.

559 Koheleth 2.26.

560 BHM II, 108; *Likkutim*, I, 22b–23a; Targum Yerushalmi Num. 16.19; Sanhedrin 110b, and Yerushalmi 10, 27d (bottom); Mishle 11, 70; Pesahim 119a; PRE 50; Gorion 46. Concerning Joseph's treasures, see vol. II, p. 125; vol. III, p. 11. On Korah's riches see also Josephus, *Antiqui.*, IV, 2.2 and 4; BaR 18.13 and 22.7; Tan. B. IV, 160; Tan. Mattot 5; Aggadat Esther 56.

561 BaR 18.2 and 8; Tan. B IV, 85 and 89; Tan. Korah 1 and 5; *Likkutim*, IV, 39b and 41b; Yelammedenu in Yalkut II, 1080. On Samuel, as the descendant of Korah and his comparison with Moses and Aaron, see notes 242, 492 and Tehillim 99, 424. Comp. further vol. III, p. 293; vol. IV, p. 69.

562 Sanhedrin 109b; Mishle 11, 71. Comp. also Sekel II, 35–36; *Likkutim*, IV, 40b.

563 Tan. B. IV, 88 and 93 (for the proverb, "woe to the wicked, etc.", very frequently quoted in talmudic and midrashic literature, see references given by Buber, note 38, as well as note 116 on p. 12); Tan. Korah 4 and 10; *Likkutim*, IV, 40b; Sanhedrin 110a. According to some authorities, the Reubenites were angry with Moses for having conferred so many honors on the tribe of Judah and not on them, who were the descendants of Jacob's first-born; see *Likkutim*, IV, 42b, as well as Josephus, *Antiqui.*, IV, 2.2; *Pa'aneah*, Num. 16.1. Among

the rebels there were to be found representatives of all tribes, with the exception of that of Levi. Each tribe was represented by twenty-three men, corresponding to the number of the members constituting the lower courts. Accordingly, the congregation of Korah consisted of two hundred and fifty-three men, of whom only three are mentioned by name: Dathan, Abiram, and On (Num. 16.1–2), while the rest remained unnamed; *Imre No'am* Num. 16.2. According to the Midrash quoted by Shu'aib, Num., *loc. cit.*, the men who rebelled together with Korah knew the Name, and hence Moses was afraid of them, since he realized that he could not use the Name against them. This is based on the midrashic explanation of the words אנשי שם (Num., *loc. cit.*), which is taken to mean "masters in the use of the Holy Name". Concerning Moses' employment of the Name in punishing sinners, see vol. II, p. 280 and vol. III, p. 240. Comp. Manzur, 8–9; Tan. IV, 86; PR 7, 27b–28a.

⁵⁶⁴ Sanhedrin 110a; Midrash Aggada, Num. 16.8. This legend is a doublet of the one which follows it immediately; see references in the following note. Comp. these references also with regard to Korah's wicked wife.

⁵⁶⁵ BaR 18.4; Tan. B. IV, 86–87; Tan. Korah 3. Comp. also Zohar III, 49a and references in the following note.

⁵⁶⁶ Yerushalmi Sanhedrin 10, 27d–28a; Tan. B. IV, 85 (it is said here that the outbreak of the rebellion took place during the banquet given by Korah to his friends, when certain parts of the slaughtered animals were seized by Eliezer as his priestly share); Tan. Korah 2; Mishle 11, 70; Aggadat Esther 56 (in this passage it is stated that it was Korah's wife who called her husband's attention to the absurdity of some of the laws promulgated by Moses; comp. the preceding two notes); *Likkutim*, IV, 39b–40a. Ps.-Philo 16.1 likewise remarks: At that time did He give him the commandment concerning the fringes; and then did Korah rebel, and two hundred men (read: and fifty) with him, and spoke saying: "What if a law which we cannot bear is ordained for us?" One fails to see the hardship of this commandment concerning the fringes, whereas its absurdity under certain circumstances is very clearly shown by the Rabbis. The connections of the commandment concerning the fringes and the rebellion of Korah was assumed by the Haggadah in accordance with the hermeneutical rule of סמוכין "juxtaposition", which implies that there is some connection between two passage of Scripture which are "near" one another. The Haggadah therefore presupposes that the rebellion of Korah, the

narrative of which follows the commandment concerning the fringes, must be connected with the passages preceding it. Philo, *Moses*, 2(3).21 and 38, is of the same opinion as the Midrashim just quoted that Korah denied the divine origin of Aaron's priesthood. Comp. also Zohar I, 17.

⁵⁶⁷ Tehillim 1, 14 (read בא אהרון after נר); Midrash Aggada, Num. 7.19; Manzur 7-8. A short version of this legend, lacking the fine humor of the longer version, is found in *Likkutim*, I, 23a-23b; BHM VI, 107-108; *Hibbur Ma'as*. No. 6; *Neweh Shalom*, 56. Comp. also Matthew 23.14.

⁵⁶⁸ Tan. B IV, 86; Tan. Korah 3; BaR 18.4; Yelammedenu in Yalkut I, 752 (which reads: Korah said: "We received the ten commandments on Mount Sinai, but no law concerning the gifts to the priests, nor concerning the fringes, which thou hast devised thyself"); *Likkutim* IV, 40b. Comp. also references given in note 566. Concerning the fifteen thousand men who died annually, see vol. III, p. 282 (top). The Haggadah presupposes that the rebellion of Korah took place after the return of the spies, and this is explicitly stated in Seder 'Olam 8, and in many other passages referred to by Ratner, *ad loc.* Midrash Aggada, Num. 14.22, on the contrary, maintains that the sending of the spies took place after the rebellion of Korah.

⁵⁶⁹ Mo'ed Katan 18b; Tan. B. IV, 92; Tan. Korah 10; Targum Yerushalmi Num. 16.4; BaR 18.20; Tehillim 106, 455.

⁵⁷⁰ BaR 18.4. Comp. Josephus, *Antiqui.*, IV, 2.3.

⁵⁷¹ Tan. B. IV, 90, 92, and 96; Tan. Korah 6; BaR 18.9 and 12; Yelammedenu (?) in Yalkut I, 752; *Likkutim*, IV, 40a and 42b-43a; Tehillim 2, 25; Yerushalmi Sanhedrin 10, 28a. Moses (Num. 16.29), Elijah (1 Kings 18.36), and Micah (1 Kings 22.28) are the prophets who asked that a miracle should be wrought for them, otherwise they would be declared as impostors; see Sanhedrin, *loc. cit.* Comp. also Mishle 11, 71; *Likkutim*, I, 23b.

⁵⁷² BaR 18.6-7; Sanhedrin 52a; Tan. B. IV 88; Tan. Korah 4-5; *Likkutim*, IV, 41a; Midrash Aggada Num. 16.5.

⁵⁷³ BaR 18.7-9; Tan. B. IV, 88-90; Tan. Korah 5-6; *Likkutim*, IV, 41a. On the idea of selection in nature and history, see also Pesahim 104a; Tehillim 24, 203, and the liturgical formula of the Habdalah recited at the termination of the Sabbath. The oneness of Israel's God, Law, and Sanctuary, as contrasted with the multitude of gods, laws, and sanctuaries of the heathens, is a favorite topic with the Haggadists; comp., *e.g.*, Philo, *Special. Leg.*, 1 (*de Sacrif. Offeren.*11); Josephus,

Contra Apionem, 2.23, and *Antiqui.*, IV, 8.5; Apocalypse of Baruch 48.24; Sifre D., 354; Midrash Tannaim 218–219; vol. IV p. 32. Concerning the prophetic presentiment of Korah, see vol. III, p. 287.

574 Mo'ed Katan 16a; Targum Yerushalmi Num. 16.12. Moses was rewarded for his attempt to make Dathan and Abiram abandon their evil designs, although he did not succeed in saving them. The three sons of Korah, as well as On, were saved because they repented of their sin; see Yelammedenu in Yalkut I, 752, and *Likkutim*, IV, 41b. Comp. also vol. III, pp. 300–303.

575 BaR 18.10; Tan. B. IV, 90; Tan. Korah 6; Yelammedenu in Yalkut I, 752 (the sentence ואין אנו וכו׳ is to be taken as an unconscious prophecy); *Likkutim*, IV, 41b and 42a.

576 BaR 18.10–11; Tan. B. IV, 90–91; Tan. Korah 6–7. Comp. also Yelammedenu in Yalkut II, 292, on Jer. 15, and in Makiri, 215 (on Is. 56), as well as 29 (on Amos); ER 17.73; ShR 4.1; DR 11.2; Tehillim 24, 206. Josephus, *Antiqui.*, IV, 3.32, makes Moses deliver, on this occasion, a long oration, in which he gives a survey of his life history; this oration is addressed to God.

577 BaR 18.11; Tan. B. IV, 91; Tan. Korah 7 (end); Targum Yerushalmi Num. 16.24.

578 BaR 18.12; Tan. B. IV, 91; Tan. Korah 8; comp. also 4 Maccabees 2.17.

579 Targum Yerushalmi 16.26. On this pair of wicked brothers, see vol. II, p. 281; vol. III, pp. 13, 84, and the references given in the notes appertaining to these passages. Comp. also Targum Yerushalmi Exod. 14.11.

580 BaR 18.12; Tan. B. IV, 92 and 94; Tan. Korah 8; *Likkutim*, IV, 42b; Nedarim 39b; Mishle 11, 71. Comp. also the references given in the following note, as well as in note 571.

581 Nedarim 39b; Sanhedrin 110a; Tan. B. IV, 94; Mishle 11,71. On the sun and moon being forced to do their duty, see vol. I, p. 25, and vol. IV, p. 309. The designation of Moses as "son of Amram" in this passage is not to be taken in a derogatory sense (comp. note 163); it rather expresses pity for Moses, who is thus described as being helpless. In view of the fact that "there is nothing new under the sun", the Rabbis maintain that the mouth of the earth which swallowed up Korah was created in the twilight between the sixth day of creation and the first Sabbath (comp. vol. I, p. 83), and that at the time of the punishment of the congregation of Korah it approached the spot where the sinners stood, and swallowed them up; see Abot 5.6, and the references given

in note 99 on vol. I, p. 83. A dissenting view is given in Sanhedrin 37b,which states that the earth did not open its mouth from the time it swallowed up the blood of Abel until it swallowed up Korah. Th very same remark is also found in ps.-Philo, 16, where the translator from the Hebrew committed an amusing error. The words "*et locutus sum Sion, dicens: Non adicias ut deglutias sanguinem*" (16, bottom) are a mistaken rendering of the Hebrew ולציון דברתי אל תוסף לבלע דם "And I spoke unto the dry land, saying: Thou shalt not any more swallow up blood." In view of the rare occurrence of the word ציון the translator may be forgiven for misreading it as ציון "Zion".

⁵⁸² BaR 18.13; Tan. B. I 96–97 (in this passage the view is also given that the earth was cleft asunder at different places wherever one of the sinners stood); Yelammedenu in Yalkut I, 752; *Likkutim*, IV, 43a–43b; Yerushalmi Sanhedrin 10, 28a.

⁵⁸³ Shemuel 5, 62; Yerushalmi Sanhedrin 10, 28a.

⁵⁸⁴ Targum Yerushalmi and Lekah on Num. 16.22–34; Tan. B. IV, 97; *Likkutim*, I, 23b; BHM VI, 108; vol. III, 299–300. The Christian legend tells of similar punishments of sinners. Comp. *The Acts of Philip*, towards the end.

⁵⁸⁵ Tan. B. IV, 93; BaR 18.19 (*op. cit.* 15 speaks of the fire which consumed Korah's wife); Sanhedrin 110; Sifre N., 117. According to Josephus, *Antiqui.*, IV, 3.4, Korah was consumed by fire, whereas the *Protevangelium of James* 9.2 declares that Korah was swallowed up by the mouth of the earth.

⁵⁸⁶ Baba Batra 74a; Sanhedrin 110a–110b; Tan. B. IV, 94; BaR 18.13; Targum Yerushalmi Num. 16.34; Shemuel 5, 61–62; Mishnah Sanhedrin 10.3 (in this passage the view is also given that they were punished with eternal damnation); Tosefta 13.89; Babli 109b; Yerushalmi 10, 29c (here it is stated that Moses prayed for them that they should be saved from the torments of hell, with reference to Deut. 33.6, the Reubenites being identified with the congregation of Korah, whose leaders belonged to the tribe of Reuben; comp. Num. 16.1); ARN 26, 107 (here it is said that they do not suffer torments of hell, but will not come to life at the time of the resurrection; this is also the view of ps.-Philo, 16.3); BHM VI, 108; *Likkutim*, I, 23b–24a; Alphabet of R. Akiba 16–17 (here it is said that at the day of final judgment, Metatron, the holy Hayyot, as well as Korah and his congregation, will bear witness that there is only one God in heaven, on

earth, and in hell); *Neweh Shalom*, 55–56; comp. note 590; vol. I, p. 23; vol. III, pp. 298 and 476; vol. IV, pp. 60 and 321.

⁵⁸⁷ Tan. B. IV, 87; Tan. Korah 3(end); BaR 18.4; *Likkutim*, IV, 43b. Concerning the twentieth year as the age of majority, see above, note 546.

⁵⁸⁸ Sanhedrin 109b–110a; Tan. B. IV, 93; BaR 18.20; Manzur 8–9.

⁵⁸⁹ Quotation from an unknown Midrash, as recorded from a manuscript, by Schechter in *Semitic Studies*, 493; Tehillim 45, 270. According to another legend, the sons of Korah had decided in their hearts to repent when Moses attempted to persuade their father to desist from his evil work, and they indicated their adherence to Moses by rising in his honor in the presence of Korah; see Yelammedenu in Yalkut I, 752 (Tehillim 1,14 is to be emended accordingly); *Likkutim*, IV, 41b–52a. According to ps.-Philo, 16.4 Korah asked his seven (six) sons to join him in his revolt against Moses; but they refused to follow his counsel, and endeavored to dissuade him from his evil designs. Comp. also the following note.

⁵⁹⁰ Tehillim 45, 269–270; 46, 272–273; 1, 14–15 (here also the view is expressed that the earth was only cleft around the spot upon which they stood, but not beneath it); Sanhedrin 110a; quotation from an unknown Midrash, as recorded, from a manuscript, by Schechter in *Semitic Studies*, 493; Yelammedenu in Yalkut I, 752 and in II, 924, on Job 38. In the last passage and in Tehillim 49, 278 a view is quoted, according to which the sons of Korah were saved by "flying in the air". In a similar manner the righteous will be saved on the day of judgment, when the Lord will "take hold of the ends of the earth, and the wicked will be shaken out of it." Concerning the "flying of the righteous" at the time of the destruction of the world, see also Sanhedrin 92b(top). The legend recorded in vol. III, p. 300, to the effect that Korah and his congregation were appointed the custodians of the sunken portals of the Temple, was originally applied to the sons of Korah who repented at the last moment, and hence, though they are in hell, they are not tortured, but take charge of the remnants of the Temple. According to the Midrash quoted in Yalkut II, 376, on Ezekiel 28, the sons of Korah entered into paradise alive. The statement that the world rests on three pillars (comp. Abot 1.2), means, according to some authorities, that the world owes its existence to the three sons of Korah. Other authorities, however, are of the opinion that the three pillars are the three patriarchs. Still other authorities maintain that the three youths, Hananiah, Mishael, and Azariah, are the three pillars

supporting the world; Tehillim 1, 15. As to the pillars (i. e., righteous men) upholding the world, see note 28 on vol. I, p. 11. In the legends concerning the sons of Korah it is assumed that the sons of Korah, mentioned in the book of Psalms as the authors of many psalms, are identical with the sons of that Korah who led the revolt against Moses; but with regard to the psalmist Asaph opinions differ as to whether he was related to this Korah or not. Some authorities maintain that Asaph was the son of this Korah, while others are of the opinion that he flourished at a much later period than Korah, but that he belonged to the family of Korahites. According to a third view, this Asaph was in no way related to this Korah. See WR 17.1; ER 30, 150–151 (this passage contains the midrashic basis for the legend that the sons of Korah are the custodians of the sunken portals of the Temple); comp. vol. IV, p. 321: Shir 4.4.

⁵⁹¹ Sanhedrin 52a. Comp. vol. III, p. 187.

⁵⁹² Lekah Num. 17.2.

⁵⁹³ Tan. Zaw 13; Makiri Is. 6, 54–55; Targum Yerushalmi Num. 17.5. For other versions of this Haggadah, see Yelammedenu in Yalkut II, 271 on Is. 6; Tan. B. III, 19–20; *Likkutim*, IV, 43b–44a. Comp. vol. IV, p. 262.

⁵⁹⁴ Josephus, *Antiqui.*, IV, 4.1.

⁵⁹⁵ Shabbat 89a. Whenever Israel deserved to be punished for its sins, the punishment came forth from the sanctuary; and since Moses lived near the sanctuary, he was the first to notice the appearance of the destroying angel. Whereupon Moses would hasten to Aaron and urge him to protect Israel against the approaching visitation; BaR 5.6. According to Targum Yerushalmi Num. 7.11, it was the angel Kezef ("Wrath"), the one who fought against Moses in Horeb, who came forth to destroy Israel; comp vol. III, pp. 124–125. See also below note 598.

⁵⁹⁶ Rashi and Midrash Aggada on Num. 16.11, probably based on Mekilta Amalek 6, 52a; comp. vol. III, p. 52, top.

⁵⁹⁷ Tan. B. III, 19; Tan. Zaw 9; Lekah Num. 17.11.

⁵⁹⁸ Tan. Tezawweh 15 (end); *Likkutim*, IV, 44a–44b; Targum Yerushalmi Num. 17.12–13. According to 4 Maccabees 7.11, the angel caused the death of the people by fire.

⁵⁹⁹ Lekah, Num. 17.13. Prayer can only have the power to ward off half of the punishment decreed by God, whereas repentance averts the entire punishment. Hence Moses' prayer saved only two of Aaron's sons from the death decreed on Aaron's four sons; see WR 10.5 and 18.1; BaR 9.47; DR 8.10; Tan. B. III, 67; Tan. Ahare 8; PR 47, 188b–189a;

comp. also vol. III, p. 192 (top); Sifra 10.12; Yoma 87a, where it is stated that it was for the merits of Aaron that two of his sons escaped death.

⁶⁰⁰ BaR 18.23, which contains the statement that Aarons's rod is identical with the rod of Judah; Tan. B. III, 66–67, which reads: Aaron's rod was placed in the middle, so that the people should not say that its proximity to the Shekinah (*i. e.*, the ark) caused it to blossom; Tan. Ahare 8; *Likkutim*, IV, 44b. The rod which blossomed is the very same with which Jacob crossed the Jordan (comp. note 125 on vol. I, pp. 347–348), which later came into the possession of Judah (Gen. 48.18; comp. above, and vol. II, p. 34), and which Moses took with him on his journey to Egypt (Exod. 4.17). It is the same rod with which Aaron performed the miracles before Pharaoh (Exod. 7.9, *seq.*), and which David held in his hand in his encounter with Goliath (1 Samuel 18.40). It remained in the possession of the Davidic kings until the destruction of the Temple, when it was hidden. It will again be made use of in the time of the Messiah when it will be taken out from the place where it is hidden. See Yelammedenu in Yalkut I, 763, and II, 869, on Ps. 110; Midrash Aggada, Gen. 32.11 (in this passage it is said that Moses divided the Red Sea with this rod); Makiri, Prov. 20.3 and Ps.110, 183. In this legend Aaron's rod is identified not only with that of Moses (comp. note 88 on vol. II, p. 292), but also with the staff of the kings (*i. e.*, Judah, David, and the Messiah), so that the blossoming of this rod proved not only the justice of Aaron's claim to the priesthood, but also established David's claim to the kingdom. See also *Zerubbabel* (Jellinek's edition, 55; Wertheimer's edition 10b), as well as vol. III, p. 310.—The rod brought forth blossoms on one side and almonds on the other, and when the blossoms turned into almonds, there were sweet almonds on one side and bitter ones on the other. As long as Israel walked in the ways of the Lord, the sweet almonds were fresh (literally, *moist*); but when they departed from the right path, the bitter ones were fresh; see Shu'aib and *Hadar* on Num. 17.23. The first-named source quotes, from an unknown Midrash, a symbolic explanation, according to which the buds represent the first Temple, the blossoms the second, and the fruit—that is, the almonds—the third, *i. e.*, the Temple to be built by the Messiah. Comp. also Yerushalmi Horayyot 42a; Shekalim 6, 49c; references given in note 112 concerning the "hiding" of Aaron's rod (מקלו), with its blossoms and fruit, by Josiah. See further vol. IV, pp. 234, 282. Legendary amplifications of the biblical narrative of the blossoming of the rod are also recorded by Josephus,

Antiqui, IV, 4.2, as well as in Clemens' Letter to the Corinthians 43.
The latter is very likely based on the Jewish legend. Ps.-Philo. 17.3–4
comments on the miracle of the blossoming of the rod in the following
words: And this likeness which was born there was like unto the work
which Israel (= Jacob) wrought, while he was in Mesopotamia with
Laban the Syrian, when he took rods of almonds, and put them at
the gathering of waters (comp. Gen. 30.37). This remark of ps.–Philo
seems in some way connected with the rabbinic legend which identifies
Aaron's rod with that of Jacob. On the Christian and Mohammedan
legends concerning Aaron's rod, see Ginzberg in *Jewish Ecncyclopedia*,
I, 5–6, and Salzberger, *Salomo-Sage*, I, 66, *seq.*

⁶⁰¹ Seder 'Olam 8. Comp. note 568 and ps.-Philo 16.7. The
latter maintains that immediately after Korah had been swallowed
up, the people asked Moses for permission to move away from that
place.

⁶⁰² Yelammedenu (?) in *Batte Midrashot* III, 8–10; comp.
Yelammedenu in Yalkut I, 7.3. See also vol. III, pp. 48–49, and
note 498. The death of the righteous possesses atoning power, and
hence, in Scripture, the report of Miriam's death (Num. 20.1) follows
immediately the law concerning the red heifer which was used for
the "purificarion of sin"; see Mo'ed Katan 28a; Yelammedenu in
'*Aruk*, s. v. פר 2; *Likkutim*, I, 19a–19b, and IV, 48a–48b. Concerning
the women of this generation, see vol. III, p. 281.

⁶⁰³ Yelammedenu in Yalkut I, 673; *Likkutim*, IV, 50a. Comp.
vol. III, p. 262 (bottom).

⁶⁰⁴ Lekah, Num. 20.3. Concerning the number of deaths every
year, see vol. III, pp. 282 and 291. The number fifteen thousand is
a round one; see Tosafot on Baba Batra 121a.

⁶⁰⁵ Yelammedenu in Yalkut I, 763, and in *Batte Midrashot*
III, 10; Esfah in Yalkut, *loc. cit.*; comp. also Lekah, Num. 20-35.
Concerning Aaron's love of peace, and about the people's affections
for him, see vol. III, p. 328.

⁶⁰⁶ Yelammedenu in Yalkut I, 763; Lekah, Num. 20.6; comp.
also vol. II, p. 228 (end of section). Yelammedenu, *loc. cit.*, remarks
that the righteous are as concerned about the welfare of their beasts
as about themselves. This may be inferred from the fact that Jacob
told Joseph to find out "whether it is well with thy brethren and well
with the flock." Comp. also Mekilta Amalek 6, 52a; Tan. B. IV,
120; vol. II, p. 9; Nedarim 81a.

⁶⁰⁷ Yelammedenu in Yalkut I, 763; Targum Yerushalmi Num.

20.8, which reads: God said unto Moses and Aaron: "Adjure the rock by the Name, and only in case of its refusal should ye smite it" (on תריכון "adjure", see Targum Is. 65.9, where יקלל=יתרך); Lekah Num., *loc. cit.* Comp. vol. III, p. 320.

⁶⁰⁸ Targum Yerushalmi and Lekah on Num. 20.8. Comp. the preceding note, as well as notes 600 and 625.

⁶⁰⁹ Yelammedenu in Yalkut I, 763, and in II, 879, on Ps.78; Lekah Num. 20.10.

⁶¹⁰ Tan. B. IV, 120–121; Tan. Hukkat 9; BaR 19.9; PK 14, 118b; PR 11, 42b; Hashkem 19b–20a; Shir 1.6; comp. also ER 13 65, and Midrash Tannaim 14, where it is said that Moses' delinquency was a mere oversight. Comp. note 870.

⁶¹¹ Yelammedenu in Yalkut I, 763; BR 5.7; BaR 19.9; Tan. B. IV, 120; Tan. Hukkat 79. Comp. vol. III, p. 180 and note 410.   The rod upon which the Name was engraved was taken away from Moses , as a punishment for his having used it to smite the rock; Zohar I, 6b. On the identification of Aaron's rod with the staff of Moses, see note 600.

⁶¹² BaR 19.19; Tan. B. IV, 20; Tan. Hukkat 9; Tehillim 78, 345; Yelammedenu in Yalkut I, 763, and II, 819, on Ps. 78. The final portion of the last-named passage is taken from Tehillim, *loc. cit.*, and does not form part of the Yelammedenu.

⁶¹³ Yelammedenu in Yalkut I, 763. Comp. note 490, according to which this passage of Yelammedenu is to be understood in the following manner: Moses' sin consisted in his having used words which might have been misunderstood by the people to mean that it was Moses, and not God, who made the water flow from the rock. See also Nahmanides, Num. 20.1–11, who fully discusses the different opinions concerning the sin committed by Moses at the Waters of Meribah. Comp. further vol. III, pp. 317–320. Concerning Moses (and Aaron) as leaders of Israel in the time of the Messiah, see vol. IV, pp. 302, 373, and vol. III, pp. 35, 313, 481.

⁶¹⁴ Yelammedenu in Yalkut I, 764. Comp. vol. III, pp. 16, 51, and 310.

⁶¹⁵ BaR 19.13–14 (שמקדם is correct; comp. PK 5, 46a, which reads: At the crossing of the Red Sea it became known to Moses that he would not enter the Holy Land); Tan. Hukkat 10.11; Tan. B. IV, 121–122. These Midrashim point out that Moses on several other occasions had employed worse expressions in addressing God (comp. note 285), and yet was not punished for them. The reason given for this is because on those occasions he did not commit the offence publicly

but privately. Concerning the question whether the "generation of the wilderness" shall have a share in the world to come, see Sanhedrin, Mishnah 10.3; Tosefta 13.10; Babli 110b; Yerushalmi 10, 29c; ARN 26, 107–108; references in notes 177 and 586 (the references in the last note deal with the congregation of Korah); 'Abodah Zarah 4b–5a, which reads: The commission of that grievous sin (*i. e.*, the worship of the golden calf) was out of harmony with Israel's nature; but God willed it so, in order to show thereby that even a whole nation might be forgiven the most grievous of sins, if it only repents.

616 Tan. B. IV, 121–122; Tan. Hukkat 10; BaR 19.12; Yoma 86b; Sifre D., 26; Sifre N., 137; Midrash Tannaim 13; Sifre Z., 160; DR 2.6.

617 Yelammedenu in Yalkut I, 764; BaR 19.13–14; Tan. Hukkat 11. Comp. BR 42.7.

618 BR 4.6. Comp. vol. I, p. 15.

619 BaR 19.9; Tan. B. IV, 121; Tan. Hukkat 10; Yelammedenu (?) in *Likkutim* IV, 526; comp. vol. III, p. 457. According to Lekah, Num. 20.12, Aaron's sin consisted in his not having tried to prevent Moses from using angry words against Israel. For other legends about the Waters of Meribah, see vol. III, pp. 317–320.

620 Lekah, Num. 20.14; BaR 19.15; Tan. B. IV, 122; Tan. Hukkat 12. Comp. vol. I, p. 379, and note 234 appertaining to it.

621 Yelammedenu in '*Aruk*, s. v. פטריקון (comp. *Likkutim*, IV, 53b); Tan. B. IV, 122 and 129; Tan. Hukkat 12; BaR 19.15. Of the patriarchs, it is Jacob in particular who suffers with his descendants; see Tehillim 14, 115; PR 40 (end); Ekah 2.111. Comp. Vol. V, p. 275. Concerning the "inheritance", see vol. III, pp. 55 and 332 (bottom).

622 BaR 19.15–16; Tan. B. IV, 122–123; Tan. Hukkat 12–14; Mekilta Beshallah 2, 28a; Mekilta RS, 45–46. Moses assured the king of Edom that the Israelites would not attack the Edomite women (Targum Yerushalmi Num. 20.17); but although the king knew that God commanded the Israelites not to destroy the Edomites, he feared lest they should subjugate them and make them pay tribute, so that in this manner the debts which Esau owed Jacob might be paid by the descendants of the former. See Mekilta Shirah 11, 49a (read אנמות "annonae"); Mekilta RS, 68. Great is the importance of blood-relationship; if not for their kinship with Israel, the Edomites would have been excluded from "entering into the congregation of the Lord", since their sin was greater than that of the Moabites and the Ammonites, who were punished in this manner; see Midrash Tannaim 146, with

regard to Deut. 23.5–8.   Edom threatened Israel with the sword; even so will God destroy Edom with the sword (see Is. 34.5) in the time to come; Yelammedenu in Yalkut II, 439, on Is., *loc. cit.*   Concerning the cloud that went before Israel, see vol. II, p. 375.

⁶²³ Petirat Aharon beg.(read ובו ביום "on that day", forty years before, Aaron's sons died at the dedication of the Tabernacle, see vol. III, pp. 187, *seq*); Ta'anit 9a; Sifre D., 305; Seder 'Olam 10; Yelammedenu in Yalkut II, 907, on Job 16.   Concerning the day of Miriam's death, see Ratner, note 20 on Seder 'Olam *l. c.*

⁶²⁴ *Batte Midrashot* III, 8–9.   Comp. Tehillim 24, 219, as well as Tosefta Sanhedrin 9.9.   For a different view, see vol. III, p. 283.

⁶²⁵ Petirat Aharon 91.   Comp. vol. III, pp. 310–311.   On the great mourning for Miriam, see Josephus, *Antiqui.*, IV, 4,6.

⁶²⁶ Rashi and Midrash Aggada on Num. 20.10; PetiratAharon 92.   Comp. vol. III, p. 63.   An allusion to this legend is perhaps to be found in Targum Yerushalmi Num. 20.8 where תריכון is to be taken literally.   Comp. note 607.

⁶²⁷ Petirat Aharon 92, where אינו מוציא מים is to be read.   Concerning the blood flowing from the rock, see Targum Yerushalmi Num. 20.11; ShR 3.13; Tehillim 78, 344.   See also Sibyll. 3.803 and 4 61; vol. II, p. 322.   Concerning the honey flowing from the rock, see vol. II, p. 257, according to which גדלם "on which they were brought up" is to be read in Petirat Aharon, *loc. cit.*   Comp. vol. III, pp. 308–311.

⁶²⁸ PK 14, 118b 119a; Tan. B. V 14; DR 2.2 and 8; *Likkutim* V, 97a–97b (on this passage see II, p. 340, bottom, and note 610); Petirat Aharon 92.

⁶²⁹ Petirat Aharon 92.

⁶³⁰ Tan. B. IV, 123–124; Tan. Hukkat 14; BaR 19.17.

⁶³¹ Petirat Aharon 93.   Comp. the following note.

⁶³² Yelammedenu in Yalkut I, 764; *Likkutim* IV, 54a.   "Difficult in the sight of the Lord is the death of His saints" (comp. Ps. 116.15; יקר is taken to mean "heavy", "difficult"), and if Abraham, Isaac, Jacob, Moses, and David had not spoken, in a heedless moment, of their death, they would never have died; Yelammedenu in Yalkut II, 874 (end); Tehillim 116, 477–478; Tan.Wayehi 4, which reads: The righteous never die, except when they have expressed their desire to do so.   DR 9.1; Hallel 104.

⁶³³ Petirat Aharon 92–93 (line 22 of 92 read פועל נאמן; the following line seems also to be corrupt); Tan. B. IV 131.   On Aaron's love

of peace, and the people's affection for him, see vol. III, pp. 309, 328–329. Concerning the ceremonies connected with the reception of the leaders of the people by Moses, see vol. III, p. 144.

⁶³⁴ ER 13, 63; 20, 112, and 25,128.

⁶³⁵ ER 13,68. See also EZ 1, 169–170, where the three patriarchs, Moses, Aaron, and David, are praised for their kindness as their highest virtue.

⁶³⁶ Petirat Aharon 93–94 (read לפניכם instead of 'לפני ה); Tan. B. IV, 131–132. Concerning the conception that the soul is a pledge entrusted to man by God, see Vol. V, p. 255, note 259 and Index, s. v. "Soul". The story about Aaron's preparations for his death is related differently in Yelammedenu in Yalkut I, 764. One early morning Moses called upon his brother, and informed him that he had spent a sleepless night pondering over a difficult passage in the Bible and asked him whether he would not assist him in solving the difficulty. Moses added that in his excitement he had forgotten the exact place, and that he only remembered that the passage occurred in the Book of Genesis. They read the first chapter of the Bible, and at the perusal of the creation of each day, Moses exclaimed, "How beautiful and good is the creation of this day!" When they reached the narrative concerning the creation of Adam, Moses remarked: "I do not know what to say of the creation of man. How can I call it beautiful and good, knowing that the end of man is death?" Aaron, however, replied: "Far be it from us not to resign ourselves to the will of God." These words of Aaron gave Moses the desired opportunity to inform his brother of his imminent death. At the very moment Aaron became aware of his approaching death, his stature shrank, and all the people knew that he had reached the end of his life. In *Likkutim*, IV, 54a–54b, the text of Yelammedenu was taken from the later editions of the Yalkut, in which entire sentences are missing. Comp. also Zohar III, 183a.

⁶³⁷ Sifra Milluim 8.7, and comp. the notes of R. Jacob David, *ad loc.*, in the Warsaw edition. Vol. III, p. 445, contains a different legend concerning the undressing of Aaron and the dressing of Eleazar. Yelammedenu I, 787, describes Aaron's last hour in the following manner: The brothers had nearly reached Mount Hor, and Moses did not yet find courage to inform Aaron of his approaching death. Finally Moses took heart, and said to Aaron: "If a hundred years from now God would decree thy death, what wouldst thou say?" Aaron replied: "I would only say: The Judge is just" (comp. note 256 on vol. I, pp. 286–287). Without any hesitation Moses then said: "Now that

thou didst resign thyself to God's will, let us ascend the mount, since God has decreed that thou shouldst die in that place". Reconciled to his fate, Aaron followed his younger brother "as a lamb that is led to the slaughter." God spoke to the angels, saying: "Ye were astonished at Isaac when he put himself on the altar to be slaughtered in obedience to his father's will. Marvel ye now all the more at Aaron who submits himself to death at the words of his younger brother." Three different views are given in Yelammedenu concerning the undressing of Aaron. Moses began to undress him from below; as soon as one part of the body was laid bare, it was immediately covered by a "cloud of glory" (*i. e.*, a celestial garment; comp. Index, s. v. "Celestial Garments") so that by the time Aaron was completely undressed his body was covered with the cloud of glory, and he was no longer among the living. According to the second view, every part of Aaron's body, as soon as Moses removed the garment from it, was "swallowed up" by the mouth of the mount, and thus his naked body was not exposed to anyone's eye. The third view maintains that the undressing of Aaron and the dressing of Eleazar took place simultaneously: while Moses undressed his brother, the angels dressed his nephew Eleazar. At the very moment of his death, Aaron was asked by his brother: "How is the death of the righteous?" The answer given was: "I cannot tell thee that; all I can say is: I wish I had come sooner to the place where I am now."

⁶³⁸ Petirat Aharon 94. Comp. vol. II, p. 328 (bottom); vol. IV, p. 201.

⁶³⁹ Baba Batra 17a. This passage contains also the statement that the three patriarchs, as well as Moses and Miriam, died by a kiss from God. Comp. vol. II, p. 330.

⁶⁴⁰ Petirat Aharon 94–95 (read לנן עדן=לנ'ע, instead of לב'ע); Yelammedenu in Yalkut I, 764 and 787.

⁶⁴¹ Petirat Aharon 95; Yelammedenu in Yalkut I, 674 and 787 (the phrase דרך שמים מת, 764, means "he died a natural death"; but the text is hardly correct, and in view of the explicit statement of Petirat Aharon that Moses feared lest the people should deify Aaron, it may best be assumed that the words דרך וכו' refer to Aaron's translation); Tan. B. IV, 124; PRE 17; BaR 20.20; Tan. Hukkat 17; Zohar III, 183a (which reads: All the people in the camp saw what was happening on Mount Hor); Sifre D., 304. Moses did not inform the people of Aaron's approaching death, because he feared lest, out of their love for Aaron, they might attempt to prevent God's decree from being carried out

by praying for his life. In this way they would act contrary to God's wise plan. See Yelammedenu in Yalkut I, 764. On Aaron's over-powering the Angel of Death, see vol. II, p. 305; on his popularity, see vol. III, p. 328, *seq.*; concerning his suspicion of Moses, see vol. III, p. 330.

⁶⁴² Yelammedenu in Yalkut I, 787; Petirat Aharon 95; Lekah, Deut. 31.14.

⁶⁴³ ARN 12, 48–51, and second version 24, 48–51, as well as sup-plement, 161 and 163; Kallah 2.6 (read שצהבת "thou quarrellest", instead of שתרצית); WR 3.6; Sanhedrin 6b; Tan. B. IV, 130 1–131; Yelammedenu in Yalkut I, 787. The description of Aaron as the ideal of kindness and love of peace is found in sentences attributed to Hillel and his masters Shemaiah and Abtalion; see Abot 1.12; Yoma 71b; comp. Ginzberg's remarks in Geiger, *Kebuzzat Maamarim*, 160. See also vol. III, pp. 323 and 327. The statement found in Targum Yerushalmi Num. 20.29 (whence it was borrowed by Rashi and Lekah) that men as well as women mourned for Aaron, whereas for Moses only the men mourned, is taken from PRE 17. The other statement of Targum that the weeping and mourning of Moses and Eleazar for Aaron made all the rest of the people do the same is found also in ARN 12, 49.

⁶⁴⁴ Yelammedenu in Yalkut I, 787, and (in abridged form) 764. According to another view, the people mourned very deeply for Miriam, see note 625. Concerning the statement that Moses desired a death simi-lar to that of his brother, see vol. III, pp. 445–446. On the disappearance of Aaron's grave, see vol. III, p. 326 (bottom), and note 792. On "death by a kiss", see note 639.

⁶⁴⁵ Petirat Aharon 95; Midrash Aggada on Deut. 4.26. On convincing the people of Aaron's death, see vol. III, p. 327. Concern-ing the clouds that were sent down for Aaron's sake, see vol. III, pp. 48–49, and the following note.

⁶⁴⁶ Seder 'Olam 9; Tosefta Sotah 11.1; Sifre N., 82; Rosh ha-Shanah 3a; Ta'anit 9a; Yerushalmi Yoma 1, 38b; PK 19, 138a; PR 13, 55a; Tan. B. IV, 124–125 (only in this passage and in the sources dependent upon it is Arad identified with Amalek; comp. to the contrary vol. III, p. 340); Tan. Hukkat 18; BaR 19.20; Shir 4.5; Ekah 1.93; Targum Yerushalmi Num. 20.1 and 33.40. It is noteworthy that the Septuagint and Philo, *Moses*, 1.45, take כנעני in Num. 21.1 as the name of a person, and not as a *gentilicum*; they perhaps presuppose the rab-binic legend which considers that the King of Arad was an Amalekite

and not a Canaanite. Comp. also note 669. The Haggadah concerning the death of Aaron which gave courage to the enemy to attack Israel is also known to Aphraates, 452, who undoubtedly had it orally communicated to him by Jews.

⁶⁴⁷ Yelammedenu in Yalkut I, 763, and II, 549, on Obadiah; *Likkutim*, IV, 55a–55b, as well as in '*Aruk*, s.v. פתח; Targum Yerushalmi Num. 21.1, and somewhat differently on 33.4, where it is stated that Amalek joined Canaan in his attack on Israel (comp. the preceding note); BaR 19.20; Tan. B. IV, 125; Tan. Hukkat 18. On the idea that Amalek carried out the counsel given him by Esau, see also *Rokeah* 234; Lekah, Gen. 27.45; vol. III, p. 31; vol. IV, p. 315. According to an unknown Midrash quoted by Rashi and Kimhi on 2 Chron. 20.11, the enemies who waged war against Jehoshaphat were really Amalekites disguised as Ammonites.

⁶⁴⁸ BaR 19.20; Tan. B. IV, 125; Tan. Hukkat. The complete destruction of this enemy by the Jews is explained by Philo, *Moses*, 1.45, in the following manner: As every pious man offers the first fruits unto God...., so did the Hebrews dedicate the whole of this mighty country (*i. e.* Arad) unto the Lord. The very same reason is given by *Rokeah*, 221 (on the authority of an old source?) for devoting Jericho to God; comp. note 22 on vol. IV, p. 8.

⁶⁴⁹ Yelammedenu in Yalkut I, 764 (in the later editions of the Yalkut the reference to Yelammedenu as a source is missing); Lekah, Num. 21.1. Comp. 2 Kings 5.2.

⁶⁵⁰ Yerushalmi Yoma 1, 38b, and Sotah 1, 17b; BaR 19.20; Tan. B. IV, 125; Tan. Hukkat 18; Seder 'Olam 9; Mekilta Wayyassa' 1, 22b; Targum Yerushalmi Num. 21.1, and Deut, 10.6; Yelammedenu (?) in *Batte Midrashot*, III, 14; Midrash Aggada, Num. 26.12. It is noteworthy that the tannaitic sources, Seder 'Olam and Mekilta, know nothing of the quarrel between the Levites and the other tribes; they only state that the Israelites, after having continued to march for eight stations, returned to the place where Aaron died to arrange for a great mourning in his honor. Concerning the Benjamite and Simeonite clans who were entirely annihilated, see vol. II, p. 189; vol. III, p.390.

⁶⁵¹ Rashi on Num. 21.4, which is very likely based upon an old midrashic source. As long as Aaron lived the Hebrews were protected by "the cloud" against the burning sun of the wilderness; but immediately after his death the cloud disappeared (see vol. III, p. 330, and note 645), and they suffered greatly from the sun; they therefore became peevish and impatient; Yelammedenu (?) in *Batte Midrashot*, III, 17. They

did not give expression to their vexation at the long journey through the wilderness; they were nevertheless punished for having harbored evil thoughts concerning God and Moses; Sanhedrin 110a; Targum Yerushalmi Num. 21.5.

⁶⁵² Tan. B. IV, 125–126; Tan. Hukkat 19; BaR 19.21. These sources further remark that life in the wilderness was vexatious and difficult only to those against whom God decreed that they should die in the wilderness.

⁶⁵³ Targum Yerushalmi Num. 21.6; Tan. B. IV, 126; Tan. Hukkat 19; BaR 19.22; Ephraem I, 263. Comp. vol. III, pp. 245–246.

⁶⁵⁴ BaR 19.22; Tan. B. IV, 126; Tan. Hukkat 19; PRE according to the text of *Batte Midrashot*, III, 34. Concerning the kind of death caused by the serpent, see Zohar III, 183b. On the slanderous serpent, see vol. II, p. 321; vol. V, p. 95, note 62. Concerning the clouds that marched before Israel burning the serpents, see vol. III, p. 374. Comp. *Likkutim*, IV, 56a.

⁶⁵⁵ Lekah, Num. 21.

⁶⁵⁶ Tan. B. IV, 126; Tan. Hukkat 19; BaR 19.22, which reads: Just as Israel sinned against two, God and Moses (comp. also Sanhedrin 110a), so also two kinds of serpents were sent to execute God's punishment on them, in order that they might thereby learn how grievous was their offence against their leader Moses; *Hadar*, Num. 21.8. BaR and Tan., *loc. cit.*, on the contrary, maintain that all the havoc was caused by one serpent. Concerning the speedy forgiveness granted to the sinners by God and Moses, see vol. I, p. 260.

⁶⁵⁷ Yerushalmi Rosh ha-Shanah 3, 59a; BR 31.8. Several other explanations for making the serpent of brass are given by Philo, 2 *Leg. Alleg*, 20. Comp. also Midrash Aggada Num. 21.9.

⁶⁵⁸ Rosh ha-Shanah 3.8; Mekilta Amalek 1, 54a; Targum Yerushalmi Num. 21.8–9; PRE in *Batte Midrashot*, III, 34; Wisdom 16.10–13. In the patristic literature the serpent of brass "put upon a pole" is symbolic of the crucified Jesus; comp. *e. g.*, Justin *Dialogue*, 91, 94, 112, and 1 *Apologia*, 60; Tertullian, *De Idol.* 5; *Adversus Marcion*. 3.8, and *Adversus Judaeos* 10. The rabbinic explanation of the setting up of the serpent upon a pole must not be taken as an anti-Christian Haggadah, as may be seen from the fact that it was known to the author of Wisdom. It is at the same time true that in the polemic literature of the Jews in the Middle Ages the correct explanation of the serpent of brass plays an important part. Comp., *e. g.*, *Peletat Soferim* 32, which records the reply given by R. Nathan Official to a Christian with regard to the

setting up of the serpent (the text is corrupt; read שאל אחד instead of סובל אחד; at the end read אלא זה instead of ולא זה); the statement of R. Nathan that this serpent was nothing else but Moses' rod which was turned into a serpent (comp. Exod. 4.3) is found in no other source. See vol. III, pp. 60–61 and note 145.

⁶⁵⁹ Yerushalmi Rosh ha-Shanah 3, 59a; Tan. B. IV, 126; Tan. Hukkat 19; BaR 19.23.

⁶⁶⁰ Targum Yerushalmi Num. 33.4–42. Comp. Lekah and *Hadar* on Num. 21.10.

⁶⁶¹ Tan. B. IV, 126–127; Tan. Hukkat 19; BaR 19.24.

⁶⁶² Tan. B. IV, 127; Tan. Hukkat 20; BaR 19.25; DZ 23–24. According to Berakot 59a–59b, the miracle was caused by the pillar which preceded the Israelites on their marching, and prepared the way for them, elevating the valleys and levelling the mountains and hills; comp. vol. II, pp. 374–375 and vol. III, p. 156. These sources further state that the Israelites would never have known of this miracle had it not been for two lepers who, marching outside the cover of the clouds (see vol. III, p. 57), had the opportunity to observe the levelling of the mountains and the annihilation of the Amorites. The proverb "if you give, etc." occurs also in Shabbat 10b. As to the mountains meeting persons, see vol. II, p. 303 (top).

⁶⁶³ Yelammedenu in Yalkut I, 763–764; Tan. B. IV, 127; Tan. Hukkat 21;BaR 19.26. That the song at the Red Sea was composed by Moses and sung by Israel is also the view of Ephraem I, 216B. For a different opinion, see vol. III, pp. 31 and 33.

⁶⁶⁴ Targum Onkelos and Yerushalmi on Num. 21.17–20 (the places named in the verses are haggadically explained to refer to the Torah and to those who study it; see also 'Erubin 59a). Midrash Aggada and *Hadar* on Num., *loc. cit.*, as well as Sabba', Hukkat (end), have other explanations of this song. Comp. also Tan. B. IV, 127–128, Tan. Hukkat 21; BaR 19.26; vol. III, p. 53. In all these sources, the well praised by Israel is identified with "Miriam's well" (comp. vol. III, p. 50), which disappeared after the death of the prophetess (comp. vol. III, p. 308). This well subsequently reappeared, and its reappearance was greeted with a song by the people; see Seder 'Olam 9.10, and the parallel passages cited by Ratner, *ad loc.* Philo, *Moses*, 1.46, on the other hand, is of the opinion that the well greeted with a song was the first well the Israelites found on entering a cultivated land after their long journey in the wilderness.

⁶⁶⁵ Yelammedenu in Yalkut I, 763. The great miracles performed

for Israel in Egypt and in the wilderness were, in one way or another, connected with water. The first plague inflicted upon the Egyptians was the turning of the water into blood. Then there was the dividing of the Red Sea. At Marah the bitter waters were made sweet. Later on many other miracles were performed in connection with water. Israel therefore was moved to sing the praise of water at the end of their wandering through the desert. Moses at the same time informed the Israelites that when they enter the Holy Land another miracle connected with water would take place, namely, the dividing of the Jordan; see DR 2.8.

⁶⁶⁶ Seder 'Olam 9; Tan. B. IV, 130; Tan. Hukkat 34; BaR 19.32, which reads: Aaron died in the month of Ab, and the war against Sihon took place in the following month, that is in Elul. Comp. note 669.

⁶⁶⁷ Niddah 61a. According to an unknown Midrash, quoted by R. Bahya, Hukkat (end), they were the sons of Shemhazael. Comp. vol. I, pp. 150 and 160, as well as vol. III, p. 343.

⁶⁶⁸ Tan. B. V, 3 and 6; DR 1.24; DZ 24–25; Makiri Amos 10–11; Niddah 24b. The above sources do not agree as to the selection of their hero, some expressing their predilection for Sihon and others for Og. Comp. vol. III, p. 343. Sihon's mother was Ham's wife, who committed adultery with Ahiah before and after the deluge, and bore him two sons, Og, who was born before the deluge (see vol. I, p. 160), and Sihon, born after it; *Hadar* and *Da'at* Hukkat (end). Concerning the enormous stature of the giants, see vol. I, pp. 125 and 151, as well as vol. III, p. 268.

⁶⁶⁹ Rosh ha-Shanah 3a, where it is stated that Sihon, Arad, and Kenaani are three names of the same person; comp. also Baba Batra 78b and Midrash Aggada Num. 21.23. In the last-mentioned source כנעני is said to be the name of a person. This is in agreement with the Septuagint, Num. 21.1 and Philo, *Moses*, 1.45. Comp. note 646. The victory over Arad took place in the month of Ab, shortly after the death of Aaron; Aggadat Esther 29; comp. also vol. III, p. 331, as well as notes 666 and 682, dealing with the victory over Sihon.

⁶⁷⁰ DR 1.22–23; DZ 26; Yelammedenu in Yalkut I, 764. Comp. vol. III, pp. 25 and 277.

⁶⁷¹ Ta'anit 20a; 'Abodah Zarah 25a; Targum Yerushalmi Deut. 2.25. Comp. note 245.

⁶⁷² Yelammedenu in Yalkut I, 764; Tan. B. III, 16, and V, 6–7; Tan. Zaw 3; DR 5.13 (which states that Moses sent messengers

117

without consulting God; comp. notes 191, 239); BaR 19.33. Comp. vol. III pp. 80 and 405.

⁶⁷³ Targum Yerushalmi Num. 21.22. Concerning the explanation that "field and vineyard" are metaphors for woman, see PRE 21; BR 63.12 and Theodor's note 4 on BR 22.7; Sanhedrin 74 b (קרקע = שדה); Zohar I, 36b. Comp. also Ps. 128.3. See note 622.

⁶⁷⁴ Tan. B. IV, 129; Tan. Hukkat 23; BaR 19.29; DZ 26. The negotiations took place between the people of Israel and Sihon, as it was beneath Moses' dignity to deal directly with this small potentate, but to the king of Edom the Hebrew ambassadors were sent as the representatives of Moses, Lekah, Num. 20.21, which offers this as an explanation of the difference in the wording between this verse and Num. 20.14. The three Midrashim quoted at the beginning of this note do not share this view, and maintain that the "leader of a generation is equal to the entire generation." Comp. Tosefta 'Abodah Zarah I, 4, and hence Scripture considers the undertakings of Moses as those of the people, and speaks of them promiscuously.

⁶⁷⁵ 'Abodah Zarah 38a; Targum Yerushalmi Deut. 2.28. In view of the fact that Jews are forbidden to eat food prepared by Gentiles, all that they wanted was food stuffs.

⁶⁷⁶ Tan. B. IV, 129; Tan. Hukkat 230; BaR 19.29; DZ 26.

⁶⁷⁷ Tan. B. IV, 130 (comp. Buber, *ad loc.*); Tan. Hukkat 25; BaR 19.32; DZ 27; Yelammedenu (?) in *Likkutim*, V, 96b.

⁶⁷⁸ Tan. B. IV, 129; Tan. Hukkat 230; BaR 19.29; DZ 26–27; Yelammedenu in Yalkut I, 810; Sifre D., 3; Midrash Tannaim 4; comp. vol. III, p. 376.

⁶⁷⁵ DZ 27.

⁶⁸⁰ Yelammedenu in '*Aruk*, s. v. פרמא 3; comp. *Likkutim*, V, 96b. See also vol. IV, p. 26.

⁶⁸¹ DZ 27; Tan. B. IV, 130; Tan. Hukkat 24; BaR 19.31. Philo, *Moses*, 1.47, likewise dwells upon the complete annihilation of Sihon's army in the first encounter with Israel. That Caleb and Phinehas were the spies is found only in Targum Yerushalmi Num. 21.22. Comp. vol. IV, p. 5.

⁶⁸² Tan. B. IV, 130; Tan. Hukkat 24; BaR 19.32; Seder 'Olam 9; Josephus, *Antiqui.*, IV, 5.2. Comp. note 666, and vol. IV, p. 400.

⁶⁸³ Shir 4.8; Midrash Tannaim 4; for the contrary view, see Josephus, *Antiqui.*, IV, 5.3.

⁶⁸⁴ DR 1.25; BR 42.8; Niddah 61a; Tan. B. IV, 130; Tan. Hukkat 25; BaR 19.32; comp. vol. I, pp. 160 and 341 as well as vol.

III, p. 340. The Haggadah assumes that Og was a contemporary of Abraham (comp. vol. I, p. 160), and this accounts for the statement that he was five hundred years old at the time of his death, which took place in the last year of Israel's wandering through the wilderness, or two years prior to this; comp. Seder 'Olam 9, and Ratner note 13. Abraham was born 1948 A. M., and the forty years of the wandering through the wilderness ended in the year 2488, hence Og was by fifty years the junior of Abraham. According to another view, however, Og was born before the deluge (comp. note 667), so that he lived more than eight hundred years.

685 DR 1.24; DZ 25; Makiri on Ps. 136, 260 (the text is corrupt, and should be emended in accordance with DZ). Comp. note 668. Concerning Edrei, see *Kaftor wa-Ferah*, ed. Lunz, Index, s. v.

686 Niddah 24b; Tan. B. V, 6; DZ 27. Comp. note 668.

687 DZ 27 (the giant Goliath was very big and tall but his breadth was proportionate to his height); Targum Yerushalmi Deut. 3.11; comp. note 704. Maimonides, *Guide*, II, 47, strongly repudiates this view of Og's monstrosity, but does not mention the fact that Targum and Midrash are the authorities for this opinion. Comp. also Onkelos Deut., *loc. cit.*

688 Soferim 21, where it is also stated that Abraham received him as a present from Nimrod. Comp. vol. I, pp. 125, 203; Index, s. v. "Eliezer, the Slave of Abraham", and the following note.

689 PRE 16, where it is also stated that he was the slave (according to another reading, the son) of Nimrod, from whom Abraham received him as a present; comp. the preceding note. The version of this legend, as given in Soferim 21, presupposes that Abraham manumitted his slave when he knocked his tooth out, in accordance with the law as recorded in Exod. 21.26.

690 Soferim 21.

691 Tan. B. IV, 130; Tan. Hukkat 25; BaR 19.32; Zohar III, 181a. Moses was afraid of Og who had been circumcised by Abraham, whose slave he was. Comp. notes 688, 689.

692 Tan. B. IV, 130; Tan. Hukkat 25; BaR 19.32; DZ 27; comp. Niddah 61a and the remark of Tosafot, *ad loc.*

693 BaR 19.32; Tan. B. IV, 130; Tan. Hukkat 25. Comp. vol. I, 380 (bottom). The battle against Og took place on a Sabbath, and Moses feared lest the desecration of the Sabbath (though forced by necessity) should result in misfortune for Israel; see David Luria on BR 70.16.

⁶⁹⁴ Yelammedenu in Yalkut I, 810.

⁶⁹⁵ Berakot 54b (Moses was ten cubits high, and by jumping ten cubits he reached Og's ankles); Targum Yerushalmi Num. 21.35, where תלתא is to be read instead of שיתא. Another version of this legend is to be found in DR 1.24 and Midrash Aggada, Num., *loc. cit.* This version reads: Og tore up a mountain, and lifted it up to cast it upon the camp of Israel, but Moses wrote the Name upon a potsherd, and threw it at the mountain which was about to fall upon Israel. The result was that the mountain remained suspended in the air. Parhon, s. v. דוכיפת, quotes a Midrash to the effect that it was the hoopoe which perforated the mountain, whereas the Midrash Aggada ascribes this feat to the raven. The statement in Sekel 178 that Og's teeth were sixty cubits long is taken from Megillah 15b. Comp. also ER 26, 133. The legend given in vol. III, p. 469, maintains that Moses slew Sihon and Og with his rod.

⁶⁹⁷ Niddah 61a; Tan. B. IV, 130; Tan. Hukkat 25; BaR 19.32; PRE 23; Targum Yerushalmi Deut. 3.11. Comp. vol. I, p. 160, and vol. III, p. 343. The description of Og as the "last of the giants" in Deut. 3.12 is found by the Haggadah also in Gen. 14.13 (that is how the Haggadah explains הפליט) and it refers either to the escape from the deluge, in which all the giants perished, or to his escape from Amraphel's sword.

⁶⁹⁸ Yelammedenu in Yalkut I, 810. Comp. vol. III, p. 342. Yelammedenu, *loc. cit.*, adds that whereas after the victory over Sihon the Israelites had been very anxious to get as much spoil as possible, they were quite indifferent to the spoil after the victory over Og. The riches the Israelites had acquired by the first victory had satisfied their desire for spoil. Comp. *Likkutim*, V. 97a.

⁶⁹⁹ Tan. B. I, 6. Concerning the giant's measuring eighteen cubits, see vol. III, p. 340. On the Amorites as giants, see *Recognitiones* I, 29. Comp. also Jub. 29.9.

⁷⁰⁰ Tan. in Makiri on Ps. 136, 257; *Likkutim*, V, 96a; Tan. B.V., 3 and 6 (the victories over Sihon and Og were greater—*i. e.*, more miraculous—than those over Pharaoh); DZ 25; Midrash Tannaim 4.

⁷⁰¹ Tan. B. V, 6; DZ 27; BaR 18.22; Sotah 36a; Midrash Aggada Deut. 7.20 (the hornets used to track the Amorites to their hiding-places and kill them there; in this manner they frustrated the sudden attack upon Israel planned by their enemies); Philo, *Quaestiones*, Exod. 2.24. See also Wisdom 12.8–10 which reads: And sentest wasps as forerunners of their host, to destroy them.... executing judgment upon them little

by little, Thou gavest them a place of repentance. The use of τόπος literally "place", in the sense of "opportunity," is of frequent occurrence in Jewish-hellenistic literature, and is a Hebraism, being a translation of מקום which has both meanings in mishnaic Hebrew; comp., *e. g.*, Berakot 4.2.

⁷⁰² Sotah 36a, which also gives the dissenting view that there were two kinds of hornets, one which killed the trans-Jordanic enemies of Israel, and another which destroyed the inhabitants of the Holy Land proper; Tosefta Sota 11.10; Shir 4.5.

⁷⁰³ Tan. B. V, 6; Aggadat Bereshit 8.19. Comp. vol. III, p. 131 (bottom), and vol. IV, p. 7.

⁷⁰⁴ Targum Yerushalmi Deut. 3.11. Comp. note 687. Josephus *Antiqui.*, IV, 5.3, dwells upon Og's beauty and high descent.

⁷⁰⁵ Midrash Aggada Deut. 3.11.

⁷⁰⁶ Tan. B. V, 4–6; DR 1.15–20; Yelammedenu in *Likkutim*, V, 91a–94b; DZ 20–24; Makiri on Ps. 36, 227; 60, 309 (where David is censured for having engaged in war against Edom); 137, 264; on Is. 41, 125, and on Obadiah 18–19. Concerning Esau's filial piety, see Zohar I, 146, and Index, s. v.

⁷⁰⁷ Midrash Tannaim 1 and 4(which reads: Before the victory over Sihon, the mind of the people was too distracted to pay proper attention to the words of Moses); Sifre D., 3. Comp. vol. III, p. 118 (bottom).

⁷⁰⁸ Midrsh Tannaim 1–3; Sifre D., 1–2; Targum Yerushalmi Deut. 1.1. The ten temptations (mentioned in as early a source as Abot 5.4) are enumerated in different ways; comp. ARN 9, 39, and 34, 98–99 (second version 38, 98–99; a view is quoted here according to which there were eleven temptations; comp. Num. 14.22); Tehillim 95, 420–421; 'Arakin 15a; DZ 13–14. On God's intentions to bring them quickly to Palestine, comp. vol. III, p. 243 and note 459.

⁷⁰⁹ DR 1.13. As a reward for their having listened to his reprimand with reverence, they were blessed by Moses; DR 1.9; DZ 18.

⁷¹⁰ Sifre D., 4; Midrash Tannaim 4.

⁷¹¹ Lekah, Deut. 1.5. Comp. vol. III, p. 97; vol. IV, p. 6.

⁷¹² Baba Kamma 38a–38b (here it is stated that the prohibition "not to vex Moab" remained valid even after the latter had attempted to destroy Israel by means of Balaam's curses); Nazir 23b; Horayyot 10b; BR 51.11; BaR 20.3; Tan. B. IV, 133; Zohar III, 188. Comp. also Yelammedenu in Yalkut II, 418, on Is. 40 (the reference to the source is only given in the first edition), which reads: As a reward

for Lot's hospitality by giving the angels one night's lodging in his house, the Israelites were forbidden to wage war against his descendants.

⁷¹³ BaR 20.3. Comp. note 717.

⁷¹⁴ Tan. B. IV, 129; Tan. Hukkat 24; BR 20.7. Concerning the view that Balaam caused the defeat of Moab, see vol. III, p. 354. Ps.-Philo, 18.2 maintains, on the other hand, that Balak sent to Balaam, saying: "Behold, I know how that in the reign of my father Zippor, when the Amorites fought against him, thou didst curse them and they were delivered into his hands." On Balaam's father, see note 722.

⁷¹⁵ Lekah, Num. 21.29, whence this statement found its way in Sekel and Ziyyoni on Num. *loc. cit.* These authorities regard Chemosh as the Moabite Ka'bah.

⁷¹⁶ BaR 20.3; Tan. B. IV 133; Tan. Balak 2. These Midrashim also remark that the defeat of Sihon and Og, "the sentinels of Palestine", (see vol. III, p. 341, bottom) was the cause of the great fear of the Moabites.

⁷¹⁷ Hullin 69b; Gittin 38a; Tan. B. IV, 129; Tan. Hukkat 24; BaR 19.30. Josephus, *Antiqui.*, IV, 6.2, likewise calls attention to the fact that Balak was ignorant of God's command to Israel not to wage war against the Moabites.

⁷¹⁸ BaR 20.4; Tan. B IV, 134; Tan. Balak 4. On Balaam's father, see vol. III, p. 383 and note 722. According to Targum Yerushalmi Num. 22.4, Moab and Midian formed a confederate state, and the king was alternately a Moabite and a Midianite; hence the predecessor of Balak the Moabite was a Midianite, and not his father. Comp. also Koheleth 2.9. Zohar III, 196b–197a, reads: Balak was the grandson of Jethro, and the only one of the latter's family who was not converted to the true religion of Israel (comp. vol. II, p. 289, and vol. III, pp. 75–76). The Moabites and Midianites therefore elected him king as a reward for his steadfastness to the faith of his people, comp. note 721. The text of Lekah 23.18 is corrupt, and is to be emended in accordance with Koheleth, *loc. cit.*

⁷¹⁹ Lekah, Midrash Aggada, and *Ba'al ha-Turim* on Num. 22.1. In Lekah מצפיר is the same as משכים, from the Aramaic צפרא "early morning", and Balak ia said to have started the day with hostile plans against Israel. Comp. also vol. II, p. 328, which deals with the etymology of the name Zipporah. Philo, *De Confusione Ling.* 15, explains the name Balak as one who is "void of sense", in accord-

ance with Is. 24.1, where the Septuagint has ἐρημώσει for בולקה of Hebrew text.

⁷²⁰ Zohar III, 184b. The use of the bird Yaddua' for magical purposes is referred to in very early sources; comp. the explanation of ידעוני (Lev. 19.31) in Sanhedrin 66b. A comparison of Zohar with Maimonides, commentary on Mishnah Sanhedrin 7.4, will prove the dependence of the former on the latter. The Franco-German school of talmudic commentators identify Yaddua' in Sanhedrin, *loc. cit.*, with the "vegetable man", see Rashi, *ad loc.*, R. Samson of Sens, Kil'ayim 8.5; comp. Ginzberg's full discussion on this point in *Schwarz Festschrift* 329–333. Comp. also vol. I, pp. 31–32, and the notes appertaining to them. Philo, *Moses*, 1.48, describes Balaam as a great master in the art of augury. Did he confuse Balaam with Balak "the son of the bird"? Concerning Balak's magical art, see also Zohar III, 198b, which reads: He sank a magical mixture consisting of herbs and heads of scorpions fifteen hundred cubits deep into the ground. This mixture was subsequently found by David; see vol. IV, p. 96. For further details concerning Balak's magic, see vol. III, pp. 370, 376, 378.

⁷²¹ Tan. B. IV, 134; Tan. Balak 3; BaR 20.4; Sifre N., 157; Sanhedrin 105a; MHG I, 546; Zohar III, 189b–190a. In the last-named source the Midianites are chiefly blamed, and are said to have incited the Moabites against Israel. Comp, vol. II, p. 164 (bottom), and vol. III, p. 405. Josephus, *Antiqui.*, IV, 6.2, writes: Balak the king of the Moabites, who had from his ancestors a friendship and a league with the Midianites; comp. notes 718 and 842.

⁷²² Sanhedrin 105a (Beor is taken here as an epithet of Balaam; this explanation is against that of Rashi); Targum Yerushalmi Num. 22.25; BR 57.3 (Balaam is identified here with Kemuel; see Theodor *ad loc.*, *Hadar*, Exod. 1.10, and Num 22.5; *Da'at*, Gen. 22.23, and Exod., *loc. cit.*, Mahzor Vitry 549); Yeammedenu in Yalkut I, 766. Comp. also vol. I, pp. 376, 424; vol. II, pp. 159, 163,165, 254, 272, 277, 287, 296, 332, 334, 335; vol. III, pp. 364, 373, 411; vol. IV, p. 30. In the sources quoted above three different views can be easily recognized: Balaam is identified with Laban; Balaam is Laban's grandson; Balaam is Laban's nephew. But there is still a fourth view which maintains that Balaam died at the age of thirty-three, and accordingly could not have been a close relative of Laban, and certainly not identical with him, see Sanhedrin 106b. The view held by many modern authors, Jewish as well as Christian, that in Sanhedrin, *loc. cit.*, as well as in

many other passages of the legendary literature of the Jews, Balaam is used as an *alias* for Jesus (comp. the literature on this point given by Laible, *Jesus in Talmud*, IV, 50, *seq.*, Schorr, *He-Haluz* X, 32-46; Herford, *Christianity in Talmud*, 65 *seq.*) is decidedly wrong; comp. Ginzberg, *Journal Biblical Literature*, 41.121, note 18. On the descent of Balaam, see also Lekah, Num. 22.6, where he is described as belonging to the family of Kemuel.

⁷²³ Sotah 11a; Abba Gorion 30, which reads: Balaam incited Amalek to attack the Israelites as soon as they left Egypt, telling him that as a descendant of Abraham he might count upon God's assistance. Comp. vol. II, pp. 254, *seq.* and the references to vol. II given in the preceding note. It was due to Balaam's magic that the Israelites could not flee from Egypt (comp. Zohar III, 212a, which was excerpted in Yalkut Reubeni on Num. 23.22; see also note 3). Although they finally succeeded, by the help of God, in gaining their liberty, Balaam did not give up hope to bring them back to the house of bondage. The seven weeks between the exodus and the revelation on Mount Sinai Balaam spent with the fallen angels Azza and Azzazel, endeavoring, with the help of these angels, to force Israel back to Egypt; *Emek ha-Melek* 107b–107d. This passage also gives a detailed description of Balaam's magic.

⁷²⁴ Sanhedrin 105b (on the text comp. *Aruk*, s. v. בלעם); Midrash Aggada and Targum Yerushalmi on Num. 22.5.

⁷²⁵ Tan. B. IV, 134; Tan. Balak 4; Sanhedrin 105a; Koheleth 2.9; Targum Yerushalmi Num. 22.5 and 24.3. Comp. also Josephus, *Antiqui.*, IV, 6.2, who writes: These Midianites, knowing that there was one Balaam....the greatest of the prophets at that time....sent some of their honorable princes to entreat the prophet to come to them, *etc.* As to Balaam's relation to the Moabites and the Amorites, see notes 714, 718. As long as the Israelites were in Egypt, Balaam was considered the wisest of men, and all nations came to him for advice; but after the exodus (*i. e.*, after the revelation of the Torah; see vol. III, p. 106) a Jewish bondwoman possessed more wisdom than Balaam. He therefore hated the Israelites out of envy, 2 ARN 45, 124–125. As to the question whether Balaam was a prophet, or merely an interpreter of dreams, or a magician, see note 784.

⁷²⁶ BaR 20.1; Tan. B. IV, 132 (read ונבדקו instead of ונדבקו); Tan. Balak 1; Koheleth 3.18. On the "rulers over all the world", see note 82 on vol. I, p. 178. Concerning Balaam as the one who counselled the allurement of Israel to lewdness, see vol. III, pp. 380, *seq.*

⁷²⁷ ER 18, 141–147, and 6, 35; EZ 10–11, 191–192; Yelammedenu
in Yalkut I, 766. This passage maintains that Balaam, Job and
his four companions, were descendants of Abraham's brother Nahor.
See above, note 722; note 3 on vol. II, p. 225; vol. II, p. 236.
Concerning Job as a prophet, see Ecclesiasticus 39.9. Comp., however,
vol. IV, p. 411, where Balaam is said to have been the only prophet
the Gentiles had ever produced. Moses, the greatest prophet of the
Jews, and Balaam, the greatest prophet of the Gentiles, are often
contrasted with one another in the haggadic literature; see Sifre D.,
and Midrash Tannaim at the end; Sifre Z., 58–59; comp. also WR
1.13; BaR 14.20; Zohar II, 22a; vol. II, p. 366 and 371–372. As to
the refusal of the Torah by the Gentiles, see vol. III, p. 80. On the
non-Jewish prophets, see also Abodah Zarah 3a; vol. III, p. 205.

⁷²⁸ Tan. B. IV, 134–135; Tan. Balak 4–5; BaR 20.7–8; Zohar
III, 198a and 209b; comp. note 720.

⁷²⁹ Sanhedrin 105a, which was followed by Lekah and Midrash
Aggada on Num. 22.8.

⁷³⁰ BaR 20.6 and 9–12; Tan. B. IV, 136–137; Tan. Balak 5–8;
2 ARN 45, 125 (here Adam is counted as the fourth who failed to pass
the test to which he was put by God; comp. Gen. 3.9); BR 19.11;
Zohar III, 200a; *Batte Midrashot*, IV, 5: (Balaam hated Israel, because
he had hoped that God would select him to accomplish the exodus from
Egypt and to deliver the Torah; comp. vol. VI, pp. 421-422). In connection with the question put by God to Balaam, the following remark
is made by ps.–Philo, 18, 173. Balaam said: "Wherefore, O Lord, dost
Thou tempt the race of men? They cannot sustain it; for Thou knowest more than they, all that was in the world before Thou didst found it.
And now enlighten Thy servant if it be right that I go with them."
Balaam's answer, according to ps.–Philo, is identical with the one he
ought to have given according to the Rabbis. Concerning the idea that
God never appears to Gentiles save at night, see BR 52.11; Mekilta
Bo 1.1 (God made the moon appear during the day to instruct Moses
in the regulations of the calendar, as He never spoke to him except by
day); WR 1.13; note 221 on vol. I, p. 373. All the Midrashim quoted
above, as well as Philo, *Moses*, 1.48, maintain that Balaam was from
the very beginning anxious to carry out Balak's invitation and was
ready to curse Israel. Opposed to this view is the statement in Aggadat
Bereshit 65, 130, according to which Balaam said to Balak's messengers:
"I cannot undertake to do any evil against Israel, with whom the Lord
is." Comp. note 766. In ps.–Philo, *loc. cit.*, it is God who reminded

Balaam of His love for Abraham and Jacob, whose descendants He chose as His people; "and now, behold, thou thinkest to go with these, and curse them whom I have chosen;" comp. note 744. On Balaam's blindness, comp. Niddah 31a, where it is said that he became afflicted with blindness as punishment for an impure thought. See also Zohar III, 147b.

731 Sotah 10a; Sanhedrin 105a.

732 Tan. B. IV, 136–137; Tan. Balak 6; BaR 20.10; Targum Yerushalmi Num. 22.12.

733 Lekah and Midrash Aggada on Num. 22.12.

734 BaR 20.19-20; Tan. B. IV, 136–137; Tan. Balak 6–8; Midrash Aggada, Num. 22.19–20; *Likkutim* IV, 61b–62a. Balaam's three bad traits are contrasted with Abraham's three good traits. These are: a good eye, a loving soul, and a humble spirit; Abot 5.19. See also 2 Peter 2.15, and Jude 11. Concerning unconscious prophecy, see vol. V, 250, note 239, and Index, s. v.

735 Sanhedrin 105b; BaR 20.12; Tan. B. IV 137; Tan. Balak 8. God exalted Balaam in order to make his humiliation all the more noticeable, He therefore did not permit him to go with Balak's first messengers, who were not men of high rank, so that he should be disgraced in the presence of the second messengers, who were men of great prominence; Lekah, Num. 22.20. Comp. vol. III, p. 362, which gives another reason why God did not permit Balaam to go with the first messengers, but allowed him to go with the second.

736 BaR 20.9 and 12; Tan. B. IV, 136–137; Tan. Balak 5 and 15. Comp. also ps.-Philo, 18.8; 17B, which reads: and God said unto him: "Go with them, and thy journey shall be an offence, and Balak himself shall go to destruction."

737 Midrash Aggada, Num. 22.7. Concerning the magicians sent by Balak; see vol. III, 357, and note 735.

738 Sanhedrin 105a; Mekilta Beshallah 1, 27a; Mekilta RS, 44; BR 45.8; BaR 20.12; Tan. B. IV, 137; Tan. Balak 8; Ozar Midrashim 42. Sabba', Wa-Yera, 22b, quotes an unknown Midrash to the effect that before Abraham there had been none who saddled his ass by himself, *i. e.*, who was anxious to fulfil the divine command given to him.

739 Midrash Aggada Num. 22.21. This passage presupposes the identity of Balaam with Laban; see note 722. Concerning Balaam as the counsellor of Pharaoh, see note 723. The old sources quoted in note 99 on vol. I, p. 83, speak of the "mouth of Balaam's ass" as having been created in the twilight between the sixth day and the first Sabbath of creation.

⁷⁴⁰ Targum Yerushalmi, Num. 22.22. The later legends likewise consider these two magicians to have been Balaam's sons; comp. vol. II, pp. 177 and 282. According to vol. III, p. 28, they were drowned in the Red Sea; comp., however, vol. III, p. 120, where they are made responsible for the fashioning of the golden calf.

⁷⁴¹ BaR 20.13; Tan. B. III, 81–82, and IV, 137; Tan. Emor 2 and Balak 8; BR 55.8; WR 26.7; Shemuel 24, 118. Abraham and Saul (comp. Gen. 22.3 and 1 Samuel 28.8) are quoted as proof that this is the proper conduct. Comp. also Sotah 7a.

⁷⁴² ER 28, 142 (which dwells also upon Balaam's eagerness to curse Israel; he spent a sleepless night, excited over the opportunity offered to him. That God did not appear to Balaam in his dream, but while he was awake, may be inferred from the fact that Num. 22.20 does not have the word בחלום, as in Gen. 20.3 and 21.24); Lekah and Targum Yerushalmi on Num. 22.22.

⁷⁴³ BaR 20.13; Tan. B. IV, 137; Tan. Balak, 8; Rashi on Num. 22.23 (partly based on Berakot 6a, which reads: If the eye of man were permitted to see all that surrounds him, he could not exist for a moment, as he would be instantly killed by the fear of the myriads of evil spirits around him); Zohar III, 207b. In the last-named source the purpose of the legend is entirely misunderstood, and the statement is made that the "Angel of Mercy" attempted to prevent Balaam from proceeding on his journey. The angel thereby wished to save Balaam from destruction. "Woe unto the wicked who turn the attribute of mercy into the attribute of justice" is a favorite expression of the Haggadah (comp. *e. g.*, BR 30.3), and in this sense one is to understand the statement that Balaam made the "Angel of Mercy" (Num. 22.23 reads מלאך־ה' and not מלאך־אלהים; comp. note 6 on vol. I, p. 4, which deals with the use of the tetragrammaton to describe God as merciful) turn against him. According to Tan. B. I, 187; ShR 2.3: Aphraates 57; Theodoretus, Num., *loc. cit.*, this angel was Michael. But according to *Imre No'am*, Num., *loc. cit.*, it was Gabriel. On the rivalry of these two angels, see note 8 on vol. I, p. 5, and Index,s. v. Michael, Gabriel.

⁷⁴⁴ BaR 20.14; Tan. B. IV, 138; Tan. Balak 8; Targum Yerushalmi Num. 22.24 and 30; Al-Barceloni, 57 (a somewhat different interpretation of the two "sides of the road"). Comp. vol. III, p. 373. The legend that Balaam's wall is identical with that erected by Jacob and Laban is found only in Targum Yerushalmi, *loc. cit.* But many medieval authors quote this statement from the Midrash; comp. *Hadar*, Wa-Yeze, end, (they stuck a sword into the wall, and with this sword Balaam

was killed); Num. 22.24 and 21.8; *Da'at* and *Pa'aneah* Wa-Yeze **(end);**
Imre No'am, Num. 22.24; Ziyyoni, Gen. 38.8 (towards the end);
Midrash Aggada, Num. 22.24–25; *Gan*, quoted by Poznanski, *Mebo*,
102–103, who strangely enough did not notice that *Gan* reproduces a
widespread legend. Whether this legend presupposes the identity
of Balaam with Laban (comp. note 722) is doubtful. On Levi as one
of the very pious men in the pre-Mosaic times, see Index, s. v. Concerning God's wrath at Balaam's attempt to curse the descendants
of Jacob, see note 730, end, where the same remark by ps.-Philo is quoted.

⁷⁴⁵ Midrash Aggada and Targum Yerushalmi, Num. 22.27–28.
Comp. vol. I, p. 83, and note 739. Tan. B. IV, 138, and BaR 20.14,
dwell upon the ridiculous position into which Balaam was brought by
his ass, and which enraged him against the animal. It is worth while
noticing that Josephus, *Antiqui.*, IV, 6.3, twice emphasizes the fact
that Balaam's ass "spoke with the voice of a man". It may well be
assumed that as early as the time of Josephus the allegorists and
rationalists attempted to explain the speaking of the ass in an allegorical
or symbolical manner, and it is against such views that Josephus' words
are directed. On a similar attempt made by the Jewish philosophers
of the Arabic period, see Ibn Ezra, Num. 22.28, and Maimonides,
Guide, II, 42, who maintain that the episode with the ass is nothing but
a vision.

⁷⁴⁶ Tan. B. IV, 138; Tan. Balak 9; BaR 20.4. Balaam's imper-
fect knowledge of Hebrew is evidenced by his use of the word התעללת
Num. 22.29, whicn had an obscene meaning; comp. Lekah, Num. 22.6.

⁷⁴⁷ Sanhedrin 105a-105b; Tan. B. IV, 138-139; Tan. Balak 9; Yerushalmi Targumim Num. 22.30. In the Talmud and 1 Targum Yerushalmi Balaam is said to have committed buggery with his ass; comp.
also Zohar III, 209b–210a.

⁷⁴⁸ Tan. B. IV, 139; Tan. Balak 9–10; BaR 20.14–15; Yelammedenu
in Yalkut I, 765 (Yelammedenu is given as the source in the first edition only). Concerning the conception that God does not wish to have
sinners publicly disgraced, see Sanhedrin 7.3; PK 9, 75b, and parallel
passages cited by Buber.

⁷⁴⁹ Targum Yerushalmi Num. 24.3; PRE 29 (this passage also
states that even Abraham before he was circumcised could not listen
to the words of God and remain standing); Zohar I, 96b; BaR 20.15;
Tan. B. IV, 39; Tan. Balak 10. Comp. also the references in note 727
to the sources dealing with the differences between Moses and Balaam;

see also vol. IV, p. 146; note 131 on vol. I, p. 241; note 318 on vol. I, p. 306.

⁷⁵⁰ BaR 20.13; Tan. B. IV, 137–138; Tan. Balak 8; Midrash Aggada, Num. 22.23 (elaborated). Comp. vol. III, p. 316, and note 855.

⁷⁵¹ BaR 20.5; Tan. B. IV, 139 (Balaam who boasted of knowing the plans of the Most High—vol. III, p. 356—had now to admit that he knew nothing thereof); Tan. Balak 10; Yelammedenu (?) in Yalkut I 766.

⁷⁵² Midrash Aggada, Num. 22.35; Tan. B. IV, 140; Tan. Balak 10; BaR 20.15; *Likkutim*, IV, 62b–63a. Josephus, *Antiqui.*, II, 63, in agreement with the rabbinic Haggada (see vol. III, pp. 361–362) maintains that Balaam after having heard the words of the angel, intended to return home, but was advised by God to proceed on his journey. Philo, *Vita Mosis* 1.39, agrees with the view of the Rabbis as given in the text that the words spoken by Balaam, "if it displease Thee, I will get me back" (Num. 22.34), prove his insincerity (if he were sincere, he would have returned without asking), and God therefore became angry with him, and allowed him to go to his destruction.

⁷⁵³ MHG, Num. 22.35 (in manuscript); comp. note 735.

⁷⁵⁴ Tan. B. IV, 140; Tan. Balak 10; BaR 20.16. Concerning the boundary lines fixed by Noah, see vol. I, p. 172.

⁷⁵⁵ BaR 20.16; Tan. B. IV, 140; Tan. Balak 10.

⁷⁵⁶ ER 28.142. Concerning the seven altars and seven sacrifices, see vol. III, p. 371.

⁷⁵⁷ BaR 20.16–18; Tan. B. IV, 140; Tan. Balak 11; 2 ARN 23,48. For an illustration of the truth of the proverb concerning the liberality of the pious, see vol. I, p. 243 (top). Concerning Balak's magic art, see vol. III, pp. 353, 357, 376, 378; Zohar III, 112b; 304a.

⁷⁵⁸ Berakot 7a; 'Abodah Zarah 4a–4b; Zohar I, 95b; III, 113a; *Batte Midrashot*, IV, 16. Comp. also Yerushalmi Berakot 1.2d (in connection with the smallest fraction of an hour). See Bornstein in *Hatekufah* VI, 271–272, according to whom this fraction (one 56848 of the hour) is to be read in Babli too. In vol. III, p. 371, top, eighty-five is a misprint for fifty-eight.

⁷⁵⁹ BaR 20.18; Tan. B III, 12; IV, 140–141; Tan. Zaw 1 and Balak 11–12; Tehillim 17, 125, and 90, 385. Comp. also Tan. B. III, 16, and Tan. Zaw 4, which reads: The nations of the world asked Balaam, "Why did God command Israel, and not us, to bring sacrifices?" He answered: "The purpose of sacrifices is to establish peace; but peace

without the Torah is impossible.   The Israelites accepted the Torah; they were therefore commanded to bring sacrifices, but ye who rejected it are not to bring any sacrifices."   The verse "the sacrifice of the wicked is an abomination" (Prov. 21.27; comp. also 15.8) is said to refer to the sacrifices brought by Balaam and the wicked nations, which were not acceptable to God.   Comp. Tehillim, *loc. cit.* See also Midrash Aggada and Rashi on Num. 23.1; vol. III, p. 369.

⁷⁶⁰ BaR 20.18; Tan. B. IV, 141; Tan. Balak 11; Midrash Aggada and Lekah on Num. 23.4; WR 1.3; *Likkutim*, IV, 63b–64a; Zohar III, 200b (top).   Concerning the contrast between Moses and Balaam, see vol. III, p. 356.

⁷⁶¹ Tan. B. III, 12, and IV, 141; Tan. Zaw 1, and Balak 12; BaR 20.18; Yelammedenu (?) in *Likkutim*, IV, 64a; Midrash Tannaim 146–147.   Comp. Aggadat Shir (end), and note 759.

⁷⁶² Sanhedrin 105b; Yelammedenu in Yalkut I, 765 (the source is given in the first edition only); Tan. B. IV, 141; Tan. Balak 12; BaR 20.18; *Likkutim*, IV, 64a–64b; *Batte Midrashot* IV, 15a.

⁷⁶³ Yelammedenu in Yalkut I, 765. Comp. also references in the preceding note.

⁷⁶⁴ BaR 20.19; Tan. B. IV, 141–143; Tan. Balak 12; *Batte Midrashot* IV, 15a–15b; Yelammedenu in Yalkut I, 765–766.   Concerning the blessing which came to Laban through Jacob, see vol. I, pp. 370 and 376. On Balaam's descent from Laban, see note 722 (end).   Concerning the view that Balaam was deprived of the gift of prophecy, see note 784.   In the Midrashim quoted above there are many other haggadic interpretations of Balaam's orations.   Other kinds of explanations are given by Josephus, *Antiqui.*, IV, 6.5, and ps-Philo, 18.10–12; 18C-D. It is noteworthy that Josephus' interpretations are based upon the Hebrew text of Scripture, and not upon the Septuagint. If, *e. g.*, Josephus makes Balaam say: "There is not any nation among mankind, but ye will be esteemed superior to them in virtue," it is obvious that it is a haggadic rendering of Num. 23.9, where יתחשב is taken in the sense of "being esteemed", in accordance with the mishnic use of this verb (comp., *e. g.*, Shebi'it 8.11).   Num. 23.7 is paraphrased by ps.-Philo as follows: "Lo, Balak hath brought me....,saying: 'Come, run into the fire of these men.'"   This of course, is a haggadic interpretation of ארה connecting it with אור "fire".   The following sentence in ps.–Philo runs: It is easier to take away the foundation and all the topmost parts of the earth (read "terra" instead of "erorum") and darken the light of the sun....than to uproot the planting of the Most

High.   This Haggadah on Num. 23.9 is similar to that given by Yelam
medenu in Yalkut I, 766. Comp. vol. III, p. 374. Josephus, as
well as ps.-Philo, combined Balaam's four orations into one.

⁷⁶⁵ Yelammedenu in Yalkut I, 766. Comp. *Likkutim*, IV,
65a–65b. Concerning the statement found in these Midrashim that
Israel's strength lies in words (*i. e.*, the Torah), see vol. III, pp. 366–367.

⁷⁶⁶ BaR 20.19; Tan. B. IV, 142; Tan. Balak 12; Wa-Yekullu
18; *Batte Midrashot* IV, 16; Yelammedenu in Yalkut I, 766; *Likkutim*,
IV, 66a–66b. The conception that God does not associate Himself
with the evil brought upon Israel has, properly considered, no bearing
upon any special privilege of Israel. The idea that God, as the source
of the good, cannot be the direct source of evil is Philonic as well as
rabbinic; see Tan. B. III, 39–41 and the discussion on this point in
note 9 on vol. I, p. 5, and note 176 on vol. II, p. 70.—In the quotation
from Aggadat Bereshit given in note 730 the words בשעה ששלח are
perhaps not to be taken literally. Concerning the idea that the manna
was given to Israel even after they had worshipped the golden calf,
see vol. III, p. 123, and note 270.

⁷⁶⁷ Yelammedenu in Yalkut I, 766; *Likkutim*, I, 67a.   Comp.
vol. I, pp. 3 and 132, as well as note 764.

⁷⁶⁸ Tan. B. IV, 143; Tan. Balak 12; BaR 20.17; Yerushalmi
Targumim Num. 23.9; *Batte Midrashot* IV, 16; Yelammedenu in
Yalkut I, 765; Mekilta Amalek 1, 54a; Mekilta RS 82; PR 12, 49a;
Lekah, Num. *loc. cit.* (quoting a tannaitic source?). Comp. vol. III, p.
134.

⁷⁶⁹ Yelammedenu in Yalkut I, 768;   *Batte Midrashot* IV, 16–17;
Tan. B. IV, 143; Tan. Balak 12; BaR 20.19; Yerushalmi Targumim
and Lekah on Num. 23.9. On the judging of the nations in the darkness
of the night, see Tehillim 9, 87; Yerushalmi Rosh ha-Shanah 1, 57a;
BR 50.3; PR 40, 167b. The last-named source reads: God does not
desire the destruction of the sinner, He therefore judges the nations at
night, the time of rest, when they cease from doing evil. The Israelites,
on the other hand, are judged by day, the time when they perform
good deeds, in remembrance of which God is merciful unto them. This
view is entirely different from that of the old Haggadah, according to
which the judging of the nations at night is a form of severity; see note
170 on vol. I, p. 253, and note 216 on vol. II, p. 366.

⁷⁷⁰ Tan. B. IV, 143; Tan. Balak 12; BaR 20.19. These Midrashim
take the words "the dust of Jacob" to refer to the fulfilling of the
commandments connected with the soil (*i. e.*, agricultural laws),

131

whereas Targum Yerushalmi, *ad loc.*, and Wayekullu 18 consider this phrase as an allusion to the performance of circumcision, when dust is strewn over the wound (on this custom see Hilluf Minhagim 18–19). Yelammedenu in Yalkut I, 765, and ER 21,116 refer this phrase to the purity of the young men in Israel, who are thus described as עפר "young gazelles."

⁷⁷¹ Yerushalmi Targumim and Midrash Aggada Num. 23.10; ER 21,116. The translation of Num., *loc. cit.*, by Septuagint seems to presuppose a similar haggadic interpretation; comp. also Philo, *Moses*, 1.50. That Balaam lost his share in the world to come is stated in Sanhedrin 10.2. Comp. also the quotation from a Midrash (on Job?) in Makiri, Is. 57,217.

⁷⁷² Tan. B. IV, 144; Tan. Balak 12–14; BaR 20.20; Yerushalmi Targumim 23.19, *seq.* On Balak as a great sorcerer, see note 757. Philo, *Moses*, I, 51, explains the change of place by Balaam as an attempt to influence God thereby. Comp. Rosh ha-Shanah 16a, which reads: Change of place brings change of luck. See also note 122 on vol I, p. 239. Josephus, *Antiqui.*, IV, 6.5, gives a lengthy address by Balaam, in which he excuses himself and explains his failure to curse Israel.

⁷⁷³ Gittin 68b; Lekah, Num. 23.22. Concerning the invisiblity of the demons, see vol. I, p. 83, and note 743.

⁷⁷⁴ Tan. B. IV, 144–145; Tan. Balak 14; *Likkutim*, IV, 70a–70b. Concerning Israel's superiority over the angels, see Nedarim 32a; Yerushalmi Shabbat 6 (end); DR 1.12. On the warding off of the evil spirit by the recitation of the Shema', see Berakot 5a.

⁷⁷⁵ Rashi and Midrash Aggada, Num. 23.29. Comp. vol. III, p. 376, which has a similar statement concerning the choice of Pisgah. According to Targum Yerushalmi, Num. 22.41, Balak led Balaam at the very beginning to the top of Peor, which is also called Bamot-baal.

⁷⁷⁶ Targum Yerushalmi, Rashi, and Lekah on Num. 24.1. See also Targum Yerushalmi Num. 22.41–23.1, which reads: Balaam, from the top of Peor, observed the Danites, who, on account of their sins, were not covered by the clouds of glory (comp. Index, s. v. "Danites"), and he rejoiced, hoping that he would be able to induce God to curse Israel on account of these sinners. That Balaam, despite the clear indication of God's unwillingness to curse the Israelites, continued to hate them, is emphasized also by Philo, *Vita Mosis*, 1.52.

⁷⁷⁷ Yelammedenu in Yalkut I, 771; Targum Yerushalmi Num. 24.2; Baba Batra 60a; BaR 2.4. The strict separation of the tents was proof of the purity of their family life.

778 Yelammedenu in Yalkut I, 765, and II, 782, on Ps.62. In another passage of Yelammedenu (I, 771) it is shown in detail that Balaam worded the blessings which he was forced to pronounce upon Israel in such a way that they might be turned into curses. The same view is also found in Ta'anit 20a. Comp. also note 780.

779 Yelammedenu in Yalkut I, 766; Makiri, Prov. 27, 86b. On Balaam's voice, see note 781.

780 Sanhedrin 105b. This passage contains also the following remark: The blessings which Balaam was forced to pronounce upon Israel indicate the nature of the curses which he attempted to call down on them; for God made him speak exactly the opposite of what he had intended. Balaam wished to say: "May the Shekinah never dwell among them", but he was forced to say: "How beautiful....are the dwellings(=the sanctuaries)of Israel,etc." Comp. also Yelammedenu in Yalkut I, 771. Talmud, Yelammedenu, ER 21, 116–117, as well Yerushalmi Targumim Num. 24.5, take the "tents of Jacob" (Num. 24.5) to refer to the houses of study. All the worldly bliss that Israel enjoyed was the fulfilment of Balaam's blessings, while the "benedictions of the patriarchs" will be fulfilled in the world to come; DR 3.4.

781 Yelammedenu in Yalkut I, 765; Tan. B. IV, 146; Tan. Balak 15; BaR 20.21. The anti-Christian passages occur only in Yelammedenu and, partly, also in Makiri, Prov. 68b–69a. Another legend concerning Balaam's powerful voice is found in Yelammedenu I, 771, whence it has been incorporated in Koheleth 7.5, which reads: Balaam's voice carried as far as sixty miles (במחנה ישראל is a variant which is not found in Yalkut I, 765), and when the Israelites heard it, they became very proud. Jacob's blessing contained reproaches against some of the tribes; Moses' blessings administered admonitions and reprimands; but Balaam uttered nothing but praises and blessings. Their pride over it became a stumbling-block to the Israelites, who were enticed to lewdness immediately after Balaam had pronounced his benedictions. Comp. vol. III, pp. 380–381.

782 Targumim Num. 24.7–9 and 17–24; Yelammedenu in Yalkut I. 771; PR 13, 54a, and 41, 173b; ER 21, 117; Sanhedrin 106a; the Messianic Midrash in Lekah on verse 17; Josephus, *Antiqui.*, IV, 6.5. It is noteworthy that Ephraem I, 153E, explains verse 17 to refer to Zerubbabel, though as early an authority as R. Akiba finds in it a Messianic prophecy; comp. Yerushalmi Ta'anit 4, 68d. This view was later shared by Jewish as well as Christian authorities; comp. *e. g.*, Targum Yerushalmi and Theodoretus, *ad loc.* It is quite likely that

Ephraem reproduces the view of a Jewish rationalist, as it is rather strange for a Christian to ignore this messianic passage. Ephraem's explanation of כתים (Num. 24.24) as Rome is found in Targum Yerushalmi, *ad loc.*

⁷⁸³ Unknown Midrash quoted in Makiri on Is. 52, 145. On the descendants of Jonadab, see vol. III, pp. 76–77, and note 57 on vol. IV, p. 318. Yelammedenu in Yalkut I, 771 likewise identifies the Kenite spoken of in 24.21 with the descendants of Jonadab the Rechabite; it reads: When Balaam saw the sons of Jonadab occupying seats in the Chamber of Gazit (= the great Synhedrion), he exclaimed in astonishment: "The law prescribes that only priests, Levites, and (pure-blooded) Israelites are qualified to become members of the Synhedrion (Sanhedrin 4.2), and yet these descendants of Jonadab were found worthy of this high position as a reward for the hospitality of their sire Jethro, who offered bread to Moses." Comp. also Sanhedrin 106a. Concerning the superiority of Jethro's descendants to all other proselytes, see Bikkurim, Tosefta 1.2 and Yerushalmi 1, 64a.

⁷⁸⁴ Yelammedenu in Yalkut I, 771; Sanhedrin 106a; see also ps.-Philo 18.11; 17D, where the following words are put into Balaam's mouth: "For but a little is left to me of the holy spirit which abideth in me since I know that through having been persuaded by Balak, I lost the days of my life." In 18. 2 ps.-Philo describes Balaam as "the interpreter of dreams, who dwelt in Mesopotamia." This is in agreement with Targum Yerushalmi Num. 22.5 and Tan. B. IV, 134, according to which פתורה means "the interpreter of dreams", from the Hebrew-Aramaic root פתר "to interpret dreams". Balaam was thus, as Tan., *loc. cit.*, points out, first an interpreter of dreams, and then a prophet; but when he proved unworthy of his high calling, he sank to the low level of sorcerer; he remained a sorcerer for the rest of his life, see Josh. 13.22 and note 852.—"Moses committed Balaam's prophecy to writing, and while it was in his power to claim this glory for himself and make people believe that the predictions were his own, there being no one who could contradict him and accuse him of doing so, still he gave attention to Balaam, and did him the honor to make mention of him on this account," Josephus, *Antiqui.*, VI, 6.13. The statement of the Baraita, Baba Batra 14b, that Moses wrote his own book (= the Pentateuch) and the section of Balaam is to be understood in the same sense as the words quoted from Josephus. Comp. note 38 on vol. IV, 253.

⁷⁸⁵ Sanhedrin 106a. Balaam's wicked counsel to entice Israel to idolatry by means of unchastity (see Num. 24.14 and 31.16) is de-

scribed at full length by Philo, *Moses*, 1.54–55, and *De Fortit.*, 7; Josephus, *Antiqui.*, IV, 6.6–9, and ps.-Philo 18.18–19. Comp. also
Revelation 2.14, where this legend is very likely presupposed. The
rabbinic sources offer several versions of this legend; see Sifre, N.,
131 and 157; Yerushalmi Sanhedrin 10, 28d (top); Tan. B. IV, 147;
Tan. Balak 15 and Mattot 3; BaR 20.23 and 22.4; ARN 1.3; Yelammedenu
in Yalkut I, 785; PRE 47; Yerushalmi Targumim Num. 24.4. On
the severe punishment which God inflicts for unchastity, see vol. I,
p. 153; vol. IV, p. 369 (bottom).

⁷⁸⁶ BaR 20.23; Tan. B. IV, 146, and Tan. Balak 17, which, in
the main, follow earlier sources; see Sifre N., 131; Sanhedrin, Babli
106b; Yerushalmi 10, 28d; see also references in preceding note. New
is the statement in BaR and in the Tanhumas that Balaam instructed
them not to allow the Jewish young men to commit idolatry while drunk,
because they would not be held responsible for acts committed while
in a state of drunkenness. This sounds like a learned reflection on
the popular legend as given by the old sources, to make it agree with
the Halakah concerning the irresponsibility of the inebriate; see
'Erubin 65a. The proverb "Throw the stick, etc." is also found in
vol. II, p. 44. Concerning the description of the worship of Peor,
found in rabbinic sources, see Chajes, *Marcus Studien*, 24. Israel
became subjected to the "four kingdoms" through the worship of
Peor; Tehillim 106, 456.

⁷⁸⁷ Tan B. I, 146–147; Tan. Balak 16–17; BaR 20.22. Concerning the effect of the water on the body and soul of those who partake
of it, see Zohar I, 125a. Herodotus III, 23; Tertullian *De Anima*
50 . On the identity of the well of Shittim (the etymological explanations of this name are found in Sanhedrin 106a; Yelammedenu in Yalkut
I, 771; Tan. Terumah 10) with the "well of lewdness", out of which
the inhabitants of Sodom drew water, see note 184 on vol. I, p. 256,
and Zohar Ruth 1.4.

⁷⁸⁸ Tan. B. IV, 148; Tan. Balak 19; BaR 20.23; *Likkutim*, IV,
73b. The midrashic basis of this Haggadah is to be found in the words
of Scripture (Num. 24.4): "And hang them up...in the face *of the sun*."
On the view that the cloud of glory did not protect the sinners, see
vol. III, pp. 57, 413; vol. IV, p. 11, and note 776.

⁷⁸⁹ Yerushalmi Sanhedrin 10, 28d. On the number of the officers
and judges, see vol. III, p. 70.

⁷⁹⁰ Targum Yerushalmi and Rashi, Num. 25.4 (נגד השמש is taken
to mean as long "as the sun shone"); Sanhedrin 34b (bottom), and

Yerushalmi 10, 28b; Sifre N., 131.   Comp. vol. III, p. 241.   According
to the standard Halakah (Sanhedrin 6.4), only the bodies of the blasphemers and idolaters were hung upon gallows, but not those of other
criminals who were executed.   Josephus, *Antiqui.*, IV, 6.9, likewise
is of the opinion that the crime for which these sinners suffered death
was apostasy from the Jewish religion, from which they were led stray
by the Midianite women (comp. Num. 31.16; the Rabbis speak of
the Moabite women in accordance with 31.1), who would not consent
to marry Jews unless they abandoned their faith.   It is to be noted
that Josephus speaks of intermarriage between Jewish men and Moabite-
Midianite women, whereas the Rabbis (comp. the references in note
785), in agreement with Philo, *Moses*, 1.5, and ps.-Philo, 18.18–19,
maintain that the great sin committed at Shittim consisted in Israel's
complete surrender to illicit passion; see, however, Philo, *De Monarchia*
7, where he seems to share Josephus' view.   Comp. note 40 on vol.
IV, p. 31.

⁷⁹¹ Sanhedrin 82a, and Yerushalmi 10, 28a; Tan. B. IV, 148;
Tan. Balak 20; BaR 20.24; ShR 33.5; Targum Yerushalmi Num. 25.6.
According to Josephus, *Antiqui.*, IV, 6.10–11, Zimri, at the instigation
of his wife (notice the description of Cozbi as Zimri's wife, and comp.
end of preceding note), sacrificed publicly to an idol; but Moses, fearing that by severe measures he might make a critical situation still
worse, preferred not to proceed against this criminal nor against others
who acted in a similar manner.   All that Moses did was to exhort
the people to remain faithful to God.   Zimri, encouraged by the apparent weakness of Moses, called upon the people to throw down the
fetters of the law, which Moses imposed upon them, and he publicly
confessed that he had married a non-Jewish woman.   As a free man
he did not care for the law promulgated by Moses against intermarriage,
nor for any other of his laws.—On the identification of Balak with
Zur, see vol. III, p. 353, top.   On Jethro as the former idolatrous priest,
see vol. II, p. 289.   Zimri's sarcastic remarks on Moses' marriage with a
Midianite woman were without foundation.   Moses married Zipporah
before the revelation of the Torah; when the law forbidding intermarriage was promulgated, Zipporah had already for a long time been a
pious proselyte; comp. quotation from a Midrash in *Imre No'am*,
Balak (end).   On Moses' lack of energy, on certain occasions, see vol.
III, p. 404.

⁷⁹² Tan. B. IV, 148; Tan. Balak 20; BaR 20.24.   For the opposing
view comp. vol. III, p. 330, where it is stated that a great distinction

was conferred upon Moses by God, who did not reveal his burial-place to any man. Comp. vol. III, p. 330 and note 644.

⁷⁹³ Sanhedrin 82a.

⁷⁹⁴ ShR 33.5; see also Sanhedrin 82a, where it is said that Phineas attempted to ward off the plague by performing a very pious act, the slaying of the sinners at the great risk to his own life. See also note 799.

⁷⁹⁵ Unknown Midrash quoted by Sabba', פנחס 128a; comp. PRE 47. A somewhat different version of this Haggadah is given in Lekah, Num. 25.7 (at the end), which is partly based on Sifre N., 131, and Yerushalmi Sanhedrin 10, 29a.

⁷⁹⁶ Sanhedrin 82a–82b, and Yerushalmi 10, 29a; BaR 20.25; Tan. B. IV, 148–149; Tan. Balak 21; Sifre N., 131; PRE 47 (here it is said: Phineas seized the spear from Moses' hands); Targum Yerushalmi Num. 25.7.

⁷⁹⁷ Sanhedrin 82b, and Yerushalmi 10, 29a; Sifre N., 131; Ephraem, I, 166b.

⁷⁹⁸ BaR 20.25; Tan. B. IV, 149; Tan. Balak 21; Targum Yerushalmi Num. 25.8; Sifre N., 131 (in this passage two versions have been combined into one); Sanhedrin 82b, and Yerushalmi 10, 29a; PRE 47. According to the legend given in vol. III, p. 385, the plague broke out before Zimri was slain by Phineas. See also Josephus, *Antiqui.*, IV, 6.12, and Philo, *Moses*, 1.55. The latter, combining Num. 25.5 with 25.9, speaks of the twenty-four thousand sinners slain by the pious who followed the example of Phinehas. In *De Fortit.*, 7, Philo maintains, on the other hand, that the sinners were slain by God. PRE, *loc. cit.*, seems to assume that Phineas himself killed many (or all?) of the sinners. Comp. the following note.

⁷⁹⁹ Sanhedrin 82b, where it is said: The mixed multitude took to themselves wives from among the daughters of the tribe of Simeon, and the offspring of these intermarriages were the sinners who fell a prey to the allurements of the Moabite women. The plague that broke out in consequence of the sins committed by them purged Israel of this element. Etymological explanations of the names of Zimri and Cozbi, as well as of the names of their fathers, are given in Sanhedrin 82b; Yelammedenu in *'Aruk*, s. v. זמר; Targum Yerushalmi Num. 25.14. Although these etymologies differ from one another, they are all based on the assumption that the names of these sinners indicate the unchaste and lewd life led by their bearers. According to Sanhedrin, *loc. cit.*, Zimri bore different names, as he is identical

with Saul, the son of a Canaanite woman (Gen. 46.10), and with Shelumiel (Num. 1.6) the prince of the tribe of Simeon.

⁸⁰⁰ Sanhedrin 82b, and Yerushalmi 9, 27b (in this passage it is stated that they intended to excommunicate Phineas on account of his rashness); Sifre N., 13; WR 33.4; Sotah 43a; BaR 21.3; Tan. B. IV, 151; PR 13, 115 (Sabbaʿ Balak, 127c, reads בזויה in the Pesikta); comp. vol. I, p. 289. According to Julius Africanus, *Epistola ad Aristidem*, Putiel, the maternal grandfather of Phineas (comp. Exod. 6.25), belonged to the tribe of Judah; but the Rabbis are of the opinion that Putiel is another name for Jethro or Joseph. See references at the beginning of the note; MHG II, 55 = Yelammedenu in ʿ*Aruk*, s. v. פט 2.

⁸⁰¹ Yelammedenu in ʿ*Aruk*, s. v. זרוע; Midrash Aggada Num. 25.13 (from ʿ*Aruk*?); Sifre D., 165; Midrash Tannaim 107–108; Hullin 134b; Targum Yerushalmi Num. 25.13; Ephraem I, 166D. For another symbolical explanation of the priestly gifts, see Philo, *Special. Leg., De Praem. Sacerd.* 3.

⁸⁰² Sifre N., 131; Zebahim 101a. For the opposite view, see vol. III, p. 187, according to which Phineas became priest at the same time as his father and grandfather.

⁸⁰³ *Batte Midrashot* IV, 32 (this is the only passage which contains the legend concerning the daily sacrifice offered by Phineas-Elijah; comp. vol. IV, p. 202); Sifre N., 131; BaR 31.3; Tan. Phineas 1. Comp. the following note.

⁸⁰⁴ Yelammedenu in ʿ*Aruk*, s.v. זרוע and in Yalkut I, 771 = Midrash Aggada, Num. 25.13, where no source is indicated; Targum Yerushalmi Num., *loc. cit.* (on the text, see *Imre Noʿ am, ad loc.*). On Phinehas = Elijah, comp. note 3 on vol. IV, p. 195. As a reward for his zeal Phinehas received the greatest gift granted to man, and this only by God, namely, "peace"; Philo, *Vita Mosis*, 1.55; an almost identical statement is found in BaR 21.1. On the decree issued by Phinehas against "the wine of Gentiles", see vol. III, p. 414.

⁸⁰⁵ Esfah in Yalkut I, 773. Comp. vol. III, pp. 238–239. On the census, see Tan. B. IV, 152; Tan. Pinehas 4; BaR 21.7.

⁸⁰⁶ Midrash Aggada, Num. 26.12, 38, and 40; BaR 21.8; Tan. Pinehas 5. Concerning those who perished in Egypt during the three days of darkness, see vol. II, p. 345, and vol. III, p. 42. According to ps.-Philo, 14.15–16, only one-fiftieth part of Israel left Egypt, because they believed not in God. This is a midrashic explanation of וחמשים (Exod. 13.1-8). See Mekilta Beshallah (פתיחתא) 1, 24a, and

Mekilta RS, 38, where it is said that forty-nine fiftieths died during the the three days of darkness. Comp. also Jerome, *Epistola ad Damasum*, 36 (ed. Migne, I, 458). On the losses sustained by the tribes of Benjamin and Simeon, see vol. III, p. 333, and note 799.

⁸⁰⁷ BaR 21.7; Tan. B. IV, 152; Tan. Pinehas 4. Concerning the census after the exodus, see vol. III, p. 146; BaR 1.10; Lekah, Num. 1.1.

⁸⁰⁸ Baba Batra 117a–118a and 121b (the opposite view is given here to the effect that the land was divided according to the numbers of those who left Egypt); Sifre N., 132; BaR 21.8. Comp. Friedmann on Sifre, *loc. cit.*

⁸⁰⁹ Tan. Pinehas 6; BaR 21.9; Sifre N., 132.

⁸¹⁰ Yelammedenu in Yalkut I, 773; Tan. Pinehas 6; BaR 21.9. Comp. vol. IV, p. 15.

⁸¹¹ Sifre N., 133; Sifre Z., 155–157; Targum Yerushalmi Num. 27.1; BaR 21.11; Tan. B. IV, 153; Tan. Pinehas 7.

⁸¹² Yelammedenu in Yalkut I, 773 (end); BaR 21.11; Tan. B. IV, 153; Targum Yerushalmi Num. 27.4; Pinehas 7; Baba Batra, Mishnah 8.16, and Talmud 119b. The sisters were all of equal learning, wisdom, and piety; hence in approaching Moses and the elders, each one of them addressed one sentence to the leaders, and accordingly Num. 27.3–4 consists of five sentences. See Yelammedenu, *loc. cit.*; Sifre N. 133; Sifre Z., 157; Baba Batra 120a.

⁸¹³ Sifre N., 133; Sifre Z., 157; Baba Batra 118b; Targum Yerushalmi Num. 27.3. Comp. the following note.

⁸¹⁴ Sifre N., 113 and 133; Sifre Z., 103–104 and 157. Comp. vol. III, pp. 240 and 284. According to Zohar III, 157a and 205b, Zelophehad, though of noble descent, was an ignorant man, and therefore was not appointed prince of his tribe. Disappointed in his hopes, he joined those who complained against God and Moses (see Num. 21.5–6), and was killed by the serpents, thus atoning with his death for his sin.

⁸¹⁵ Sifre N., 133; Sifre Z., 155; BaR 21.10; Tan. B. IV, 153; Tan. Pinehas 7. Comp. Baba Batra 119b, and note 546.

⁸¹⁶ BaR 16.10; Tan. B. IV, 153; Tan. Pinehas 7. Comp. vol. III, p. 121 and note 546.

⁸¹⁷ Seder 'Olam 9. Comp. vol. III, pp. 200, 300, and 436. On Otah, see note 33 on vol. II p. 261.

⁸¹⁸ Sifre Z., 157; BaR 21.12; Tan. B. IV, 153; Tan. Pinehas 9; Targum Yerushalmi 27.2. In Sifre N., 133 and 68, as well as in Baba

Batra 119b, is given a dissenting view, according to which Zelophehad's daughters placed their case before Moses and the elders, while they were sitting in the "house of study." An entirely different view is found in Zohar III, 205. Zelophehad's daughters did not place their case before Moses, because they feared lest he should be prejudiced against them on account of the enmity their father showed toward Moses (comp. note 814). They therefore preferred to have their case decided by the lower authorities. But when none of the judges was able to render a decision, and the case was brought before Moses, he, in his great modesty, did not wish to display his superior knowledge, and said that he would put the case before God. Comp. also the remarks of R. Bahya on the long ן of משפטן (Num. 27.5). According to another version, God took it ill of Moses for having withdrawn himself from the case of Zelophehad's daughters, and therefore, immediately after this episode, He informed him of his impending death, saying unto him: "Thou couldst withdraw thyself from acting as a judge in the case of Zelophehad's daughters; but thou wilt have to submit thyself to My judicial decree against thee." See Shir 1.10; Midrash Aggada, Num. 27.5 (as an explanation of the long ן in משפטן). Comp. note 822.

⁸¹⁹ Sifre N. 134; Sifre Z., 157–158; Baba Batra, Mishnah 8.3; Babli 118b–119a; Yerushalmi 8, 16a. The tannaitic sources just quoted as well as Philo, *Moses*, 2(3).31, find in Num. 27.7 words of high praise for Zelophehad's daughters. Comp. note 821.

⁸²⁰ Baba Batra 119b. For the contrary view see Sifre Z., 157, where strong objections are raised against the opinion which considers them to have been old spinsters.

⁸²¹ Baba Batra 119b (top); Shabbat 32a. The proverb "God works good, etc." is of frequent occurrence; see Tosefta Yoma 5(4).12; BaR 3.18. Comp. also vol. III, p. 7 (with regard to Jethro's counsel concerning the appointment of Judges).

⁸²² BaR 21.11–13 (this passage has also the dissenting view that Moses had hoped to lead Israel into the Holy Land); Tan. Pinehas 7–11; Tan. B. IV, 153, and I, 192; Sifre D., 17; Midrash Tannaim 10; Mekilta RS, 91; Koheleth 8.17; Shemuel 14, 88. Comp. vol. IV, pp. 83 and 96, as well as vol. III, p. 194. According to *Otiyyot Gedolot* in *Leket Midrashim*, 23a, and *Eshkol*, 45a, 118, the long ן at the end of the word משפטן indicates Moses' punishment for his boastful words; comp. note 818. On Moses' continence, see vol. III, p. 256. As to the four legal questions which he was unable to decide, see vol. III,

p. 242; *Ozar Midrashim,* 47 (this passage counts six cases). Comp. note 862.

[823] 2 ARN 30 (first version 17), 65; BaR 21.14; Tan. Pinehas 11; Yelammedenu in Yalkut I, 776; Sifre Z., 161. As to Moses' wish to have Joshua as his successor, see vol. III, p. 400.

[824] Yelammedenu in Yalkut I, 776. More amplifications of the prayers of Moses for a right leader of the people are given in Sifre N., 139; Shir 1.7; Midrash Shir 10b–11a; Targum Song of Songs 1.7–8.

[825] Sifre N., 138; Midrash Shir 1.10b–11a.

[826] BaR 21.15; Yelammedenu in Yalkut I, 776. On Moses' hesitation to undertake the leadership of Israel, see vol. II, pp. 316–326.

[827] Sifre N., 138–139; Sifre Z., 160–162 (בני דויה means here "those in misery"); Sifre D., 26; Midrash Tannaim, 15. On the *Jewish* Kings participating in the combat themselves, see vol. IV, p. 72.

[828] Yelammedenu in Yalkut I, 776, on Num. 27.16 and 22; BaR 12.9 and 21.15; Tan. Pinehas 11. Comp. vol. IV, p. 3. Concerning the future prophets and judges shown to Moses, see vol. III, pp. 154, 443–447.

[829] Sifre N., 140, and Sifre D., 305; Sifre Z.; 162, BaR 21.15; Tan. Pinehas 11; Midrash Tannaim 185.

[830] Sifre D., 305; BaR 21.15. See also Enoch 89.39, where the two leaders who were at the head of Israel at the entry into the Holy Land refer to Joshua and Eliezer. Comp. also vol. III, p. 414.

[831] Sifre N., 141; Sifre Z., 62.

[832] Sifre N., 140; Sifre D., 305; Midrash Tannaim 180; Assumption of Moses 12.2. According to Megillah 21a, from the time of Moses until Rabban Gamaliel the Elder, it was customary, both for the master and the disciple, to study the Torah, standing. Comp., however, Mo'ed Katan 16b (bottom); Baba Mezi'a 84b; Sanhedrin 17a; ARN 6, 27–28. See note 893, and Ginzberg's discussion of this point in *Hazofeh* III, 121.

[833] Sifre N., 140.

[834] Midrash Aggada, Num. 27.20. On the herald, see vol. III, p. 437. It is a wise rule "to tell a man part of his praise in his presence, but not all of it;" accordingly Moses assembled all the people while Joshua was absent, and spoke to them of their new leader's great virtues; Lekah, Deut. 31.6.

[835] Sifre N., 141; Sifre Z., 163 (only the first edition of the Yalkut indicates the source); Philo, *De Caritate,* 3. Comp. vol. III, p. 251.

[836] Tehillim 21, 179. This passage also states that the rays

which will emanate from the countenance of the Messiah will spread a stronger lustre than those of Moses and Joshua. Does this mean that the Messiah will be greater than Moses? See Tan. B. I, 139, where it is said: The Messiah is greater than the (three) patriarchs, more exalted than Moses, and superior to the angels. Maimonides, *Yad ha-Hazakah, Teshubah* 9.2, on the other hand, explicitly states that the Messiah will be "a great prophet, akin to Moses." Concerning Joshua's rays, see vol. III, p. 441; note 6 on vol. IV, p. 4; note 14 on vol. IV, p. 5.

⁸³⁷ Sifre Z., 162; Sifre N., 139, where it is said: It was Moses' sincerest desire to have Joshua as his successor, and yet he did not give expression to it in his prayer, in order not to arouse animosity between the new leader and Aaron's sons, who might feel offended at not having been selected to succeed their uncle. Comp. also Philo, *De Caritate*, 1–3. As to Moses' punishment for his reluctance to accept the office offered to him, see vol. II, p. 326.

⁸³⁸ Assumption of Moses 1, *seq.* The uniqueness of Moses' leadership is emphasized also Sotah 14a and Tan. B. V, 13.

⁸³⁹ Tan. B. IV, 145; Tan. Balak 14; BaR 20.20; *Likkutim*, IV, 70b.

⁸⁴⁰ Yelammedenu in Yalkut I, 783, on Num 31.2 (the first edition contains the unintelligible words וכן במנין after אש); *Likkutim* IV, 81a.

⁸⁴¹ Yelammedenu in Yalkut I, 785, on Num. 31.1–2; *Likkutim*, IV, 79b. Comp. vol. III, p. 384.

⁸⁴² Yelammedenu in Yalkut I, 785. Comp. also Sifre N., 157, where מדינים is likewise used to describe the Moabites. This identification of the Midianites with the Moabites is very likely presupposed by Phillo, *Moses*, 1.56, who speaks of this campaign as being directed against Balak, the king of Moab; but comp., on the other hand, his remarks in *De Fortitud.* 7. See reference to Josephus in note 721.

⁸⁴³ BaR 31.4–6; Tan. B. IV, 151–152; Tan. Pinehas 3; Sifre D., 252; Midrash Tannaim 147; *Likkutim*, V. 147a. Comp. vol. III, p. 341.

⁸⁴⁴ Yelammedenu in Yalkut I, 785. On the fear of the Moabites, see vol. III, p. 351. According to the sources in note 842, the last campaign of Moses was against Moab. But against this view comp. Baba Kamma 38a–38b, and the following note.

⁸⁴⁵ Yelammedenu in Yalkut I, 875, where it is assumed that the prohibition to wage war against the Moabite extended only till David's birth; comp. Tosafot Baba Kamma 38a and note 59 on vol. IV p. 94. According to Yelammedenu, the reason why the prohibition against intermarriage with Moab (Deut. 23.4) applied to Moabite males

only is to be found in the fact that the Moabite Ruth had been destined to become the mother of David. Abraham succeeded in bringing many "under the wings of the Shekinah" (on Abraham's proselytizing activity, see vol. I, pp. 203 and 217), and yet he failed to influence Lot; the descendants of the latter were therefore precluded from entering into the congregation of the Lord; Yelammedenu, *loc. cit.*

846 Yelammedenu in Yalkut I, 785.

847 Sifre N., 157; Yelammedenu in Yalkut I, 785; Tan. B. IV, 158; Tan. Mattot 4; BaR 22.6; *Likkutim* IV, 82a. According to another view, Joshua lost ten years of his life on account of his forwardness to give advice to Moses without having been asked for it; see Tan. Tezawweh 9; vol. III, p. 253; note 526; comp. also note 19 on vol. IV, p. 7.

848 Sifre N., 157; BaR 22.2; Tan. B. IV, 158–159; Tan. Mattot 3; Philo, *Moses*, 1.56. Concerning the idea that the hatred of the nations for Israel is due to their hatred for God and the Torah, see vol. IV, p. 406.

849 BaR 22.4 (this passage has the dissenting view that Midian against which Moses waged war was located near Moab, and is to be distinguished from the country of the same name whither he took refuge when fleeing from Egypt); Tan. B. IV, 159; Tan. Mattot 3; Sifre N., 157; Sotah 43a. Concerning the view that Phineas was (on his maternal) side) a descendant of Joseph, see vol. III, p. 388. According to Sotah, *loc. cit.*, Phineas acted in the campaign as field-chaplain (משוח מלחמה literally, "anointed for war"), whereas Philo, *Moses*, 1.56, and Josephus *Antiqui.*, IV. 7, are of the opinion that he was commander of the army, and this view is shared by many of the Rabbis; see note 860. The sacrifices preparatory to the undertaking of war, of which Philo, *loc. cit.*, speaks, are unknown in rabbinic sources. See, however, note 145.

850 BaR 22.3 (this passage has also the dissenting view that each tribe sent two thousand warriors); Tan. B. IV, 158–159; Tan. Mattot 3; Sifre N., 157; Targum Yerushalmi Num. 31.6; Sotah, Tosefta 7.17, and Babli 43a. On the taking of the ark to the battle, see note 331; vol. IV, pp. 62 and 276.

851 BaR 20.20 and 22.5; Tan. Mattot 4; Sifre N., 157; Sanhedrin 106b and Yerushalmi 10, 29a. For a full description of Balaam's gruesome end, see vol. III, pp. 410–411.

852 Sifre N., 157; comp. references given in the preceding note. On the sword with which Balaam was killed, see note 744. Israel regretted having slain Balaam, and exclaimed in despair: "Woe unto

us! We have slain a prophet." But a heavenly voice was immediately heard proclaiming: "Ye slew not a prophet but a sorcerer"; PRK, 33a. Comp. note 784.

⁸⁵³ Yelammedenu in Yalkut I, 785. In this source Balaam is said to have performed his feat by means of the Name. Phinehas, who also knew the Name, flew after him and caught up with him at God's throne, where he was begging for mercy. Phinehas held up to him the high priest's plate of pure gold, upon which the Name was engraved, and thus caused him to descend (comp. vol. III, p. 409), and brought him before the Synhedrion, who sentenced him to death. Targum Yerushalmi Num. 31.8 and *Aguddat Aggadot* 78-79 follow Yelammedenu in the main. What is meant by the statement of Yelammedenu that Balaam, while flying through the air, stretched out his arms like the two tables of stone? In Jewish and Christian legends, flying through the air is one of the accomplishments of the sorcerers; comp., *e. g.*, vol. III, p. 28 (the same expression תפשו בציצית ראשו is used in *Aguddat Aggadot*, *loc. cit.*, with regard to Balaam, as in Abkir in connection with Jannes and Jambres; comp. note 53), and the Christian legend concerning Simon Magus. Comp. the following two notes.

⁸⁵⁴ Zohar III, 194a-194b, where two different versions of the legend are combined into one. According to one version, Jannes and Jambres were killed shortly after they had fashioned the golden calf; see vol. III, p. 120. Zohar remarks that the tribe of Dan produced four heroes: Samson, Zaliah, Ira, David's friend (see 2 Sam. 20.26), and Seraiah who, as assistant of the Ephraimite Messiah, will cause great havoc among the Gentiles. The connection between this Seraiah and the Christian legend concerning the Danite descent of the anti-Christ is obvious, although it is difficult to trace the exact nature of this connection. Comp. Index, s. v. "Danites."

⁸⁵⁵ Targum Yerushalmi Num. 31.8, where, in accordance with Sanhedrin 106b, it is said that Phineas killed Balaam; comp. note 853. On the identity of Balaam with Laban, and on the long list of his crimes, see vol. III, p. 354. On the sword, see notes 44 and 852, as well as vol. III, p. 367 (top) and note 59 on vol. IV, p. 94. See Index, s. v. "Methusalem, Sword of", and "David, Sword of". The different legends concerning the death of Balaam show many points of resemblance to those about the death of Jesus (comp. the rich collections of such legends by Krauss, *Leben Jesu*). But this does not furnish any basis for the hypothesis that Balaam is used as a cryptic name for Jesus; see note 722. According to the legend given in the Masorah,

(ב"כ לו) it was Joshua who killed Balaam. Is this based upon the read-- ing יהושע instead of פינחס in Sanhedrin 106b? Comp. note 34 on vol. IV, p. 10.

⁸⁵⁶ Zohar III, 194. Onkelos, the son of Titus's sister, succeeded by means of necromancy to have a talk with Balaam, who told him that his punishment consisted in being boiled in scalding *semen virile* corresponding to his sin, for he was responsible for the unchaste acts committed by the Israelites with the daughters of Moab; Gittin 57a. The same passage stated that Balaam advised Onkelos not to adopt the Jewish religion. His words were: "Seek thou not their (Israel's) peace and prosperity all thy days for ever." And he gave this advice to Onkelos, though he had to admit that Israel is the foremost nation on earth.

⁸⁵⁷ Sifre N., 157; Tan. B. IV, 159; Tan. Mattot 3; BaR 22.4; Philo, *Vita Mosis*, 57.

⁸⁵⁸ Shir 4.4 and 6.6. On the piety of those warriors, see Aggadat Shir 4, 35 (here (ף‎לא=דחא) and quotation from an unknown Midrash in *Kimha Dabishuna* on תהלות לישב (morning prayer for the Day of Atonement).

⁸⁵⁹ Shir 1.6 and 4.4; Targum Yerushalmi Num. 31.50. Accord-ing to Philo, *Moses*, 1.57, they were in need of atonement, because he who kills a man, even though justly and in self-defence, appears to be guilty of bloodshed by reason of the relationship of all mankind to a common father.

⁸⁶⁰ Midrash Aggada, Num. 31.9 (which is introduced with the formula חכמינו אמרו, but in the rabbinic literature now extant nothing is found about this Jewish apostate); Sifre N., 157. In these sources Phineas is supposed to have been the commander-in-chief of the army. Comp. PRE 47, and note 849.

⁸⁶¹ Yebamot 60b; Targum Yerushalmi and Midrash Aggada, Num. 31.9 (here the holy ark takes the place of the high priest's plate). Comp. vol. IV, pp. 111 and 146. In the Christian legendary work *Protevangelium of James*, 5.1, it is related how Joachim the father of Mariah observed the high priest's mitre to ascertain whether he (Jo-achim) was free from sin or not.—As to the captives who escaped death, see Philo, *Moses*, 1.57, who is of the opinion that the very young boys were also spared. See, however, his remarks on this subject in *De Fortitud.* 8. Comp. also Sifre N., 157.

⁸⁶² Sifre N., 157, (end); here attention is called to two other cases of fits of anger which caused Moses to forget the words revealed to

him by God: In his anger at the sons of Aaron he forgot the law concerning sacrifices, see vol. III, pp. 191–192; when he grew wrathful against the people at Meribah, he smote the rock instead of talking to it, as he was commanded, see vol. III, p. 312; ARN (both versions) 1,3; WR 13.1; Pesahim 66b; 'Erubin 63a; PRE 47; Mishle 25, 97. Comp. also notes 110, 387 and 830.

863 PRE 47. Comp. note 786.

864 Tan. B. IV, 160; Tan. Mattot 5; BaR 22.7. Comp. also Aggadat Esther 56, as well as Koheleth 4.6 and 5.12. On the riches of Korah and Haman, see vol. III, p. 286; vol. IV, 393. On the view that Balaam and Ahitophel forfeited their share in the world to come, see vol. III, p. 375, and note 72 on vol. IV, p. 97.

865 BaR 22.9; Tan. Mattot 7.

866 Midrash Aggada, Num. 32.38. Comp. also the paraphrase of the names of the conquered places in Yerushalmi Targumim (on the text of 2 Targum Yerushalmi, see *Hadar* and R. Bahya, *ad loc.*). See the following note.

867 Rashi on Num. 32.28; comp. also Targum Yerushalmi and Lekah, *ad loc.*

868 Rashi, Lekah, and Midrash Aggada on Num. 32.41–42. Comp. also Ruth 2.13.

869 DR 2.26–27; Koheleth 5.8. On the relation of Deut. 4.41–49 to Joshua 20, see Makkot 9b and 11a. According to a quotation from Yerushalmi Makkot in Makiri on Is. 9, 74, Joshua, at the command of God, introduced many new regulations concerning the cities of refuge. In our texts of Yerushalmi Makkot II, 31a (bottom) the omission of this passage is indicated by גר"שה, which is an abbreviation of גמר שיטה "the continuation of this passage" (see Ginzberg, *Yerushalmi Fragments*, I, 128); but this discussion is not resumed in any part of the Yerushalmi.

870 Yelammedenu in Yalkut I, 743, on Num. 14.11 (read with RSBM on Deut. 3.23, שנה instead of מ'שנה, as the episode of the water at Meribah took place one year before the death of Moses; see vol. III, p. 311), which is followed by Midrash Tannaim 18; Mahzor Vitry 531; 'Aruk, s. v. אל; Nehemias, *Perush Pirke Abot* 44b, who cites Tanhuma as his source. Comp. Ginzberg, *Hazofeh* III, 127, and Taylor, *An Appendix to Sayings of the Jewish Fathers*, 161–162.

871 DR 1.5.

872 DR 11.10; Petirat Mosheh 120; 2 Petirat Mosheh 376. On the sealing of the heavenly decree, see Elleh Ezkerah 6; vol. III, p. 418; vol. IV, p. 416.

873 Midrash Tannaim 15; Mekilta Beshallah 2, 55a. Comp. also Sifre D., 26.

874 BaR 13: Tan. B. IV, 154; Tan. Pinehas 9.

875 DR 11.19; Petirat Mosheh 120–121; 2Petirat Mosheh 376–377, where the name Akraziel "Herald of God" is corrupted to Azkariel. Concerning the circle drawn by Moses, see vol. III, p. 260. On Zagzagel see vol. V, p. 417 (top) and note 898. On God's justice as revealed in his dealings with Moses, see vol. III, p. 436.

876 DR 11.10; Petirat Mosheh 121; 2Petirat Mosheh 377; Midrash Tannaim 15 and 179; Nispahim 44 = Yalkut II, 284, on Jer. 9 (in the first edition פ'פרה is given as source; this, however, must be emended to פ"ר אליעזר; comp. *op. cit.* 285). The sources cited at the beginning of the note state that Moses prayed five hundred and fifteen prayers, until God heard him and granted him the privilege to look at the promised land from the top of the mountain.

877 Yelammedenu in Yalkut I, 815 (on the proverb "no mercy in justice", see Ketubot 9.3, and Mishle 22, 93, where it refers to justice administered by a terrestrial court); *Likkutim*, V, 79b. Comp. also Yelammedenu in Yalkut I, 813.

878 DR 2.1; Tan. B. V, 9; Tan. Wa-Ethanan 3 (מצוה = "alms"). Comp. also vol. III, pp. 135, 280, and 426.

879 Tan. B. V, 14; Sifre D., 27; Midrash Tannaim 16; DR 2.8; Petirat Mosheh 117; 2 Petirat Mosheh 375. That the death of Moses in the wilderness was a punishment for his calling Israel "rebels" is inferred from Num. 20.10–12. Comp. vol. III, pp. 311, *seq.*, and 320. According to ps.-Philo, 19.6-7, God spoke to Moses, saying: "Behold, thou goest to sleep with thy fathers, and this people...will forget My Law...but thou shalt not enter therein (into the Holy Land) in this age, lest thou see the graven images whereby this people will be deceived and led out of the way." This novel view concerning God's refusal to allow Moses to enter the Holy Land is inferred from Deut. 31.16.

880 Tan. B. V, 10; *Likkutim*, V, 79b–80a. The tannaitic Midrashim Sifre D., 27, and Midrash Tannaim 16 remark: Abraham, Jacob, Moses, David, and Isaiah described themselves as "servants of the Lord", and so they were called by Him, whereas Samson and Solomon were never recognized by God as such, though they called themselves "servants of the Lord"; Joshua, Job, Caleb, Eliakim, Zerubbabel, Daniel and his three companions, as well as the early prophets, were described by God as His servants, but they never applied this designation to themselves. The Midrashim quoted above cite the biblical

passages where the title "servant of God" is applied to the above-mentioned persons by God and by themselves.

⁸⁸¹ Sifre D., 27; Midrash Tannaim 17; Petirat Mosheh 118; Yelammedenu in '*Aruk*, s. v. אנטפתא; Mekilta Amalek 2, 55a.

⁸⁸² Midrash Tannaim 16; Sifre D., 28; Tan. B. V, 9; Targum Yerushalmi Deut. 3.25.

⁸⁸³ Sifre D., 27; Midrash Tannaim 16. For other explanations of החלות in Deut. 3.24 (according to the Haggadah, it is to be translated: "thou didst absolve"), see the sources quoted above, as well as Sifre N., 134. Comp. vol. III, p. 128; *Pa'aneah*, Deut. 3.24.

⁸⁸⁴ Midrash Tannaim 17, 19, and 178; Sifre N., 135; Mekilta Amalek 2, 55b; comp. vol. III, pp. 424 and 442.

⁸⁸⁵ Midrash Tannaim 178; DR 2.8. Comp. vol. II, p. 293.

⁸⁸⁶ DR 9.6; Tan. B. V, 10–11 and 56; Tan. Wa-Ethanan 6, Wa-Yelek 3, and Berakah 7; Midrash Tannaim 179–180; 2 Petirat Mosheh 374; *Likkutim*, V, 161a; Ziyyoni, Wa-Yelek; Manzur 52. In the last-quoted Midrash, as well as in many others (see Grünhut on *Likkutim*, *loc. cit.*), the word הן is interpreted as having the meaning of the Greek ἕν "one", God thus describes Himself as the "One" and Moses as the "One (*i. e.*, greatest) prophet".

⁸⁸⁷ Midrash Tannaim 178; Sotah 13b; BaR 18.18; Tehillim 18, 150–151. On the reluctance of Moses to accept the leadership of the people, see note 837. The Haggadah offers many explanations of the words רב לך in Deut. 3.26; comp. Midrash Tannaim 17–18; Sifre D., 29; Sotah 13b; Sifre N., 135; Mekilta Amalek 2, 55b; Tan. B. V, 10 and 14; *Likkutim*, V, 101b-102a.

⁸⁸⁸ DR 9.8; Koheleth 7.13; Tan. B. V, 11 (read in line 3 הן כבר קנסתי); Tan. Wa-Ethanan 6; 2 Petirat Mosheh 374 (two different sources are made use of); Petirat Mosheh 116. On the view that Adam's sin was the cause of the death of Moses and of those who like him were free from sin, see Sifre D., 339; Shabbat 55b; note 142 on vol. I, p. 102; Index,s. v. "Death", "Sin".

⁸⁸⁹ Tan. B. V, 11; Tan. Wa-Ethanan 6; 2 Petirat Mosheh 374–375 (on the two leaders of Israel one of whom, Moses, wished his sin to be recorded, while the other, David, desired to keep his sin secret, see the sources quoted in note 616 on vol. III, p. 313, bottom). Concerning Moses' superiority to all other mortals, see vol. III, pp. 427–428 and 479–480. On the sins of Moses, see vol. II, pp. 316, *seq.*, and 339; vol. III, pp. 311, *seq.*, 317, *seq.*, and note 571. As a punishment for having used the hasty words "Ye are risen, etc", Moses' grandson (comp. vol. IV, p. 50)

became a priest to an idol; Hasidim 71. Moses was commanded by God to ask the fathers of Israel for pardon for having offended them by describing his contemporaries as having "risen up in their fathers' stead an increase of sinful men", which words stamped the past generations of Israel as sinful men. In accordance with this command given to Moses, it is customary that one who has slandered those who are "in the grave" should beg their pardon; *Imre No'am* and *Pa'aneah* on Mattot (end); Aguddah 17b.

⁸⁹⁰ Tan. B. V, 11, Tan. Wa-Ethanan 6; 2 Petirat Mosheh 375. For the description of Moses' praying for mercy, see vol. III, p. 420. On the angel of death, see vol. III, p. 436.

⁸⁹¹ Petirat Mosheh 118–119; Makiri, Ps. 71, 345. On the parable of the king and his servant, see Yelammedenu in Yalkut II, 86, on 1 Sam. 2, *seq.*, and on Is. 2. Concerning Moses' claim that he was free from sin, whereas all other men died on account of their sins, see vol. III, p. 425, and note 889. According to Yelammedenu in Yalkut II, 873, on Ps. 115, God spoke to Moses as follows: "All creatures descend to Sheol, but thou shalt ascend (to heaven) after thy death." On Noah, see vol. I, p. 165. On the slaying of the Egyptians, see vol. II, p. 280.

⁸⁹² Petirat Mosheh 119–120; 2 Petirat Mosheh 377–378. On the great distinction conferred by God upon Moses, see vol. III, pp. 118, 141, 235, and 243.

⁸⁹³ Midrash Tannaim 18; DR 9.5. Comp. also Midrash Tannaim 19, which reads: God said to Moses: "I exalted thee above the angels, which remain standing in My presence and are not permitted to sit, whereas thou wast permitted to remain sitting." On Moses' sitting in the presence of God, see Megillah 21a and note 832.

⁸⁹⁴ Petirat Mosheh 121 (רבוא is to be omitted; see 'Okazin (end), and Sanhedrin 100a, which reads: Every righteous man will receive three hundred and ten words from God); 2 Petirat Mosheh 376. In the last-mentioned source, DR 11.9 is made use of, hence the statement that in the days to come Moses will appear at the head of fifty-five myriads of pious men. This is also found in Manzur 14. On the rod of Moses, see vol. II, p. 291, and Index, s. v. On the creation of the world by means of the Name, see Yerushalmi Hagigah 2, 17, and Index, s. v. "God, Name of".

⁸⁹⁵ Tan. B. IV, 11–12; Tan. Wa-Ethanan 6; Petirat Mosheh 125–126 (על עצמינו‎=ע״ע); 2 Petirat Mosheh 379–380; Manzur 15; quotation from Midrash in *Eshkol* 137a–137b, 364. The three last-

named sources are independent of Tan., and the appeals addressed by Moses to the different parts of the universe are given in these sources in a more elaborate form than in Tan.   Comp. note 908.

⁸⁹⁶ 2 Petirat Mosheh 380; Manzur 15–16 (the text is not in an entirely satisfactory state); quotation from Midrash in Eshkol 137b, 364.   Some elements of this legend are found in very early sources; comp. Mekilta Amalek 2, 55b; Midrash Tannaim 179; DR 3.11 and 7.10. On the "sixty blows of fire", see '*Aruk*,ס. v. פלס 4, and accordingly the reading of Eshkol פולסין דנורא is the correct one, whereas in Manzur the text is somewhat abridged.   פולסא is nothing but the Syriac בלצציחא "sparks".   Comp. note 84 on vol. IV, p. 220.

⁸⁹⁷ Tan. B. V, 12 (the text is not in a satisfactory state; read מדת הדין instead of רוח הקדש and חרבו instead of חבלו); Tan. Wa-Ethanan 6; Petirat Mosheh 120 (this source is the only one which contains the passage about the two vows); 2 Petirat Mosheh 375; Mishle 14, 77.   That Moses finally became convinced that his request could only be granted at the cost of Israel's destruction, is clearly brought out in the version of this legend as given in *Hadar*, Deut., 3.25.   On the effect of the reciting of God's thirteen attributes, see vol. III, p. 138. On the view that Moses was not delivered into the hands of the Angel of Death, see vol. III, pp. 426, 448, 471, *seq.*   That Jochebed survived her illustrious son is also stated in vol. III, p. 393.   On the view that Moses' death was the highest expression of God's justice, see vol. III, p. 419

⁸⁹⁸ Petirat Mosheh 123–124.   As to the different elements of which this legend is composed, see DR 9.9; Tan. B. V, 12–13; Tan. Wa-Ethanan 6; Mishle 14, 77.   On Moses' willingness to become Joshua's servant, if he were only permitted to continue to live, see vol. III, pp. 421, 440, 442, 465.   Concerning the herald, see vol. III, pp. 390, 440. On God's love for the innocent youth, see vol. IV, p. 295; on the words exclaimed by the earth, see Yebamot 16b, where these words are said to have been uttered by "the prince of the world", comp. note 75 on Vol. I, p. 19; on the rays of Moses and Joshua, see vol. III, p. 400, and Index, s. v.   According to Sefer Hanok 116, Zagzagel (comp. also vol. II, p. 309, and vol. III, p. 469) is no other than Metatron, and consequently one is inclined to explain this strange name (the variant סגנואל occurs several times) as סגן סגניאל "the prince of the heavenly princes."

⁸⁹⁹ Petirat Mosheh 122: 2 Petirat Mosheh, 378; DR 9.9.   Comp. also Josephus *Antiqui.*, IV, 8; vol. III, pp. 350–351.

⁹⁰⁰ DR 9.9; Petirat Mosheh 122; 2 Petirat Mosheh 378; comp. vol. IV, p. 114

⁹⁰¹ Petirat Mosheh 122–123 (line 14 of p. 123, beginning with יצתה is the continuation of line 5); 2 Petirat Mosheh 378–379; quotation from Midrash in *Eshkol* 137a–137b, 379. On the praying of the departed souls, see vol. I, p. 23, and vol. IV, p. 219. The part of the Meturgeman is ascribed to Caleb on account of his strong voice; see vol. III, p. 273. On the shining of the countenances of Moses and Joshua, see vol. III, p. 400, and note 898; see also note 6 on vol. IV, p. 3.

⁹⁰² Sifre D., 357; Sifre N., 135–136; Mekilta Amalek 2, 55b–56a (according to this passage, the past history of the human race was shown to him); Midrash Tannaim 19, 206, 207, 293–294; Targum Yerushalmi Deut. 34.1–4. A very lengthy description of the mysteries revealed to Moses shortly before his death is found in ps.–Philo 19.10–13, whereas "The Assumption of Moses" containing the future history of Israel from the time of Moses' death until the days of the Messiah is given as the last words of Moses to Joshua. Comp. vol. III, pp. 401–403. The haggadic literature contains many references to the cosmic as well as historic revelations made to Moses. But the occasion on which they took place is not stated. The election of Moses at the burning bush, the revelation on Sinai, and the vision on the top of Pisgah are the three outstanding moments in the life of the great prophet, and accordingly the legend connects the revelations of the cosmic and historic mysteries, granted to Moses, with one of these three events. See Tan. B. III, 83, and IV, 162; WR 26.7; EZ 6, 183; BaR 23.5; vol. III, pp. 154 and 398; vol. V, p. 417. Among the Church Fathers it is Aphraates, 420 who, in agreement with the Rabbis and ps.-Philo, finds in Deut. 34.1–4 an allusion to the revelation of the future history of Israel.—Concerning the line of prophets from the house of Rahab, see vol. IV, p. 5.

⁹⁰³ Sifre N., 37; Sifre D., 338; Midrash Tannaim 206. Comp. Vol. IV, p. 9 (bottom); Hullin 60b.

⁹⁰⁴ Sifre D., 337–339; Midrash Tannaim 206–207; Sotah 13a; Ozar Midrashim 41–42; BR 47.9. The last two sources add that Abraham performed the ceremony of circumcision on himself and the members of his family in broad daylight (comp. Gen. 17.26), to show his fearlessness and his trust in God. With regard to Moses' burial, ps.-Philo, 19; 20D, remarks: And He buried him…in the light of the whole world. A similar statement is found in the Assumption of Moses 1.15: And

I am now going in the presence of all the people to rest with my fathers.
The emphasis laid by all these authorities on the fact that Moses'
death took place "in public" has very likely the aim to combat the view
that he did not die at all, but was translated to heaven; comp. note 951.
That this hypothesis is not without sound ground may be seen from
Josephus, *Antiqui.*, IV, 8.48, who describes the last moments of Moses
as follows: Now as he went thence to the place where he was to vanish
out of their sight, they all followed him weeping; but Moses beckoned
with his hand...and bid them stay behind...All those who accompanied
him were, the senate and Eleazar the high priest and Joshua the commander.   Now as soon as they were come to the mountain called Abarim...
he dismissed the senate, and as he was going to embrace Eleazar and
Joshua, and was still discoursing with them, a cloud stood over him
on the sudden, and he disappeared in a certain valley, although he wrote
in the holy books that he died (comp. note 951), which was done out of
fear lest they should venture to say that because of his extraordinary
virtue he went to God.   The later legend concerning the translation
of Enoch is similar to that given by Josephus with regard to "the disappearance" of Moses.   Comp. vol. I pp. 129–130.

⁹⁰⁵ BHM VI, Introduction 22; a superior text (but even this one
is not entirely correct; read שמי אותך ואלמד; at the end read ולא instead of או) is given by Epstein, *Eldad*, 67–70.   The legend that God
showed Jacob (and also Abraham, Isaac, Moses, and David) the
terrestrial as well as the celestial temple is very old; see Midrash Tannaim 216; Sifre D., 352; BR 56.10.   On the view that Moses surrendered
his soul only to God, see vol. III, pp. 436, 471 *seq.*

⁹⁰⁶ Midrash Tannaim 179; Petirat Mosheh 125; 2 Petirat Mosheh
379.

⁹⁰⁷ DR 11.9; Petirat Mosheh 125 (read ואפרח אנתר); 2 Petirat
Mosheh 379.   On the struggle between Sammael and Moses, see vol.
III, pp. 466, *seq.*

⁹⁰⁸ Petirat Mosheh 125–126 and 2 Petirat Mosheh 380, both
of which are based on old sources; see Sifre D., 305; quotation from Tan.
in Makiri, Prov. 23.13; *Likkutim*, V, 161a–161b; ARN 17, 65, and the
parallel sources cited by Schechter.   Concerning the appeal made by
Moses to the "works of creation", see vol. III, pp. 431–432, and
'Abodah Zarah 17a.   The Midrashim very likely made use of this
talmudic passage.   Concerning "the acknowledging of God's justice"
(צדוק הדין) by Moses, see vol. I, p. 286, vol. II, p. 27.   Comp. Sotah
40a and Sanhedrin 8a.

⁹⁰⁹ Petirat Mosheh 126. Comp. vol. IV, p. 4. Moses further said to Joshua: "Thou shalt have to carry a burden which proved too heavy for three (Moses, Aaron, and Miriam). May God be with thee! I implore thee to take care of my mother, who has the terrible misfortune of losing all her children in her life-time. Now thou art to be her son. Be kind to the poor proselyte (Zipporah), and see that no evil is done to her. In memory of our friendship treat my orphans, to whom it was not granted to be my successors, as members of thy household." See 2 Petirat Mosheh 380 (bottom). On Jochebed, see vol. III, p. 393.

⁹¹⁰ Tan. B. V, 13; Tan. Wa-Ethanan 6; Petirat Mosheh 126; 2 Petirat Mosheh 380–381; PK 32, 197a.

⁹¹¹ PK 32, 198b; DR 11.5; DZ 9. As to the victory of Moses over the angel of Death (=Sammael), see vol. III, pp. 456, *seq.*

⁹¹² PK 32, 198b–199b; Tan. B. V, 52–54; Tan. Berakah 1. Comp. also DR 11.1. As to Abraham's refraining from blessing Isaac, see vol. I, p. 299. On the relation of the blessings of Moses to those of Jacob, see vol. II, p. 147. Jacob bestowed upon his sons the blessings he had received from God, from the angel with whom he had wrestled, and from his grandfather; the two blessings he had received from his father (comp. Gen. 27.28–29 and 28.1); he also added one blessing of his own. He thus gave six blessings to his son. Comp. also BR 94.5. The blessings given by Moses to each tribe corresponded to the pious deeds of the progenitor of the tribe, and accordingly they supplemented the blessings which Jacob bestowed on his sons, the sires of the tribes; see quotation from Midrash in Sabba', Berakah, 165b. Comp. further Sifre D., 357 (on עֵין יַעֲקֹב); Hasidim 18. Jacob's sons took turns in attending on their father on week-days, while on the Sabbath they all together attended on him. As long as their grandfather Isaac was alive, they, together with their father, spent the Sabbath with Isaac. The blessings bestowed by Jacob on his sons corresponded with the services rendered on the days when they attended on him; Hasidim 171. On other blessings of Moses, see vol. III, pp. 69 and 178.

⁹¹³ Sifre D., 343; Midrash Tannaim 208–209. Following Moses' example, David, Solomon, and the wise men who instituted the prayer (comp. vol. IV, pp. 359–361) began with the glorification of God's name, and then proceeded with their requests.

⁹¹⁴ Midrash Tannaim 209. On the west as the place of the Shekinah, see Baba Batra 25a and Index, s. v. "West".

⁹¹⁵ Sifre D., 343; Midrash Tannaim 209; Targum Yerushalmi Deut. 32.2. Comp. vol. III, p. 80.

⁹¹⁶ Midrash Tannaim 212. For other haggadic interpretations of Deut. 33.3, see Targumim, *ad loc.*; Sifre D., 344; Midrash Tannaim 212-213.

⁹¹⁷ Sifre D., 345; Midrash Tannaim 212-213. On the Torah as the bride, or rather "betrothed" of Israel, see Friedmann on Sifre, *loc. cit.*; vol. III, p. 92 and note 200.

⁹¹⁸ Midrash Tannaim 313; Targumim Deut. 33.5. According to another view, this verse of Deut. speaks of God as the King of Israel; comp. Sifre D., 346, and Midrash Tannaim, *loc. cit.* On Moses as king see note 170. On the Seven Shepherds, see note 142, on vol. I, p. 102.

⁹¹⁹ Midrash Tannaim 210. According to Sifre D., 343, the appearance of God against Gog will be the third and the fourth at the advent of the Messiah. An old tannaitic tradition speaks of "God's ten descents on earth". He descended to punish Adam (Gen. 3.8); to look at the tower (*ibid.* 11.5); to convince Himself of the wickedness of the sinful cities (*ibid.* 18.21); to deliver Israel from Egypt (Exod. 3.8); to drown the Egyptians in the Red Sea (2 Sam. 22.10); to reveal the Torah (Exod. 19.20); to make His spirit rest upon the seventy elders (Num. 11.5); to make the Shekinah dwell in the Temple (Ezek. 44.2). He will also descend in the time to come when He will appear to execute judgment upon Gog. See Mekilta Bahodesh 3, 64a; Sifre N., 33; ARN 24, 102 (in this passage the ascents are also described), and second version 37, 96-97, which contains some variants; BR 38.9. According to PRE 14 and 24, God descended to reveal Himself unto Moses in the bush, to perform the miracle of making the water flow from the rock (twice); He also descended twice on the tabernacle. Comp. note 206.

⁹²⁰ Sifre D., 347; Midrash Tannaim 213-214. Comp. also Philo, *De Caritate*, 4, which reads: And the things which were entreated for in the petitions were real blessings, not only that such things might fall to their share in this mortal life, but still more so when the soul should be released from the bondage of flesh. Philo was very likely acquainted with the interpretations given by the Rabbis of the blessings bestowed upon Reuben and Judah. The genuineness of this sentence is however very doubtful; it is very likely an addition by a Christian reader. The further remarks of Philo, *ibid.* and *Moses*, 2(3).39, that some of the blessings have already been fulfilled, and that "the rest will certainly be accomplished", are in full agreement with the

Haggadah of the Rabbis, who find in these blessings the history of Israel from its very beginning until the days of the Messiah. The statement of Josephus, *Antiqui.*, IV, 8.44, that "the song (*i. e.*, Deut. 32.1–43) contains a prediction of what was to come afterwards, agreeably whereto all things have happened all along, and so still happen to us", is in perfect agreement with the view of the Rabbis; see Sifre D., 307–333; Midrash Tannaim 192–204; Yerushalmi Targumim, *ad loc.*—That Moses prayed for Reuben's life in the future world is also stated by Aphraates, 420, and Epiphanius, *Ancoratus*, 97.

⁹²¹ DZ 10. Comp. vol. III, pp. 172–173; vol. IV, p. 8; vol. II, p. 41.   When in accordance with the command of God, the tribe of Reuben was charged to pronounce the curse upon mount Ebal against him who committed incest with his father's wife (comp. Deut. 27.13 and 20), all Israel knew then that Reuben's sin was forgiven; *Shitah* 2; the very lengthy quotation from an unknown Midrash in Sabba', Wa-Yeze 36b, Ki-Tabo, 152a. This unknown Midrash adds that Reuben never asked his father's pardon, and therefore his sin, notwithstanding his life-long repentance, was not forgiven until Moses prayed for him. Comp. note 60 on vol. II, p. 24.

⁹²² Baba Kamma 91b; MHG I, 689; Sifre D., 348; Midrash Tannaim 214.   Comp. vol. II, p. 36.

⁹²³ Sifre D., 348; Midrash Tannaim 214; Targum Yerushalmi Deut. 33.7; Tehillim 86, 372, and 102, 430; PK 32, 197b.   As to the sins committed by the tribe of Simeon, see vol. III, p. 390, and note 794. PK, *loc. cit.*, adds that because the tribe of Simeon had not received any blessing from Moses, it did not furnish Israel with a king, whereas each of the other tribes produced one king or more.   It is true that Zimri was of the tribe of Simeon; but having only reigned for seven days (comp. I Kings 16.15), he may be disregarded.   The fact that this tribe did not furnish any kings is mentioned also in the Testaments of the 12 Patriarchs, Simeon, 5.6. and Tadshe 8; but comp., to the contrary, Sukkah 27b, where it is stated that "there was not one tribe which did not furnish kings and judges"; comp. also vol. II, p. 142.   Philo, *De Conf. Ling.*, 35, is of the opinion that Moses included Simeon in Levi's blessing.   Comp. the following note.

⁹²⁴ Sifre D., 349–352; Midrash Tannaim 214–215; comp. vol. II, p. 188; vol. III, pp. 211, 281, 314.   Ephraem I, 191 A-C, in agreement with the Rabbis, remarks that Moses failed to bless the tribe of Simeon on account of its sin committed at Shittim.   His observations on the difference between the tribes of Simeon and Levi, as contrasted with

the similarity of the character of their sires, the sons of Jacob, are found, almost verbatim, in the tannaitic sources quoted.

⁹²⁵ Targum Yerushalmi Deut. 33.11. According to a later tradition, the father of Mattathias the Hasmonean was the high priest Johanan (Soferim 20.8; comp. Müller, *ad loc.*), and it is very likely that Targum Yerushalmi refers to this alleged high priest and not to John (Johanan) Hyrkanus. The older haggadah never alludes to the Hasmoneans (it was too near the time of the strife between the Pharisees and the Hasmoneans to be impartial to the latter). The later Haggadah of the Amoraim (comp., *e. g.*, Megillah 11a; Tehillim 93, 413; vol. III, p. 218) hardly knew of the Hasmoneans more than that at a certain period they played a glorious part in the history of Israel, for which they deserve praise and honor. The reference to "John the high priest" in Targum Yerushalmi, far from being "remarkable proof" of the high antiquity of this Aramaic paraphrase of the Pentateuch, as Geiger (*Urschrift*, 479) maintains, is clear evidence of its comparatively recent date.

⁹²⁶ Sifre D., 352; Midrash Tannaim 216-217. According to one view, even the temporary central sanctuaries, as those at Gibeon and Nob, were in the territory of Benjamin; Yerushalmi Megillah I, 72d and Zebahim 118b. The description of Benjamin as the "host of the Shekinah" (comp., *e. g.*, Yoma 12a) very likely refers to the fact that the Shekinah during her wanderings found temporary rest in the territory of this tribe. Three reasons are assigned for this great distinction conferred upon the tribe of Benjamin. The sire of this tribe, Benjamin the son of Jacob, was the only son of the patriarch born in the Holy Land (comp. Gen. 35.16, *seq.*). Furthermore he was the only one of Joseph's brethren who took no part in selling the latter. If the central sanctuary had been located in the territory of any other tribe, God would not have heard the prayers addressed to Him in such a place, even as Joseph's brethren turned a deaf ear to their brother's supplications when they sold him. Finally, just as Jacob found solace by leaning on "the shoulders" of his youngest son Benjamin, even so did the Shekinah "dwell between his shoulders"; see Sifre and Midrash Tannaim, *loc. cit.*; Mekilta Bahodesh 4, 65b; BR 99.1. Comp. note 262 on vol. I, p. 390. According to some authorities, the site of the Jerusalem Temple was partly in the territory of Benjamin and partly in the territory of Judah; see Yoma and BR, *loc. cit.*

⁹²⁷ Sifre D., 353; Midrash Tannaim 217-218; Targum Yerushalmi Deut. 33.16-17. The statement that Joseph will be the first to appear in the Holy Land very likely refers to the Ephraimitic Messiah who

will inaugurate the future redemption; see Ginzberg, *Unbekannte Sekte* 337. The statement in Sifre with regard to "the mountains of Joseph" is to be emended in accordance with Midrash Tannaim in the following manner: The mountain of the Temple antedates the mountains of Joseph; the mountains of Joseph antedate the mountains of the land of Israel. The Temple mount was created first (see vol. I, p. 12), then the mountains of Joseph (the hill-country of Ephraim הר אפרים, or the mountains Ebal and Gerizim), and finally the other mountains of the Holy Land.

⁹²⁸ Sifre D., 345; Midrash Tannaim 218–219; Targum Yerushalmi Deut. 33.18–19; Megillah 8a.

⁹²⁹ Sifre D., 354; Midrash Tannaim 218; BaR 13.17; Targum Yerushalmi 33.18. On the relation of "the tribe of merchants" (Zebulun) to "the tribe of scholars" (Issachar), comp. vol. II, p. 154.

⁹³⁰ Sifre D. 355; Midrash Tannaim 219–220; Targum Yerushalmi Deut. 33.20; comp. Sifre N., 106, and the parallel passages given by Friedmann. The activity of the tribe of Gad in "the time to come" very likely alludes to the activity of the Gadite Elijah (see vol. I, p. 365), who will appear in "the time to come" as the forerunner of the Messiah. However as may be seen from Targum Yerushalmi, *loc. cit.*, and Aggadat Bereshit 67, 133, הוא in Sifre was taken by some authorities to refer, not to the tribe of Gad, but to Moses, who will lead Israel back to the Holy Land; see vol. III (end).

⁹³¹ Sifre D., 355; Midrash Tannaim 220.

⁹³² Sifre D., 355; Midrash Tannaim 220. Comp. vol. I, p. 365; vol. II, p. 145.

⁹³³ Sifre D., 355; Midrash Tannaim 220; Targum Yerushalmi Deut. 33.24.

⁹³⁴ ER 9, 52. Comp. vol. II, p. 145.

⁹³⁵ PK 32, 198a; Tehillim 90, 387.

⁹³⁶ Tehillim 1, 7; Baba Batra 14b–15a (in this passage ten psalmists, besides David, are enumerated, adding Heman and Jeduthun, but excluding Solomon); Shir 4.4 (here Ezra is counted instead of Melchizedek), 8.9. Comp. note 590 (end).

⁹³⁷ PK 32, 198a; Tehillim 90, 387. On Reuben, see vol. II, p. 24; on Gad, vol. I, p. 365; on Issachar, vol. II, p. 144. Comp. Shebu'ot 1, 33b, l.38.

⁹³⁸ Tan. B. V, 13; Tan. Wa-Ethanan 6; Petirat Mosheh 126; 2 Petirat Mosheh 381.

⁹³⁹ Sifre D., 356; Midrash Tannaim 222–223. Comp. vol. III, pp. 92–93 and 132.

⁹⁴⁰ Tan. B. V, 13; Tan. Wa-Ethanan 6; Petirat Mosheh 126; 2 Petirat Mosheh 381. Comp. the following note.

⁹⁴¹ Midrash Tannaim 14–15, where מתנעעין is to be read instead of מתעננין. As to the view that it is "the people", and not the individual (not even the genius), who decides the current of history, see vol. III, p. 283, and Assumption of Moses 12.

⁹⁴² Petirat Mosheh 125–126; 2 Petirat Mosheh 381. As to the great mysteries revealed to Moses immediately before his death, see note 902. Comp. also DR 11.8 which reads: Moses requested God that before his death the gates of heaven and the abyss should be opened, that all men might see that there is only one God. See vol. III, p. 96. The supplication of Moses to be allowed to enter the Holy Land was not prompted by his longing for earthly pleasures, but by his great desire to be in a position to fulfil those commandments which cannot be observed outside the Holy Land; see Sotah 14a; Midrash Tannaim 17; 2 Petirat Mosheh, 381–382, where this point is elaborated at full length. Comp. vol. III, p. 436.

⁹⁴³ DR 11.10; Petirat Mosheh 127; 2 Petirat Mosheh 381. "The book of song" is identical with the poetic piece in Deut. 32.1–43, on which see notes 920 and 946. In Petirat Mosheh "the book of song" became "the book of Yashar", through the error of a copyist who confused שיר "song" with ישר "Yashar". The author of 2 Petirat Mosheh seems to have had before him the corrupt reading ס'ה'ישר, and not being able to explain it, wisely omitted the entire sentence.

⁹⁴⁴ Tan. B. V, 12–13; Tan. Wa-Ethanan 6; Mishle 14, 77; Makiri, Prov. 14; Likkutim VI, 17a–17b; Petirat Mosheh 127. Another version of this legend is found in DR 9.9 which reads: When Moses, with Joshua at his right, reached the tabernacle, God revealed Himself unto Joshua in a cloud of glory. Moses thereupon asked Joshua of what nature the revelation was. Joshua answered: "Were the revelations granted to thine ear made known to me?" Thereupon Moses exclaimed: "A thousand deaths are preferable to one jealousy." Strong as death was Moses' love for Joshua; but cruel as the grave was his jealousy. Comp. vol. III, pp. 436, 442; Sotah 13b. On the explanation of the midrashic passages referred to at the beginning of the note, see Ginzberg, Rivista Israelitica VII, 93–94.

⁹⁴⁵ Petirat Mosheh 127 (read אמר הקב"ה לגבריאל); 2 Petirat Mosheh 381; Manzur 16; DR 11.1. On Sagsagel, see note 898.

946 2 Petirat Mosheh 381–382. On the superiority of Moses to all other pious men, see vol. III, pp. 423–424, 427, 479, 480. The Christian booklet, the Revelations of Esdras, is a poor adaptation of this part of Petirat Mosheh. Notice, *e. g.*, the following words of Ezra addressed to the angels who wanted to take out his soul through his mouth: "Mouth to mouth have I spoken with God". But where has it ever been stated that Ezra, or anybody else but Moses, spoke mouth to mouth with God? In changing the name of the hero, the Christian compiler was not aware of the fact that he makes Ezra use words which can only be attributed to Moses. DR 11.10, Petirat Moshe, *loc. cit.*, and Manzur 16 have retained some traces of the old legend concerning the struggle between Michael and Satan (=Sammael) about the body of Moses, to which the pseudepigraphic and early Christian literatures allude quite frequently; see Jude 9, and the references to the Church Fathers given by Fabricius, *Codex Pseudepig. Vet. Test.* 842, *seq.*, and Charles, Assumption of Moses, 105, *seq.* According to this old legend, Michael asked God for permission to bury Moses (comp. vol. III, pp. 471–472). But Satan objected to this request, first on the ground that Moses did not deserve this last honor because he killed the Egyptian (comp. vol. III, p. 428), and then on the general ground that everything corporeal may be claimed by him (Satan) as his due. Satan's claim was refuted by Michael with the following words: "The Lord rebuke thee! For it was God's spirit which created the universe and all mankind." Not satisfied with refuting Satan's claims, the archangel accused his adversary of having caused the serpent to seduce Adam and Eve (comp. vol. I, p. 95). He finally succeeded in achieving a complete victory over Satan, with the result that the body of Moses was not delivered up into the hands of Satan. The controversy between Michael and Sammael reads in DR, *loc. cit.*, as follows: Sammael, head of the Satans (=evil spirits; comp. Tosefta Shabbat 17.3: "the angels of Satan"), waited impatiently for the moment of Moses' death, exclaiming: "O for the moment when Michael shall weep and I will open my mouth with laughter!" Hearing these words, Michael replied: "I weep, and thou laughest; but 'rejoice not against me, O mine enemy, though I am fallen, I shall arise; though I sit in darkness, the Lord is light unto me.'" *Though I am fallen* through the death of Moses, *I shall arise* with the leadership of Joshua; though *I sit in darkness* through the destruction of the first and second Temples, *the Lord shall be a light unto me* in the days of the Messiah. The last sentence does not continue Michael's reply to Satan, but is a haggadic

159

interpretation of Micah 7.8, the first half of which verse is alleged to have been uttered by Michael on the occasion of Moses' death. Comp. vol. III, p. 449. It is noteworthy that the rabbinic sources speak of the attempt of Sammael or Satan to come into possession of Moses' soul, whereas in the old legend Satan claims his body. See, however, Yelammedenu in Yalkut II, 873, on Ps. 115, which reads: God said to Moses: "All creatures descend into Sheol, but thou shalt ascend unto Me." Comp. notes 892, 951.—The statement that Gabriel was the first angel called upon to fetch the soul of Moses is perhaps connected with the view that this angel is one of "the six angels of death"; see Ma'aseh Torah 98; PRK, 14b; *Huppat Eliyyahu* 46. According to these sources, it is Gabriel's task to take the life of kings. Comp. note 187 on vol. I, p. 41. See also Zohar I, 99a (סתרי תורה), where Gabriel appears as the assistant of the angel of Death. As to the latter's (= Satan's) claim on all living, see vol. I, p. 40.

⁹⁴⁷ DR 11.10; Petirat Mosheh 127–128 (read ומראהו instead of ומאמרו); 2 Petirat Mosheh 382; Manzur 16–18 (the text is very corrupt); quotation from Midrash by Hadassi, *Eshkol*, 137c, 364. Concerning the various elements of this legend, see note 318 on vol. I, p. 306; vol. II, pp. 264, 270, 272, 332; vol. III, pp. 25, 109, *seq.*, and 340. Short versions of a legend about Sammael's futile attempts are found in early sources; see Sifre D., 305; ARN 12, 50 (second version 25.51; comp. also p. 150, which agrees with 2 Petirat Mosheh); DR 11.5 (on the text see *Hadar*, Deut. 32.1); Tan. Berakah 3. In the two last-named Midrashim it is stated that Moses rebuked the Angel of death with the following words: "Begone from here, as I intend to praise the Lord." The latter replied: "Heaven and earth declare God's glory incessantly, and He does not need thee for this purpose." Whereupon Moses said: "Give ear, ye heavens, and I will speak, and let the earth hear the words of my mouth. Ye two be silent, that I may praise the Lord." When the Angel of Death came a second time, Moses forced him again to retire and made him do his bidding by means of the Name. But when the Angel of Death appeared for the third time, Moses became convinced that his last hour was come, and he resigned himself to his fate, saying: "Now I shall acknowledge the justice of the Lord, and submit myself to it." Comp. note 908 and 911. Concerning the view that the Song of Moses (see note 920) caused heaven and earth to keep silent, see Sifre D., 306, 131 (middle of page); Midrash Tannaim 182; DR 10.2; *Likkutim*, V, 163a; Yelammedenu in Yalkut I, 729; Philo, *De Carit.* 3; note 245; note 102 on vol. I, p. 25 and note 43 on vol. IV, p. 11.

⁹⁴⁸ DR 11.10 (on the text, see *Hadar* and *Da'at*, Deut. 34.5, and Ziyyoni, 10); Petirat Mosheh 128–129 (read לא היתה בו צרעת מעולם, and comp. Yalkut I, 540); 2 Petirat Mosheh 382; ARN 156 (read line 10, bottom, בסתרקי של מילח); Targum Yerushalmi Deut. 34.6 which reads: Michael and Gabriel arranged Moses' couch, while Metatron, Yofiel, and Yefifiyyah placed him upon it; quotation from Midrash in Hadassi's *Eshkol*, 137a, 364. On the various elements of this legend, see vol. I, pp. 149–150; vol. II, p. 316; note 132 on vol. II, pp. 321–322; vol. III. pp. 436 and 445, as well as note 12 on vol. IV, pp. 242–243. It is noteworthy that Targum Yerushalmi follows on the whole the midrashic description of the last act in the life of Moses, whereas on Deut. 32.49–52 it gives an independent Haggadah concerning Moses' reluctance to submit to death. In this passage we read: When Moses was commanded by God to ascend unto mount Abarim, he greatly rejoiced, thinking that he was going to receive there revelations as on mount Sinai, and he made himself ready to prepare the people for the new revelations. God, however, did not permit him to retain his illusions very long, and explained to him that the purpose of his ascending unto mount Abarim was to die there. Moses thereupon began his supplications that he might be permitted to enter the Holy land. A similar Haggadah is also found in 2 Petirat Mosheh 378, which is probably dependent on Targum Yerushalmi, since it fits rather badly in the description of Moses' last days as given in this Midrash.

⁹⁴⁹ DR 11.5; 2 Petirat Mosheh 383; *Likkutim*, V, 169b; Midrash Tannaim 225; comp. note 946 (towards the end).

⁹⁵⁰ Baba Batra 17a; DR 11 (end); Petirat Mosheh 129; 2 Petirat Mosheh 383. As to "the death by a kiss", see vol. III, pp. 326 and 330. According to Baba Batra, *loc. cit.*, this kind of death differs from all others because it is not caused by the Angel of Death, and hence it is a privilege granted only to a very few people. A rationalistic view is given in Sifre D., 357, and Midrash Tannaim 225–226, according to which it means no more than a painless death.

⁹⁵¹ Sifre D., 357; Midrash Tannaim 224; Sotah 13b. In all these three sources it is given as the opinion of "some who maintain that Moses did not die, but continues to administer above". This view was known to Josephus, *Antiqui.*, IV, 8.48, who emphasizes the fact that Moses wrote in the holy book that he died (as to the question whether the narrative concerning the death and burial of Moses was written by himself or by Joshua, see Baba Batra 15a, where different opinions of the Tannaim are recorded; see also Philo, *Vita Mosis*, 2.39) out of fear

lest they should venture to say (comp. vol. III, p. 327, with regard
to Aaron) that because of his extraordinary virtue he went to God.
Comp. note 904 and note 58, towards the end, on vol. I, p. 127.   Philo
though insisting on the literal meaning of the biblical narrative concerning Moses' death and burial (see Moses 2[3], end), also seems to
have been acquainted with the view that Moses ascended to heaven;
see *De Sacrif. Abeli*, 3.   Comp. also the following note and note 25,
towards the end, on vol. I, p. 317.

⁹⁵² Sifre D., 357; Midrash Tannaim 224; Sotah 14a; Tan. B. V.
132 (where it is stated that the graves of the three patriarchs are on
Mount Nebo; on the identification of Mount Nebo with Mount Abarim,
see vol. III, p. 444); Berakot 18b, which reads: God said to Moses
before his death: "Go to Abraham, Isaac and Jacob, and inform them
that I have fulfilled my promise made unto them to give the
Holy Land to their descendants."—God himself buried Moses;
Sanhedrin 39a; ps.-Philo, 19; 20D. According to other authorities,
Moses buried himself; see Sifre N., 32; BaR 10.17; Septuagint Deut.
34.6. A third view is that of Philo, *Moses*, 2(3), end, according to which
he was buried by celestial beings.   The following legend of the Falashas,
partly found also in Mohammedan literature, is an attempt to explain,
at full length, the manner in which Moses buried himself.   Moses,
so the legend runs, adjured God by His Name to indicate to him the
day of his death.   God informed him that he would die on a Friday
(this is in accordance with Seder 'Olam 10; comp. Ratner's note 11).
Accordingly, Moses put on his shrouds every Friday and waited
for the Angel of Death.   But many years elapsed, and the Angel of
Death did not appear to Moses, who thus entirely forgot the information
imparted to him concerning his last day.   One Friday while praying on
mount Sinai, Moses was startled by the words of greeting addressed to
him by a youth.   The youth's voice sounded very strange, and in
great fear he asked him who he was.   The youth introduced himself
as Suriel, the Angel of Death, and told him that he had come to take his
life.   Moses asked him for a few hours' grace to enable him to take
leave of those who were near and dear to him.   This request was
granted by Suriel.   Descending from the mountain, Moses hesitated
in his walk, as he did not know whether to go first to his mother (comp.
vol. III, p. 474), or to his wife.   A heavenly voice was heard, saying:
"To thy mother."   Having bidden farewell to his mother, he betook
himself to his wife and sons.   The latter wept so bitterly that heaven
and earth, as well as Moses himself, could not refrain from weeping

with them. God asked Moses: "Weepest thou because thou art re-
luctant to depart from the earth or because thou fearest death?"
Moses replied: "My father-in-law Jethro is dead, and so is my brother
Aaron; who then will take care of my widow and children?" But
God reminded him of the care He had taken of him when thrown into
the water by his mother. Just as He provided for him, even so will
He not fail to provide for those left behind. God then commanded
Moses to divide the Red Sea with his rod. Moses did as he was bidden,
and a stone rolled out of the depth of the sea. He then cleft the stone,
wherein two worms, a big one and a small one were found. The latter
spoke, saying: "Praised be God who forgot me not in the depth of the
sea." Turning to Moses God said: "I did not forget the small worm
in the depth of the sea; how then couldst thou think that I would forget
thy children?" Whereupon Moses left his house, not knowing whither
to turn. On the way he met three angels (comp. vol. III, pp. 471–
472), who assumed the appearance of three young men, busying themselves with the digging of a grave, "For whom is the grave?", asked
Moses. "For the beloved of God", was the reply. "If so", said Moses,
"I will assist you in your work." The angels rejoined: "We know
not whether the grave is big enough. Wouldst thou go down into it?
The person to be buried therein is of thy size." As soon as Moses
descended into the grave, he was met there by the Angel of Death,
who greeted him with the words: "Peace unto thee, O Moses the son
of Amram!" Moses replied: "Peace be with thee"—and he died.
The angels then buried him in the grave in which he met death. See
Faitlovitch, *Mota Musa*, 9–20; Arabic text, *ibid.*, 29–21; 36–37. Comp.
also Grünbaum, *Neue Beiträge*, 183. The legend concerning the death
of David, as given in vol. IV, pp. 113–114, shows many points of
similarity to this legend. The legend concerning the death and burial
of Solomon in *Rev. d. Trad. Pop.* II, 513 is almost identical with this
Moses legend. See also *Weil, Bible Leg.* 142. On Suriel, see Index, s. v.
Moses' grave was created in the twilight between the sixth day of creation and the first Sabbath (see Abot 5.6, and the references given in note
99 on vol. I, p. 38), and although its location is accurately described in
the Bible (Deut. 34.6), no one was ever able to find it. The Roman government attempted once to establish the exact spot, but failed. To the
officers looking at the grave from the mountain it appeared to be in the
valley; to those in the valley it appeared to be on the mountain. See Sifre
D., 359; Midrash Tannaim 226; Sotah 14a. Comp. also Josephus,
Antiqui., IV, 8.48, which reads: And as he was going to embrace Ele-

azar and Joshua... a cloud stood over him on the sudden, and he disappeared in a certain valley. The quotations from a lost version of the Assumption of Moses (comp. Origen, *In Josuam*, homily 2.1, Lommatzsch's edition 11.22, and references in note 946) speak of Joshua and Caleb as having been present at "the disappearance of Moses"; Caleb believed that he saw Moses' grave in the valley, whereas Joshua saw him ascend into heaven; the former saw Moses' body, the latter beheld his spirit. Concerning the visions seen by Joshua and Caleb at the moment of Moses' death, comp. the description of the vision of Seth at Adam's death as given in the Apocalypse of Moses. See vol. I, pp. 99–101. That a cloud came down and separated Moses from Joshua is also stated in Midrash Tannaim 225. The grave of Moses was concealed from the eye of man, so that the Hebrews should not turn it into a sanctuary and the Gentiles into an idolatrous place of worship; see Lekah Deut. 34.6. A similar view is expressed by the Christian authors Aphraates, 162; Origen, *Selecta in Num.* Migne's edition. 12, 578B; Theodoretus, *Interr.* 43, Deut. For further details concerning the grave of Moses, see vol. III, p. 125, as well as note 274.

953 Sifre D., 357; Midrash Tannaim 227. Comp. Geiger, Kebuzzat Maamarim 44, and Ginzberg in Geiger, *op.cit.* 383; Lekah Deut 34.7 reads: Moses received six distinctions which were not granted to any one else: His voice could be heard through the entire camp (comp. note 210); he looked at the entire extent of the Holy Land with one glance (comp. vol. III, p. 433); God spoke to him face to face (on this point see DZ 10, which reads: God fulfilled all the wishes of Moses, including the request to "see the glory of God", which was granted to him at the time of his death; comp. vol. III, 137); there never arose a prophet in Israel equal to him (on Moses' superiority to the Messiah, see note 836); his eye became not dim when he died, his countenance forever retained the brightness it received on mount Sinai (comp. vol. III, pp. 93 and 119), so that he appeared as though he had been administering before the living God. On the last point, see also ps.-Philo, 19.20D, who remarks: And his likeness was changed gloriously, and he died in glory.

954 Sifre D., 357; Midrash Tannaim 227; Josephus, *Antiqui.*, IV, 8.3 and 48–49; Philo *Moses*, 2(3), end. For a different view concerning the mourning for Moses, see BR 100.4; vol. III, p. 328.

955 Tan. B. IV, 13; Tan. Wa-Ethanan 6; quotation from Tan. in Makiri, Ps. 12.71; ARN 156; DR (end); Sotah 13b and 14a, as well as Yerushalmi 1 (end); Sifre D., 355, 357; Midrash Tannaim 219, 224; Tosefta Sotah 4.8–9; Petirat Mosheh 129; 2 Petirat Mosheh 383.

Ps.-Philo, 19.20D, strongly emphasizes the fact that the angels mourned for Moses. He writes as follows: And the angels lamented at his death... and on that day the hymn of the hosts was not chanted (comp. vol. I, pp. 17–18) because of the departure of Moses. Neither was there a day like unto it . . neither shall there be any such for ever, that He should make the hymn of the angels to cease because of a man. The last words perhaps indicate that on another occasion God made the hymn of the angels to cease, but not on account of the mourning for "a man", but on account of the Temple. See vol. VI, p. 397, note 32. On the mourning of the angels for Moses, see also vol. III, pp. 460–461; ARN 25.51. On the view that by the death of Moses the Israelites lost the intermediary between them and God, see also ps-Philo, 19.3; 19A. Comp. note 248. See Krauss in *Ha-Goren* VII, 29 with regard to the statement, found in Sifre, *loc. cit.*, and parallel passages that the angel Semalion announced the death of Moses with the words: "The great scribe is dead." Comp. also note 66 on vol. II, p. 275.

⁹⁵⁶ Piyyut אזלת יוכבד in the Italian Mahzor for the Rejoicing of the Law, which is undoubtedly based upon an unknown version of Petirat Mosheh. See the quotation given by Epstein, *Mikkadmoniyyot*, 128, from a work by R. Eleazar Ashkenazi. Jochebed's futile search for Moses is a doublet to Sammael's futile search; see vol. III, pp. 475, *seq.*

⁹⁵⁷ Midrash Tannaim 225; ARN 12.51 and 57; Sifre D., 305. Comp. also ps.-Philo 20.2; 20D, who remarks: Then said God unto Joshua: "Wherefore mournest thou, and wherefore hopest thou in vain, thinking that Moses shall yet live? Now therefore thou waitest to no purpose, for Moses is dead."

⁹⁵⁸ ARN 156–157 (in line 8 of p. 157 read: אצל עץ החיים instead of אצל היים); Manzur 19. The old sources (Sifre D., 305; Midrash Tannaim 224–225; ARN 12, 50–51, and second version 26, 52) give this legend in a very abridged form. On the Holy Land as "the land of the living", see Ketubot 111a. On the dividing of the sea, see vol. III, p. 22. Concerning the idea that Pharaoh is keeping guard at the gate of Hell, see vol. III, p. 30. On the sons of Korah who dwell within the abyss, see vol. III, pp. 300 and 302. Concerning Moses' visit to paradise, see vol. II, p. 210; on his staff (=rod), see vol. II, p. 291, where a different story is told, according to which a branch from a tree in paradise became the rod of Moses. On the reed used by Moses in writing the Torah, see note 99 on vol. I, p. 83. Comp. Nispahim 28–29.

⁹⁵⁹ Tan. B. III, 29; IV, 46–47. Concerning the animate and in-

animate things pointed out by God to Moses , see Buber's note to Tan., as well as note 202 on vol. II, p. 362.

⁹⁶⁰ ARN 157 (in this passage it is very likely supposed that Moses did not die, but was translated to heaven; see note 951); Manzur 19; Midrash Tannaim 225; ARN 20, 50, and second version 25.52.

⁹⁶¹ 3 Petirat Mosheh 71, *seq.* Comp. the references given in the following note. Josephus, *Antiqui.*, IV, 8.49. writes: He (Moses) excelled all men that ever were in understanding, and made the best use of what that understanding suggested to him. Philo likewise (*Moses*, 1, beginning) describes Moses as the greatest and most perfect of all men. The rabbinic sources, however, place the three patriarchs higher than Moses; see notes 490 and 836.

⁹⁶² Quotation from Tan. (Yelammedenu?) in Makiri, Prov. 31,29, and Ps. 49, 270; 68, 330; DR 11.3 (on the text see *Hadar*, Deut., end); DZ 9; *Likkutim* V, 166b–167a. On Adam, see vol. I, p. 86; on the view that Isaac's loss of eyesight was caused by his having looked at the Shekinah, see vol. I, pp. 328–329; on Moses' victory over the angels, see vol. III, p. 109. Concerning Moses' superiority to all other pious and righteous men, see vol. III, pp. 423–424, and note 961.

⁹⁶³ 3 Petirat Mosheh 72. Comp. vol. II, p. 416.

⁹⁶⁴ 3 Petirat Mosheh 72–73. On the view that Abraham was the cause of Israel's bondage in Egypt, see note 110 on vol. I, p. 235. On the flight of the angels at beholding Moses in heaven, see vol. III, p. 110. Concerning the celestial light that shone for the Israelites during their wandering through the wilderness, see vol. II, p. 37; vol. III, p. 331.

⁹⁶⁵ DR 11.4; PK 32, 198b; Tehillim 90, 388. In the text the literal translation of the Hebrew is given. The purport of the passage in a less literal but more accurate form is: Moses was half terrestrial, half celestial. The sources just quoted contain several other explanations of the designation of Moses as איש אלהים ordinarily translated "a man of God". According to the Haggadah, it means "master of the angels" (comp. note 962); "master of God" (God was willing to do the bidding of Moses); "master of justice", since the principle of Moses was that justice be done, even "if mountains have to be bored through." Comp. note 877. Philo, like the Rabbis, gives many explanations of the expression "man of God"; comp. *De Mut. Nom.* 3. 22 (this agrees literally with the explanation given in Tehillim, *loc. cit.*); 2 *De Somniis* 35–36 (which reads: "The perfect man is neither God nor man, but something between the uncreated—God— and the perishable

nature); *Quod Omnis Probus Liber*, 7 (which reads: The man who is wholly possessed of the love of God..is no longer a man, but actually—God). Comp. also Aristeas 140. According to *Imre No'am*, Naso (end), Moses' importance was as great as that of the Cherubim. As to those whom Scripture calls "man of God", see Sifre D., 342; Midrash Tannaim 208; ARN 37.95, where the following are enumerated: Moses, Elkanah, Samuel, David, Iddo, Shemaiah, Elijah, Elisha, Micaiah, and Amos. With the exception of Elkanah, all these personages are described as "men of God" in the Bible. On Elkanah, see note 28 on vol. IV, p. 61.

⁹⁶⁶ DR, end, and 3, end, with the addition that God promised Moses to send him, together with Elijah, at the end of the days. Messianic activity in co-operation with Elijah or the Messiah, is ascribed to Moses in Sifre D 355; Targum Yerushalmi Deut. 33.21; Aggadat Bereshit 67, 133 (see note 930); Midrash Tannaim 219. Comp. also vol. II, pp. 302, 315, 373; vol. III, pp. 35, 312; Sanhedrin 92a. In Mahzor Vitry 164 it is said that Moses will be the cupbearer at the messianic banquet. Moses, who was one hundred and twenty years old at the time of his demise, lived less years than any of the patriarchs, from Adam until his own times, with the exception of Joseph, who died at the age of one hundred and ten years. The reason for the premature death of these two righteous men (on Joseph comp. vol. II, p. 221) is as follows: "Long life" is promised in the Torah as a reward for studying the Torah and for honoring parents (see Deut. 5.16 and 30.20). Men would be inclined to believe that a long "terrestrial life" is meant by this promise. This is, of course, not the case, as the reward promised is eternal life in the world to come. Therefore Moses, who more than any other man devoted himself to the study of the Torah, and Joseph, who distinguished himself greatly by honoring his father, died at an early age. It thus becomes clear that the reward for good deeds does not consist in temporal things. See Hasidim, 225, which is partly based on Kiddushin 39b. On the day of Moses' death see Wistinetzki's note on Hasidim, *loc. cit.*, and Ratner's note 11 on *Seder 'Olam* 10. All opinions agree that he died in the month of Adar (Seder 'Olam, *loc. cit.*, Kiddushin 38a, and many parallel passages cited by Ratner). With the exception of Josephus, all authorities are also unanimous that it was on the seventh of that month. Josephus is of the opinion that it was on the first of that month. The authorities, however, differ greatly as to the day of the week on which Moses died. Sunday, Wednesday, Friday, and Saturday compete for the distinction of being the day on which Moses died. The prevalent opinion among the post-

talmudic authorities is that Moses (like Joseph and David) died on Sabbath afternoon. On the day of Moses' birth, see note 44 on vol. III, p. 264. Moses' reward for interceding for the Israelites and saving them from destruction (see note 284 and vol. III, p. 435 toward end) consists in the fact that Scripture speaks of him as though he had created Israel; ER 4.19. Comp. note 70 on vol. II, p. 278 and note 259.

I. JOSHUA.

Vol. IV, (pp. 1-17).

[1] Esther R., introduction; Abba Gorion 2.

[2] *Rab Pe'alim*, 12a, giving as source a Midrash quoted by the Kabbalist R. Nathan (*i. e.*, R. Nathan Shapiro, author of מגלה עמוקות), but the published writings of this Kabbalist do not to my knowledge contain this form of the Oedipus legend, nor is it found in any other Jewish source. The reference to ס' מעשיות of R. Nissim Gaon by the editor of *Rab Pe'alim* is a poor guess, as this narrative does not occur in that book. The name of Joshua's father, Nun, "fish", is hardly sufficient to account for this legend, though it is given as an explanation thereof. With regard to Joshua's parents, the above-cited source relates the following details: They were very pious, but for a long time they were not blessed with children. After many prayers and supplications, Nun's wife became pregnant. But instead of rejoicing at the approaching fulfilment of his great desire, Nun kept on weeping and lamenting day and night. Pressed by his wife to explain his strange behavior, he informed her of the revelation made to him from heaven that his own child would cut his head off .To prevent this, Joshua's mother exposed him immediately after his birth. The infant was swallowed by a whale and subsequently carried out what heaven had decreed against his father. The insultihg name hurled at Joshua by the spies (comp. note 526 on vol. III, p. 272) was "cutter of heads", alluding to his having been the official executioner, and as such having cut off his father's head. Very strange is the statement that Joshua's father lived in Jerusalem; yet the king who had him executed (read קוסטינר "quaestionarius", instead of סנדטור) is described as king of Egypt. On the view that Palestine was an Egyptian dependency in pre-Mosaic times; see note 10 on vol. III, 8. Comp. note 33.

[3] Yelammedenu in Yalkut II, 959 on Prov. 21 (towards the end) Midrash Tannaim 227; Alphabet R. Akiba II, 16; 2 ARN 11, 28 and 18.39; *Likkutim*, IV, 76b, and V, 106a. Comp. vol. III, pp. 398–399. The Kabbalists describe the charms applied by Moses for the strengthening of Joshua's intellect; comp., *e. g.*, Raziel (ס'המזלות), 31a.

[4] Mekilta Amalek 1, 55a. Friedmann, *ad loc.*, calls attention to the view of several Tannaim, according to which the war against

Amalek took place towards the end of Israel's journey through the wilderness, when it was decreed that Moses should not enter the Holy Land.

⁵ Zohar II, 66a; comp. PK 3, 22a; Luria's note 28 on PRE 44; note 144 on vol. III, p. 60.

⁶ Sifre N., 140; Baba Batra 75a; Zohar 114b; vol. III, pp. 400, 441. The metaphorical description of Joshua as the moon gave rise to the popular belief, common among Jews of Eastern Europe, that Joshua is the man in the moon; comp. Perez, *Schriften* III, 75 (English translation 155) Mandllin *Urquell* IV, 122; Dähnhard, *Natursagen*, I. 319. On the legend concerning the plant Arum (= Aaron's rod) discussed by Dähnhardt, *loc. cit.*, see vol. III, p. 269, according to which Moses gave the spies his rod to protect them against the attacks of the Canaanites (the legend very frequently confuses, or identifies, the rod of Moses with that of Aaron; see Index, s. v. "Aaron, Rod of"). On the man in the moon, see note 35 on vol. I, p. 317, and Index, s. v.

⁷ Temurah 16a; comp. vol. III, pp. 451–452; vol. IV, p. 29. Joshua is the ideal type of the "disciple of the wise", and hence the talmudic phrase "even if Joshua the son of Nun had told me, etc." Comp. Hullin 124a; Yebamot 45a; Berakot 24b (comp. the reading given by Rabinovicz, note 50); Yerushalmi Yebamot 4,6a, where שקול כמשה is perhaps to be read instead of קשור למשה; Epstein, Eldad. 88. See also Yerushalmi Peah 1, 15a, which reads: Joshua by means of deep reasoning succeeded in establishing laws which were revealed to Moses on Sinai.

⁸ Temurah 16a. The revelation of the Torah to Moses was final and could not be abrogated nor altered by the prophets who succeeded him; comp. Chajes, *Torat Nebiim, passim.* See further note 97 on vol. IV, p. 40; note 42 on p. 64 and note 13 on p. 197.

⁹ BR 6.9. On the designation of Deuteronomy as "the book of the Law" ספר התורה, see Ginzberg, *R.E.J.*, LXVII, 135 (= *Compte Rendu* 21). On Joshua as the ideal type of the scholar, see note 7. According to ps.-Philo, 20; 20D, God spoke to Joshua after the death of Moses, saying: "take the garments of his wisdom (those worn by Moses?) and put them on thee, and gird thy loins with the girdle of his knowledge; then shalt thou be changed and become another man." And it came to pass when he put them on, that his mind was kindled, and his spirit was stirred up. Of a famous teacher of the Mishnah it is said that he ascribed his learning to the fact that he used a staff

which belonged to the great master R. Meir; see Yerushalmi Nedarim 9, 41b and comp. 1 Kings 19.19–20.

¹⁰ Tan. B. IV, 62; Tan. Shelah 1; BaR 16.1. According to another opinion, the spies were Perez and Zerah, the sons of Judah; comp. vol. II, pp. 36–39. Ps-Philo 20, 21, is of the opinion that the two spies were Kenaz and Seenamias (the Hebrew original had either שמע or משע; comp. 1 Chron. 2.42 and 43), the two sons of Caleb, whom Joshua admonished "to do like unto their father", and not to follow the example of the other spies, who slandered the Holy Land.

¹¹ *Kinat Setarim* 31c and 44d. Owing to the ambiguity of the word חרש in Josh. 2.1, the opinions in the Midrashim differ as to how the spies succeeded in avoiding the suspicion of the inhabitants of Jericho. According to some, the spies pretended to be deaf and dumb (חָרָשׁ is reads as חָרָשׁ), while others say that they disguised themselves as merchants of pottery (חרש is read as חרס); still others say that they were disguised as carpenters (חרש is read as חָרָשׁ); comp. Sifre Z., 74; Ruth R. 1.1; Tan. B. IV, 62; Tan. Shelah 1; BaR 16.1; Yelammedenu in 'Aruk, s. v. חרס; *Likkutim* IV, 27a

¹² Sifre N., 78; Sifre Z., 75; BaR 8 (end); Megillah 14b; EZ 22, 37 (here it is said that Rahab's descendants were seven kings and eight prophets); PR 40, 167b; Midrash Aggada Num. 167 (below). Comp. vol. III, p. 443; vol. IV, p. 282. The eight prophets and priests are: Jeremiah and his father Hilkiah, Seraiah and his grandfather Mahseiah (Jer. 51.59), Baruch and his father Neriah, as well as Hananel and Shallum, Jeremiah's cousin, or according to some (comp. Rashi and Kimhi on Jerem. 32.12) his uncle. According to some authorities, Ezekiel and his father Buzi (who, too, was a prophet) were likewise descendants of Rahab. As to the immoral life led by Rahab until the time of her conversion, see, in addition to the sources cited above, also Mekilta Yitro 57a; Mekilta RS, 85; Zebahim 116b. In the last passage it is asserted that she led an immoral life from the age of ten years until fifty. The legend paints Rahab in very black colors to bring out the effect of repentance; but it has in Josh. 2.1 biblical authority for that. It is true that Josephus, *Antiqui.*, V. 1.2, and Targum *ad loc.* interpret זונה to mean "keeper of an inn" (from זן "he fed"), but comp. Kimhi, a d *loc.*, and Büchler, *Priester und Cultus*, 63–64 who call attention to the identity of פונדקיתא with זונה; comp. note 106 on vol. IV, 43.

¹³ Tan. B. IV, 62; Tan. Shelah 1; BaR 16.1; WR 1.1. As to the

miracle of becoming invisible, see also vol. II, p. 261, vol. IV, pp. 25, 391. The medieval legends frequently allude to the miracle of invisibility, and know of the charms which render one invisible; see Raziel, at the end of ד ואחר. The Christian legends are also acquainted with this idea; comp. *Acts of Matthew*, towards the middle; see Index, s. v. "Invisibility".

14 Sotah Tosefta 8.1–4; Babli 33b–34a; Yerushalmi 7, 21d–22a; comp. vol. III, p. 400. The division of the waters of the Jordan is said to have taken place as a reward for the good deeds of Abraham (Yelammedenu in Yalkut II, 15); according to others, for the good deeds of Jacob (BR 76.5; Shir 4.4; comp. Vol. V, p. 275). Still others think that it was on account of Joseph (comp. vol. II, p. 3, bottom).

15 Sotah, Mishnah 7.5; Tosefta 8.5–11; Babli 34a, 35b–37b; Yerushalmi 7, 22a; Seder 'Olam 9; Sifre D., 55–57; Midrash Tannaim 56, 57–58; Mekilta Deut., 189–190 (line 5 read ובסדרים instead of ובסתרים, and comp. Mekilta Bahodesh 2, 62b, top as well as Seder 'Olam, *loc. cit.*; כה כסדר means "in proper order"); Targum Yerushalmi Deut. 27.9 and 25. According to Josephus, *Antiqui.*, V, 1.19, the ceremonies on the mountains Gerizim and Ebal took place after the conquest of the Holy Land, and not on entering it. R. Ishmael (Midrash Tannaim 58) is of the same view. On the miracle that the narrow space contained all the people, see BR 5.7, and parallel passages cited by Theodor as well as vol. III, p. 180. On the ark moving by itself, see ShR 36.4; BaR 4.20 (27b); vol. III, p. 395. As to what part of the Torah was written upon the stones, see Mekilta Deut., *loc cit.*; Ginzberg, *R.E.J.*, LXVII, 35 (= *Compte Rendu* 21); vol. III, pp. 350–351, note 9. As to the conditions under which Israel was willing to refrain from attacking the heathens, see vol. IV, p. 9.

16 Yebamot 71b–72a; Midrash Shir 15a–15b; Shir 4.6. See also Midrash Aggada Gen. 17.8, which reads: Israel would never have been able to enter the Holy Land, had not Joshua circumcised those born in the wilderness, since this land was promised the patriarchs on the condition that their descendans would observe the rite of circumcision; comp. BR 46.9; vol. III, p. 282; note 196 on vol. II, p. 358. The statement of Josephus, *Antiqui.*, V, 1.11 that Gilgal means "liberty" is a haggadic rendering of Josh. 5.9, and perhaps presupposes the view quoted above that by performing the rite of circumcision at that place they definitely won their liberty.

17 Tosefta Sotah 11.2 (the manna which came down on the last day sufficed them for the following thirty-nine days); Seder 'Olam

10; Mekilta Wa-Yassa' 5, 51b (where different views are given as to how long they ate manna after the death of Moses; one authority is quoted to the effect that the last manna sufficed them for "the fourteen years of the conquest and the dividing of the Holy Land"); Kiddushin 38a. An allegorical explanation of Josh. 1.11 is found in ER 18, 101, and reads as follows: Joshua's command to Israel to prepare victuals did not refer to the preparation of food to eat (for there was no need for that as long as the manna came down); but he urged them to prepare spiritual food, to repent from their sins, that they might be found worthy to enter the Holy Land. Here is presupposed that the manna continued to come down after the death of Moses, and only ceased after they had crossed the Jordan. Comp. vol. III, p. 41, which gives a similar legend concerning the bread which the Israelites took with them from Egypt. That the manna was given to Israel as a reward for the good deeds of Moses is a widespread haggadah, comp. ps–Philo, 21A (end); vol. III, pp. 48–49 and 246.

¹⁸ ER 18, 101–102.

¹⁹ 'Erubin 63b, and parallel passages on the margin; Aggadat Esther 80. In these sources Joshua is further reproached for having kept the warriors in camp (separated from their wives) when there was no need for it. Comp. note 526 on vol. III, p. 273; Yerushalmi Ketubot 5, 30a–30b. Joshua is also blamed for having married Rahab (comp. vol. IV, p. 5), and for not having prayed to God on entering the Holy Land to have the "evil inclination removed from Israel"; see *Pa'aneah*, Haazinu (end). Comp. Index, s. v. "Joshua".

²⁰ BR 97.3; Tan. B. II, 87; Tan. Mishpatim 18; Aggadat Bereshit 32, 64–65. On the view that Moses refused the help of an angel and insisted on God's direct guidance for Israel, see also Midrash Tannaim 222; ShR 32.3–8; Tehillim 90, 390; Philo, *Quaestiones*, Exod. II, 13; vol. III; pp. 131–132 and 347.

²¹ Aggadat Bereshit 32.64; Zerubbabel (Jellinek's edition, 55; Wertheimer's edition, 10); R. Hananel as quoted by R. Bahya, Exod. 23.20; Lekah and Midrash Aggada on Exod. *loc. cit.*; BR 97.3, where the text is to be emended in accordance with ShR 2.5. That the angel who appeared to Joshua was Michael is also asserted by Aphraates, 57. In Tan. B. I. 17, Michael is declared to be the "angel of the face", whereas in Sanhedrin 38b the angel whose services Moses refused, and who is none other than the "angel of the face" (comp. Tan. Mishpatim 18), is identified with Metatron. The identity of Michael with Metatron in Zerubbabel, *loc. cit.*, is due to an attempt at harmoni-

zation. Comp. Index, s. v. "Angel of the Face", "Michael", "Metatron".
²² Tan. B. IV, 42; Tan. Naso 28; BaR 14.1. That the fall
of Jericho took place on the Sabbath is frequently stated in rabbinic
literature; comp. Seder 'Olam 11; Yerushalmi Shabbat 1, 4a–4b;
BR 47.9 and 70.15; Tan. B. IV, 9 and 163; Tan. Bemidbar 9 and Mass'e
5; BaR 2.9 and 23.6. Among the Church Fathers it is Tertullian who
attempts at great length to explain this desecration of the Sabbath
by Joshua; comp. *Adversus Marc.*, 2.21 and 12. In *Adversus Judaeos*,
4, the abrogation of the Mosaic law is argued from this incident and
this is a further proof that this work is wrongly ascribed to Tertullian.
It is very likely that this Christian (and Karaitic; comp. Hadassi,
Eshkol, 45b) polemic prompted Sa'adya Gaon, *Emunot we-De' ot*, 3,
95, to assert that Jericho was not captured on the Sabbath. According
to a Midrash quoted by Sabba' Wa-Yehi, 59a–59d, Joshua would not
even allow the trumpets to be blown on the Sabbath (the production
of music on the Sabbath is forbidden by the Rabbis only; see Rosh
ha-Shanah 29b) before he heard the sounding of the heavenly trumpets.
Just as the first of all the products of the earth belong to the Lord,
even so did Joshua consecrate unto Him the first city conquered; comp.
the sources cited at the beginning of this note. See also note 648
on vol. III, p. 33; Josephus, *Antiqui.*, V, 1.15. The statement of
Josephus that Jericho fell on the seventh day of Passover is not in
agreement with the view of the Rabbis, according to whom this event
took place after the festival; see Seder 'Olam 11.—Not only Rahab
and the members of her family escaped the fate of the inhabitants of
Jericho, but all the families allied to her by marriage; Yerushalmi Berakot
4, 8, Sanhedrin 10, 28c; BR 1.1; Koheleth 5.6; Ruth R. 1.1. Israel
was forced to spare the lives of all those inhabitants of Jericho in comp-
liance with the oath given by the two spies to Rahab. However,
there was no justification for the spies to grant Rahab's request, and as a
punishment for this it was a descendant of Rahab, the prophet Jeremiah
(see note 12), who was charged to prophesy about the destruction of
the Temple and the exile of Israel; PK 13.112a; Ekah Z., 75. According to some authorities, Rahab did not belong to one of the "seven
nations", whose extermination God had commanded. The spies were
therefore justified in granting her request; comp. Tosafot Megillah
14b (bottom); Kimhi, Josh. 6.25; Halakot Gedolot (Venice edition,
108b; Hildesheimer's edition, 443). In the last-named source רוסתקיאתא
means "foreigner" (=*rustica?*) and not farmer, as maintained by
Perles, *Etymologische Studien*, 84. Another view is also quoted in To-

safot to the effect that since Rahab had adopted Judaism before
the Israelites entered the Holy Land, the laws relating to the "seven
nations" did not apply to her; comp. however Sifre N., 78; Sifre Z., 75.
The victory over Jericho was of very great importance, as the inhabitants of that city were valiant warriors, so that Israel's first victory
equalled all the later victories put together (Sifre D., 52, and Midrash
Tannaim 45) which were won by an army of seventy thousand Jewish
warriors; Shir 6.4. Comp. also Josephus, V. 125. The great miracle
which happened at Jericho was not that the walls fell, but that they
disappeared in the bowels of the earth; Berakot 54a, 54b; Targum
Joshua 6.20.

²³ WR 11.7; Baba Batra 121b; Yerushalmi Sotah 7, 22a (top);
Alphabet of Ben Sira 2a-2b. In the last source it is said that when
Abraham journeyed in Ai it was announced to him that all his descendants, with the exception of one (Jair), would fall in the battle of Ai.
He then prayed that this misfortune should be averted from Israel,
and his prayer was granted. In the battle of Ai the Jewish army suffered only one casualty, the death of Jair. A somewhat different version
of this legend is found in BR 39.16, and Sanhedrin 44b. The prominence of those slain at Ai is also emphasized by Josephus, *Antiqui.*,
V, 1.12. Joshua is responsible for this defeat, because he remained in
camp and did not march at the head of the army as he had been commanded by God. Comp. vol. III, p. 397. Others say that Joshua's sin
which caused this defeat consisted in his having delayed to erect the stones
and write the Torah upon them. Instead of doing so immediately after
the crossing of the Jordan, he waited till he was sixty miles away from
the river. Another opinion blames Joshua for having declared Jericho
devoted to the Lord and thereby led the Israelites to temptation; comp.
Sifre D., 29; Mekilta RS, 26; ER 18, 102; Sanhedrin 44a; vol. IV, p. 6. On
Jair, comp. 2 Alphabet of Ben Sira 27a, where it is said that he declared
the raven (=עורב =ע, the first letter of ע'‎, Ai) clean, but the dove (=יונה
=י, the second letter of ע'‎, Ai) unclean. This wishes to convey that he
was of such a keen mind that he could by clever dialectics demonstrate
the exact oposite of the law; comp. Sanhedrin 17a-17b, and 101a (top).

²⁴ Sanhedrin 43b; Yerushalmi 6, 23b; BR 85 (end); Tan.
B. IV, 163; Tan. Mass'e 5; BaR 23.6.

²⁵ Sanhedrin 44a; Tan. B. IV, 163; Tan. Mass'e 5; BaR 23.6.
The crime of which he is accused are: unchastity with a betrothed
woman, desecration of the Sabbath, and *epispasmos.*

²⁶ Sanhedrin 43b (below); Shebuot 39a (this is the *locus classicus*

of the statement that all Jews are responsible for one another); Yerushalmi Sotah 7.22 (top). Comp. also WR 1.10, and Shir 2.3. That Achan stole an idol is asserted in PRE 38 and Tan. Wa-Yesheb 2. Comp. note 33.

²⁷ Sanhedrin 43b, and Yerushalmi 6, 23b; ER 18, 102. Joshua's prayer and God's reply to it (Josh. 7, *seq.*) are embellished with many additional passages in the Haggadah; comp. Sanhedrin 44a; Yerushalmi Ta'anit 1, 65d; Tan. B. IV, 163; Tan. Mass'e 5; BaR 23.6; ER, *loc. cit.*; Josephus, *Antiqui.*, V, 1.13. The Rabbis, as well as Josephus, emphasize the fact that "Joshua used freedom with God". See also ps.–Philo, 21B.

²⁸ PRE 38; Tan. Wa-Yesheb 2; comp. vol. III, 455, and vol. IV, p. 566. An unknown Midrash quoted by Kimhi on Josh. 8.3, reads: Joshua caused the people to pass before the ark; the sinners remained rooted to the soil, without being able to move a step; comp. vol. IV, p. 111 (top) and note 861 on vol. III, p. 413.

²⁹ Sanhedrin 43b, and Yerushalmi 6, 23b; Tan. B. IV, 163; Tan. Mass'e 5; BaR 23.6; ER 18, 102.

³⁰ Tan. B. IV, 163; Tan. Mass'e 5; BaR 23.6.

³¹ Sanhedrin Mishnah 6.2; Tosefta 9.5; Yerushalmi 6, 23b; PRE 38; Tan. Wa-Yesheb 2. Comp. ARN 45, 126, which reads: Three men, by their confessions, lost this world, and gained the world to come: the gatherer of wood on the Sabbath (comp. vol. III, p. 240); the blasphemer (comp. vol. III, p. 239–240); Achan. See further WR 9.1. That Achan by his confession gained the world to come is also presupposed in ps.–Philo, 25.7; see the quotation therefrom in vol. IV, p. 22 (top). On the question whether the members of his family were executed with him, as Scripture seems to indicate (comp. Josh. 8.24–25), or not, see Sanhedrin 44a; PRE *loc. cit.*; *Neweh Shalom* 75–76. According to the Talmud only Achan was executed, but his execution took place in the presence of the members of his family, and that is how Josh. 8.24 is to be understood. The Midrashim, on the other hand, maintain that, together with Achan, all the members of his family were executed, because they had not informed the authorities of the crime committed by him. The statement of Josephus, *Antiqui.*, V, 1.14, that Achan was buried at night in a disgraceful manner, suitable for a condemned criminal, is in harmony with the regulations concerning the burial of criminals described in Sanhedrin 6.5, and Babli 46b (top). According to Sanhedrin 44b and WR 9.1, this Achan is identical with Zimri mentioned in 2 Chron. 2.6, and the different names borne

by this sinner are explained haggadically. The derivation of the name
Achan, עָכָן, from עָכִינָא "serpent" (Greek ἐχῖνος) is also given by
ps.-Jerome on 2 Chron. 2.7.

³² On the reason for the defeat at Ai, see note 23.

³³ Yerushalmi Shebi'it 7, 36c; WR 17.6; DR 5.14. On foreign
kings who acquired possessions in Palestine, see also vol. III, pp. 443, 444.
In connection with the story of Achan this legend is employed to explain how it came about that he found in Jericho a Babylonian garment
(see Josh. 7.21). Comp. Sifre D., 37; BR 85 (end); Tan. Mishpatim
17 and Re'eh 8; Shir 8.11; Tan. B. II, 86–87, and IV, 86 (this is the
source of Makiri, Ps. 84.61); Yelammedenu (?) in Yalkut II, 271, on
Jer. 3; ShR 32.3; Tehillim 5, 51. Most of these sources state that
the Palestinian viceroy of the king of Babylon resided in Jericho.
The former used to send to his overlord Palestinian dates, in exchange
for which he would receive articles manufactured in Babylon, like
garments and similar things. It is hardly likely that the Haggadah
has preserved reminiscences of the time when Palestine stood in
political and commercial relations with Babylon, as maintained by
Jastrow, *Zeitschrift für Assyriologie*, VII, 1–7. On the relations of
Palestine with Egypt, according to the Haggadah, see note 2; note 12 on
vol. II, p. 251, and note 10 on vol. III, p. 8—The large number of kings in
such a small country as Palestine is explained by the Haggadah by
assuming that they were representatives of the foreign kings, who
were desirous of owning possessions in the Holy Land.

³⁴ Yerushalmi Shebi'it 7, 36c; WR 17.6; DR 5.14; BaR 17.3;
Mekilta Bo 18, 21b–22a; Tosefta Shabbat 7(8).25. In the tannaitic
sources it is the Canaanites, or, to be more accurate, the Amorites,
who emigrated to Africa, and this is very likely the haggadic way of
stating that the Phenicians (=כנען) founded Carthage in Africa. Procopius, II, 20, p. 135, and Suidas, s. v. χαναάν likewise report the
emigration of the Canaanites from Palestine at the time of Joshua, and
that on a pillar found in Tangiers, Africa, the following inscription was
engraved: "We are Canaanites who were driven out from our country by
the robber Joshua." Comp. Fabricius, *Codex Pseud. Vet. Test.*, 889–893
and Bacher, *J.Q.R.*, III, 354. On the designation of Joshua as "robber,"
comp. note 855 on vol. III, p. 411, where it is suggested that some read
Sanhedrin 10b ישוע ליסטאה "Joshua the robber." Tosefta Shabbat
7(8).23 records also a view very unfavorable to the Amorites who are
said to have been the "hardest people" on earth (*i. e.*, morally insensible)
so that even today the word "Amorite" is used to designate a "hard

person". Superstitious practices are designated in tannaitic, as well as in amoraic texts, as the "ways of the Amorites" (comp., *e. g.*, Shabbat, Mishnah 6, end; Tosefta 7[8], passim; Babli 67a–67b). This indicates that the Amorites were considered as magicians and sorcerers. The Apocalypse of Baruch 60.1 and ps.–Philo, 25.10, 26, (bottom) share this opinion with regard to the Amorites.—In the legend concerning the emigration of the Girgashites, the place where they are alleged to have settled is perhaps not Africa (אפריקא), but the land of the Iberians (אבריקא = 'Ιβηρική) in Caucasia; comp. Krauss in *Monatsschrift*, XXXIX, 2, *seq.*; Harkavy, *Ha-Me'assef*, 1912, 470; Munk, *Palestine*, 81; vol. III, p. 269; note 45.

³⁵ Gittin 46a. Comp. Tosafot (beginning כיון). Josephus, *Antiqui.*, V, 1.17, dwells upon the inviolability of an oath, as illustrated by the way Israel dealt with the Gibeonites.

³⁶ Yerushalmi Kiddushin 10, 65c; Shemuel 28, 134; BaR 8.4. Comp. vol. IV, p. 110.

³⁷ BaR 8.4; Shemuel 18.133; comp. vol. III, p. 64, and vol. IV, p. 110.

³⁸ Berakot 54b; Tan. Wa-Era 16; Ephraem I, 21OF. Comp. vol. II, p. 357.

³⁹ PRE 52. On the "seven great miracles", of which the standstill of the sun is one, see note 272 on vol. I, p. 291.

⁴⁰ PRE 52, and comp. vol. III, p. 61. Opinions differ as to how long the sun stood still; see 'Abodah Zarah 25a; Targum Hab. 3.11, according to the reading of Mahzor Vitry 171; Shu'aib, Bereshit (end). The miracle took place on a summer's day in the month of Tammuz; comp. Seder 'Olam 11; Aggadat Esther 29.

⁴¹ Tan. B. III, 68; Tan. Ahare 9; BR 6(end). Comp. vol. III, pp. 18–19. Opinions differ as to what is meant by the "Book of Yashar" of which Joshua spoke on that occasion (Josh. 10.13). Gen., Num., Deut., and Jud. are named by one authority or another as the book to which Joshua referred; comp. BR, *loc. cit.*; 'Abodah Zarah 25a; Yerushalmi Sotah 1, 17; Targum 2 Sam. 1.18 (here the "Book of Yashar" = Pentateuch); Jerome, Is. 44.2 and Ezek. 18.4. Comp. Ginzberg, *Haggada bei den Kirchenv.*, 39–41.

⁴² Tan. B. III, 68; Tan. Ahare 9; BR 6(end).

⁴³ Tan. B. III, 68; Tan. Ahare 9. On the conception that the praise of God rendered by the pious might take the place of the song chanted by nature to the glory of God, see DR 11.5, and note 947 on vol. III, p. 471.

⁴⁴ Yashar Joshua, 135b–136a. As during the war for the defence of the Gibeonites a great miracle was wrought for Joshua, so also later in his war against the united kings of Canaan (see Josh. 11), when the enemies of Israel at the prayer of Joshua "became still as a stone"; Mekilta Shirah 9, 43a. Comp. note 515 on vol. III, p. 269.

⁴⁵ Shulam in his appendix to his edition of Zacuto's Yuhasin, following a Samaritan chronicle (=*Chronicon Samaritanum*, ed. Juynboll, XXVI–XXXII); see also Yalkut Reubeni, Debarim (end), which follows Shulam. That the Canaanites fleeing from Joshua settled in Armenia is asserted also by Moses Choronensis (comp. p. 53); but it is not unlikely that the original form of the legend spoke of Arameans and not of Armenians. Observe the name of the hero Shobah, which is identical with that of an Aramean general; see 2 Sam. 10.16 and 18. There is perhaps also some connection between this legend and the one concerning the emigration of the Girgashites (comp. vol. IV, p. 10, top), if we accept the hypothesis that in the latter legend the Georgians (Γεώργιοι) in the Caucasus are identical with the biblical Girgashites; comp. references to Krauss, Harkavy, and Munk, in note 34.

⁴⁶ Seder 'Olam 11; Mekilta Wa-Yassa' 5, 51b; Zebahim 118b, and in many more talmudic and midrashic passages, where the "seven years of conquest" and "seven years of division" are spoken of. Josephus, *Antiqui.*, V, 1.19, and the Assumption of Moses 2.3 maintain that the war of conquest lasted only five years.

⁴⁷ Baba Batra 122a, and, in a somewhat different form, Yerushalmi Yoma 4, 41b, where it is stated that the division of the land was carried out by lot, the decision of the Urim and Tummim, and the valuation of the different kinds of the soil allotted. On the last point, see also Josephus, *Antiqui.*, V, 1.21, and vol. III, p. 391. The small stones used in casting the lots proclaimed aloud the share allotted to each tribe, crying out: "This is the share of the tribe of Judah, etc." Comp. vol. III, p. 391. Comp. Ma'asiyyot (Gaster's edition, 114); Yalkut Reubeni, Gen. 1.1, quoting *Sode Raza* as his authority, whereas in Num. 26.56 *Hakam ha-Razin* is given as the source. Comp. Raziel 11a–11b; note 70 on vol. IV, p. 96.

⁴⁸ On this plant (=*urginea maritima*) and its use, see Löw, in *Lewy-Festschrift*, 47–53, and Ginzberg, *R.E.J.*, LXVII, 139–140 (*Compte Rendu*, 26).

⁴⁹ Baba Batra 56a; Bezah 25b; Yerushalmi Peah 2, 16d; Tehillim 87, 377.

⁵⁰ Baba Kamma 81a, where several other ordinances are as-

cribed to Joshua by some authorities; Tosefta Baba Mezi'a 11.32;
Yerushalmi Baba Batra 5, 15a (top).   Comp. Bloch, *Sha'are Torat
ha-Takkanot* I, 54–68.   The second benediction of Grace after Meal
is said to have been composed by Joshua; Berakot 48b; comp. vol.
III, p. 50.   On Joshua as the author of *'Alenu*, see note 53 on vol.
IV, p. 361.

⁵¹ Seder 'Olam 11.   Comp. note 46.

⁵² BR 98.15.   Comp. vol. III, p. 222.   The rabbinic Haggadah
has nothing to add to the biblical narrative concerning the erection
of the altar by the two and a half tribes (Josh. 22.9, *seq.*), whereas
ps.–Philo, 22: 22D, *seq.* embellishes this story with many new details.   In
the days of Joshua the Israelites "took upon themselves the kingdom
of heaven" with love, and as a reward God treated them for three
hundred years (the period of the judges) with love and patience as a
father deals with his children, not as a teacher with his disciples;
ER 17, 86.

⁵³ Seder 'Olam 12; Comp. Ratner, *ad loc.*, and Ginzberg, *Haggada
bei den Kirchenv.*, 1–2.

⁵⁴ To commemorate his great victories, the coins struck by
Joshua bore the figure of a bullock on the obverse, and a wild ox (Re 'em)
on the reverse, in allusion to Moses' blessing to his tribe (comp. Deut.
33.17); thus his fame spread through all the world; BR 39.11; Baba
Kamma 97b.   Comp. note 46 on vol. I, p. 206.

⁵⁵ Septuagint Josh. (end).

⁵⁶ An unknown Midrash quoted by Rashi, Josh. 24.30.   Comp.
also Kimhi, *ad loc.*   According to Zohar I,53a, Joshua was one of the
few mortals who "died free from sin"; comp., to the contrary, vol.
III, pp. 407–408, and notes 19, 23.

⁵⁷ Shabbat 105b; Shemuel 23, 114; Ruth R., introduction; Koheleth 7.1.   The high priest Eleazar died not long after Joshua, but
not before he had completed the Book of Joshua, to which he added
the report about the author's (Joshua's) death; see Baba Batra 15a;
Seder 'Olam 12.   Comp. Ginzberg, *Unbekannte Sekte*, 27.   On the
burial place of Eleazar, see Midrash Tannaim 107.

II. JUDGES

Vol. IV, (pp. 21–54)

[1] The elaborate Kenaz legend is found in ps.–Philo pp. (25–32) only, and therefrom in Yerahmeel 57, 165–173, in a somewhat abridged form. It is worthy of note that Josephus, *Antiqui.*, V, 3.3, calls the first judge (after Joshua) Kenaz, and not Othniel, as the Hebrew text and the Septuagint of Jud. 3.2 have it. Ps.–Philo and Josephus, however, do not agree as to who the father of Kenaz was; according to the former, it was Caleb, whereas the latter seems to think it was Othniel; see statement of contents of *Antiqui.*, V. The Christian literature of the Middle Ages contains many references to Cenec (this is the most frequent form of this name; but there are more than a dozen corruptions thereof), who was the successor of Joshua in the leadership of the people, and who distinguished himself by his deep mastery of lithology; see the references given by Steinschneider, *Hebräische Bibliographie*, XVI, 104–106; *Hebräische Uebersetzungen*, 237, note 922, and 963, note 105. This Cenec or Zenek is, of course, none other than Kenaz קנז transliterated Cenez by ps.–Philo. The view which ascribes the mastery of lithology to Cenec (=Kenaz) is connected with the legend about the precious stones (as recorded by ps.–Philo), the hero of which is Kenaz; see vol. IV, pp. 23–24. The holy Getha, whose grave is described by a traveller in Palestine in the Middle Ages, is not Jephthah (so Nestle, *Zeitschrift des deutschen Palästina Vereins*, XXX, 210–211), but Kenaz-Cenec, which name is also spelt Cethel (see Steinschneider, *loc. cit.*), of which Getha is a slight corruption. Comp. James, *Biblical Antiquities of Philo*, 146; note 10 on vol. IV, p. 5.

[2] In Yerahmeel the number of the sinners of the tribe of Benjamin fell out, and the numbers of the sinners of the other tribes are different from those given by ps.–Philo. Comp. the following note.

[3] The sum total of the numbers given is 5480, and not 6110 as Yerahmeel and ps.–Philo have it; but in these two sources the numbers of the sinners of the tribes of Dan and Naphtali have fallen out. It is to be noted that Simeon has the largest number of sinners, and Levi the smallest. This is in keeping with the view of the Jewish legend

concerning these two tribes.   See vol. III, pp. 457–458, and note 924 appertaining thereto.

4 Achan's confession saved him from losing his share in the world to come; see vol. IV, p. 176, note 32.

5 According to Gen. 35.4, Jacob hid the foreign gods under the terebinth (אֵלָה in Hebrew, and hence Elah, Elas, in ps.–Philo, is the sinner who hid the foreign gods in his tent).   On the identity of the terebinth of Jacob with the one mentioned in Josh. 24.26, see quotation from an unknown Midrash in Rashi and Kimhi, Josh., *loc. cit.*

6 Yerahmeel 57, 166.   In ps.–Philo Elah's words read: "Shall not death come upon us, that ye shall die by fire?   Nevertheless I tell thee, my lord, there are no inventions like unto those which we have made wickedly.   But if thou wilt search out the truth plainly, ask severally the men of every tribe, and so shall some one of them that stand by perceive the difference of their sins".

7 Yerahmeel 57, 167, whereas ps.–Philo reads somewhat differently: We would inquire by the evil spirits to see whether they revealed plainly. On the tribe of Issachar as the tribe of scholars and wise men, see vol. II, p. 144, and Index, s. v.

8 So Yerahmeel 57, 167, whereas ps.–Philo has the "tent of Elas" (=Elah), instead of mount Abarim.   The texts of both sources are corrupt; the former ascribes to the tribe of Naphtali the same sin as that committed by the tribe of Dan, while the latter source ignores Naphtali altogether.   As to the books of the Amorites, see note 34 on vol. IV, p. 10.   Ps-Philo has: The Amorites taught us that which they did, that we might teach our children.   But later ps.–Philo refers to the books of the Amorites which were destroyed in a supernatural way, and therefore the text of ps.–Philo made use of by Yerahmeel is the correct one.

9 According to ps.–Philo, the seven sinners are: Canaan, Put, Selath, Nimrod, Elath, Desuath.   James, *ad loc.*, adds Ham, to make up the required seven; but Yerahmeel shows that the last name is Suah (שׁוּחַ), and accordingly it is safe to assume that Desuath is a corruption of De'dan, Suah.   Comp. Gen. 10.7.   On the making of idols in the time after the deluge, see vol. I, pp. 174–175.   On the hiding of the idols under Mount Shechem, see vol. I, p. 412.

10 Ps.–Philo gives some more details concerning these stones, not found in Yerahmeel.

11 On the ice in paradise (an allusion to Ezek. 1.22?), see vol.

I, p. 9. Yerahmeel seems to have had before him a corrupted text of ps.-Philo.

¹² On the twelve stones in the breast-plate of the high priest, see vol. III, pp. 169–172.

¹³ Ps.-Philo, 28 (bottom) reads: *Donec exurgat Jahel, qui aedificet domum in nomine meo et tunc ea proponet ante me supra duo Cherubin.* That Solomon is here referred to cannot be doubted and Yerahmeel substitutes Solomon for Jahel. The puzzling Jahel can easily be explained by retranslating this passage into Hebrew as follows: עד אשר יקום אתיאל והוא יבנה בית לשמי "Until Ithiel will arise and build a house for My name." It is quite natural that in this oracle the wise king should not be called by his ordinary name, but by one of his numerous other names. The writer's fancy decided to use אתיאל (comp. vol. IV, p. 125 on Solomon's ten names), but the translator misread it as אֵת יָאֵל, and hence *exurgat Jahel* in the present text. Quite puzzling is also the end of the sentence, as one fails to see any connection between the stones of the high priest and the Cherubim.

¹⁴ On the hiding of the temple vessels, see vol. III, p. 480 vol. IV, pp. 320–321. On the "illuminating stones" in Mesianic times, see PK 18, 135b–137b, as well as the numerous references cited by Buber *ad loc.* Comp. also vol. IV, p. 222, and further vol. I, p. 162.

¹⁵ According to ps.-Philo, the Amorites were the enemies, whereas at the beginning of the Kenaz legend the *Allophyli* (*i. e.*, the Philistines) were the enemy.

¹⁶ Ps.-Philo enumerates them all by name, but the names are mutilated.

¹⁷ This is in accordance with the abridged text of Yerahmeel, whereas ps.-Philo speaks of two angels who came to the assistance of Kenaz: Gethel (or Ingethel), "who is set over the hidden things and worketh unseen", and the angel Zeruel, who "is set over strength". The former smote the Amorites with blindness so that every man who saw his neighbor counted him his adversary and they slew one another, while the second angel "bare up the arms of Kenaz" in order to remain unperceived. Gethel is a fairly accurate transliteration of עטיאל or עטהאל from עטה (Arabic *ghata*), "covered, hid", and hence Gethel is an appropriate name for the angel "who is set over the hidden things and worketh unseen." The name of the angel who "is set over strength" is Zeruel, זרועאל from זרוע "strength", and as this word in Hebrew also means "arm", it is said that Zeruel "bare up the arms of Kenaz", in

order to be unperceived. Comp. note 43 on vol. IV, p. 88. On the miracle of invisibility, see note 13 on vol. IV, p. 5, and Index, s. v. On the blinding of the enemy by angels, see II Kings 6.18; vol. III, p. 342; vol. IV, p. 421.

¹⁸ On the view that the blood that was stuck to the hand loosened the sword, see vol. IV, p. 100.

¹⁹ The name Jabez יעבץ (on the rabbinic legend concerning him, see notes 22 and 30) is transliterated in ps.-Philo by Jabis, which Yerahmeel took to be the equivalent of Hebrew יבין, and thus the wicked king of Hazor is made to be the namesake of the prophet. The dependence of Yerahmeel upon the Latin text of ps.-Philo is thereby proved beyond doubt. Yerahmeel had before him the incorrect Latin text: "*Jabis et Phineas duos prophetas et filium Eleazari sacerdotis*", whereas there can hardly be any doubt that the last four words are a gloss, explaining that Phinehas "the prophet" is identical with Phinehas the son of Eleazar the priest. This is, of course, quite correct, since according to ps.-Philo (see quotation in vol. IV, p. 53–54 and note 140) Phinehas the son of Eleazar is none other than the prophet Elijah. But when the gloss crept into the text, it made ps.-Philo speak absurdly of Phinehas the prophet and Phinehas the priest.

²⁰ Besides the vision of Kenaz, ps.-Philo gives also one by Eleazar the priest, which he revealed on his death-bed to his son Phinehas, who, in his turn, communicated it to the dying Kenaz and the elders surrounding him. On the view that the "shepherd must perish for the iniquity of his flock", see Shabbat 33b. As to the conception that the world is to exist seven thousand years, see note 140 on vol. I, p. 102. The sentence concerning the shepherd and the flock reads in ps.-Philo as follows: "Shall the shepherd (God) destroy His flock (Israel) to no purpose, except that it continues to sin against Him?"

²¹ Zebul is a corruption of Iehud, *i. e.*, Ehud, the second judge in Israel; see Jud. 3.15. On p. 33 (towards the end) this name is spelt Iebul. For the interchange of *Z* and *I* in ps.-Philo, see 47A, where Jambri stands for Zambri זמרי; on the confusion of *d* and *l*, see 44D, which has Dedila instead of Delila דלילה; in old Latin MSS. it is difficult to distinguish between *b* and *h*, and between *d* and *l*. Yerahmeel, following the masoretic text of the Bible, according to which Othniel was the first judge, makes him the successor of Kenaz, instead of Ehud; but there can be no doubt that ps.-Philo knows nothing of

Othniel, and considers Kenaz as the first judge. Comp. note 1, and the following note.

²² BR 58.2; Shemuel 8,73; Koheleth 1.5; Shir 4.7; Temurah 16a. In all these sources Othniel is supposed to be the direct successor of Joshua, and not Kenaz, as ps.-Philo has it; comp. note 1, and the preceding note. According to the Rabbis, Judah, who was commanded by God to go up first against the Canaanites (Jud. 1.1), was a person so named (*i. e.*, Othniel, the first judge), and does not refer to the tribe of Judah. Aphraates, 481, shares this view of the Rabbis. The statement of Lactantius, *Institut.*, 4.10, that the country of Judea was called after a certain Judah who was the leader of Israel after Moses, presupposes the rabbinic view that the first judge was called Judah. Josephus, *Antiqui.*, V, 2.1, paraphrases the passage of Jud. 1.1 by "the tribe of Judah". He adds that priority was given to this tribe in accordance with the command of God through Phinehas. Comp. Seder 'Olam 20, according to the reading of Rashi on Jud. 2.1; Targum Jud., *loc. cit.*, and the references cited by Ratner. All these sources maintain that "the messenger of God" sent to Israel after the death of Joshua was none other than Phinehas. See also Septuagint on Josh. (end); Ginzberg, *Haggadah bei den Kirchenv.*, 2-4.

²³ Temurah 16a. Comp. vol. IV, p. 4. As to the learning and devotion to the Torah displayed by Othniel-Jabez, see also ShR38.5; BHM V, 69; Yelammedenu in Yalkut II, 936; Tan. Tezawweh 9; ER 5,30. In the last passage it is said that Jabez (=Othniel) had never experienced pain nor committed sins; this was granted to him as a reward for his having travelled through the entire land of Israel to instruct the people in the Torah, for the sake of God's glory. Comp. also the references in the following note.

²⁴ Sifre N., 78; Sifre Z., 76–77; Mekilta Yitro 2,60a–60b; Mekilta RS, 92; Temurah 16a; ER 5,30–31; Targum 1 Chron. 2.55 and 4.9–10; vol. III, pp. 75–76..

²⁵ Temurah 16a. The identity of Caleb the son of Jephuneh, one of the spies, with Caleb the son Kenaz (Jud. 1.13; according to the Septuagint, it is Kenaz who is described in this passage as the younger brother of Caleb), whose daughter was the wife of Othniel, is presupposed in many places of the Talmudim and Midrashim. Comp., *e. g.*, Sanhedrin 69b; Sotah 11b: Caleb's father was Hezron, his step-father was Kenaz, but he was called "the son of Jephuneh", because he deviated (the name Jephuneh is here connected with פנה "turned aside") from the evil counsel of the spies, and did not slander the Holy

Land. On Caleb's first marriage with Miriam, see vol. II, p. 253; on his second marriage with Bithiah, Moses' foster-mother, see Megillah 13a; Targum 1 Chron. 4.18; Index, s. v. *Hadar*, Wa-Yelek (end),75a, quotes from Temurah, *loc. cit.*, a statement concerning the great devotion to the Torah evinced by the generation of Othniel-Jabez. This is, however, not found in our texts of the Talmud. The description of the devotion to the Torah evinced by the disciples of R. Judah ben Ilai (Sanhedrin 20a) agrees verbatim with that concerning the generation of Othniel quoted in *Hadar* from Temurah.

²⁶ Seder 'Olam 12, and the parallel passages cited by Ratner. Comp. also Ginzberg, *Haggadah bei den Kirchenv.*, 1–2. According to the Rabbis, Othniel followed almost immediately upon Joshua as the leader of the people. It is true that between Joshua and Othniel there were the "elders", to whom the leadership was entrusted; but these elders outlived Joshua (Jud. 2.6) only for a short while. Their short duration was a punishment for their not having mourned for Joshua in a manner befitting his merits; comp. vol. III, p. 17. According to some authorities, however, the time intervening between Joshua and Othniel was twenty, or, as others maintain, seventeen years. It was during this interval that the events recorded in the book of Ruth took place. Comp. the references cited by Ratner, note 5 on Seder 'Olam, *loc. cit.*, and Shir 4.6, where Boaz is identified with Judah mentioned in Jud. 1.1. See note 22.

²⁷ Sifre D., 353 (end); Midrash Tannaim 218. An unknown Midrash quoted by R. Bahya, *Kad ha-Kemah* ודוי, 78b, and Sabba', Bereshit, 8d, remarks thar Adoni-bezek was forgiven his sin because he confessed it. Comp. vol. IV, pp. 9 and 22.

²⁸ BR 69 (end); Sotah 46b; Nispahim 14–15 (=EZ 16); Sukkah 53a; PRK (Schönblum's edition, 43b); Zohar II, 151b. Comp. also Sanhedrin 97a, which gives the story concerning the place called Kushta ("Truth"), where nobody died "before his time", *i. e.*, before reaching old age, because the inhabitants thereof never spoke an untrue word. It is not quite clear whether there is any connection between the city of Luz, over which the angel of death has no power, and the little bone in the human body called Luz which never decays and out of which the new body will be formed in the time of resurrection (see vol. V, pp. 184, note 44 and 365, note 345; Index, s. v. "Luz"); but it can hardly be regarded as accidental that the immortal city and the immortal bone of the human body bear the same name. The above-cited sources

contain the obscure statement that purple (תכלת) was made in the city of Luz; a play on לח and נג woven?

29 Sanhedrin 105a; Yerushalmi Nazir 9,57c. On Laban's enmity towards the descendants of Jacob, see vol. III, p. 354. The Israelites suffered oppression at the hands of Cushan on account of their sins; but Othniel pleaded to God in their behalf, saying: "Thou hast promised Moses to redeem Israel from their enemies, whether they fulfil Thy will or not; now, I pray Thee, redeem Israel." Tan. Shemot 20(on the text, comp. Rashi, Jud. 3.10); ShR 3.2.

30 2 Alphabet of Ben Sira 29a and 36a, where by Jabez the judge Othniel-Jabez is very likely meant, though later sources maintain that "the immortal Jabez" was a grandson (son?) of R. Judah the patriarch, the redactor of the Mishnah; comp. Derek Erez Z., 1 (end), the parallel passages cited by Tawrogi, *ad loc.*, and Epstein, *Mik-kadmoniyyot*, 111-112, as well as PRK (Grünhut's edition, 83); Carmoly *Aggadat Aggadot*, 12. It is probable that the original form of the Haggadah concerning Jabez read ויעבץ הוא יהודה, referring to the identity of Othniel-Jabez with Judah mentioned in Jud. 1.1 (comp. note 22). Later this remark was misunderstood, and was emended to ויעבץ [בן] בנו של יהודה, which presupposes that this Judah is the patriarch, the redactor of the Mishnah. Kallah 2,9b explicitly states that Jabez who was one of the seven who entered paradise alive was none other than the one mentioned in the Bible. Comp. Index, s. v. "Paradise, Entering Alive into."

31 Seder 'Olam 12; comp. the references cited by Ratner, note 13. According to Baba Batra 91a, Boaz is identical with the judge Ibzan who was a contemporary of Samson's father (comp. note 47), whereas according to Josephus, *Antiqui.*, V, 9.1, the story of Ruth took place at the time of Eli. Other authorities consider Boaz a contemporary of Deborah; see Ruth R. (beginning), and We-Hizhir I, 87; comp. also note 26. The rather puzzling reference to the judge Jahshun (= Nahshon) by Hamzah al-Ispahani (comp. Steinschneider, below) is based on a confusion of Nahshon with his grandson Boaz who, as mentioned above, is identical according to some of the Rabbis, with Ibzan. The confusion of Nahshon with his grandson Boaz is found also in *Schatzhöhle*, 176, where it is stated: Ibzan is identical with Nah-shon; comp. Ginzberg, *Haggada bei den Kirchenv.*, 10, and Steinschneider, *Zeitschrift für die religiösen Interessen des Judenthums*, II, 321.

32 Baba Batra 15b; Targum Ruth 1.1; Ruth R., 1.1; Ruth Z., 345. Comp. Matthew 7.4.

³³ BR 25.3; Targum Ruth 1.1. On the famines, comp. vol. I, pp. 220–221; on the famine in the time of Boaz, see Baba Batra 91a; Ruth R. 1.1. According to Ruth Z., 45, this famine was not a "famine for bread only, but for the heavenly words of the Lord."

³⁴ According to a widespread tradition Nahshon had four sons: Elimelech, Shalmon (the father of Boaz), Naomi's father, and Tob (comp. note 16); see Tan. B. III, 107; Tan. Behar 3; Baba Batra 91a; Seder 'Olam 12. According to the view of Ruth R. 3.12, Elimelech, Boaz, and Tob were brothers.

³⁵ Haggadic etymologies of their names and those of their wives are given in Ruth R. 1.4; Ruth Z. 46–47; Tan. B. III, 107; Tan. Behar 3; Berakot 7b.

³⁶ Targum Ruth 1.1–2; Tan. Shemini 9 (here שׁופט stands for דיין "judge of a community") and Behar 3 (Elimelech was the head of his generation); Tan. B. III, 107; Ruth R. 1.1–2; Baba Batra 91a.

³⁷ Ruth R. 1.1; Baba Batra 91a; Zohar Ruth 1.1, which is based on Ruth Z., 46–47. In the last source it is observed: They felt themselves drawn to the Moabites, whom they resembled. They were mean and ungenerous like the Moabites who "did not meet Israel with bread and water in the way, when they came forth out of Egypt." (Comp. Deut. 23.5).

³⁸ Targum Ruth 1.1.

³⁹ Ruth R. 1.4: When Ehud said unto Eglon, King of Moab: "I have a message from God unto thee", the King arose from his seat (Jud. 3.20) to show honor to God. His reward was that his descendant Solomon (by his daughter Ruth) "sat on the throne of the Lord" (1 Chron. 29.23); see Tan. B. I, 220; Tan. Wa-Yehi 14; Sanhedrin 60a; Ruth R., *loc. cit.* On the similarity between the "throne of God" (the heavenly mode of ruling) and the "throne of Solomon" (his wise and just ruling), see ShR 15.26; Shir 1.1. Comp. note 70 on vol. IV, p. 157. Good deeds though lacking good intention, have their reward; Balak offered up unto God forty-two sacrifices (see Num. 23.1, 14, and 29), and he was rewarded in that Ruth, the granddaughter of his grandson (son?) Eglon, became the mother of the Davidic dynasty; see Nazir 23b; Sanhedrin 105b; Targum and Lekah on Ruth 1.4. Comp. note 4 on vol. IV, 240.

⁴⁰ Lekah, Ruth 1.4. The old sources take it for granted that the sons of Elimelech did not convert their wives to Judaism, either at the time of their marriage or later; see Ruth R. 1.4, where (that is how the obscure passage is to be understood) it is said that the sons

of Elimelech were of the opinion that the prohibition against intermarriage with the Moabites (Deut. 23.2) applied also to the marrying
of Moabitish women after their conversion to Judaism. Accordingly
their wives' conversion would not have rendered marriage legitimate
(comp. note 64). See Tan. B. III, 108; Tan. Behar 3; Zohar III, 190a
(in this passage Elimelech is held responsible for the sinful actions of
his sons); Targum Ruth 1.4. Against this view Zohar Ruth 1.4
(שאל ר׳פדת) and 14 maintains that the wives of Elimelech's sons were
converted to Judaism before their marriage; but no sooner was Orphah's
husband dead than she returned to her idols, for her conversion to
Judaism was only a matter of policy with her. See also Ruth Z., 47,
where the death of Mahlon and Chilion was a punishment for their
father's sin (avarice). Here their marriages were considered to have
been in accordance with the law, or in other words, this passage presupposes that their wives were proselytes. See also the supplement
to Lekah, Ruth 48, 49, where special stress is laid on the fact (read
שנתיהדו instead of שנתיהדו) that Orphah and Ruth became converted to Judaism prior to their marriage to the sons of Elimelech.
Comp. note 44; note 790 on vol. III, p. 383; note 16 on vol. IV, p. 129.

⁴¹ Ruth R. 1.5, which reads: The Merciful One does not take away
the life of the sinner before warning him with some other punishment.
WR 17.4; PK 8,66b; PR 17, 89a; Tan. B. III, 108; Tan. Behar 3.

⁴² Targum Ruth 1.8. Comp. also Ruth R., *ad loc.*, which reads:
Naomi's daughters-in-law not only saw to it that the last honors
paid to their husbands should be in keeping with their station in life,
but also renounced their claims to the estates of the deceased (their
dowery rights) in favor of their mother-in-law. Naomi decided to
return to the Holy Land after she had heard from the Jewish merchants
who came to Moab that the famine had disappeared. Other authorities
think that this fact was revealed to her by the holy spirit; see Ruth
R., Targum (this passage speaks of an angel instead of the holy spirit),
and Lekah on Ruth 1.6.

⁴³ Ruth Z, 47–48. This passage also states that in Jerusalem
each class of the population inhabited its own district, and the higher
classes did not permit the lower ones to dwell in their midst. Similarly
the classes were distinguished by different dress, and in view of the
class consciousness among the Jews, Naomi feared to expose her daughters-in-law to humiliation and disgrace, especially as they were very poor
and clad in rags. Naomi herself, however, was anxious to return
to the Holy Land, and barefoot, and in rags she continued her home-

ward journey, without stopping to rest even on the eve of Sabbath (Holy Day? comp. note 48) Ruth R. 1.7; Ruth Z. 49. On the text of this passage of Ruth R. comp. Lekah, *ad loc.*, according to which we have to read שהוצדה.....ביחד; for ביחף is a poor variant instead of ביחד, whereas שהוצדה is the Hofal of צדה "feared"; see Rosh ha-Shanah 1.9, and the explanation of this passage by Geiger, *Kebuzzat Ma'amarim*, 15–20.

⁴⁴ Ruth R. 1.14; Shemuel 20, 106–107; Sotah 42b; Ruth Z., 49; vol. IV, pp. 85 and 108. The law prescribes that one asking to be admitted as a proselyte is to be refused, unless he persists and presents his request a second time. Accordingly Naomi refused Ruth's first request, but admitted her as a proselyte when Ruth repeated her request a second time, after the laws appertaining to a proselyte were expounded to her; Ruth R. 1.7 and 13; Ruth Z. 48.

⁴⁵ According to Yebamot 47a, the attention of one desirous of adopting Judaism must be called to these ceremonial laws.

⁴⁶ Ruth R. 1.16–17; Yebamot 47b; Ruth Z., 49 (on the phrase שאני קונה עולמי, see 'Abodah Zarah 17a, which has קונה עולמו); Targum Ruth 1.16–17; Mishle (end).

⁴⁷ Midrashic fragment published by Hartmann, *Ruth in der Midrasch-litteratur*, 97. Comp. vol. III, p. 293.

⁴⁸ Baba Batra 90a; Yerushalmi Ketubot 1,25a; Ruth R. 1.19. In the last source several other views are given concerning the day on which Naomi arrived. Some say that it was on the day when the marriages of the sixty children of the judge Ibzan took place (comp. Jud. 12.9), whereas other authorities maintain that the people flocked to Beth-lehem on that day for the preparation of the 'Omer, and accordingly Naomi's arrival occurred (see Menahot 10.3) at the "termination of the first day of Passover." A somewhat different view is given by Targum Ruth 1.22, where the beginning of the barley harvest, spoken of in Ruth, *loc. cit.*, is referred to the day preceding Passover (ערב פסח), when the first preparations for the reaping of the 'Omer are made (comp. Menahot, *loc. cit.*). One is, however, inclined to read במפקי יומא א'דפסחא "at the termination of the first day of Passover", instead of במעלי יומא דפסחא of our texts of Targum; see also note 43. Comp. also Ruth R. 1.22.

⁴⁹ MHG I,336, maintains that she is one of the twenty-two pious women whose piety was praised by Solomon in the last chapter of Prov., where the words "she reacheth forth her hand to the needy," refer to Naomi, who brought Ruth under the wings of the Shekinah. Comp. note 271 in Vol. I, p. 291.

⁵⁰ Ruth R. 2.5–6; on the text see Lekah and Yalkut, *ad loc.* As to the law appertaining to gleanings, see Peah 6.5.

⁵¹ Ruth Z., 50; Ruth R. 2.5–6. It was an angel who led Ruth to the field of Boaz; see Lekah, Ruth 2.3.

⁵² On Timna, see vol. I, pp. 422–423, and Index, s. v.

⁵³ Midrashic fragment published by Hartmann, *Ruth in der Midrasch-Litteratur*, 98; Targum Ruth 2.11–13. Ruth in her modesty described herself as one of the "handmaids of Boaz"; whereupon he assured her that she would be counted as one of "the mothers of Israel"; see PK 16, 124a; Ruth R. 1.14. According to PK, *loc. cit.*, the Halakah that the biblical law excluding the Moabites "from the congregation of the Lord" (Deut. 23.4, *seq.*) applies only to the males, but not to the females, was promulgated at that period and was still unknown to Ruth, who learned it from Boaz. Comp. notes 40, 64, and vol. IV, p. 89. The greeting, "The Lord be with you" (Ruth 2.4), was first introduced by Boaz, and sanctioned by a heavenly voice (see note 193 on vol. IV, p. 448). This sanction was absolutely necessary, as it was against the law that forbids to mention God's name under ordinary circumstances. This greeting continued to be in vogue until the time of Athaliah (according to some authorities, until the days of the three youths, while according to others, until the time of Mordecai and Esther), when the name of the Lord was forgotten. See Berakot Mishnah 9 (end); Babli 63a; Yerushalmi 9, 14c; Makkot 23b; Ruth R. 4.4. The Haggadah very likely presupposes that the innovation of Boaz consisted in the use of the Tetragrammaton; see Geiger, *Urschrift*, 262, *seq.*; Schwarz in his notes on Tosefta Berakot 9; Jacob, *Im Namen Gottes*, 174. What Kohler, *Journal of Jewish Lore and Philosophy* I, 26–38, has to say on this subject does not deserve serious consideration, as he evidently did not grasp the point made by Geiger. In this connection it may be mentioned that the phrase "Thanked be God" is said by ps.-Matthew, 6 to have been coined by Mary the mother of Jesus.

⁵⁴ Shabbat 113b; Ruth R. 2.14; Ruth Z., 51. God put His blessing in the few ears of corn Boaz gave her, and they sufficed for her meal; see PK 6, 59a–59b (it is not explicitly stated whether the blessing was on account of Boaz or Ruth); PR 16, 82a; WR 34.8; BaR 21.20; Mishle 13, 74; Tan. Pinehas 13.

⁵⁵ Ruth R. 2.20. Boaz took great pains to impress upon his numerous workmen (he employed so many of them, that each group

of forty-two had a foreman; Ruth R. 2.4) to be kind and polite to Ruth. He also told them to drop sheaves in her way, that she might take them home, as she was very strict in observing the law (comp. vol. IV, p. 32) and would not take anything to which she was not entitled. The workmen did even more than they had been commanded by their master, and threshed for her the grain she gleaned. But she was contented with very little, and would not take home more than was required for her daily need. This daily supply aroused the suspicion of Naomi, who feared her daughter-in-law was leading an immoral life, obtaining her daily needs from her lovers. See Ruth Z., 51. The story in that passage about the pious man goes back to Tosefta Peah 3.8.

56 Ruth Z., 52. Naomi had taken an oath to provide for Ruth, and was therefore anxious to see her married; comp. Targum Ruth 3.1.

57 Shabbat 113b; Ruth R. 3.3; Yerushalmi Peah 8, 21b; PR 23, 115b; Ruth Z., 52; Tan. B. III, 108; Tan. Behar 3; Targum and Pe-shitta Ruth 3.3. Some of these sources state that Naomi, to allay Ruth's apprehensions, said to her: "My merits will accompany thee"; comp. also Haserot 4a, and Lekah, Ruth 3.5. Ruth was extremely afraid to walk at night all by herself, as she was of such extraordinary beauty that no man could look at her without becoming passionately enamoured of her; Ruth R. 2.4. On the haggadic explanation, given in this passage, of ויקר (Ruth 2.4) as קרא or rather קרה "had a night pollution", see Megillah 15a.

58 Demons, both male and female, have their bodies and faces covered with hair, but their heads are bald; see 'Emek ha-Melek, 140 b. According to Hasidim (Bologna edition, 1161), the male demons have hair on their heads, but not the females. Comp. Yalkut Hadash, Keshafim, 55.

59 On Ruth's extraordinary beauty, see note 57.

60 Ruth R. 3.7–10 (Boaz retired after praying and studying the Torah); Ruth Z., 52; Sanhedrin 19b; Tan. B. III, 108; Tan. Behar 3; midrashic fragment published by Hartmann in *Ruth in der Midrasch-Litteratur*, 98–99; Targum Ruth 3.7–12, which reads: Boaz retired after having thanked God for having removed the famine from Israel at his prayer; comp. also Targum Ruth 1.6. On the chastity of Boaz, highly praised in the above-cited sources (Boaz, Joseph, and Palti, the husband of Michal, are declared to have been the highest types of chastity) comp. note 85. See also ER 24, 131; WR 23.11; BaR 15.16; Ruth R. 3.13; Ruth Z., 53; PRE 39. The Karaite Hadassi, *Eshkol* 45b, No. 118, accuses the Rabbis of slandering Boaz, because they maintain

that he did not resist the temptation to which he was exposed. But the Rabbis on the contrary are full of praise for his steadfastness and chastity. On similar Karaitic fabrications, see note 43 on vol. IV, p. 64.

⁶¹ According to the prevailing opinion, טוב (Ruth 3.13) is taken to be the name of the kinsman, who in 4.1 is addressed by Boaz: "Ho, such a one", because he was not conversant with the law, and Boaz did not deign to call him by his name; see Ruth R. 3.11 and 4.1; Ruth Z., 53; Tan. B. III, 108; Tan. Behar 3; Baba Batra 91b. On the relationship between Boaz and Tob, see note 34. Targum Ruth 3.13, however, takes טוב to mean "well." By the six measures of barley which Boaz gave Ruth on her return home, he indicated to her that she was destined to become the ancestress of six pious men who would be endowed with six spiritual gifts (comp. Is. 11.2). These men are: David, Daniel, Hananiah, Mishael, Azariah, and the Messiah (others count Daniel's three friends as one, and add Hezekiah and Josiah); see Ruth R. 3.14; Ruth Z., 53; Sanhedrin 93b; PRK 36b; BaR 13.11; Targum Ruth 3.15.

⁶² Targum Ruth 4.1; Ruth Z., 53 (סנהדרין=בית המדרש in this passage and in many others). Comp. also Josephus, *Antiqui.*, V, 9.4.

⁶³ Ruth R. 4.1–2. On the text, comp. Lekah and Yalkut on Ruth, *ad loc.*

⁶⁴ Ruth R. 4.1-2 and 5 (the Ketib קניתי, Ruth 4.5, is explained as second person feminine: Tob did not act like a man, but like an ignorant woman. See the similar Haggadah in Berakot 32a on Num. 14.16); Haserot 6. On the view that through Boaz the prohibition against intermarrying with the Moabites was limited to the males only, see note 53, and vol. IV, p. 89. It was Boaz too who introduced the ceremony of pronouncing the benedictions on the bridal couple in the presence of ten men; see Ketubot 7a, and Yerushalmi 1, 25a; Ruth R. 4.2. In view of the fact that at weddings and on similar festive occasions young people are apt to forget what morals and decorum require of them, Boaz ordained that "elders" should be appointed to supervise over such festive celebrations, and this ordinance continued in force until the time of the Palestinian patriarchate; Yerushalmi and Ruth R., *loc. cit.*

⁶⁵ Josephus, *Antiqui.*, V, 9.4, combining Ruth 4.6 with Deut. 25.89, maintains that Ruth performed the ceremony of "taking off the shoe" (חליצה) of the kinsman who refused to marry her. The same view is alluded to in Zohar Ruth 4.6. It is very likely that Targum paraphrases נעל by "glove" to combat this view which is against the

Halakah enjoining only that a sister-in-law should take off the shoe of the brother of the deceased, and Ruth was certainly not Tob's sister-in-law. The Halakah explains Ruth 4.7 to refer to the form of acquisition known in rabbinic jurisprudence as Halifin (חליפין), consisting in the handing over of an object by the purchaser to the seller, as a symbolical substitute for the object bought. See Baba Mezi'a 47a; Yerushalmi Kiddushin 1, 60c; Ruth R. 4.8; Shemuel 28, 100.

⁶⁶ Ruth R. 3.10.

⁶⁷ Ruth R. 3.10. Comp. Tosafot Yebamot 48b (bottom).

⁶⁸ Ruth R. 4.12. Apart from her advanced age at the time of her second marriage (comp. however vol. IV, p. 34, top), Ruth's physical condition was not fit for bearing children, had not a miracle been wrought for her. On the pious Obed ("servant", *i. e.*, servant of God), see also Targum Ruth 4.21 and Lekah on Ruth 4.17. According to the midrashic fragment published by Hartmann, *Ruth in der Midrasch-Litteratur*, 100, Obed was one of the pious men who were born with the sign of the Abrahamic covenant on them; comp. note 318, towards the end, on vol. I, p. 306.

⁶⁹ Ruth Z., 55; Lekah, Ruth 4.17 (this passage gives a detailed description of the death of Boaz in the bridal chamber); comp. also Josephus *Antiqui.*, V, 9.4, which reads: Obed was born within a year after the marriage of Ruth. Lekah, 4.16, adds that Naomi in her youth was "a nurse" to Boaz, as she was later a nurse to his son Obed. The view that Ruth lived to see the glory of Solomon (this already in Baba Batra 91b) very likely assumes that the story of Ruth took place at the end of the period of the Judges. Comp. note 31. Boaz became the ancestor of kings (the Davidic dynasty), as a reward for "his taking a wife for the sake of Heaven"; EZ, 3, 178.

⁷⁰ Ps.-Philo, 33; 30.1–2. On the erroneous reading "Zebul" (32 bottom) instead of Iehud (=Ehud), see note 21. The activity of Shamgar who succeeded Ehud (comp. Jud. 3.31) is entirely ignored by ps.-Philo, whereas Yerahmeel 58.2 refers at least to the fact recorded in Scripture that Shamgar's activity fell between the time of Ehud and Deborah.

⁷¹ Ps.-Philo 33, where Jabel is a corruption of Jabin, see Jud. 4.1. Jabin's capital, Hazor, was completely burned down by Joshua (Josh.11.11), who carried out the divine command given to Moses with regard to its complete destruction, and thus fulfilled the desire of Jacob (in this sense is מסורת to be understood) who had waged war against it; see BR 81.4; vol. I, p. 410, bottom.

⁷² Aguddat Aggadot 77–78 (read בקרונין instead of בתנורין);
Abba Gorion 27–28; Neweh Shalom, 47–48. On the enormous size
of Sisera's army see note 80.—The Haggadah sees in Sisera (the name
occurs among the pagan inhabitants of Palestine as late as the third
century C. E.; comp. Yerushalmi Dammai 2, 22c) not only the enemy
of the Jews, but also the blasphemer of God and the mocker of the
Jewish religion; see Shemuel 13, 85; Tehillim 2, 24; WR 7 (end); Tan.
B. III, 14; Tan. Zaw 2; Aggadat Bereshit 1.2; Esther R. 2.4; comp.
also vol. IV, p. 422. In all these sources it is pointed out that God
sent the heavenly fire against Sisera (comp. note 81) to punish him for
his blasphemy. The view that Sisera at the age of thirty years was the
conqueror of the whole world is very likely a reminiscence of the history
of Alexander the Great. On the falling of the walls at the sound of his
voice, see vol. II, p. 16. According to Tan. Wa-Yakhel 8, Shemaiah
and Abtalion, the two famous leaders of the Pharisees towards the
end of the first century B. C. E. were descendants of Sisera; according
to Gittin 57b, their ancestor was Sennacherib, whereas Sisera's descendants are said to have been "ordinary school teachers". As remarked above, the name Sisera was in use among the pagan population
of Palestine as late as the third century C. E., and accordingly the
statement that Sisera was the ancestor of some scholars who were of
Gentile descent may be historical, though of course, not the Sisera
mentioned in Scripture. Comp. vol. VI, p. 462, note 93.

⁷³ Megillah 14a (on the text see Rabbinovicz, *ad loc.*, and Aggadat
Esther 48); ER 10,48, which reads: Deborah's husband had three names.
He was called Barak because his countenance shone like lightning;
Lappidoth because he used to make the lamps for the sanctuary at
Shiloh; Michael after the angel Michael, or because he was very modest
(in Hebrew מך is modest). The statement that he was called Michael
after the angel very likely wishes to convey that Barak received the
divine revelation through the angel. Comp. vol. II, p. 303, on Michael
as the intermediary between the Shekinah and Moses. That Barak
was a prophet is explicitly stated in Targum Jud. 5.23, where the correct
text is that of the editions, Kimhi, *ad loc.*, and not of Codex Reuchlin,
and Leiria edition of Targum who have not ברק נביאה. Comp.,
however, Seder ʿOlam 20, where Barak is not counted among the prophets. That Barak was the husband of Deborah is maintained also
by ps.-Jerome on Jud. 5.1, and the same author (on 5.25) speaks also
of the revelations communicated to Deborah by the angel Michael;
comp. Ginzberg, *Haggadah bei den Kirchenv.*, 5 and 8–9, where note

2 on p. 5 is to be corrected in accordance with the above remark. Another Haggadah about Barak is given in ER 10, 50–51, where it is said that he attended on the "elders", who were the leaders and teachers of the people after the death of Joshua. For his faithful service to them he was rewarded by God, and was chosen to assist Deborah in her work of delivering Israel from the hands of Sisera. God revealed to the prophetess that the work of salvation can only be achieved by men who devote themselves to the study of the Torah and the service of God, or by those who (like Barak) place themselves at the disposal of the students of the Torah. According to Tehillim 22, 180, and Tobit 1.8, Deborah belonged to the tribe of Naphtali, whereas Clemens Alexandrinus, *Stromata*, 1.21, maintains that she was of the tribe of Ephraim. This latter view is shared by Tadshe 8, where the reading should be דבורה מאפרים וברק מנפתלי "Deborah belonged to the tribe of Ephraim, Barak to that of Naphtali." According to Ambrosius *De Viduis*, 1; 8.45 and 16; 248 Barak was Deborah's son. That the victory over Sisera was won by the tribes of Naphtali and Zebulun (comp. Jud. 5.8) was due to the fact that Naphtali was a very obliging son to his father Jacob as Zebulun was a very obliging brother to Issachar; see ER 10,50–51; comp. vol. II, pp. 144–145.

⁷⁴ ER 10, 48–49; Megillah 14a. On the legal question whether women are eligible to the office of judge, see Tosafot Niddah 50a. Comp. also Zohar III, 19b, which reads: Woe unto the generation whose leader (judge) is a woman. Targum Jud. 4.5 calls attention to the wealth of Deborah who had possessions throughout the country, and dispensed justice without receiving any remuneration for it.

⁷⁵ Megillah 14b. Here it is also stated: Pride is unbecoming to women; the prophetesses Deborah and Huldah were proud women (on Huldah, see note 117 on vol. IV p. 282), and both bore ugly names (Deborah = "bee", and Huldah = "weasel").

⁷⁶ Barak not only obeyed her command, but also insisted on her going with him to the battle to protect him with her merits against dangers; see Zohar III, 21.

⁷⁷ Pesahim 66b; Zohar III, 21b–22a; BR 40.4, and parallel passage cited by Theodor.

⁷⁸ Ps.-Philo, 33–34; 30.4–7, which contains also a lengthy address by Deborah delivered to the people on this occasion.

⁷⁹ Tan. B. IV, 164; Tan. Mass'e 5; BaR 23.7. These kings were foreign potentates who were so charmed with Palestine that they de-

sired to own possessions there. See BR 53.1.0; note 33 on vol. IV, p. 9.

⁸⁰ Abba Gorion 27; Aguddat Aggadot 77; *Neweh Shalom*, 47. Comp. also ps.-Philo, 34; 31.2, which reads: And the number of them (of Sisera's army) that were gathered and slain in one hour was ninety times nine hundred and seventy thousand men. This number seems to be connected with the "nine hundred chariots", of Sisera spoken of in Jud. 4.2, where, however, ps.-Philo, 33; 30.3, reads "eight thousand." On the army of Sisera, see also Josephus, *Antiqui.*, V; 5, 1 and vol. IV, p. 407.

⁸¹ The Haggadah takes Jud. 5.20 literally, and accordingly maintains that "the hosts of Sisera" were annihilated by the "hosts of heaven", the stars and angels; comp. WR 7 (end). Ps.-Philo, 34C and D; 31.1 and 2; Josephus, *Antiqui.*, V, 5.4, and Yerahmeel 58.174 (which is based on Josephus or on a text of ps.-Philo different from ours) rationalize in the following manner: God sent rain, storm, and hail against Sisera. Pesahim, 118b reads: The iron chariots of Sisera melted on account of the intense heat emanating from the stars. Comp. vol. III, p. 27. See also Abba Gorion 27; Aguddat Aggadot 77; *Neweh Shalom* 47. Comp. Aggadat Bereshit 1,2; Tosefta Sotah 3.14. On the identification of the stars with angels, see Mo'ed Katan 16a. Comp. vol. IV, p. 407.

⁸² Mo'ed Katan 16a, which cites also another view to the effect that Meroz is the name of a prominent personage who refused to participate in the war against Sisera and was therefore excommunicated by Barak. Ps.-Jerome, Jud. 5.23, reads: *Meros. i, e. potestati angelicae.*

⁸³ Pesahim 118b; PRE 42. Comp. vol. III, p. 31. A somewhat different view is given by ps.-Jerome, Jud. 5.1. An allusion to this legend is to be found in the paraphrase of Targum which renders נחל קדומים by "the brook at which miracles have been wrought for Israel in ancient times." It should be observed that Targum agrees with ps.-Jerome who likewise refers נחל קדומים to the Red Sea, and not to the Brook Kishon. The remarks by Ginzberg, *Haggada bei den Kirchenv.*, 8, are to be corrected accordingly. The victory over Sisera was won in the first night of Passover; *Panim Aherim* 74 (comp. note 76 on vol. I, p. 224). Sisera was killed within a very few hours of the beginning of the battle; Koheleth 3.14. Similarly ps.-Philo, 34; 31.2. reads: And...they were slain in one hour. On Mount Tabor, where the battle took place, see vol. III, pp. 83–84.

⁸⁴ Ps.-Philo, 34; 31.3; according to this ברגליו (Jud. 4.17) is to be translated "by himself" and not "on his feet."

197

⁸⁵ Ps.-Philo, 34; 31.3; Megillah 15a. The former source, like the Palestinian Midrashim, speak only of the great fascination which Jael's beauty exerted over Sisera; comp., *e. g.*, WR 23. 10, which reads: God attached His name to the names of Joseph (=יהוסף), Paltiel (=פלטיאל), the husband of Michal, and Jael (=יהאל), to testify that these pious persons withstood the temptation to which they were exposed (comp. note 60 on vol. IV, p. 34) and remained chaste. Comp. also MHG I, 336, which reads: When Sisera, in a state of intoxication, asked her to submit to his passion, she killed him. The Babylonian Talmud goes much further, and maintains that Jael surrendered herself to Sisera's passion, as this was the only sure means to get hold of him and kill him; see Yebamot 103a–103b; Nazir 23b; Horayyot 10b. *Rimze Haftarot* quotes a Haggadah to the effect that Jael gave Sisera to drink "the milk of her breast"; comp. Niddah 55b and Tosefta Shabbat 8.24, where this legend is perhaps presupposed. Ps.-Philo, 35; 31. 6, reads: And Jael took wine and mingled it with the milk. Similarly MHG, *loc. cit.*, speaks of Sisera's intoxication, which presupposes that he was served by Jael with something stronger than milk.

⁸⁶ Ps.-Philo, 34–35; 31.3–7; this was reproduced, in abridged form, by Yerahmeel 58, 172. On the fire of the stars contending for Israel, see notes 72, 81. According to the law, Deut. 22.5, a woman is forbidden to use weapons, and that is the reason why Jael slew Sisera with a hammer, and not with a spear or sword; see Targum Jud. 5.26; *Hadar*, Deut., *loc. cit.*; Mishle 31, 111. This Midrash is the source of Yalkut II, 456, where the first edition refers to מדרש and not to אבכיר as in later editions. Deborah's words "like women in the tent shall she (Jael) be blessed" (Jud. 5.24) contain the blessing that Jael may be like unto Sarah, Rebekah, Rachel, and Leah (whose tents are mentioned in Scripture; see Gen. 24.67 and 41.33), since if it were not for Jael, the descendants of these four women would have perished by the hand of Sisera; see BR 48.15; Nazir 23b, and parallel passages. Comp. also Targum Jud. 5.24.

⁸⁷ *I. e.*, תמחה=תמח "may she be destroyed." The same name was borne by Cain's wife; ps.-Philo, 1; 2.1. Yerahmeel misread or "emended" the text of ps.-Philo, and has Tamar as the name of Sisera's mother.

⁸⁸ Ps.-Philo, according to Yerahmeel 58, 184, while our text of ps.-Philo, 35; 31.8, reads somewhat differently. On the magic of Sisera's mother, see Zohar III, 119a, and Sabba', Wa-Yeze, 27d.

⁸⁹ Yerushalmi quoted by many medieval authors but not found in

our rexts; comp. R. Hananel in Rosh ha-Shanah (end); '*Aruk*, s. v. ערב 1; Manhig 54, No. 21; *Shibbale ha-Leket* 282, No. 301 (end); *Pardes* 42b (bottom). On the "hundred cries", comp. also WR 27.7; PK 9, 77b, and parallel passages cited by Buber. The connection between the "hundred cries" of Sisera's mother and the "hundred sounds" of the Shofar, alluded to in Yerushalmi, *loc. cit.*, is obscure and should probably read אמנו שרה instead of אמא דסיסרא; comp. Reifmann in *Or Torah*, 205; Ratner, *Ahawat Zion*, Rosh ha-Shanah 57; note 256 on vol. I, p. 287. Comp. note 92.

⁹⁰ Ps.-Philo, 35–36; 32.1–17, and a shorter paraphrase in Targumim on Jud. 5.1, *seq.*

⁹¹ Ps.-Philo, 37; 33.1–6. According to Seder 'Olam 12, the forty years of Deborah's rule included the twenty years of Israel's subjection to Jabin and Sisera. On the doctrine that the pious who are dead cannot interecede for the living sinners, see vol. IV, p. 416; vol. V, pp. 160–161 and note 118, towards the end, on vol. II, pp. 314–315. This, however, has nothing to do with the strong faith in the "merits of the fathers", which ps.-Philo frequently emphasizes. Comp. Index, s. v. "Fathers, Merits of".

⁹² Tehillim 18, 137; Shemuel 19, 135. Comp. note 58 on vol. III, p. 31. Ps.-Philo, 37; 32.18, speaks of a great sacrificial festival celebrated by Deborah and the people at Shiloh, after the victory over Sisera. On this occasion "they sounded the broad trumpets", and Deborah said: "This shall be for a testimony of the trumpets between the stars and their Lord." The meaning of the last sentence is not clear, but it seems that ps.-Philo explains the ceremony of sounding the trumpets (the sounding of the Shofar on New Year?) as a memorial of the victory of Israel over Sisera. Comp. the quotation from Yerushalmi in note 89.

⁹³ Ps.-Philo 37; 34.1–5. Comp. Sifre D., 84, where it is said that God will enable the false prophet to cause the sun and moon to stand still in order to test the strength of Israel's faith.

⁹⁴ Yelammedenu in '*Aruk*, s. v. בבואה, and Yalkut II, 62, where Tan. is given as source; this is, however, not found in our text of the Tanchumas. Comp. Tan. B. I, 138, and note 98.

⁹⁵ Tehillim 106 (end).

⁹⁶ Yelammedenu in Yalkut II, 62; Zohar Hadash, Noah, 29a. The victory over the Midianites took place on the second night of Passover; see note 100.

⁹⁷ Ps.-Philo 38; 35.6–7; Yerahmeel 58, 175. On a similar miracle

see vol. III, p. 195. With regard to the miracles which, according to Scripture (Jud. 6.37–40), were wrought for Gideon, the following remark should be noted: The first miracle, the non-appearance of the dew upon all the ground, was not performed directly by God, whereas the second one was direct from God. The reason is because God enters into direct connection with good, but not with evil; comp. Yelammedenu in Yalkut II, 62; B. I. 138; note 9 on vol. I, p. 5. The Angel who appeared to Gideon looked like a youth; Josephus, *Antiqui.*, V, 6.2. The Haggadah points out that Gideon, in making use of an altar dedicated to an idol and of sacrifices set aside for idolatrous practices, acted contrary to the law (he transgressed no less than seven commands), but he obeyed a special revelation that came to him on this occasion. See Yerushalmi Megillah 1, 72c; WR 22.9; Shemuel 13, 83; Comp. note 8 on vol. IV, p. 4.

⁹⁸ Ps.-Philo, 38; 36.1–2. The Haggadah offers several explanations of the water test referred to in Scripture (Jud. 7.5, *seq*). The sinners of this generation used to worship their own images reflected in the water (see vol. IV, p. 39, bottom), and accordingly those who "bowed down upon their knees to drink water" betrayed themselves as idolaters by bowing down to worship their images in the water; Yelammedenu in '*Aruk*,s. v. בבואה and Yalkut II, 62; somewhat differently Tan. B. I, 183, which reads: "As idolaters they were accustomed to bow down", and they followed their custom while drinking water. According to Josephus, *Antiqui.*, V, 6.3, God desired to show that He was able to accomplish the defeat of Israel's enemies with a small army of faint-hearted people who were too timid to "bow down and drink water quietly."

⁹⁹ MHG I, 722–723, and, in a somewhat different form, in the later editions of Yalkut II, 62. This story is found in a Genizah fragment of Tan., and it is very likely that R. Abraham Gedaliah, who inserted this legend in his edition of Yalkut (Leghorn 1656), was in possession of a MS. of Tan. similar to that of the Genizah.

¹⁰⁰ PK 8, 71a; PR 18, 92b; WR 27.6. These sources only say that the victory over the Midianites was the reward for the fulfilment of the commandment of the 'Omer; the later sources, however (*Panim Aherim*, 73; the paitan Yannai in piyyut ובכן ויהי בחצי הלילה), expand this Haggadah, and maintain that this victory was won on the first night of Passover or according to some on the very day on which the 'Omer was brought. See Aggadat Esther 29, where it is stated that the war against the Midianites took place in the month of Elul. Comp. note 83 and note 76 on vol. I, p. 224. MHG I, 722, finds in

the "cake of barley, which turned the camp of the enemy upside down," an indication that this victory was gained by Gideon as a reward for his filial piety towards his father, whom, at the risk of being captured by the Midianites (see vol. IV, pp. 39–40), he provided with bread of barley. Josephus, *Antiqui.*, V, 6.3, sees in the cake of barley the symbol of Israel's low state. Comp. Sifre N., 8; Sotah 15a; Jerome, Hosea 3.2.

101 Yalkut II, 64 (the source is not given). It is very likely that on account of the making of the Ephod Gideon is disparaged by the Haggadah which considers Gideon, Jephthah, and Samson as the three least worthy of the judges; see Rosh ha-Shanah, Tosefta 2(1).3; Babli 25a–25b. Comp. also Zohar Hadash, Noah, 29a, which reads: Gideon was neither a pious man himself not the son of a pious man, and yet he was found worthy of being the liberator of Israel, because he pleaded for them to God; see Jud. 6.13–14, and vol. IV, p. 40. Very severe is the censure of Gideon in ps.-Philo, 38; 36.3–4, and a reason is given why he was not punished for his idolatry. God said: "...when he (Gideon) destroyed the sanctuary of Baal, then all men said: Let Baal avenge himself. Now, therefore, if I chastize him for the evil he did against Me, ye (men) will say: It was not God who chastized him but Baal because he sinned aforetime against him." For a similar view, see vol. IV, pp. 156–157.

102 Shabbat 83b. Comp. also Yerushalmi 9, 11d, and 'Abodah Zarah 3, 43a, where attention is called to the smallness of the images of this idol, which is said to have been of Priapean form. On the sinfulness of this generation, see also Bezah 25b.

103 Tan. B. I, 103. The parable of Jotham is said here to refer to the prominent judges Othniel (= olive-tree), Deborah (= fig-tree), Gideon (= vine), and Elimelech (= bramble). Tan. also states that Abimelech reigned three years, as a reward for the modesty of his father Gideon, who in a "tripartite" sentence refused the royal crown offered him by the people; see Jud. 8.23. Abimelech, in contrast to his father (Jud. 8.27), was very greedy for riches, and his end therefore came speedily; Aggadat Bereshit 26, 54; see also *ibid.*, 52–53, where Abimelech's wickedness and greed are contrasted with the piety and liberality of his namesake Abimelech, the King of Gerar. The ingratitude of the Israelites who permitted Abimelech to murder the children of their benefactor Gideon was counted unto them as though they had forsaken God; ingratitude is as grave a sin as idolatry; Yelammedenu in Yalkut II, 64. On the blessings pronounced on Mount Gerizim, see vol. IV., p. 6, according to which the blessings were pronounced in the valley,

whereas Tan., *loc. cit.*, maintains that they were uttered on the mountain. The reading in Tan. *loc. cit.*, should be הר גריזים שלנו מבורך הוא; comp. טורא בריכא in BR 32.10, and parallel passages. The name of Abimelech's mother was Drumah, comp. Josephus, *Antiqui.*, V; 7,1.

¹⁰⁴ Ps.-Philo 39; 38.1–2; Yerahmeel 68, 175. The names of the seven pious men are badly mutilated in ps.–Philo, and not quite correct in Yerahmeel. This legend about Jair and the pious men recalls in many details the story of Abraham as given in ps.–Philo 6–8; 6.16–18. Jair is said to have perished in fire. This is a haggadic interpretation of בקמון (Jud. 10.5), which is taken to mean "furnace" from קמין = καμίνιον, of frequent occurrence in the Talmudim and Midrashim.

¹⁰⁵ Ps.-Philo, 39, and Yerahmeel 48, 175. The name Nathanel given to the "angel who is over fire" (only in ps.-Philo) is rather strange. Is perhaps Atuniel (from אתונא "furnace") to be read? In rabbinic angelology Gabriel is the angel appointed over fire; see Index, s. v. As to Baal, the following statement of Zohar I, 49a, is rather interesting: Baal is the sun; Asherah the moon; the former is the husband, the latter the wife. On the rescue of the pious from the furnace, see Dan. 3.22 and vol. I, p. 176.

¹⁰⁶ Targum (Tosefta) Jud. 11.1 in Leiria edition, and in Kimhi; comp. also Josephus, V, 7.8, who remarks: They (Jephthah's brethren) cast him off, because he did not have the same mother as the rest, but was born of a strange mother, who was introduced among them by his father's fondness. Did Josephus read זרה instead of זונה in Jud., *loc. cit.*? Of course, it is possible, and even very likely, that Josephus for apologetic reasons did not care to describe a prominent personage in Israel as the son of a γυναικὸς πόρνης as the Hebrew זונה is rendered by Septuagint. Our Targum paraphrases it by פונדקיתא ("inn-keeper"); comp. Büchler, *Priester und Cultus*, 63; Krauss, *Lehnwörter*, s. v. פונדקית; note 12 on vol. IV, p. 5. That in olden times it was considered improper to marry out of one's tribe is maintained also by Origen, Num. 36.8. This is very likely presupposed also in Ketubot 28b and Yerushalmi 2, 26d. Comp. Freund, *Schwarz–Festschrift*, 180.

¹⁰⁷ Yerushalmi Shebi'it 6.36c where the land of Tob is identified with the city of Hippos in the Decapolis. It is on account of the fertility of its soil that it is described in Scripture as "good land". The editions of Targum also have בארעא טבא, but Codex Reuchlin and Kimhi read טוב, in agreement with Septuagint. Ps.-Philo seems to take טוב as the name of a person, and this is also the view suggested

by Kimhi. "As each bird seeks its kind, so does man his equal find"; the "vain fellows" who gathered around Jephthah show what kind of a man he was; Baba Kamma 92b. Josephus, *Antiqui.*, V, 7.8, for apologetic reasons (see the preceding note), represents Jephthah in a favorable light, and as a true aristocrat he adds that Jephthah's father was a very prominent personality. The Rabbis, on the other hand, are rather severe in their opinion of this judge; comp. notes 101, 109.

¹⁰⁸ Ps.-Philo, 40–42; 39. 6–40.4; Yerahmeel 59. 176. On Getal, see note 1. Concerning Isaac's joyful readiness to be brought as a sacrifice, see vol. I, pp. 279–280. Mount Telag or Selac (also written Thelac) is, of course, nothing but Hermon, Hebrew הר שלג, Aramaic טור תלג. Comp. Onkelos on Deut. 3.9, and Sifre N. 131. Accordingly Stelac is a faulty reading, combining the Hebrew form *selac* (=שלג) with the Aramaic *thelac* (=תלג) "snow". What ps.-Philo has to say about the "shutting up of the mouth of the wise" becomes intelligible only in connection with the statement of the Rabbis (comp. the following note) that, were it not for the ignorance of the people, Jephthah's daughter would never have been sacrificed, for his vow was not according to the law. On the text of ps.-Philo, see the fragment published by James, *Text and Studies*, II, 3.

¹⁰⁹ WR 37.4; Br 60.3; Tan. B. III, 112–114; Tan. Behukkotai 5; Koheleth 10.15; Ta'anit 4a; Midrash Tannaim 100; Sifre D., 148; Targum and Tosefta Targum on Jud. 11.39; PRK 32b; ER 11, 55–57; We-Hizhir, Behukkotai (end). Although Jephthah was severely punished for having slain many thousands of the Ephraimites, they deserved their fate, for they were addicted to idolatry, particularly to the worship of an idol called Sibboleth, which name was so much on their lips that they involuntarily said Sibboleth when they intended to say Shibboleth; Tosefta Targum Jud. 12.6; ER 11, 456. In the last-named source Phinehas is blamed for not having prevented the war between Jephthah and the Ephraimites. He ought to have remonstrated with those proud men who did not intercede in behalf of Jephthah's daughter, though they were ready to go to war for an alleged insult. The view that Jephthah did not offer his daughter as a sacrifice, but merely made her live in seclusion far from all earthly intercourse, devoting herself entirely to the service of God, is first found in the writings of medieval Rabbis (comp., *e. g.*, Kimhi on Jud. 11.39). The midrashic and talmudic literature does not know of this rationalistic view, and it strongly condemns Jephthah and his contemporaries for having offered a human sacrifice. Josephus, *Antiqui.*, V, 7.10, shares the view of the old rabbinic

authorities. "Woe unto the wicked and unto those who come near them"; Jephthah, originally a pious man, dwelled among the wicked Ephraimites, and followed their example. They offered human sacrifices to Baal, and he sacrificed his daughter to God. Murder was common among the Ephraimites, and the slaughter of twenty-two thousand men was considered a light thing by Jephthah. The earth refused to receive the corpse of this evil doer, and its decaying parts were found scattered here and there; comp. Alphabet of Ben Sira 4a–4b.—An old legend connects "the poisoning of the water" during the "four turnings of the sun" (*i. e.*, vernal equinox, summer solstice, autumnal equinox, and winter solstice) with the sacrifice of Jephthah's daughter. In the vernal equinox God turned the waters of Egypt into blood (comp. note 174 on vol. II p. 347) and from that time on every year, at the time when the vernal equinox takes place, a drop of blood is thrown into the waters, which poisons them. The same thing happens at the summer solstice, the time when Moses smote the rock, and blood began to flow therefrom (see vol III, p. 319); at the autumnal equinox, the time when Abraham stretched out his hand to slay Isaac (comp. note 248 on vol. I, p. 285) and the knife began to bleed (comp. note 242 on vol. I, p. 282); at the winter solstice, the time when Jephthah offered his daughter as a sacrifice, and his knife began to bleed. On these four days of the "turn of the sun" the maidens of Israel went to lament Jephthah's daughter. According to some authorities, however, the poisoned state of the water during the "four turns of the sun" is due to different causes. At each "turn of the sun" a different angel is appointed over the world, but for a moment "the world remains without a leader", and this is the moment when the change of heavenly officials takes place. Availing himself of this opportunity, Scorpio throws gall and a drop of blood into the water to cause death to mankind. See Mahzor Vitry, supplement 14; *Ginze Yerushalaim* III, 18b; Abudrahim סדר תקופה; Aptowitzer in *Ha-Zofeh* II, 122–126; Ginzberg, *ibid.*, III, 184, and IV, 98. In the last-quoted passage attention is called to the myth concerning the weeping for Belti for seven days in the month of Tebeth, as well as to the Jewish legend, according to which Jephthah's daughter was sacrificed and wept for in this month; comp. *Z.D.M.G.*, LXVI, 176.

¹¹⁰ Ps.-Philo, 42; 41.1. Josephus, *Antiqui.*, V, 7.15, on the other hand, maintains that Abdan ruled during a very peaceful time, which did not offer him any opportunity to display his qualities as a warrior.

¹¹¹ Tan. B. IV, 160, and parallel passages cited in note 864 on vol. III, pp. 414–415; Baba Batra 91a; BaR 10.5; Aggadat Bereshit

52, 106–107 (which reads: A miracle was wrought for seven sterile women, and they bore children; they are: Sarah, Rebekah, Leah, Rachel, Hannah, Hazlelponit, and Zion); MHG I, 337, says: Hazlelponit is one of the twenty-two virtuous women who are praised in the last chapter of Proverbs. Comp. note 271 on vol. I, p. 291. The MSS. of the Talmud have Hazlelponit, which is very likely the correct reading, since there can be no doubt that the reference is to הצללפוני in I Chron. 4.3. The obscure sentence in Baba Batra, *loc. cit*, ואחתיה נשיין is very likely to be translated: "And sister means the same as wife". The Talmud identifies Etam mentioned in Chron., *loc. cit.*, with Manoah, the father of Samson on the basis of Jud. 15.8, and hence the remark that ואחותם הצללפוני means the same as ואשתו הצללפוני, or in Aramaic נשיין ואחתיה. On נְשִׁיָין "wife"

(secondary form of the plural נשי), see Targum Yerushalmi Deut. 22.5. On "sister" = "wife", comp. Song of Songs 4.9–10; Tobit 5.22; Jub. 27.14; Shir 3.11; MHG. I. 341. The explanation given by Güdemann, *Religionsgeschichtliche Studien*, 49–55, of the name Hazlelponi and of נשי is untenable. BaR, *loc. cit.*, explains this name as "The shadow of God (*i. e.*, the angel) turned to her" (and not to her husband), as it was her piety and virtue which were rewarded with a son like Samson, whereas her husband was an "ignorant man"; comp. BaR and MHG, I, 337; Berakot 61a; Midrash Mishle (end). Josephus, on the other hand (comp. his statement with regard to Jephthah, notes 106, 107), maintains that Manoah was one of the greatest men of his generation. Ps.-Philo, 42–43, 42.1, enumerates the names of Samson's ancestors up to Dan, the son of Jacob, and it is worthy of note that the judge was the tenth from the patriarch. Samson's mother is called Eluma (עלומה = עלמה), the daughter of Remac. Ps.-Philo knows some other details concerning Samson's parents. Manoah and his wife contended for some time as to who was responsible for their childless union. Finally God heard the prayer of Manoah's wife, and sent to her the angel Phadihel (very likely פחריאל, and not פריאל), who said unto her: "Thou art the barren one... but now... thou shalt conceive and bear a son, and shalt call his name Samson, for he shall be holy unto the Lord." The etymology of the name Samson as given by ps.-Philo is rather obscure, since there is no Hebrew word meaning "holy" which can in any possible way be connected with the word Samson. Possibly "holy unto the Lord" is an inaccurate rendering of "anointed to the Lord", in allusion to שמן "oil". Josephus, *Antiqui.*, V, 8.4, explains Samson as "the mighty one", and this is still less satisfactory. The Rabbis, on the other hand, connect this name with שמש "sun", remarking that Samson spread light over his generation like the sun; comp. Sotah 10a (where read, with Makiri on Ps. 84, 61, האיר בדורו), which says: Samson received the name of God, as it is written: "For the Lord God is a sun and shield" (Ps. 84.12). Although the angel told Manoah's wife that it was she herself, and not her husband, who was responsible for their childless union, she did not reveal this to Manoah, "for the sake of peace"; BaR 10.5 and 11, 88a; WR 9.9; Derek Erez, Perek ha-Shalom. According to Josephus, *Antiqui.*, V, 8.2–3, Manoah "was fond of his wife to distraction (he did not divorce her, though she bore him no children; nor did he marry another wife), and was therefore extremely jealous of her. Now when his wife informed him of what the angel, who resembled a young man (comp. note 97), beautiful and tall, had told her, he became beside himself for jealousy". The angel's command to Manoah's wife, "and eat not any unclean thing", was a warning to her not to follow the advice of the women who had counselled her to eat of a hare's stomach as a remedy against sterility. This cure is ascribed to the hare's stomach, because this animal changes its sex: it is a male for a time and then changes into a female. See Tosefata 'Atikata 5.19; *Rimze Haftarot*, Naso; note 177 on vol. I, p. 39. Comp. also Index, s. v. "Hare".—The angels who visited Abraham partook of the food offered to them by the patriarch (comp. note 143 on fol. I, p. 243), but the angel who came to Manoah refused. The different attitudes are to be explained in the following manner: The angels visited Abraham as wayfarers, and they revealed the divine message to him only after they had partaken of his food; but this was not the case with the angel who came to Manoah and his wife. He appeared to them as the bearer of a divine message, and if he had taken anything from them it would have looked like compensation for his service. He said to them: "The prophets of God do not take presents as the false prophets do." BaR 10.5; comp. also ER 12, 60, and Index, s. v. "Angels." What ps.-Philo 43; 42.8, has to say about the angel's refusal to receive gifts is unintelligible to me.

[112] BR 98.13 and 99.11; BaR 10.5. Comp. the preceding note with regard to the identification of Samson's mother with Hazlelponi in 1 Chron. 4.3, who is described as belonging to the tribe of Judah.

[113] Baba Batra 91a; Tosefta-Targum Jud. 12.9. These sources presuppose the identity of Ibzan with Boaz; see note 31 and note 3 on vol. IV, p. 81.

[114] Sotah 10a. Comp. vol. I, p. 59. Samson's superhuman

strength is presupposed in the haggadic interpretation of כאחד (Gen.
49.16), as "like unto the One (= God)". Comp. ןBR 98.13; Tan.
Wa-Yehi 12; Sotah, *loc. cit.* See also note 123.

¹¹⁵ Sotah 10a; Nispahim 44; BaR 14.9. The enormous size
of Samson's body is inferred from the fact that he carried the gates
of Gaza on his shoulders (see Jud. 16.3), which, "according to tradition
measured sixty cubits." Ps.-Philo, 43; 43.4, describes Samson's feat
at Gaza in the following terms: One of the gates he held in his right
hand as a shield and the other he laid upon his shoulders, and bore it
away, and because he had no sword, he pursued the Philistines with
it, and killed therewith twenty-five thousand men.

¹¹⁶ Sotah 9b and Yerushalmi 1, 17b; WR 8.2. On the conception
that God's holy spirit might manifest itself in man's hair, see BR 4.4 and
vol. II, p. 319. The Rabbis speak of Samson as one upon whom God's
spirit rested, but do not consider him a prophet. Josephus, *Antiqui.,*
V, 8.4, however, does not hesitate to describe him as a prophet.

¹¹⁷ BR 98.13. According to the Haggadah, the blessing given
to Dan by Jacob (Gen. 49.16–18) refers to Samson the Danite. See
vol. II, p. 144.

¹¹⁸ Tosefta-Targum Jud. 15.15. For other interpretations of this
verse, see BR 98.13; 1) a three-day-old ass; 2) a she-ass pregnant with
two. For the latter interpretation of חמור חמרתים, see also Targum,
ad loc.

¹¹⁹ BR 98.13. which reads: Samson would have perished even
if there were water near him, as he was too exhausted to stretch out
his hand; he prayed to God: "Even if I have no other merit than
that of being circumcized, whereas the Philistines are not, I ought not to
fall into the hands of the uncircumcized." Samson who was proud of
his superhuman strength came near dying by thirst, that he might learn
that a man's strength avails him nothing without God's help; Josephus
Antiqui., V, 8.9. The remark of BR, *loc. cit.,* that "the babbler becomes thirsty", wishes very likely to convey the same idea as Josephus.
The latter's (*loc. cit.*) rationalistic explanation of the miracle narrated
in Jud. 15.19, according to which Samson noticed water flowing from
a rock, is known also to the Rabbis; comp. BR, *loc. cit.* According to
some authorities, however, לחי (Jud., *loc. cit.*) means the "jaw-bone"
(of the ass). God said: He likes that which is unclean (Philistine
women), and his life shall be saved by the water coming from an unclean
thing (the jaw-bone of an ass); Sotah 9b; BaR 9.24.

¹²⁰ Sotah 10a; BaR 9.24.

¹²¹ Sotah 9b–10a (on טחן as a euphemism for sexual intercourse, see also Jerome, Is. 47.2); BaR 9.24. Samson's parents at first attempted to dissuade him from marrying a Philistine woman, saying to him: "As the fields of the heathen are sown in mixed seeds (this is forbidden in Lev. 19.19), so are their offspring. "Samson, however, did not heed their wise counsel, and married a Philistine woman from Timnah (according to some authorities this place is not identical with Timnah mentioned in Gen. 38.12), with whom he lived only one week, because she betrayed his secret to his companions who pretended to be his friends, while in reality they watched him that he should not attack the Philistines. It is with good reason that Samson, after his first experience of married life, exclaimed: "There is nothing more deceitful than a woman!" (Josephus, *Antiqui.*, V, 8.6). When, however, the father of the Philistine woman gave her into marriage to another man, Samson became so infuriated at the Philistines for their connivance at the breach of marriage vows (שחזרו בשבועתן refers perhaps to the breach of the covenant made between the Philistine Abimelech and Abraham), that he destroyed their fields by means of the torches put between the tails of the foxes; they acted like sly foxes, and their punishment was therefore carried out by foxes. Samson went from bad to worse: He started by marrying a heathen woman, and finished by becoming a captive of a heathen harlot at Gaza. It was therefore at this place that he met his fate at the hands of Delilah, who deserves this name, "she who makes poor", as it was through her that Samson became poor: he lost his strength, his wisdom, and his piety. See Sotah, Mishnah 1.8 (the sentence, "he who went astray after his eyes lost his eyes", is found almost verbatim in ps.-Philo, 43, bottom; 43.5); Tosefta 3.15; Babli 9b–10a; Yerushalmi 1, 17b and Ketubot 5, 30b; MHG I, 752; Mekilta Shirah 2, 36a; BR. 52.12; BaR 9.24. "Wine leads to unchastity", and therefore Samson was commanded to be a Nazirite all his life (on the nature of his form of Naziriteship, see Nazir, Mishnah 1.3–4; Babli 4b), otherwise his conduct would have been still more licentious; BaR 10.5. Josephus, *Antiqui.*, V, 5.11 and 12, attempts to exonerate Samson to some extent. On the vile means employed by Delilah, see Sotah 9b.

¹²² ויתן לך האלהים (Gen. 27.28) is translated: "And He shall give thee that which is divine."

¹²³ BR 66.3. Comp. note 115.

¹²⁴ Yerushalmi Sotah 1, 17b; BaR 9.24; Sotah 10a. On the reading of Babli in Jud. 16.31, see Ratner on Seder 'Olam 12, and

Schnitzer in *Ha-Zofeh* III, 137. According to BR 98.14, the number
of the slain by far exceeded three thousand. Scripture (Jud. 16.27)
speaks only of those who were in the building which Samson pulled
down. There was, however, a vast multitude, much in excess of that
number, standing around the building, and they all perished when it
fell on them. The same view is shared by ps.-Philo, 44; 43.8, which
reads: And the house fell and all that was in it, and slew all those
that were round about it, and the number of them was forty thousand
men and women. Samson's last words read in ps.-Philo: "O Lord,
God of my fathers, hear me yet this once, and strengthen me that I
may die with those Philistines, for the sight of the eyes which they have
taken from me was fully given unto me by Thee." He then added:
"Go forth, O my soul, and be not grieved. Die, O my body, and weep
not for thyself."

¹²⁵ Ps.-Philo 44; 44.2; Tosefta-Targum Jud. 17.2; a quotation
from an unknown Midrash in Rashi and Kimhi, *ad loc.* There can be
no doubt that in ps.-Philo, *l. c.*, we ought to read Delila instead of
Dedila. Ps.-Philo has a very strange statement to the effect that this
Dedila or Delila was not only the mother of Micah but also of Heliu
i. e., Eli. According to Eldad, 4–5, the descendants of Samson from
his marriage (?) with Delilah live among the Danites (comp. vol. IV,
p. 182), and are distinguished by their gigantic strength and great valor.
Their war-cry is: "Salvation belongeth unto the Lord; Thy strength
over Thy people, the tribes of Jeshurun, Selah." The text, however,
is not quite clear, and this war-cry is probably that of the Danites,
and not of the descendants of Samson. Comp. also note 27 on vol.
IV, p. 85.

¹²⁶ Tan. Ki-Tissa 19 (on children as building material, see vol.
II, p. 250); Sanhedrin 101b (see Rashi on נתמכך בבנין); Alphabet
of Ben Sira 4d; Shu'aib, *Hadar*, and Ziyyoni on Exod. 32.4, *seq.*
According to another version of this legend, Micah stole the silver
plate by means of which Moses had made Joseph's coffin come to the
surface of the water (comp. vol. II, p. 182; vol. III, p. 122), and employed
it first to fashion the golden calf, and later to make a graven image;
Teshubot Hakme Zarefat, 42, No. 67; Ziyyoni, *loc. cit.* The latter quotes
from Midrash Shir ha-Shirim (not found in any of the three Midrashim
on Song of Songs), still another legend about Micah's share in the
fashioning of the golden calf. Comp. the following two notes and note
266 on vol. III, p. 122. See also ShR 41.1.

¹²⁷ Mekilta Bo 14, 16a. For a full discussion of this point, comp.

note 72 on vol. III, p. 37. The Mekilta and many other sources pre-suppose that Micah's activity took place shortly after the death of Joshua. Comp. the following note and note 136.

[128] Seder 'Olam 12, which reads: In the days of Cushan-Risha-thaim Micah set up the graven image (comp. Jud. 3.8, *seq.*). This, of course, does not preclude the possibility that Micah made this image in Egypt. On his share in the fashioning of the golden calf, see note 126, and note 72 on vol. III, p. 37.

[129] Sanhedrin 103b reads: From Gareb to Shiloh is a distance of three miles, and the smoke of the holy altar at Shiloh mingled with the smoke proceeding from the altar erected by Micah to his graven image at Gareb. This occurs also in Aggadat Bereshit 49, 100; PR 29, 137b. The statement about Gareb is rather puzzling, as this locality is in the neighborhood of Jerusalem, not of Shiloh. The Talmud *l. c.* adds: the angels wished his doom but God said to them, "Leave him; his bread is offered to the wayfarers."

[130] Tosefta Sanhedrin 14.7–8; Baba Batra 109b; Yerushalmi Berakot 9, 13d; Shir 2.5; ARN 24, 99. In all these sources the Levite mentioned in Jud. 17.7 is identified with Jonathan of 18.30. The suspended Nun in Jud. 18.30 is accordingly explained in these sources in the following manner: This priest of the graven image was a grand-son of Moses; but out of respect for the great prophet, he is described, by means of the suspended Nun, as the grandson of Manasseh, to whom he was related through their kindred actions, both having been idolaters. See Blau, *Masoretische Untersuchungen*, 46–49. Comp. also the refer-ences cited in note 133. This priest was not only a grandson of Moses on his paternal side, but on his maternal side, too, he was of prominent descent, as his mother belonged to the tribe of Judah. He is therefore described in the very same scriptural verse (Jud. 17.7) as a Levite and Judean. The soundness of the rule that "children take after their mother's brothers" can be proved by the difference between the descendants of Moses and those of Aaron. The latter married the sister of Nahshon, the prince of Judah, and his descendants were priests and high priests unto the Lord; but the former married the sister of idolaters (the sons of Jethro), and his grandson was a priest of Micah's graven image; Baba Batra 109b–110a.

[131] Ps.-Philo, 44; 44.2–9; Yerahmeel 59, 180. The first source contains also a lengthy Midrash showing how Israel, by worshipping Micah's graven image, transgressed all the ten commandments. The statement of Yerahmeel that Micah's activity took place in the

days of the judge Abdon agrees neither with the view of the Rabbis, nor with that of ps.-Philo. Comp. notes 125, 127, 128, and 136.

¹³² Baba Batra 109b; Tosefta-Targum Jud. 18.18. Comp. also the references cited in the following note.

¹³³ Yerushalmi Berakot 9, 13d; Sanhedrin 10, 30b–30c; Shir 2.5; Baraita de-Yeshua 46b; Alphabet of Ben Sira 4b. The first three sources quote also a different view to the effect that Amaziah the priest of Beth-el (Amos 7.10) is identical with the "old prophet" of Beth-el (1 Kings 13.11, *seq.*). As to the man of God out of Judah (*ibid.* 14.1), the prevalent opinion is that he was none other than the prophet Iddo (2 Chron. 12.15 and 13.22); comp. Seder 'Olam 10; Tosefta Berakot 10.19; Sifre D., 177; Midrash Tannaim 112; Sanhedrin 89a–89b; Josephus, *Antiqui.*, VIII. 8.5. נביאי הבעל (Sanhedrin 104a) refers perhaps to Amaziah the priest of Beth-el. Comp. also Targum 1 Chron. 26.24, which is entirely dependent on Yerushalmi, *loc. cit.* In Alphabet of Ben Sira, *loc. cit.*, " the priest of Micah" is confounded with Micah himself, who is thus said to have been the priest of Beth-el.

¹³⁴ Ps.-Philo, 44; 45–47, and, in abridged form, Yerahmeel 59, 180–181. It is very strange that in ps.-Philo the crime of the Benjamites is tranferred from Gibeah to Nob. When the man of the tribe of Levi came to Gibeah, he desired to abide there, as the sun had set; but the inhabitants of this place did not suffer him to lodge in their midst. He was therefore obliged to proceed to Nob, where hospitality was offered to him by Bethac (on this name, see note 26 on vol. IV, p. 61) who, like himself, was of the tribe of Levi. The rabbinic sources know of no direct connection between the sin of Micah and the calamity that befell Israel in consequence of the crime of the Benjamites. They do, however, maintain that both events took place about the same time; according to some, Micah's graven image was set up on the very same day on which the war against the Benjamites began, that is, on the twenty-third of Shebat, which, in that year, fell on a Sabbath. See Seder 'Olam 12, and Ratner, note 9, as well as Esther R. 37.7. It is also said that the defeats suffered by the other tribes, in their campaign against the tribe of Benjamin, was their punishment for "having gone to war to avenge the honor of a woman, while they paid no heed to God's honor, which was outraged by Micah and his followers." See Sanhedrin 103b; PRE 48. Comp. further Yerushalmi Yoma 1, 38c; Megillah 1, 72a, where Phinehas' indifference towards the "crime of the Benjamites" is unfavorably contrasted with his zeal displayed in his early career. A similar remark is found in ER 11, 56–57, where

the Synedrion and the high priest Phinehas are held responsible for the death of the several thousands who fell in the war with the Benjamites. The crime which caused the war would never have been perpetrated if they, the leaders of the people, had done their duty and not neglected the moral education of Israel. There is also a view to the effect that the Israelites addressed themselves first to the idols for counsel (אלהים in Jud. 20.18, *seq.*, is taken to mean "gods", not "God"), and therefore suffered defeat; but when they called upon God, victory was granted them. Attention is also drawn to the difference in the answers given by God to Israel. The first and second answers did not contain any promise of help and assistance from God; hence the defeats of Israel. But the third answer was: "Go up, for to-morrow I will deliver him into thy hand"; and God fulfilled His promise. See Shebu'ot 35b; Soferim 4.17. That the first two answers were not favorable was due to the fact that they were addressed to God by one who was not worthy of performing the ceremony of inquiring of the Urim and Tummim; the last answer was favorable because the question was asked by the pious Phinehas; see Hasidim 122. The men who fell in the war to avenge the outraged and murdered woman deserved their fate; the woman, too, deserved her death, for she had at one time broken faith with her husband by sinning with the Amalekites; it was for this reason that God delivered her into the hands of sinners; ps.-Philo, 46; 45.3. The Rabbis are by far more considerate of the poor woman, and maintain that it was all the fault of her husband who was of a very harsh nature, so that his wife could not bear his treatment any longer and ran away from him. Thus his history "teaches us that one must not attempt to overawe the members of his family", for this man's severity led to bloodshed, unchastity, and desecration of the Sabbath; Gittin 6b; Targum Jud. 19.2 (on the text of Targum, see Nahmanides in his commentary on Gittin, who writes: ויונתן תירגם והזנה...לשון מזון); Ratner on Seder 'Olam 12; note 9. On the desecration of the Sabbath as the cause—not the effect— of this calamity, comp. the Midrash fragment in *J.Q.R.* New Series, VIII, 132.

¹³⁵ Midrash quoted by Kimhi, Jud. 20.5. The reading נרמניא, "Germany", is not certain, as some texts have רומניא "Romania" (Byzantium, or the Roman Empire?). For a full discussion of this legend comp. Brüll, *Jahrbücher*, IV, 34–40. A haggadic interpretation of רמון (Jud. 20.46) as Romania is perhaps the origin of the widespread legend among the Jews of the Middle Ages that the fleeing Benjamites settled in Romania. Ps.-Philo, 48; 57.11, gives the names of the

Benjamite clans and their chiefs who escaped death. The other tribes first decided to exclude the tribe of Benjamin from Israel; but changed their minds, for they found in Scripture an indication that it was God's will that Israel should consist of twelve tribes; see Yerushalmi Ta'anit 4, 69c; BR 84.4; Ekah, introduction, 33, 36. In these sources, as well as in Babli, Ta'anit 30b, and Baba Batra 116a, the great popular feast on the fifteenth of Ab is said to have originally been celebrated to commemorate the day (it was the fifteenth of Ab) on which Benjamin was re-admitted into the community of Israel. To enable the handful of Benjamites to develop normally, it became necessary to change some old laws of inheritance; Baba Batra, *loc. cit.*, and Midrash Aggada, Num. 36.4. The punishment meted out to the inhabitants of Jabesh-Gilead (comp. Jud. 21.5, *seq.*) was well merited. After the disastrous defeats sustained by the other tribes at the hands of the Benjamites, they threw themselves before the holy ark, and repented of their sins, whereupon God's grace turned to them. All Israelites were called to arms under threat of excommunication, and all responded to the call, with the exception of the inhabitants of Jabesh-Gilead. These were excommunicated, and death was their punishment. See PRE 38; Tan. Wa-Yesheb 2; *Orehot Hayyim*, II, 509. As to the means by which they ascertained which of the women of Jabesh-Gilead were virgins, who should thus escape death (Jud. 21.11–12), see Yebamot 60b and vol. III, p. 413. The festival on which the Benjamites went up to Shiloh and captured wives (Jud. 21.19) was Passover; see ps.-Philo, 48; 48.2. This is an interesting example of the use of midrashic Haggadah by this author, as it is based upon the hermeneutic rule of analogy נזרה שוה according to which מימים ימימה (Jud., *loc.cit.*) has the same meaning as in Exod. 13.10, where it undoubtedly refers to Passover. See Targum and Kimhi on Jud., *ad loc.*; Menahot 36b; Mekilta RS, 34; note 9 on vol. IV, p. 58.

¹³⁶ Ps.-Philo, 45; 44.9, and 48, 47.12. On the view that blasphemers and other grave sinners are punished by being eaten up alive by worms, see note 552 on vol. III, p. 283 and Vol. VI, p. 242, note 106. This author is obviously of the opinion that Micah's activity and the "crime of the Benjamites" took place towards the end of the period of the judges, whereas the Rabbis and Josephus, *Antiqui.*, V, 8.2, maintain that they occurred at the beginning of that period. Comp. notes 127, 134. See also ER 11, 57, which reads: In Scripture the crime of Gibeah is given at the end of the history dealing with the times of the judges, that the Gentiles should not say: The Israelites were already morally corrupt when they entered Palestine.

¹³⁷ Sanhedrin 103b; Alphabet of Ben Sira 4d.

¹³⁸ Konen 31. Nahmanides, Sha'ar ha-Gemul. 97c, reads Posiel (from פסל, Micah's graven image) instead of Hadriel.

¹³⁹ Sanhedrin 101b. Here also it is said that the rebel Sheba the son of Bichri is none other than Micah. Comp. vol. IV, p. 179.

¹⁴⁰ Ps.-Philo, 48; 48.1; Yerahmeel 59, 180. Danaben is undoubtedly a corrupt reading, though it is hard to suggest the correct form of this name. It may be a corruption of Lebanon, Abarim, or some other word. Ps.-Philo is the oldest source for the widespread legend which identifies Phinehas with Elijah; see note 803 on vol. III, p. 389 and note 3 on vol. IV, p. 195. Of interest is ps.-Philo's statement that Phinehas-Elijah (and, of course, all other "immortals") will "taste death" in the time to come. The same view is also shared by 4 Ezra, 7.29; comp. also vol. V, 21, note 61 (end) with regard to the disappearance of the angels before the creation of the new world. According to the Septuagint (Josh., end), the death and burial of Phinehas are recorded in Scripture.

III. SAMUEL

Vol. IV, (pp. 57-77).

[1] Megillah 13a. On Samuel as the descendant of Korah, whose sons were prophets, see Seder 'Olam 20, and Ratner, *ad loc.*; vol. III, pp. 297 and 301–303. According to PR 43, 181b, Tohu, the great grandfather of Elkanah, is none other than the psalmist Asaph. On the many haggadic interpretations of Ramathaim-Zophim and Ephrathi (1 Sam. 1.1), see Shemuel 1, 44–45; WR 2.3; Ruth R. 1.2; PRE 45; Targum 1 Sam. 1.1 (צופים = prophets, in accordance with Megillah *loc. cit.*); ps.-Jerome and Ephraem on 1 Sam. 1.1. Comp. Ginzberg, *Haggada bei den Kirchenv.*, 12–13, and Kellermann, *Der Midrasch zum 1 Buche Samuelis*, 7–12.

[2] Seder 'Olam 20 and 21; Megillah 14a. Comp. also Shemuel 1, 45, and note 28. The name of Hannah's father was Batuel (Bethuel); ps.-Philo, 51; 61.6.

[3] Aggadat Bereshit 49, 100–101. See also Shemuel 1, 44; BaR 10.5, which reads: Elkanah was equal in importance to thirty-one pious men. On a lengthy legend concerning Elkanah in ps.-Philo, see note 17,

[4] "A man of moderate means" is found only in Josephus, *Antiqui.*, V, 16.2. This is perhaps a haggadic interpretation of הרמתים (1 Sam. 1.1), "between the heights". Comp. Megillah 14a, and references given in note 1.

[5] ER 7, 47–48; Koheleth 5.19; Yerushalmi Berakot 9, 14; PR 43, 179a (which reads: Hannah used to go up to the sanctuary for prayer); Shemuel 1, 45; Targum and ps.-Jerome on 1 Sam. 1.3. The last mentioned Midrash points out that prayer is vastly superior to sacrifices, and therefore maintains that Elkanah's purpose in visiting the sanctuary was to pray there. On the meaning of מימים ימימה, see also note 9.

[6] PR 43, 181a; ER 18, 99. According to the law (Mishnah Yebamot 6, end), ten years of married life without children is a ground for divorce or gives the husband the right to take a second wife. The Rabbis who looked with disfavor on polygamy attempt therefore to

215

explain why the pious Elkanah had two wives; comp. PR 43, 181b; Shemuel 1, 45; Aggadat Bereshit 49, 101.

⁷ PR 43, 181b; Shemuel 1, 45–46. On the conception that barren women may change their unfortunate state by self-denial, see vol I, p.364. Peninnah's taunting words read in ps.-Philo, 49–50, 51.1–2, as follows: "What profiteth it thee that Elkanah thy husband loveth thee? But thou art a dry tree. I know moreover that he will love me, because he delighteth to see my sons standing around him like the planting of an olive-yard...A woman is not indeed beloved, even if her husband love her for her beauty. Let not Anna therefore boast herself of her beauty; but he that boasteth let him boast when he sees his seed before his face; and when it is not so among women, even the fruit of their womb, then shall love become of no account. For what profit was it unto Rachel that Jacob loved her? Except that there have been given unto her the fruit of her womb, surely his love would have been to no purpose." On the several interpretations of מנות and אפים (1 Sam 1.4–5) given by the Haggadah, see PR 43, 182a; Shemuel 1, 46; Targum and ps. Jerome, *ad loc.* Comp. Ginzberg, *Haggada bei den Kirchenv.*, 14–15, and Kellermann, *Midrasch zum 1 Buche Samuelis*, 20–21.

⁸ Baba Batra 16a; PR 43, 182b. A less favorable opinion of Peninnah is expressed by the sources referred to in the preceding note and in note 22.

⁹ Berakot 31b; MHG I, 391–392. In ps.-Philo, 50; 50.4, the prayer of Hannah reads: Hast not Thou, O Lord, examined the heart of all generations before Thou formedst the world? But what is the womb that is born open, or what one that is shut up dieth, except Thou will it? And now let my prayer go up before Thee this day, lest I go down hence empty. For thou knowest my heart, how I have walked before Thee from the days of my youth. The last sentence is a combination of 2 Kings 20.3 and 1 Kings 18.12. Other versions of Hannah's prayer are found PR 43, 179b–180a; Shemuel 1, 48 and 49; PRK (Grünhut's edition, 42a; here עלילה, "ruse", amounts to ואם לאו הרי אני מסתרת ונו' of the parallel passages); Aggadat Bereshit 19, 60. The last-named Midrash takes the "memorable day" (1 Sam. 1.4) to refer to the day of Passover which is spoken of in the preceding verse as מימים ימימה, in accordance with the use of that phrase in Exod. 13.10. The same view is shared by ps.-Philo, 49–50; 50.2, which reads: *Die bono paschae* (a Hebraism = יום טוב של פסח); whereas Shemuel 1, 46, maintains that it was "the Feast of Weeks", the only one of the "three festivals" consisting of one day, and is therefore described as "the

day". On מימים ימימה as the term for Passover, see note 135 (end) on vol. IV, p. 53. Comp. also references cited in note 5.

¹⁰ PR 43, 179b; Shemuel 1, 48–49. Aggadat Bereshit 52, 106. On the statement in Shemuel that Hannah was the first to call God "the Lord of hosts", see also Shemuel 9, 75, and Berakot 31b.

¹¹ Shemuel 2, 51–52. According to ps.-Philo 52; 50.7–8, Eli assured her that her prayer was heard, as he was acquainted with the prophecy concerning the birth of Samuel; but he did not tell her that it had been foreordained that she should give birth to a prophet; comp. note 17. Hannah's prayer is considered by the Rabbis to have been "correct and in accordance with the regulations concerning prayer" (='Amidah). The reason why Eli thought her drunk was because she came to prayer straight from a festival banquet. Comp. Berakot 31a; Shemuel 2, 50–51. According to ps.-Philo 50; 50.5–6, Hannah did not pray aloud, as all men do, because she thought: "Perchance I am not worthy to be heard, and it shall be that Peninnah will taunt and reproach me yet more (*"plus me zelans improperet mihi Phenenna"* is a faulty translation of פנינה לקנאני ותוסף), as she daily saith: Where is thy God in whom thou trustest?" Her praying in a low voice and the way she deported herself at prayer caused Eli to say to her: "Go, put away thy wine from thee." The Rabbis, on the other hand, maintain that one must follow the example of Hannah, and pray (the 'Amidah) in a low voice. Comp. Talmud and Midrash as quoted above. See, however, *Hilluf Minhagim*, No. 43, 40, where it is said that the saying of the 'Amidah in a low voice is a Babylonian custom, whereas in Palestine it is uttered aloud. Josephus, *Antiqui.*, V, 10.2, is of the opinion that it was the length of Hannah's prayer which made Eli suspect that she was drunk. Comp. the similar statement Yerushalmi Berakot 4, 7b, and Shemuel 3, 72.

¹² Shemuel 2, 52; comp., however, ps.-Philo, 50; 50.2, where Hannah's beauty is highly praised.

¹³ Rosh ha-Shanah 11a (here it is assumed that Hannah's prayer in the sanctuary took place on Passover; comp. note 9); Shemuel 3, 52. Like Samuel, Isaac, too, was a "seventh-month child" (Rosh ha-Shanah, *loc. cit.*), and "for this reason every child brought forth in the seventh month shall live, because upon him (Isaac) did God call His glory, and showed forth the new age;" ps.-Philo 24; 23.8. Another seventh-month child was Ichabod, the gransdon of Eli; Josephus, *Antiqui.*, V, 11.4. According to MHG II, 13, all prophets were seventh-month children. Comp. note 44 on vol. II, p. 264.

¹⁴ PR 43, 181a; ER 18, 99. Comp. note 6.

¹⁵ Shemuel 3, according to the reading of Yalkut II, 80 (1 Sam. 1, end). It is, however, possible that the reference אגדת שמואל (so ed. princeps) in Yalkut belongs to the preceding sentence. *Rimze Haftarot*, Rosh ha-Shanah 1, reads: A miracle was wrought for her, as for Abraham and Sarah, and she gave birth to a child when she was old. Each woman who enters into a holy union (not to statisfy the desires of the body) receives a pious son for her reward, as may be seen from the history of Hannah; Tan. B. IV, 31.

¹⁶ Hagigah 6a.

¹⁷ Shemuel 3, 52. Comp. also *Rimze Haftarot*, Rosh ha-Shanah 1, where the name Samuel is explained as שמו של אל עליון, which very likely means:"his name is given to him by the Most High God" and not "his name is the same as that of the Most High God". Here it is likewise presupposed that not only the birth of the prophet, but also his name was made known by God. An amplified form of this legend is given by ps.-Philo 49, 51, 53; 49.1, 51.1–2. At the end of the period of the judges the people began to inquire of the Lord, and said: "Let us cast lots, that we may see whether there is one who can rule over us like Kenaz." But when they cast lots, no man was found worthy of the office. Grieved at this token of divine displeasure, they again cast lots by tribes, but the lot did not fall on any tribe. And Israel said: "Let us choose one of ourselves; for we perceive that God abhorreth His people, and that His soul is displeased with us." At the advice of a man named Nethez (perhaps a corruption of Nebez, Aramaic נבזין "lots". Comp., however, the Jewish name נחזה, Sanhedrin 74a), they tried for the third time, and cast lots by cities, and the lot fell on Armathem. They then cast lots by the men of that city, and the lot "leaped out" (*cecidit sors*, a Hebraism = נפל הגורל) on Elkanah. The people took him, and said: "Come and be ruler over us." He, however, could not be induced to become either prince or judge. Greatly disconcerted, the people prayed again unto the Lord for guidance. God answered them as follows: "Know ye that Elkanah upon whom the lot hath fallen cannot rule over you; but it is rather his son that shall be born of him; he shall be prince over you, and shall prophesy; and from henceforth there shall not be wanting unto you a prince for many years." The people inquired again of the Lord which of Elkanah's ten sons by Peninnah shall be the ruler and prophet, and the reply was: "None of Peninnah's sons can be a prince over the people; but he that shall be born of the barren woman, whom I have given Elkanah to wife, shall be a prophet before

Me for ever. And I will love him, even as I loved Isaac (comp. note 13), and his name shall be before Me for ever." And when Hannah bore a son, she "called his name Samuel, which is interpreted Mighty, according as God called his name when He prophesied of him." The original Hebrew of the last sentence very likely read: ותקרא אותו שמואל שמו אל כאשר קרא אותו יי וגו' (comp. the rabbinic interpretation of the name Samuel given above), and is to be translated: She called his name Samuel, *i. e.* his name was given by God. On names given by God, see note 112 on vol. I, p. 239. See also the quotation from ps.-Philo in note 13, where it is stated that Eli knew of this prophecy about Samuel, but not Hannah. But if so, how did she know the name given by God to the prophet?

¹⁸ Shemuel 3, 53; Berakot 31b. As to the slaughtering of a sacrifice by a non-priest, see also Josephus, *Antiqui.*, III, 9. 1, who agrees with the rabbinic Halakah, whereas Philo, *De Special. Legi.*, *De Sacrifican.*, 5, and *Quaestiones in Exod.* 10, is of the opinion that the slaughtering is a priestly function; comp. Schürer, *Geschichte* (4th edition), II, 239, note 39. There seems, however, to have been a difference of opinion among the Rabbis on this point; comp., *e. g.*, WR 22.7, where R. Ishmael (himself a priest) speaks of the slaughtering of the sacrifices by priests. Zohar III, 124a, maintains that the slaughtering must *not be done* by a priest. Comp. R. Ezekiel Feivel, *Toledot Adam*, I, 52a–52b.

¹⁹ Shemuel 3, 53. This passage contains also the remark that Hannah uttered an unconscious prophecy when she said: "I also have lent him to the Lord" (1 Sam. 1.28). Samuel remained among the living as long as Saul (= "lent to the Lord") was alive, and departed this life shortly before Saul's death. Comp. note. 70.

²⁰ Targum 1 Sam. 2.1–11; Shemuel 4–6, 55–65; *Batte Midrashot*, IV, 6–9, as well as ps.-Philo, 51; 51.3, *seq.*, contain lengthy homiletical paraphrases of Hannah's prayer of thanks. It should be observed that Targum finds in verse 4 a prophecy concerning the victory of the Maccabees over the Greeks; comp. note 925 on vol. III, p. 458. The Haggadah considers Hannah's second prayer (on the first, see note 11) as an abridged form of the 'Amidah. See Yelammedenu in Yalkut II, 80.

²¹ Sanhedrin, Mishnah 10.3; Tosefta 13.9; Babli 109b; Yerushalmi 10, 28a and 29c; Shemuel 5, 61–62; BR 98.2; Targum 1 Sam. 2.6. Comp. vol. III, p. 300.

²² Shemuel 5, 61; PR 43, 182a; *Batte Midrashot*, IV, 7. Hannah

bore, besides Samuel, who was equal to two, two other sons, as well as two daughters (she prayed for sons as well as for daughters; Shemuel 2, 49); to these should be added her two grandsons (Samuel's sons), who were born during her life-time; she thus had eight children, corresponding to the number of children lost by her rival Peninnah. Comp. also ps.-Jerome, 1 Sam. 2.5, and the remarks on this point by Ginzberg, *Haggada bei den Kirchenv.*, 15–16. That Peninnah had ten children (= sons) is also maintained by ps.-Philo; comp. note 17, and this view is based on I Sam. 1.8.

²³ Shemuel 1, 46, which is very likely based on Seder 'Olam 13 (see parallel passages cited by Ratner, *ad loc.*), stating that Eli ruled the people for forty years, and Samuel, who died at the age of fifty-two, for twelve. Comp. notes 25, 26, 69.

²⁴ Tan. Shemini 2; Tan. B. III, 23; Aggadat Bereshit 41, 83; MHG I, 413. According to Tagin 1, it was Eli who copied from the Torah written on the stones of Gilgal (comp. vol. IV, p. 6) the "crowns" and embellishments of the Hebrew letters. He transmitted their exact form to Palti (= Paltiel, Michal's husband; see Index, s. v. "Paltiel"); the latter handed them over to Ahitophel, who transmitted them to Ahijah the prophet of Shiloh, who in turn transmitted them to the high priest Jehoiada, from whom the prophets received them. The prophets buried the copy of the Torah provided with the "crowns" under the threshhold of the Temple, where Ezekiel found it, when during the reign of Jehoiakim, the Temple was torn open. He took this copy to Babylon, whence it was subsequently brought to Jerusalem by Ezra.

²⁵ Ps.-Philo 50; 52.2, and accordingly we ought to read 48D; *Heli* instead of *eum*. That Eli was the immediate successor of Phinehas (comp. note 40) is presupposed by ER 11, 57; Origen *in Joan.* and Aphraates, 272. Comp. Ginzberg, *Haggada bei den Kirchenv.*, 10–11. 6.7. All these sources very likely presuppose the identity of Phinehas and Elijah (comp. vol. IV, pp. 53–54); they accordingly see no difficulty in the fact that this "immortal" exercised the high-priestly functions for several centuries. Josephus, *Antiqui.*, V, 11.5, has the high priests Abiezer, Bukki, and Ozi between Phinehas and Eli (comp. 1 Chron. 5.30–31), but he is also acquainted with the tradition that Eli was the first high priest of the priestly line of Ithamar. According to ps.-Philo, 44D; 44.2, Eli's mother was Dedila (read Delilah; comp. note 125 on vol. IV, p. 49), whose son Micah fashioned the graven image. This statement seems very strange in view of the favorable picture of Eli given by this author.

²⁶ Yerushalmi Sotah 16a and Ketubot 13, 35c; BR 85.12; Yoma 9a–9b; Shabbat 55b; Tosefta-Targum 1 Sam. 2.22; Shemuel 7, 66; Zohar I, 176a; Aggadat Bereshit 41, 84. The last-named source maintains that the women, tired of waiting, used to return home without having brought the sacrifices, and hence were made to have conjugal relations in a state of impurity. The same view is expressed by Ephraem as well as ps.-Jerome, and is very likely presupposed by Peshitta 1 Sam 2.22. This interpretation is based on an old (Sadducean?) Halakah which forbids conjugal relations with women before they have brought their purification offerings. Comp. Geiger, *Jüdische Zeitschrift*, II, 28, and Ginzberg, *Haggada bei den Kirchenv.*, 17–19. Attention is to be called to the fact that neither the Septuagint nor ps.-Philo has the slightest reference to the improper conduct of Eli's sons with the women who came to the sanctuary. The latter, 51; 52.1, writes: The two sons of Eli…began to act wickedly toward the people, and multiplied their iniquities. And they dwelt hard by the house of Bethac, and when the people came together to sacrifice, Hophni and Phinehas came and provoked the people to anger, seizing the oblations before the holy things were offered unto the Lord. Although Bethac occurs in another passage of ps.-Philo (comp. note 134 on vol. IV, p. 53), one feels inclined to reconstruct the original text of this passage in the following manner: והם גרו בבית קרוב לבית א'ק (אלהים=) וכאשר יבואו האנשים לזבח ונו'. The sanctuary is here, as in Scripture, described as "the house of God", but the translator misread the abbreviation (א'ק)=אלהים, and hence mistranslated בית א'ק by "Bethac". On this abbreviation, see note 60 on vol. I, p. 137 =vol. V, p. 160. In MHG I, 414–415, the sons of Eli are exculpated of the charge of improper conduct with women, but their disgraceful treatment of the sacrifices is painted in black colors. Comp. also Shemuel 6, 64, and Tosefta Menahot (end). Pesahim 57a reads: A voice was heard from the Temple hall crying aloud: "Be gone, ye sons of Eli, who defile the sanctuary." It is very likely that in this passage the Sadducean priests are meant by the sons of Eli.

²⁷ Aggadat Bereshit 41, 83; MHG I, 413–414; Shabbat 55b; Josephus, *Antiqui.*, V, 11.12. The view that Eli had to relinquish his office of high priest does not seem to agree with the opinion concerning the duration of his office as given in note 23. It is, however, true that according to the law, he could hardly perform his priestly functions while blind; see Lev. 21.18, and Bekorot 43b–44a. As to his sons, see also vol. IV, p. 158, where they are described as two pious priests. This, however, may be explained by the fact that they died as martyrs

(in the war for God and Israel), and hence all their sins were forgiven them. Ps.-Philo, 51–52; 52.2–4, has a lengthy paraphrase of Eli's words of rebuke addressed to his sons, at the conclusion of which he remarks that "when Eli said to them: 'Repent you of your evil way', they said: 'When we grow old, we will repent.'" And for this reason the opportunity was not granted to them to repent. Comp. Yoma 85b, which reads: If one says: "I shall continue to sin, and later repent," the opportunity to repent is not granted to him. Comp. Index, s. v. "Repentance".

²⁸ Shabbat 55b; Seder 'Olam 20, and parallel passages by Ratner on "Elkanah, the man of God" (= prophet); Shemuel 8, 69; Midrash Tannaim 208; ps.–Jerome on 1 Sam. 2.27 which, reads: *Hunc virum Dei Judaei Phines dicunt.* Comp. Ginzberg, *Haggada bei den Kirchenv.*, 19–20, where attention is called to the unanimous view of the old rabbinic sources that the man of God was Elkanah and not Phinehas; see also note 2, and note 965 on vol. III, p. 481.

²⁹ Rosh ha-Shanah 18a; Yebamot 105a; BR 59.1; Shemuel 8, 71; ER II, 53; Tosefta Targum 1 Sam. 2.32. On the haggadic interpretation of 1 Sam. 2.27–36, see Kellermann, *Midrasch zum 1 Buche Samuelis*, 56–63.

³⁰ Ahimelech, the father of Abiathar, was identical with Ahijah the great grandson of Eli (1 Sam. 14.3), according to a Haggadah found in ps.-Jerome, 1 Sam. 21.1. On the appointment of Zadok as high priest to succeed Abiathar, see ER 12, 57, and EZ 10, 190. Zadok was the only priest who was anointed (this statement, of course, disregards Aaron and his sons who were consecrated as priests by anointment); PRK (Grünhut's edition, 87–88). Here it is also stated that Saul, David, Solomon, Joash, and Jehoahaz were the only kings who were anointed. Comp. Ginzberg, *Unbekannte Sekte*, 319–320 and note 371 on vol. III, p. 179.

³¹ Shekalim 6, 49c. On the view that the ark accompanied Israel to the camps, see fol. III, p. 409. When at war with the Philistines they took the ark with them; God said: "Ye did not think of the holy ark when the sons of Eli provoked Me by their iniquities; but now, going to battle, ye bethink yourselves thereof." See ER 12, 57; comp. also ps.-Philo, 53; 54.2, which reads: And as the ark went up with them...., the Lord thundered (haggadic interpretation of תהם הארץ, 1 Sam. 4.5), and said: "This time shall be like the time when they were in the wilderness; then they took the ark without My commandment (a strange interpretation of Num. 14.44), and destruction befell them; even so shall it be now: the people shall fall, and the ark

222

shall be taken, that I may punish the adversaries of My people because of the ark, and rebuke My people for their sins."

³² Josephus, *Antiqui.*, V, 11.2.

³³ Sifre N., 88; Sifre Z., 196; Tosefta Sotah 9.4; Shemuel 10, 77. The two sons of Eli were slain by Goliath who took the holy ark with his left hand, and slew Hophni and Phinehas with his right. When Eli heard from Saul (who was light on his feet and fled from the battle) that the ark had been taken, he said: "Behold, Samuel prophesied about me and my sons that we should die together, but he made no mention of the ark unto me." In his great despair Eli fell off from his seat and died on the same day as his sons. On the very same day another member of Eli's family died: his daughter-in-law, while giving birth to a son whom she called Ichabod, said: "Where is the glory? for the glory of the Lord is departed from Israel, since the ark of the Lord was taken." See ps.-Philo, 52–53; 54.3–6. On the parts played by Goliath and Saul in this campaign , see vol. IV, p. 65. The first part of the name Ichabod (א) is explained as אי "where"? (the same explanation is also found in Kimhi on Sam. 4.21). The Septuagint renders this verse: And she called the child Οὐαιβαρχαβώθ, both because of the ark of God, and because of her father-in-law, and because of her husband. The Septuagint very likely takes אי in the sense of וי "woe" (Aramaic), whereas Josephus, *Antiqui.*, V, 11.4, reads: Ichabod, which name signifies "disgrace", and this because the army received a disgrace at this time. Comp. the etymology of the name Aaron in note 36 on vol. II, p. 261.

³⁴ Sifre N., 88; Sifre Z., 96; Tehillim 93, 414; Shemuel 10, 77. According to Septuagint on 1 Sam. 5.6, *seq.*, the punishment of the Philistines consisted in being smitten in "their secret parts". Furthermore mice sprang up in the midst of their country, and there was a great "confusion of death" among them when God smote the men of their cities, great and small. It is interesting that ER 11, 58, likewise speaks of the visitation of the mice, as well as of the plague causing death among men, women, and children. Josephus, *Antiqui.*, VI, 1.1, very likely following Septuagint, writes: God sent a very destructive disease upon the city and country of Ashdod, for they died of dysentery or flux, a sore distemper that brought death upon them very suddenly; for before the soul could, as usual in easy deaths, be well loosed from the body, they brought up their entrails, and vomited them up, entirely corrupted by the disease. And as to the fruits of their country, a great multitude of mice arose out of the earth and hurt them, and spared neither

the plants nor the fruits.   It is doubtful whether ps.-Philo's (53–54; 55.2.9) elaborate account of the plague is based on a text different from that of the Masorah or not.   According to this writer, the plague consisted of scorpions and all kinds of noisome creeping things, which particularly attacked the children and the mothers.   The number of them that died with child was seventy-five thousand, and of the sucklings sixty-five thousand, and of those that gave suck fifty-five thousand, and of men twenty-four thousand.   The wise men of the Philistines therefore of said: "Whereas all that are with child and give suck die,...and they that are suckled perish, we also will take kine that give suck and yoke them to a new cart, and place the ark upon it, and shut up the young of the kine. And it shall be, if the kine go forth.... we shall know that we have suffered for the ark's sake."   At the advice of their sages the Philistines set the kine at the head of the three ways that are about Ekron; for the middle way leads to Ekron, and the way on the right hand to Judea, and the way on the left hand to Samaria.   The kine, albeit they lowed and yearned for their young, went forth nevertheless by the right-hand way which leads to Judea.   And they knew that it was for the ark's sake that they were laid waste.   And all the Philistines assembled and brought the ark again into Shiloh with timbrels and pipes and dances.   And because of the noisome creeping things that laid them waste, they made seats of gold, and sanctified the ark.   The "seats of gold" (*sedilia aurea*) correspond literally to αἱ ἕδραι αἱ χρυσαῖ of the Septuagint, 1 Sam. 6.17 = טחרי הזהב of the Hebrew text, whereas in 5.9 and 6.5 the Hebrew equivalent of ἕδραι is עפלים.   It is not unlikely that the substitute used in the time of the Septuagint and ps.-Philo for עפלים (this word was considered obscene) was מושב = "*sedilium*" and "*podex*" (for מושב in the sense of "*podex*" see Sanhedrin 82b).   Accordingly there is no proof that ps.-Philo made use of the Septuagint.   Very strange is the statement of ps.-Philo that the Philistines brought the ark to Shiloh.   This contradicts not only the Bible (see 1 Sam. 6. 12), but also the story about the kine so minutely described by this author.   It is very likely that Allophili (54D, line 6) is a copyist's error for *Israel* or *populi*.   After the kine brought the ark to Judea all the people assembled, and took it to the sanctuary.   "Israel" and not "the Philistine" is required as subjects of "*sanctificaverunt arcum*".   When the ark returned from the Philistines it was "re-sanctified" by the people.   With regard to the accident that befell the idol Dagon, ps.-Philo narrates that its priests were crucified by the people when they found it fallen on its face and its hands and feet lying before the ark. Kimhi quotes an opinion (of the Midrash?) that the upper part of the idol had a human form, the lower that of a fish. Comp. R. E. J. IV, 56 *seq.* and 269–271.

³⁵ Josephus, *Antiqui.*, VI, 1.2; ps.-Philo (as quoted in the preceding note). Comp. also sources cited in note 33 which likewise mention the difference of opinion among the Philistines.

³⁶ BR 54.4 (this passage has many other "songs of the kine"); 'Abodah Zarah 24b; ER 11, 58; Shemuel 12, 82; Tan. Wa-Yakhel 7. That the kine were set at the head of the three ways (a haggadic interpretation of 1 Sam. 6.12) is asserted not only by ps.-Philo (comp. note 34), but also by Josephus, *Antiqui.*, VI, 1.2.

³⁷ ER 11, 58 (the unseemly behavior of the Jews is contrasted with the great respect shown to the ark by the Philistines, who covered their faces that they should not behold the holy vessel); Sotah 35a; BaR 5.9; Tan. Wa-Yakhel 7 (the wind pushed back the cover from the ark, and the people did not refrain from looking at the uncovered ark); Josephus, *Antiqui.*, VI, 1.4, reads: And the wrath of God overtook them, and struck seventy persons dead . . . . . who, not being priests, and so not worthy to touch the ark, had approached it. Josephus did not forget for a moment that he was a priest. As to the sin committed by the inhabitants of Beth-Shemesh, see also Yerushalmi Sanhedrin 2, 20b; Septuagint Targum and Tosefta-Targum on 1 Sam. 6.19. On the rejoicing of the people at the return of the ark, see the quotation from ps.-Philo in note 34.

³⁸ Yerushalmi Sanhedrin 2, 20b (another opinion has it: the loss of the seventy members of the Synedrion was as grave a loss as the death of fifty thousand men); Targum on 1 Sam. 6.19; BaR 5.9; ER 11, 58; Sotah 35b. In the last-named source two views are given: 1) seventy men, each one of whom was as important to Israel as fifty thousand other men; 2) fifty thousand men, each one of whom was as important as the seventy members of the Synedrion. Comp. Mekilta RS 26 and Ginzberg, *Haggada bei den Kirchenv.* 20–21, where reference is made to ps.-Jerome 1 Sam 4, 19 who remarks: *Hos septuaginta viros judices septuaginta Hebraei intelligunt.* See also the similar haggadic interpretation of Joshua 7.4–5, vol. IV, p. 8 and note 23 appertaining thereto.

³⁹ Sotah 35a–35b. Comp. also sources referred to in preceding note.

⁴⁰ Ps.-Jerome, 1 Sam. 7.6, *seq.*, quoting this legend as "*Hebraei tradunt*". The extant rabbinic literature knows of such an ordeal in

connection with the worshippers of the golden calf, but not with regard to the sinners in the days of Samuel; see Ginzberg, *Haggada bei den Kirchenv.*, 21–23; vol. III, p. 130.—A lengthy description of the "call of Samuel" is given by ps.-Philo, 52; 53.1, *seq.* When Samuel was only eight years old, God decided to reveal Himself to him; but, in order not to frighten the child, the voice that came to him was as that of a man and not as of God. Samuel at first thought that he heard the voice of Eli, and ran to him. The latter thought that an unclean spirit was attempting to deceive Samuel, and he warned him with the following words: "In thee do I behold the sign that men shall have from this day forward for ever (it is very likely an inaccurate translation of the Hebrew ועתה ראה את זה לכל האדם מהיום ולעולם "And now behold that sign for all men from this day forward and for ever"; the translator, however, read, ואתה ראה instead of ועתה ראה), that if one call unto another twice in the night or at noonday (very likely an inaccurate translation of חצות which here means "midnight", and not "noonday"), they shall know that it is an evil spirit. But if he call a third time, they shall know that it is an angel." The second time the voice of heaven which called Samuel sounded to him like the voice of his father Elkanah, and awakening from his sleep, he ran again to Eli. The latter said to him: "In those two voices, wherewith God hath called upon thee, He likened Himself to thy father and to thy master; but now on the third time (He will speak) as God." Eli then instructed Samuel as follows: Attend with thy right ear, and refrain with thy left. For Phinchas the priest commanded us, saying: The right ear heareth the Lord by night, the left ear an angel. Therefore if thou hear with thy right ear, say thus: "Speak what Thou wilt, for I hear Thee, for Thou hast formed me." But if thou hear with thy left ear, come and tell me. A third time a voice resembling that of Elkanah's awoke Samuel from his sleep, and "filled" his right ear. He now knew that God was revealing Himself to him. The content of this revelation was the announcement of the doom decreed upon the "flower that came forth of the rod of Aaron" (the punishment of the priests). Because they transgressed the law concerning the "nest with birds" (comp. Deut. 22.26) it shall happen to them that the mothers shall die with the children, and the fathers with the sons. Samuel at first would not reveal the prophecy to Eli, saying: "How shall I prophesy the destruction of him that fostered me?" But Eli insisted on knowing the truth. Samuel was afraid, and told him all the words he had heard. And Eli said: "Can a thing formed answer him that formed it? Even so cannot I answer Him when He takes away that which He hath given; He who is the Faithful Giver, the Holy One who hath prophesied. I am subject to His power." That Samuel began to prophesy at a very early age is also the view of Josephus, *Antiqui.*, V, 16.4, who gives the age of twelve as the beginning of his activity. The statement of the Rabbis (comp. notes 23, 25, and 27, as well as Midrash Tannaim 89) that Samuel's leadership lasted only twelve years, from his fortieth years until his death, refers to his activity as judge and head of the nation, and does not preclude the possibility of his having exercised his prophetic calling many years more. On the view that God addressed Samuel in the voice of his father, in order not to frighten him, see vol. III, p. 305, where the same statement is given with regard to Moses. On the relation between Phinehas and Eli, see note 25. That the priests were punished for their transgression of the law concerning the "bird's nest", is a very strange statement, especially in view of the explicit words of Scripture (1 Sam. 2.12, *seq.*, and 22). It seems therefore likely that the Hebrew original read: וכשם שהם עברו על מצות קנים שציויתי למשה כך ימותו וגו'. The reference was not to the commandment given in Deut. 22.26, but to that of Lev. 12.6, in accordance with the tannaitic use of קנים to designate the purification offering of a woman after child-birth. Ps.-Philo, in agreement with the Rabbis (see note 26), is of the opinion that the sons of Eli were negligent in the sacrifices of the "birds" brought by the women. The translator, or perhaps a later glossator, not acquainted with the mishnaic use of the word קנים (the treatise dealing with the law given in Lev., *loc cit.*, bears the name of קנים), took it in the sense of קן צפור of Deut., *loc. cit.* Eli's words, at hearing the doom of his family, express his resignation to the will of God, or, as the Rabbis term it, his "acknowledgment of God's justice" (צדוק הדין); this is an obligation incumbent upon any one who hears bad "tidings"; comp. Berakot Mishnah 9.2 and vol. V, p. 255, note 256. Samuel was chosen prophet by God as a reward for his humility. Three times he arose from his bed in response to what he thought was Eli's summons. Had he not been so humble, he would never have found out through Eli that it was God who called him; *Batte Midrashot*, IV, 34; a quotation from a Midrash in *Reshit Hokmah* שער ענוה 7. Samuel did not sleep in the sanctuary, as one might erroneously infer from the words of Scripture (1 Sam. 3.3), but in the "hall of the Levites". The voice calling Samuel went forth from the sanctuary, and passed Eli, who did not hear it, though he was near the holy place; see Shemuel 9, 75; Targum 1 Sam. 3.20 Comp. Rashi and Kimhi, *ad loc.*

⁴¹ Yerushalmi Ta'anit 2, 65d; Shemuel 13, 83; Tehillim 119, 503; Baraita de-Yeshu'a, 47a; Targum 1 Sam. 7.6; ER 17, 86–87.

⁴² Josephus, *Antiqui.*, VI, 2.2. On three occasions God wages a "war of confusion" against the enemies of Israel: in the battle of Gibeon (Josh. 10.10); in the battle against Sisera (Jud. 4.15); in the battle which Samuel fought against the Philistines. In the time of the Messiah Israel's enemies will be destroyed by God in the same way. The Egyptians were likewise annihilated at the Red Sea in the same manner. See Shemuel 13, 84; Tehillim 18, 147. Before going into action, Samuel brought a sacrifice, and though not a priest, he performed the sacrificial rites. A divine command suspended on this occasion the laws pertaining to sacrifices, bidding a non-priest to perform the functions of a priest, and making him transgress seven other sacrificial laws; see Yerushalmi Megillah 1, 72c; Shemuel 13, 83; BaR 14.1; WR 22.9; Tehillim 27, 227; Tan. B. IV, 41. On similar suspensions of the law, see note 8 on vol. IV, p. 4.—This was the first war in which Samuel participated, as he did not take part in that disastrous campaign which resulted in the capture of the ark and the death of Eli's two sons. Three days before that battle God sent him away, saying: "Go and look upon the place of Arimatha (=Ramathaim); there shall be thy dwelling". When, at his return, he heard of the great calamity that befell Israel, he was deeply grieved. God consoled him, saying: "Before thou diest, thou shalt see the end which I will bring upon Mine enemies, whereby the Philistines shall perish and be destroyed by scorpions and by all manner of noisome creeping things." Ps-Philo, 53–54; 55. 1–2. As to the sending away of Samuel, see a similar legend about Jeremiah vol. IV, p. 303.

⁴³ Nedarim 38a; Tan. B. IV, 91; BaR 18.10. When Samuel spoke the words: "Witness against me.....Whose ass have I taken, etc." (1 Sam. 12.3), a heavenly voice proclaimed: "I witness." Makkot 23b; BR 85.1; Shemuel 14, 90–91; comp. also Yelammedenu in Likkutim, V, 90b–91a, and vol. IV, p. 69, with regard to Samuel's disinterestedness and incorruptibility, wherein he was equal to Moses. Philo, *De Inebrietate* 34, describes Samuel as the greatest of kings (=rulers, *i. e.*, judges) and prophets. As to Samuel's Naziriteship, see Nazir Mishnah, Babli, and Yerushalmi (end), as well as Shemuel 1, 49–50; Targum 1 Sam. 1.11. According to some authorities quoted in these sources, he was no Nazirite, and the words of Scripture (Sam. *loc. cit.*) are to be translated "And he shall know of no fear (of man) all his life." On Samuel as the "master of the prophets", see Yeru-

shalmi Hagigah 2, 77a; Tan. B. IV, 82; Shemuel 24, 120; Tehillim 90, 387. He is said to have been equal to Moses and Aaron put together PR 43, 182a; *Batte Midrashot*, IV, 7. On the view that Samuel was Moses's equal, and in some respect his superior, see also Shemuel 9, 74–75; Tehillim 25, 212 (see Buber, note 24); BaR 3.8; PK 4, 38b; ShR 16.4 note 561 on vol. III, p. 287. Comp. also Ecclus. 46.11, which reads: The Nazirite of God among the prophets, Samuel who judged and performed the service of priests. On the last point see the preceding note. The Karaite Hadassi, *Eshkol*, 45b, No. 119, quotes a statement of the Rabbis to the effect that Samuel acted proudly in proclaiming in the presence of all the people his incorruptibility as a judge and his disinterestedness. No such remark is found in the rabbinic literature still extant, and in view of the extraordinary glorification of Samuel by the Haggadah, it is very unlikely that it brought this accusation against him. Hadassi either misunderstood his source, or deliberately invented a statement unfavorable to Samuel, that he might be able to reprove the Rabbanites for their lack of reverence towards the heroes of Israel. A late Karaitic writer (see Neubauer, *Beiträge*, Hebrew part, 65), drawing upon Hadassi, maintains that the Rabbanites accuse Samuel of having been a corrupt judge. What the Rabbis do say is that Samuel acted proudly in saying: I am the seer; comp. vol. IV, p. 83 (bottom). Comp. note 60 on vol. IV, p. 34.

⁴⁴ Shabbat 56a (it contains several attempts to tone down the biblical report concerning Samuel's sons); Hullin 133a; Tosefta Sotah 14.5–6; BR 85.12; Shemuel 7, 67; Yerushalmi Sotah 1, 17a, and Ketubot 13, 35d (top). Comp. note 46, and Tosefta-Targum 1 Sam. 12.2.

⁴⁵ Makkot 11a. The Haggadah finds in 1 Sam. 3.7 the curse uttered by Eli.

⁴⁶ Shemuel 1, 45 (the views differ; accrding to one opinion, both were wicked; while others maintain that when they repented, both were found worthy of receiving the gift of the holy spirit); BaR 10.5; Ruth R. 2.1; Tehillim 80, 361. See also ps.-Jerome., 1 Chron. 6.13; who (following Jewish tradition?) maintains that Ahijah was an unworthy judge, but not his brother Joel, though he too is censured by Scripture for not having attempted to restrain his brother from his evil deeds. See a similar view with regard to the two sons of Eli, vol. IV, p. 61. Comp. Rahmer, *Ein lateinischer Commentar... zu den Büchern der Chronik*, 29–30, and references given in note 44. It is very likely that, in agreement with ps.-Jerome, we are to read in Tehillim, *loc. cit.*: הוא יואל הוא ושני.

⁴⁷ Sanhedrin, Tosefta 4.5, and Babli 20b; Sifre D., 156; Midrash Tannaim 103–104; Mekilta D., 5–6; DR 5.8–11. All these sources cite a difference of opinion among the Rabbis with reference to Deut. 17. 14. According to some, the institution of a monarchy was commanded by God to Israel, and therefore the sin committed by Israel in Samuel's time consisted in the manner the common people formulated their demand for a king, or in asking for a king before the time was ripe for one. Others maintain that God never commanded the appointment of a king, but knowing Israel's inclination towards a monarchy, He permitted the establishment of such a rule, should the people desire it. This request made by Israel in Samuel's days was granted by God, who, however, did not approve of it. But the prevalent opinion is that Israel, after entering the Holy Land, had three national duties to discharge: the establishment of a monarchy, the annihilation of Amalek, and the building of the Temple. According to Sanhedrin 20b, these duties were to be fulfilled in the order given herewith, whereas Mekilta D., *loc. cit.*, is of the opinion that the first national duty was the building of the Temple, and then the appointment of a king (first the establishment of the kingdom of heaven on earth, and then the organization of the earthly kingdom). In Samuel's days the people committed the sin of asking for a king before the Temple had been erected. The same view seems to be shared by ps.-Philo, 54; 56.1–3, who makes Samuel utter the words: "Behold, now I see that there is not yet for us the time of a perpetual kingdom, nor of building the house of the Lord our God, inasmuch as they desire a king before the time." The last expression "*petentibus regem ante tempus*" is practically identical with the one found in Sifre, *loc. cit.*, שהקדימו על ידן or שהקדימו עליהן (comp. Tosefta, *loc. cit.*) in describing Israel's sinful action in Samuel's days. After Saul had been appointed king, the people attempted to excuse their demand for a king by saying to Samuel: "We, as well as our king with us, are thy servants; because we are unworthy to be judged by a prophet, therefore we said: Appoint a king over us to judge us." See ps.-Philo, 55; 57.4; comp. also 55; 58.4. Josephus, *Antiqui.*, VI, 3,3, reads: These words (the people's demand for a king) greatly afflicted Samuel on account of his hatred of the kingly government; for he was very fond of aristocracy, which is divine and makes men who possess it of a happy disposition. In Sanhedrin, Tosefta and Babli, *loc. cit.*, a difference of opinion is cited with regard to the picture drawn by Samuel of the king's powers. According to one view, the law accedes to the king all this arbitrary power, but another maintains that Samuel

tried to "frighten the people" by picturing to them what a lawless king might do.

⁴⁸ Shemuel 11, 78–79; Tehillim 7, 63; Tosefta-Targum 1 Sam. 4.12 (an angel assisted Saul to cover the long distance in a short time); ps.-Philo, 53; 54.3–4. Comp. note 32 and note 34 on vol. IV, p. 86.

⁴⁹ Sotah 10a; comp. vol. I, p. 59.

⁵⁰ Berakot 48b; Shemuel 13, 86; Tehillim 7, 70.

⁵¹ Tosefta Berakot 4.18; Tan. B. III, 4; ARN 10 (second version 20), 43; a quotation from a Midrash in *Reshit Hokmah*, שער ענוה 7. When Saul refused to accept the crown offered to him on account of his youth (comp. 1 Sam. 9.2; but here he dwells on the insignificance of his tribe and family), the prophet replied: "Who will grant that the word should come into accomplishment of itself, that thou mayest live many days? But consider this that thy words shall be likened unto the words of a prophet, whose name shall be Jeremiah." See ps.-Philo, 55; 56.6. The statement in ps.-Philo that Saul met Samuel walking hard by Baam (*ille autem ambulabat juxta Baam*; 54, bottom; 56.4) goes back to 1 Sam. 9.14: והנה שמואל יוצא לקראתם הבמה where the Septuagint has εἰς Βαμά, as if במה were the name of a place. On Saul's modesty and other virtues, see also note 80, and note 86 on vol. IV, p. 309, as well as Josephus, *Antiqui*, VI, 4.5.

⁵² Tan. B. III, 4; Tosefta-Targum 1 Sam. 10.22. Saul, however, had a presentiment that he was destined to become king. For in a vision he saw himself on top of a palm-tree, which indicates accession to royal dignity; see ps.-Jerome, 1 Sam. 9.20, who gives it as a "Hebrew tradition." Comp. Berakot 57a (towards the end) about dreaming of ascending a roof. In the incidents which happened to Saul on his way from Samuel to his father, the history of his life was shown to him. The three goats (comp. 1 Sam. 10.3, *seq.*) indicated to him that he would be the father of three sons, and the two loaves of bread which were given to him signified that two daughters would be born unto him; Tan. as quoted in Makiri, Is. 46.161. Comp. Tan. B. I, 22. On the haggadic interpretation of Zelzah (1 Sam. 10.2), comp. BR 82.9; Shemuel 14, 89; Tosefta Sotah 11.11.

⁵³ Yoma 22b (1 Sam. 13.1 is explained to mean, innocent like a one-year-old child); PR 195a; Targum 1 Sam. 13.1; Yerushalmi Bikkurim 3, 65d; Shemuel 17, 95. The two last-named sources read: The bridegroom on the day of his wedding, the king on the day of his coronation, and the elder on the day of his ordination are forgiven all their sins up to that day. That Saul was free from sin is also men-

tioned by ps.-Jerome on 1 Sam. 13.1.   Comp. Ginzberg, *Haggada bei den Kirchenv.* 23–24.   See also Targum 1 Chron. 8.40, and note 80.

⁵⁴ Ps.-Jerome, 1 Sam. 10.6, giving this view as a Jewish tradition. Comp. Ginzberg, *Haggada bei den Kirchenv.* 117.

⁵⁵ Yerushalmi Shebi'it 3, 34d; WR 9.2; Tan. Tezawweh 8; Targum 1 Chron. 8. 33; comp. vol. III, 218.   Saul was one of the Benjamites who were told to get a wife by capturing one of the daughters of Shiloh (Jud. 21.21); but being very shy by nature, he had no courage to come near the dancing maidens.   One of them, however, attracted by Saul's beauty (comp. vol. IV, p. 64), suggested to him that he should capture her; Rashi, 1 Sam. 20.30, and *Rimze Haftarot*, Rosh ha-Shanah, 1.

⁵⁶ Shemuel 14, 89 (other opinions are: he wanted them to slay the Jewish archers, or the members of the Synedrion); Tosefta-Targum 1 Sam. 11.2; comp. also Josephus, *Antiqui.*, VI, 5.1, who remarks that if Nahash had accomplished what he wanted, he would have rendered Israel powerless in war, as the left eye of the warrior is covered with the shield.

⁵⁷ PRE 38; Shemuel 17, 96.   On the dimness of the stone of Benjamin, indicating the sin of that tribe, see vol. IV, p. 8,

⁵⁸ Zebahim 120a, as an explanation of 1 Sam. 14.34.   On the explanation of this verse by ps.-Jerome, see Ginzberg, *Haggada bei den Kirchenv.*, 24–26.   It is quite possible that ps.-Jerome has correctly transmitted the Haggadah to the effect that no meat except that of a sacrifice could be eaten in time of war, when all the people were near the holy ark that followed them to the battle-field; Saul prevented the use of other meat by the people.   Comp. sources quoted in note 519 on vol. III, p. 270 with regard to the use of meat during the journey of Israel in the wilderness.

⁵⁹ WR 25 (end); BaR 11 (towards the end); Shemuel 17, 95–96.

⁶⁰ Yoma 22 b; Koheleth 7.16; Shemuel 18, 100; Alphabet of Ben Sira 4c; Jerome, Eccles. 7.16.   Quite correct was Saul's attitude towards the Kenites, whom he had warned of the danger threatening them in case they should not separate themselves from the Amalekites.   He owed this to them for the hospitality offered by the Kenite Jethro to Moses. Although this hospitality was prompted by selfish motives (he wanted Moses to marry one of his daughters), one ought to be grateful for a good deed, even if the motive thereof is not a pure one; Berakot 63b; WR 34.8; PRE 44; Shir 2.5; Shemuel 18, 99; ps.-Jerome on 1 Sam. 15.6; Josephus, *Antiqui.*, VI, 7.2–3.

⁶¹ Tehillim 52, 284; Shemuel 18, 99–100.   On the contrast be-

tween the kindness of the law concerning animals and the severity of war, see vol. I, p. 381, and the quotation from ps.-Philo, note 40. The Amalekites were great sorcerers (comp. vol. III, p. 60), and used to transform themselves into animals to escape the attacks of the enemies in war. God therefore commanded Israel to kill all the animals of the Amalekites; see *Ketab Tamim*, 61, and R. Bahya, Ki-Teze (end), both of whom had that legend in their text of PRE 39.

⁶² Yoma 22b; Shemuel 18, 99; Targum 1 Sam. 16.4. Comp. also vol. III, p. 146. Ps.-Philo, 55; 58.2-4, on the other hand, maintains that Saul had spared Agag and his wife because of the hidden treasures promised by the Amalekite king. But Saul never saw the hidden treasures which Agag had promised to show him, as the latter was shortly after killed by Samuel.

⁶³ Yoma 22b; comp. the favorable opinion of Saul in vol. IV, pp. 65-66 and 72, as well as Josephus, *Antiqui.*, VI, 4.1 and 12.7.

⁶⁴ Tehillim 57, 297-298; Ephraem, 1 Sam. 15.27. Opinions differ as to the meaning of Scripture that Saul on his return from the campaign against Amalek set up a יד on Carmel (1 Sam. 15.12). According to some, Saul erected on Carmel, an altar, the one which was later used by Elijah (1 Kings 18.30, *seq.*); but according to others, Saul deposited the spoils on Carmel. See Midrash quoted by Rashi and Kimhi, *ad loc.* These two interpretations of יד are also known to Ephraem, *ad loc.*, 362E. Comp. Ginzberg, *Haggada bei den Kirchenv.*, 27.

⁶⁵ PK 3, 25a-26b (comp. Buber, note 90); PR 12, 52b; Ekah 3, 139; Tan. B. V, 39-40; Tan. Ki-Teze 9; Shemuel 18, 101. In these sources opinions differ as to the way Samuel executed Agag. According to some, Samuel cut Agag's body into pieces, which he threw to the ostriches (מעדנות in 1 Sam. 15.32 is taken to mean the same as־ נעמיות, because the roots עדן and נעם are synonymous); but others maintain that he bound him on four poles, and killed him by pulling the poles apart. It is obvious, though none of the commentators noticed it, that this Haggadah attempts to solve the difficulty involved in the fact that Samuel who was a Nazirite would not have been permitted to slay Agag, since a Nazirite is forbidden to touch a dead body. The old view which denies the Naziriteship of Samuel was probably prompted by this difficulty; comp. note 43. Ps.-Philo, 55; 58 (end), maintains that Samuel slew Agag with a sword. Josephus, *Antiqui.*, VI, 7 (end) writes: He (Samuel) gave orders to slay him. This is a simple way out of the difficulty.

⁶⁶ ER 20, 115 and 21, 117; Alphabet of Ben Sira 11c; Targum

Sheni 4.13; comp. vol. IV, p. 422. A similar legend is related in ps.-
Philo, 55, 58.3–4. When Saul in his greed (see note 62) had spared
Agag, God decided to punish him, and made this very sin to become
the cause of his death. God therefore said to the prophet Samuel:
"Suffer Agag and his wife to come together this night, and slay him to-
morrow; but preserve thou his wife until she has given birth to a male
child, and then she, too, shall die. The child born of her shall be an
offence unto Saul." This posthumous child of Agag, called Edad,
later became Saul's armor-bearer, and in the battle of Gilboa it was
Agag's son who delivered the death blow to the Hebrew king. Comp.
also ps.-Philo (end). Comp. note 107.

⁶⁷ On the view that Samuel was the equal of these two, see note
43, and vol. III, p. 108. The evil spirit which afflicted Saul was "one
born of an echo in chaos", and David composed a psalm which when
sung by him had the power to make the evil spirit depart; ps.-Philo
56; 60, where the text of the psalm is given.

⁶⁸ *i. e.*, his premature death will be declared to be due to his sins.

⁶⁹ On Samuel's age at the time of his death and the duration of
his activity, see references cited in notes 23, 25, 27. In opposition to
the prevalent opinion that Samuel ruled only twelve years, there is
found in Tehillim 25, 212 (see Buber, *ad loc.*) the view that his activity
lasted as long as that of Moses, forty years. This view is shared by
Julius Africanus, 1, 93. This author very likely combined the statement of Josephus, *Antiqui.*, V, 10.3 (to the effect that Samuel began to
prophesy at the age of twelve), with that of the Rabbis that he died
at the age of fifty-two. Comp. also BaR 3.8; ER 6, 37; Tehillim 92
411; Josephus, *Antiqui.*, VI, 13.5; Tabari I, 414.

⁷⁰ Ta'anit 5b; Yerushalmi Berakot 4, 7b; Shemuel 25, 122 (מטעת
שלו, *i. e.*, Saul, "the planting of Samuel"; the planter would not have
survived the destruction of his planting; accordingly, Samuel died
about the time when Saul's death was decreed; the reading of Yalkut
II, 141, and Makiri, Ps. 51, 282, is not acceptable); BaR 3.8. "Hannah's
long prayer shortened the days of Samuel." In her prayer she consecrated her son to the service of the sanctuary for his entire life (see
1 Sam. 1.11 and 22); but as a Levite Samuel could not perform any holy
service after the age of fifty (Num. 8.24), and hence he died after having
spent this number of years at the sanctuary, from the age of two (see
1 Sam. 1.24; she weaned him at that age; comp. Ketubot 60a) until
the age of fifty-two. See Yerushalmi Berakot 4, 7b, and Ta'anit 4,
67c, as well as Bikkurim 2, 64c and Shemuel 2.50 and 3.52.

⁷¹ Tosefta Sotah 11.5. On the text, see Ginzberg, *Haggada bei den Kirchenv.*, 35–36, where it is suggested that we ought to read וימת שמואל מיתה ודאי ושמואל מת אלא לענין שאול. Tosefta, in agreement with the "Hebrew tradition" given by ps.-Jerome, 28.8, explains that 1 Sam. 25.1 contains the report concerning Samuel's death and burial, whereas in 1 Sam. 28.3 Samuel's death is merely referred to by the way, in connection with Saul's visit to the witch of En-Dor, which would not have happened, had the great prophet still been alive. Comp. the following note.

⁷² Koheleth 7.1 and Shemuel 23, 111, 115, 117–118 (according to these sources, Samuel's death is mentioned in 1 Sam. 25.1 by the way only, in connection with the story of Nabal; comp. the preceding note); Yerushalmi Bikkurim 2, 64a (the "ten days" mentioned in 1 Sam. 25. 38 refer to the "ten days of penitence", from New Year to the Day of Atonement, granted to the sinners as days of grace before their final doom is decreed on the Day of Atonement); Tehillim 26, 219–220; ER 18, 109; 2 ARN 43, 118. Nabal's untimely death was due to his failure to assist the poor; EZ 1, 170. Greedy as he was, he was ashamed to refuse flatly the requests and petitions of the needy, but employed great cunning in avoiding his duty. He lived in Maon, but his possessions were in Carmel (1 Sam. 25.2); the poor who came to Maon were told that if they applied in Carmel, their wishes would be granted; those who came to Carmel were told that Nabal's residence was in Maon where he transacted his affairs; quotation from a Midrash by Shu'aib, 'Ekeb, 104b. Comp. also Tehillim 14, 113. Pride was another vice of Nabal. He was so proud of his aristocratic descent that he despised David, the descendant of Ruth the Moabite, and claimed the honor and privileges due to the tribe of Judah for himself, the representative of the noble clan of Caleb; Yerushalmi Sanhedrin 2, 20b; Baraita de-Yeshu'a, 45a. In his pride he not only denied David's claim to royal dignity, but also God, in whose name Samuel anointed David; denying God, Nabal led a loose life; Tehillim 53, 287–288.—On Samuel as the ideal type of judge, see vol. IV, p. 64.

⁷³ WR 26.7; Tan. B. III, 81; Tan. Emor 2; Shemuel 24, 118. As to "the rule of conduct" to take two companions on a journey, see vol. III, p. 363. The Midrashim mentioned above (see also PRE 33) dwell also upon Saul's strange action, in that he first destroyed the sorcerers, and then sought the advice of the witch of En-dor. Ps.-Philo, 59; 64.1, maintains that Saul "scattered all the sorcerers out of the land" not out of zeal for God and His law, but that "men should remember him

after his death." For this he was punished by God that he himself sought help from the sorcerers.

⁷⁴ PRE 33; ps.–Jerome, 1 Sam. 28.7. On the view that Abner accompanied Saul on his visit to the witch, see the references given in the preceding note. Comp. also Ginzberg, *Haggada bei den Kirchenv.*, 36–37. Ps.-Philo, 59; 64.3–5, calls the witch Sedecla (= צדק לא "unrighteous"; comp. the explanation of the name Tobal by Rashi, Is. 7.6), the daughter of Adod (the reading Debin is hardly acceptable), the Midianite (see vol IV, p. 39), and maintains that she deceived the people of Israel with her sorceries for forty years. In PRE the name of the witch is Zephaniah = "the hidden one".

⁷⁵ WR 26.7; Tan. B. III, 82 (here it is supposed that necromancy can only be performed during the day, and accordingly לילה in 1 Sam. 28.8 is to be taken in the sense of gloom; comp. a similar explanation of לילה in Tan. B. I.93; note 163 on vol. I, p. 253); Tan. Emor 2; Shemuel 24.119. Septuagint, 1 Sam. 28.14, very likely read זקף instead of זקן, but the legend about the dead walking with their heads downwards and feet in the air is found in sources independent of this passage; see the references given in note 301 on vol. I, p. 297. Frankel's remarks in *Vorstudien*, 188, and Wellhausen, *Text der Bücher Samuelis*, 13, are to be corrected accordingly. When Saul noticed that the witch did not recognize him, though she had seen him often, he wept and said: "Lo, now I know that my beauty is changed, and the glory of my kingdom is passed from me;" ps.-Philo, 59; 64.4. This author, however, does not explain how the witch, seeing Samuel rise from among the dead, knew that it was Saul who asked her services. Josephus, *Antiqui.*, VI, 14.2, maintains that Samuel informed her of Saul's presence.

⁷⁶ Comp. 1. Sam. 15.28 with 28.17.

⁷⁷ WR 26.7; Tan. B. III, 82–83; Tan. Emor 7; Shemuel 24, 119–120; Yerushalmi Ta'anit 2, 77a; Hagigah 4b; PRE. 23. The story of the witch of En-dor as narrated by ps.-Philo, 59; 64.5,8, offers many parallels to the rabbinic legends, but in some respects this author's description differs from that of the Rabbis. When Saul asked the witch to describe to him the form of the apparition, she replied: "Thou inquirest of me concerning the gods; for behold, his form is not the form of a man. He is arrayed in a white robe...and two angels lead him." We have here two haggadic explanations of אל' עולים (1 Sam. 28.14); Samuel is like a God (so also Josephus, *Antiqui.*, VI, 14.2), and with him two angels (see vol. V, p. 76, middle of page, and Index, s. v. "Guardian Angels"), whereas according to the Rabbis, "two men of

God" (Moses and Samuel) ascended. Saul, continues ps.-Philo, recognized the mantle Samuel had rent; comp. 1 Sam. 15.27. On the views of the Rabbis as to whose garment was torn on this occasion, Samuel's or Saul's, see Ruth R. 41.8 and Shemuel 18, 100. In agreement with the Rabbis, ps.-Philo makes Samuel utter the words: "I thought that the time was come for me to receive the reward of my deeds (*i. e.*, in the terminology of rabbinic theology, the day of judgment). Ps.-Philo and the Rabbis (comp. Shemuel 10.76; PRE, *loc. cit.*), as well as Eccles. 46.20, dwell upon Samuel's great distinction in having "prophesied after his death". PRE and ps.-Philo maintain that the purpose of the "prophecy after death" was to call Saul to repentance, to atone by his heroic death for his sins. This throws light upon Ecclus., *loc. cit.*, where "to remove the sins" (λαοῦ of the Greek is not represented in the Syriac, and is based on a misunderstanding) refers to those of Saul, who, on hearing Samuel's words, went to his death, to atone thereby for his sins, as is explicitly stated by the Rabbis and ps.-Philo. The latter writes: And Saul heard the words of Samuel..and said: "Behold, I depart to die with my sons, if perchance my destruction may be an atonement for my iniquities". Josephus, *Antiqui.*, VI, 14.2, likewise dwells upon Saul's heroic spirit, who, knowing what awaited him at the battle, did what duty demanded of him, and even took his sons with him to certain death. According to a Midrashic Genizah fragment, Saul in going into battle followed the advice of his son Abinadab ("father of the free-will offering"). The same statement is made by ps.–Jerome, 1 Sam. 31.6, with the additional remark that this son of Saul was also called Ishvi (1 Sam. 14.41), because of his being worthy (שָׁוֶה) to be mentioned with his father.—The witch of En-dor succeeded in making Samuel appear, because he had only been dead a few months (comp. note 70), and the first year the bodies of the pious remain intact in the grave, while their souls "ascend and descend"; as soon as the bodies begin to decay, the souls remain above and descend no more; Shabbat 152b. The rationalistic view that necromancy, like sorcery in general, is nothing but a fraud, is first met with among authors who flourished about 900 C. E.; comp. the references given by Kimhi on 1 Sam. 18.25; R. Hananel on Sanhedrin 67b quoted by R. Bahya, Exod. 22.7. R. Bahya himself considers necromancy possible, and knows many things about it. See also Ziyyoni, Kedoshim (end). As to the view that the dead will rise in the garments in which they were buried, see Yerushalmi Shebi'it 9, 32b; BR 90 (beginning); Tan. B. I, 208–209; Koheleth 5.10. On the punishment of those who were worshipped as gods, see vol. II, p. 129.

⁷⁸ Tan. B. III, 45, which reads: The thought of having caused the death of the priests of Nob drove him into the arms of death; he had executed eighty-five priests who were worthy to be high priests; Yerushalmi Sanhedrin 10, 29a; Targum 1 Sam. 22.18. Kimhi, *ad loc.*, seems to have misunderstood the meaning of this passage of Targum; comp., however, note 92 which cites the unfavorable opinions on these priests expressed by ps.-Philo. This author nevertheless remarks (58; 63.3) that the defeat of Israel and the death of Saul and his sons at the hands of the Philistines were the punishment for the crime committed against the priests of Nob. God said: "Behold, in the first year of Saul's reign, when Jonathan sinned and was about to be put to death by his father, the people rose up and saved him. Now when the priests were slain, even three hundred and eighty-five (this number is found in Septuagint, whereas the Hebrew has only eighty-five; comp. Kimhi, *loc. cit.*), they kept silence and said nothing. Therefore...they shall fall down wounded, they and their king."

⁷⁹ Berakot 12b; 'Erubin 53b (top); Yoma 22b (which reads: David committed more sins than Saul, and yet they did not cause his fall); Alphabet of Ben Sira 3b. In the last passage Saul's severity toward his children is contrasted with David's leniency towards the sins and evil deeds of his children. On the virtues of Saul, see vol. IV, pp. 65–66, 68, and the following note.

⁸⁰ Tehillim 7, 62–63; Shemuel 24, 122; Yerushalmi Nedarim 10 (end; here a view is cited according to which, 2 Sam. 1.24–25 refers to Saul's great devotion to the Torah and its exponents; comp. 'Erubin 53a, bottom); PRK 5, 44a–44b; PR 15, 68a–68b; BaR 11.3; Tosefta-Targum 1 Sam. 10.23. The distinction of being the first Jewish king Saul owed to the tribe of Benjamin, which was rewarded in this way for its great faith in God displayed at the Red Sea, when it was the first to jump into the water; Targum 1 Sam. 15.7, and comp. vol. III, p. 21. In contrast to these Haggadahs glorifying Saul, see ER 31, 159, where he is described as having been of a proud and distrustful nature, which led him to sin and finally to ruin. See also Yerushalmi Sotah 1, 17b; Shemuel 13, 85, and BaR 11.3, where the statement is made that Saul and Absalom possessed beauty of body but not of soul. Opinions differ as to whether Saul in taking away his daughter Michal from David and giving her to another man (comp. 1 Sam. 25.44) committed a crime or an error, the latter consisting in his thinking erroneously that his daughter's marriage to David was void according to the law;

comp. Sanhedrin 19b, and the list of Saul's sins in WR 26.9; Tan. B. III, 83; Tan. Emor 2; Shemuel 24, 120–121. ER, *loc. cit.*, censures Saul severely for his taking away Michal from David, and according to Tosefta Sotah 11 (end) he did the same with his daughter Merab, whom he first gave unto marriage to David, and then took her away from her lawful husband to make her marry another man. Comp. also vol. IV, pp. 76 and 116. Instructive is the remark of BR 32.1 and 38.1, that Saul considered David's marriage to Michal void the moment he became an outlaw and legally dead. On the observance by Saul of the priestly laws of purity, see also Josephus, *Antiqui.*, VI, 11.9. According to Seder 'Olam 12, Saul ruled two years, but Eupolemus, 477b maintains that he reigned twenty-one years. Josephus, *Antiqui.*, VI (end) states that Saul reigned forty years. Comp. also Alphabet of Ben Sira 4a; Septuagint 1 Sam. 13.1; note 53, beginning.

[81] Berakot 62b. David was all the more to be blamed for this act, as he cut off the fringes ("Zizit") from Saul's garment; Tehillim 7, 64, and somewhat differently in ראבי״ה I, 163, No. 162. Comp. also *Toledot Adam we-Hawwah* I; 19.3 and vol. VI, p. 374.

[82] Berakot 12b; 'Erubin 53b. Comp. vol. IV, p. 110.

[83] PRE 33. Comp. note 74.

[84] Koheleth 9.11.

[85] 2 Alphabet of Ben Sira 24b; Yalkut II, 285, on Jer. 9.22, which reads: The entire camp of Israel found place between Abner's knees. Comp. vol. IV, p. 91.

[86] Yalkut II, 285, on Jer. 9.22. The text is not quite certain. The first edition reads: תפש בן אבנר, which, of course, must be emended to תפ׳ בו אבנר, whereas the later editions have תפ׳ אבנר. According to the second reading, it is Joab who laid hold of Abner, and the words שכבה את נרי were spoken by the former, who thus describes the killing of his brother by Abner as "extinguishing my light". Abner's words, "If I could, etc.", remind one of the famous saying of Archimedes: "Give me a place to stand and I will move the earth (δός μοι ποῦ στῶ καὶ κινῶ τὴν γῆν)."

[87] PRK (Grünhut's edition, 72); PRE 53. Comp. vol. I, pp. 59–60, and the note appertaining thereto. The loss caused to David by the death of Ashael was equal to that caused by the death of the nineteen men who were killed by Abner at the same time with him; Sifre D., 52; Midrash Tannaim 55.

[88] Koheleth R. 9.11; Yalkut II, 285, on Jer. 9.22. For a similar remark concerning the swift runner Naphtali, see vol. II, p. 109.

[89] Sanhedrin 49a. Comp. vol. IV, p. 126.

⁹⁰ BR 82.4; Yerushalmi Sotah 1, 17b.

⁹¹ Yerushalmi Peah 1, 16a; PK 4, 31b; Tehillim 7, 67; Tan. B. IV, 106; Tan. Hukkat 4; BaR 19.2; WR 26.2. In all these sources Abner and Amasa are described as "the two lions in the Torah" during the reign of Saul. Comp. Vol. IV, p. 127. The name Abner signifies "father of light", and Saul's cousin bore this name on account of his having been the head (father) of the Synedrion, which illuminates the world by its wisdom; *Rimze Haftarot*, Mahar Hodesh; comp. Baba Batra 4a.

⁹² Yerushalmi Sanhedrin 10, 29a, which reads: Abner and Amasa declared to Saul that they would rather resign the high position held by them than accede to the king's demand. The fate that overtook the priests of Nob was, however, well merited by them. These priests were polluting the holy things of the Lord, and making the first-fruits a reproach. God was wroth, and said: "Behold, I will wipe out the priests who dwell in Nob, because they walk in the ways of the sons of Eli." Ps.-Philo, 58; 63.1. Comp. note 78.

⁹³ Sanhedrin 20a, which cites also the different view to the effect that Abner tried in vain to restrain Saul from his bloody act. See also Yerushalmi Sotah 1, 17b and the references cited in the following note.

⁹⁴ Yerushalmi Peah 1, 16a, and Sotah 1, 17b; PK 4, 32b–33a; WR 26.2; Tan. B. IV, 107–108 and 168; Tan. Hukkat 4 and Mass'e 12; BaR 19.2 and 23.13. These sources cite four different opinions on the nature of the sin for which Abner paid with his life: 1) He did not try to restrain Saul from slaying the priests of Nob; 2) he prevented a reconciliation between Saul and David; 3) he was guilty of lése-majesté in using the words "from Abner to David" in writing to the latter (2 Sam. 3.12), instead of "to David from Abner"; 4) he thought little of human life, and for his amusement he arranged a tournament resulting in the death of many men; see 1 Sam. 2.14, *seq.* Comp. also Sanhedrin 20a.

⁹⁵ BR 82.4; Tan. B. I, 177; comp. vol. I, p. 414.

⁹⁶ Ps.-Jerome, 1 Chron. 8.38, quotes the Hebrew tradition that Doeg accompanied Saul when he went to seek the asses. Septuagint, 1 Sam. 21.8 reads הארמי "Aramean", instead of האדמי "Edomite". It is worth noticing that according to the view of the Rabbis (Tehillim 52, 284), Doeg was not at all of foreign extraction (indeed he belonged to the tribe of Judah like David), but he was blood-thirsty by nature, and hence his epithet אדמי "the bloody one". According to others,

he acted like an Edomite; the Edomites were revengeful, so was he. A third view is that he hailed from the country south of Nob, and that part of the Holy Land was called Idumea. Ps.-Philo, 58; 63.1, and Josephus, *Antiqui.* 6.12, 1, follow Septuagint, and speak of "Doeg the Syrian". Comp. note 98.

⁹⁷ Sanhedrin 69b and 106b. In the last passage Ahitophel is said to have died at the same age as Doeg. Comp. note 100.

⁹⁸ Tehillim 52, 184–185 and 284 (in 284 many explanations of the epithet האדמי are given, see note 96); Tan. B. V, 29; Tan. Shofetim 1; Yerushalmi Sanhedrin 10, 29a; Babli 106b. The "Hebrew tradition" in ps.-Jerome, 1 Chron. 8.38, to the effect that Azrikam the first-born of Azael (this is in agreement with Septuagint and Peshitta which read בכרו instead of בכרו) is identical with Doeg, presupposes a haggadic explanation of *Edomi*, as this Azrikam is described as a descendant of the Benjamite Saul; Comp. note 96. On the names given in 1 Chron., *loc. cit.*, see Pesahim 62b.

⁹⁹ Sanhedrin 106b; Hagigah 15b; BaR 18.17. Ahitophel shared this moral weakness as well as Doeg.

¹⁰⁰ Sanhedrin, Mishnah 10.1; Tan. B. III, 43 and 45; Tan. Mezora' 1 and 2; ARN 40, 133, and 36, 108. The rule laid down in these sources is that all Israelites have a share in the world to come, with the exception of the three kings Jeroboam, Ahab, and Manasseh, as well as the four "private men" Balaam, Doeg, Ahitophel, and Gehazi. See also Tosefta Sanhedrin 12.11, where Ahaz is counted among the hopeless sinners; Babli 101a–107b; Yerushalmi 10, 28b–29b; ARN 36, 108, which reads: Absalom and all the wicked kings of Israel (but not those of Judah) have no share in the world to come; but 41, 133 has: Five kings have no share in the world to come (these are: Jeroboam, Ahab, Manasseh, Ahaz, and Ahaziah; comp. Sanhedrin 103b); ER 3, 16. The view of the allegorists (דורשי רשומות) is quoted, according to which all the abominable sinners enumerated above have their share in the world to come; comp. Sanhedrin 104b–105a; Yerushalmi 10, 29b (end of section). Comp. also Yelammedenu in '*Aruk*, s. v. גלעד=MHG I, 479, and note 93 on vol. IV, p.172. As to the popular, but untenable, hypothesis that the "four private men" mentioned above stand for Jesus and some of his apostles, see note 722 on vol. III, p. 354.

¹⁰¹ Zebahim 54b. This learned discussion, in which Samuel, David, and Doeg partook (see Targum 1 Sam. 19.19, 23, and 20.1), was about the explanation of Deut. 12.14. David carried his point that

"the place which the Lord will choose", spoken of in the Torah, refers to Jerusalem.

¹⁰² Sanhedrin 83b; Ruth R. 2.1; Shemuel 19, 104; BaR 13.10. These sources dwell upon the cunning of Doeg, who knew how to arouse Saul's jealousy by pointing out to him that neither the king himself nor his son Jonathan, though they are great masters of the Torah, succeeds as often as David in "rendering decisions according to the law". The young man mentioned in 1 Sam. 16.18 is none other than Doeg, who praised David before Saul to arouse the latter's jealousy. David surpassed Saul not only in knowledge, but also in his great success as a teacher, 'Erubin 53a (end). He was so marvellous, that when his pupils looked at his face their memory became unfailing; WR 20.1; Koheleth 9.2. Comp. 'Erubin 13b; vol. VI, 170–171.

¹⁰³ Yebamot 76b. Comp. vol. III, pp. 88–89; note 53 on vol. IV, p. 33, and Index, s. v. "Moabites."

¹⁰⁴ Yelammedenu in Yalkut II, 131, on 1 Sam. 22; Tehillim 52, 284. Comp. also Yerushalmi Sanhedrin 10, 29a (on the text of Yerushalmi, see *Batte Midrashot* I, 34–35). The death of the priests of Nob was the last act in the execution of the divine decree against the house of Eli; Josephus, *Antiqui.*, VI, 12.6. Comp. note 78 and note 92. Abiathar, the only priest of Nob who escaped the massacre, is described in 1 Kings 2.26 as "a priest of Anathoth, which means "a priest of poverty". He who, during David's life-time, lived in affluence and wealth, was reduced by Solomon to poverty. Zohar I, 63b.

¹⁰⁵ BR 32.1 and 38.1; Tehillim 52, 284. Comp. note 80.

¹⁰⁶ Sanhedrin 106b; Yelammedenu in Yalkut II, 131, on 1 Sam. 22. Comp. also ps.-Philo, 58–59; 63.4, which reads: And as to Doeg the Syrian (comp. note 96), thus said the Lord: "Behold, the day shall come quickly when the worm shall come upon his tongue, and shall cause him to pine away, and his dwelling shall be with Jair (see vol. IV, pp. 42–43) forever in the fire that shall not be quenched." According to the Rabbis, Doeg and Ahitophel will not be resurrected, nor will they (on the great judgment) be given over to punishment (BR 32.1 and 38.1; ER 18, 107; comp. references in note 100), and the burning of the soul amounts to the same thing. Ps.-Philo decrees eternal punishment for Doeg in fire, *i. e.*, Gehenna. On being eaten alive by worms, see note 552 on vol. III, 283; and vol. VI, p. 213, note 136. It is the punishment for blasphemers and slanderers. The Haggadah links Doeg and Ahitophel together, because of the similarity of their sins: both were "men of evil tongues". See BR,

loc. cit.; Tan. B. I, 51–52, and III, 43; Tan. Noah 17 and Mezora' 1.
[107] Tan. B. V, 44; Tan. Ki-Teze 11; PK 2, 28b–29a; PR 12, 51a;
ps.-Jerome, 2 Sam. 1.2. Our texts of the Pesiktas read as though it
were Doeg himself and not his son who was Saul's armor-bearer slain
by David. But see Ginzberg, *Haggada bei den Kirchenv.*, 39. R.
Solomon b. ha-Yatom, in his commentary on Mo'ed Katan 9b, quotes
a Midrash to the effect that Saul split Doeg like a fish (a haggadic play
on the word דיג in 1 Sam. 22.18; see Yerushalmi Sanhedrin 10, 29a,
where נתפשתה כדג is to be read in the text, with *Batte Midrashot* I, 35),
which would support the view that Doeg was Saul's armor-bearer
slain by David. It seems certain that in Ben ha-Yatom שאול is a scribal
error for דוד. Ps.-Jerome, 1 Chron. 9.44, mentions the Hebrew tradition that Doeg was Saul's armor-bearer; but in the last battle in which
the king fell it was Doeg's son who acted as his armor-bearer. On the
death of the latter at the hands of David, see also vol. III, p. 63. According to Yelammedenu in Yalkut II, 130, on 1 Sam. 21, David came
to the high priest Ahimelech on a Sabbath, just when he found the priests
occupied with the baking of the shew-bread. Astounded at their
desecration of the Sabbath, he was told by them that they were acting
in accordance with the instructions given them by Doeg, who taught
them that the baking of the shew-bread, being a Temple ceremony,
superseded the Sabbath. David, however, called their attention to
the grave error of Doeg, who confused the arranging of the shew-bread,
which must take place on the Sabbath, with the baking thereof, which
ought to be done on the previous day. Comp., however, Menahot
95b–96a, where an opinion is quoted that the error of the priests of Nob
consisted in baking the shew-bread on Friday; whereupon David
pointed out to them that it must be done on the Sabbath. In this
passage it is also said that David and his men were at the point of
starvation, and therefore partook of the holy bread, as there is no
ceremonial law which one is bound to observe at the risk of death.
They received the holy bread which had been removed from the table
of the sanctuary to be distributed among the priests; but David pointed
out to the priests that whenever it is necessary to preserve life, it is
permitted to take the shew-bread from the holy table. The statement of ps.-Jerome, 1 Sam. 21.6, that, according to Jewish tradition,
David did not partake of the holy bread, is very strange, for the explicit
words of the Talmud and Yelammedenu, *loc. cit.*, are to the contrary.
The view of Matth. 12.3–4 is shared by the Rabbis and not, as ps.-
Jerome maintains, opposed by them.

[108] Mo'ed Katan 26a. On Jonathan's scholarship, see also note 102.

[109] Baba Mezi'a 85a; Yerushalmi Pesahim 6, 33a; comp. on the other hand, Baraita de-Yeshua' 46a which reads: He who regrets having performed a good deed delays the (Messianic) salvation. Such a man was Jonathan, who used to say: "If I had not been kind to David, he would never have had designs on the life of my father."

[110] Ps.-Jerome, 1 Sam. 31.6. On Abinadab, see also note 77.

[111] Berakot 4a; 'Erubin 53b; comp. vol. IV, pp. 101, 111, 118.

[112] Yoma 22b; ps.-Jerome, 2 Sam. 19.29. Comp. also Yerushalmi Yebamot 2, 4a, where allusion is very likely made to the wrong done by David to Mephibosheth in granting one half of the latter's possessions to Ziba. This wrong was all the more grievous because David granted Ziba one half of Mephibosheth's personal property, besides his real estate. The Temple was destroyed because David gave ear to Ziba's slander against Mephibosheth. See Alphabet of Ben Sira 11b.

IV. DAVID
Vol. IV, (pp. 81–121).

[1] 2 ARN 43, 121. Comp. note 35 on Vol. I, p. 317 = vol. V, p. 275, towards beginning. Besides David, the following are described in Scripture as "the elect of God": Abraham, Jacob, Israel (the people of), Saul, Levi (the tribe of), Moses, the Messiah, Joshua, Judah, Solomon, and Jerusalem. Just as Moses was "the elect" among the prophets, so was David "the elect" among the kings; Tehillim 1, 3, and parallel passages cited by Buber. These sources point out the great similarity between the life of the great king and that of the great prophet. Comp. vol. V, p. 404.

[2] Sifre N., 78. On the view that the kings of Judah (including the Messiah) were descendants of Judah, the royal tribe, and Levi, the priestly tribe, see vol. II, p. 253.

[3] Baba Batra 91a; Targum Ruth 1.6, 3.7, and 4.21. Comp. note 31 on vol IV, p. 30.

[4] Sifre N., 78; Sotah 11b; PRE 45. Comp. vol. II, p. 253.

[5] Targum Ruth 4.21. Comp. vol IV, p. 34.

[6] Berakot 58a and Yebamot 76b, which read: Jesse went to the front at the head of an army of sixty myriads, returned from the front with such an army, and delivered his lectures before a similar multitude. See also Makiri on Ps. 118, 214.

[7] Shabbat 55b (hence the name Nahash, "serpent", by which Jesse is known; he died merely because death was decreed for all men in consequence of the serpent's seduction of Eve); Baba Batra 17a; Targum Is. 14.29; Targum Ruth 4.22; ps.-Jerome 2 Sam. 17.25. Comp. Ginzberg, *Haggada bei den Kirchenv.*, 58–59. The four men untainted by sin are, according to Baba Batra, *loc. cit.*: Benjamin, Amram, Jesse, and Kilab the son of David. Zohar I, 57b, has Levi instead of Kilab. Allusion to the great piety of Jesse is made by ps.-Philo, 57–58; 62.5, who makes David say to Jonathan: "Yet the righteousness of my father shall help me that I fall not into thy father's hands." The Hebrew original perhaps, read: וצדקת אבות=וצדקת אבו 'אבו "and the righteousness of my fathers" (in rabbinic Hebrew the phrase used is זכות אבות), which the translator misread as וצדקת אבי "and the righteousness of my father." Comp. note 30 on vol. II, p. 260 and vol. V, p. 129.

⁸ BR 96.4. Comp. Lekah, Gen. 46.29.

⁹ BaR 14.1. Josephus, *Antiqui.*, VI, 12.3, on the other hand, maintains that the king of Moab was very kind to David's parents. Comp. also Zohar III, 190a. The Haggadah attempts to excuse David's cruelty towards the Moabites (comp. 2 Sam. 2.2) by accusing them of having killed his parents.

¹⁰ Sukkah 52b. On "the Messianic princes", see note 142 on vol. I, 102.

¹¹ An unknown Midrash quoted by Makiri, Ps. 118, 214. On the references to this legend by the medieval authors, see Zunz, *Synagogale Poesie*, 129. Comp. also *Kele Yakar*, 1 Sam. 17; Azulai, *Midbar Kedemot*, s. v. שׁי, No. 20; R. Elijah Wilna in his commentary on Yoreh De'ah, 157.24. Comp. note 23. Josephus, *Antiqui.*, XII, 4.6, narrates a similar story about Hyrcanus the son of Joseph the tax collector. As to the names of Nazbat and Adiel (which occur only in Baba Batra 91a), see Güdemann, *Religionsgeschichtliche Studien*, 49, *seq.* The reading עראל and עדה, instead of עדיאל are incorrect; see 1 Chron. 27.25, where a son of Adiel is mentioned as King David's treasurer.

¹² PRE 19; BaR 14.12; Tehillim 92, 409; Midrash in Yalkut I,41; Aggadat Bereshit (introduction), XXXVIII; Zohar I, 55a–55b, 140a, 248b; II, 235a. In Zohar I, 168a–168b, the legend reads that Abraham presented David with five years, Jacob with twenty-eight, and Joseph with forty-eight; all of which amount to seventy-one, *i. e.*, David died in his seventy-first year. Comp. also Epstein, *Eldad*, 67, and Zohar Hadash, Ruth, 98b, beginning דבר אחר עיר קטנה. On the Mohammedan version of this legend, see Grünbaum, *Neue Beiträge*, 64; vol. I, 69 and note 28 appertaining thereto. The Mohammedan writers misunderstood the point made by the legend, and state that Adam donated forty of his years. Of course, the point is that David lived seventy years, corresponding to the number missing in Adam's life to make up a thousand years = a "day of the Lord". As to the deeds signed by God and the angels, see also the quotation from Tosafot in manuscript given by Poznanski, *Kommentar…von Eliezer aus Beaugency, Einleitung*, CX. Here a deed is drawn up on the sixth day of creation between the Most High, called the Almighty God, and the earth, in which the latter takes upon itself the obligation of furnishing every day "one hundred dead men like Adam". The witnesses are Michael, the prince of wisdom, and Gabriel, the prince of strength. On the daily

deaths, see note 123. The legend in Seymour, *Tales of Solomon* 15–16, applies to Solomon what really belongs to his father David.

¹³ Makiri, Ps. 118, 214. Verses 22–24 of this psalm are put by this Midrash into the mouth of David's mother and brothers. This is a very old Haggadah; comp. Pesahim 119a and Shemuel 19, 104, where it is said that verses 21–27 were uttered on the occasion when David was anointed by Samuel. David said: "I will give thanks...for Thou hast afflicted me (עניתני from ענה "afflicted"), but now Thou art become my salvation." Jesse said: "The stone which the build ers, etc." David's brothers said: "This is the Lord's doing, etc." Samuel said: "This is the day, etc." David's brothers said once more: "O Lord, save now." David joined in their singing: "O Lord, make us prosper", and Jesse continued their prayer with the verse: "Blessed be he that cometh in the name of the Lord." Where-upon Samuel responded: "We bless you out of the house of the Lord." Then they all exclaimed: "The Lord is good, and hath given us light." Ps.-Philo 56.59.4 also gives a psalm by David composed on the occasion of his anointment, in which the new king contrasts his good fortune with the sad fate of Abel who was slain by his brother out of envy. "But it is not so with me", David is alleged to have said, "for God hath kept me, and hath delivered me unto His angels and His guardians to watch over me. For my brothers envied me, and my father and my mother made me of no account." David's ruddy complexion (comp. 1 Sam. 16.12; according to Septuagint, this verse speaks of the reddish color of David's hair. See also Josephus, *Antiqui.*, VI, 8.1) was due to Jesse's great passion at the time of begetting his youngest son. And this unusual color nearly caused the death of David and his mother, as his brothers suspected her of adultery. Jesse, however, restrained them from carrying out their evil designs, and they yielded to his wish on the condition that David should be considered as a slave, and thus for twenty-eight years he was shepherd of his father's flock. See Makiri, *loc. cit.* where בנים 'ו is to be read for בנים 'ס; David's age at the time of his anointment is said to have been twenty-eight years; comp. Seder 'Olam 13; note 18. The older sources maintain that David's ruddy complexion indicated that he was destined to shed blood, and accordingly Samuel was terrified when he beheld the "red David", whom he thought a second Esau. God, however, informed him that David would shed much blood, but only of those who by their iniquity have forfeited their lives. One could see at David's birth that he was destined for great

things, as he was born with the sign of the Abrahamic covenant on him; Sotah 10b; Tehillim 9, 58; note 318 on vol. I, p. 306.

¹⁴ Tehillim 78, 357; ShR 2.2. Comp. Grünbaum, *Neue Beiträge* 193–194, and vol. II, p. 300.

¹⁵ Shemuel 20, 107; Baraita of 32 Middot 3. Of the fleece of the sheep saved from the claws of the wild beasts David made himself a garment, that he should always remember the miracle wrought for him; see quotation from an unknown Midrash by R. Elijah Wilna in *Toledot Adam* I, 59. According to ps.-Philo, 56; 59.5, a lion came out of the wood and a she-bear (the female of this species is considered more ferocious than the male, comp. BR 87, beginning) came from the mountain, and took the bulls of David (did this author read שׁר instead of שׁה in 1 Sam. 17.34 ?). Whereupon David said: "Lo, this shall be a sign unto me for a mighty beginning of my victory in the battle"; and he went after the wild beasts with stones, and slew them. God then said unto him: "Lo, by stones have I delivered unto thee these beasts...and this shall be a sign unto thee that hereafter thou shalt slay with stones the adversary of My people." Comp. also Mekilta Amalek 2, 56a, where, with reference to David's slaying of the wild beasts, it is said "that a sign was given unto him of which he took notice." David was of such unusual strength that he could bend a "bow of brass"; Tehillim 18, 155. The first battle in which David engaged took place shortly after the encounter with the wild beasts, while he was still feeding his sheep, when the Midianites came and would have taken his sheep; but he fought against them, and slew of them fifteen thousand men; ps.-Philo 56; 61.1.

¹⁶ This designation of the lion is very frequent in Jewish literature; comp., *e. g.* Hagigah 13b.

¹⁷ Tehillim 22, 195; 91, 395; 92, 408. Comp. vol. IV, p. 333.

¹⁸ Seder 'Olam 12 (on the variant "twenty-nine", see Ratner, *ad loc.*); Makiri, Ps. 118, 24. Comp. note 13.

¹⁹ Sifre D., 17; Midrash Tannaim 10; Tan. Wa-Yera 6; Shemuel 14, 88. Comp. note 322 on vol III, 396. See also ps.-Philo 56; 59.2, which reads: And the Lord said unto him: "Where is thy vision which thy heart hath seen? Art not thou he that saidst: I am that seeth? And how knowest thou not him whom thou must anoint? And now let this rebuke suffice thee, and seek out the shepherd, the least of them all, and anoint him." Samuel, though sure of God's help, kept his journey to Beth-lehem a secret (1 Sam. 16.2, *seq.*), and did not betray to any outsider the purpose of his visit. This teaches

us that one must not expose himself to danger (as far as it can be avoided) even while carrying out God's command. See Pesahim 8b; Yoma 11a; Yebamot 65b (here it is said: For the sake of peace Samuel told an untruth); Zohar I, 209a; Maimonides, *Shemonah Perakim*, 8. Comp. also MHG I, 519, and Yalkut II, 123. In the last source the statement about the importance of peace, the same almost verbatim as MHG, is quoted from Yerushalmi Yoma, but our texts do not have it. On Samuel's self-consciousness, see note 43 on vol. IV, p. 64.

²⁰ Pesahim 66b; Shemuel 14, 88. The Haggadah finds that Eliab's violent character is indicated in 1 Sam. 17.28.

²¹ Yalkut II, 124, wheren Tan. is erroneously given as source instead of Yelammedenu; see Yalkut II, 750. on Ps. 45.8.

²² On the "holy oil" (Josephus, *Antiqui.*, VI, 8.1), see Shemuel 19, 102, and vol. III, p. 179. In anointing David Samuel used a "horn" filled with oil, but in anointing Saul he took a cruse: the horn was the symbol of David's everlasting kingdom, whereas the cruse represented Saul's temporary rule. Comp. vol. IV, p. 257. See Megillah 14a, and also Hippolytus, 5.4 (end).

²³ Makiri on Ps. 118,214; Yelammedenu in Yalkut II, 124 (comp. note 21), and 750, on Ps. 45.8; Ephraem, 1 Sam. 16.13. Comp. Ginzberg, *Haggada bei den Kirchenv.*, 28. As to the secret of David's mother, see vol. IV, p. 82 and note 11. While still a youth, David began to prophesy that he would slay Goliath the Philistine and erect the house of God. His father thought him weak-minded, and therefore made him keep the sheep, the only occupation for which he considered him fit. When Samuel arrived at Jesse's house, he, too, was struck by David's insignificant looks, and hardly took notice of him. But God said to Samuel: "Arise; My anointed one stands, and thou sittest." It is with reference to the low esteem in which he had been held that David praised God with the words: "The stone which the builders rejected is become the chief corner-stone" (Ps. 118.22); see Midrash Tannaim 10, and comp. references cited in note 13. David was not the youngest son of Jesse, as one might be inclined to infer from Scripture (1 Sam. 16.11), but "the least esteemed of his sons". Comp. note 88, end. Jesse's youngest son was Elihu; see Midrash Tannaim *l. c.* and comp. 1 Chron. 27.18.

²⁴ Josephus, *Antiqui.*, VI, 8.2, and comp. the quotations from ps.-Philo in note 13. Although the Psalms, the book of David, does not form part of the prophetic section of the Bible, he was nevertheless a prophet, see Seder 'Olam 20; Mekilta Bo (פתיחתא) 2a. According to Sotah 48, Yerushalmi 9, 24b, the term "the first prophets" refers to Samuel and

David. Some, however, maintain that by this term Gad and Nathan are meant, while others think that it stands for Jeremiah and Baruch. Comp. note 358 on vol. III, p. 173.

²⁵ Sanhedrin 93b. Comp. note 102 on vol. IV, 75.

²⁶ BHM IV, 150–151; Ma'aseh-buch, No. 199, 67d. In many sources the hero of this legend is Solomon. Comp. Gaster, *Exempla*, No. 403; Seymour *Tales of Sol.* 17 and 33; note 27 on vol. IV, p. 131.

²⁷ Sotah 42b (here several etymologies of the names ערפה Orpah, Naomi's daughter-in-law, and הרפה 2 Sam. 21.16, are given, to show their identity); Tan. B. I, 208; Ruth R. 1.14; Ruth Z. 49; Shemuel 20,106–108; ps.-Philo, 57; 61.6. In the last source *mater tua* ("thy mother") very likely means " thy ancestress", since David describes Ruth as "my mother", which, of course, cannot be taken literally. On the meaning of the name Goliath, and his designation as איש הבנים, see Sotah, *loc. cit.*, and Targum Ps. 9.1. In the latter source איש הבנים=לבן Goliath. On Orpah, Goliath's mother, see vol. IV, pp. 31 and 108

²⁸ Ruth R. 1.4; ps.-Philo, 57; 61.6. Comp. vol. IV, p. 31.

²⁹ Sotah 42b; Ruth R. 1.14; Ruth Z., 49; Vulgate 1 Sam. 17.4. Comp. Ginzberg, *Haggada bei den Kirchenv.*, 30–31. According to Tosefta-Targum Sam., *loc. cit.*, Goliath's father (ancestor?) was Samson, and his mother was Orpah.

³⁰ See, on the other hand, vol. IV, p. 31, according to which Orpah accompanied her mother-in-law a long distance.

³¹ Sotah 42b; Ruth R. 1.14; Shemuel 20, 106–107; Tan. B. I, 208. The forty days are explained by ps-Philo, 57; 61.2, as corresponding to "the number of days wherein Israel feasted when they received the law in the wilderness." Goliath said: "For forty days I will reproach them, and after that I will fight with them." Similar is the meaning of the statement in Sotah, *loc. cit.* כנגד מ' יום שנתנה בהן תורה. For other explanations of the forty days, see Shemuel 20, 106.

³² Sotah 42b (Scripture hints at Goliath's extraordinary strength and powers, that we might properly appreciate David's achievement); Shemuel 20, 106; Tosefta-Targum 1 Sam. 17.9–10 and 16. Targum has the morning and evening sacrifice instead of the morning and evening prayer. See also ps.-Philo, 57; 61.2, where Goliath challenged Saul to fight him, and "if not, he will come unto him and cause him to be taken captive, and his people will be forced to serve the gods of the Philistines."

³³ Tan. V. I. 207 and 208; Haserot 44. This Haggadah is given

as an explanation of Jesse's words, who told David to "take the pledge" of his brothers; comp. 1 Sam. 17.18. According to another view, David was bidden by his father to see to it that his brothers send their wives bills of divorce, so that in case they do not return from the battle, their wives would have no difficulty in remarrying. See Ketubot 9a; Shabbat 56a; ps.-Jerome, 1 Sam., *loc. cit.* Comp. Ginzberg, *Haggada bei den Kirchenv.*, 31–32, and vol. IV, p. 103.

³⁴ Shemuel 11, 78–79; ps.-Philo, 53; 54.3–4, and 56–57; 61.2. Comp. vol. IV, p. 65.

³⁵ Tan. B. III, 84; Tan. Emor 4; Shemuel 21, 108. Saul suspected that David must have been anointed with "holy oil" (see vol. IV, p. 84), which had the effect of changing the body of the anointed one; if he was short he bacame tall; if he was black, he became white, etc; Tanhumas., *loc. cit.*, and Yelammedenu in Yalkut II, 750, on Ps. 45.2. It is very likely that Philo was acquainted with the legendary qualities of the holy oil, and in his way attempted to rationalize this legend. Comp. *De Nobilitate*, 5.

³⁶ Shemuel 21, 108.

³⁷ Zohar III, 272a; comp. vol. I, p. 350.

³⁸ Shemuel 21, 108, and somewhat differently in the unknown Midrash quoted by Kimhi on 1 Sam. 17.40. According to ps.-Philo, 57; 61.5, David wrote upon seven stones "the names of his fathers Abraham, Isaac, Jacob, Moses, and Aaron, and his own name, and the name of the Almighty." See also 2 Maccabees 10.29, where the five men are very likely the three patriarchs, and Moses and Aaron. Comp. further Aggadat Bereshit 50.102–103 (only in manuscript not in printed text).

³⁹ WR 21.2; PK 27, 175a; Shemuel 21, 109; Zohar II, 206a– 206b. The last-named source gives many details about the power of David's eye. Comp. vol. III, p. 214.

⁴⁰ WR 21.2; PK 27, 175a; Shemuel 21, 108. The sources dwell upon the fact that the beauty of David aroused an impure passion in Goliath.

⁴¹ Shemuel 21, 109, according to the reading of Kimhi, 1 Sam. 17.44.

⁴² A Midrash quoted by Kimhi, 1 Sam. 17,49. According to others, a miracle was performed, and the small pebble pierced the hard metal of which Goliath's visor was fashioned; see Shemuel 21, 109 and Tehillim 78, 350, which read: On five occasions God made the "soft" conquer the "hard": the frogs crawled through the marble buildings

of the Egyptians (comp. vol. II, p. 349); the hornets penetrated through the rocks to the hiding-places of the Amorites, and killed them (vol. III, p. 347); the mice sent upon the Philistines gnawed through the metal vessels (vol. IV, p. 63); the pebble which David threw at Goliath and the missile which struck Ahab (see vol. IV, p. 188) penetrated through the hard metal to the bodies of Goliath and Ahab, respectively. Comp. also Tehillim 105, 452.

⁴³ Tehillim 18, 160, and 144, 533; WR 10.7; Shir 4.4; Shemuel 21, 109. According to ps.-Philo, 57; 61.4–8, it was the angel Ceruihel, the angel appointed over strength (*i. e.*, זרועאל; comp. note 17 on vol. IV, p. 25), who gave David strength to slay Goliath. While there was still life in him, Goliath said unto David: "Hasten and slay me, and rejoice." But David said: "Before thou diest, open thine eyes and behold the slayer who hath killed thee." And the Philistine looked and saw the angel, and said: "Thou hast not killed me by thyself, but he that was with thee, whose form is not like the form of a man." Ps.-Philo, *loc. cit.*, makes David harangue Goliath as follows: "Were not the two women, of whom thou and I were born, sisters (comp. notes 27, 28)? Thy mother was Orpah, and mine was Ruth. Orpah chose for herself the gods of the Philistines, and went after them, but Ruth chose for herself the ways of the Almighty, and walked in them. And now...I that am born of thy kindred am come to avenge my people. For thy three brothers also shall fall into my hands after thy death."

⁴⁴ The Uriah story is quoted, from an unknown Midrash, by R. Moses Al-Sheikh, on 2 Sam. 13, and by R. Samuel Laniado on 1 Sam. 17.50. Comp. vol. IV, p. 103. The controversy between the scholars of that time concerning David's admission to "the congregation of the Lord" is found in Ruth R. 2.5; Shemuel 22, 109–110, and, in a somewhat different form, in Yebamot 76b and Ephraem, 1 Sam. 17.55. Comp. Ginzberg, *Haggada bei den Kirchenv.*, 32–33. This Haggadah is an attempt to harmonize 1 Sam. 16.18, *seq.*, with 1 Sam. 17.55, *seq.* Another solution of this difficulty is given by ps.-Philo, 57; 61.89, who remarks: And the angel of the Lord "lifted up the face" of David and no man knew him, and when Saul saw David, he asked him who he was, and there was no man who knew who he was. There can be no doubt that *erexit faciem* ("lifted up his face") is a mistranslation, and I would suggest that the original Hebrew read שִׁנָּא [ה=] פָנָיו "changed his face", which was misread as נשא פָניו "lifted up his face." On the "changing of the face" in ps.-Philo, see the quotation in note 75 on vol. IV, p. 70.

⁴⁵ Yebamot 77a; Yerushalmi 8, 9c; Tehillin 9, 87; Ruth R. 1.21; Targum and ps.-Jerome on 1 Chron. 2.17. Comp. Ginzberg, *Haggada bei den Kirchenv.*, 124, and Index, s. v. "Moabites." With regard to Ithra, another view is given in Tehillim, *loc. cit.*, according to which, he was an Ishmaelite, but became converted to Judaism when he heard Jesse recite the verse: "Look unto Me, and be ye saved, all the ends of the earth" (Is. 45.22).

⁴⁶ ⸰Tehillim 34, 294; 2 Alphabet of Ben Sira 24a–24b: *Kimha Dabishuna* שבת בראשית.

⁴⁷ 2 Alphabet of Ben Sira 24b; Targum Ps. 57.3. Comp. Grünbaum, *Neue Beiträge*, 195.

⁴⁸ 2 Alphabet of Ben Sira 24b; comp. vol. IV, p. 73. Abner, however, never believed David that he had been near him while he was asleep, and therefore tried to convince Saul that David found the cruse of water lost by the servant; Yerushalmi Peah 1, as quoted in 'Aruk, s. v. בר 7, but not in our texts; comp. note 94 on vol. IV, p. 74.

⁴⁹ Tehillim 18, 138; 9, 85; comp. also 142, 532, which reads: David was within the cave, and Saul was watching outside at the entrance.

⁵⁰ WR 21.3; PK 27 175b; Ekah, introduction, XXX; Tehillim 18, 162.—The legend tells of many things (not mentioned in Scripture) which happened to David during the time he was pursued by Saul. Although his position on the day of his flight was precarious (1 Sam. 21.35, *seq.*), he nevertheless insisted on saying his morning prayers with the quorum required for the service, and he requested his friend Jonathan to bring eight men (the quorum מנין, consists of ten) to the hiding-place; *Rimze Haftarot*, Mahar Hodesh. The prolix description of the last meeting between David and Jonathan in ps.-Philo, 57–58; 62.3, *seq.*, hardly contains any other legendary material except the statement that Jonathan knew already then that David was destined to possess "the kingdom in this world." If Jonathan had thought of giving his departing friend a few loaves of bread on his journey, Nob, the city of the priests, would not have been destroyed, Doeg would not have been excluded from the community of the pious, and Saul and his three sons would not have been slain. This teaches us that the refraining from giving a departing guest the necessary provisions for his journey is accounted to one as a deliberate sin, even though it might be due to forgetfulness, as in the case of Jonathan; Sanhedrin 104a. David, who started on his journey without provisions, arrived in Nob almost in a state of collapse, and was forced to partake of the holy bread to save his life. On

that occasion he ate bread baked of seven seah of flour; Yelammedenu
in Yalkut II, 130.   Comp. note 107 on vol. IV, p. 76. From Nob he fled
to Adullam, where fourteen hundred scholars joined him; EZ 5, 181.
Later he was forced to leave the Holy Land, and this caused him extreme pain, as "he who leaves the Holy Land to settle in another
country is considered as though he worshipped idols".   It is in this
sense that we have to understand David's words: "Cursed be they
before the Lord, for they have driven me out this day that I should not
cleave unto the inheritance of the Lord, saying: Go, serve other gods"
(1 Sam. 26.19).   See ARN 26, 85; Ketubot 110b; Tosefta 'Abodah
Zarah 4(5).5; Sifra 25.38.   David was so much attached to the Holy
Land, that he used to say: "I prefer to stand at the threshhold of
the house of my God and live in the Holy Land, though lacking all necessities of life, even the carob, rather than dwell in any other land in
affluence and prosperity."   Yelammedenu in '*Aruk*, s. v. סטסימה and
ספף. He showed his devotion to his country when immediately after
he married Michal he went to war against the Philistines, who had
hoped that he would stay home, availing himself of the privilege granted
by the law (Deut. 20.7) to newly-married men.   David went still
further, and promulgated the law that nobody is exempt from military
duty in a defensive war, as the exemptions mentioned in the Torah
refer to an offensive war only; Shemuel 22, 110; Sotah, Mishnah 8(end);
Babli 44b; Yerushalmi 8, 23a; Tosefta 7 (end).   In his zeal to expand
the confines of the Holy Land he engaged in offensive wars against
Syria before he conquered all that belonged to the Holy Land.   This
mistaken zeal resulted in the fact that the Syrian provinces conquered
by him never received the holy character of Palestine proper; Sifre
D., 52; Midrash Tannaim 44; Yerushalmi Hallah 2, 58b; Tosefta
Kelim, Baba Kamma, 1.5.; Gittin 8a; Baba Batra 90b.

    ⁵¹ PRE 36.   According to another view, the Jebusites were the
descendants of Abimelech, king of Gerar, who later settled in Jerusalem,
where he built a strong fortress (Zion), which for many centuries had
withstood all attacks until David captured it; Yalkut Reubeni 44c,
giving ספר הקבלה as his authority; but neither ספר הקבלה of R. Abraham ibn Daud, nor שלשלת הקבלה of Ibn Yahya, has this legend.   The
Jebusites had, on the top of a high tower, two monuments, one representing a blind man (Isaac), the other a lame man (Jacob).   Attached to
these monuments was the text of the covenant between Abraham and
the Philistine king Abimelech, some of whose descendants inhabited
Jerusalem.   The Jews respected the covenant as long as some of Abi-

melech's descendants were still in existence, but in David's time
Abimelech's family became extinct, and there was no longer any reason
for refraining from driving out the Jebusites from Jerusalem.   See
Midrash quoted by Rashi and Kimhi, 2 Sam. 5.6, as well as Yalkut
Reubeni, *loc. cit.* According to Targum, *ad loc.*, "the blind and the
lame" mentioned in this verse refer to the sinners (*i. e.*, the Jebusites).

52 Tehillim 18, 152; PRE 36; MHG I, 351; comp. note 268 on
vol. I, p. 290.

53 Tehillim 18, 152; PRE 36; Shemuel 32, 139; Sifre N., 52;
Sifre D., 62; Zebahim 116b; BaR 11.7; Baraita of 32 Middot, 15;
ps.-Jerome, 2 Sam. 24.24; Midrash 13 Middot, 70–71.   Only the
last source has the statement that David himself contributed as much
as all the twelve tribes together.   The money given to the Jebusites,
according to the sources just cited, was for the site of the Temple (comp.
2 Sam., *loc. cit.*, and 1 Chron. 21.25); but PRE, *loc. cit.*, maintains that
it was for the city of Jerusalem.   As to the miracle of the wall lowering
itself, see also Baba Mezi'a 95b; Yerushalmi Mo'ed Katan 3, 81d;
ps.-Matthew 20.   According to a Christian legend, the Jebusites,
after having been driven out from Palestine by David, settled in
Cyprus.   Comp. Acts of Barnabas (towards the end); see also note
57 on vol. IV, p. 154.

54 Ps.-Jerome, 2 Sam. 5.24, which very likely follows a Jewish
tradition.   On the judgment inflicted upon the guardian angels of
the nations, see vol. III, p. 25 and note pertaining thereto.   According to
Rashi, 2 Sam., *loc. cit.*, the motion of the tops of the trees indicated the
approach of the angels who came to David's assistance.   With regard
to the meaning of בכאים in 2 Sam., *loc. cit.*, and 1 Chron. 14.14, ps.-
Jerome, on the latter passage, quotes a Jewish tradition, according to
which the Philistines used to bring human sacrifices to their idol (Moloch),
and hence בכאים is the same as בכאים "the weeping ones", because they
wept when they offered up their human sacrifices.   Another explanation
of בכאים is given by ps.-Jerome on 2 Sam., *loc. cit.*: All idols deserve
this name, "the weeping", for they are the cause of the tears of their
worshippers. Quite similar is the remark of the Rabbis 2 ARN 28,
101, and Tehillim, 96, according to the reading of Makiri on Ps. 96, 112.

55 Tehillim 27, 222–223; PR 8, 30b.   On the view that Saul
lacked trust in God, see 1 Sam. 14.19.

56 Sotah 42b; Tehillim 3, 38.

⁵⁷ PRE 36. On the covenant between Jacob and Laban, see Yalkut Reubeni on Deut. 12.2, and vol. I, pp. 374–375.

⁵⁸ PRE 36; MHG I, 410.

⁵⁹ Tehillim 60, 304; Tan. B. V, 2; Yelammedenu in 'Aruk, s. v. שׁשׁע; Targum Ps. 60. 1; BR 74.15. The last source dwells upon the fact that the Moabites, the Ammonites, and the Edomites, the moment they attacked the Israelites, forfeited the claim they might have had to be treated kindly. See also Jub. 24.28–33; note 77 and vol. I, p.257. David engaged in eighteen campaigns (WR 1.4), and was forced to defend himself against the attacks of ten adversaries: Saul, Doeg, Ahitophel, Sheba, Shimei, Shobach and Goliath and the latter's three brothers (Tehillim 18, 139); yet there was nothing for which he was so grateful to God as for the help granted him against Saul. During his flight from Saul he prayed to God for two things: that he should not be delivered into the hands of his enemy, and that the latter should not be delivered into his hands, so that he should not be led into temptation to slay the anointed of the Lord; Tehillim 6, 69. David used a sword upon which the name of God was engraved. He was therefore accustomed to swear by his sword. He did not, however, use this sword to slay Uriah, but employed for this purpose the sword of the children of Ammon (2 Sam. 12.9), upon which was engraved a serpent, the idol of the Ammonites. David had some excuse for slaying Uriah (see vol. IV, p. 103), but not for using this "unclean" sword; Zohar II, 107a–108a. As to the sword used in slaying Uriah, see also vol. I, p. 321; vol. III, p. 411. These passages record similar legends concerning the swords of Esau and Phinehas. In Gaster, *Exempla* No. 351 reference is made to the sword of David upon which the Name was engraved; see note 32 on vol. IV, p. 136.

⁶⁰ Berakot 3b, which reads: David did not engage in any war before he took counsel with Ahitophel. Targum Ps. 141.10 describes Ahitophel as the head of the Synedrion.

⁶¹ Sanhedrin 101b; ps.-Jerome 2 Sam. 11.3. Ahitophel was at first David's best friend; Tehillim 55, 290.

⁶² Nedarim 37b; Yerushalmi Sanhedrin 10, 29a; Tehillim 3, 38, which reads: His wisdom was superhuman, like that of an angel. Comp. also Tehillim 55, 391, which reads: David feared nobody except Ahitophel, who was his master and teacher in the knowledge of the Torah. According to some, David learned two things only from Ahitophel, to acquire colleagues with whom to study the Torah, and to walk quickly to the house of God for prayer and service; see Abot 6.2;

Nispahim 18; Kallah 6, 16; Mahzor Vitry 556; Nehemias, Commentary on Abot, 77; BaR 18.17.

⁶³ Sanhedrin 69b; comp. note 97 on vol. IV, p. 74.

⁶⁴ Sanhedrin 106b; Hagigah 15b; Tehillim 55, 292–293, and 119, 495 and 500. Comp. vol. IV, p. 75, where a similar characteristic is attributed to Doeg. Ahitophel used to compose three prayers for each day; Yerushalmi Berakot 4, 8a (bottom), which is a play on the name Ahitophel אחיתפל=תפלה אחי "brother of prayer", *i. e.* "man of prayers"; comp., however, Ratner, *Ahabat Ziyyon, ad. loc.* It was his pride which brought destruction upon him, as may be seen from his haughty behavior towards David at the removal of the ark (comp. vol. IV, p. 75); ER 31, 157.

⁶⁵ Sanhedrin Mishnah 10.1. Comp. note 100 on vol. IV, p. 75.

⁶⁶ Sanhedrin 101b; an unknown Midrash in Yalkut II, 151 on 2 Sam. 16. Comp. note 52 on vol. IV, p. 63, and note 2 on vol. IV, p. 180.

⁶⁷ Yalkut II, 151 on 2 Sam. 16. Ahitophel thought that David was fallen from the grace of God for ever since he had committed the sin with Bath-sheba. But he did not know that "no sin can efface the merit acquired by the study of the Torah", and these merits stood David in good stead in the time of his disgrace; see Sotah 21a; comp. also Baba Mezi'a 59a; PK 2, 10b; Tan. B. II, 106; Tan. Ki-Tissa 4; Tehillim 2, 38, which reads: Doeg and Ahitophel used to remark mockingly: "Is it conceivable that he who took the sheep and slew the shepherd should be able to make good?" On the reading "Doeg" in this passage, see Tosafot שעיר on Sotah, *loc. cit.*

⁶⁸ Yerushalmi Sanhedrin 10, 29a; BaR 4.20; ER 31,157, which reads: The ark was suspended in the air, and Uzzah "put forth his hand" to take hold of it. The sinners in Israel then said: "Were it not for Uzzah, the ark would have dropped down to the ground". No sooner did they utter these blasphemous words than Uzzah dropped dead. All then became convinced that the ark was able to support itself without human help. According to Sotah 35a, Uzzah eased himself near the ark, and as a punishment was smitten dead, whereas according to *Rimze Haftarot*, Shemini, he brought his death upon himself by uncovering the ark. Comp. notes 37 and 39 on vol. IV, p. 63. As to the grave error committed by David in putting the ark on a wagon, see Josephus, *Antiqui.*, VII, 4.2; Aphraates, 363; Ephraem, 2 Sam. 6.7; vol. III, pp. 194 and 395–396; Ginzberg, *Haggada bei den Kirchenv.*, 47–48. On the number of functionaries appointed by David, see vol.

III, p. 70. The king chose pious men, and therefore passed over Ahitophel, who was wise but not pious; Hasidim 416.

⁶⁹ Ahitophel ended his life by strangling himself; see 2 Sam. 17.18. A somewhat different reason for Ahitophel's death by strangling is given in ER 31, 157.

⁷⁰ Yerushalmi Sanhedrin 10, 29a; Sukkah 53a–53b; Makkot 11a; Shemuel 26, 125; Ma'asiyyot (Gaster's edition, 113–114); Raziel והן סדר שמושן; *Sode Raza* as quoted in Yalkut Reubeni, Gen. 1.1; *Hakam ha-Razim* in Yalkut Reubeni, Num. 26.56; Al-Barceloni, 72–73; Zohar III, 198b. In the last source it is stated that David found a pot filled with magic herbs at the abyss where it was placed by Balak; comp. vol. III, p. 99, and note 47 on vol. IV, p. 15. As to the waters below the holy of holies, see Middot 2.6, and Yoma 77b–78a. All these Haggadahs belong to the cycle of legends concerning the Eben Shetiyyah; see Index, s. v.

⁷¹ 2 Sam. 17.23 is quoted as proof for the law that the last wish of the dying has legal validity; comp. Baba Batra 147a.

⁷² Yerushalmi Sanhedrin 10, 29a–29b; Baba Batra 147a (here the first rule of conduct reads: Do not engage in dissension, which is very likely a doublet to rule 2; comp. ER 31, 157); PRK 23a (as in Baba Batra, with the addition: When you begin to suffer the "travail of the Messiah", start to prepare gifts for him).   Comp. also Tosefta 'Arakin 1.9.

⁷³ R. Moses Isserles, *Torat ha-'Olah* 1.11, quoting an "old source".

⁷⁴ On the fortune-book, see Steinschneider, *Hebräische Ueber-setzungen*, 870.

⁷⁵ Sanhedrin 49a; Yerushalmi Makkot 2,31d; ps.-Jerome, 1 Kings 2.34.

⁷⁶ Yerushalmi Makkot 2, 31d; Tan. B. IV, 166; Tan. Mass'e 12; BaR 23.13; PR 11, 43b. In these sources the Tahchemonite (2 Sam. 23.8) is said to refer to Joab who bore this name, "the wise", because of his having been the head of the academy. Allusion to this Haggadah is made in Chronicle of Ahimaaz, 112, line 12 where מבית יואב = of the house of the head of the academy. According to Mo'ed Katan 16b and Targum, 2 Sam., *loc. cit.*, as well as 1 Chron. 11.11, Tahchemonite is an attribute of David, who was as famous a scholar as a warrior.

⁷⁷ The first Joab legend is found in BHM V, 52–53 (on the text see Löw, *Monatsschrift* XXVI, 240), and comp. VI, introduction, XVI–XVII; the second legend of which Joab is the hero is found in several sources independent of one another; see Gaster, *Exempla* No. 304; BHM V, 146–

148; Makiri, Ps. 18, 115 (here correctly קסרין=קנסרי Caesarea and not קינסלי as in BHM; comp. Megillah 6a קסרי בת אדום); Mahzor Vitry 332, giving Tehillim as source; Ma'aseh-book 42d–43c, No. 145. The last two call the city, captured by Joab, Rabbah of the children of Ammon, and this is very likely the correct reading, as the story ends with the incident that the crown of the captured king was given to David. This obviously refers to the biblical narrative (Sam. 12.30) concerning the crown of the king of Rabbah. On the effect of the blood upon the sword, see vol. IV, p. 26. The old sources contain many details concerning the war against Edom waged by David and Joab, some of which have been made use of in this Joab legend. It is said in Baba Batra 21a–21b that Joab had first slain the men of Edom only, sparing the women. This action was based on a faulty reading of Deut. 25.19, where the Bible speaks of "blotting out the remembrance of Amalek"; but instead of זֵכֶר "remembrance", Joab's teacher had made him read זָכָר "male". When Joab found out the grave consequences of the faulty reading, he was so enraged that he was about to slay his teacher. ER 11, 54, on the other hand, maintains that Joab exterminated all the Edomites, with the exception of one pregnant woman; as proof for this assumption 1 Kings 11.16 is quoted, and this is only intelligible if we suppose that the Midrash read in 1 Kings, *loc. cit.*, זָכָר (= Deut., *loc. cit.*), and not זֵכֶר as the Masorah has it. In his campaign against Edom Joab almost despaired of victory, and in a moment of despondency he addressed the following words to God: "O God, Thou hast cast us off, Thou hast broken us down, Thou hast been angry". No sooner did he utter these words than the earth began to tremble and quake because of Joab's lack of trust in God. David became so enraged by Joab's lack of faith that he intended to slay him. The shaking and trembling of the earth ceased at Joab's prayer: "Heal the breaches thereof, for it tottereth." See Tehillim 60, 305; the text is slightly corrupt, but by reading שאמר יואב we get the proper meaning of the passage, which has baffled the commentators. Notwithstanding the great victory over Edom it was not as great as David had wished; Rome did not, like the rest of Edom (on Rome = Edom, see note 19 on vol. I, p. 314), fall into his hands. The entire annihilation of Edom, including Rome, will not take place before the advent of the Messiah. Until then the descendants of Esau enjoy power and prosperity as a reward for the filial piety of their ancestor. See BR 1.16; DZ 21–23 and 24; Makiri, Ps. 60, 309; comp. Index, s. v. "Edom", "Rome", and "Esau". David though fierce in battle, treated the bodies of the fallen warriors with piety, and cared for their burial. These human acts spread his fame throughout the world. See the quotation, from an unknown Midrash, in Rashi and Kimhi on 2 Sam. 8.13.

⁷ ⁸ Mo'ed Katan 16b; Targum 2 Sam. 20.26. As to the supposition that in Sam., *loc. cit.*, as well as in many other places, כהן means "master", "teacher", and not "priest", see also Mekilta Amalek 1, 57b; Comp. note 141 and note 82 on vol. II, p. 289. David is the bearer of many names in Scripture, some of which characterize him as a great warrior and others as a prominent scholar. See Mo'ed Katan, *loc. cit.*: Targum 2 Sam. 21.19 and 23.8; ps.-Jerome on Sam., *loc. cit.*, and 1 Chron. 11.11; Ruth R. 1.1; Targum Chron., *loc. cit.* Comp. also note 76. By assigning a multitude of names to David, the Haggadah harmonizes the contradictions between 2 Sam. 21.19, where the slayer of Goliath is called Elhanan, and 1 Sam. 17.1–54, where the slaying of this Philistine is ascribed to David. These two names belong to one person: David was called Elhanan, "he to whom God was gracious". In 2 Sam. 23.8 it is David himself who is the greatest warrior of his time, "who slew at one time eight hundred," and were it not for the sin he committed with Bath-sheba, he would have slain a thousand of his enemies at one time, as promised in the Torah to the pious; see Lev. 26.8; comp. Moed Katan *l. c.*; Targum and ps.-Jerome *ad loc.* Just as Amram received the priesthood as a reward for his zeal in the study of the Torah, even so did David receive the kingdom as a reward for his zeal in the study of the Torah, 2 ARN 48, 131; comp. also ER 2, 8;3, 13, 15–16; Tehillim 25, 211. His devotion to the fulfilment of the Torah (see note 102 on vol. IV, p. 75) was equal to his zeal in the study thereof, so that he felt disappointed at the thought that there were moments in the life of a man when the body requires his entire attention, disturbing him from his religious activity. He, however, consoled himself with the thought that the Jew has the sign of the covenant of Abraham on his body, and may therefore be said to be constantly fulfilling God's command; see Sifre D., 36; Midrash Tannaim 29; Tosefta Berakot (end); Yerushalmi 9,14d; Menahot 43b; Tehillim 6, 38; Makiri, Ps. 119, 230. Lovingkindness was one of David's chief virtues; he would not permit a day to pass without giving alms to the poor. He would usually distribute charity before entering the house of prayer (Alphabet of Ben Sira 8a). But above all virtues he prized justice. In his capacity as judge he never decided a

case in favor of a poor man, if he was guilty, but insisted on justice being done (comp. vol. III, p. 71), though after the poor man had satisfied the law, he could count without fail on the liberality and generosity of the king. See ARN 33, 94; DR 5.3; Tosefta Sanhedrin 1.2 and Babli 6b. The last two sources maintain that it was David's rule to arbitrate between the litigants; but when he failed in his effort, he let justice take its course. His respect for justice was so great that he never availed himself of his constitutional rights as king (on these rights see note 47, end, on vol. IV, p. 65), which permitted him, under certain circumstances, to disregard the right of private property. If interests of the state compelled him to make use of his royal prerogative, he would first apply to the court for a permit, and even then he would indemnify those whose property he seized. A case of this kind is hinted at in 2 Sam. 23.13–17. David was in need of such a permit, but the Synedrion which could grant him one was not near him; so three of his valiant warriors volunteered to break through the battle-lines of the enemy and put the case before the Synedrion. According to another view, however, the passage in 2 Sam., *loc. cit.*, refers to something entirely different. The three valiant warriors risked their lives to fetch water for libation, as it was the feast of Tabernacles, when the ceremony of the water-libation is performed. See Yerushalmi Sanhedrin 2, 20b–20c; Baba Kamma 60b; Shemuel 20, 105; Ruth R. 2.9; ps.-Jerome, 1 Chron. 11.18. Notwithstanding the great care David took in meting out justice, he nevertheless once committed a judicial murder, and had a very pious man executed on the false testimony of two witnesses, who accused him of buggery; Yerushalmi Sanhedrin 6, 23b–23c. This legend with many elaborations is also found in Arabic literature; comp. Salzberger, *Salomo-Sage*, I, 55, who is not acquainted with the Jewish prototype of the legend given by him. That David described himself as "godly" (Ps. 86.2, חסיד) was not due to conceit, which would have been pardonable in his case, but he wished to say that he was "like God", inasmuch as he bore the insults heaped upon him, like the Lord who patiently bears the blasphemies of the heathen. See Tehillim 16, 123, and 96, 372. This Haggadah derives חסיד "godly" from חסד "insult"; as to the etymology of this word, see vol. V, p. 59 towards the middle. David was called "the servant of the Lord" (comp. note 880 on vol. III, p. 421) after he repented of his sin because the Lord exalts the honor of the repentant sinner. See Tehillim 18, 136.

79 Berakot 4a; comp. vol. IV, p. 76. According to a Jewish legend in ps.-Jerome, 2 Sam. 4.2, it was Mephibosheth who instigated the

slaying of his uncle Ishbosheth in the hope of succeeding him as king.

⁸⁰ Sukkah 26b; Zohar I, 206b–207b, which reads: The deep sleep after "sixty breaths of the horse" is a foretaste of death, and therefore David would never indulge in a deep sleep. Comp. Berakot 57b. It is said that "sixty breaths" are a little more than half an hour. Comp. Lewysohn, *Zoologie d. Tal.* 137, note 2.

⁸¹ Opinions differ as to the number of these strings. Some maintain that David's harp had only seven strings, whereas the harp to be used in Messianic times will have eight; but according to others, the strings of David's harp numbered ten. See Tosefta 'Arakin 2.7; Babli 13b; PR 21 (beginning); Tan. B. IV, 50; BaR 15.11; Tehillim 81, 366, and 92, 406; PRE 19. David would never have composed the Psalms without the aid of music, as the Holy Spirit came over him only when he was put in a state of ecstasy by music, see Tehillim 24, 204, and comp. also Josephus, *Antiqui.*, VII, 12.3, as well as vol. II, pp. 115–116. The Psalms, to a great extent, consist of revelations made to David by the Holy Spirit concerning the future history of Israel; see Tehillim 4, 40, and 24, 204; Pesahim 117a–118a; Gittin 57b; Ekah 2, 111. Comp. note 24. The passages in Psalms dealing with Israel's salvation refer to the Messianic salvation; see quotation from Midrash in Mahzor Vitry 8; Pardes 57d; Siddur Rashi 9.

⁸² PRE 21 (on the text see R. Bahya, Exod. 19.13); comp. vol. I, p. 283.

⁸³ Berakot 3b; Yerushalmi 1, 2d; PK 7, 62b–63a; PR 196a; Tehillim 22, 185; 57, 298; 108, 464; Ekah 2, 121; ER 18, 96; Zohar III, 175b. Comp. Löw, *Lebensalter*, 315–316, who fully discusses this legend and its relation to the Aeol's harp of the Greeks. See also R. Schmidt, *Pancantantram*, 21, on the Indian form of the legend. A rationalistic explanation of the legend concerning David's harp is given by R. Hai Gaon; see Löw *op. cit.*, 317, and Shu'aib, Bo, 28c. The Talmudim and Midrashim often speak of the night as the proper time for prayer and study (comp., *e. g.*, 'Abodah Zarah 3b, and note 254 on vol. III, p. 117), but the praying at midnight (*Hazot*) is first found in the mystic literature of the Middle Ages. Comp. note 194 on vol. I, p. 44. Great praise is bestowed upon David for the devotion with which he prayed; see Berakot 30b; PR 9, 32a.

⁸⁴ Perek Shirah; Yalkut on Ps. (end); Zohar III, 222b and 232b (as to the remark made here concerning the frogs, see vol. II, p. 350); Zohar Hadash, Ahare Mot חיד הא (end); comp. Steinschneider, *Hebräische Bibliographie*, XIII, 104. On the parables, see vol. I, p. 141,

and IV, 130. David prayed to God that the reading of his Psalms might be accounted to men as meritorious as the reading of the Torah, so that "his lips should move gently in the grave" while the people occupy themselves with his work, and in this manner he would have eternal life as his share; Tehillim 1, 9; 30, 334; 61, 306; Yerushalmi Berakot 2, 4b, and parallel passages. On the composition of the Psalms, see vol. III, p. 462, and further Tehillim 1, 8 (parallel passages are cited by Buber); Zohar II, 101a; Berakot 9b-10a. In the last passage it is stated that the favorite psalms of David are those beginning with Ashre, "Happy is he", whereas according to others the alphabetic ones have this distinction. Comp. the quotation from an unknown Midrash in Shu'aib, Shelah (beginning); Kimha Dabishuna שאמר ברוך for Sabbath morning. According to Josephus, *Antiqui.*, VII, 12.3, David being freed from wars and dangers, and enjoying for the remainder of his life a profound peace, composed songs and hymns to God in several sorts of meters: some of those which he made were trimeters, and others pentameters. He also made instruments of music, and taught the Levites to sing hymns to God, both on the Sabbath day and on festivals. It is rather strange that Josephus limits the songs in the Temple to the Sabbaths and festivals, though there can be no doubt that in his time the song was a daily feature; comp. Tamid (end). See, however, Sifre N., 77 and Sifre Z., 72.

⁸⁵ BR 39.11; Baba Kamma 97b. The money coined by Solomon bore his own and his father's names (figures?) on the obverse, and Jerusalem (figure or name?) on the reverse side. Comp. note 46 on vol. I, p. 206.

⁸⁶ Sotah 10b; Megillah 11a; Mo'ed Katan 16b. On the reverence shown by David to the scholars, and particularly to his master Ira, see also Shir 1.2, and ps.-Jerome, 2 Sam. 20.26. When, however, the interests of the state demanded resolute and decisive action, David knew how to play the master and lord; Sotah 40b; comp. vol. III, p. 451. After he had slain Goliath, the women hailed him with the words: "Saul hath slain his thousands, and David his ten thousands." But David with true humility, spoke: "O Lord of the universe, Thou wagest war, and unto Thee belongs the victory." See Tehillim 36,249. As a truly modest man, he even doubted whether the promises of honor and glory made to him by God would ever be fulfilled. Not that he doubted the power of God, but being aware of his sinfulness, he feared that he forfeited them. Comp. Berakot 4a, and see vol. I, p. 380.

⁸⁷ Hagigah 12b; comp. vol. I, p. 9. David's prayer for "exiled

Israel" had the effect that even when subjected to foreign powers, Israel never occupies a despised state. Were it not for David's prayer, the Israelites in exile would have been "sellers of wax" (= poor peddlers); Sotah 49a. Juvenal, *Saturnalia*, 6, 542, alludes to the Jews selling wax-candles in Rome. Comp. Sanhedrin 95a; note 110, end; vol. VI, p. 466.

⁸⁸ Shemuel 26, 125. It is a prerogative of the Davidic kings that they (according to some sources, they and the high priests) are permitted to sit in the Temple court (עֲזָרָה), whereas all others must remain standing. Hence Scripture (2 Sam. 7.18) mentions the fact that David, on receiving the divine revelation concerning the building of the Temple by his son, "went and *sat* before the Lord." Comp. Tehillim 1, 1–3; Yerushalmi Pesahim 5, 32d and parallel passages on the margin; Yoma 25b, and parallel passages on the margin, as well as note 9 on vol. IV, p. 181. David desired so ardently to erect the house of God, that he was full of joy when he heard the people say: "O that the time would soon come when the old man (David) will die, and Solomon will proceed with the building of the Temple." See Makkot 10a; Yerushalmi Berakot 21, 4b; DR 5.3. Nathan the prophet before receiving the revelation concerning the building of the Temple by Solomon strongly encouraged David in his plan to erect a permanent house of God; Tehillim 62, 308–309. This prophet, by the way, was the son of one of David's brothers, but was brought up by his grandfather Jesse, and is therefore counted sometimes as a son of the latter. Accordingly there is no contradiction between 1 Sam. 16.10 and 1 Chron. 3.13. Comp. ps.-Jerome on Sam., *loc. cit.* See also note 23, and note 11 on vol. IV, p. 128.

⁸⁹ PR 2, 7a–7b; Tehillim 62, 309. Comp. also Mekilta Shirah 1, 34b; which reads: The Temple, though built by Solomon, is nevertheless called the "house of David" (see Ps. 30.1), because the latter had set his heart upon the building of the Temple; had not God prevented him, he would have carried out his plan. Comp. note 59 on vol. III, p. 32.—David was engaged in war all his life. He never had a pleasant dream, being always troubled by bad dreams, whereas Ahitophel always had pleasant dreams; Berakot 55b; Zohar I, 200a.

⁹⁰ Baba Batra 17a. Comp. vol. I, p. 292.

⁹¹ ʿAbodah Zarah 4b–5a. Comp. also quotation from an unknown Midrash in Shuʿaib, *Kippurim*, 121a.

⁹² Shabbat 56a; Ketubot 9b; Kiddushin 43a. In contrast to this exoneration of David, comp. Shemuel 25, 122–123, where he is severely censured not only for his sins attributed to him in Scripture,

but for many others. The Midrash maintains that Uriah was not the only one whose death was caused by David. Even Nathan the prophet would have been killed by him, if he had dared to talk about the king's crime. The prophet was continually watched by the king's spies that he should not "divulge" anything. See also quotation from an unknown Midrash in Shu'aib, *Kippurim*, 121a; vol. IV, p. 72, and note 33.

⁹³ Quotation from an unknown Midrash in Al-Sheikh, 2 Sam. 12. Comp. vol. IV, p. 88. Sanhedrin 107a reads: Bath-sheba was destined to become David's wife from the creation of the world; but he took her while she was not mature. This is a play on the name Bath-sheba, which in later Hebrew denotes "a fine quality of figs" (comp., *e. g.*, Ma'aserot 2.8), with פגה "an unripe fig". A brilliant defence of David by God against the accusations of the angel Duma(= prince of hell; comp. Index, s. v.) is given in Zohar I, 8b (on the "three months" in this passage, see Ginzberg, *Haggada bei den Kirchenv.*, 31, note 2), 94a; II, 107a; III, 78b. The question about the shepherd and the lambkin in Yoma 66b refers, according to a geonic tradition, to David (comp. R. Hananel and Tosafot, *ad loc.*, as well as Ginzberg, *Geonica* II, 19), and was very likely addressed to R. Eliezer by Jewish Gnostics who condemned David. Comp. Ginzberg, *Unbekannte Sekte*, 28-30. Comp. also note 67.

⁹⁴ Sanhedrin 107a; Tehillim 18, 157; 26, 216; midrashic Genizah fragment in the University Library at Cambridge. As to David's wish to be considered like the three patriarchs, see also Justin Martyr, *Dialogue*, 141; Pesahim 117b; Shemuel 26, 126; Tehillim 18, 139; Yerushalmi Rosh ha-Shanah 4, 59c; Zohar I, 82a; ps.-Jerome, 1 Chron. 17.8. Comp. Ginzberg, *Unbekannte Sekte*, 295-297, with regard to the relation of God to the three patriarchs as shown in the expression "the God of Abraham, etc." and see further note 304 on vol. I, p. 414, as well as note 4 on vol. II, p. 226. The liturgy has the expression "God, the shield of David", but it is used only in the benediction after reading the Haftarah. Did the Haftarah, in olden times, close with a passage from the Psalms? According to Mo'ed Katan 16a, God spoke to David: "I shall reward thee for thy humility, and shall make thee like unto Me, inasmuch as thou shalt be able to annul my decrees (David's prayer will avert the decreed punishment). I shall further make thee 'the head of the three' (patriarchs)". Comp. also vol. I, p. 414; vol. II, p. 225.

⁹⁵ ER 2, 7. Comp. also Apocalypse of Sedrach 14, which reads: David was saved by tears.

⁹⁶ Yoma 22b; Yerushalmi Rosh ha-Shanah 1, 56b; Sanhedrin 107b; Shemuel 26, 127. On the basis of this Haggadah, 2 Sam. 5.5 is brought in harmony with 1 Kings 2.11. According to the last source, the six months during which David was isolated physically and spiritually are disregarded in giving the number of the years of his reign. Other authorities (Yerushalmi, Shemuel, *loc. cit.*; Ruth R. 2.14) maintain that the six months during which David was in flight from Absalom are disregarded in 1 Kings, *loc. cit.* Both these views are also given in ps.-Jerome, 2 Sam. 5.4–5. Comp. Ginzberg, *Haggada bei den Kirchenv.*, 43–46. The word נמרצת (1 Kings 2.8) is to be taken as the initials of the five insulting names hurled at David by Shimei; he called him "adulterer" (נואף=נ'), Moabite (מואבי=מ'), "murderer" (רוצח=ר'; according to others, רשע "wicked"), "leper" (צרוע=צ'), and "abomination" (תועבה=ת'). See Shabbat 105a; Tehillim 3, 36; BaR 9.7; ps.-Jerome, 1 Kings, *loc. cit.* Comp. Ginzberg, *ibid.*, 72. On the view that David was punished with leprosy for committing adultery, comp. also vol. II, p. 190, where it is said that Reuben was punished in the same manner for a similar sin, and see further vol. VI, p. 305, top; Index, s. v. 'Leprosy'. Comp. also Josephus, *Antiqui.*, VII, 9, 4.

⁹⁷ Niddah 24b; BaR 9.24.

⁹⁸ Tosefta Sotah 3.16; Nazir 4a; BaR 9.24; Shemuel 27 (here two conflicting views are also given, according to one Absalom clipped his hair monthly; according to the other, once a year only); Josephus, *Antiqui.*, VII, 8.5; Vulgate and ps.-Jerome on 2 Sam. 14.26. Comp. Ginzberg, *Haggada bei den Kirchenv.*, 54.

⁹⁹ Tan. B. I, 155–156; BaR 9, 24 (the elders who joined Absalom soon found out his true character); Yerushalmi Sotah 1, 17b. Comp. also Tehillim 55, 292, which reads: The prayers of the members of the Synedrion for David had the effect that the counsel given by Ahitophel was not followed by Absalom. Comp. vol. IV, p. 181.

¹⁰⁰ Berakot 7b; Tehillin 3, 34. Owing to an incorrect reading in Tehillim, *loc. cit.* (עם instead of אצל), Zohar, I, 151b, maintains that David felt some consolation in the fact that the leaders of the people remained faithful to him, and did not join Absalom; comp. the preceding note. In the Book of Psalms the psalm which David composed "when he fled from Absalom" follows the one concerning Gog and Magog (the "nations in uproar against God and the Messiah;" comp. Ps. 2 and 3). The reason is that if one should say: "How is it possible that the

slave should rebel against his master?", he will receive the answer: "Behold, it even happened that the son rebelled against his father." See Berakot 10a.

¹⁰¹ Sanhedrin 107a; DR 4.4; Zohar III, 24a; EZ 3, 177; ps.-Jerome, 2 Sam. 15.25. Comp. Ginzberg, *Haggada bei den Kirchenv.*, 53–54. David served an idol because he wished to make his fate appear just in the eyes of men, who would say: "Behold, he merited his punishment." That David on this occasion had his head covered and went barefoot (2 Sam. 16.30) was due to the fact that the Synedrion excommunicated him (on account of his sin with Bath-sheba?), and one who is excommunicated is forbidden to put on shoes or to have his head uncovered. The ban was removed from him by his master Ira. Comp. Shemuel 8, 70; BaR 3.2; Zohar II, 107b. See also Moʿed Katan 15a.

¹⁰² Tehillim 2, 34–36, where also the different kinds of food sent by David's friends (2 Sam. 17.28–29) are described in detail.

¹⁰³ Shabbat 152a, which reads: Barzillai had led a lascivious life, and having spent his strength, he could not enjoy life any more when he became old; comp. 2 Sam. 19.36. In Tehillim 2, 35–36 it is stated that David had feared these very men who came to his assistance. Barzillai was a proselyte; see Jerushalmi Kiddushin 4.65b.

¹⁰⁴ Sotah 10b; BaR 9.24; PRE 53. Absalom's miserable end is often referred to in the Haggadah to illustrate the rule that God "punishes measure for measure," and it is shown in detail how Absalom's fate corresponded to his sins. Comp. Sotah, Mishnah 1.8; Tosefta 3.16–17; Yerushalmi 1, 17b; Babli, and BaR, *loc. cit.*; Mekilta Shirah 6, 40a.

¹⁰⁵ Sanhedrin 103b. Comp. Yoma 66b, and note 100 on vol. IV, p. 75.

¹⁰⁶ Maʿaseh de Rabbi Joshua b. Levi in BHM II, 50–51.

¹⁰⁷ Sotah 10b. This passage records also the different view that David's prayer brought Absalom into paradise. David, however, was punished for his great love for his wicked son, and eight of his sons (Bath-Sheba's first child, Amnon, Absalom, Adonijah, and four others; comp. vol. IV, p. 113) died a premature death, corresponding to the eight times he cried out in agony: "My son", about the wicked Absalom (2 Sam. 19.1 and 5). Eight rulers of the Davidic dynasty likewise died a violent death. These are: Joram, Ahaziah, Athaliah, Jehoash, Amaziah, Amon, Josiah, and Jehoiakim. See the quotation, from an unknown Midrash, in Hasidim 107; comp. also vol. IV, p. 72. As to Jehoiakim's violent death, see vol. IV, p. 285. The death of

David's sons and descendants was also a punishment for his having kept himself in a place of safety, while his army fought against Absalom. Comp. 2 Sam. 18.3, *seq.* See further vol. IV, p. 72. David's great love for Absalom may be judged from the way he acted towards the Ethiopian and Ahimaaz. The former who informed him of Absalom's death he had executed, and the latter, who attempted to keep it a secret for a time, was appointed to a high office. Comp. PK 32, 196a–196b; see also PRE 53.

¹⁰⁸ Sotah 11a. This passage records also the different opinion that Absalom left sons, but that they were so insignificant that Scripture (2 Sam. 18.18) speaks of them as though he died childless. Ps.-Jerome, 2 Sam., *loc. cit.*, mentions both views in a somewhat confused manner. Comp. Ginzberg, *Haggadah bei den Kirchenv.*, 60–61, where attention is drawn to Targum 2 Sam., *loc. cit.*, which paraphrases בן of the text by בר קימא: Absalom had children, but they died at an early age. In view of 2 Chron. 11.21 there can be no doubt that Absalom had a daughter, and accordingly בנים in the sources quoted is to be taken literally "sons".

¹⁰⁹ By his lack of precaution he caused Saul's suspicion against the priests of Nob; comp. also vol. IV, pp. 257–258. Against this view, see Sanhedrin 104a; ER 12, 60. Comp. also note 92 on vol. IV, p. 72.

¹¹⁰ Sanhedrin 95a; BR 59.11; Tan. B. I, 150–151; Tan. Wa-Yeze (according to the Tanhumas, Joab and Abishai hastened to David's assistance from the land of the Ammonites; comp., however, Tehillim, 60, 305); Hullin 91b; Tehillim 18, 157–159; BHM IV, 140–141; Hibbur Ma'as. No. 5; Likkutim, I, 21b–22b; *Neweh Shalom* 55–56; Zohar Ruth 1.14. Comp. also Gaster *Exempla*, 111–113 which offers some interesting variants to our texts of Sanhedrin. On the withering of the wreath as a sign of death, see note 20 on vol. II, p. 236. On the Persian elements in this legend see *R. E. J.* II, 300, and XVII, 202, *seq.* On the dove as Israel's symbol, see Berakot 53b; Shir 2.14 and 4. 1; 4 Ezra 5.26; ps.-Philo, 40; 39.5. On David's saddle-beast, see vol. IV, p. 125. On the miracle of the contraction of the earth, see note 287 on vol. I, p. 294. On Orpha the mother of the giants, see vol. IV, pp. 31 and 85. As to the saying, "Let thy children sell wax", see note 87.

¹¹¹ BR 25.3. Comp. vol. I, pp. 220–221, and vol IV, p. 30. David caused the famine by bestowing all the priestly gifts on one person, his master Ira, instead of distributing them among severa lpriests; 'Erubin 63a. On Ira, see also note 78 beginning, according to which he

was not a priest. This famine was so grievous that the people were forced to eat bitter vetches (כרשינה *ervilia*; comp. Löw, *Erve und Wicke*, in *Zeitschrift für Assyriologie* XXX) which is ordinarily used only as fodder. David then ordained that the priestly gifts should be set aside from vetches, since in case of necessity it can be used as food for men; Yerushalmi Hallah 4, 60b; ER 13,67.

¹¹² Yerushalmi Ta'anit 3, 66c, and Kiddushin 4, 65b–65c; Yebamot 78b; PRE 17; BaR 8.4. The last-named source contains a glowing praise of the proselytes; see the similar remarks of the Rabbis concerning proselytes in Tan. B. I, 63, and ShR 19.4. As to the sins which keep back the rain, see Ta'anit 7b; Mishle 25, 97–98; Yelammedenu in Yalkut I, 771; quotation from Yerushalmi (?) in Sabba', Bereshit, 5a (not in our texts); ps.-Philo, 45; 44 (end), which reads: Therefore if they shall speak lies before Me, I will command the heaven and it shall defraud them of rain. This is based on a midrashic interpretation of Prov. 25.14. Comp. Ta'anit and Midrash Mishle, *loc. cit.* See also Ta'anit 10b, which reads: Just as the Babylonians are deceptive, even so are the clouds of their country.

¹¹³ PRE 17; BaR 8.4. See also Shemuel 28, 132–133, and the references cited in the preceding note. On the piety of Saul, "Samuel's companion in paradise", see vol. IV, pp. 71 and 72. According to ps.-Philo, 57; 62.2, the spirit rested on Saul, and he prophesied, saying: "Why art thou deceived, O Saul? Whom dost thou persecute in vain? The time of thy kingdom is at an end. Go to thy place, for thou shalt die, and David shall reign. Shalt not thou and thy sons (read *filios tuos*, instead of *filius tuus*) die together? And then shall the kingdom of David appear." And the spirit departed from Saul, and he knew not what he had prophesied.

¹¹⁴ Yerushalmi Kiddushin 4, 65c, and Ta'anit 3, 66c; Shemuel 28.134; Tehillim 1, 100; ShR 39.16; Yebamot 78b–79a; BaR 8.4; WR 22.6; Tan. B. IV, 23. In the last four sources the view is expressed that Saul did not kill any of the Gibeonites; but the destruction of Nob, the city of the priests, caused great misery to their servants, the Gibeonites, and this was accounted to Saul as though he had brought about their death. On the Gibeonites, see also vol. IV, p. 10. On the three qualities God gave to Israel, see also PRK 33b; Abot 4.19; John 8. 39–44; note 240 on vol. III, p. 107.

¹¹⁵ Yerushalmi Kiddushin 65c; Yebamot 79a; Shemuel 28, 133; BaR 8.4. Comp. note 28 on vol. IV, 8; vol. III, p. 413; vol. IV, p. 146.

¹¹⁶ Berakot 4a.   Comp. further references in the preceding note, and vol. IV, p. 76.

¹¹⁷ Yebamot 79a; Yerushalmi Kiddushin 65c; BaR 8.4; Shemuel 28, 134; comp. vol. IV, p. 444.   According to Yebamot 76a, no proselytes were admitted into the Jewish fold during the time of David and Solomon, because there was good reason to suspect the sincerity and religious convictions of those who wished to become Jews.

¹¹⁸ Ruth Z., 51; PR 6, 26a.   Comp. vol. IV, pp. 156–157.

¹¹⁹ PR 11, 43b–44a; Shemuel 30, 136.   David's sin consisted not so much in taking the census, but in taking it without making "every man give a ransom for his soul unto the Lord", half a shekel for an offering, as God had commanded Moses.   See Exod. 30.11, *seq.*   God made David forget this law as a punishment for using unbecoming words in speaking of God as the one who had "stirred up" Sau lagainst him (1 Sam. 26.18); see Berakot 62b.   On the view that David forgot a commandment of the Torah, see vol. III, pp. 194, 395; vol. IV, p. 96.   Josephus, *Antiqui.*, VII, 13.1, is likewise of the opinion that David's sin consisted in not paying half a shekel for each man that was numbered, whereas according to PK 2, 18b, and BaR 2.17, he sinned in taking the census without having any valid reason for doing so.   On the idolatrous Danites, see vol. III, p. 57 and Index, s. v. "Danites".

¹²⁰ PK 2, 18b; PR 11, 43b; Shemuel 30, 137; ps.-Jerome, 2 Sam. 24.9.   The contradiction between Sam., *loc. cit.*, and 1 Chron. 21.5 disappears if we assume that the number given in the first passage is not the complete one.

¹²¹ PR 11, 44b; Targum 1 Chron. 21.13; ER 7, 39; Tehillim 17, 126; Josephus, *Antiqui.*, VII, 13.2.

¹²² Opinions are unanimous that the plague lasted only a few hours, but they differ as to the exact number; comp. Berakot 62b; PR 11, 44b; Tehillim 17, 126–127; Shemuel 30, 137–138; Targum, Peshitta, and ps.-Jerome on 2 Sam. 24.15.   Comp. also Josephus, *Antiqui.*, VII, 13.3, and the following note.

¹²³ Tehillim 18, 126; Shemuel 30, 38; Berakot 62b; Targum 1 Chron. 21.15.   A detailed description of the plague is given by Josephus *Antiqui.*, VII, 13.3.   A widespread legend states that one hundred youths died daily during the plague (but comp. the preceding note; on the one hundred deaths, see note 12), whereupon David instituted that one hunderd benedictions should be recited in the daily prayers (for the oldest enumeration of the one hundred benedictions, see Ginzberg,

Geonica II, 116–117). The plague ceased as soon as this change in the liturgy was introduced. See BaR 18.21; *Eshkol* of R. Abraham b. Isaac I.56 (geonic source); *Orehot Hayyim* 1, 4c; Kad ha-Kemah ברכה 36b; Mahzor Vitry 3, and the parallel passages given by Hurwitz, *ad loc*. The plague was a punishment for Israel's lack of enthusiasm for the building of the Temple; Tehillim and Shemuel, *loc. cit.* Abishai, though distinguished for his piety and learning, was not free from the sin of having been an accomplice of his brother Joab in the killing of Abner. To indicate his sin, Scripture (2 Sam. 10.10) spells his name defectively. See the Jewish tradition in ps.-Jerome, *ad loc.*, and Ginzberg, *Haggada bei den Kirchenv.*, 50–51. Comp. also note 267 on vol. I, p. 290.

124 ER 7, 39; Aggadat Bereshit 38.77 (comp. Buber, note 9). Against this, see ShR 15.20, which reads: The "board of intercalaion" at the time of Solomon consisted of ten members, three of whom were Solomon, Nathan the prophet, and Gad the seer. The angel who caused the death of so many men in Israel was nevertheless an "angel of mercy"; he hoped that the dreadful calamity brought upon Israel would pacify God's anger kindled against them. This angel pleaded with God for Israel, and entreated Him that He should remember His covenant with the patriarchs and be merciful to Israel. God looked at the terrestrial sanctuary, the place where Isaac was tied to be sacrificed (see vol. I, p. 284), and at the celestial sanctuary, where the souls of the pious are (vol. I, p. 9) and where Jacob's image is engraved (see vol. III, p. 351), and He caused the plague to cease. See Aggadat Bereshit, *loc. cit.*, and 30, 61; Berakot 62b; Targum 1 Chron. 21.15.

125 Shabbat 30a–30b; Ruth R. 1.17; Koheleth 5.10. As to the conception that God never reveals to man the time of his death, see also Pesahim 54b (top), PRK 35b, and 4 Ezra 5.25. God said to David: "I delight more in thy acts of justice than in the multitude of sacrifices brought by Solomon; Yerushalmi Berakot 2, 4b, and Rosh ha-Shanah 1, 56b; Makkot 10a. As to the cnception that the angel of death has no power over those who are occupied with the study of the Torah, see also Mo'ed Katan 28a; Baba Mezi'a 86a; vol. III, p. 439; vol. IV, p. 239.

126 Ruth R. 1.17; Yerushalmi Bezah 2, 61b. In the last source it is presupposed that David died on a week-day. David, it is stated there, died on the feast of Pentecost, and as all Israel was in a state of mourning, the festive offerings were brought on the following day. Comp. also Koheleth 5.10.

¹²⁷ Ruth R. 1.17. For the contrary view, see Shabbat 30b; Kohelet 5.10, where it is said that the removal of the corpse was accomplished without any miracle. Comp. also Mirkhond, 72 on the birds sheltering the crowds from the sun at the funeral of David.

¹²⁸ BHM V, 167–168, and VI, 25–26; Or Zarua I, 39a, and II, 18b. As early an authority as R. Akiba (Sanhedrin 38b, and parallel passages) speaks of the throne upon which David will sit on the Day of Judgment. Comp. vol. V, 418–419. See also ER 18, 89–90, where it is said that David will sit at God's right hand on the Day of Judgment. There can be no doubt that these legends about David are connected with the view that he is the promised Messiah; see Sanhedrin 98a; Rosh ha-Shanah 25a which reads: David, the king of Israel, lives for ever; Tehillim 5, 52; 57, 298; 75, 340; 2 ARN 45, 125; *Shitah Hadashah* 2 (which reads: David is the first and the last of the Jewish rulers); Zohar I 82b; III, 84a. The last passage is a kabbalistic rendering of the statement (Sanhedrin 98b) that in the days to come God will raise "another David" to be the Messiah, whose viceroy will be the first David. See also Mishle 19, 87, where David is given as one of the names of the Messiah. One of David's distinctions which he shares with the three patriarchs, and Moses, Aaron, Miriam, and Benjamin is that his corpse was not touched by worms; Baba Batra 17a; Tehillim 119, 492; Derek Erez Z., I (end). Comp. also Acts 13.36. Baba Batra, *loc. cit.*, states that David is one of the few over whom the evil inclination had no power; comp. note 276 on vol. I, p. 292. Somewhat different is the statement of Yerushalmi Sotah 5, 20c: Abraham turned the evil inclination into the good inclination, but David was unable to do that, and he therefore slew the evil inclination. This wishes to convey that David (as repentance for his sin with Bath-sheba) denied himself the pleasures which are permitted by the law, and lived like an ascetic, whereas Abraham served God in enjoying life. On David's ascetic life, comp. the remark in Yerushalmi Sanhedrin 2, 20a, with regard to 2 Sam. 20.30. The world was created for the sake of David; Sanhedrin 98b, where Moses and the Messiah are regarded by some authorities as those for whose sake the world was created. See the similar statement in Berakot 61b, which reads: The world was created only for the very pious or for the extremely wicked; for the former the world to come, and this world for the latter. See note 8, end, on vol. I, p. 50.

¹²⁹ BHM V, 45–46, and VI, 47 (in this passage David is said to be on a horse of fire), which is based on older sources; see Pesahim 119b; Yoma 76a; Tehillim 23, 202; Nispahim 32–33. In ShR 25.8 Michael

is first requested to say the blessing; but with "angelic" modesty passes on this honor to Gabriel, who likewise refuses the honor, and asks the patriarchs to say the blessing. They in turn ask Moses and Aaron, who pass on the honor to the elders, and the latter find David to be the one deserving of this great distinction. Comp. however, vol. VI, p. 167. In the world to come there will be no company of righteous of which David will not be a member; Shemuel 19, 104. On the throne of David see the preceeding note, and Index, s. v. "Thrones of the Righteous."

130 BHM V, 46; Nispahim 33. Comp. also *Visio Pauli* 29.

131 Sanhedrin 21a; BR 82.7; BaR 4.8; Shemuel 11, 79, and 22.111; Tehillim 59, 303; Tosefta-Targum and ps.-Jerome on 2 Sam. 3.5. All these sources agree on the identity of Eglah and Michal, but they differ as to the reason why the designation "little calf" was given to Michal; comp. Ginzberg, *Haggadah bei den Kirchenv.*, 41–42. According to an unknown Midrash quoted by Kimhi, 2 Sam. 21.10, David also married (took as concubine ?) Rizpah, whom he greatly admired for the reverence and devotion she displayed for Saul's unlucky descendants; see Sam., *loc. cit.* Comp. also Yerushalmi Yebamot 3, 3d, which reads: David married Rizpah. On Rizpah's noble deeds, see also Yerushalmi Kiddushin 4, 65c, and BaR 8.4.

132 Megillah 15a. This passage contains different views as to who were the most beautiful women. The unanimous opinion seems to be that there were only four women of perfect beauty, but there is no agreement on their identification. Sarah, Rachel, and Abigail are three of the undisputed beauties. As to the fourth, Esther, Vashti, Jael, and Michal are the competitors. Comp. also note 24 on vol. I, p. 60.

133 Sanhedrin 19b–20a. As to the legality of David's marriage with Michal, or rather Michal's second marriage to Palti, see note 80 on vol. IV, p. 72, and note 105 on vol. IV, p. 76. Palti, Michal's second husband, is highly praised for his control of his passions; see Sanhedrin, *loc. cit.*, and many other places; note 85 on vol. IV, p. 37. Obeying Saul's command, he went through the ceremony of marriage with Michal, and as far as the outside world was concerned, they lived as a married couple; but he never came near her, knowing that she was David's lawful wife. He placed a sword between her and himself, saying: "The one who will dare to do it (*i. e.*, have conjugal relations) will be slain with this sword." On the expression נעץ חרב ....ידקר בחרב, comp. also Shabbat 17a; Yebamot 77a. Accordingly there is not the slightest reason to assume, with Heller, *R.E.J.* XLIX, 190, that this legend

is dependent on Indian sources. Comp. also Gaster, *Exempla* 242, *col.* 2. On the view that God was the witness to Palti's continence (hence he is called Paltiel), see PRE 39; WR 23.10; ps.-Jerome 1 Sam. 25.44; note 85, on vol. IV, p. 37; Ginzberg, *Haggada bei den Kirchenv.*, 33–35 and 64. On the children of Merab, see Josephus, *Antiqui.*, VII, 4.3, and ps.-Jerome, 2 Sam. 21.8. The latter shares the views of the Rabbis that Michal brought up her sister's orphaned children, and this is why Scripture speaks of Michal as being their mother. As to the means employed by Michal to save David (1 Sam. 19, *seq.*), see Shemuel 22, 110–111; Tehillim 59, 303; Josephus, *Antiqui.*, VI, 11.4. According to MHG I, 337, Michal boldly declared to her father that she enabled David to escape because she was convinced of his innocence.

¹³⁴ Mekilta Bo 17, 21; 'Erubin 96a; Yerushalmi Berakot 2, 4c; PR 22, 112b. With the exception of 'Erubin, *loc. cit.*, Michal is described in these sources as "the daughter of Cush", which is another name for Saul, who was called Cush, "Ethiopian" (comp. Ps. 7.1), antiphrastically. Saul was distinguished for his beauty as the Ethiopian for his (dark) color; see Sifre N., 99; Sifre Z., 204 (here it is said: Distinguished for his looks and pious deeds); Mo'ed Katan 16b; Tehillim 7, 69, 70, 71–72 (this passage gives a different explanation of this designation of Cush); 2 ARN 43, 12; Targum and Ibn Ezra on Ps. 7.1. The legend about Michal using phylacteries is of midrashic origin. The last section of Prov. is said by the Haggadah to refer to the twenty-two pious women mentioned in the Bible (comp. MHG I, 344, *seq.*; Mishle 31; note 271 on vol. I, p. 291), each of the twenty two verses of this section containing the praise of each of these pious women. It was therefore quite natural for the Haggadah to find in verse 25 an allusion to Michal, of whom one might have rightly said: "And she rejoices at the last day" (this is the literal translation of the Hebrew), as it was in her very last day that she had the joy of motherhood (comp. vol. IV, p. 117). The first half of this verse reads: "Strength and dignity are her clothing". Now since in the Haggadah "strength" עֹז is equivalent to "phylacteries" (comp. Berakot 6a), it follows that the woman whose praise is sung in this verse (*i. e.*, Michal) is lauded for having clothed herself with phylacteries. It should also be mentioned that לובש תפלין, which literally means "clothing oneself with phylacteries", is the technical expression in Palestinian sources for putting on phylacteries; comp. Yerush. Berakot 2, 4c.

¹³⁵ Sanhedrin 21a. The narrative given in 2 Sam. 4.20, *seq.*,

was adorned with many legends by the Haggadah; comp. Yerushalmi Sukkah 5, 55c, and Sanhedrin 2, 20b; Shemuel 25, 124; BaR 4.20. The legend about Obed Edom in the last-named source is very old, see Berakot 63b–64a; Yerushalmi Yebamot 4.6b; 2 ARN 11, 27; Shir 2.5; ps.-Jerome, 2 Sam. 6.11. The reward of this pious Levite, who lit the lamp twice a day before the ark which had been placed in his house, consisted in his having been blessed with many children. The women in his house gave birth after a pregnancy of two months only, and bore six children at one time. Israel became now convinced that the ark, far from bringing misfortune, as they thought, upon those who are near it, was a source of blessing and good fortune. It is true the people at Beth-Shemesh (see vol. IV, p. 63) and Uzza (see vol. IV, pp. 95–96) were punished when they came near to the ark, but this was on account of not having shown due reverence to the holy ark. See Mekilta Wa-Yassa‘ 6, 52a–52b. On Obed-Edom see also Josephus, *Antiqui.*, VII, 4.20.

¹³⁶ Megillah 15a; Seder ‘Olam 21. See also Mishnah Sanhedrin 2, 4, where Abigail is described as the highest ideal of the pious woman

¹³⁷ Megillah 14b; Yerushalmi Sanhedrin 2, 20b, and 4, 22b; Shemuel 23, 116–117; Tehillim 53, 287–288. The expression הלכו לאורה in the three first-named sources is to be taken literally. On the conception of the "bright light" emanating from the body of persons (men as well as women) distinguished for their beauty, comp. Berakot 5b and Ketubot 65a. For further details concerning Nabal, see Tehillim, *loc. cit.*, and 14, 113; vol. IV, p. 70. On Abigail's beauty, see note 132, and comp. further Josephus, *Antiqui.*, VII, 13.6 and 8, who has many embellishments of this biblical story about her and Nabal her husband.

¹³⁸ BHM III, 136.

¹³⁹ Sanhedrin 21b; comp. vol. IV, p. 258. On the similarity of Adonijah's and Absalom's characters which made both act in like manner, see Baba Batra 109b; Tehillim 2, 28; ps.-Jerome, 1 Kings 1.6.

¹⁴⁰ Yelammedenu in Yalkut II, 141, and in ‘*Aruk*, s. v. כלאב; Wa-Yekullu in Likkutim, II, 16a–17a; comp. also VI, 82b–83a; Tan. Toledot 6; Targum I Chron. 3.1. On the similar legend concerning the striking likeness of Isaac to Abraham, see vol. I, p. 262.

¹⁴¹ Berakot 4a(the real name of this son of David's was Daniel); ps.-Jerome, 1 Chron. 3.1. This author remarks (2 Sam. 20.26) with reference to כהנים in 2 Sam. 8.19 that some of David's sons were the masters of their brothers; but comp. Targum, *ad loc.*; Josephus, *Antiqui.*, VII, 5.4 and note 78, beginning.

¹⁴² Derek Erez Zuta 1 (end), and parallel passages cited by Taw rogi. Comp. Index, s. v. "Paradise, Entering Alive into."

¹⁴³ Sanhedrin 21b; Kiddushin 76b; ps.-Jerome 2 Sam. 13, 37; comp. vol. IV, p. 106. To prevent such misdeeds as the one committed by Ammon, David and his Synedrion ordained that even an unmarried woman must not be alone with a man; though the biblical law prohibits only a married woman to be alone with a man. See Sanhedrin 21a–21b and Excursus II, Reuben. The description of David's vanguard in rabbinic sources reminds one of that given by Josephus, *Antiqui.*, VIII, 7.3, of Solomon's guard.

¹⁴⁴ Josephus, *Antiqui.*, VII, 15.3. This statement of Josephus is quoted by Yahya in *Shalshelet ha-Kabbalah*, 16a (bottom; headed אחיה השלוני), with the following additions. Herod after having abstracted large sums from the cave where David's tomb was located, wished to enter the tomb itself, but fearing that some misfortune might befall him, ordered two young men to try it first. They were, however, destroyed by a fire that went forth from the tomb, and Herod who stood outside, watching them, fled for his life. To make atonement for the attempted sacrilege, Herod erected a beautiful monument over the tomb; nevertheless from that time on none of Herod's undertakings succeeded. Comp. also R. Benjamin of Tudela, 35 and Nallino, *Tomba di Davide.*

¹⁴⁵ *Sha'are Yerushalayim* 47a–47b. The beadle of the synagogue (usually one of the poorest men of the congregation) as the most worthy member of the community, is also found in the legend given in vol. I, p. 307.

¹⁴⁶ *Sha'are Yerushalayim* 47b. Until David's time man's average span of life was much longer than in later generations. He died at the age of seventy years, and this came to be considered a good age; Yebamot 64b.—To David's heroic deeds we must add his victory over Lahmi, the brother of Goliath, both of whom he slew in one day; see Targum, Kimhi, and ps.-Rashi on 1 Chron. 20.5, as well as Targum 2 Sam. 21.19, and note,78, toward the beginning.

V. SOLOMON.

Vol. IV, (pp. 125–176).

¹ Seder 'Olam 14. Comp. the parallels cited by Ratner, as well as Nazir 5a; Temurah 15a; Sanhedrin 69b; Targum Sheni 1.2 (which remarks: About thirteen years old, *i. e.*, after having completed his twelfth year); Jerome, *Epistola*, 72, (22, 674); Eupolemus, 452. According to Josephus, *Antiqui.*, VII, 7.8, Solomon ascended the throne at the age of fourteen, and reigned eighty years. The Masorah and Septuagint read "forty", and not "eighty", in 1 Kings 11.42.

² Targum Sheni 1.2, 4; Shir 1.1 (here the real names are: Koheleth, Solomon, and Jedidiah, whereas Agur, Jakeh, Lemuel, and Ithiel are attributes); BaR 10.4; Mishle 30, 103–104; Tan. Wa-Era 5; Tan. B. II, 18; Yelammedenu in *'Aruk*, s. v. אגר; Koheleth 1.1; Jerome, Eccles. 1.1. Comp. also Ephraem, 2 Sam. 12.24–25, who remarks: He was later called Solomon because of the peace that prevailed during his reign. According to the Rabbis, Solomon is one of the names of God, and in Song of Songs God is designated by that name; comp. Shabbat 35b; Shir, *loc. cit.* On the view that Solomon received his name before he was born, see vol. I, p. 122, and comp. further Tan. B. I, 21; Josephus *Antiqui.*, VIII, 4.2. On Ithiel, see note 13 on vol. IV, p. 26.

³ Yerushalmi Kil'ayim 8, 31c; Tosefta 5.7. According to Josephus *Antiqui.*, VIII, 4.2, God revealed to David, before the birth of Solomon, that this son promised to him would succeed him as king and build the Temple; comp. 1 Chron. 22.9. A rabbinic legend tells us that after the death of Bath-Sheba's first child David swore unto her that her next child would be his successor; see ps.-Jerome, 1 Kings 1.17, and Kimhi, 2 Sam. 12.24. The anointing of Solomon served the purpose of counteracting Adonijah's claim to the throne, otherwise this move would not have been necessary, since Solomon succeeded to the throne by the law of inheritance; see Midrash Tannaim 106; Tosefta Sanhedrin 4.11; Horayyot 11b. See note 371 on vol. III, p. 179 and Index, s. v. "Anointing of Kings". The request made by Adonijah to be permitted to marry Abishag (1 Kings 2.13, *seq.*) clearly indicates that he still considered himself David's legitimate successor, as it is only the king who is allowed to make use of the servants of the deceased king. Solomon

therefore ordered the execution of Adonijah for this attempt at rebellion. That David did not marry Abishag was not due to his advanced age and impotence, as some mockingly remarked to him, but to his respect for the law which does not permit a king to marry more than eighteen wives, and David already had that number. See Sanhedrin 22a.

⁴ On Joab's pious descendants, among whom were priests and prophets, see Targum 1 Chron. 2.54.

⁵ Yerushalmi Makkot 2, 31c; Tan. B. IV, 166. Comp. note 76 on vol. IV, p. 97.

⁶ On this point see vol. IV, pp. 73–74. The people had suspected David of having conspired the death of Abner, but they became convinced of the king's innocence by the genuine grief which he expressed at Abner's funeral. It was fortunate for David that the people realized their error, otherwise they would have killed him in their rage against the murderer of Abner. The king, to show his respect for the dead hero, participated in the funeral, though, according to the law, a king must never be present at a funeral: see Sanhedrin, Mishnah 2.3; Tosefta 4.2; Babli 20a; Yerushalmi, 2, 20c. See note 275 on vol. I, p. 394. In the last source it is said that David addressed first the men then the women, to convince them that Joab acted entirely without his knowledge. As to the suspicion against David, see also the references in the following note.

⁷ Tan. B. IV, 167; Tan. Mass'e 12; BaR 23.13.

⁸ Yerushalmi Makkot 2, 31a; Shemuel 35, 123. As to the question whether the sanctuary at Jerusalem offered asylum to criminals, and under what conditions, see also Babli Makkot 12a, and Mahzor Vitry 33. The latter made use of a version of Midrash Tehillim in which the trial of Joab was dealt with at full length; but our texts of this Midrash have preserved no reference to it; comp. also note 10.

⁹ Sanhedrin 49a; comp. also Josephus, *Antiqui.*, VII, 1.5 and 11.7; vol. IV, pp. 73–74.

¹⁰ Sanhedrin 48b–49a; Jerushalmi Kiddushin 1.61a, Shemuel 25.123–124; Tan. B. IV, 167; Tan. Mass'e 12; BaR 23.13. A poetic description of Joab's tragic end, partly based on an unknown Midrash, is found in Mahzor Vitry 341–342; comp. also *ibid.* 331–332 (the commentary on the poem); see further note 8. In this poem Joab first laments his innocent death, and then proceeds to ask Solomon and Israel to have pity on him. When, however, he saw that his pleadings were in vain, he called his son Joel, to give him his last message. He said to him: "Observe the Torah, educate thy (younger) brothers, and honor

thy mother." Solomon first called upon his son Rehoboam to slay Joab, and in this way avenge the death of Absalom caused by Joab (see 2 Sam. 18.14–15); but Rehoboam could not muster enough courage for the deed, when he saw all Israel weep. Benaiah was therefore sent by the king to carry out this command instead of his hesitating son. When Joab saw him approach with his sword in his hand, he said: "Benaiah, Benaiah, attempt not what will end in a great disappointment (this is how לא תשנק רוחך is to be understood, and is not to be emended as done by the editor); my neck is strong and thy sword too weak, and thou canst not kill me." Joab, however, was mistaken. Benaiah succeeded in carrying out the king's command to the great consternation of Israel who out of fear of the king dared not give expression to the deep sorrow in their heart for the bitter end of Joab. As to the great loss sustained by Israel through Joab's death, see also Yerushalmi Makkot 2, 31a; Shemuel 25, 124. The high priest Abiathar was not slain by Solomon. The king merely removed him from his high position, and appointed Zadok to the office of high priest; see Josephus, *Antiqui.*, VIII, 1.4. According to the views of the Rabbis, Abiathar was removed from his office by David, on his flight from Absalom, when the Urim and Tummim refused to give answer to Abiathar; when Zadok succeeded in obtaining a response, he was appointed high priest; see Yoma 73b; Sotah 48b; Seder 'Olam 14. Zadok was the man best fitted for holding the office of high priest in his time, as his ancestor Aaron in his time. See Koheleth 1.1, and comp. also ps.-Jerome 1 Chron. 21.7, where Zadok is said to have been a second Aaron, and, like his great ancestor, had stopped a plague by his prayers. As to the anointing of Zadok, see note 371 on vol III, p. 179.

11 Berakot 8a; Tosefta-Targum 1 Kings 2.36 and 3.1; comp. vol. IV, pp. 381–382. As to the insults heaped by Shimei on David, and the reconciliation of these two men, see Tehillim 3, 36–37; note 96 on vol. IV, p. 104. According to Josephus, *Antiqui.*, VIII; 5.1, Shimei was executed by Solomon for breaking the oath he had given to him. On death as a punishment for perjury or similar offences, see Ginzberg, *Unbekannte Sekte*, 135–137. Solomon slew Shimei by pronouncing God's Name upon him (comp. vol. II, p. 280); Shimei sinned by the word of mouth, and his punishment, in accordance with his sin, was executed by a word. See Zohar II, 108. Comp. also *ibid.*, 107b, where Berakot, *loc. cit.*, and perhaps also Kimhi, 1 Kings 2.8, are made use of. That Nathan the prophet was Solomon's teacher, as maintained in Zohar, is found nowhere in rabbinic literature, nor are Septuagint and

Vulgate, 2 Sam. 12.25, to be understood in that sense. On the view
of ps.-Jerome, 1 Chron. 20.7, that Nathan is identical with Jonathan,
David's nephew, who slew one of the Philistine giants (1 Chron. 20.7),
see note 88 on vol. IV, p. 102. On the founding of Rome, see Shabbat
56b; Yerushalmi 'Abodah Zarah 1, 39c (here it is Michael who inserted
the reed in the sea; comp. note 8 on vol. I, p. 5); Sifre D., 52; Shir
1.6. Comp. Grünbaum, *Gesammelte Aufsätze*, 169; Schlatter, *Verkanntes Griechisch* 64 and Ginzberg, *Jewish Encyclopedia*, s. v. "Abba Kolon". This Abba Kolon ("Father of Colony", or Abba Ka-
lon, "father of shame"?) is said in Shir, *loc. cit.*, to have made the
settlement of Rome possible. The first settlers of Rome found that
the huts collapsed as soon as built. Whereupon Abba Kolon said to
them: "Unless ye mix water from the Euphrates with your mortar,
nothing that ye build will stand." He then offered to supply such water,
and for this purpose journeyed through the east as a cooper, and returned with water from the Euphrates in wine-casks. The builders
poured this water into the mortar, and built new huts which did not
collapse. Hence the proverb: "A city without Abba Kolon is not worthy
of the name." The newly-built city was therefore called Babylonian
Rome. On Babylon = Rome, see Rev. 14.8, 17.18, and the references to
rabbinic literature in Ginzberg, *Geonica*, I, 29, note 1, as well as
Hekalot, ed. Wertheimer, 32, 39, and Mahzor Vitry 520. The babylonian myth about the origin of the city of Babylon (see King, *Creation
Tablets*, 132) resembles the Jewish legend about the founding of Rome.
Comp. also Zohar III, 251b–252a, and Nehemias מכתבי דודים, 161.

   12 Comp., however, Seder 'Olam 15, according to which Solomon's
marriage with Pharaoh's daughter took place at the time when he started
to build the Temple; hence the word of God (Jer. 32.31) that this city
(Jerusalem, *i. e.*, the Temple) has been to Him a provocation from the
day that they built it. The first four years of Solomon's reign were the
only ones during which he walked in the ways of the Lord; comp.
also Niddah 70a and EZ 8, 185. The last passage reads: The first
Temple existed four hundred and ten years, but Israel was free from
idolatry for twenty years only. This number very likely refers to the
twenty years of the reign of the pious king Josiah; comp. Ginzberg,
Unbekannte Sekte, 302. According to Josephus, *Antiqui.*, VIII, 7.5,
Solomon "fell into an error about the observance of the laws, when he
made the images of the brazen oxen, which supported the brazen sea
and the images of the lions about his own throne." The Rabbis, on
the other hand, are far from blaming him for these images, and the

images of the throne occupy a very important position in the rabbinic legend; com. vol. IV, pp. 157, *seq.*

¹³ Shabbat 56b; Sanhedrin 70b; Yelammedenu in 'Aruk, s. v. בטני; Tan. Shemot 1; WR 12.5; BaR 10.4; Mishle 30, 107–108. למחות in Prov. 31.3, is derived from חיה "he lived". The warning against drunkenness on this occasion had its good reasons. Solomon had not touched any wine all the years he was engaged in building the Temple. To celebrate his marriage with Pharaoh's daughter, which took place on the day when the building of the Temple was completed, he changed his mode of life, and drank wine, with the effect that he was overpowered by a heavy sleep; see WR, *loc. cit.*—Bath-sheba is here, as elsewhere in the Haggadah, well spoken of, and is counted as one of the twenty-two virtuous women, whose praise is sung in the last chapter of Prov. Comp. Mishle, 31, 112, and MHG I, 337. Comp. note 271 on vol. I, p. 291. In the latter source it is maintained that she had, by means of the holy spirit, foreseen that her son would be the wisest of men.

¹⁴ רוזנים in Prov. 31.4, is connected with the Aramaic רז "a secret". The secret refers to the secret lore of the Torah.

¹⁵ BaR 10.4. Comp. also Sanhedrin 70b; WR 12.5, and the references given at the beginning of note 13.

¹⁶ Yerushalmi Sanhedrin 2, 20c; PK 27, 169a; Tan. B. III, 55; Tan. Ahare 1; Shir 1.1 ('); Koheleth 2.2. Wealth came to Solomon in a miraculous way. God commanded the sea to cast up all the valuable things that had ever been thrown into it; see *Tub ha-Arez*, 37c. As soon as Solomon married Pharaoh's daughter, his wealth began to diminish, though he remained very rich all his life; Niddah 70b. With regard to the foreign women whom he married, the following views are found: 1) He married women belonging to the nations with which it is forbidden to enter into marriage relations (the so-called "seven nations") even when converted to Judaism; 2) he did not marry the foreign women, but had illicit relations with them; 3) the women he married were converts to Judaism, but as their conversion was not prompted by love for God, they did not observe the commandments of the Torah, and particularly neglected those which are incumbent on married women, and yet Solomon did not remonstrate with them; 4) he married those women to convert them to Judaism; but though his intentions were good, he is blamed for having done it, as one should not take a wife without being certain of her piety and virtue. Comp. the sources cited at the beginning of the note, and further Seder 'Olam 15; Yebamot 76a; Josephus, *Antiqui.*, VIII, 7.5. Kimhi, 1 Kings 3,3,

quotes from an unknown midrashic source the view that the biblical prohibition against intermarriage with Egyptians refers only to the marriage of Egyptian males and Jewish females, but not *vice versa*; comp. Index, s. v. "Moabite Women". The difference of opinion concerning Solomon's marriages reflects not only the difference in estimating Solomon's character (comp. note 59), but also in the attitude toward intermarriage. Solomon's favorite wife was Pharaoh's daughter, whom he loved as much as all the others put together. But she led him astray, and made him commit as many sins as all the others put together. See Sifre D., 52, and Midrash Tannaim 45; the sources quoted at the beginning of the note refer also to the sin of Solomon in marrying a multitude of wives; comp. note 81 and vol. VI, pp. 188–189.

¹⁷ BR 44.8; Aggadat Shir 1.5; Tehillim 2, 29; 12, 179; 119, 494; 2 ARN 43. According to the dissenting view given in these sources Abraham and Jacob shared this distinction with the three other men mentioned there.

¹⁸ PR 14, 59a; Shir 1.1 ('ט). Solomon fasted forty days, that God should grant him wisdom, and as a reward for his modesty and humility his wish was fulfilled so that he became "the father of wisdom". See Mishle 1, 1, where אבי הנבואה "father of prophecy" is to be struck out as a copyist's error, who while writing of Solomon put down the title of Moses, who is often called the father of wisdom and the father of prophecy. Comp. vol. V, p. 404, note 68 towards the end. Glowing descriptions of Solomon's wisdom are found in Ecclus, 47.13, *seq.*; Wisdom 7. 15, *seq.*; Josephus, *Antiqui.*, VIII, 2.5. According to the Hellenistic writers, Solomon's wisdom consisted in his great knowledge of science and philosophy. But for the Rabbis there is no other wisdom than the knowledge of the Torah, and accordingly, Solomon's great mastery of the Torah is praised; see references in note 24. He attempted to find not only the reasons of the divine commandments, but also the profound secret of divine retribution for the fulfilment of the commandments. He further attempted to discover the "end" (the time of the advent of the Messiah). See Tehillim, 9, 80–81. As to Solomon's wisdom, see also Shir 1.1; Koheleth 1.1 and 13; 'Erubin 21b; Shabbat 14b; Yebamot 21a. In the three last passages Solomon is said to have contributed a great deal to the further development of the Torah by his introducing new ordinances and ceremonies. The institution of the 'Erub and the ceremony of washing the hands before meals as well as the extension of the prohibited marriages (שניות לעריות), are attributed to him. When Alexander the Great conquered Jerusalem, he found there Solomon's

books of wisdom which he gave to his teacher Aristotle, who drew all
his knowledge from them. The wisdom of the Greeks is accordingly
entirely dependent upon Solomon. See *Derek Emunah* 46b; *Shalshelet
ha-Kabbalah* 102b (שמעון הצדיק); *Iggeret Ba'ale Hayyim* 3.7; Ginzberg,
Aristotle in Jewish Literature in *Jewish Encyclopedia*, s. v.

¹⁹ Jewish tradition identifies Ethan the Ezrahite (Ps. 89.1) with
Abraham. Comp. Baba Batra 15a.

²⁰ Heman, "the confidant" (of God), *i. e.*, Moses; comp. Num. 12.7.

²¹ Calcol, "the giver of food", *i. e.*, Joseph; comp. Genesis 47.12.

²² Dar-Da; *"Dor"* = "generation", and *Da* = "wisdom"; they
are called "the sons of Mahol", that is, the "sons of pardon", because
their sins were forgiven; comp. vol. III, p.79.

²³ האדם (= man), in this verse, is taken to mean Adam.

²⁴ PK 4, 33a–33b; PR 12, 59a–60b; Tan. B. IV, 109–112;
Tan. Hukkat 6; BaR 19.3; Koheleth 7.23; Mishle 1, 39; Midrash Shir
23a; ps.-Jerome, 1 Kings 4.31–32. On the variants of this Haggadah
in ps.-Jerome, see Ginzberg, *Haggada bei den Kirchenv.*, 73. On the
three thousand parables of Solomon, see also 'Erubin 21a; Shir 1.1;
vol. IV, p. 102, and Ginzberg, *ibid.*, 74. As Solomon excelled all
Israel in wisdom, even so did he excel all the wisest men among other
nations, the dwellers in the east, who were renowned for their wisdom (on
these, see also Yerushalmi Shabbat 12, 13d, towards the end), the Egyptians, who were famous as masters of astrology and magic. In his great
wisdom Solomon was not only able to supplement the wise words of his
father David, but sometimes also to correct them, and accordingly
the views expressed in the Book of Proverbs are not always in harmony
with those of the Book of Psalms, notwithstanding the great reverence
Solomon had for his father, to whose glorification he devoted his entire
life. See Mishle 1, 42, 43; 15, 79; Shir 1.6 (here the parallels between
the lives of David and Solomon are dwelled upon) and 1.10; Baba
Batra 10b. To the opinions wherein David and Solomon differed belongs also this: the former holds that the heart (= feeling and will)
is the seat of wisdom, whereas the latter declares that the head
(intellect) generates wisdom. See Mishle 1, 42, and the Mohammedan
legend in Salzberger, *Salomo-Sage*, 66, who, strangely enough, did not
see the dependence of this legend on the rabbinic Midrash, comp. note
27 (middle). On Solomon's literary products, see note 93.

²⁵ Rosh ha-Shanah 21b. According to another version, Solomon's
wisdom was in one respect akin to the divine wisdom; like God he

could give judgment without the evidence of witnesses, for he penetrated into the secrets of man's thoughts.   See Tehillim 72, 324 (with regard to Solomon's decision in the case of the two women); Targum Shir 1.2, followed by Zohar II, 78a; Shir 1.1; ShR 15.26; Wisdom 7.20.   As to the "forty-nine gates of wisdom", which were open to Moses and Solomon (according to one view in Rosh ha-Shanah, *loc. cit.*, however, the former only had that privilege), see the numerous passages containing the Haggadah that each statement of the Torah admits of forty-nine correct interpretations ("and as many incorrect ones" in PR 21.101a is a later addition). Comp. PR 14, 58a–58b, 60b, and 21, 101a; Yerushalmi Sanhedrin 4, 22a; Ekah, introduction, XXIII, 20; PK 4, 31a–31b; Soferim 16.6; 'Erubin 13b. The reading "sixty gates of wisdom" in *Hinnuk*, No. 152 is very likely a copyist's error. A different Haggada is given in Alphabet of R. Akiba 16, according to which no less than five thousand gates of wisdom, eight thousand gates of understanding, and eleven thousand gates of knowledge were opened to Moses on Sinai.   These numbers correspond to the number of the books of the Bible multiplied by a thousand. This Scripture consists of the five books of Moses, eight of the prophets (the Minor Prophets are counted as one book), and eleven of the Hagiographa (counting Ezra and Nehemiah as one book; see Baba Batra 14b; Sanhedrin 93b). See also Norzi, Num. 28.5.

[26] Tehillim 72, 324–325; Shir 1. 1,10; Koheleth 1.1; Makkot 23b; BR 85.12; Yalkut Reubeni on Gen. 4.8, which reads: These female spirits were Lilith and Naamah. It is hardly admissible to assume dependence upon the similar Indian legend (comp. Salzberger, *Salomo-Sage*, 52–53). This Haggadah very likely has its origin in the quite natural supposition that no woman, and particularly no mother, would have a child killed to satisfy a grudge.   Comp. Shu'aib, Shekalim, 34c. Tehillim, *loc. cit.*, has the fine remark that the Bible, in describing the procedure in Solomon's court, is employing forensic style, and therefore 1 Kings 3.23 is not superflouous, as it is the duty of the judge to sum up the claims of the litigants before rendering his decision.

[27] BHM IV, 145–146; Hibbur Ma'as. No. 10; Hasidim 91, where the wise judge is R. Sa'adya Gaon.   On the widespread legend concerning the test of kinship, see Steinschneider, *Hebräische Bibliographie*, XIII, 133, and XVIII, 39; Kohut, *Journal of American Oriental Society*, XXIX, 84–85; Davidson, *Sepher Sha'ashuim*, LXII; Gaster, *Exempla* No. 391; Gaston Paris, *R. E. J.* XI, 7.   The legend in vol. IV. pp. 88–85, about young David's discovery of the thief very likely be-

longs to the cycle of legends clustering around Solomon, a copyist erroneously putting the name of the father instead that of the son. Comp. Steinschneider, *op. cit.* XVIII, 40; Salzberger, *Salomo-Sage*, 57; note 8; note 26 on vol. IV, 85. The legend is very fond of showing the great wisdom of the youth Solomon, who even then often overruled the seemingly just decisions of his father David. A poor servant of David once borrowed an egg with the promise to return all that might come from it. When his creditor insisted upon the fulfilment of the promise, David, before whom the case was tried, condemned him to an enormous amount of money, in view of the fact that from the egg a chicken could be hatched which would lay eighteen eggs, from which eighteen chickens could be hatched, each of which would lay eighteen eggs, etc. On the advice of Solomon the debtor sowed boiled peas, and when seen by David and asked how he could expect these to grow, he replied: How can a boiled egg be hatched and produce chickens? David had neglected to find out before giving judgment whether the egg borrowed was boiled or not. Levi, R.E.J. XXXIII, 65 *seq.* Gaster, *Exempla*, Nos. 329 and 342. Seymour, *Tales of King Solomon*, 18 *seq.*, gives a considerable number of legends all of which have the same aim, to show the superiority of Solomon's wisdom to that of his father. The earlier Jewish literature hardly knows of this rivalry between father and son, though we find there some remarks to the effect that certain views expressed by Solomon in his writings do not always agree with those of his father, comp. Shabbat 30a and note 24. Some of these legends however, contain old material. Comp. *e. g.* the tale about the treasure (Seymour 18–19) which belongs to the circle of Alexander legends, comp. note 35 on vol. IV, p. 251. Great as was Solomon's wisdom, he nevertheless was not free from human limitations. Once a poor man was carrying a sack of flour in his hand when a wind came and blew it into the sea. He complained to David about the wind, but all that the King could do was to make his loss good and send him home. Solomon, however, was not satisfied with his father's action in this matter and insisted on calling the wind to justice and David finally yielded to the wish of his son. He conjured the spirit of the wind and asked him to explain why he had blown the poor man's flour into the sea. The answer was as follows: a ship, on high sea with many people on board had sprung a leak and was on the point of foundering; the flour, however, stopped the leak and all were saved. A few days later the ship came into port and they gave the poor man a third of their possessions which they had vowed

as a thank-offering; Gaster, *Exempla*, No. 444; Jacob Saphir אבן ספיר
I, 26 *seq.*; Seymour, *Tales of King Salomon* 18.

²⁸ On the dwelling-place of the Cainites, see vol. I, p. 114.

²⁹ *Hibbur ha-Ma'asiyyot*, No. 11; BHM IV, 151–152; Ma'asiyyot
(Gaster's edition), 113, 75; Al-Barceloni, 173; Mordecai, *Tefillin*, who
gives PRE as his source. See Gaster, *Exempla*, No. 113; Steinschneider.
Hebräische Bibliographie, XVIII, 16, and Salzberger, *Salomo-Sage*, 58.

³⁰ Rabbenu Nissim 38; Midrash 'Aseret ha-Debarim in Hibbur ha-
Ma'asiyyot (eighth commandment) and BHM I, 86–87; Ma'asiyyot
ed. Gaster 73–75; Baraita de-Yeshua (end); Hegyon ha-Nefesh, 10a.
Comp. Steinschneider, *Hebräische Bibliographie*, XVIII, 40.   The
legend given in BHM *ibid.* 87–88, and Hibbur Ma'asiyyot (third commandment) concerning the thief who betrayed himself is brought into
relation with Solomon in the version thereof in the Constantinople
edition of משלים של שלמה.   This legend is as follows: A man arriving
in a strange place shortly before the beginning of the Sabbath, hastened
to bury the money he had with him, as it is forbidden to carry about
any money on the day of rest.   For he had no friend in that place to
whom he could entrust his purse.   At the termination of the Sabbath
he went to get his money, but it was not there; his host had watched
him on the previous day, and stole the purse.   The stranger suspected
his host, but having no evidence, he thought it best to ask the wise
Solomon for advice, and he did not regret it.   On the king's advice,
he went up to his host, and told him that he had lately buried a large
sum of money for safety, but having retained a still greater sum on his
person, he would like to be advised whether he should put it in the same
place as the other sum, or should entrust it to somebody.   The dis-
honest host, greedy for the stranger's money, advised him to bury
the larger sum in the same place, and hastened to replace the stolen money
so that the owner should add more thereto.   The latter, however, joy-
fully took his money and went his way.   Comp. Steinschneider. *op.
cit.* XIII, 129, *seq.* Gaster, *Exempla*, No. 111.

³¹ Tan. B. Introduction, 157, and in a very elaborate form,
Ma'aseh-Buch, No. 144. Comp. Gaster, *Exempla*, Nos. 441a–441b.
On the view that the serpent knew the place of the hidden treasures,
see vol. I, p. 71.

³² Rabbenu Nissim 14; Meshalim No. 3; BHM IV, 146–147;
Zabara, Sepher Sha'ashuim, Davidson's edition, XLIX–XXLII; Gas-
ter *Exempla* Nos. 328, 401. Another legend illustrating the truth of
Solomon's words, "a woman, etc." (Eccles. 7.28) is given in Meshalim,

No. 2, and BHM IV, 146; but this source does not attribute any part in it to the wise king. On the other hand he plays a very important part in the following two legends. Once Solomon had to make use of his knowledge of magic to convince people of the truth of his words against women. Once he warned a man against the faithlessness of his wife, but the latter did not believe him. Solomon gave him as a present a silver goblet, which the man took home. The paramour of his wife came, saw the goblet and asked the woman to drink out of it together with him. They did so and their lips remained attached to the goblet. When brought before Solomon, the wise king said: "The spell can only be broken if their heads be pierced with red hot iron. The wronged husband pleaded, however, for the culprits. Solomon took David's sword (comp. note 59, end, on vol. IV, p. 94) on which was engraved the Name, poured water over it and sprinkled their faces with this water. They were thus released. Others say that two scholars passed a scroll of the Torah between them which released them; Gaster, *Exempla* 351a. The variant of this legend (No. 351b) in which Bath-sheba is introduced, to illustrate the wickedness of women, has some relation to that given by Seymour, *Tales of King Solomon*, 14-15. Here it is told that the mother of Solomon decided to kill him because of his slighting remark about women made by him while still an infant of three years, when he said that "a woman's soul is not as heavy as a handful of chips of wood."

³³ Meshalim No. 4; BHM IV, 148-150; Gaster, *Exempla* No. 402. Comp. Steinschneider, *Hebräische Bibliographie*, XVIII, 39-40. As to the three rules of conduct imparted by Solomon to his disciple, see vol. II, pp. 9. 99, and 115, where the first one is referred to; the second is a verbal variant of the proverb: "he who throws himself against a wave is overthrown by it" (comp. BR 14.15); the third is found verbatim in *Musar Haskel* beginning (Steinschneider's edition), and comp. also Eccles. 7.26, according to the Greek. On hundred as a round number see note 316 on vol. I, p. 417, and comp. also Yerushalmi Sanhedrin 4, 22b (middle of column).

³⁴ *Ben ha-Melek we-ha-Nazir*, XXIV, and in abridged form in Prym and Socin, *Der Dialekt des Tur Abdin*, LXVI. There are several versions of this legend, in some of which Solomon does not play any part. Comp. Gaster *Exempla*, Nos. 381, 449; Neuhoff, *Afrikanische Märchen* 51; vol. V, pp. 57-58. The conception that he who knows the language of animals must keep it secret at the peril of his life seems to be presupposed also in the Arabic legend given by Salzberger, *Salomo-Sage*, 60. The view that Solomon understood the

languages of all animals is based upon 1 Kings 5.13, and is often referred
to in the midrashic literature; comp. Shir. 1.1; Koheleth 1.11 (here
an attempt is made to rationalize the popular belief. Comp. also Tan.
B. IV, 112 top, and parallel passages cited by Buber); Targum Sheni
1.2, 5. Solomon's knowledge of the languages of the animals plays
an important part in Mohammedan legends; see note 58 on vol. I, p. 71.
The following legend given by Sabba', Wa-Yeze, 33b, is very likely
of Mohammedan origin: Solomon once overheard a male bird say
to his mate: "If thou desirest it, I shall forthwith destroy the throne
upon which Solomon sits." Astonished at its impudence, the wise
king had this bird appear before him, and asked it to explain what it
meant by these boasting words. The bird replied: "O Solomon, where
is thy wisdom? Knowest thou not that one utters foolish things to
gain the admiration of the woman one loves?" A similar tale is found
in Hanauer, *Folklore of Holy Land* 48.

³⁵ PK 4, 34a; PR 12, 59b; Tan. B. IV, 110; Tan. Hukkat 6; BaR
19.3.

³⁶ Josephus, *Antiqui.*, VIII, 5.3. The correspondence between
the two kings is given by Josephus, *op. cit.*, VIII, 2.6–7, and by Eupolemus, 448–449, in a very lengthy form, whereas Scripture only refers
to it in a few words. Eupolemus, 451, speaks of a golden pillar which
Solomon presented to Hiram, and which the latter dedicated to Zeus;
comp. Josephus, *Antiqui.*, VIII, 5.3. Another legend relates that Hiram
fashioned his daughter's statue of the gold which Solomon presented to
him; comp. Theophilus in Eusebius, *Praep. Evang.*, 452. This is also to be
supplemented by the legend that Solomon married Hiram's daughter;
see Clemens Alexandrinus, *Stromata*, 1.21. In the kabbalistic literature
the legend concerning the rivalry between Solomon and Hiram in solving riddles is connected with the Hiram legend given in vol. IV, pp.
335–336; comp. Zohar II, 159a, and II, 61a; Sabba', Tezawweh, 84,
and wa-Ethanan, 134a. As to the possessions given by Solomon to
Hiram (1 Kings 9.13), see Shabbat 54a, where several opinions are
given why the king of Tyre was dissatisfied with the gift. According
to one view, the inhabitants of these cities "were laden with gold and
silver", so that Hiram apprehended that they would not be willing to
engage in warlike expeditions; see also Josephus, *Antiqui.*, VIII, 5.3

³⁷ In Baba Batra 15b an opinion is quoted that a "queen of Sheba"
never existed, and that the expression מלכת שבא means "dominion of
Sheba" (מַלְכַּת). This statement very likely refers to Job. 1.15, where

the Rabbis seem to have read שבא מלכת; comp. Targum, *ad loc.* See, however, MHG I, 379; note 311 on vol. I, p. 298; Schechter in *Folk-Lore*, 1890, pp. 350–351.

³⁸ Solomon's knowledge of the languages of the animals is hardly referred to in the older literature; comp. the references given in notes 24 and 34 to the Midrashim, where 1 Kings 5.13 is interpreted in a rationalistic manner. But Solomon's dominion over the entire creation, men, animals, demons, and angels, is not disputed; comp. ShR 15.6 and 30.16; BaR 11.3; BR 34.12 (which reads: The power over the animal world, lost by Adam through his sin, was regained by Solomon); Sanhedrin 20b (which reads: Solomon before his fall was lord over all the terrestrials and celestials); comp. also vol. IV, pp. 149, *seq.*, and 165, *seq.*

³⁹ For details concerning this bird, see Grünbaum, *Gesammelte Aufsätze*, 139, *seq.*; note 85 and note 696 on vol. III, p. 346.

⁴⁰ Solomon is one of the few (three or ten) monarchs who ruled over the entire world; see Shir 1.1, 10; Mishle 20, 88, and 30, 104; PRE 11; Esther R. 1.1 (here David is also said to have been a "Cosmocrator"); Megillah 11b (top). Comp. vol. I, p. 178; vol. III, pp. 196, 355. The Church Fathers are at pains to contradict this assertion of the Jewish legend, not out of dislike for Solomon, but for polemical reasons, maintaining that the scriptural passages speaking of man's dominion over the entire creation can only refer to Jesus. See Justin Martyr, *Dialogue*, 34; Tertullian, *Adversus Judaeos*, 7.

⁴¹ Certain particulars concerning the relations between the queen of Sheba and Solomon have been omitted here because of their too realistic character. In the Arabic legend in which the queen bears the name Bilkis (Hebrew פילגש "concubine"?), we are told that the genii wanted to hinder the marriage of Solomon and the queen of Sheba; they therefore called the king's attention to the growth of hair on her legs. To convince himself that they spoke the truth, Solomon had a glass palace built, and when he found that their allegation was confirmed, he ordered them to make Nurah, a mixture of arsenic and unslaked lime, which he used as a depilatory. Comp. Grünbaum, *Neue Beiträge*, 219, and Seymour *Tales of King Solomon* 146–148. The legend concerning the hair on the queen's legs very likely supposes that she was of the genii (this is explicitly stated by the Arabs), and hence the hair, for the bodies of demons are covered with hair; comp. note 58 on vol. IV, p. 33. That Solomon married the queen of Sheba is stated also in 2 Alphabet of Ben Sira, 21b, where the depilatory is also

mentioned. Comp. note 311 on vol. I, p. 298 and note 21 on vol. IV, p. 300.

⁴² Targum Sheni 1.3, 8–10. Read either לשמשא instead of ליומא, or "day" is here used instead of "sun"; comp. BR. 6.7. The description of Benaiah (concerning whom see vol. IV, pp. 166, 172) reminds one of that given of the high priest Simeon in Ecclus. 50.6, *seq*. It is, however, possible that Targum Sheni made use of the old piyyut מה נהדר (Musaf of Day of Atonement), the author of which was acquainted with the Hebrew original of Ecclus. Comp. Rapoport, *Bikkure ha-'Ittim* IX, 116.

⁴³ Those who are not sons of the covenant of Abraham cannot bear the divine presence; comp. note 131 on vol. I, p. 241, and note 727 on vol. III, p. 356. See also vol. IV, p. 111.

⁴⁴ The living tree had no motion; the trunk from which the crowning branches have been severed supplies the material for the moving vessels.

⁴⁵ As to the question whether the angels who visited Abraham actually ate, or only "feigned to eat", see note 143 on vol. I, p. 243. The fifth riddle seems to be anti-Christian. For the sixth riddle, see PRE 10 and Midrash Jonah 98, where it is said that the fish showed Jonah the "roads of the Red Sea" through which Israel passed. The ninth riddle refers to the story of Judah (comp. Gen. 38.25).

⁴⁶ These nineteen riddles found in the MS. Midrash ha-Hefez were translated and explained by Schechter in *Folk-Lore* I, 349–358. It is noteworthy that the fifth and eighth riddles are introduced by the words, "and furthermore she asked him", from which it may be inferred that three different sources have been made use of by the compiler of this Midrash. The first four occur in Mishle I, 40–41. It is further noteworthy that the seventh and eighth are in Aramaic while the others are in Hebrew. This would probably show that the former belonged to some Targum. Comp. Herz, *Die Rätsel d. König. von Saba;* Grünbaum, *Neue Beiträge,* 220–221, and the following note. On the fourteenth riddle, see note 61 on vol. I, p. 140.

⁴⁷ Targum Sheni 1,3, 10. The second riddle is given in Hebrew (מבים literally "look", means here "lights"), though the Targum is of course in Aramaic. The following points may contribute to the understanding of the third riddle. The sail of the boat is made of flax, in a storm it waves to and fro, and when beaten by the wind, it emits sounds; the rich wear byssus, the poor have rags, and shrouds are usually made of linen (comp. Ketubot 8b); the birds steal the flax-seed, and the

fish are caught with nets made of flax, comp. Wünsche, *Räthsel-Weisheit bei den Hebräern*; Cassel, *Zweites Targum*, 21–22. The meaning of ארקלין in Targum Sheni is a riddle which the lexicographers attempted to solve; but not being as wise as Solomon, they failed. Comp. Krauss, *Lehnwörter*, s. v., and *Ha-Shiloah*, XIV. 92. According to Josephus, *Antiqui.*, VIII, 6.5, the "queen of Egypt and Ethiopia" (that is how he designates the queen of Sheba) was inquisitive about philosophy, and was "a woman that on other accounts also was to be admired." She showed her admiration of Solomon by many and precious gifts she made to him, and it is said that the root of that balsam which Palestine produces (comp. Berakot 43a, where balsam oil, אפרסמון, is described as שמן ארצנו, "the oil of our land") was the gift of this woman; Josephus, *Antiqui.*, VIII, 6.6.

⁴⁸ Josephus, *Antiqui.*, VIII, 2.5. The recognized authorities of rabbinic Judaism condemn the use of the conjuring books ascribed to Solomon (comp. note 90 on vol. IV, p. 277), whereas the early Church held them in high esteem, and preserved considerable fragmets of them; see Schürer, *Geschichte*, III, 407–414. Comp. note 93, and *Jewish Encyclop.*, s. v. Solomon.

⁴⁹ Koheleth 2.5. On Solomon's dominion over the spirits and demons, see PK 5, 45b, and the parallel passages cited by Buber, as well as the references given in note 38. In agreement with the view given in Testament of Solomon (comp. vol. IV, p. 150, *seq.*), Shir 1.1, 5, and ShR 52.4 limit Solomon's power over the world of spirits to the time of the building of the Temple, when they were forced by him into service, since "all creatures contributed their share to the glory of God".

⁵⁰ Koheleth 2.25; Apocalypse of Baruch 87.26; comp. also vol. IV, pp. 114 and 319.

⁵¹ The "mountains of darkness" are mentioned in the Alexander legend of the Talmud (Tamid 32a), and play an important part in the later folklore of the Jews.

⁵² On these angels see vol. I, pp. 148, *seq.*, and vol. III, p. 274.

⁵³ Zohar III, 233a–233b. Palmyra is said to be the place where the queen of Sheba was buried by Solomon; comp. Seymour, *Tales of King Solomon* 148, and hence the remark of Zohar on Palmyra, the city of magic. For another version of the visits paid by Solomon to the fallen angels, see Zohar III, 112b; comp. also Aggadat Bereshit (end of introduction); '*Emek ha-Melek* 107c; Zohar III, 208a; Zohar Ruth (beginning ר' נחמיה פתח); note 55.

⁵⁴ This, five A's interlaced, is somewhat different from the Magen David, "the shield of David", to whose magic power the Karaite Judah Hadassi (Eshkol, 92c, No. 242) is the earliest authority to make reference. Comp. *Monatsschrift*, 66, 1–9.

⁵⁵ On Sheba as the land of sorcerers, see also MHG I, 378–379; note 311 on vol. I, p. 298. It is possible that the substitution of "Egypt" for "Sheba" by Josephus, who consistently speaks of the "queen of Egypt" (comp. note 47), is to be ascribed to the fact that in the Haggadah Egypt is the land of magic and witchcraft *par excellence*; comp. Index, s. v. "Egypt". In the Arabic legend the "sorceress" became the daughter of a female jinn (Peri); comp. Grünbaum, *Neue Beiträge*, 219. As to the Jewish sources, where the queen of Sheba appears as a female demon, see Zohar III, 309b; note 41; note 20 on vol. II, p. 233. As she was a sorceress or demon, it is quite natural that the question she asked Solomon had reference to magic and witchcraft; see Zohar III, 194b. Comp., on the other hand, Aggadat Shir 1, 65, where it is said that the queen of Sheba praised Solomon for the wisdom he displayed in rendering justice and providing for the poor.

⁵⁶ Testament of Solomon, which is a pseudepigraphic book of Jewish origin, but with many Christian layers, and it is therefore often difficult to distinguish between the Jewish and the Christian elements of this work; comp. Conybeare, *J.Q.R.* XI, 1–45, and Salzberger, *Salomos Tempelbau*, 12–15. The following are the rabbinic parallels to the Solomon legend of this pseudepigraph. The demons assisted Solomon in the erection of the Temple; see the references cited in note 49. For Solomon's magic ring in the Ashmedai legend of the Talmud, see vol. IV, p. 166. Beelzeboul (= Beelzebul) holds in this writing the same position as Sammael in the rabbinic legend, and the statement that the name Beelzeboul describes its bearer as the dweller of the first heaven (chapter 25) is to be explained in accordance with the view of the Rabbis that Zebul is the name of one of the heavens (comp. Hagigah 12b), though it is to be noticed that it is the fourth heaven which is called Zebul in the Talmud. On the son of Beelzeboul, see the Jewish legend concerning the son of Sammael (vol. I, p. 154). It should also be noticed that Cain is said to have been the son of Sammael; see vol. I, p. 105. The green stone which Solomon needed for the building of the Temple is very likely identical with the Shamir of the rabbinic legend; see note 82. The episode related by Ornias is only a slightly different version of the rabbinic legend, vol. IV, p. 167, where Ashmedai takes the place of Ornias. As to the sacrifices of the locusts, see vol. I.

p. 264, and comp. also *Kebra Negast*, 60 (German translation), where this incident is told about Solomon and the daughter of Pharaoh. The idol Rephaim is probably a reminiscence of רפאים "the shades" in Sheol; comp. also the etymology of תרפים, "images of idols", in ARN 38, 101. The name Abezi-thibod, borne by a very powerful spirit, is probably the Hebrew אַב עֲצוֹת אוֹבֵד, "the father who is devoid of counsel"; comp. Deut. 32.28 (גוי אוֹבֵד עֵצוֹת). This evil spirit is said to have fought against Moses in Egypt by means of magic, hardened Pharaoh's heart, assisted Jannes and Jambres, caused the Egyptians to pursue the Israelites after having permitted them to leave Egypt, and finally been drowned with the Egyptians in the Red Sea, where he is kept a prisoner under a pillar. In the rabbinic legend it is Sammael, in the Book of Jubilees Mastema, who is the great adversary of Moses and Israel in Egypt and at the Red Sea; but there is also a rabbinic legend which ascribes this part to Uzza, the angel of Egypt, who like Abezi-thibod was thrown into the Red Sea. Comp. vol. III, pp. 13–14, 16–18, 239, and see also Index, s. v. "Mastema". See also *Zadokite Fragm.* 5.18, which reads: And Belial raised Johanan (=Jannes) and his brother. That Ornias has the form of a lion (9) is very likely to be explained by the fact that he is said to have been the offspring of Uriel, whose name is taken to be identical with Ariel, "lion of God", hence the form of a lion is ascribed to him. Comp. Zohar III, 32b, where Yoma 21a is made use of; vol. V, pp. 70–71. The Testament of Solomon, though containing a great many Jewish elements, is on the whole of a strongly syncretistic character. The pagan element is obvious in the fact that the angels (not only the fallen ones) are made to have offspring. This is neither Jewish nor Christian, but pagan.

⁵⁷ Costa, *Mikweh Israel*, No. 59, based perhaps on Berthold Auerbach, who refers to this legend in his Village Stories. It is not sure whether these sources have been made use of by the writer in *Ha-Zefirah*, 1897, No. 172. It is possible that he drew upon an oral legend current among the Jews of Russia of today as it was among those of Germany at the time of Auerbach. This legend seems to be based on a midrashic exposition of Ps. 133.1. According to old sources, the site of the Temple had been known before Solomon, see note 101 on vol. IV, p. 75, and note 53 on vol. IV, p. 92. See further Sifre D., 62, where it is said that the prophet Gad made known the holy site to David. See also PR 43, 179b; Eupolemus, 447d; Josephus, *Antiqui.*, VII, 13.4. As to the original possessor of the site, Araunah the Jebusite, see Josephus *loc. cit.*, who seems to have been

acquainted with some legends concerning the Jebusite. According to 'Abodah Zarah 24b, he was "a proselyte of the gate". Araunah is described in Scripture as king (2 Sam. 24.23), which means that he was the legitimate owner of the site of the Temple, for every one is "king" of his possessions; Zohar II, 214b. Just as David transmitted to Solomon the tradition about the site of the Temple, even so did he give him the necessary instructions about the furniture and vessels of the Temple; these traditions were handed down to him by Moses, through the long chain of authorities (Joshua, the elders, and the prophets). See Shemuel 16, 92–93; Yerushalmi Megillah 1, 70a. Just as a woman after giving birth to a male child remains impure for thirty-three days (see Lev. 12.4), even so did the earth after giving birth to Adam remain impure for thirty-three generations, that is, until the time of Solomon; Aguddat Aggadot 77, and comp. Vol. V, p. 72. Another Haggadah reads: Just as the moon acquired its complete light after fifteen days, even so did the light which began to shine at the time of Abraham reach its full strength in Solomon's time, the fifteenth since Abraham; as the moon loses its light completely on the thirtieth day, even so did this light become dark after thirty generations during the time of Zedekiah, when the Temple was destroyed and Israel sent into exile; see ShR 15.26; PR 15, 76b–77a; BaR 13.14. A parallel to this Haggadah is perhaps Matth. 1.17; comp. however, Moore, *Harvard Theological Review*, XIV, 97–103, and Ginzberg, *op. cit.* 196.

⁵⁸ Yoma 39b; Yerushalmi 4, 41d; BaR 12.4; Tan. B. IV, 33; Tan. Naso 9; Shir 3.9. A rationalistic rendering of this legend is found in Josephus, *Antiqui.*, VIII, 5.2. On the "gold that grows", see also BaR 13.18, and vol. III, p. 163.

⁵⁹ Sanhedrin 104b; Yerushalmi 10, 29b (as to the meaning of הדר עלה, see the remarks of R. Abraham Schiff in ספר יראים, note 140, end; but comp. the explanation given further below); PR 6, 23b–24a; Tan. B. III, 43; Tan. Mezora' 1; Mishle 22, 93 (on this passage see *Ketab Tammim*, 63); BaR 14 (beginning); comp. also Shabbat 56b; Yoma 66b; note 100 on vol. IV, p. 75. The sin on account of which some of the Rabbis were inclined to count him among the wicked kings is the one committed by him in marrying foreign women, particularly Pharaoh's daughter; see note 16 about the different views on this question, and comp. further Josephus, *Antiqui.*, VIII, 7.2. See also Sanhedrin 103b; where it is stated that Ahaz, Ahaziah, and all the kings of Israel concerning whom Scripture uses the words, "and they did that which was evil in the sight of the Lord" have no share in the world to come.

Notice the emphasis laid upon the "kings of Israel", to exclude Solomon from this class of the wicked, though Scripture employs the words "and he did that, etc." with regard to him; see 1 Kings 11.16. When the authors of the Mishnah decided to count Solomon among the kings who have no share in the world to come, David appeared to them in a vision, and prostrated himself before them that they should change their decision. Others narrate that a fire broke out from the holy of holies, and consumed everything around them, forcing them to interrupt their discussions. Later they intended to take it up again (this is how הדר עלה, read הדרו עלה, is to be understood in Yerushalmi; comp. חזרו לשנות in the Tanhumas), but finally they gave it up, as they found that their prayers which used to be granted remained now unanswered or, according to another view, because a heavenly voice pleaded for Solomon; comp. the references at the beginning of the note. Targum Sheni 1.2, 5, seems to take Solomon as the promised Messiah. On the controversy among the Church Fathers concerning the salvation of Solomon, see Seymour *Tales of King Solomon* 187–188.

⁶⁰ PR 6, 25a. Here it is also stated that the Temple "had built itself," the stones broke loose from the quarries and placed themselves in layers on the site of the Temple. The same view is also given in Shir 1.1, 5; Tehillim 24, 208; BaR 14.13; Zohar I, 74a. A similar statement concerning the tabernacle erected by Moses is found in ShR 52.4. For the symbolism of the Temple, see Midrash Tadshe 2, and vol. III, p. 165–167.

⁶¹ To harmonize the contradiction between 1 Kings 7.14 and 2 Chron. 2.13, it is assumed that the architect Hiram was a Naphtalite on his father's side and a Danite on his mother's side, a descendant of the Danite Oholiab, the assistant of Bezalel in the errection of the tabernacle; comp. 'Arakin 16a; PR 6, 26a; Josephus, *Antiqui.*, VIII, 3.4; ps.-Jerome on 1 Kings 7.14. As to the view of ps.-Jerome on 2 Chron. 2.13, according to which צרי in this passage of Chron. means "artist" (צָיָר), see Ginzberg, *Haggada bei den Kirchenv.*, 74–75.

⁶² Derek Erez 1 (end). Comp. the parallel passages cited by Tawrogi, *ad loc.*, and Epstein, *Mikkadmoniyyot*, 111. See also vol. V, pp. 95–96 and Index, s. v. "Paradise, Entering Alive".

⁶³ PR 6, 24b–25a. Comp. vol. III, p. 176; note 65. On the brazen altar which was withdrawn from use by Solomon on the occasion of the dedication of the Temple (1 Kings 8.64), see Midrash Tannaim 54; Mekilta Bahodesh 11, 73a.

⁶⁴ Tan. B. I, 43; Tan. Noah 11. As to the blessings which came upon the world at the erection of the Temple and disappeared at its destruction, see ARN 4, 19–20 (second version 5, 18–19); Tan. B. IV, 5, and the parallel passages cited by Schechter and Buber.

⁶⁵ Mo'ed Katan 9a; Shabbat 30a; Sanhedrin 107b; Tan. B. II, 22 (here it is said that the door of the holy of holies did not open of itself until Solomon had David's coffin brought into the sanctuary), and IV, 83; ShR 8.1 (here it is said that the ark measured exactly ten cubits, and the opening of the door of the sanctuary was exactly the same measure; hence it was impossible to bring in the ark; comp. note 330 on Vol. III, p. 158), and 44.2; BaR 14.3 and 15.13; Tehillim 7, 66, and 24, 207–208; PR 2, 6b; Koheleth 4.2; Targum Ps. 76.17 and 132.10; Targum 2 Chron. 7.10. Comp. also BR 35.3; Justin Martyr, *Dialogue*, 36; vol. III, p. 159.

⁶⁶ PR 6, 25b. Comp. note 102, end, on vol. IV, p. 41. According to another legend, David begrudged himself food and other necessities of life, so that Solomon should have plenty of gold and silver for the vessels of the temple; but God would not allow him to make use of the money left him by his father, because the latter kept his treasures in the time of the great famine, instead of using them to alleviate the sufferings of the poor; comp. vol. IV, p. 111, and DR. 2.27.

⁶⁷ אינקא "a goat", from ינק "sucked"; comp. Hebrew יונק and Aramaic ינוקא, as well as Hebrew טלה "lamb", and Aramaic טליא "lamb", "youth". The Assyrian *uniku* is to be explained in the same manner. As to the prosthetic א, it is to be remarked that in primae yod verbs the use of such an א is the rule in Syriac, whereas in Judeo-Aramaic it is not very frequent.

⁶⁸ Read שורינקא "falcon" instead of שונרא "cat".

⁶⁹ Targum Sheni 1.2, 5–7. Other versions of the description of the throne (more or less different from that given in Targum Sheni) are found in Abba Gorion 4–8; *Panim Aherim* 57; *Kolbo*, No. 119, republished from there by Jellinek in BHM II, 83–85; Ma'asiyyot (Gaster's edition) 78–79; Midrash on the Throne of Solomon, published from a MS. by Perles in *Monatsschrift* XXI, 128–133, and hence in BHM V, 34–37 (a very fantastic description, in which also the demons play a part; they fly with Solomon through the air "between heaven and earth" before he takes his seat); Yerahmeel 84, 251–253; Esther R. 1.2, 12; Midrash Shir 31b. Comp. also Shu'aib, who quotes from Targum (Sheni) a description of the throne different from that found in our texts, and further R. Bahya's introduction to his commentary,

who seems to have been acquainted with the Midrash published by
Perles; comp. also the following note. On the "seven patriarchs" see
PR 7, 29b, and on the other distinguished men whose images were en-
graved on the throne, see Index, under the respective names.

⁷⁰ BaR 12.17; Shir 6.4; Esther R. 1.1, 12; DR 5.6; PK 1, 7a–7b.
The descriptions of the throne as given in the later sources state that
there were inscriptions on the throne or on the animals thereof which
reminded him of his duties as king and judge. BaR, *loc. cit.*, contains
many symbolic explanations of the six steps of Solomon's throne.
According to one explanation, Solomon's throne was fashioned after
the pattern of the divine throne; now since God's throne is in the seventh
heaven, therefore the seat Solomon occupied was also above six
elevations; Comp. note 39 on Vol. IV, p. 31. The legends concerning
Solomon's throne are treated in detail by Cassel, *Der Thron Salomos*
and in his edition of Targum Sheni, as well as by Salzberger, *Salomos
Thron*. Comp. also Gaster, *Exempla*, No. 115.

⁷¹ This etymology of the name Necho, connecting it with Hebrew
נכה רגלים "lame", is very old, as may be seen from the Peshitta and
Targum on 2 Kings 23.29. Comp. also PK 27, 168a. The daughter
of Pharaoh (= Shishak), whom Solomon took as wife, is called Bithiah
in Targum on 2 Chron. 8.11. This is very likely due to a confusion of
Shishak's daughter with the one of his predecessor, the foster-mother
of Moses; comp. note 60 vol. II, p. 271 and Index, s. v. "Bithiah".

⁷² Abba Gorion 2–4; Esther R. 1.2, 10.; Aguddat Aggadot 57–59
(on p. 59, top, read של מ׳=מצרים של; "Alexandria of Egypt" is the usual
way in which the Rabbis refer to Alexandria); *Panim Aherim* 57–59;
Kolbo 119 (= BHM II, 83); WR 20 (beginning); Koheleth 9.2; Tan.
B. V., 7; Targum 1 and Targum Sheni 1.2. Comp. further vol. IV, pp.
182 and 368. The sources quoted differ with regard to the details
of the "wandering of the throne", but agree that none but Solomon and
his descendants were able to make use of the throne, whereas the pagan
rulers who attempted to ascend it not only failed of their purpose, but
were punished for their efforts.

⁷³ Esther R. 1.2, 12, where the Tanna R. Eleazar the son of R.
Jose, who visited Rome about 170 C. E., states that he saw fragments
of Solomon's throne in Rome. On this Tanna's visit to Rome, see
Graetz, *Geschichte*, IV, 191. Here also it is stated that only "Cosmocrators", like Nebuchadnezzar and Cyrus, had the privilege of making
use of this throne; Ahasuerus had therefore to be satisfied with a rep-

lica and was not permitted to sit on the original, because he ruled only over one hundred and twenty-seven provinces. Comp. vol. VI, p. 454, top.

74 The great animal race was under the supervision of the official mentioned in 1 Kings 4.19, whose duties are explained in this manner. See also Sanhedrin 12a, where he is said to have been the superior of the other twelve, each of whom served one month. Others maintain that he exercised his functions only in leap years, performing his duties during the additional month.

75 Midrash published by Perles from a MS. in *Monatsschrift*, XXI, 134–136, and reprinted by Jellinek in BHM V, 37–39. On pp. 38–39 read לכרות כחדקל ופרת "He will dig channels as deep as the Tigris and Euphrates"; the subject is קטן שבישראל mentioned before. The Naphtalites were swift runners (see vol. II, p. 245), and the Gadites excelled in military skill; see note 393 on vol. II, p. 145. Index, s. v.

76 PK 6, 58a–58b; PR 16, 81b; BaR 21.19; Tehillim 50, 280; Baba Mezi'a 86b; Tan. Pinehas 12; Koheleth 2.7 and 9.11; comp. also DR 1.5 (parallel passages are cited on margin); Baba Mezi'a Mishnah 7.1; Matthew 7.29.

77 This hero of the Arabic legend is known in Jewish sources only as the father of "medicine"; comp. note 75, on vol. I, p. 174. The attempt of Venetianer, *Asaf Judaeus*, 18. *seq.*, to distinguish between the legendary Asaph and the author of medical books bearing the same name is not to be taken seriously.

78 "To prepare for a journey" in Jewish parlance means "to do good as long as life lasts, before the great journey to the great beyond is begun;" comp. Ketubot 67b.

79 Ma'aseh ha-Nemalah published several times separately and also in BHM V, 22–26. The Arabic origin of this legend is obvious, and the Arabic original is still in existence, though less known than the Hebrew translation; see *Hebräische Bibliographie*, XIII, 105, and Jellinek, Introduction to BHM V, 11–13. Salzberger, *Salomo-Sage*, 90, published an Arabic text containing the first part of Ma'aseh ha-Nemalah, but did not recognize the nature of the text. Comp. also Gaster, *Exempla*, No. 343 and Seymour *Tales of King Solomon* 80–99. See further *Ben ha-Melek*, XVI, where David is said to have found an inscription upon which a king told of himself that he had ruled a thousand years, destroyed a thousand cities, annihilated a thousand armies, and married a thousand princesses. This is only a somewhat different version of the inscription by Shadad supposed to have been found by Solomon.

[80] That means: He fails to pay attention to the Yod in לא ירבה (Deut. 17.16–17); comp. also Matthew 5.18.

[81] Yerushalmi Sanhedrin 2, 20c; WR 19.2; ShR 6.1; Tan. Wa-Era 5; Tan. B. II, 18; Aggadat Bereshit 75, 146. It is worthy of notice that Solomon is censured for having married many wives, but ʌot for having married foreign women. Comp. note 16.

[82] On the Shamir, see vol. I, p. 34, and the notes appertaining thereto. The Tannaim speak of the Shamir as having been created (in the twilight between the sixth day and the Sabbath of creation; see references in note 99 on vol. I, p. 83) *ad hoc*, that is, for the use of the sanctuary. Accordingly it disappeared after the destruction of the Temple. See, *e. g.*, Tosefta Sotah 15.1. The old sources do not state explicitly whether it was a mineral, plant, or animal; but the tradition which considers it to have been some kind of an insect represents the view of the old authorities; see note 165 on vol.. I, p. 34. The Testament of Solomon, however, seems to regard the Shamir as a stone; see note 56. In an Abyssinian legend the Shamir is supposed to have been a kind of wood; see Seymour, *Tales of King Solomon*, 149.

[83] For Ashmedai in the Solomon legend, see Ginzberg, *Jewish Encyclopedia*, s. v. "Asmodeus". The Aramaic origin of the name Asmodeus is pointed out there.

[84] As to the demons being present at the debates of the scholars in the academies, see Berakot 6a (top). The demons are divided into three classes: 1) the angel-like; 2) the human-like; 3) the animal-like. Asmodeus and his family are "Jewish demons", *i. e.*, they profess the true religion, and observe the Torah. See Zohar III, 253a and 277a (below). According to the Arabs, there are different religions among the genii, as among men, and this view is "Judaized" by the Zohar. The older view considers the demons to be either fallen angels, or at least spirits akin to them. See Index, s. v. "Demons".

[85] The guardian bird of the Shamir is called תרנגולא ברא, "the wild cock", in the Talmud, where it is identified with the biblical דוכיפת (Lev. 11.19), usually rendered by "hoopoe". The important part played by the hoopoe in the later Solomon legend (comp. note 39) is very likely to be explained by Arabic folk-lore; comp. Grünbaum, *Gesammelte Aufsätze*, 39, *seq.* According to some it was the eagle which brought the Shamir from paradise, see Tehillim 78.351 = Yalkut II.182; vol. I, p. 34.

[86] Gittin 68a–68b (for a correct text use must be made of Maʻ-asiyyot 75–78 (Gaster's edition and Makiri, Prov. 20, beginning);

Tehillim 78, 351–353; Likkutim I, 20b–21b; BHM VI, 106–107; *Neweh Shalom*, 53–55; *Hibbur Ma'asiyyot*, No. 4; Manzur al-Dhamari, 13–14; Targum on Eccles. 1.12; Midrash Shir 29a–30a.   In contrast to Babli and the above-mentioned sources dependent upon it, the Palestinian sources maintain that it was an angel who, disguised as Solomon, occupied the throne during the time that the real Solomon wandered about through the world as a beggar; comp. Yerushalmi Sanhedrin 2, 20c; PK 27, 168b–169a; Tan. B. III, 55-56; Tan. Ahare 1 and Wa-Ethanan 2; Shir 1.1, 10 and 3.17; Ruth; R. 2.14; Koheleth 1.12, 2.2, and 9.12.   Comp. also Megillah 11b (top; on the text see Aggadat Esther 7); Sanhedrin 29b; ShR 30.16; Aggadat Shir 3,33. In the Babylonian version of the legend Persian influence is apparent. It is, however, doubtful whether one is justified in assuming Persian influence in the Palestinian version.   Comp. *R.E.J.* XVII, 59, *seq.*; Ginzberg, *Jewish Encyclopedia*, II, s. v. "Asmodeus" and Gaster, *Exempla*, No. 114.

⁸⁷ Mishle 15, 78–79; on the text, see R. Bahya, Pekude (beginning).

⁸⁸ The marrying of foreign women is not accounted as a sin unto him; comp. notes 16 and 81.

⁸⁹ According to 1 Kings 14.21, Naamah the Ammonitish woman was the mother of Rehoboam; hence the ancestress of the Messiah, who is to be a descendant of the Davidic kings.   Comp. Baba Kamma 38b; BR 50.10; Index, s. v. "Messiah".   The text explicitly states: שיצא ממנה משיח בן דוד.

⁹⁰ This city is called משכמם, probably an intentional corruption of עם כמש, which, though it stands for Moab in Num. 21.29, might be taken for Ammon in accordance with Jud. 11.24.

⁹¹ *'Emek ha-Melek* 14d–15a and 108c–109d, whence it is incorporated in BHM II, 86–87.   Comp. also Azulai, *Midbar Kedemot*, 96, No. 24.   The relation of the Jewish legend to the Arabic one, published by Salzberger, *Salomo-Sage*, 124, *seq.*, needs careful examination; see Midrash Shir 29b–30a, Steinschneider, *Hebräische Bibliographie*, XVIII, 57–58 and Gaster, *Exempla*, No. 404.   The old Jewish sources often speak of the "two precious doves", Ruth the Moabitish woman and Naamah the Ammonitish woman, on whose account Ammon and Moab escaped destruction; comp. BR 50.10; Baba Kamma 38a, Yebamot 63a. But the authors of the Talmud (comp. Yebamot 77a) speak of David playing with his grandson Rehoboam, and accordingly are of the opinion that Solomon married Naamah the Ammonitish woman, the mother of Rehoboam, during his father's lifetime.   This view is shared by Aphraates,

461. The assertion of Ephraem on 1 Kings 14.25 that Naamah misled her son into idolatry is not found in the talmudic-midrashic literature. Kimhi, 1 Kings, *loc. cit.*, is the first to mention it. Comp. note
18 on vol. IV, p. 184.

⁹² The feet of demons resemble those of the cock; see Berakot
6a; Zohar III, 309a. On the feet of angels, see vol. I, p. 302.

⁹³ Gittin 68b; Tehillim 78, 353. Comp. also the references cited
in note 86. A different view is given in the Talmud, *loc. cit.*, and elsewhere, to the effect that Solomon never regained the throne, but died
(in his wanderings?) as a private man. It is said that Solomon was at
first the ruler over the entire world, then over Tadmur only (on Tadmur,
see vol. IV, p. 149), then over Israel only, and finally he only possessed
the couch upon which he slept; even this possession he did not enjoy
entirely, as he was terrified by evil spirits in his sleep. See Aggadat
Shir 3, 33–34, and (somewhat differently) 1, 6; Shir 3.6; comp. also the
parallel passages cited by Schechter. It was towards the end of his life
that the holy spirit came to him (according to some, he was a prophet;
see Sotah 48b, top; Targum 1 Kings 5.13; Ratner on Seder 'Olam 20;
notes. 8, 25), by means of which he composed three books: Song of Songs,
Proverbs, and Ecclesiastes; see Seder 'Olam 15. On the reasons for
this trilogy, see Aggadat Shir 1, 6. It is the first book, the "holiest of
holy books" (=Hagiographa) upon which Solomon's glory is based,
whereas the last had for a long time to encounter the opposition of
the sages against its admission into the Canon, because the passages
thereof, owing to their obscure language, seem to contradict the dogma
or reward and punishment and other essential doctrines of Judaism;
see Yadayim 3.5; Tosefta 2.14; Shabbat 30b; Mishle 25, 97; PK 8,
68b; PR 18, 90b; WR 28 (beginning); ARN (both versions) 1, 2–3;
Jerome, Eccles. 12.13. On the great esteem in which Songs of Songs
was held (it was taken as an allegorical presentation of the history of
Israel from the beginning of its career until the advent of the Messiah),
see Targum Shir 1.1; Aggadat Shir 1, 4–6 and 10; Midrash Shir 1b;
Shir 1.1; Zohar I, 98b and 135a; quotation from an unknown Midrash
in the anonymous Arabic commentary on Songs of Songs published
by Friedlaender in *Steinschneider—Festschrift*, 54, *seq.* Those who
recite this book like a (love) song will be severely punished for their
sacrilege. See Sanhedrin 101a; Kallah 1, 1b. Solomon composed
his first book while he was still young, songs having a special attraction
for the youth; when he reached the age of manhood he wrote Proverbs,
containing the ripe fruit of a man who knows life; but when he became

old he composed Ecclesiastes, the key-note of which is the vanity
of all human pleasures and desires. See Shir. 1.1; Aggadat Shir 1.6.
In the Zohar reference is made to the following books of Solomon:
1) The book which Ashmedai gave Solomon, from which something bearing on magic is quoted in III, 194b; 2) the book of the wisdom of Solomon,
from which three sayings are quoted (the first is found in Shabbat 33a)
in III, 193b; 3) the book on physiognomy, from which a lengthy passage
is quoted in II, 70a, *seq.*; comp. Davidson, *Sepher Sha'ashuim*, Introduction, LXXXII, *seq.*; 4) Solomon's book on the knowledge of
precious stones in II, 127a (top). The book of Solomon's wise counsels
referred to in I, 225b, is very likely identical with No. 2. Solomon is
probably the author, or rather the redactor of the book (or books)
of the Sons of the East; see Zohar I, 99b, and II, 171b. Comp. note
70 on vol. IV, p. 270. Comp. notes 18 and 24.

⁹⁴ Berakot 18b; Targum 2 Sam. 23.20–25; Zohar I, 105b–106b;
2 Alphabet of Ben Sira 20a. See also the undoubtedly Jewish Haggadah
in ps.-Jerome on 2 Sam. *loc. cit.*

⁹⁵ Berakot 4a = Sanhedrin 16b (on the text see Tosafot and Rabbenu Hananel, *ad loc.*; *Aruk*, s. v. אחר; R. Nissim in *R.E.J.* XLIV, 29
295–296), where the assertion is made that the Cherethites and Pelethites
whose chief was Benaiah (2 Sam. 8.18), represent the Great Synhedrion,
whose president was Benaiah. Mahzor Vitry, 332, is of the opinion
that this Benaiah is not identical with his namesake, the commander-
in-chief of Solomon's army (1 Kings 2.35). The reason for this is probably to be found in the fact that Benaiah, the general of Solomon, was
not a priest (see 1 Kings 2.34, where he acts as executioner, which work
cannot be done by a priest on account of the Levitical laws of purity),
whereas according to the Haggadah, Benaiah, the head of the Synhedrion
was a priest; see Midrash Shir 30a, and 1 Chron. 37.5. Comp. also
Tosafot, *loc. cit.*

⁹⁶ *Ma'aseh-Buch*, No. 230; translated into Hebrew in BHM VI,
124–126; Comp. Gaster, *Exempla*, No. 426.

⁹⁷ Tehillim 39, 255. The legend about the rivalry of the human
organs, without any reference to Solomon and Benaiah, is also found
in Makiri, Prov. 18, 3a; *Orehot Zaddikim*, 25; Shu'aib, Shelah, 83d-
84a. The last-named author offers several other variants for our
texts of Tehillim.

⁹⁸ On Luz see vol. IV, p. 30.

⁹⁹ Sukkah 58a. Another version is found in Yerushalmi Kil'ayim
9, 32c; Ma'asiyyot (Gaster's edition 100). The two servants of Solo-

mon are described in Babli as סופרים "scribes", and hence in Yerushalmi as איסקבטירי, which is ἐσκέπτωρ = *"exceptor"*, "copyist", correctly spelled אסקפטריא in Ma'asiyyot. The words אליחרף ואחיה in Babli are very likely a later addition from Yerushalmi, whereas the original version of Babli spoke of Solomon's "two slaves". Rashi's explanation of כושאי is not acceptable.

100 Tan. B. Introduction, 136; Arabic parallels to this legend are cited by Grünbaum, *Neue Beiträge*, 233, *seq.*, and Salzberger, *Salomo-Sage*, 80. In another version of this legend many new points of interest are introduced; it reads as follows. During a war between Solomon and Hiram the Jewish soldiers were attempting to cross a river on a very hot day. Solomon called upon the birds to protect his soldiers from the heat (comp. note 126 on vol. IV, p. 124), and when Hiram came to see this miracle he was received peaceably, and the war thus ended. While the two kings were conversing, an eagle removed his wing from over Solomon's head, informing him at the same time that the High Priest Joshua (sic!) would die and the king's daughter would marry a bastard. This information the eagle gave to Solomon as he had received it from his spouse. Solomon shut his daughter up in a high tower, etc. as given in the text. Gaster, *Exempla*, No. 336.

[1] WR 12.5. On the delay caused by Solomon's long sleep, see vol. IV, pp. 128–129. See also ER 24, 125, which reads: Jeroboam received the rulership over the tribes as a reward for his courage in calling Solomon to account.

[2] Sanhedrin 101b; vol. IV, p. 53. As to the legal question whether the inhabitants of Abel of Beth-maacah acted in accordance with the law when they surrendered Sheba, who had taken refuge with them, see Tosefta Terumot 7.20; Yerushalmi 8, 46b; BR 94.9; Shemuel 32, 140; Koheleth 9.18. The only excuse given for the inhabitants of this city is that Sheba as a rebel against the "throne of David" had no claim upon them. The Midrashim just quoted (as well as Tan. B. I, 92; PK 10, 87a; Aggadat Bereshit 22, 45–46) maintain that the woman at whose counsel Sheba was killed by the inhabitants of Abel of Beth-maacah was Serah the daughter of Asher, concerning whom see vol. II, p. 116, and Index, s. v. "Paradise, Entering Alive". The Midrashim cited above give, in full, her pleadings with the inhabitants of the city to yield to the demands of Joab for the surrender of Sheba. On the confusion of Sheba with Shemi the son of Gera by ps.-Jerome on 2 Sam. 16.10, see Ginzberg, *Haggada bei den Kirchenv.*, 56–57. About the early history of Jeroboam, comp. the following addition to 1 Kings 12.24 found in Septuagint. There was a man...a servant to Solomon, and his name was Jeroboam, and the name of his mother was Sarira, a harlot...And he built for Solomon Sarira in mount Ephraim, and he had three hundred chariots of horses. He built the citadel with the levies of the house of Ephraim, fortified the city of David, and aspired to the kingdom. And Solomon sought to kill him, and he escaped to Sousakim king of Egypt, and was with him until Solomon died. And Jeroboam heard in Egypt that Solomon was dead, and he spoke in the ears of the king of Egypt, saying: "Let me go, and I will depart into my land"; and Sousakim gave to Jeroboam Ano, the eldest sister of Thelkemina his wife, to be his wife. She was great among the daughters of the king, and she bore to Jeroboam Abijah...And Jeroboam departed out of Egypt, and came into the land of Sarira...And hither the whole tribe of Ephraim assembled, and Jeroboam built

a fortress there. The description of Jeroboam's mother as a harlot is perhaps an old haggadic explanation of her name Zarua צרוע, literally "leper". Comp. Yebamot 63b: אשה רעה צרעת לבעלה "A shrew is like leprosy to her husband," and see also vol. VI, p. 266, note 96.

³ According to Sanhedrin 102a, Jeroboam left Palestine with the intention never to return there again.

⁴ Seder 'Olam 1, and the parallel passages cited by Ratner; Baba Batra 121b. Ahijah is one of the seven whose terms of life overlapped one another, so that they form a chain extending from the creation of the world until the end of time. These seven are: Adam, Methuselah, Noah, Shem, Jacob, Amram, Ahijah, and Elijah, the last of whom continues to live. According to Septuagint 1 Kings 12.24, Ahijah was sixty years old when Ano the wife of Jeroboam (comp. note 2) made him inquire about the outcome of her son's illness; see 1 Kings 14.1, *seq.* Septuagint further differs from the masoretic text of 1 Kings 11, 29, *seq.*, by making the prophet Shemaiah, instead of Ahijah, the bearer of the divine message to Jeroboam.

⁵ BR 35.2; Yerushalmi Berakot 9, 13d (bottom); PK 10, 88a. In the legends of the Hasidim Ahijah figures as the teacher of R. Israel Baal Shem Tob, the founder of the sect; comp. Ginzberg, *Jewish Encyclopedia*, II, 389; see also vol. IV, p. 264. Ahijah suffered a martyr's death: He was executed by Abijah (the wicked king of Judah and not his namesake, the son of Jeroboam, who is praised in the Haggadah for his piety; comp. vol. IV, p. 183), as was his contemporary Shemaiah by Basha the wicked king of Israel. See Midrash Aggadah Num. 30.5.

⁶ Jeroboam was as distinguished a scholar as his master, the prophet Ahijah; see Tehillim 5; 55, and comp. also MHG I, 412.

⁷ Sanhedrin 102a. Ahijah and Jeroboam discussed the mysteries of the divine throne (מעשה מרכבה). The angels therefore asked God: "Dost Thou reveal the secrets of the Torah to this man who is going to set up two calves to be worshipped?" God rejoined: "Is this man at present righteous or wicked?" "Righteous", replied the angels. Whereupon God said: "I deal with a man as he is, not as he will be". See Tehillim 5, 55. Comp. note 215 on vol. I, p. 265. The opposite view is given in Zohar Hadash, Bereshit (end) and Ahare (end), where it is said that God had intended to take away Jeroboam from this world while he was still young and pious; but at the pleading of the angels He did not carry out His intention. Later, when Jeroboam forsook God

and His Torah, the angels realized that in their short-sightedness they pleaded for the life of a terrible sinner.

⁸ Seder 'Olam 15. That Jeroboam persisted in his evil ways, notwithstanding the miracle performed by the prophet of Judah (on this miracle, see Tan. B. III, 10; Tan. Tehillim 12), was the fault of the false prophet of Beth-el (1 Kings 13.11, *seq.*) who persuaded the king that no miracle took place at all, and supported his words by the fact that the prophet of Judah was killed by a lion, from which incident one ought to conclude that he was not a true prophet; Josephus, *Antiqui.*, VIII, 9. For further details concerning the true prophet of Judah and the false prophet of Bethel, see PK 2, 14b–15a, and the parallel passages cited by Buber, *ad loc.*, and Ratner's note 29 on Seder 'Olam 20, as well as the references cited in note 133 on vol. IV, p. 51. One might infer the great merit of hospitality from the fact that the false prophet of Beth-el received a revelation (see 1 Kings 13.20) as a reward for his kindness towards the prophet of Judah to whom he offered hospitality; Sanhedrin 103b; ER 12, 60–61.

⁹ Sanhedrin 101b; comp. vol. IV, p. 257. As to the view that only members of the house of David were privileged to sit down in the Temple (*i. e.*, עורה "Temple court"), see note 88 on vol. IV, p. 102 and comp. also Josephus, *Antiqui.*, VIII, 4.2, who takes pains to point out that on the occasion of the dedication of the Temple Solomon sat down and then rose for his prayer. Another legend charges the people rather than Jeroboam with the sin of idolatry. Intoxicated with wine at the coronation of Jeroboam, they urged him to erect idols; but not being sure that they would not change their mind on becoming sober, he delayed his decision till the following day. When he saw that the people persisted in their demand, he yielded to them on the condition that the members of the Synhedrion be killed (or, according to others, removed from office), so that one might worship idols without fear of being executed for the offence. Jeroboam then sent emissaries through the entire country to entice the pious to worship idols. These emissaries used to address the people in the following manner: The most illustrious generation was that of the wilderness (see vol. III, p. 79), and it worshipped the golden calf, without receiving severe punishment. Our king therefore desires to follow the example set by this generation. It was Jeroboam's pride and ambition which made him forsake his God. He knew that in the Sabbatical year the king is commanded to read the word of God to the people in the Temple (see Deut. 31.10), and as long as Israel should make pilgrimages to Jerusalem, Rehoboam would in-

306

evitably appear to the entire nation as the real king. Jeroboam therefore established the worship of the calves, and in this way prevented the people from going up to Jerusalem. He abolished not only the three festivals, when pilgrimages were made, but also the Sabbaths; Yerushalmi 'Abodah Zarah 1, 39b; Jerome on Hos. 7.4–7. See also the quotation from an unknown Midrash in Shu'aib, Nizzabim 114a, where it is likewise said that Jeroboam claimed to be the legitimate king of Israel on account of his Ephraimitic descent. At first, however, he refused to accept the offered crown because of his poverty; whereupon the people (or, according to some, Ahijah) bestowed great wealth upon him; Aggadat Shir 95, according to the reading of Makiri, Is. 7, 105.

¹⁰ Koheleth 2.11, 3. On Jeroboam's father see vol. IV, pp. 179–180. At Shechem Israel renounced not only his allegiance to the house of David, but also his loyalty to God and his sanctuary, (see 1 Kings 12.16, where לאהליך is taken to be an "emendation of the Scribes" for לאלהיך "to thy gods"); the salvation of Israel will therefore not come before Israel "seeks the Lord their God, David their king, and the sanctuary" which God in His great goodness had given to His people; Shemuel 13, 84.

¹¹ According to the Rabbis, the Bible forbids one to dwell in Egypt. Comp. Mekilta Beshallah 2, 28b; Yerushalmi Sukkah 55b; Esther R. 1.3 (פתיחתא).

¹² Eldad 25–26.

¹³ His real name was Zebub, "fly", and he is called Shishak (from *Shuk*, "desire"), because he longed for the death of Solomon whom he feared to attack; Seder 'Olam 20; Aggadat Shir 7, 43. Comp. Esther R. 1.2, 13.

¹⁴ On the history of the throne, see vol. IV, pp. 159–160.

¹⁵ Pesahim 119a. On the further history of these treasures see vol. II, pp. 125–126. Three returned to the place whence they came: Israel, the Torah, and the treasures. Israel came originally from Babylon (Abraham from the other side of the river), and returned thither after having been exiled from the Holy Land; the Torah came from heaven, and the letters of the tables ascended to heaven after Moses broke the tables (see vol. III, p. 129); the treasures which came from Egypt returned thither; Pesahim 87a; Mekilta Amalek 1, 53b; ARN 41, 132–133; second version 47, 130.

¹⁶ Seder 'Olam 16; Yerushalmi Yebamot 16, 15a; BR 56.20; WR 33.5; Ruth R. 4.8; Shemuel 18, 100; comp. Josephus, *Antiqui.*, VII, 11.3, who also maintains that Abijam (= Abijah in 2 Chron. 13.1)

died directly after his victory over Jeroboam. Abijah, in speaking of the supporters of Jeroboam as "sons of Belial" (see 2 Chron. 13.7, where the Hebrew representing "vain men" is בני בליעל), insulted the prophet Ahijah, who more than anybody else contributed to the elevation of Jeroboam to the throne of Israel.

¹⁷ Mo'ed Katan 28b. According to the Kabbalists, the son of Abijah will be the Ephraimitic Messiah; Zohar Hadash Balak (end). Besides Abijah there were others who, like him, disregarded the command of Jeroboam against pilgrimages to Jerusalem, and by clever ruses fooled the guards at the frontier. The descendants of these pious men celebrated the fifteenth of the month of Ab as a festival by bringing sacrifices to the Temple; see Yerushalmi Ta'anit 4, 68b; Targum 1 Chron. 2.54. Comp., however, Babli Ta'anit 28a, and Megillat Ta'anit 5.9–10, where the pious men, who at the risk of their lives made pilgrimages to Jerusalem, are said to have lived at the time when the Greek government decreed against the Jews ordinances "like those of Jeroboam". With regard to Jeroboam's edict against pilgrimages to Jerusalem, see Yerushalmi 'Abodah Zarah 1, 39b, where the text seems to be corrupt, though Yalkut II, 542, on Hos. 7, has the same reading as our texts.

¹⁸ 'Abodah Zarah 44a; Vulgate 1 Kings 15.13; Jerome on Hos. 4, 14. The assonance of "Phallus" and מ[ו]פלצת may have suggested this assumption. Comp., however, Josephus, *Antiqui.*, VIII, 10.3, who quotes Herodotus of Halicarnassus to the effect that the king of Egypt (*i. e.*, Shishak, who, shortly before Asa, conquered Jerusalem) left behind him pillars upon which were engraved the secret parts of women. To reconcile the contradiction between 1 Kings 15.10 and 2 Chron. 13.2, it is asserted that after repenting of her idolatrous practices, the name of Asa's mother was changed; her father's name, too, was changed; the latter was none other than the wicked Absalom. See Targum 2 Chron., *loc. cit.*, and 15.16. Comp. also Josephus, *Antiqui.*, VIII 10.1, and ps.-Jerome on 2 Chron. 15.16. The latter quotes the Jewish tradition, according to which the water of the brook of Kidron turned into fire, and burned the image of the idol which Asa threw into it. The commentators Kimhi and Gersonides on 1 Kings 15.2, as well as ps.-Rashi on 2 Chron. 13.2, call attention to the fact that it was not the mother, but the grandmother, of Asa who had been addicted to idolatry. This is another attempt to reconcile the contradiction between 1 Kings 15.2 and 15.10. Comp. note 91 on vol. IV, p. 171.

¹⁹ Pesahim 119a; Seder 'Olam 16; Esther R. 1.2. Comp. vol. II, pp. 125–126, and vol. IV, pp. 159, 192. The number in the hostile army (comp. 2 Chron, 14.8) was established by Asa from the number of the chariots; comp. Mekilta Beshallah 1, 27b. Most historians identify Zerah with Osorchan I, the successor of Sesanchis (Shishak). It is noteworthy that Seder 'Olam merely states that Zerah restored to Asa what Shishak had won in the battle with Rehoboam, and does not mention that Zerah had in turn taken it from Shishak in war. This latter statement appears first in the Talmud.

²⁰ Pesahim 119a; Seder 'Olam 16. Comp. the references at the beginning of the preceding note.

²¹ Ekah, introduction, XXX, and Tehillim 79, 358, which read: Four kings expressed four different wishes, and God granted to each of them his desire. David prayed for strength to attack his enemies (Ps. 18.38), and God granted his prayer (1 Sam. 30.17). Asa said: "I have no strength to attack my enemies; but if God so wills, I shall defeat them by pursuing them"; his prayer was heard (2 Chron. 14. 11–12). Jehoshaphat said: "I can neither attack the enemy nor pursue him; but I shall leave the carrying on of the war to God, whom I shall continue to praise and glorify"; God defeated the enemies of Jehoshaphat, while the pious king was engaged in praising Him (2 Chron. 20.21–22). Hezekiah said: "I cannot attack the enemy, nor pursue him, nor engage in continually praising God; but I pray that He should annihilate him while I sleep"; God destroyed the army of the Assyrians while the Jews were asleep (2 Kings 19.35). According to the Haggadah, the words addressed by the prophet Azariah to Asa and his people (2 Chron. 15.3, *seq*.) contain a prophecy and are to be translated: And for long seasons Israel will be without the true God, etc.; WR 19. 9; Josephus, *Antiqui*., VIII, 12.2.

²² Sotah 10a. See also Nedarim 31b,where it is stated that the servitude of Israel in Egypt was a punishment for Abraham's having made the scholars engage in war against the kings. On the view that Asa was distinguished for having his strength in his feet, see vol. I, p. 59.

²³ Seder 'Olam 16; Tosefta Sotah 12.1–2.

²⁴ Seder 'Olam 17; Tosefta Sotah 12.13.

²⁵ Pesahim 119a; comp. vol. II, pp. 125–126; note 19.

²⁶ Tehillim 15.118 הצפירה is very likely a gloss to הדירינון.

²⁷ BaR 21.6; Tan. B. IV, 152; Tan. Pinehas 3. According to another view quoted in these sources, Jehoshaphat did not don his royal

robes from the moment he heard that God had decreed the punishment of Asa's descendants; see note 24, as well as the following note. Jehoshaphat had to pay dearly for his friendship and close connection with the wicked house of Omri; his commercial undertakings ceased to prosper from the time he associated himself with the godless; ARN 9, 42; Alphabet of Ben Sira 14a, as a comment upon 2 Chron 20.37.

²⁸ Ketubot 103b; Makkot 24a; Tehillim 15, 118. Comp. also Yerushalmi Sotah (end), where the king's humility is praised (read שרץ מן). Notwithstanding his lack of regard for scholars (vol. IV, p. 184), Asa nevertheless married the daughter of the prophet Hanani (2 Chron. 16.7), and the issue of this marriage was Jehoshaphat. The prophet Eliezer, who was active during the reign of Jehoshaphat (2 Chron. 20.37), was a grandson of Hanani, and accordingly בן דודוהו in the verse referred to is to be translated "the son of his uncle"; ps.-Jerome, 2 Chron. 20.31 and 37.

²⁹ Yebamot 7b, given as a haggadic interpretation of החצר החדשה of 2 Chron. 20.5. For another Haggadah on this verse see ps.-Jerome. *ad loc.*

³⁰ Yerushalmi Berakot 9, 13b; Tehillim 4, 3. See also Babli Berakot 10a (bottom), which contains an allusion to it not recognized by Rashi (caption מקובלני).—In reality God had condemned Jehoshaphat to death for having joined Ahab in war, and he was only saved by his prayer. He lived seven years longer, a period which Scripture puts to his son's account, not to his own. Seder 'Olam 17; notes 24 and 27.

³¹ Megillah 11a; PRE 11. Comp. note 82 on vol. I, p. 178. See also Septuagint 1 Kings 18.10, where Obadiah's words to Elijah read: "There is not a nation or a kingdom, whither my lord hath not sent to seek thee; and if they said: He is not here, then hath he (Ahab) set fire to the kingdom and its territories, because he hath not found thee." This undoubtedly presupposes that Ahab had power over all the kingdoms. Comp. Index, s. v. "Cosmocrators".

³² Esther R 1.1. ER 9, 49, counts only two hundred and thirty-two, who, according to 1 Kings 20.15, are supposed to be the sons of the conquered kings whom Ahab held as hostages. Of them it is said that life in the midst of Jewish surroundings made them pious, and through them God granted victory to Ahab in his war with Benhadad. According to Esther R., *loc. cit.*, twenty of the satrapies owing allegiance to Ahab were devastated by the famine which took place

in his time, and therefore only two hundred and thirty-two hostages are mentioned in 1 Kings, *loc. cit.*

³³ Shemuel 2, 47; Koheleth 6.3; Esther R. 1.1; Nispahim 44. On the winter and summer residences of the rich, see Midrash Shir 24a; on Ahab's great wealth see Berakot 61b; ER 9, 49. On Ahab's wicked children, see Koheleth 1.18.

³⁴ Sanhedrin 102b: 103b. Comp. also Tan. Shemot 29 and Gaster, *Exempla* pp. 184–185. In Tanḥuma the story of the Talmud is elaborated. In the latter passage the great learning of Ahab and of the two other wicked kings (Jeroboam and Manasseh) is emphasized. See also MHG I, 412; vol IV, pp. 180 and 278.

³⁵ Yelammedenu in Yalkut II, 219; Tan. B. II, 16; Tan. Shemot 29. During the reign of Ahab Israel was addicted to idolatry, but possessed the great virtue of keeping away from slander and backbiting. During the time of Samuel and Saul the Israelites were just the reverse: they were devoted to the study of the Torah (even young boys and girls were learned in the law), but they had "evil tongues". The former were victorious in their wars, the latter were unfortunate in their military expeditions. One may infer from this that one is severely punished for the "evil use of his tongue". See Yerushalmi Peah 1, 16a; WR 26.2; DR 5.10; Tehillim 7, 67; PK 4, 31b; Tan. B. IV, 106; Tan. Hukkat 4; BaR 19.2. Ahab's generation did not reveal the hiding-place of Elijah and the other hundred prophets; but David's abode in his flight from Saul was betrayed many a time. The great victory of Ahab and his people over the Syrians was the reward for their obervance of the Sabbath. Likewise under Ahab's son it was because of the observance of the Sabbath that Israel was victorious in the war against Mesha. See Mekilta RS, 162 = Midrash Gadol 124.

³⁶ Seder 'Olam 20; Tosefta Sanhedrin 14.15; Babli 89b; Josephus, *Antiqui.*, VIII, 14.15. The first and the last sources take the prophet mentioned in 1 Kings 20.13, 22 and 28 to be Micaiah, whose activity at the time of Ahab is spoken of in 1 Kings 22.8.

³⁷ WR 26.8; Tan. B. III, 84; Tan. Emor 3; Shemuel 24, 121; Yerushalmi Sanhedrin 11, 30c. Comp. also Baraita di-Yeshua' 46, where בן הדד should be read instead of חזאל.

³⁸ Sanhedrin 48b; Tosefta 4.6. Two views are given there with regard to Ahab's claims upon Naboth's possessions. According to one, the king and Naboth were cousins, and when the latter died without issue, his possessions reverted to the nearest of kin, that is, Ahab.

According to the other view, the property of those executed for lèse majesté fell to the royal treasury; comp. vol. IV, p. 126. That Naboth was of noble descent is asserted by Josephus, *Antiqui.*, VIII, 13.7.

[39] PR 25, 127a. Josephus, *Antiqui.*, VIII, 13.7, speaks of the *three* false witnesses who testified against Naboth. This presupposes the old Halakah according to which in cases involving capital punishment three witnesses (or to be more accurate, one accuser and two witnesses) are necessary. Comp. Ginzberg, *Unbekannte Sekte*, 170, note 5. Naboth's fate illustrates the saying, "Woe unto the wicked and woe to his associate; " Naboth paid with his life for having been on friendly and close relations with the wicked Ahab; Alphabet of Ben Sira, 4b.

[40] PK 25, 160b; Yerushalmi Sanhedrin 10, 28b; Sotah 3, 18d; Ta'anit 25b; PRE 43; Shir 1.5.

[41] Commenting on 1 Kings 22.19, the Rabbis remark that in the heavenly court there were some who pleaded for Ahab's life and others who demanded his death; this is the meaning of Scripture in speaking of the host of heaven standing by God on His right and on His left; Tan. B. I, 96; II, 8 and 84; Tan. Shemot 18 and Mishpatim 15; Yelammedenu in *'Aruk*, s. v. שמאל.

[42] Sanhedrin 89a; Shabbat 102b. But Naboth's soul had to leave the abode of the pious, which is near God, for God tolerates not in His presence those who resort to lies; Sanhedrin and Shabbat *loc. cit.*; Tosefta-Targum 1 Kings 22.21 and 23. On the view that no two prophets express themselves in the same words, see also Aggadat Bereshit 14, 30; Josephus, *Antiqui.*, VIII, 15.4. The last-named author writes: Zedekiah exhorted him (the king) not to hearken to Micaiah, for he did not speak the truth at all. To support his words, he instanced the saying of Elijah, who was a greater prophet to foretell the future than Micaiah. Now Elijah prophesied that the dogs would lick his (Ahab's) blood in the field of Naboth (see 1 Kings 21.19). It was therefore plain that Micaiah was a false prophet, since he contradicted the words of a prophet greater than himself, and asserted that Ahab would be slain in a place three days' journey distant from there. It was, however, subsequently seen that Micaiah did not contradict Elijah: Ahab fell in Ramoth Gilead, but his blood was licked by the dogs in Samaria, when they washed the king's chariot there (1 Kings 22.38). See Josephus, *ibid.*; comp. also Sanhedrin 39b; Tosefta-Targum 1 Kings 22.34. Ahab's sad end illustrates the truth of the sayings: "He who honors his enemy

is like an ass", and "He who honors his enemy will meet his death through him". Ahab honored his enemy Ben-hadad, and was slain in the war against him; Alphabet of Ben Sira 10b–11a.

⁴³ Tehillim 78, 350; Shemuel 11, 80. That it was Naaman's missile which struck Ahab is also mentioned by Josephus, *Antiqui.*, XVIII, 15.5; in Targum 2 Chron. 18.33; by Ephraem, 2 Kings 6.1. On the nature of this miracle, see note 44 on vol. IV, p. 88. Ahab was the only Jew slain in this battle; the suffering of the prophet Micaiah who had himself wounded to bring home the truth of his prophecy concerning the fatal result of the war against the Syrians (1 Kings 22. 37; comp. note 36) atoned for the sins of Israel, who were spared further punishment. See Yerushalmi Sanhedrin 11, 30c. This passage, however, is very obscure, and its purport probably is that the suffering of the pious Jehoshaphat (see vol. IV, p. 186) had the atoning power.

⁴⁴ Megillah 3a; Mo'ed Katan 28b; Targum Zech. 12.11. Comp., however, Sanhedrin 39b, where 1 Kings 22.36 is explained: And a jubilant song was heard through the battle arrays; the army rejoiced in the final execution of the divine punishment on Ahab.

⁴⁵ Baba Kamma 17a. On the baring of the shoulders as a sign of mourning, see Büchler, *Zeitschrift für alttest. Wissenschaft*, XXI, 81. *seq.*

⁴⁶ Sanhedrin, Mishnah 10.1. On the persons who have no share in the world to come, see note 100, on vol. IV, p. 75. Comp. also note 65 on vol. IV, p. 95.

⁴⁷ Konen 31. Comp. vol. IV, pp. 53 and 107.

⁴⁸ Yerushalmi Sanhedrin 10, 28b, Comp. also ER 9, 49, and Babli 102b, where several authorities are quoted to the effect that Jezebel was mainly responsible for Ahab's wicked life.

⁴⁹ Sanhedrin 39b.

⁵⁰ Sanhedrin 100b, and somewhat different Yerushalmi 10, 28b. On the custom to devote to the Temple gold corresponding to one's increase in weight, see Yoma 38b; Sifra 26.29; Ekah 1, 86–87; comp. further 'Arakin Mishnah 5.1.

⁵¹ Esther R. 1.9. Among the heathen Semiramis and Vashti are considered the two reigning queens. Shemuel 2 (beginning) calls Jezebel "the daughter of a priest", while 1 Kings 16.31 describes her father as a king.

⁵² PRE 17.

⁵³ ShR 31.9; Tan. Mishpatim 9; Tehillim 15.6. Comp. vol. IV, pp. 240–241. According to Gaster, *Exempla*, p. 185, however, Joram

was wicked only "from without", but within he was good, as shown by the sympathy he felt with the sufferings of his people. Comp. 2 Kings 6.30.

54 PK 2, 13; Tan. Ki-Tissa 9; Tosefta-Targum 2 Kings 3.27; Ta'anit 4a; Midrash Tannaim 100; Sifre D., 148; Ephraem, 2 Kings 3. 26–27; Jerome, Micah 6.7; Josephus, *Antiqui.*, IX, 3.2. Comp. Ginzberg, *Haggada bei den Kirchenv.*, 83–86. According to one view (Sanhedrin 39b), the king of Moab brought his son as a sacrifice to an idol and not to God.

55 Ta'anit 5a; comp. also PR 29, 136b–137a; Sanhedrin 12a; Tosefta 2.9; Yerushalmi 1, 18d; Nedarim 6, 39d.

56 Ta'anit 45a; Yerushalmi 1, 64a. Others identify this Joel with Joel the son of Samuel (see note 46 on vol. IV, p. 65), whereas Seder 'Olam 20 (but see Ratner, *ad loc.*) maintains that Joel, Nahum, and Habakkuk were contemporaries of Manasseh. A fourth view found in PK 16.128b declares Joel, Amos, Zephaniah, Haggai, Zechariah, Malachi, Ezekiel, and Jeremiah to have been the eight post-exilic prophets. The reading is not certain; some texts have Micah and Habakkuk instead of Joel and Jeremiah. Jerome, Joel 1.1, very likely on the authority of his Jewish masters, maintains that Joel lived shortly after Hosea, and therefore their books follow one another. Besides the literal interpretation of Joel's prophecy, according to which a grievous famine took place in his time which was caused by the locust (see Ta'anit, *loc. cit.*, and Jerome 1.6), there is also a symbolic explanation maintaining that the prophet refers to the devastations brought upon Israel by the "four kingdoms" (comp. Index, s. v.), and therefore he speaks of four kinds of locusts. See Targum and Jerome on Joel 1.4 (he writes: *Hebraei interpretantur*); WR 5.3. Comp. Rahmer, *Die Commentarii zu den XII Kleinen Propheten*, Joel, 4–6.; note 20 on vol. IV, p. 260. On the etymologies of the names Joel and his father Pethuel given by Jerome, Joel 1.1, see Rahmer, *ibid.*, 1–3, and the references in note 20 on vol. IV, p. 260. For an interesting description of the different kinds of locusts which devastated the Holy Land in Joel's times, see PRK 43a. Comp. also MHG II, 80. As to the statement in PRK that the heart of a certain kind of locust has the shape of the letter Heth, it is to be remarked that to this day this kind of locust is believed to be the only one permitted to be eaten by the Jews of North Africa. On the war against Moab, which took place during the reign of Joram, the contemporary of Joel, see vol. IV, p. 10. This war was caused by the inhuman cruelty of the Moabite king, who

had the bodies of the Edomite kings exhumed and their bones burned to lime. God could not permit such an evil deed to pass unpunished, and the Moabites suffered a crushing defeat at the hands of the allied kings. See Baba Batra 22a; Targum and Jerome (who introduces it by *tradunt Hebraei*) on Amos 2.1. Comp. also Rashi, *ad loc.*

VII. ELIJAH

Vol. IV, (pp. 195–235).

¹ Popularly he is always called Elijah the Prophet (אליהו הנביא); but in the talmudic-midrashic literature Elijah alone, without any qualification, is of more frequent occurrence. The eulogy זכור לטוב "remembered to good" is often added to his name; comp. Berakot 3a; Yerushalmi Terumot 1, 40a; PK 18, 136a; PR 22, 111b; Tan. B. I, 20; II, 7 and 28. In Ecclus. 45.1 this eulogy is added to the name of Moses. See Zunz, *Zur Geschichte*, 321, *seq*.

² Elijah was one of the original inhabitants of Jabesh-Gilead who escaped the war of annihilation waged against this city by the rest of Israel (see Jud. 21.10, *seq*.), and who called themselves "the inhabitants of Gilead" when they returned to their native city after the war, to indicate the difference between themselves and the new settlers. See Tosafot Ta'anit 3a (beginning ויאמר), and, without giving his authority, Bahur, *Tishbi*, s. v. תשבי. Elijah never married, and therefore nothing is said in Scripture concerning his family. Zohar Hadash Ruth 2.1 (beginning ר' נתן); ps.-Matthew 7. Comp. (against it?) the responsum of R. Judai Gaon in תשובות הגאונים (Lyck edition, 19, No. 45); Mishle 30, 105.

³ Baba Mezi'a 114b and Tosefta-Targum 1 Kings 17.13 consider Elijah to have been a priest, but do not identify him with Phinehas. This view is shared by several Church Fathers; comp. Aphraates, 314; Epiphanius, *Haereses*, 55.3; ps.-Epiphanius, *De Vitis Prophetarum*, s. v.; the Armenian pseudepigraph in *Apocrypha Anecdota* II. 164. The identification of Elijah with Phinehas is first met with in ps.-Philo. 48; 48 1–2, and this view prevails in the later Midrashim; comp. PRE 44; Targum Yerushalmi Exod. 6.18; Num. 25.12; Deut. 30.4; BaR 21.3; Tan. Pinehas 1. Comp. Buber on Tan. B. III, 151, note 19. This identification is very liekly presupposed in Sifre N., 131. Comp. vol. III, p. 458; vol. IV, pp. 53–54, and the notes appertaining to them. The tribes of Gad and Benjamin compete with the tribe of Levi for the honor of counting Elijah as theirs; see BR 71.9; ShR 40. 4; ER 18, 97; EZ 15, 199. See the full discussion on this point by Friedmann, introduction to ER 2-12, and Ginzberg, *Haggada bei den Kir-*

chenv., 76–80. The designation of Elijah as "the disciple of Moses" in talmudic literature (Tosefta Sotah 4.8 and Eduyyot, end; Mekilta Beshallah פתיחתא, 24b) is not to be taken literally, since all prophets may aptly be described as the disciples of Moses,"the father of prophecy"; see note 68 on vol. II, p. 276. The real teacher of Elijah was Ahijah the Shilonite; see Yerushalmi 'Erubin 5, 22a, in accordance with Seder 'Olam 1 and Baba Batra 121b; comp. note 4 on vol. IV, p. 180. The description of Elijah as התשבי מתושבי גלעד in 1 Kings 17.1 is said in PRE *loc. cit.*, to mean: Elijah whose name was changed (from Phinehas) and who is destined to bring Israel back to their heavenly Father. The identification of Elijah with Phinehas is also known to Origen, John 6.7; Petrus Damascus (Migne's edition CXLV, 382B); ps.-Jerome on 1 Sam. 2.27. Comp. Ginzberg, *op. cit.* On the identification of Elijah with Khadir by the Arabs, see Friedlaender, *Die Chadhirlegende*, index, s. v. "Elias".

⁴ Phinehas is "the angel of God" mentioned in Jud. 2.1, as well as the prophet in Jud. 6.8. See Seder 'Olam 20; WR 1. Comp. also Ratner's remark on the Seder 'Olam passage referred to. See also Josephus, *Antiqui.*, V, 2.1; note 22, on vol. IV, p. 29.

⁵ Yerushalmi Sanhedrin 10, 28b; Babli 113a; Tosefta-Targum 1 Kings 16.34; EZ 8, 185–186; 2 Alphabet of Ben Sira 36a–36b (Addenda); Midrash 'Aseret Melakim 41. It was love for his people that prompted Elijah to request God for the famine; he hoped that the sufferings of the people would turn God's wrath from them; PR 44, 183a. The people mocked at Elijah, not only on account of the unfulfilled threat hurled at them by him because of their wickedness, but they also derided him for his looks. Elijah was a hairy man (2 Kings 1.8), and when they saw him they would say: "Behold, Elijah curls his locks" PR 26, 129a. Comp. vol. VI, p. 358, note 32.

⁶ Some early rationalists, however, deny that Elijah was fed by ravens; they explain ערבים (1 Kings 17.4) to mean "the inhabitants of the city of Oreb;" BR 33.5; Hullin 5a; Jerome on Is. 15.7 (who gives it as a Jewish tradition). Comp. also Kimhi on 1 Kings, *loc. cit.*, who quotes the opinion according to which ערבים denotes "merchants."

⁷ Tan. B. IV, 165; Tan. Mass'e 8; BaR 23.9; WR 19.1. In opposition to this view it is said in Sanhedrin 113b and Hullin 5a, as well as in BR 33.5, that the ravens brought the meat from the slaughter house of Ahab. According to Aphraates, 314, the ravens brought Elijah his priestly portion (comp. note 3) from the Temple of Jerusalem. Aphraates very likely follows a Jewish tradition.

⁸ Sanhedrin 113 b. When God sent Elijah to inform Ahab of the impending rain (1 Kings 18.1), the prophet exclaimed: "How could rain come, when Israel did not repent of his sins?" God replied: "I sent rain upon the earth when Adam was the only man on it." See Tehillim 117, 480.

⁹ Yerushalmi Sukkah 5, 55a; PRE 33; Jerome, introduction to his commentary on Jonah (he gives the midrashic interpretation of the name Amittai אמיתי, as being connected with אמת in 1 Kings 17.24); BR 98.11. Koheleth R. 8.10 maintains, on the other hand, that the son of the widow at Zarephath was a sinner. Comp. also Luke 4.26, where emphasis is laid on the fact that this widow was not a Jewess. The sources cited at the beginning of this note are of the opinion that she belonged to the tribe of Asher and her deceased husband to that of Zebulun. As to the view that the son of the widow was the future "Messiah of the tribe of Joseph", see note 38 on vol. IV, p. 253. The midrashic basis for this statement is found in the words of Elijah addressed to the widow to the effect that he should receive his portion first and afterwards her son should receive his (see 1 Kings 17.13). By this he wished to convey that at the end of time he would appear as the forerunner of the "Messiah of the tribe of Joseph". According to Tosefta-Targum, *ad loc.*, however, Elijah told the widow that he, being a priest, must receive his priestly portion first (see Num. 15.20), before she and her son could partake of the bread. See ER 18, 97–98 (read לבשר, instead of לבבל), where both explanations of 1 Kings, *loc. cit.*, are given.

¹⁰ BR 50.11; PR 3, 10a. Comp., however, PRE 33, which mentions the insinuating reproaches made by the widow of Zarephath to Elijah for having taken his lodging with her, a single and unprotected woman.

¹¹ A man owes his life to one who opens his door hospitably for him to enter. Hence Elijah exercised his resuscitating powers not upon his own dead parents, but upon the child of the hostess; ShR 4.8.

¹² Yerushalmi Berakot 5, 9b; Ta'anit 1, 63d. There is a different version of this Haggadah: God entrusted the "key of rain" to Elijah who asked for it, and God Himself retained the "keys of quickening the dead" and the "key of birth". When Elijah further requested that the "key of quickening the dead" should also be given to him, God said that it was not seemly that the master should hold only one key and the servant two. Whereupon Elijah returned the "key of rain". See Sanhedrin 113a; DR 7.6; PR 42, 178a; Tehillim 78, 346; BR 73.4; Ta'anit 2b; Tan. B. I 106 (which says: There are four

keys with which God does not part: the key of sustenance, the key of rain, the key of graves, and the key of the womb of a barren woman), 139, and 135; Targum Yerushalmi Deut. 28.12; 2 Targum Yerushalmi Gen. 30.22; BHM VI, 62. Comp. note 177 on vol. I, p.364. On the dew of resurrection of the dead, see vol. I, pp. 10, 336; vol. IV, p. 333. As to the similarity of the "reviving of the soil by rain" and the quickening of the dead, see Ta'anit 7a; vol. V, p. 119, note 113.

¹³ Tehillim 68, 318. Comp. vol. III, p. 84. The altar upon which Elijah sacrificed had been erected by Saul on his victorious return from the war against Amalek, but was destroyed by the sinful inhabitants of Samaria, and Elijah "repaired the altar of the Lord" (see 1 Kings 18.30). See quotation from an unknown Midrash by Kimhi on 1 Sam. 15.12. Comp. note 64 on vol. IV, p. 68. The law forbidding to sacrifice outside the Temple of Jerusalem was suspended temporarily by Elijah at the command of God. Prophets have no right to abrogate the law, but only to suspend it temporarily; Yebamot 90b; Yerushalmi Ta'anit 2, 65a; WR 23.9; Shemuel 13 (end); BaR 14.1, 113a; Tan. B. IV, 41. Comp. also the references cited by Buber on Shemuel, *loc. cit.* and note 8, on vol. IV, p. 4. According to an unknown Midrash quoted in Midrash Aggada Deut. 12.9, Elijah permitted himself the temporary suspension of this law on the strength of the words of God spoken to Jacob when He announced to him the approaching birth of Benjamin. He said: "A nation among a multitude of Gentiles shall be of thee (Gen. 35.11; גוים =ובקהל=וקהל = Gentiles, *i. e.*, idolatrous and sinful Jews). By these words God revealed to Jacob that Benjamin would have a son (Elijah belonged to this tribe, see note 3), who would perform a great deed among a multitude of Gentiles (=sinful Jews) and would erect an altar outside the holy place.

¹⁴ Tan. B. IV, 165; Tan. Mass'e 8; BaR 23.9. On the talking of animals, see vol. I, pp. 17, 39.

¹⁵ Yalkut II, 214 on 1 Kings 18.26, giving מדרש as source (see the first edition); ShR 15.15; PR 14, 13a. This Haggadah is also known to Christian authors; see Ephraem, 1 Kings 18.19; Chrysostomus, *In Petram et Eliam* I, 765 (edition Fronto Ducaeus); Armenian pseud-epigraph, *Apocrypha Anecdota*, II, 164. Comp. Ginzberg, *Haggada bei den Kirchenv.* I, 80–82.

¹⁶ ShR 29 (end). On a similar "silence of nature", see vol. III, p. 97.

¹⁷ Aggadat Bereshit 76, 148, and from there in Yalkut II, 215, on 1 Kings 18 (first inserted in Leghorn edition, and accordingly R.

Elijah ha-Kohen in his *Midrash Talpiyyot*, s. v. אליהו quotes this Haggadah from Yalkut).

¹⁸ ER 17, 87. Here it is also stated that the miracle or rather the miracles (besides the fire, the small quantity of water poured by Elisha over the hands of Elijah caused ten springs to gush forth) performed by Elijah brought Israel back to God; they gave up their idolatry, and became God-fearing with all their hearts. The afternoon prayer (Minhah) is the most acceptable to God, and it was therefore in this Minhah prayer that Elijah besought God to grant his wishes. See Berakot 6b and Aggadat Bereshit 76, 147, with reference to בעלות המנחה (1 Kings 18.36). He began his prayer with the words: "O Lord, the God of Abraham, Isaac, and Israel". He did not employ the liturgical formula: "God of Abraham, God of Isaac, God of Jacob" (= Israel), that the people should not be misled to believe that there are three gods (anti-Christian). He therefore did not repeat the word God. Elijah further said: "If Thou grantest not my request for the merits of the fathers, do it for the merits of the tribes." See Aggadat Bereshit 76, 148–149. On the merits of the tribes see note 3, on vol. II, p. 187. Elijah, in his great love for Israel, spoke the very bold words: "For Thou didst turn their heart backward" (1 Kings 18. 37), as if God were the cause of Israel's apostasy. See Berakot 31b–32a (which reads: God admitted that He was partly the cause of man's sin, by having created the evil inclination); Yerushalmi Sanhedrin 10, 28c (top); Tan. B. IV, 96; BaR 18.12. Comp. note 571, on vol. III, p. 292. Other explanations of 1 Kings 18.37 are given in Targum and Kimhi, *ad loc.*

¹⁹ Berakot 9b. It is an interpretation of Elijah's double exclamation, "Hear me, hear me!" (1 Kings 18.37). Another interpretation of the double exclamation is found in Yerushalmi Ta'anit 2, 65d: Elijah said: "Hear me for my own merits; hear me for the merits of my disciples." Targum, *ad loc.*, and Aggadat Bereshit 76, 149 offer still other explanations. As to Elijah's desire not to have the miracle misinterpreted by the people, see also Josephus, *Antiqui.*, VIII, 13.5.

²⁰ Midrash Shir 25a; Aggadat Bereshit 76, 149.

²¹ Yoma 21b, where six different kinds of fire are enumerated; comp. vol. I, p. 16. "The majority decides everything"; the fire would never have fallen from heaven, were it not for the fact that the majority of Israel exclaimed on mount Carmel: "The Lord, He is God;" Yerushalmi Ta'anit 3, 66c (towards the end).

²² WR 31.4; Shir 7.6; PK 30, 192a, and Koheleth 11.2, which

read: Elijah prayed that God might remember to Israel the merits of observing the commandments of circumcision and of Sabbath. The words: "and Elijah put his face between his knees" (1 Kings 18.42), are thus explained to mean that he besought God to remember the sign of the covenant, comp. WR *loc. cit.* As to the observance of the Sabbath by the "generation of Ahab", see note 35 on vol. IV, p. 187. Elijah did not for a moment forget the honor due to a king, and he ran before Ahab's chariot as a precursor; Mekilta Bo 13, 14a, with reference to 1 Kings 18, 46. Comp., on the other hand, Josephus, *Antiqui.*, VIII, 13.6, which reads: And the prophet was under a *divine fury*, and ran along with the king's chariot. Against this interpretation of יד ד׳, see Targum *ad loc.*

²³ Yelammedenu in Yalkut II, 219; they are identified with Gideon warriors (their descendants? Jud. 7.5) in Tan. B. I, 138. Comp. also Jerome, Obadiah 1.1, who quotes a Jewish tradition that the hundred prophets hidden by Obadiah (1 Kings 18.4) did not "bow unto Baal", and belonged to the seven thousand whom "Elijah is accused of having ignored". On this rather obscure statement, see Rahmer, *Die Commentarii zu den XII Propheten, Obadja*, 2–3.

²⁴ WR 36 (end); Shabbat 55a; Yerushalmi Sanhedrin 10, 27d; Aggadat Bereshit 10, 24. These sources quote different views as to the time when the "merits of the fathers" ceased to be effective. The times of Elijah, Hosea, Jehoahaz, and Hezekiah are mentioned in this connection. On the different explanations given by the medieval authorities of the statement about the "end of the merits of the fathers", see Tosafot Shabbat, *loc. cit.* (beginning ושמואל); Or Zarua I, 39, No. 106, and II, 12b, No. 23. Comp. also Index, s. v. "Fathers, Merits of".

²⁵ PRE 29. On the zeal displayed by Elijah for the observance of the law of circumcision, see note 103. Elijah was zealous for the honor of God, and hence was ready to appear as the accuser of Israel before God (comp., however, note 18). Jonah was zealous for the honor of Israel, but less so for the honor of God (see note 27 on vol. IV, p. 274). Jeremiah, however, was as zealous for the honor of God as for the honor of His people. Jeremiah therefore remained a prophet all his life, while Elijah was commanded to appoint Elisha as his successor, and Jonah received but two revelations from God. See Mekilta Bo (פתיחתא), 2a; ARN 47, 129. Elijah had no fear of man, and did not flee to the desert to escape Jezebel, but to ascertain his fate at the holy mount of Horeb, for he had noticed that the angel of death had no power

over him, and was anxious to know what God had decided concerning his person. See Zohar I, 209a.

²⁶ Megillah 19b; Josephus, *Antiqui.*, VIII, 13.7. Comp. vol. III, p. 137.

²⁷ Shir 1.6; Aggadat Shir 8, 45; EZ 8, 186; Zohar I, 209a–209b; II. 90b; Zohar Hadash, Noah (towards the end, beginning ר' אליעזר (ור' יהושע.

²⁸ Shir 1.6.

²⁹ This wind was so strong that it nearly brought about the ruin of the entire world, which was swept by it. Of the same violence, but limited to certain places, were the winds which God sent on the sea when Jonah was on his way to Tarshish (Jonah 1.4), and the wind which "smote the four corners of the house" in which Job's sons were (Job. 1.19; vol. II, p. 234). Yerushalmi Berakot 9, 13c; BR 24.4; WR 15.1; Koheleth 1.6; Koheleth Z., 87.

³⁰ Tan. Pekude 2; Yezirat ha-Walad 155. According to Targum 1 Kings 19.11, *seq.*, God first showed Elijah three different classes of angels ("angels of wind", "angels of storm", and "angels of fire"), and then appeared Himself. Comp. also Zohar I, 16; 2 Alphabet of Ben Sira 22a; Berakot 58a. On the four worlds through which man must pass, see Ginzberg, *Hazofeh* IV, 27, and 98. Comp. also 4 Ezra 3.19, which reads: And Thy glory went through the four gates of fire, earthquake, wind, and cold. It is obvious that this author, in describing the theophany at Horeb on the occasion of the revelation of the Torah, uses as his pattern the theophany at Horeb in the time of Elijah. Accordingly, *gelu* "cold" is out of place here, and *vox* "voice" must be one of the four gates. The misreading of קל "voice" for קר "cold" in the Hebrew original is responsible for the present text.

³¹ Seder 'Olam 17. On the day on which Elijah was taken from this world, the first king of Edom was appointed; Shir 1.6; Yerushalmi 'Abodah Zorah 1.39c.

³² Septuagint, as well as Targum, on 2 Kings 2.1, seems to oppose the popular view of Elijah's translation to heaven. Josephus, *Antiqui.*, IX, 2.2, explicitly states: Elijah disappeared from among men...It is written in the Sacred Books that they (*i. e.* Elijah and Enoch) disappeared, but so that nobody knew that they died. R. Jose, living a generation after Josephus, definitely states that neither Moses (at the time of the revelation on Sinai) nor Elijah ascended to heaven (Mekilta Bahodesh 4, 65b; Sukkah 5a), and according to the Talmud, it is the opin-

ion of this Tanna that the temporary abode of Moses and the permanent one of Elijah are to be looked for in the close vicinity of heaven but not in heaven itself. In 'Erubin 45a it is unqualifiedly assumed that Elijah "dwells on high", which refers to heaven, or the vicinity thereof. Paradise is often spoken of as the abode (permanent?) of Elijah (comp., *e. g.*, Derek Erez Z. 1, and the numerous parallel passages cited by Tawrogi concerning Elijah and the others who entered paradise alive; vol. IV, pp. 205, 219), but in view of the confused notions of the location of paradise prevailing in the midrashic and talmudic writings, this does not give us any clue as to whether these passages assume Elijah's translation to heaven or not. That Elijah never "tasted death" (on this phrase see BR 21.5; Mark 9.1; Hebrews 2.9), but continued "to live for ever", is the almost unanimous opinion of the talmudic-midrashic literature and (disregarding a few rationalists; see *e. g.*, Kimhi on Malachi 3.23) also of the medieval Jews; see Seder 'Olam 2 and 17; Mo'ed Katan 26a; BR, *loc. cit.*; PK 9, 76a; WR 27.4; Koheleth 3.16; Tan. B. III, 90; Tan. Emor 9. Comp. also the references cited by Friedmann, introduction to ER 14–20. His statement that some of the old sources refer to the translation of Elijah's soul, but not to his body, is a rationalistic conception entirely alien to the old sources, and there can be no doubt that Elijah was considered to have been translated, body and soul, to a place beyond the earth, that is, to heaven or paradise, or in the vicinity of heaven. Zohar II, 197a, asserts that Elijah received a celestial body which enabled him to ascend to heaven; but when he descends to earth to reveal himself, he resumes his ter-restrial body. Comp. Index, s. v. "Celestial Garments". See also notes 34 and 37. For Christian views concerning Elijah's translation, see Bollandi, *Acta Sanctorum*, July 20, V, 1.9. There is no cogent reason for assuming that the view of R. Jose mentioned above was prompted by an anti-Christian tendency, to combat the Christian doctrine of the ascension of Jesus. This view seems to be shared not only by Septuagint but also by Ecclus. 48.9, where the Hebrew text has מעלה and מרום but not שמים "heaven", and there can hardly be any doubt that the substitution of the words "upwards" and "on high" for שמים "heaven" was intentional. Comp. vol. V, p. 59, note 58.

³³ Zohar Hadash Ruth 1.1 (beginning אמר רבי אשרי משכיל). On the struggle between Elijah and Sammael on the Day of Judg-ment, see note 275 on Vol. I, p. 394, and comp. also the struggle be-tween Moses and Sammael in Vol. III, pp. 466, *seq.*

³⁴ Seder 'Olam 1; Baba Batra 121b; 2 ARN 38, 103. See the

full discussion on Elijah's immortality in note 32, and comp. further the words quoted from ps.-Philo in Vol. IV, pp. 53-54.

³⁵ WR 34.8; Ruth R. 2.14, which reads: Elijah and the Messiah write down the good deeds of man, and God affixes His seal to this record. See also Kiddushin 70a, which says: Every marriage is recorded in writing by Elijah (Rashi's explanation of the contents of the writing is unacceptable, as may be seen from the parallel passages cited further below; the sentence לו אוי‎, etc. is a remark by the author of the Baraita and not the text of the writing of Elijah), and God affixes His seal to the marriage record. He who marries a woman not worthy of him (*i. e.*, not of pure descent) will be put in stocks on the pole by Elijah, and flogged by God. Some quote a similar statement from Abot 5 (end; comp. Taylor, *Appendix to Sayings of the Jewish Fathers*, 172), but this addition to Abot is found in none of the extant texts of Abot. See also Derek Erez R. 1, which reads: He who marries a woman worthy of him is loved by God and kissed by Elijah; but he who marries an unworthy woman is hated by God and flogged by Elijah. For the correct text of Derek Erez see *Halakot Gedolot* 52b (Hildesheimer's edition, 254). That Elijah in these passages is not the prophet Elijah, but an angel called Elijah, is maintained by Rashi to Kiddushin, *loc. cit.* But there is no good reason for this assumption. Elijah's zeal for the purity of the family is perhaps connected with the view that he is identified with Phinehas who slew a man and a woman for their unchastity. Comp. also note 107.

³⁶ Seder 'Olam 7. It is possible that the phrase מעשה כל הדורות‎ means: "the deeds of all living". Comp. the quotations from WR and Ruth R. in the preceding note.

³⁷ PRE 15, which reads: Elijah sits at the crossways; one road is that of justice, the other of love. On the arrival of a righteous person, Elijah calls out: "Open ye the gates, that the righteous nation that keepeth faithfulness may enter in."

³⁸ Yalkut Reubeni (Addenda), s. v. אליה‎. See also MaHaRil, hilkot shabbat (end; Frankfort edition, 76b), where it is said that Elijah is seated under the tree of life and records the good deeds of those who observe the Sabbath. MaHaRil cites Tosafot (or Tosefta?) as his source; but in Tosafot on the Talmud and Pentateuch (and still less in the Tosefta) no such passage can be found. I doubt whether he is right in connecting the popular belief as to Elijah's occupation at that hour with the custom of reciting piyyutim in his praise at the con-

clusion of the Sabbath. For further details, see Kohn, *Monatsschrift*, XII, 287–288.

³⁹ R. Moses De Leon quoted by Cordovero, *Pardes*, 24.4, whence Yalkut Reubeni, Gen. 1.26, 9d (Amsterdam edition). This conception cannot be found in any old source, but its resemblance to the teaching of the Melchizedekites is so striking that one is warranted in assuming a connection between them. It must be borne in mind that Ambrosius (*De Fide*, III, 11.88; Migne's edition XVI, 607) assigns a Jewish origin to the doctrine of the Melchizedekites. It is also noteworthy that Epiphanius, in his polemic against this sect (*Haer.* 15; Migne's edition XLI, 976), uses the expression "As for Elijah, we have the following tradition about his descent, etc." Epiphanius, as may be seen, deemed it necessary to prove, in opposition to the Melchizedekites, that Elijah was not an angel sent from heaven. The designation of Elijah as an "angel in heaven" מלאך בשמים (in Zohar Hadash Ruth 2.1, beginning רבי נתן שאל) refers to his state after his translation. The celestial body of Elijah spoken of in Zohar II, 197, likewise refers to his body after his translation.

⁴⁰ *'Emek ha-Melek*, 175c. Sandalphon is explained as a compound of σύν = "with" and ἀδελφός = "brother"; Elijah is the "brother" of Enoch-Metatron, both of whom were changed to angels after their translation.

⁴¹ Zohar II, 58a, based in the main on Hagigah 13b and PR 20.79a. In the old sources Elijah has nothing to do with Sandalphon. Comp. vol. III, p. 111.

⁴² *'Emek ha-Melek* 65 (end); comp. vol. III, p. 389.

⁴³ Seder 'Olam 17. Comp., however, Josephus, *Antiqui.*, IX, 5.2.

⁴⁴ PRE 50; Esther R. 7.9.

⁴⁵ The origin of this Haggadah is as follows: The prayer after the reading of the Megillah closes with the words: "May Harbonah, too, be remembered unto good" (Yerushalmi Megillah 3, 74b, bottom; Soferim 14.6). Now the expression זכור לטוב "remembered unto good" is the ancient eulogy attached to Elijah (see note 1), and accordingly its application to Harbonah in the prayer for Purim was interpreted to mean that he was identical with Elijah. The last words of the prayer וגם חרבונה זכור לטוב were thus understood to mean: "And as for Harbonah, he is the one (Elijah) who is remembered unto good". As to Elijah's participation in the delivery of the Jews from the hands of Haman, see vol. IV, p. 416.

⁴⁶ Berakot 4b, which reads: Michael traverses the world with one stroke, Gabriel with two, Elijah with four, the angel of death with eight (this is only in ordinary cases, but in the time of plague with one). Comp. also Zohar I, 13a.

⁴⁷ On the ability of the angel to assume the most varied appearances and forms, see vol. I, p. 16 (bottom). In the note appertaining thereto it is pointed out that an angel never assumes the form of a woman, and in this respect Elijah is their superior, as he, at least once, appeared as a harlot; see 'Abodah Zarah 18b. On Elijah as an angel comp. notes 34 and 39–40.

⁴⁸ גם זו לטובה. This favorite expression of the Rabbis was supposed to have given rise to his appellation Gamzu (גמזו). But in fact it is the name of his birthplace.

⁴⁹ Ta'anit 21a; Sanhedrin 108b. Comp. vol. I, p. 232.

⁵⁰ Berakot 58b.

⁵¹ 'Abodah Zarah 18b. In the legend given *ibid.* 17b, concerning R. Eliezer b. Parata, Elijah assumed the appearance of a high official for the purpose of silencing the accusers of the Rabbi in court. Failing in this, he made the Rabbi disappear (the Rabbi suddenly found himself in a place four hundred parasangs away from court).

⁵² Shabbat 33b, and, with additions, Zohar Hadash Ki-Tabo (beginning). In the Zohar, which claims to be the work of this Rabbi and saint, Elijah's conversations with the pious, particularly the masters of the Kabbalah, are frequently referred to. Friedmann, introduction to ER, 38–40, gives an almost complete list of these Zohar passages. Comp. note 98.

⁵³ Kiddushin 40a. Palestine, as well as Egypt, extends over four hundred parasangs (Pesahim 94a; Index, s. v. "Palestine", "Egypt"), and therefore the expression "four hundred parasangs" is often used to describe a great distance. Comp. note 51.

⁵⁴ Baba Mezi'a 114a–114b. אכל לעלמיה in this passage, as well as דליכליה לעלמא in Gittin 68b means: "he used up his share in the world to come during his life-time." Grünbaum, *Gesammelte Aufsätze*, 49, and many other scholars misunderstood the passage in Gittin. On the fragrance of paradise, see vol. I, p. 21.

⁵⁵ *Hibbur Yafeh*, 57–59, and hence in later sources; comp., *e.g.*, BHM V, 140–141. The relation of this Jewish legend to the Christian one, as elaborately set forth in the *Acta Thomae*, ought to be examined. A poetic version of this Elijah legend by R. Jesse b. Mordecai was incorporated in the liturgy and is sung at the conclusion of the Sabbath.

Comp. Zunz, *Literaturgeschichte*, 486 and Gaster, *Exempla*, No. 415.

⁵⁶ Ruth Z., 55; *Hibbur Yafeh* 82–84. On Elijah assuming the guise of an Arab, see also note 62. Another legend about Elijah as the one to bring succor to the needy is found in *Hemdat ha-Yamim* III, 14b, and hence in *'Oseh fele* II, 52, *seq*. Once upon a time there lived a pious and learned Rabbi in Jerusalem, who was in the habit of providing the poor with food and other necessities for Passover. But it happened once that he entirely forgot to provide for the needs of a very poor but worthy scholar, who on the day before Passover had neither mazzot nor wine for the feast. In his miserable state he decided to leave his home rather than see his family dying of hunger. Walking aimlessly in the streets, he was addressed by a venerable looking old man with the following words: "I am a stranger in this place; I beg of you to take me to your house for the days of the festival, and here is the money to furnish us with all our needs. The poor scholar, though depressed by his inability to be the host to the stranger without payment, did as he was requested, and with the ample funds now at his disposal prepared a really supmtuous meal for the first night of Passover. But when the time of the Seder arrived, the stranger did not appear; all the searching was in vain, as no trace could be found of him. The poor scholar then realized that the stranger was none other than Elijah the prophet who came to his assistance. On the very same night Elijah appeared to the Rabbi of the place, and awakened him by seizing him by his throat and nearly choking him to death. Elijah chided him for having neglected the poor scholar, and told him that if it were not for his quick action, God would have destroyed the entire community for not having taken care of the worthy man. He then commanded the Rabbi to hasten to the poor scholar and beg his pardon for not having provided him with the necessities of life.

⁵⁷ Nedarim 50a. Comp. Ginzberg. *Jewish Encyclopedia*, s. v. "Akiba in Legend".

⁵⁸ Luzzatto, *Kaftor wa-Ferah*, 7b; collection of Ma'asiyyot published from MS. in *R.E.J.*, XXXIII, 58–60. A shorter form of this legend is found in Ruth Z. 50. Four other versions of this legend are found in Gaster, *Exempla*, Nos. 301, p. 193, and 307, pp. 206–207; Comp. also No. 334. On Elijah assuming the guise of an Arab, see note 62. The following is a widespread legend about Elijah as a helper in need. Shortly before the arrival of the Sabbath a man came to a town where he had no friends at all, and did not know what to do with his money, as it is prohibited to carry money on the

day of rest (see the same motive vol. IV, p. 133, top). He betook himself to the synagogue, where he found a man praying with his phylacteries on his forehead and arm. Deeming him a pious man, he entrusted the money to him. At the termination of the Sabbath the stranger asked him for the money. But the hypocrite denied that he had ever received any money from him. In his distress he prayed to God as follows: "O Lord, I did not trust that man, but Thy name (the letter ש as an abbreviation of שדי "almighty", is written on the phylactery for the forehead), believing that a man who bears Thy name on him would not defraud people." After praying he fell asleep, and in his dream Elijah appeared unto him, saying: "Go to the wife of this man and tell her that her husband commands her to return the money to you. That she may believe your words, say unto her: Your husband, to show his confidence in me, revealed unto me the secret that you both ate the meat of a swine on the Day of Atonement." The stranger did as he was advised by Elijah, and the woman returned the money to him. See PR 22, 111b; Yelammedenu in Or Zarua I, 149; Ma'asiyyot, ed. Gaster 83. For the later version of this legend, see Ma'asiyyot ed. Araki, Nos. 96 and 105; *Hebräische Bibliographie*, XIII, 129–130; Gaster, *Exempla* No. 123. In the profuse legend concerning the "two faithful friends" (*'Oseh Fele* II, 44a, *seq.*), Elijah appears in a dream to the Rabbi, and informs him of the fraud perpetrated by one of the "two faithful friends" against the other.

⁵⁹ The legend concerning R. Shimi is found in Shabbat 109b; that about R. Judah is in Yerushalmi Kil'ayim 9, 32b; BR 33.3 and 96.5; Tan. B. I, 215; Tan. Wa-Yehi 3. Elijah plays the rôle of a physician also in the legend about the "woman with the animal face" in *'Oseh Fele* II, 36a, *seq.* The medicine given by him changes the monstrosity into a beauty. Comp. also Ginzberg, *Hagoren*, IX, 34 *seq.*

⁶⁰ DR 5 (end). The parallel passages in Yerushalmi Sotah 1,198a; WR 9.9 and BaR 9.30 have "the holy spirit" instead of Elijah. Comp. also Gaster, *Exempla* No. 145, the text of which is different from those of the Midrashim and Jerushalmi. On spittle as a remedy for sickness, see also Mark 8.22 and John 9.6.; Comp. Ginzberg, *Journal Bibl. Literature*, XLI, 123, note 20.

⁶¹ Ma'aseh-buch, No. 157, 47d, and No. 169, 52c. The animals notice the presence of Elijah; when dogs bark gleefully it is a sign that Elijah is not far from them; when they whine, the angel of death is near them. See Baba Kamma 60b; comp. *Imre No'am*, Bo (end) and note

on vol. I, p. 294. On a different version of this legend, see Gaster, *Exempla*, No. 355.

⁶² Mishle 9, 62; Elleh Ezkerah 68; Ma'aseh Haruge Malkut 27–28. Mishle is the source of MHG (Ms.), whence Gaster, *Exempla* No. 245. On the cave in the vicinity of Caesarea, see vol. IV, p. 222, and on the furniture thereof see vol. III, p. 325; comp. also 2 Kings 4.10.

⁶³ Berakot 6b, where it is also stated that on this account Elijah assumed the guise of an Arab. Comp. note 56. He often took the opportunity to point out the importance of prayer and devotion to the saints and scholars to whom he revealed himself. R. Eleazar the son of R. Jose once met Elijah driving four thousand camels heavily laden, and at his question concerning the nature of the load, he received the following answer from the prophet: "These camels are laden with wrath and fury for those who talk during their prayers". He further informed this Tanna that prayers of this kind are never granted, whereas those who pray with devotion and do not talk in their prayers will be heard by God. To the father of this Tanna Elijah once gave the same piece of information. The legend is quoted by many medieval authors from the Yerushalmi or Midrash respectively but is not found in the extant Midrashim and not in the Yerushalmi. See the references cited by Buber, *Yerushalayim ha-Benuyah*, No. 33, 18, and Friedmann, introduction to ER 32. This legend is further quoted from the Midrash by Shu'aib, 33b; R. Bahya, *Kad ha-Kemah* II, 57b קדושה; Abudrahim ישתבח; Treves, *Kimha Dabishuna* ישתבח. To his friend R. Jose (comp. note 74) Elijah imparted the following piece of information: As often as Israel, in the houses of worship, praise God, He exclaims: "Happy the King who is praised in His house; but woe unto the father (מה לו is a euphemism for אוי לו) who exiled his children, and woe to the children who were exiled from their father's table." See Berakot 3a.

⁶⁴ Tendlau, *Sprüchwörter*, 14–15, who took down this legend in the form he found it current among German Jews. It is the Jewish version of a widespread legend among European nations. Comp. Dähnhardt, *Natursagen*, II, 140. *seq.* Comp. also Gaster, *Exempla*, No. 435.

⁶⁵ Baba Mezi'a 84a. A contemporary of this Rabbi, who subsequently became famous under the name of R. Eleazar b. R. Simeon, was in his earlier days very ignorant, but of a very strong physique. On account of sturdiness he was appointed overseer of the laborers employed by the government. Elijah appeared to him once as an old man, and after convincing him of the uselessness of his life, advised

him to take up the profession of his fathers and to study the Torah. R. Eleazar objected, as he had no teacher to instruct him, and Elijah became his master for thirteen years. See PK 10, 92b–93a (for the text use Gaster, *Exempla*, No. 94), and with additional embellishments Zohar Hadash, Lek (end of וישמע).

⁶ Yerushalmi Terumot 8, 96b; BR 94 (end). According to the law, the Rabbi was permitted to surrender one man, that all the inhabitants of the place might be saved; but a pious man is expected to do more than the strict law requires of him. On another occasion this Rabbi, to his great humiliation, had found out that too much rigor in ceremonial matters was far from being commendable. Elijah pointed out to the disciple of the Rabbi the unpleasant consequences of a too rigorous decision by the master. See Yerushalmi Shabbat 9, 39a; Dammai 2, 22c.

⁶⁷ Ketubot 61a. Comp. Rashi, who has a somewhat different interpretation of this passage.

⁶⁸ Baba Batra 7b.

⁶⁹ Makkot 11a.

⁷⁰ Ketubot 106a. The conclusion of this narrative is: Hence the titles "the great order of Elijah" and "the small order of Elijah", that is, the collection of teachings imparted by Elijah to R. Anan before this occurrence is called the "great order", and that imparted after is called "the small order." The nature of these works attributed to Elijah is entirely unknown, as there can be no doubt that the extant Midrashim Seder Eliyyahu Rabba and Seder Eliyyahu Zutta date from post-talmudic times, and may have nothing in common but the titles with the works referred to in the Talmud. The nine haggadic Baraitot cited by the Talmud from Tanna de be Eliyyahu (see the references in Friedmann, Introduction to ER 45) are very likely taken from a haggadic compilation by a Tanna called Elijah. On the use of this name in the time of the Tannaim and Amoraim, see Ratner, *Ahabat Ziyyon*, Pesahim, 61. In the above-mentioned Midrashim attributed to Elijah these nine Baraitot are incorporated (see Friedmann, *loc. cit.*), and in three passages the talmudic תנא דבי אליהו is changed to משום דבי אליהו הנביא by the author (authors?) of these Midrashim. This shows that at a comparatively early date דבי אליהו of the Talmud was misunderstood to refer to the prophet Elijah. These Midrashim quite often introduce the prophet as narrating events and incidents of his life, but they lack the simplicity of legend, and one immediately sees that the author puts into the mouth of Elijah his own views concerning

God, Israel, and the Torah. Another work by Elijah is ספר אליהו, an apocalyptic book, in which Elijah reveals the secrets made known to him by the angel Michael concerning the Messianic times. Closely related to it is the apocalyptic writing פרקין משיח, in which Elijah imparts to R. Jose more valuable information about the Messiah and the Messianic redemption. These two apocalyptic works were very likely composed about the middle of the eighth century.

⁷¹ Alphabet of Ben Sira 9b–10a. Comp. Ginzberg, *Jewish Encyclopedia*, s. v. "Ben Sira, Alphabet", and Lévi, *R.E.J.*, LIII, 66. The pious custom to say: "If it please God" is known to the New Testament (1 Corinth. 4.19; Heb. 6.3; James 4.15) and to Plato; see the references cited by Neumark, *Geschichte der jüdischen Philosophie*, II, 292. On the use of the familiar אם ירצה השם, "If it please God", and בעזר השם, "with God's help" in medieval writings, see Zunz, *Gesammelte Schriften*, III, 268.

⁷² Aramaic ריקה "Reka"; but Ma'asiyyot (Gaster's edition 139) has רָאקָה as in Matth. 5.2.

⁷³ Ta'anit 20 (below); 2 ARN 41.131; Derek Erez R. 4, where the Tosafists (Ta'anit, *loc. cit.*) read that the "ugly man" was Elijah; Kallah 6.13a.

⁷⁴ Sanhedrin (end). Comp. James 5.17.

⁷⁵ 'Erubin 43a. On the basis of this and similar passages of the Talmud, where Elijah appears as the teacher of the wise, it was thought that he is alluded to wherever the Talmud speaks of a "certain old scholar", ההוא סבא. Comp. *Responsen der Geonim* (Harkavy's edition, No. 23) and Tosafot on Hullin 6a. As to Elijah assuming the apperance of an "old man", see also PK 10, 92b–93a. Elijah used to appear daily to R. Joseph, the Gaon of Pumbedita, but nobody knew of it until this Rabbi became very old and absent-minded (this is how ואשטיף is to be understood), so that he once remarked to the scholars of the academy: "Leave some room next to me for the 'old man' who comes to see me." They did not see anybody come, and knew that he meant Elijah. See Iggeret R. Sherira Gaon 37, lines 7–5 (from bottom.)

⁷⁶ Yebamot 63a, and more fully ER 9, 61. On certain regulations concerning prayer imparted by Elijah to this Rabbi, see Berakot 3a, and note 63. Elijah pointed out to another Rabbi that "poverty is the most precious gift which God could have bestowed upon Israel," as it leads them to be kind, self-sacrificing, and God-fearing. See Hagigah 9b; EZ 3, 176, and 6, 181.

77 Yerushalmi Berakot 9, 13c; ER 1, 15; Tehillim 18, 140–141, and 104, 447–448. Comp. also quotation from Yerushalmi (not in our texts) in Yalkut I, 836, on Deut. 6.4, and Yelammedenu in YalkutII, 862, on Ps. 104. On the causes of earthquakes and other phenomena, see also Sibyll. 4.130–135; Enoch 59.1–5; Berakot 59a. On the relation of Elijah to R. Nehorai, see Ruth R. 2.21, and Friedmann, introduction to ER 33, note 2.

78 Berakot 29b (bottom). The correct reading of the second maxim is to be found only in MHG I, 175, whereas all the other texts have חחטי instead of תְּרָיְי, which is used as a play on the preceding חָרָיִי. It is to be observed that the first two maxims are in Aramaic and the third in Hebrew. This very likely points to the use of different sources by the Talmud. The third maxim means: "Pray before thou settest out on a journey."

79 The "heavenly academy", in which the pious who departed this life and the angels study the Torah with God, is frequently mentioned in the Haggadah, as for instance Gittin 68a and Baba Mezi'a 86a.

80 Megillah 15b.

81 Gittin 6b; comp. note 134 on vol. IV, pp. 51–52.

82 Baba Mezi'a 59b. R. Nathan received from Elijah the wise counsel never to fill himself with food and drink, but to leave one third of his stomach unfilled, one third thereof filled with food and one third with beverages. See Gittin 70a.

83 For a similar function of Elijah, see Esther R. 4.9.

84 Baba Mezi'a 85b. In a similar legend (Ma'aseh-buch No. 157) it is Jeremiah who performs the function ớt the Hazzan in the congregation of the pious who departed this life. On the view that the dead pray, see also note 97 on vol. I, p. 23. In Baba Mezi'a, *loc. cit.*, it is also stated that Elijah showed to a scholar the fiery chariots in which the pious ascend to the heavenly academy. The scholar, however, lost his eye-sight, because, notwithstanding Elijah's warning, he looked at the chariot of R. Hiyyah, the lustre of which blinded him. As to the nature of the punishment inflicted upon Elijah, see note 896 on vol. III, 495. That prayer combined with repentance will bring about the Messianic redemption of Israel is also stated by Philo, *De Praemiis et Poenis* 8.

85 Hagigah 15b.

86 PRE 1; Bet Eked ha-Aggadot 8 and 14; 2 ARN 13, 30.

87 EZ 14, 195–196; Tan. Wa-Yelek 2.

⁸⁸ ER 18, 95 (read קסדור=קודור instead of קודיר), and EZ 1, 167. Comp. also Kinyan Torah 9; Mekilta RS, 98; quotation from the Midrash in *Steinschneider–Festschrift*, Hebrew section, 55.

⁸⁹ ER 14–15, 70–80, and EZ 2, 171–175 give Elijah's conversation with people who accepted the "written Torah", but not the "oral Torah", and his arguments in favor of the binding power of both, the written and the unwritten Torot. Comp. note 70.

⁹⁰ PK 18, 136; PR 32, 148b (this passage has the rare description of the prophet as "Abba Elijah" "father Elijah"; comp. Sanhedrin, (end); Ma'asiyyot, ed. Gaster 135. These stones were at the bottom of the "great sea", and the shipwreck was necessary to enable the Jewish lad to lift them and show them to the Rabbi. As to the cave where the stones were placed, see note 62. A confusion of Caesarea and Lydda seems to prevail in the sources. On the stones to be used in the Messianic times, see vol. IV, p. 24, and Jerome on Joel 4.4–12.

⁹¹ Sanhedrin 98a. In the Hebrew the reply made by the Messiah contains a play on words, which cannot be reproduced in another language.

⁹² PK 10, 87b; BR 35 (beginning). The question addressed to R. Joshua was whether he had seen a rainbow. His affirmative answer implied that his piety did not suffice to ward off the extreme punishment due to a wicked generation. For a rainbow appears only to remind God of His promise to Noah not to destroy the world on account of the iniquity of its inhabitants. Comp. Ketubot 77b and Zohar I, 72b.

⁹³ Ketubot 77b. In the numerous legends concerning the intercourse of Elijah with the sages and saints it is presupposed that these men knew his identity when he appeared to them. Other mortals, on the other hand (even those who were found worthy to be helped by Elijah in time of need and distress), were not aware of the great distinction conferred upon them until he had disappeared from among them, and sometimes did not find out at all about the supernatural company granted to them. Comp., for instance, the legend given in vol. IV, pp. 211–212 and 215–216. A third form of communication between Elijah and certain people is known as גלוי אליהו, the "appearance of Elijah," in dreams to give advice and counsel. In the old literature this is very rarely mentioned, and besides the legend quoted from PR and Yelammedenu in note 58, there is only one other in which Elijah is said to have appeared to a "Roman ruler" in a dream, and warned him against squandering the treasures left him by his ancestors;

BR 83.4. On the other hand, this "appearance of Elijah" is very frequently referred to in later literature. Comp. note 103. They favored this form of communication with wicked and cruel rulers to make them change their evil designs against the Jews. The Calif Al-Mutadhid (892–902), a veritable Haman, became a friend and protector of the Jews after Elijah had appeared to him in a dream and threatened him with a cruel death if he did not immediately change his attitude towards the Jews. See Arabic fragment published by Harkavy in *Berliner-Festschrift*, 35, seq. The same thing happened to the Sultan Sulaiman I (1545); Elijah not only prevented him from carrying out the cruel persecution of the Jews upon which he had decided, but changed him into their staunch friend. As a reward for this he was visited by Elijah (in a dream) every month. That the Sultan should have no doubt as to the reality of the appearance, Elijah first revealed himself to R. Moses Hamon, the physician-in-ordinary of the Sultan, and told him to prepare his majesty for the visit he (Elijah) would pay him. See Sambari in Neubauer's *Medieval Jewish Chronicles*, I, 147–149. Sambari, *ibid.*, 121, is the only source for the statement that Elijah was born in a village near Cairo. In view of the prevalent opinion that Elijah is none other than Phinehas (comp. vol. IV, p. 195), it was quite natural that some locality in Egypt should claim the distinction of being the birthplace of the prophet.

⁹⁴ *Hibbur Yafeh* 8–11 (reprinted by Jellinek in BHM V, 133–135). A different version is found in Ma'asiyyot 12 (reprinted by R. Elijah ha-Kohen in *Me'il Zedakah*, No. 439, and by Jellinek in BHM VI, 131–133. The latter did not know that R. Elijah ha-Kohen used Ma'asiyyot for his text). Comp. also Ma'asiyyot ed. Gaster 96–97. For Judeo-German and later German versions, see Zunz, *Gottesdienstliche Vorträge* (second edition, 138). A version agreeing with neither of the two just mentioned is given by Peter Venerabilis; comp., *R.E.J.*, XLIII, 284; See also *ibid.* VIII, 64–73 and Gaster, *Exempla*, No. 393. The antiquity of the legend is attested by Mohammed who reproduces it in the Koran (18.59–82) in his anachronistic fashion. There is no valid reason to doubt the Jewish origin of this legend, especially if one considers the fact that Elijah appears as the "vindicator of God's justice" in the old Haggadah, preceding the Koran by centuries. It may not be out of place to quote a few examples of this rôle, played by Elijah. At the destruction of Jerusalem Elijah walked about among the inhabitants of the city, who were dying of starvation, to find out whether they deserved their sad fate. Coming across a young child, he said to him: "Repeat the

words I am going to recite to you, and thou shalt live." But when the child heard the Shema' recited by Elijah, he preferred death to proclaiming God's unity. And the child died hugging and kissing his idol. See Sifra 26.30; Sanhedrin 63b. It is noteworthy that in these passages Elijah received the attribute הצדיק, literally "the righteous one", but it very likely means: "he who acknowledged God's justice." Elijah once remarked to a great saint: "You are astounded why the Messiah has not come yet. To-day is the Day of Atonement, and on this day of repentance many a virgin is deflowered in your city of Nehardea." See Yoma 19b. The young widow of a promising scholar was inconsolable at the premature death of her husband, and exclaimed all the time: "God said of the Torah: 'It is thy life and the length of thy days' (comp. Deut. 30.2); Where is the length of my husband's days, who devoted his life to the study of the Torah?" None of the great scholars could explain the premature death of their young disciple. But Elijah went to see the widow, and in his conversation with her led her to admit certain failings of her deceased husband and consequently to acknowledge that his death was a deserved punishment. See Shabbat 13a–13b; ER 15, 76; ARN 2, 8, and parallel passages cited by Schechter. Most of the incidents narrated of Elijah's life in the Midrashim ER and EZ (comp. note 70) have no other purpose but to vindicate God's justice in the history of nations and in the lives of individuals. Comp. Friedmann, introductoin to ER 31–32. For the dependence of the Arabic Khadhir legend on the Jewish Elijah Haggadah, see Friedlaender, *Die Chadhirlegende*, 255, *seq.*

⁹⁵ Ta'anit 22a. A similar lesson on the impossibility to judge things by appearances was given by Elijah to another wise and pious Rabbi when they were walking together. Passing by a carcass, the Rabbi put his hand to his nose in order not to inhale the awful stench, whereas Elijah walked hard by the carcass without taking the slightest notice of it. Shortly after a proud and haughty man passed by them, whereupon Elijah put his hand to his nose. Astonished at this strange behavior, the Rabbi asked him to explain it. Elijah replied: "The proud man is worse than the carcass; if one touches a carcass, he becomes defiled only until sunset (Lev. 11.24); but contact with the proud generates impurities lasting for a long time. Kab ha-Yashar 7, whence Ma'asiyyot (Bagdad edition, No. 89). Comp. WR (end).

⁹⁶ Tan. Haazinu 8. It is difficult to determine with certainty the relation of this legend to the story of Tobit, as it would be a rash conclusion to consider the former directly dependent upon the latter.

The legend about R. Akiba's daughter (Shabbat 156b) has obviously influenced our legend. The astrologers predicted that the daughter of this famous Rabbi would die on the day of her wedding. This prophecy would have been fulfilled, had she not, at the moment when the serpent was to sting her, hastened to the door to give alms to a beggar, and instead of being killed by the serpent, it was killed by her. As to the angel of death assuming the appearance of a beggar, see vol. I, pp. 33–34. The motive: "Charity delivereth from death" (Prov. 10.2; according to the interpretation of the Rabbis, צדקה in this verse means "charity", not "justice"; comp. Shabbat, *loc. cit.*) is also found in the legend about the youth who was saved by Elijah from the gallows as a reward for his having been very generous to his parents (*'Oseh Fele* II, 21, *seq.*; it is of very late origin); also in the diffuse legend about R. Phineas, *ibid.*, 23, *seq.* Comp. also the references in next note.

⁹⁷ Ma'asiyyot, No. 1, and, with some additions, Ma'asiyyot (Gaster's edition, 139, 100); comp. also BHM V, 152–154, where this legend is republished from *Me'il Zedakah*, No. 434. Jellinek did not know that the author of this book reproduced this legend from Ma'asiyyot. Another version of this legend occurs in Midrash 'Aseret ha-Dibrot 83–84, where, however, Elijah does not play any part at all.—Elijah's activity is not limited to the helping of the pious to save them from death, poverty, and physical pain; he sometimes comes to relieve mental pain and anguish. A very saintly man was once punished for his excessive self-consciousness by being misled to sin by a female demon God wished thus to humiliate him for his pride in his continence. Long and intense were the mental sufferings of this pious man, who could not for a moment forget his sin. But having been humiliated for a sufficiently long time, he was visited by Elijah who informed him that the beautiful woman who misled him to sin was not a human being but a spirit, and his sin was accordingly not a real one. Tan. B. I, 20. Comp. Yerushalmi Shabbat 13b. Sometimes Elijah himself inflicted punishment upon the pious for their frailities and failings, that they might mend their ways. A rich and learned young man once decided to take up some trade and profession, but not knowing what to choose, he resolved to look around before making up his mind. He first visited the market-place to study the life of the merchants, and when he saw that commerce was carried on by lying and cheating, he gave up the idea of becoming a merchant. Finally he noticed a man tilling the soil (it was none else but Elijah), and asked him what his business was. Elijah replied: "I till the soil to provide food for myself, my wife, and

children, the poor and the needy, the animals of the fields, the fowl
of the air, and the beasts of the earth." The young man thereupon
decided to stay with Elijah, and became a tiller of the soil. The latter
took him to his house, and promised to fulfil all his wishes. The young
man, however, had only one wish: to be married. Elijah knowing who
was destined to become this man's wife, took him to her (she lived in
a place a three-days' journey distant from them; but Elijah brought
the young man to her in a second), and they were married. In
his new happy state the young man entirely forgot his resolution to
become a tiller of the soil. At the end of seven days Elijah appeared
to him, and informed him that as a punishment for his having neglected
his duty for seven days, he would spend seven years in slavery. Elijah's
prediction came true. On his way to his family (אבותיך is not to be
taken literally; his father was dead), with his wife, her slaves and bondwomen, the caravan halted near a big river. While the young man was
trying to wash his feet in the river, Elijah appeared, seized him, and
carried him off to a distant country, where he sold him into slavery.
The young man's wife did not complain, but was convinced that "whatever God did was for the best." She settled down in the place where
her husband disappeared, and opened a store for the sale of corn,
in the hope that her husband would turn up in the course of time. After
five years she recognized her husband as a slave of a corn merchant.
Their joy was great, and also their trust in God. When the young man
told his wife that heaven decreed seven years of slavery against him,
of which two years were still lacking, they parted without a murmur.
At the termination of the seventh year Elijah brought the young man
to his wife, and henceforth they lived happily together. See 'Aseret
ha-Dibrot, 85–86.

⁹⁸ Zohar Hadash Ki-Tabo (beginning); Zohar Shir beginning חדי
ר"ש; Tikkune Zohar (beginning). Friedmann, introduction to ER,
38–40, gives a list of all the passages in the Zohar dealing with Elijah's
relations to R. Simeon and his son R. Eleazar. Tikkune Zohar, No.
17, contains an exposé of the Zoharic Kabbalah by Elijah. This exposé
found its way into the Sefardic prayer-book. Comp. also note 52.

⁹⁹ As for Elijah's being the teacher of R. Jacob and R. Abraham
b. Isaac, see *Shem ha-Gedolim*, 3–4; Jellinek, *Auswahl Kabbalistischer
Mystik*, 4–5. Comp. also Ginzberg, *Jewish Encyclopedia*, I, s. v.
"Abraham ben David of Posquières". As to the relation of Elijah
to Elkanah, see introduction to Peliah; Jellinek, BHM III, 38 (German
part); Graetz, *Geschichte*, VII, note 3.

¹⁰⁰ *'Emek ha-Melek*, introduction, 10a. Elijah is often conjured to give aid to women at childbirth against Lilith and the machinations of witches.

¹⁰¹ לקוטי ש״ס להאר״יז״ל 55a–59a, which is the oldest printed source of the legend about R. Joseph della Reyna found in many Hebrew, as well as Judeo-German, collections of legends. Vital, *Sha'are Kedushah* (end) refers to this legend in a few words.

¹⁰² Formerly the ceremony of circumcision was performed in the synagogue, as it still is to-day in some Oriental countries.

¹⁰³ Shibhe ha-Ari (beginning) and comp. the references in Schechter's *Studies in Judaism*, II, 323, note 117. A similar story about R. Phinehas is found in *'Oseh Fele* II, 22b–23a. During the persecution of the pious by the wicked Jezebel, Elijah displayed great zeal for the observance of the Abrahamic covenant (comp. note 25), and as his reward God promised him that he should be present at every ceremony of circumcision. Accordingly the "chair of Elijah" must not be forgotten at the ceremony of circumcision, as he is always present on these occasions, though not visible to the eyes of the ordinary man. See PRE 29; Halakot Gedolot, according to the text of *Shibbale ha-Leket*, 376, No. 6. Comp. *Jewish Encyclopedia*, s. v., "Elijah's Chair". A child was once brought in for circumcision, and all present greeted him with the customary formula of *Baruk ha-Ba*("Blessed be he that cometh"), which is at the same time a welcome to Elijah, the guest expected to come. R. Judah he-Hasid of Regensburg, the Sandek at the circumcision ceremony, remained silent. Asked for the reason of his strange silence, he answered: "I do not see Elijah seated at my side." While he was speaking, a venerable old man (comp. note 75) appeared at the window, and R. Judah was seen addressing him. The old man (of course, it was Elijah) declared to them that he refused to come because the child would one day abandon Judaism. The prophecy was fulfilled. See Ma'aseh-buch, No. 180, 54d. Elijah's ubiquity was explained in different ways; see Glasberg, *Zikron la-Rishonim*, 233 *seq.* In view of Elijah's acting as an assistant to the Sandek, it is quite natural that he is regarded as the patron of those performing the function of Sandek. See the diffuse legend concerning the help granted to the Sandek by Elijah in Rosenberg, אליהו הנביא, 34, *seq.* As his source the author gives the Midrash Wa-Yosha' in MS. But there can be no doubt that this is a pure invention. Rosenberg has the temerity to state that a part of this legend is found in the printed text of this Midrash. This is not the case.

[104] Ma'asiyyot Peliot 24–25. Comp. also *Shibhe ha-Besht* (beginning). The admirers of the Gaon, R. Elijah Wilna, the great opponent of R. Israel Baal Shem Tob, tell of their hero's intercourse with Elijah as well. Comp. *'Aliyyot Eliyyahu*, 35. I remember to have heard a temptation legend, similar to the one given in the text, told in Wilna of R. Moses Krämmer, the great grandfather of the Gaon; see *Sa'arat Eliyyahu*, 18; *'Ir Wilna*, 10. Comp. also the similar legend in Ma'asiyyot (Gaster's edition, 161, 115–116), where אביון is to be read instead of הגמון; the angel who tempted the saint assumed the appearance of a beggar. Comp. note 15 on vol. II, p. 233 and vol. IV, pp. 227, 228–229.

[105] Ecclus. 48.10–11. This is more than a free rendering of Malachi 3.25; to the author of Ecclus. Elijah is very likely the promised Messiah. Traces of this view are found in rabbinical sources, see Friedmann, introduction to ER, 25–37; Ginzberg, *Unbekannte Sekte*, 346 *seq.* The statement that Elijah is one of the names of the Messiah is inferred from Malachi, *loc. cit.*; Mishle 19, 87. This shows that even later this biblical passage was taken to refer to the Messiah. But since it later became a fixed conception that the Messiah must be a "son of David", there is no other way out of the difficulty than to give the name Elijah to the son of David. On the four Messiahs (that is: Messiah the son of David, the Messiah of the tribe of Joseph, Elijah, and the priest of righteousness), see Ginzberg, *ibid.*

[106] PRE 43 and 47. This was probably the prevalent notion in the early formative period of Christianity, as may be inferred from the New Testament account of John the Baptist (= Elijah), the alleged precursor of the Messiah. On repentance as the *conditio sine qua non* of the "final redemption", see Sanhedrin 97b; Yerushalmi Ta'anit 1, 63d; PRE 43; Tan. B. III, 111; Tan. Behukkotai 3; Philo, *De Praemiis et Poenis*, 8. Comp. also note 84.

[107] Mishnah and Tosefta at the end of 'Eduyyot, where different views are cited concerning the means by which Elijah will restore peace and harmony in Israel. All these views presuppose that Elijah's chief activity will consist in restoring the purity of the family. See the thorough discussion on this point by Friedmann, introduction to ER, 20–24. Comp. also note 35.

[108] Mishnah and Tosefta at the end of 'Eduyyot. Comp. the following note.

[109] Menahot 45a. The phrase, "This must remain undecided until Elijah comes", is of frequent occurrence in tannaitic literature.

Comp. the references given by Ginzberg, *Unbekannte Sekte*, 304, *seq.* where the meaning of this expression is also fully discussed.

¹¹⁰ Zohar III, 27b–28a.

¹¹¹ PR 35, 161. This passage also gives him the designation of "Harbinger of good tidings", which later became his favorite appellation; see Ginzberg, *Geonica*, I, 55, note 1. See also the Messianic Midrash in Lekah IV, 259, and Tefillat R. Simon, 123 (top).

¹¹² Otot ha-Mashiah, 62; Tefillat R. Simeon, 125. It is noteworthy that according to a widespread belief, Elijah, with the "rest of the righteous", will flee into the desert, whence they will return after a stay of forty-five days, led by the Messiah, who will then begin his work of redemption. PK 5, 49a–49b (משיח = Elijah; see note 105); PR 15, 72a–73a; Pirke Mashiah, 72; ShR 5.2; BaR 11.2; Shir 2.9; Aggadat Shir 5, 38; Ruth R. 2.14; Rev. 12.6. Comp. Friedmann, introduction to ER 25–26; Bousset, *Antichrist Legende*, 212–213 and 203–208. The part ascribed to Elijah in the work of Messianic redemption in Zerubbabel, 56, and Otot ha-Mashiah, 62, is rather an unimportant one compared with that assigned to him in the other Midrashim cited above. Christian authors (comp. *f. i.* Justin Martyr, *Dialogue*, 49) mention the Jewish belief that Elijah will anoint the Messiah; but the old rabbinic writings know nothing of this function of Elijah's, and the prevalent opinion in these works is that the Messiah will not be anointed at all. Only later Jewish writers, as the Karaite Joseph ha-Levi (in Neubauer, *The LIII Chapter of Isaiah* 1.21) and Nahmanides, *Wikkuah*, mention the anointing of the Messiah by Elijah, and one may be permitted to question whether these writers represent an original Jewish view or not. See Ginzberg, *Unbekannte Sekte*, 349, note 4.

¹¹³ Aggadat Shir 7, 44. In Christian legendary lore it is Elijah who demands the same sign from the anti-Christ as his credential; comp. Bousset, *Antichrist Legende*, 203. In the Jewish version of this belief it is presupposed that the resurrected dead will have the same appearance and form as they had before their death. See Apocalypse of Baruch 50.2–4; Pesahim 68a.

¹¹⁴ Pirke Mashiah, 72; Pirke R. Yoshiyyahu, 115. On the view that Moses will lead the "generation of the wilderness", see vol. II, p. 373. As to Korah's rising from the earth, see vol. I, p. 23. On the revealing of the three holy vessels which were hidden for a long time, see vol. III, p. 48. On the sceptre of the Messiah, see vol. III, p. 307. On the view that the mountains will disappear in Messianic times, see vol. I, p. 80, and note 116; vol. V, p. 142, note 31. According to a Midrash

quoted in *Rimze Haftarot*, Nahamu, Elijah and Jeremiah will hasten to the Holy Land, seize it, and give it to Israel as a possession. Jeremiah's part in the work of redemption is presupposed in Matth. 16.14. Comp. also vol. VI, p. 386, note 13.

115 It is Elijah who, during the long exile, consoles the Messiah for the suffering inflicted upon him for the atonement of Israel's sins. See Konen 29; Ma'aseh R. Joshua, 50.; vol. I, pp. 22-23.

116 Apocalypse of Daniel (towards the end). In other (earlier) sources it is God who blows the Shofar; see vol. I, p. 283 and Alphabet R. Akiba 31. Comp. also Otot ha-Mashiah 61-62, where it is said that Michael will blow the Shofar twice. On the primeval light, see vol. I, p. 86. On the levelling of the mountains, see note 114.

117 Sukkah 52b. On the eight princes see note 142 on vol. I, p. 102.

118 Koheleth 4.1. As to the doctrine that the death of young children is due to the sins of the fathers, see Hashkem 3b, and vol. III, p. 98. Opinions differ as to the age of the children who will have a share in the world to come. According to some, all children, even those who only lived a moment, have a share, while others maintain that children are not entitled to a share, unless they died at an age when they could speak (*i. e.*, say Amen after a prayer). Other authorities think that male children are entitled to a share as soon as they are circumcized. One Rabbi is very generous, and puts embryos on equal footing with grown up children. See Yerushalmi Shebi'it 4, 45c. The custom, first referred to by the Babylonian Gaon R. Nahshon (comp. Sha'are Zedek, 22a, No. 5), of circumcizing children who died before their eighth day, has its origin in the above-mentioned view that only children after circumcision are entitled to a share in the world to come. On the status of the children of the wicked and of the idolaters in the world to come, see Yerushalmi Shebi'it, *loc. cit.*; Berakot 9, 13b; Tosefta Sanhedrin 13.1, Babli 110b. Connected with the conception that God in His mercy would not have the children suffer for the sins of the fathers is the view that in the time to come "the bastards", that is, the offspring of forbidden marriages, will not be excluded from the community of Israel. See Kiddushin 72b; Tosefta 5.4; WR 32.8; Koheleth, *loc. cit.* Against this view comp. ARN 22, 53, and Wisdom 4.6.

119 Abkir in Yalkut I, 153. Comp. vol. I, p. 394; vol. IV, p. 201; note 33. Comp. also the statement: "Happy is he who met Elijah or sat next to him; such a man is destined for the world to come;" Talmud Kallah 3 (end). This is probably a praraphrase of Ecclus. 48.11, where

the author of Kallah very likely read ראך ומת כי חיה יחיה, and, according to a well-known hermeneutical rule of the Haggadah, explained the phrase חיה יחיה in the sense of eternal life, or, as the Rabbis express it, "life in the world to come." Comp., *e. g.*, the midrashic explanation of 2 Kings 20.1 in Berakot 10a. The old versions of Ecclus. have similar interpretations of the text; see Smend, *Die Weisheit des Jesus Sirach, ad loc.* The old piyyut אליהו הנביא, sung at the termination of the Sabbath, closes with the stanza: "Happy is he who saw his (Elijah's) face in a dream; happy is he whom he offered the greeting of peace, or to whom he responded the greeting of peace." It is safe to assume that the Paitan made use of Kallah, *loc. cit.*, or of a source akin to it. As to seeing Elijah in a dream, see note 93.

VIII. ELISHA AND JONAH

Vol. IV, (pp. 237–253).

[1] Seder 'Olam 21; Tosefta Sotah 12.5; Megillah 14a; Shir 4.11; Ekah 4 (end). Comp. Ratner on Seder 'Olam, *loc. cit.* The statement in the two Midrashim just mentioned, that in Elijah's time there were sixty myriads of prophets (according to some, double this number), is very likely based on a misconception of the old source given in Seder 'Olam, where so large a number of prophets refers not to the time of Elijah, but to the entire course of Jewish history. The words in the old source read: There were forty-eight prophets and seven prophetesses, whose prophecies are written down in Scripture; but besides them there were as many prophets as men delivered from Egypt (*i. e.*, sixty myriads), whose prophecies, however, were not written down. In the quotation from Seder 'Olam in Megillah the variant is found : "double the number of those who were delivered from Egypt." Four of Elijah's disciples are mentioned by name; they are Micah, Jonah, Obadiah, and Elisha. PRK (Grünnhut's edition, 64). Comp. Index, under these names. Elisha's birthplace was Abel-meholah, "mourning-dance", so called because the inhabitants of this place had the custom of performing dances in the house of mourning. But thus they expressed their trust in God's justice, who rewards the pious after their departure from this life, and who will bring them to life in the time of resurrection. Aguddat Shemuel, 1 Kings. Comp. *Zeker Natan*, 92a, אבלות No. 2. On the disciples of Elijah and Elisha, see also Targum Deut. 34.3.

[2] ER 5, 22–23. Comp. also Ta'anit 10b; Sotah 49a; Berakot 31a, and Yerushalmi 5, 8d. As to the conception that the angel of death has no power over one occupied with the study of the Torah, see vol. IV, p. 114, and note 125 appertaining thereto. The angel who came to take Elijah was not the angel of death, but his task was similar to that entrusted to the latter. Comp. Friedmann, Introduction to ER, 16–17.

[3] Baraita of 32 Middot, No. 1. For the correct text, see MHG I, XIX. As to the question whether Elisha revived two dead persons (one more than his master Elijah), or only one, see note 21. Neither the eight miracles of Elijah nor the sixteen of Elisha are enumerated in the

Midrashim extant to-day, but the reading מיכן אמרו in MHG undoubtedly refers to an old source where they were given in detail. Comp. Katzenellenbogen, *Netibot 'Olam*, 9, *seq*.

⁴ Sotah 46b–47a. According to the Haggadah, Elisha's mockers were not boys, but grown-up men who "behaved like silly boys". The leading men of Jericho were not entirely free from blame, for if they had done their duty and accompanied the prophet on his way from the city to Bethel, nobody would have dared to insult the prophet Elisha in their presence, and the regrettable incident would not have occurred. See Sotah, *loc. cit.* In this passage it is also stated that the number of men killed by the bears amounted to forty-two, corresponding to the sacrifices brought by Balak (Num. 23.1, *seq*.), since God records good deeds even if not prompted by good motives; see note 39 on vol. IV, p. 31. Comp. also the quotation from an unknown Midrash by Shu'aib 90d; *Hadar* on Num. 23.28; Zohar II, 224a–224b; Kimhi 2 Kings 2.24. The relation of the forty-two sacrifices to the forty-two persons devoured by the bears is not quite clear, and the attempted explanations of the talmudic statement by the commentators are far from being satisfactory. On the sickness of Elisha, see vol. IV, pp. 245–246.

⁵ Pesahim 66b. On Elijah's irascibility, see vol. IV, pp. 216–217. It was on account of the merit of the observance of the Sabbath that God gave victory to Joram and his allies in the war against Moab; Mekilta RS, 162. Comp. note 35, on vol. IV, p. 187.

⁶ Sanhedrin 39b; Sifre N., 133; Tan. B. I, 167; WR 13.3; Jerome, introduction to his commentary on Obadiah (who remarks: *Hunc ajunt Hebräei, qui sub rege Samariae Achab...pavit...prophetas*); ER 24, 125–126. Obadiah was reluctant to announce the doom of the nation to which he belonged by birth, but was forced to do it by the seventy-one members of the "heavenly Synedrion"; Aggadat Bereshit 14, 32 (whence *Rimze Haftarot*, Wa-Yishlah). Comp. also *ibid*. 55, 101–114, and 58, 118–119. See further vol. I, p. 422; vol. III, p. 58; vol. VI, p. 375, note 104. The Haggadah concerning Obadiah's non-Jewish descent is very likely based upon the fact that he is described in Scripture as a "God-fearing man" (1 Kings 18.3), which later was the usual name of a proselyte. See Schürer, *Geschichte* (fourth edition), III, 174, note 70. During the great famine Ahab said to Obadiah: "It seems that thou art not as worthy a man as the pious of the former generations; Laban was blessed for the merits of Jacob, and Potiphar received blessings on account of Joseph; but thou bringest no blessings to me." A heavenly voice thereupon proclaimed: "And Obadiah

feareth the Lord greatly." See Sanhedrin, *loc. cit.*; ER, 24, 126. Comp. the following note.

⁷ ShR 31.4 and Tan. Mishpatim 9 read: Jehoram stretched out his hands to receive the interest paid him by Obadiah. His punishment for taking interest was that Jehu's bow smote him "between his arms" and killed him; see 2 Kings 9.24.; Comp. vol. IV, p. 190, top. That it was Obadiah's widow for whose benefit Elisha performed the miracle with the cruse of oil is presupposed in many old sources, Jewish as well as Christian. Comp. Josephus, *Antiqui.*, IX, 4.2; PK 2, 13b (which reads: Were it not for the merits of Obadiah's widow, Israel would have been destroyed); Tehillim 16, 118; Targum and Theodoretus on 2 Kings 4.1; ps.-Epiphanius, *De Vitis Prophetarum, Obadiah;* Ephraem I, 526C. Comp. also MHG I, 338; Zohar Hadash, Ruth 1.7 (beginning רבי אלכסנדרי; read אצל אליהו instead of א' חזקיה and perhaps also בעולם הבא is to be read instead of בעוה"ז; but it is possible that בעוה"ז in the mouth of Elijah, addressed to one dwelling in paradise, is the same as בעולם הבא when used by those dwelling in "this world"). Comp. also the references in the next note. The Haggadah identifying the prophet Obadiah with Obadiah who was "over the household" of Ahab (see preceding note) is due to an inference from the Haggadah that the "certain woman of the wives of the sons of the prophets" was the widow of Obadiah, the high official of Ahab's court.

⁸ Tosefta-Targum in Kimhi on 2 Kings 4, and in several MSS.; see the text of Targum published by Luzzatto in Geiger's *Wissenschaftliche Zeitschrift* V, 132–136, and in *Kobez Debarim Nehmadim*, No. 3. The text of the Tosefta-Targum in *Tag*, Way-yera, differs from all the other texts, and contains additional legendary material. On the "four God-fearing men", see 2 ARN 10, 26, and note 332 on vol. II, p. 125, as well as Ozar Midrashim, ed. Wertheimer 42. God's blessings extend and expand that which exists, but do not make things arise "from nothing"; hence it was necessary, in order that Elisha should perform this miracle, that the widow should have some oil in her possession, though its quantity was hardly sufficient to anoint the little finger. See Zohar I, 88a.

⁹ BR 35.3.

¹⁰ PRE 33. Comp. Luria, *ad loc.*, who calls attention to the reading אמו, according to which she was the mother, not the wife, of the prophet Iddo. The old sources identify Iddo with the prophet mentioned in 1 Kings 13.1, *seq.* Comp. Seder 'Olam R. 20; Tosefta Sanhedrin 14.5; Sifre D., 177; Josephus, *Antiqui.*, VIII, 8.5, and X, 4.4. The reading Ἀχίαν in the last passage does not occur

in the better texts; comp. Niese. In PRE עודד is perhaps to be read instead of עדו. Zohar I, 7b (introduction), and II, 44a, considers the Shunammite to have been the mother of the prophet Habakkuk. The same statement is found in *Rimze Haftarot*, Shebu'ot 2. Comp. vol. VI, p. 342, bottom.

¹¹ PRE 33.

¹² Zohar II, 44a, based in the main on Berakot 10b; Baba Mezi'a 87a (comp. vol. I, p. 243); Yerushalmi Sanhedrin 10, 29b; WR 24.6. For the fragrance issuing from the bodies of the pious, see vol. II, p. 19; vol. III, p. 5. On the view that the flies cannot approach the pious, see vol. III, p. 472. The day on which Elisha "promised" a child to the Shunammite woman was New Year, when God decides the fate of all men for the coming year. See Zohar I, 64b, 160b; II, 44a; III, 231.

¹³ PRE 33; Yerushalmi Sanhedrin 10, 29b; Mekilta Amalek 1, 53b. As to Gehazi's denying the quickening of the dead and as to his sensuousness, see Sifre, Z., 202, and vol. IV, p. 244. On the heat that caused the death of the child, see Yerushalmi Yebamot 15, 14d. It is incumbent on a disciple to visit his master on festival days, and when the Shunammite told her husband on a week-day that she was going to visit Elisha (2 Kings 4.23), he was greatly surprised. See Rosh ha-Shanah 16b; Zohar III, 265b.

¹⁴ ShR 4.2; note 11 on vol. IV, p. 197. Comp. also Batte Midrashot, III, 25, which reads: The son of the Shunammite was resuscitated from death as a reward for her hospitality to Elisha. This prophet revived two persons (see note 21), whereas his master Elijah only one, and this distinction of Elisha was his reward for having given up all his possessions and joined Elijah at the command of God; see ER 5, 22–23.

¹⁵ Sanhedrin 107b (comp. Rashi, *ad loc.*), and Sotah 47a, according to the reading of Yalkut II, on 2 Kings 5. The haggadic writings dwell upon the great humility of Naaman, who appeared before Elisha in a simple manner, without any pomp, though he was commander-in-chief of a great kingdom. See Haserot 35 (as haggadic explanation of the Ketib בסוסו in 2 Kings, 5.9; comp. Yerushalmi Sanhedrin 10.29b); Tan. (or WR?) in *Kad ha-Kemah*, נאוה I, 50a but not found in our texts of the Midrashim. Before his conversion, however, Naaman was very proud, and his leprosy was a punishment for his pride. See BaR 7.5;

¹⁶ Yerushalmi Sanhedrin 10, 29b; WR 24.7; PRE 33 (on this passage see Wertheimer, Batte Midrashot, III, 19, note 46); Berakot 10b. On

the reason of Gehazi's punishment, see Sanhedrin 100a; ARN 9, 41 and 155; note 413 on vol. III, p. 214; vol. IV, p. 243.

¹⁷ Sotah 47a; Sanhedrin 107b.   In the *Zadokite Fragments* 8.20 reference is made to the "words of Elisha spoken to Gehazi", and it is probable that a pseudepigraphic work containing the history of Elisha and his wicked disciple was known to this sectarian writer. Ginzberg, *Unbekannte Sekte*, 53, calls attention to the fact that according to the talmudic passages mentioned above, Gehazi settled in Damascus, the home of this sect.

¹⁸ Mishnah Sanhedrin 11 (10).1.   Comp. note 100 on vol. IV, p. 75.

¹⁹ Yerushalmi Sanhedrin 10, 29b.

²⁰ Baba Mezi'a 87a; Sotah 47a; Sanhedrin 107b; Yerushalmi Sanhedrin 10, 29b.   Comp. vol. IV, p. 240.   As to the view that the generations before Elisha did not know of illness which was not fatal, see the references given in note 357 on vol. II, p. 131; vol. IV, pp. 274–275; Yelammedenu in Yalkut II, 874 on Ps. 116.   On Elisha's disease and severity, see also Hasidim 78, and ps.-Tertullian, *Adversus Marcionitas* 3.210 *seq.*   The prophet's severity towards his disciple is censured also in Mekilta Yitro 1, 58b, where it is said: Elisha acted against the rule: "Let thy right hand push away and thy left hand bring back."— Tosefta-Targum Kings 5.19 reads: Elisha told Naaman that it was not lawful to bring sacrifices outside the Holy Land, and accordingly if he desires to bring sacrifices to God, he must sent them annually to the holy Temple in Jerusalem.

²¹ PRE 33.   According to Koheleth 13.10, it was the false prophet Zedekiah (1 Kings 22.24) who was brought back to life by the contact with Elisha's corpse, but only for a moment, to avoid his burial near Elisha.   A similar statement is found in Sanhedrin 47a; Hullin 7b; Tosefta-Targum 2 Kings 13.21; Tehillim 26, 220.   In all these sources it is stated that the man who touched Elisha's bones "stood up on his feet", but did not go to his house, for he immediately died and was buried in another place.   Tehillim, *loc. cit.*, adds that he was the son of the Shunammite whom Elisha had once resuscitated, and when he died a second time, they threw his corpse near that of Elisha, that he might come to life again.   He revived again, but died immediately after, because he was wicked.   At all events, the promise made to Elisha by Elijah to give him "a double portion of his spirit" (2 Kings 2.9-10) was fulfilled; the master resuscitated only one person, and the disciple two.   Comp. Sanhedrin, *loc. cit.*; vol. IV, p. 229, note 3.

²² Tosefta Sotah 12.6. Comp. also ER 8, 39, where פּוּסטין =
"fossata", an allusion to כרה in 2 Kings 6.23. The Arameans esteemed the prophet so highly, that when their king Ben-Hadad became
ill, he sent a present to Elisha, the value of which outweighed all the
treasures of Damascus, and requested him to predict the outcome of
his illness. See Shir 4.8. On the contrast between the pagan ruler,
who in time of illness inquired of the prophet of the Lord, and the Jewish
king Ahaziah, who sent his messengers to inquire of Baal-Zebub
whether he would recover from his sickness (2 Kings 1.2), see Batte
Midrashot, III, 28–29; Aggadat Shir 1, 26. On the divine honors
paid to Ben-Hadad and his successor Hazael by the Arameans, see
Josephus, *Antiqui.*, IX, 4.6. Israel's victory over the Arameans, under
king Joash, was the reward of this king for his refusal to listen to
the accusations brought against the prophet Amos by Amaziah (Amos
7.10, *seq.*). The king said to Amaziah: God forfend that the prophet
should have uttered such a prophecy; but if he did, he merely obeyed
the command of God. See ER 16, 88.

²³ Ketubot 106a, which reads: Elisha was always surrounded
by at least two thousand and two hundred disciples. Comp. also
Targum Yerushalmi Deut. 34.3, and note 1.

²⁴ Seder 'Olam 19.

²⁵ Seder 'Olam 19; BR 21.5 (here very likely Jonah is identified
with the "one" of the sons of the prophets mentioned in 2 Kings 6.3,
seq.); Alphabet of Ben Sira 10b. Jonah first attempted to convey to
Jehu the divine message by signs, but the latter being somewhat
foolish by nature (comp. 2 Kings 9.20, where שגעון is taken to mean
foolishness, madness), did not understand the signs, and the prophet
had to speak plainly to him. Truly says the proverb: "For the wise
a hint, for the fool a punch". See Alphabet of Ben Sira, *loc. cit.*
Jehu belonged to the tribe of Manasseh (נמשי in 2 Kings 9.2 = מנשי),
and was the last legitimate king of the northern kingdom; those who
succeeded him were nothing else than chieftains of brigands; PR 3,
12b; Tadshe 8; Yerushalmi Horayyot 3, 47c. On Jonah's relation to
Elijah, see vol. IV, p. 197, top, and note 38.

²⁶ PRE 10; Tan. Wa-Yikra 8; Midrash Jonah 96; Yalkut on Jonah
1. According to these sources, the first prophecy of Jonah is that
mentioned in 2 Kings 14.25; against this view, see Mekilta Bo (פתיחתא),
2a, and Yebamot 98a, where it is stated that this prophet received
only two divine revelations, both concerning Nineveh (comp. Jonah
1.1 and 3.1). The passage of 2 Kings 14.25 is therefore explained as

follows: The impending punishment of Israel was averted, as in the case of the doom decreed against Nineveh.

²⁷ PRE 10; Tan. Wa-Yikra 8; Midrash Jonah 96. God conferred a great honor on the inhabitants of Nineveh by sending the prophet to them, a distinction never before granted to the "nations of the world." Asshur, the ancestor of these people, had left his native country, and founded Nineveh in honor of God (he did not wish to remain among the sinful adherents of the wicked Nimrod; comp. vol. I, p. 202, top). As he honored God, even so were his descendants honored by God. Jonah's refusal to go to Nineveh was due to his love for Israel. He knew that the Ninevites would repent of their evil doings, and this would cause the wrath of God against His people, who notwithstanding the numerous admonitions by many prophets, continued to sin. By fleeing from the Holy Land, Jonah hoped to prevent the disgrace of Israel, since the Shekinah does not reveal itself outside the Holy Land, and being removed from the place of revelation, he could no longer receive communications from God to go to Nineveh. Mekilta Bo(פתיחתא), 1b–2a; Yerushalmi Sanhedrin 11, 30b; Jerome on Jonah 1.2 and 4.1; Tertullian, *De Pudicitia* 10 and ps.-Tertullian, *De Jona* 20, *seq.* On the view that no revelations were made to prophets outside the Holy Land, see also Mo'ed Katan 25a; Mekilta RS 5–6; Zohar I, 85a, and II, 170b; John 8.52; unknown Midrash quoted by Kara, Josh. 22; 57. According to the sources mentioned at the beginning of this note, Jonah's purpose in fleeing from the dry land was to evade a further divine revelation which would send him to Nineveh. He believed that God's glory (manifestation of the Shekinah) shows itself in heaven and on dry land, but not on water.

²⁸ PRE 10; Tan. Wa-Yikra 8; Midrash Jonah 96–97; Nedarim 38a. In the last passage it is stated that "God causes the Shekinah to dwell only upon those who are physically strong, rich, wise, and humble. Jonah's wealth is quoted as a proof that the prophets were rich. As to the midrashic basis for the statement that Jonah paid for the entire cargo, see Jerome on Jonah with reference to the masoretic reading of שכרה in Jonah 1.3, in contrast to Septuagint which reads שכרו. On Tarshish, see Jerome, *ad loc.*, and Rahmer, *Die Commentarii zu den kleinen Propheten, Jonah*, 15–16.

²⁹ PRE 10; Tan. Wa-Yikra 8; Midrash Jonah 97. On the violence of this storm, see BR 24.4, and note 29 on vol. IV, p. 200. On the attempts made by the crew of the ship to save Jonah's life, see also Zohar I, 121a, and II, 230b–231a.

³⁰ PRE 10; Tan. Wa-Yikra 8; Midrash Jonah 97; Zohar II, 230b. Jonah had boarded the ship in the hope that he would lose his life on the voyage and would thus be spared the pain of seeing the heathen repent (see note 27); Mekilta Bo (פתיחתא), 2a; Jerome on Jonah 1.6. According to the Halakah, the prophet, who like Jonah, suppresses the prophecy revealed to him, will be put to death by heaven (מיתה בידי שמים); Tosefta Sanhedrin 14.15; Yerushalmi 11, 30b; Babli 89b.

³¹ Midrash Jonah (only this source contains the episode with the female fish); PRE 10; Tan. Wa-Yikra 8. As to the statements made concerning Leviathan, see vol. I, pp. 27, 28, 29. The statement that Jonah will capture the Leviathan in the days to come is perhaps connected with the Messianic part ascribed to this prophet; see note 38. All changes in nature which took place in the course of history were foreseen at the creation of the world (see vol. I, pp. 50–51), and hence it is said here that at the creation of the world God made a fish intended to harbor Jonah. The Haggadah explains סוף (Jonah 2.8) as ים סוף, and hence the statement that Jonah was shown the Red Sea. Comp. also Targum and Jerome, *ad loc.*

³² Midrash Jonah 98–99. This prayer of Jonah has the regular form of the Selihah. PRE 10, Tan. Wa-Yikra 8 and 2 Midrash Jonah 33 have a short prayer only. They add that the fish remained still while the prophet prayed. Jonah's soul left him when he was thrown into the sea, and ascended to God to be judged. The heavenly court decided that Jonah's soul should be returned to him; in possession of his soul he was swallowed up by the fish. No sooner, however, had the fish swallowed him than it died, but it came back to life when Jonah revived. See Zohar I, 121a. It is not quite certain whether the translation of the last sentence is correct. Jonah was near losing his life, because he did not fulfil the vow he had taken upon himself (did not go to Nineveh, as he had vowed to do?), and was saved from death only after he spoke the word: "I shall redeem my vow." See Yelammedenu in Yalkut I, 784, on Num. 30. On the prayer of Jonah, see Shu'-aib, 122b, and Kad ha-Kemah, Kippurim, 116, *seq.*

³³ Midrash Jonah 99. On the conversion of the ship's crew, see also PRE 10; Tan. Wa-Yikra 8. For a different explanation of Jonah 1.16, see Targum and Jerome, *ad loc.*, as well as the Midrashim just cited. All these authorities presuppose that the crew did not bring their sacrifices to God while still on board.

³⁴ Midrash Jonah 99–100; second version 25–26. According to these Midrashim the number of the population of Nineveh was

twelve times as large as that given in Jonah 4.11. The "six score thous-
and persons" refers to the population of one of the twelve districts
into which the city was divided. PRE 43 and Tosefta-Targum on Jonah
3.6 make Pharaoh king of Nineveh. Comp. vol. II, p. 150; vol. III,
p. 29.

35 Mishnah Ta'anit 2.1; Babli 16a; Yerushalmi 2, 65b; PK
25, 161a–161b; Midrash Jonah 100–102; PRE 43; ShR 45.1. It is
noteworthy that in the Yerushalmi and PK the separation of the young
animals from their mothers is described as an Arab custom. The description of the penance of the Ninevites by Tabari II, 45, is dependent
on Jewish sources. Jerome on Jonah 3.10 agrees almost literally with
the Mishnah Ta'anit. On the penance, see also Shu'aib, Jonah, 122a.
The narrative about the treasure is a variation of an Alexander legend,
which has a great vogue in Jewish literature. Comp. Yerushalmi
Baba Mezi'a 2, 8c; BR 33.1, and parallel passages cited by Theodor.
See also note 27 on vol. IV, p. 131, bottom.

36 As to the falling out of the hair, see Ibn Ezra on Jonah 4.6.

37 Midrash Jonah 102; the second version of this Midrash 34–35
gives a long prayer by Jonah in which he beseeches God to pardon his
sins. The destruction of Nineveh forty years later (Yalkut II, 550,
on Jonah 3, reads forty days, and hence the text, vol. IV, p. 253, top;
but the correct reading is years) is found only in PRE 43. Comp.
also Tobit 4.4; Josephus, *Antiqui.*, IX, 10.2, and IX, 11.3.

38 Tehillim 26, 220, where reference is also made to the widespread view that Jonah was the son of the widow of Zarephath resuscitated by Elijah; see note 9 on vol. IV, p. 197, top. Since the son of the
widow is said to be the "Messiah of the tribe of Joseph" (ER 18, 97–98),
the statement that Jonah was permitted to enter paradise alive is very
likely to be understood in the sense that he awaits there the end of
times to start on his Messianic mission. The "Messiah, the son of
David" likewise entered paradise alive, and awaits there "his time".
See Derek Erez Z. 1 (end), and parallel passages cited by Tawrogi. It
is, however, possible that the Messianic part attributed to Jonah (= the
son of the widow of Zarephath) is a Jewish adaptation of the Christian view which considers him a prototype of Jesus; see Matth. 12.39;
Luke 11.29. The statement in 3 Macc. 6.8 that Jonah returned from
Nineveh to his people is not known in rabbinic writings. The assertion that the "Book of Jonah" is a book by itself, and not a part of
the Book of the Twelve תרי עסר (BaR 18.21) wishes very likely to call
attention to the fact that this biblical book has a character of its own,

its contents dealing exclusively with the story of a heathen city. See a similar remark with regard to the "section treating of Balaam" in note 784 on vol. III, p. 380. On the time during which Jonah was active, see notes 1 and 25. Comp. also Clemens Alexandrinus, *Stromata*, 1.21, who considers Jonah to have been the contemporary of Isaiah, Hosea, and Daniel.

39 'Erubin 96a; Mekilta Bo 17, 21a (below).
40 Yerushalmi Sukkah 5, 55a.

IX. THE LATER KINGS OF JUDAH

Vol. IV, (pp. 257–287)

[1] Seder 'Olam 18; comp. note 23 on vol. IV, p. 246.

[2] Megillah 14a; Horayyot 12a; Keritot 6a. Comp. also note 22 on vol. IV, p. 84, with regard to the pitcher out of which Samuel took the oil to anoint Saul. As to the "holy oil" being used for the anointing of kings, see vol. III, p. 179. Against this, see Josephus, *Antiqui.*, IX, 6.1.

[3] Alphabet of Ben Sira 10b. Comp. note 23 on vol. IV, p. 246.

[4] Sanhedrin 102b (top). Comp. vol. IV, p. 181. Great is peace; although one performs many good deeds, he achieves nothing if he does not promote peace. This may be inferred from the life of Jehu: he abolished idolatry from among Israel, he caused the downfall of Ahab's dynasty, and killed Jezebel; but all his good deeds counted for nought because he did not promote peace. See Midrash Gadol 129–130. On the worship of the golden calves even by the pious in Israel, see vol. IV, p. 199. According to EZ 7, 184, Jehu at first was a very pious man, and did not worship the golden calves, but when he became king, he deteriorated, and followed in the footsteps of his predecessors.

[5] EZ 7, 184; ER 18, 88. A boon conferred by God upon one as a reward for a good deed remains not only with the person that merited it, but also with his descendants unto the fourth generation, whether they are good or wicked. God granted the kingdom to Jehu for his good deeds (see 2 Kings 10.30), and notwithstanding his own and his descendants' sinfulness, lasted for five generations. See EZ, *loc. cit.* Josephus, *Antiqui.*, IX, 8.5–6, describes Jehoahaz (the son of Jehu) as a repentant sinner, and his son Joash as a pious man, whereas EZ, *loc. cit.*, puts Jehu and all his descendants among the sinners.

[6] Sanhedrin 102b. According to one opinion, the Judaean kings Ahaz and Ahaziah, as well as all the kings of the northerm kingdom concerning whom Scripture uses the expression "and they did that which was evil in the sight of the Lord", have no share in the world to come, but are spared the tortures of hell; Sanhedrin 103a; comp. note 107 on vol. IV, p. 107, and note 59 on vol. IV, p. 155.

[7] Sanhedrin, 95b.

⁸ Tan. B. II, 31; Tan. Wa-Era 9; Seder 'Olam 18 (comp. Ratner, note 7); Tehillim 18, 151; Shir 1.16; Targum 2 Chron. 22.11; ShR 8.2. In the three last-named Midrashim a different opinion is given, according to which Joash was kept during the summer in the upper chamber, above the holy of holies, and during the winter in one of the cells (תא) of the Temple.

⁹ 'Abodah Zarah 44a; Targum 2 Chron. 23.11, and 1 Chron. 20.2; comp. vol. IV, p. 118. This crown, it is said, was so heavy, that it could not be placed on a person's head. David, however, engraved the "Name" on it, and this had the effect that he and his rightful successors did not feel the heavy weight thereof. According to others, the crown was suspended over the heads of the Davidic kings by means of a magnet. The child saved by Jehoash was called Joash because of the despair (יאש "he despaired") of the people of having a descendant of David occupy the throne once more. See *Rimze Haftarot*, Shekalim; comp. the similar etymology of the name Joshiah in Haserot 17a.

¹⁰ Seder 'Olam 18.

¹¹ Ps.-Sa'adya on 2 Chron., p. 54. Comp. Ratner, Seder 'Olam 19 note 14; note 95 on vol. IV, p. 173 and Index, s. v. "Benaiah". Opinions differ as to whether 2 Chron. 24.3 refers to Jehoiada marrying two wives or to his making Joash marry them. Maimonides, *Yad ha-Hazakah, Issure Biah*, 17. 13, and *Kele ha-Mikdash*, 5.10, maintains that according to the Halakah (comp. Yoma 13a) the high priest is forbidden to have two wives, and therefore the biblical verse under discussion does not speak of the two wives of the high priest Jehoiada. RABD on *Issure Biah, loc. cit.*, on the other hand, follows Rashi on 2 Chron., 24.3, and takes לו in this verse to refer to Jehoiada in agreement with Septuagint; but Josephus, *Antiqui.*, IX, 7.5, and Vulgate understand it in the same way as Maimonides.

¹² Tan. B. II, 23 and 31; Tan. Wa–Era 9; Seder 'Olam 18; ShR 8. 2; Makiri on Ps. 9(end), citing Tan.; ps.-Jerome on 2 Chron. 24.17.

¹³ Midrash Shir 3, 27a.

¹⁴ Yerushalmi Ta'anit 4, 69a; Ekah, introduction, 20–21; Koheleth 3.16 and 10.4.

¹⁵ Gittin 57b; Yerushalmi Ta'anit 4, 69a; Ekah, introduction, 20–21; Koheleth 3.16 and 10.4. Comp. vol. IV, p. 304.

¹⁶ Mekilta Amalek 1, 53a (as to the meaning of שפוטים, see Ginzberg, *Compte Rendu*, 7 = R.E.J. LXVI, 303); Tan. B. II, 23–24; Tan. Wa-Era 9; ShR 8.2; Yerushalmi Kiddushin 1, 61a; Makiri on Ps. 9 (end); ps-Jerome on 2 Chron. 24.27. The Midrashim cited remark, four kings

claimed to be gods: Hiram, Nebuchadnezzar, Pharaoh, and Joash; they ended by being treated like women (*"coitu foemineo commixantur"*). Joash was ungrateful to his benefactor Jehoiada (he killed the latter's son), and he was killed by men who were descended from the Moabites and Ammonites (see 2 Chron. 24.26), the two ungrateful nations. See Mekilta, *loc. cit.* On the characterization of these two nations as ungrateful, see vol. I, p. 257, and vol. III, p. 373.

17 Josephus, *Antiqui.*, IX, 9.3. Comp. also Seder 'Olam 19. Amaziah's violent death was the punishment for his cruelty against the Edomites; Ekah, introduction, 14.

18 BR 80.3; Tan. B. I, 171; Tan. Wa-Yishlah 7; Baraita of 32 Middot, No. 26.

19 Seder 'Olam 19. This passage also states that Amaziah did not rule the last fifteen years of his life, his kingdom having been administered by his son Uzziah, who later, in his turn, had to leave the administration of the kingdom to his son Jotham for twenty years, from the time he was afflicted with leprosy unto his death. By means of these assumptions the Midrashim and the Talmud are able to explain several chronological difficulties offered by the data found in Scripture with regard to the lives of these kings; comp. the references in Ratner, notes 24, 26. Amaziah's general is said to have ended his days in Morviedero, Spain. See Ibn Habib, *Darke Noam*, 6b and Ginzberg, *Jewish Encyclopedia*, I, 487.

20 Seder 'Olam 20; Pesahim 87b; Baba Batra 14b; PR 33, 153b (this passage reads: Hosea prophesied for ninety years); EZ 9, 86. These sources speak of the four contemporary prophets, Hosea, Amos, Isaiah, and Micah. The last-named prophet, however, was a younger contemporary of the other three, as is explicitly stated in Seder 'Olam *loc. cit.* PR 33, 150b, seems to identify the prophet Micah with Micaiah the son of Imlah who prophesied in the time of Jehoshaphat (1 Kings 22.8). Comp. PK 16.135b; Ibn Ezra on Micah 1.2; Ratner, note 6 on Seder 'Olam, *loc. cit.* Obadiah is also said to have been active as a prophet during the time of Jehoshaphat; Baraita of 32 Middot, as quoted by ps.-Rashi on BR 83.3. Comp. Ratner, *loc. cit.*, note 7, and Grünhut, *Likkutim*, II, 11b, note 3. This would agree with the widespread view that the prophet Obadiah is none else than Obadiah, the official of Ahab's court. Comp. vol. IV, pp. 240–241. Our texts of Seder 'Olam, *loc. cit.*, state that Obadiah prophesied during the time of Amaziah, "when Edom fell never to rise again." Yalkut II, Obadiah, and ps.-Rashi, *loc. cit.*, read, however, Jehoshaphat instead

of Amaziah. Grünhut, *loc. cit.*, though quoting ps.-Rashi, did not notice that this author had the same reading in Seder 'Olam as Yalkut. Clemens Alexandrinus, *Stromata*, 1.20, makes Isaiah, Hosea, Micah and Joel contemporaries, and Jerome (comp. his remarks on Hosea 1.1; Joel 1.1) partly depends upon this Christian author and partly upon Jewish tradition; hence his statement that Hosea, Joel, Amos, Obadiah, Jonah, Micah, and Isaiah were σύγχρονοι (= אחד בפרק of the rabbinical sources), contemporaries. Jerome and Clement find in the order of the biblical books a hint as to the times of the respective authors. Now as Micah (and Amos) were younger contemporaries of Hosea, it follows that Joel, Obadiah, and Jonah, whose books are placed between those bearing the names of Hosea and Micah, lived during the same period as the latter. As to the Jewish view concerning the time of Joel, see note 56 on Vol. IV, p. 191 and Index, s. v. On Micah, see also note 1 on vol. IV, p. 239.

²¹ PK 25, 159b, which reads: Beeri died in Exile, that the Godless exiles might rise with him at the time of resurrection. For a similar statement concerning the death of Moses in the wilderness, see note 615 on vol. III, p. 313.

²² WR 6.6 and 15.2. Beeri's prophecy consisted of two verses, which were later inserted in the Book of Isaiah, 8.19–20.

²³ Pesahim 87a–87b (here it is also stated that the name Gomer of Diblaim, as Hosea's wife is called in Scripture, was not her real name, but indicates her disreputable mode of life); EZ 9, 186–187; Targum as quoted in *Kad ha-Kemah*, I אהבה, 6b-7a; We-Hizhir I, 86. As to the interpretation by the Haggadah of the prophecies given in Hosea 1 and 2, see BaR 2.12–14. The view that Hosea's marriage spoken of in Scripture is to be understood as a prophetic vision is unknown in the old sources. Ibn Ezra, *ad loc.*, and Maimonides (*Guide of the Perplexed*, II, 46) are perhaps the earliest authors maintaining such a rationalistic view. On the haggadic interpretation of the name Gomer of Diblaim, see also Jerome and Targum, *ad loc.* As to the celibacy of Moses, see vol. III, p. 316.

²⁴ Shalshelet ha-Kabbalah, 19a.

²⁵ PK 16, 125b; PR 33, 150b; WR 10.2. The activity of Amos as a prophet preceded that of Isaiah by two years; the latter began to prophesy on the "day of the earthquake", the former two years before the earthquake. Comp. Seder 'Olam 20, and the references given in note 29. In Greek transliteration the names Amos (עמוס) and Amoz (אמוץ) sound alike, and hence the statement found in many Christian

356

writers, who were ignorant of Hebrew, that Isaiah was the son of the prophet Amos; see, *e. g.*, Clement, *Stromata*, 1.20; ps.-Epiphanius, *De Vitis Prophetarum*, s. v. "Isaiah". In the original of Ascension of Isaiah 1.1 the text very likely read: ישעיהו בן אמוץ הנביא, which should be translated "the prophet Isaiah, the son of Amoz," and not as the Greek translator has it, "Isaiah the son of Amoz the prophet." Yahya, *Shalshelet ha-Kabbalah*, 99b, follows Christina authors (though he does not say so) in identifying Amoz the father of Isaiah with Amos the prophet. It is, however, an old Jewish tradition that Isaiah's father was also a prophet, living in the reign of Amaziah, whose brother he was. It was at his advice that the king dismissed the army he had gathered from among the Ephraimites (2 Chron. 25.7–10). Seder 'Olam 20; Megillah 10b; Sotah 10b. Comp. also Megillah 15a; WR 6.6 (whih read: Wherever the names of the prophet and his father are given it is sure that he was a prophet the son of a prophet); Aggadat Bereshit 14, 32. In WR a different opinion is quoted, according to which all prophets mentioned in Scripture were the sons of prophets. With regard to the native places of the prophets, Megillah, *loc. cit.*, states that all those whose birthplaces are not given in Scripture were Jerusalemites. PK 16, 128b considers Amos to have been a post-exilic prophet. Comp. note 20 and note 56 on vol. IV, p 191.

²⁶ Pesahim 87b; ER 17, 88; EZ 7, 184.

²⁷ Yerushalmi Hallah 2, 58c. Comp. also EZ 7, 184.

²⁸ Yahya, *Shalshelet ha-Kabbalah*, 97, undoubtedly based on a Christian source; comp. note 25. According to ps.-Epiphanius, *De Vitis Prophetarum*, s. v. "Amos", this prophet met his death through a blow on his temples dealt him with a stick by the son of the false prophet Amaziah. Comp. Index, s. v. "Amaziah, Priest of Beth-el".

²⁹ Azariah the "chief priest" in 2 Chron. 26.20, is identified with Azariah the high priest, in 1 Chron. 5.36. Comp. Sifre Z., 112, and Josephus, *Antiqui.*, IX, 10.4. The Rabbis maintain that chapter 6 of Isaiah is the beginning of this prophetic book, and contains the first vision granted to the prophet on the day on which the impious king Uzziah attempted to sacrifice on the altar and was stricken with leprosy. As a "leper is like dead" (comp. note 177 on vol. I, p. 364), מות in Is. 6.1 does not mean death but leprosy. See Targum, *ad loc.*; ShR 1.34; Tan. Zaw 13. Comp. also Seder 'Olam 20; Mekilta Shirah 6 (beginning); Yelammedenu in Yalkut II, 404 on Is. 6; Aphraates,

362 (read ארעא instead of עמא); Jerome on Is. 7.3, *seq.*; ps.-Jerome on 2 Chron. 26.22.

³⁰ Josephus, *Antiqui.*, IX, 10.4. Tan. Noah 13 is not contented with a breach in the Temple; it says that the hall of the Temple (היכל) was rent in two parts, separated from each other by a cleft of twelve miles (a favorite number; see Index) in width, and the Midrash trans-fers to the Temple itself that which Josephus tells of the Temple mount. Comp. also Targum Is. 28.21, as well as the references given at the end of the preceding note; add ARN 9, 42. On leprosy as a punishment for arrogance see *ARN, loc. cit.*, and vol. III, p. 214. According to Tan. Noah 13, the passion with which Uzziah devoted himself to the cultivation of the soil (comp. 2 Chron. 26.10) caused him to neglect the study of the Torah. The evil consequence thereof was that he became arrogant, saying: "God is king, and so am I, and it behooves the terrestrial king to do the service in the Temple of the celestial king." As the "love of husbandry" caused the downfall of Uzziah, even so was it the cause of that of Cain and Noah. Comp. also Yelammedenu, No. 43 (here Cain, Job, and Uzziah are given); BR 22.3; Mekilta RS, 92 (where Cain, Noah, Lot, and Uzziah are described as the four men who were "greedy for husbandry", and came thereby to grief).—The statement of Josephus that a ray of sunlight caused Uzziah's leprosy is evidently based on a haggadic interpretation of והצרעת זרחה in 2 Chron. 26.19, the usual meaning of זרח being "shone" in regard to the sun. See, however, also vol. III, p. 303, and note 197 on vol. III, p. 90 (bottom) in connection with death by celestial fire as a pun-ishment for the laity usurping the priesthood.

³¹ Tan. Zaw 13; comp. vol. III, p. 303. As to the earthquake taking place on the day on which Uzziah attempted his sacrifice, see references cited in the two preceding notes; and Jerome on Amos 1.3.

³² On Isaiah's receiving the "call" on that day, see note 29. He was in his study when he heard a heavenly voice proclaim: "Whom shall I send? I sent Amos, and they (Israel) said: God found no better messenger than this stammerer (comp. vol. IV, p. 261, and Koheleth 1.1). I sent Micah, and they smote him on the cheek (I Kings 22.24; comp. note 20). Whom shall I now send, and who will go for us?" Isaiah replied: "Here am I, send me." Thereupon God said to him: "My children are rebellious and troublesome; art thou prepared to stand their abuses and blows?" But Isaiah, far from being intimidated, said: "I am willing to give my back to the smiters and my cheek to them that pluck off the hair (Is. 50.6), but am not worthy to serve as

Thy messenger to Thy children." As a reward for his trust in Israel, whom he hoped to bring back to the path of righteousness by his prophecies, Isaiah was distinguished above all the other prophets in two ways. All the other prophets received their spirit of prophecy from their masters (the spirit of Elijah came over to Elisha; the spirit of Moses was put upon the seventy elders), but Isaiah prohesied from the mouth of the Almighty." He was further distinguished by repeating the introductory words of his prophecy (comp., *e. g.*, 40. 1; 51.9, 12, 16), indicating thereby that their fulfilment was certain. See PK 16, 125b; WR 10.2. Comp. also ER 16, 82, and notes 35, 36.

³³ Jewish tradition in Jerome on Is. 6.6. This interpretation throws light on the obscure words חייב לאוכחא אנא in Targum on this passage.

³⁴ As to the conception that the sight of the divine causes death to mortals, see vol. III, p. 137.

³⁵ On Isaiah the "comforter of the mourners for Zion," see Ecclus. 48.21–25. This shows that Isaiah's authorship of the entire book now bearing his name was known at as early a time as that of Ben Sira. Comp. ER 16.82–83; Jerome, *Ad Damasum* 1.375.

³⁶ PR 33, 150b–151a. About the Seraphim which Isaiah saw, see the quotation from an unknown Midrash in BHM, V, 162, according to which the Seraph has six wings to praise God each work-day of the week with one of them, whereas on the Sabbath the Seraphim are silent, and God is praised by the terrestrials, *i. e.* Israel. Comp. also *Orehot Hayyim*, I, 18b. As to the supposition that Israel recites the Kedushah only on the Sabbath, see Ginzberg, *Geonica*, II, 48. According to PK 9, 75b, and parallel passages cited by Buber, the Seraphim praise God with two wings, they cover their faces with two wings, that they look not at the Shekinah, and with two wings they cover their feet, that the Shekinah be not reminded by them of the sin committed by Israel in worshipping the golden calf, since the "sole of their feet is like the sole of the calf's foot;" comp. Ezek. 1.7. The two prophets Isaiah and Ezekiel saw the same heavenly vision; the latter gave a fuller description thereof, than the former. "Ezekiel is to be likened to a villager, who saw the king, and Isaiah to the inhabitant of the capital city." The former, not accustomed to the sight of the divine glory, gave a detailed description of what he saw, whereas the latter, being used to it, did not care to describe it. The "wings" spoken of by Isaiah are identical with the "faces" referred to by Ezekiel. It is true that the Seraphim

which Isaiah saw had six wings, whereas the heavenly beings described by Ezekiel had only four faces. This discrepancy is to be explained by the fact that at the time of the destruction of the Temple the two wings (= faces) used by these heavenly beings to praise God with were taken from them, and hence Ezekiel, living at that time, saw "four faces" only. See Hagigah 13b. The Seraph that touched Isaiah with a live coal was Michael; Berakot 4b. On the day of judgment Isaiah will plead for the sinners that they may be permitted to look at the blissful joys of the righteous. His pleading in their behalf will not be granted, as "the congregation of Israel" (כנסת ישראל) will oppose it, insisting that the sinners are not entitled to such consideration. See Alphabet of R. Akiba ('כ), 33–34. In BHM, V, 50, an allusion is found to the view, according to which Isaiah at this memorable vision was shown the punishment of the sinners in hell.

³⁷ Seder 'Olam 19, and the parallel passages cited by Ratner.

³⁸ Sukkah 45b. Jotham's piety is also referred to in BR 63.1 and by Josephus, *Antiqui.*, IX, 11.2. Comp. further vol. IV, p. 180.

³⁹ Megillah 11a; BR 27.1; Esther R. 1.1; Tehillim 105, 449. In these sources an old tradition is given, according to which Scripture indicated with regard to five men that they were pious from "first to last", and with regard to other five that they were wicked from "first to last". The five pious men are: Abraham, Moses, Aaron, Hezekiah and Ezra; the five wicked ones are: Nimrod, Esau, the brothers Dathan and Abiram (counted as one), Ahaz, and Ahasuerus. Ps.-Jerome on 2 Chron. 23.9 quotes this Haggadah with regard to Ahaz.

⁴⁰ Sanhedrin 103b. Here, as in many other places (comp. EZ 9, 187–188; BR 42.3 and parallel passages cited by Theodor), Ahaz is said to have issued an edict against the study of the Torah. Comp. note 112.

⁴¹ Tan. B. I, 153; Aggadat Bereshit 48, 98–99; Jerome on Is. 7.12.

⁴² On the view that Isaiah was a blood-relative of the king, see note 25.

⁴³ Sanhedrin 104a; Yerushalmi 10, 27d; WR 26.3. *Rimze Haftarot*, Yitro, quotes the statement of the "wise" (אמרו חכמינו ז"ל) according to which Ahaz, when passing women who were engaged in washing, closed his eyes to avoid looking at the bare parts of their bodies. It seems fairly certain that the author confused the statement in Sanhedrin, *loc. cit.* (דכבשינהו לאפיה) with Makkot 24a (זה שאינו מסתכל וגו'), and attributed the virtue of modesty to the wicked king,

in direct contrast to the view of the Haggadah which maintains that Ahaz abolished the laws against incest; comp. Sanhedrin 103b.

⁴⁴ Sannhedrin 103b; Yerushalmi 10, 27d; WR 36.3. There are, however, also others who maintain that this wicked king forfeited his share in the world to come; comp. note 100 on vol. IV, p. 75, and vol. V, p. 419, note 118.

⁴⁵ Seder 'Olam 22; Ta'anit 30b; Yerushalmi 4, 69c; Baba Batra 121a; Gittin 88a; Ekah, introduction, 33; EZ 9, 188; 'Eser Galuyyot 2–4; Aggadat Shir 1, 28; Jerome on Hos. 10.2. The last-named author gives, on Hos. 10.5, the following somewhat humorous Haggadah communicated to him by "the Hebrews". The crafty and greedy priests at Beth-el and Dan had substituted gilded images of calves for those made of solid gold, which they appropriated for themselves. When the Assyrian kings captured the golden calves, the people mourned the loss, but the priests laughed inwardly at the trick played by them. This is the meaning of the words of the prophet (Hos. 10.5): The inhabitants of Samaria shall be in dread for the calves of Beth-aven; for the people thereof shall mourn over it, and the priests thereof shall "laugh" over it.

⁴⁶ Sanhedrin 63b. Another interpretation of the names of the idols mentioned in 2 Kings 17.30–31 is given in Yerushalmi 'Abodah Zarah 3, 42d, according to which the inhabitants of Samaria fashioned the images of Jacob and Joseph to whom they paid divine honors. This is the answer of the Jews to the Samaritans' claim to be the only legitimate descendants of Joseph. Tosefta-Targum on Kings, *loc. cit.*, contains, with slight modification, the views of Babli, as well as Yerushalmi, concerning these idols. Comp. also R. Hananel, as quoted by R. Bahya, Exod. 32.8.

⁴⁷ Sanhedrin 63b; Targum on 2 Chron. 23.3; Tosefta-Targum 2 Kings 16.3. In the last-named source it is asserted that Hezekiah was saved from death by fire through the merits of his descendants, the three youths who willingly offered themselves to be thrown into the fiery furnace for the glory of God. On Salamander, see vol. I, p. 33, and notes 156–158 appertaining thereto; comp. also Bacher, *Zeitschrift der Deutschen Morgenländischen Gesellschaft* XXVII, 15.

⁴⁸ Sanhedrin 47a; Makkot 24a; Tehillim 15, 118.

⁴⁹ Sanhedrin 96a.

⁵⁰ Sanhecrin 94b; Sifre D., 34; Sifra 9.22; 45b; ER 17, 88; Shir 1.3; Koheleth 9.18. Comp. vol. IV, p. 271.

⁵¹ Megillah 11b; BaR (end). The policy of Sennacherib was

after conquering a country, to transfer the inhabitants thereof to another country, and thus it came about that to-day no land is inhabited by its original settlers; Yadayim 4.4; Tosefta 2.17; Sotah 46b; Yebamot 76a; Tosefta Kiddushin 5.4; Seder 'Olam 23 (comp. Ratner, note 8); Berakot 28a; BaR (end); Midrash Tannaim 146. Comp. note 82 on vol. I, p. 178. On Sennacherib as "cosmocrator", see also Mekilta Beshallah 1, 26b; Sotah 9a (comp. Tosafot, caption מנימין); Tan. B. III, 37 and 38; WR 18.2; Mahzor Vitry 169; Makiri, Isa 9.11, quoting an unknown source. On other "cosmocrators", see Index, s. v.

⁵² Sanhedrin 93b, and, with variations, Tosefta-Targum Is. 10.31. Comp. also Mekilta Shirah 2, 36a; Apocalypse of Baruch 63.7; Seder 'Olam 23; Tosefta Sotah 3.18; ShR 18.5; Tehillim 79, 358–359; Tan. B. III, 38; ER 7, 44–45.

⁵³ Sanhedrin 93b; *Panim Aherim* 73; comp. also WR 5.3, where it is stated that on the very same day God decreed Uzziah's punishment (comp. vol. IV, p. 262), the delivery of the ten tribes into the hands of Sennacherib, and the latter's defeat by Hezekiah. The meaning of this Haggadah is very likely that God revealed these three things to Isaiah; comp. vol. IV, p. 262.

⁵⁴ ShR 18.5; Tosefta-Targum 2 Kings 19.35–37; Shir 1.12; Seder 'Olam 23 (comp. Ratner, note 38); Yerushalmi Pesahim 9, 36d. On the first night of Passover as the "night of miracles", see note 76 on vol. I, p. 224. *Panim Aherim* 93 = Yalkut II, 241 reads: When Rab-shakeh heard the singing of the Hallel he counselled Sennacherib to withdraw from Jerusalem, as on this night—the first night of Passover— many miracles were wrought for Israel. Sennacherib however did not accept the wise counsel given him. Here it is very likely assumed that Rab-shakeh was an "apostate"; comp. note 94.

⁵⁵ Sanhedrin 95b; Tosefta-Targum Is. 10.32; Aggadat Shir 5, 39 and 8.45; Jerome on Is. 30.2. On the other hand, ShR 18.5, Tosefta-Targum 2 Kings 19.35, and Aphraates, 58, maintain that it was Michael who destroyed the host of the Assyrians. Targum 2 Chron. 32.21 assigns this distinction to both of the archangels. On the pre-ference given to Gabriel over Michael in the Babylonian Haggadah, whereas the favorite of the Palestinian Haggadah is Michael, comp. Index, s. v. "Michael" and "Gabriel". Very obscure is the following remark of Aggadat Shir 8.45; At the time Gabriel received the power to annihilate the host of the Assyrians, Leviathan was empowered to "destroy the rivers". From the connection in which this passage is given it becomes evident that the "rivers of fire flowing from before

the Shekinah" are meant. According to Apocalypse of Baruch 63.6, it is the angel Ramael who destroyed the Assyrians. The co-operation of Gabriel and Michael in the destruction of Babylon is maintained in Tosefta-Targum Is. 21.5, and very likely also Aggadat Shir 5.39, where השומרים is to be explained in accordance with ShR. *loc. cit.* Hezekiah and Isaiah were in the Temple when the host of the Assyrians approached Jerusalem; a fire arose from amidst them, which burned Sennacherib and consumed his host. See Tehillim 22, 180. The burning of Sennacherib is not to be taken literally. See, however, vol. IV, p. 269.

⁵⁶ Sanhedrin 95b; Tosefta-Targum 2 Kings 19.35 and Is. 10.32 (only Targum makes Nebuchadnezzar the son-in-law of Sennacherib). Comp. vol. IV p. 301 (top).

⁵⁷ Sanhedrin 95b; Tosefta-Targum 2 Kings 19.35 does not mention Nebuzaradan. Sanhedrin gives different views which set the number of survivors at ten or fourteen. Jerome on Is. 10.13 has ten; 'Eser Galuyyot 7 shares the view given in the text.

⁵⁸ Sanhedrin 95b, and similarly Jerome on Is. 10.3. The latter states that Jewish tradition considers Hamon, "noise" (comp. Is. 33.3), to be the name of the angel Gabriel. This is corroborated by Aggadat Shir 5, 39. According to Sanhedrin, the angel clapped together his wings, and the noise caused by it was so terrific that the Assyrians gave up their ghosts. Another view given in Sanhedrin is that the angel blew out the breath of the Assyrians. This means that he took their souls without injuring their bodies. Comp. the following note. Here it is also stated: God asked Gabriel, "Is thy scythe sharpened?" The angel replied, "It is sharpened and ready since the six days of creation." The use of the scythe by Gabriel is very likely connected with the view that he is charged with the ripening of the products of the fields; comp. vol. IV, p. 268 (towards the end). The rabbinical sources know nothing of the mice which caused the defeat of Sennacherib by gnawing to pieces in one night the bows and the rest of the armor of the Assyrians. Comp. Josephus, *Antiqui.*, X, 1.4, who quotes Herodotus as his authority.

⁵⁹ Shabbat 113b; Sanhedrin 94a; Jerome Is. 10 16; Tosefta-Targum 2 Kings 19.35; Targum 2 Chron. 32.21. Comp. the preceding note. According to another view the bodies of the Assyrians were burned but not their garments, and this was the reward for the pious deed of their ancestor Shem who covered the nakedness of his father with a garment. See Apocalypse of Baruch 63.8; Tan. B. I, 50, and III. 13–14; Tan. Noah 15 and Zaw 2; Tehillim 11, 100; Shabbat and

Sanhedrin, *loc. cit.* Comp. also Targum Yerushalmi Num. 11.26; note 482 on vol. III, p. 253, and note 382 on vol. III, p. 187.

⁶⁰ Sanhedrin 95b–96a; Tosefta-Targum 2 Kings 19.35–37; ps.-Jerome on 2 Chron. 32.21. Sennacherib brought severe punishment upon himself by committing eight grievous sins. These were: Neglecting justice, idolatry, unchastity, bloodshed, desecration of the "Name", employment of obscene language, pride, and slander. These eight sins caused the doom of the generation of the flood, of the generation of the builders of the tower, of the inhabitans of the sinful cities, of Pharaoh, and of Nebuchadnezzar. See ER 15, 74. Arrogance is punished with "death by fire", as may be seen from what befell the generation of the flood (comp. vol. I, pp. 151, 159), Pharaoh (comp. Exod. 5.2 and 9.23–24), Sisera (comp. vol. IV, p. 37, bottom), Sennacherib (on his arrogance, see Is. 10.8, *seq.*); Nebuchadnezzar (comp. Dan. 3.15 and 22). The same punishment will be inflicted upon the "wicked kingdom" in the days to come. See WR 7.6; Tan. B. III, 13; Tan. Zaw 2; Tehillim 11, 100; Aggadat Bereshit 1.1–2. Comp. also Sanhedrin 94a–94b, which reads: Sennacherib, who instructed his messenger (Rab-shakeh) to utter blasphemies against God, was punished through a messenger of God (the angel); Pharaoh who uttered blasphemies himself was punished by God Himself. Sennacherib represents here his people who were slain by the angel. Comp. also note 55 (end).

⁶¹ Tosefta-Targum 2 Kings 19.35–37, where ומינהון must be read instead of והינון. On the pious descendants of Sennacherib's sons, see also Gittin 57a; Sanhedrin 96b; Tan. Wa-Yakhel 8. Comp. further vol. V, p. 195, note 72. Shemaiah and Abtalion are said to have been kings of Baalbek, and this seems to be connected with the legend about their descent from Sennacherib; comp. ps.-Hippolytus 705; comp. note 103. On the graves of Sennacherib's sons, see Ozar Tob, 38.

⁶² WR 5.5, which gives also the different view that Shebnah was only an Amarkol (high Temple official). The Jewish teachers of Eusebius and Jerome shared the view given in the text. Comp. the commentaries of these Church Fathers on Is. 22.15.

⁶³ Sanhedrin 26a; Jerome on Is. 22.15. The latter maintains that Shebnah delivered into the hands of Sennacherib the entire city of Jerusalem with the exception of Mount Zion.

⁶⁴ Sanhedrin 26a–26b; WR 5.5 and 17.3; Tehillim 11, 98–99; Zohar III, 199b. In Sanhedrin it is also said that Shebnah was the most prominent scholar of his time, being superior even to Hezekiah in his

learning; but he was of a very lascivious character, and for his evil
deeds he was punished with leprosy.

⁶⁵ Sanhedrin 26a–26b. On being dragged to death by horses,
see also Ekah 5, 115. A different view concerning the course of this
campaign is given in Seder 'Olam 23. Eight years after the capture
of Samaria, Sennacherib undertook his campaign against Judea, being
convinced that the punishment of Israel predicted by the prophets was
meant for the entire nation including Judea. On his march to Judea
he conquered the Moabites, Ammonites and Arabs, his former allies
in the war against Samaria, and his general Rab-shakeh succeeded in
persuading the party led by Shebnah to surrender to him voluntarily
and to follow him to Babylon. Sennacherib was forced to stop his
campaign against Hezekiah for a short time, as he had to move hurriedly
against Ethiopia. Having conquered this "pearl of all countries",
he returned to Judea. But before attacking Hezekiah, he sent his
generals Tartan and Rab-saris to make him surrender voluntarily.
Comp. also Ratner, notes 7–24. Opinions differ as to whether Sennacherib was a wise or a foolish king. See Sanhedrin 94a; Sifre D.,
37; 2 ARN 20.43.

⁶⁶ Sanhedrin 94b; PK 6, 59b–60a; PR 16, 82a; Mishle 13,74.
According to Tosefta-Targum on Is. 7, 6, the "son of Tabeel" mentioned there is no other than Pekah; but according to Yerushalmi
'Abodah Zarah 1. 39a Tabeel means "idol". The haggadic interpretation of לאם in Tosefta-Targum Is. 8.6 is taken from PK, *loc. cit.*

⁶⁷ Shir 4.8; Aggadat Shir 8, 45; Ekah, introduction, 30, and the
parallel passages cited by Buber. On Hezekiah's refusal to sing a
song of praise to God, see vol. IV, p. 272 and vol. VI, p. 309; on his great
devotion to the study of the Torah, see Sanhedrin 20a; Mishle 28, 97;
both versions of ARN 1, 2–3. Comp. further the references in note 59.
The Midrashim attempt to explain in detail the nature of Hezekiah's
activity referred to in Prov. 28.1. Comp. note 89. When Rabban Johanan b. Zakkai saw his end drawing nigh, he said: "Prepare a chair for
Hezekiah, king of Judah." See Yerushalmi Sotah 9, 24c; 'Abodah Zarah
3, 42c. This great Rabbi, whose life was devoted to the study of the
Torah and to the spreading of the knowledge thereof among the people,
expected to be met at his death by the pious king, whose life was devoted to the same ideals as his.

⁶⁸ Seder 'Olam 23; Menahot 109b; Shir 4.8. In the last passage
it is stated that Hezekiah thought that the miracle of the standstill

of the sun (comp. vol. IV, p. 275) would proclaim the omnipotence of God Almighty more than he could do by words of praise and song.

⁶⁹ According to the later mystics, the "prince of the world" is identical with Metatron. Comp. Index, s. v.

⁷⁰ Sanhedrin 94a; Shir 4.8. The Church Fathers Justin Martyr (*Dialogue*, 33) and Tertullian (*Adversus Marcionem*, 5.9) maintain that the Jews interpret Ps. 110 as referring to Hezekiah. As to the haggadic explanation of the "closed" ם in למרבה (Is. 6.6), see also the quotation from an unknown Midrash in Kimhi, *ad loc.*, according to which this "closed" ם in the middle of the word, and the open one at the end of הם (Nehem. 2.14) contain an allusion to the time of the advent of the Messiah. It is worthy of note in this connection that the old sources knew nothing of the explanation of Is. 9.5 as given by the medieval commentators, according to whom "the child" mentioned here (*i. e.*, Hezekiah) was called "prince of peace" by the wonderful Counsellor, the mighty God, the everlasting Father. The Talmud and Midrash explicitly state that the names in this verse are those of the child to whom the "names of God were given", though the authorities differ as to whether Hezekiah or the Messiah is meant by this "child". See Sanhedrin 94a; PRK (Schönblum's edition, 39a; Grünhut's edition 82. Here the child is identified with the Messiah); Ma'aseh Torah 100 (Child = the Messiah; the text is not quite correct); PR 46, 188a; Ruth R. 3.15; Makiri Is. *ad loc.*, where the text of PR reads somewhat differently As to the names of God borne by men, see Baba Batra 75b; Sifre D., 355 (אין כאל); BR 79 (end); note 282 on vol. I, p. 395. It is not quite sure whether מן קדם in Targum on Is., *loc. cit.*, is not a later "emendation" prompted by anti-Christian tendency. Comp. Aptowitzer, Ha-Zofeh, I, 81–82.

⁷¹ Yelammedenu in Yalkut II, 243 (end) on 2 Kings 20; Eusebius and Jerome on Is. 39.1; Ephraem I, 560. Seder 'Olam 23, on the other hand, maintains that the downfall of Sennacherib took place on the very same day on which Hezekiah became ill. Comp. also Yelammedenu in Yalkut II, 424 on Is. 38 (end).

⁷² Aggadat Shir 1,12; Perek R. Yoshiyyahu, 133.

⁷³ As to the point of etiquette, see Tosefta Horayyot 2.9, and Yerushalmi 3, 48b. Comp. also vol. IV, p. 46, with regard to the relation between Phinehas and Jephthah.

⁷⁴ The allusion is to Jehoshaphat; comp. vol. IV, p. 186 and note 50 appertaining thereto.

⁷⁵ Berakot 10a; Yerushalmi Sanhedrin 10, 28b (top); Hezekiah

quotes his "grandfather" David as authority for the view that prayer, alms, and repentance ward off evil decreed against one, even after it had been announced to him in a vision or dream; Koheleth 5.9; Baraita di-Yeshu'a 45a; Zohar I, 13a and 66a; ER 8, 46. In the last source Hezekiah's illness is said to have been the punishment for unseemly language used by him in his prayer of deliverance from the hands of Sennacherib. It is difficult to tell to what words in Hezekiah's prayer (as given in 2 Kings 19.15–19) the Haggadah objected.

⁷⁶ Yerushalmi Berakot 4, 8b; Babli 10b; Yerushalmi Sanhedrin 10, 28b–28c; Koheleth 5.6. This prayer of Hezekiah was considered a model as far as its formal aspect is concerned; comp. ER 8, 46 (as to the correct reading, see Rokeah, 325, and ראבי״ה 79; Aptowitzer's edition, 53); Berakot 27b. On the idea that the members of the human body were created to perform the divine commandments, see PK 12, 101a; note 210 on vol. III, p. 96. Comp. Midrash Tannaim 15.

⁷⁷ Berakot 10b. Comp. also Koheleth 1.1. As to the question whether one's good deeds could prolong one's life beyond the space of time set for him, see Yebamot 49b–50a; Koheleth 3.2; Tosefta Horayyot 1.15.

⁷⁸ Yerushalmi Sanhedrin 10, 28b; Koheleth 5.6. The last passage contains the additional remark of the king addressed to the prophet, which reads: "Did I not tell thee from the beginning that I would not be guided by thy advice but by the advice of my grandfather?" Comp. note 74.

⁷⁹ Mekilta Wa-Yassa' 1, 45b, and Beshallah 5, 32a; Mekilta RS 73; Jerome on Is. 39.1. Comp. vol. III, p. 39. The Rabbis find some difficulty in explaining the demand of the king for a sign (Is. 38.22), as it is forbidden to ask signs of a prophet; comp. Yerushalmi Sanhedrin 11, 30c. During the king's illness Isaiah made the scholars study at the entrance of the royal palace to prevent the angel of death from entering it; 'Erubin 26a, and comp. vol. IV, p. 114.

⁸⁰ BR 65.9; PRE 52 (which reads: "this was the last of the seven great miracles;" comp. vol. II, p. 131, and vol. IV, p. 246).

⁸¹ Sanhedrin 96a; Yerushalmi Yebamot 2, 4a; ER 8, 47; Zohar I, 6b; PRE 52 (with some modifications). At the funeral of Ahaz the sun set ten hours before its time (comp. vol. IV, p. 266), and at Hezekiah's recovery from his illness the sun recovered the lost hours. See Sanhedrin, *loc. cit.*, and somewhat different in PRE, *loc. cit.* Comp. also Hippolytus, *In Isaiam* 630–631; Brüll in *Bet ha-Midrash* (Hebrew periodical) II, 148.

⁸² This is a reminiscence of Merodach as sun god. Baladan's dog-face is very likely a Jewish "explanation" of the dogs seen on the Assyrian-Babylonian monuments in the company of Merodach. Comp. Roscher's *Lexicon der Mythologie*, II, 2371.

⁸³ PK 2, 13a–14a; Shir 3.4; Esther R. 1.9; Tan. Ki-Tissa 5; ER 20, 115. Another version of this legend is given in vol. IV, p. 300, according to which Nebuchadnezzar was the secretary to Merodach-Baladan, not his son. Jerome on Is. 39.1 agrees with the Palestinian Midrashim in making Nebuchadnezzar the son of Merodach.

⁸⁴ Sanhedrin 104a; Shir 3.4 (on the text, see Sachs, in introduction to *Sefer Tagin* 15 *seq.*); ER 8, 47. Comp. also Aggadat Shir 1, 26.

⁸⁵ PRE 52; Targum 2 Chron. 32.31. As to the tables comp. vol. III, p. 409.

⁸⁶ BR 19.11; BaR 20.6; Zohar III, 200a. The proper answer for the king to give to Isaiah would have been: "O prophet of God, thou surely knowest who the men are and what they want." Hezekiah like Adam (Gen. 3.9–10), Cain (*ibid.* 4.9), and Balaam (Num. 22.9), on similar occasions, was tested and found wanting. Comp. vol. III, pp. 358–359 and vol. VI, p. 421, bottom.

⁸⁷ As to the origin of these treasures, see vol. II, pp. 125–126.

⁸⁸ Sanhedrin 93b; Origen, Matth. 15.5; Jerome on Is. 39.7.

⁸⁹ Baba Batra 15a; both versions of ARN 1, 2–3; Mishle 25, 96–97. In the last two sources it is stated that the "men of Hezekiah" (Prov. 25.1) were very careful before they decided a point of law, and as a reward long life was granted to them. The Haggadah very likely identifies the "men of Hezekiah" with the members of the Great Assembly (comp. vol. IV, p. 359), and hence the statement concerning their long life. Opinions in the above sources differ as to the exact nature of the work done by the "men of Hezekiah". According to some, they "wrote down" the book of Isaiah and the three books of Solomon, whereas others maintain that they withdrew from public use the books of Solomon, because they were of the opinion that these books were not of a holy nature, and they remained "hidden" until the time of the Great Assembly. The third opinion is that these men explained the words of Solomon (ARN 1, 2: לא שהעתיקו אלא שפירשו), and owing to their explanation these books were admitted into the Canon. Hezekiah undertook six reforms; three were approved by the scholars of his time, and three were rejected. He "hid" the "books of medicine", broke in pieces the brazen serpent which Moses had made, and buried his father as though he had been a pauper (comp. vol.

IV, p. 266). All this he did with the approval of the scholars. On the other hand, they did not approve of his stopping the upper spring of the waters of Gihon, of his scraping off the gold from the Temple (comp. vol. IV, p. 272), and of his declaring a leap year by adding a second month of Nisan. See Berakot 10b; Pesahim 56a (in the editions it is given wrongly as Mishnah); Yerushalmi 9, 36c–36d; Nedarim 6, 40a; Sanhedrin 12a–12b; Tosefta 2, 10–11; Yerushalmi 1, 18d (different opinions are given here as to the nature of the error committed by Hezekiah in the intercalation of the year mentioned in 2 Chron. 30.2); ARN 1, 11–12; PRE 9. Comp. also 'Arakin 10b; Tosefta 2.6; Yerushalmi Sukkah 5, 55d. On the breaking in pieces of the brazen serpent, see also Hullin 6b; Yerushalmi Dammai 2, 22c; see also the following note. On the "books of medicine", see the following note.

⁹⁰ Berakot 10b; Pesahim 56a; Yerushalmi 9, 36c–36d (here: "tablets of medical remedies"); Nedarim 6, 40a; Sanhedrin 1, 18d. Comp. references at the end of preceding note. It is not explicitly stated in the rabbinical writings that these books had Solomon as their author, or that the people ascribed them to him. The Rabbis were very likely silent on this fact to avoid the impression of an implied unfavorable criticism on the wise king. See Josephus, *Antiqui.*, VIII. 5; Maimonides, Mishnah Commentary on Pesahim 4 (end); Schürer, *Geschichte*, III, 413, 418–419; Chajes, *Marcus Studien*, 37; Grünbaum, *Gesammelte Aufsätze* 25; Azulai in his commentary on ARN 2. The last-named authority quotes from a MS. of R. Eleazar of Worms the statement that until the days of Hezekiah a list of the healing springs was circulated among the people. In case of illness they did not pray to God for help, but made use of the healing springs. For this reason Hezekiah hid this list, which had been transmitted from generation to generation from the time of Noah. An attempt is obviously made here to connect the "stopping of the spring of Gihon" (comp. 2 Chron. 32.30, and the preceding note) with the hiding of the medical remedies. The breaking in pieces of the brazen altar by Hezekiah was due to the same reason as the hiding of the medical books. The "hissing of the brazen serpent" used to heal all sick people of Jerusalem, and the cure was so certain that in case of illness they never prayed to God for help. Hezekiah therefore broke the brazen serpent in pieces. Until his time this serpent was attached to Solomon's throne. See *Kisse we-Ippodromon*, 35. Comp. also note 74 on vol. I, p. 173.

⁹¹ Baba Kamma 17a; Ekah, introduction, 25. Comp. vol. IV, p. 188.

⁹² Baba Kamma 16b; ps.-Jerome on 2 Chron. 32.33. This pious king bore the name Hezekiah because he had been made strong by God (חזק "was strong"), and because he brought Israel nigh unto God. He had eight other names (comp. note 70), and his great adversary Sennacherib (*i. e.*, he who uttered blasphemous words against God; comp. note 60) also had eight others names; these are: Tiglath-pileser, Palnesser, Shalmanesser, Pul, Sargon, Osnappar, Rabba-yakkira ("the great and honored"). See Sanhedrin 94a; Jerome on Is. 20.1 and 36.1. On Sennacherib's eight names, see Einhorn in the supplement to his commentary on Ruth R.

⁹³ On Hezekiah's original decision to remain unmarried, comp. vol. IV, p. 273.

⁹⁴ Berakot 10a; but not in our editions; the passage is supplied by Rabbinovicz, *Variae Lectiones*, from the Munich MS. and old sources; comp. also Gaster, *Exempla*, 234. Jerome on Is. quotes the Jewish tradition, according to which Isaiah was the father-in-law of Manasseh. This is very likely a slip for the father-in-law of Hezekiah and grandfather of Manasseh, for not only Babli, but also Yerushalmi Sanhedrin 10, 28c, declares that Manasseh was the grandson of the prophet. As for Rab-shakeh, it is only said of him, in Sanhedrin 60a, that he was an "apostate". This view is shared by Ephraem, while Jerome on Is. 36.1, following a Jewish tradition, makes him a son of Isaiah. Jerome was possibly inaccurate in reporting the tradition; he may have meant to say a grandson instead of a son. In this case his tradition would tally with that in Berakot, *loc. cit.* It is, however, hard to understand the statement of the Talmud that Rab-shakeh died in his childhood, without attempting to reconcile this view with the biblical account. It would not do to assume that Rab-shakeh, the son of Hezekiah mentioned in the Talmud, is not identical with the bearer of this name in the Bible, for Targum on Eccles. 10.9, following the Talmud, explicitly states that the Rab-shakeh mentioned in the Bible was the brother of Manasseh. The emphasis laid in the Ascension of Isaiah 1.1 upon the fact that shortly before his death Hezekiah had one son only is perhaps an allusion to the rabbinic legend that his other son (Rab-shakeh) died as a child; comp. also note 54 (end). Quite obvious is the connection between this pseudepigraphic work and the Talmud with regard to Hezekiah's intention to kill Manasseh when he was informed by Isaiah of the wicked deeds his son would commit one day. He was, however, prevented by the prophet from carrying out his intention; for the latter said: "Sammael's

plan concerning Manasseh is determined upon, and words will not avail thee." These words of Isaiah remind one of the talmudic passage cited above, Berakot 10a, where the prophet is said to have refused to give his daughter in marriage to the king, remarking: "The decree is decided upon" (that Manasseh would be wicked); comp. vol. IV, p. 273. The text of Ascension of Isaiah, as given by (Ps-) Chrysostomus, *Opus Imperfectum in Mattheum*, homily I, shows still closer resemblance between the Manasseh legend as given in this pseudepigraphic work and in the Talmud.

⁹⁵ Ascension of Isaiah 2.5 and Apocalypse of Baruch 64.3, as well as the rabbinic sources (comp. the references given in the following four notes), contain detailed descriptions of the wicked deeds of this king. His name Manasseh is derived, in Ascension of Isaiah 2, 1, as well as in Sanhedrin 12b, from *nasha* "he forgot": he forgot his God and his pious father. On the act of incest committed by him, see note 112.

⁹⁶ Sanhedrin 103b. This idol was made by his grandfather Ahaz, who did not dare to set it up in the inner space of the Temple, but kept it in the upper chamber over the holy of holies. When on the seventeenth of Tammuz the idol was set up by Manasseh (Ta'anit 28b; Yerushalmi 4, 68d, top), the prophet Isaiah addressed the people as follows: "Thus saith the Lord: The heaven is My throne, and the earth is My footstool; why then do ye glory in the Temple built by you? On account of four sins I no longer take pleasure in this house, and have decreed to have it destroyed by Nebuchadnezzar, and ye shall go into captivity." These were the last words of Isaiah (the last chapter of his book begins: "The heaven is My throne, etc."), as he was forthwith killed by Manasseh, who became enraged at hearing about the destruction of the Temple and Israel's captivity predicted by Isaiah. See Tosefta-Targum on Is. 66.1; PR 4, 14a. Comp. Zunz, *Gottesdienstliche Vorträge*, 78; Bacher, *Zeitschrift der Deutschen Morgeländischen Gesellschaft*, XXVIII, 16-17; Ginzberg, *Jewish Encyclopedia* I, 81. The text of this Tosefta-Targum was printed from a MS., and privately distributed by Christian D. Ginsburg on the occasion of the International Congress of Orientalists held in Rome, 1898. That the last chapter of Is. contains the words of the prophet uttered at the time when Manasseh set up the idol in the Temple is also stated in EZ 9, 188. On the view that Isaiah met his death at the hands of Manasseh, see note 103.

⁹⁷ DR 2.20; Sanhedrin 103b; EZ 9, 188; Peshitta 2 Chron 33.7. Comp. also Apocalypse of Baruch 64.3, which reads: And he (Manas-

seh) made an image with five faces, four of which looked to the four winds, and the fifth was on the top of the image, as an adversary to the zeal of the Mighty One. Similarly it is stated in Sanhedrin, *loc. cit.*: Manasseh at first fashioned one face for it; then four (four additional ones, or three additional ones?), that the Shekinah might see and be provoked. The Talmud, as well as the Apocalypse of Baruch, connects סמל in 2 Chron. 23.7 with סמל הקנאה "image of jealousy" in Ezek. 8.5. A very obscure statement concerning the image set up by Manasseh is found in Ta'anit 28b–29a, and reads as follows: Manasseh set up two images in the Temple; but one fell down, and broke the arm of the other in its falling. On the latter this inscription was found: "Thou desirest to bring about the destruction of this house (the Temple) and I am ready to give thee my assistance." The setting up of the image in the Temple by Manasseh was the cause of Israel's captivity into Babylon. See Gittin 7a; Apocalypse of Baruch 64.4.

⁹⁸ Sanhedrin 103b. Apocalypse of Baruch 64.2–3 describes Manasseh's sins as follows: He slew the righteous, and wrested judgment, shed the blood of the innocent, and wedded women he violently polluted (this accusation is made in rabbinic sources against Jehoiakim; comp. vol. IV, p. 184), he overturned the altars, destroyed their offerings and drove forth their priests, lest they should minister in the sanctuary. And to such a degree did Manasseh's impiety increase, that he removed the praise of the Most High from the sanctuary. The last statement wishes to convey that on account of Manasseh's sins the Shekinah left the sanctuary long before the destruction of the Temple. This agrees with the view of the Rabbis, according to which the Shekinah after leaving the sanctuary had stopped at various stations, until, after the capture of the city, it finally ascended to heaven, its original abode. Comp. the different versions of the Haggadah concerning the "ten stations of the Shekinah" in Rosh ha-Shanah 31a; PK 13, 114b–115a; ARN 34, 102; Ekah, introduction, 25; Aggadat Shir 5, 39; Makiri on Ps. 115, 200. The last passage agrees with Apocalypse of Baruch that the "first journey of the Shekinah" took place in Isaiah's time, when Manasseh set up the image in the Temple. Comp. also note 96. In Ascension of Isaiah 2.4–5 it is said of Manasseh: And he (Satan) made him (Manasseh) strong in apostatizing Israel and in the lawlessness which was spread abroad in Jerusalem. And witchcraft and magic increased, and divination and auguration, and fornication, and adultery, and the persecution of the righteous.

⁹⁹ Sanhedrin 99b. On Manasseh's great mastery of the knowledge of the Torah, see the references cited in notes 109, 110.

¹⁰⁰ According to Seder 'Olam 20, the prophets Joel, Nahum and Habakkuk lived in Manasseh's days. Here it is also stated that Micah was a younger contemporary of Isaiah. For other views concerning the times of the prophets, see Index, under the corresponding names. Josephus, *Antiqui.*, IX, 11.3, makes Nahum a contemporary of king Jotham.

¹⁰¹ Ascension of Isaiah 2–3. This Samaritan is called Belchira or Belachora, which is very likely an opprobrious appellation formed of בעל "master" and חרי or rather חרא, "excrement"; comp. 'Abodah Z. 46b and Beel-zebul (perhaps=בעל זבול). Tobiah the Canaanite and John of Anathoth are mentioned as the adherents of Belchira. In view of the fact that in Nehem. 3.35, *seq.*, and 6.12, Tobiah the Ammonite appears not only as a great adversary of the Jews, but also as the supporter of a false prophet, it is very likely that we should read Ammonite instead of Canaanite in the pseudepigraphic work. The faulty reading was caused by the "Canaanite" Zedekiah mentioned a few lines below. John of Anathoth looks like a reminiscence of Jer. 28.1, where the false prophet Hananiah (= John) is mentioned. It is true that this one is described as hailing from Gibeon and not from Anathoth, but as he appears as the adversary of Jeremiah, who was a native of Anathoth, it was quite natural for the legend to make him a native of that city. Without much violence to the text, מגבעון in Jer., *loc. cit.*, might be explained to refer to the father of Hananiah and not to Hananiah himself.

¹⁰² The first charge against Isaiah occurs in Ascension of Isaiah 3 (here it is Belchira who appears as the accuser against Isaiah and the other prophets); Yebamot 49b; Origen, *In Jesajam*, homily 1.5; Jerome on Is. 1.10; *Paralipomena Jeremiae* (near the end); ps.-Jerome on 2 Chron. 33.10. The second charge is found only in Ascension of Isaiah, *loc. cit.*; ps.-Jerome, *loc. cit.*; Jerome, *loc. cit.* The last-named gives as his authority the oral information communicated to him by Jews. Comp. also Tosefta-Targum on Is. 66.1, and particularly the version thereof published by David Ginsburg (see note 96). Yebamot, *loc. cit.*, has the following two further contradictions between Moses and Isaiah. The former said: "For what great nation is there that hath God so nigh unto them, as the Lord our God is whenever we call upon Him?" (Deut. 4.7), while the latter said: "Call ye upon Him while He is near" (Is. 55.6). Moses further said: "The number of thy

days I will fulfil" (Exod. 23.24), whereas Isaiah said to Hezekiah: "I will add unto thy days fifteen years". Comp. also Tosefta-Targum on Is. 16.1, and Jerome, *Ad Damasum*, I, 369. As to the "adding of years", see note 77.

[103] Yebamot 49b; Sanhedrin 103b; Tosefta-Targum on 2 Kings 21.16, and Is. 66.1; PR 4.14; Yerushalmi Sanhedrin 10, 28c. The three last-named Palestinian sources record the legend that Isaiah was swallowed up by a tree (in PR and Targum it is a carob-tree, in Yerushalmi it is a cedar-tree), which had to be sawed in pieces before Isaiah could be killed; but there is no trace in these sources of the legend in Babli that the prophet's mouth was the only vulnerable part of his body. According to Yerushalmi, Isaiah's hiding-place was discovered through the fringes of his garment which were not swallowed by the tree. It seems that the form of the legend as given in this source is not complete. It may be suggested that this legend had a statement that the prophet had once neglected to fulfil the commandment of *Zizit*, and as a punishment his hiding-place was betrayed by the "fringes" of his garment. Comp. vol. VI, p. 239, note 81. Isaiah's martyrdom is described in Ascension of Isaiah as follows: And he (Manasseh) sent and seized Isaiah. And he sawed him in sunder with a wood-saw. And when Isaiah was being sawn in sunder, Belchira (comp. note 101) stood up, accusing him, and all the false prophets stood up, laughing and rejoicing because of Isaiah....And Belchira said to Isaiah: "Say: I have lied in all that I have spoken, and likewise the ways of Manasseh are good and right. And the ways also of Belchira and of his associates are good." And this he said to him when he began to be sawn in sunder. But the prophet refused to listen to the words of Belchira (comp. Yebamot *loc. cit.* for the reason of Isaiah's refusal to defend himself against the accusation hurled at him), and while being sawn in sunder he neither cried aloud, nor wept, but his lips spoke with the Holy Spirit, until he was sawn in twain. That Isaiah, at the time of his martyrdom, conversed with the Holy Spirit is based on the haggadic interpretation of 2 Kings 17.9; comp. Yerushalmi Sanhedrin, *loc. cit.*, and PR, *loc. cit.* To the prophets who were with him before he was put to death he said: "Go ye to the region of Tyre and Zidon; as for me only has God mingled the cup".—The legend of Isaiah's martyrdom was very likely known to so early an authority as Josephus; comp. *Antiqui.*, X, 3.1. It is generally assumed that in Hebrews 11.37 (ἐπρίσθησαν) allusion is made to the specific mode (being sawn in sunder) of Isaiah's martyrdom. In patristic literature

there are many references to Isaiah's having been sawn in sunder; but as this legend was current among the Jews for centuries (comp. the sources quoted at the beginning of note as well as in previous note), it is not always certain whether the Church Fathers made use of the pseudepigraphic work Ascension of Isaiah (more correctly, the Martyrdom of Isaiah), or drew upon the oral traditions of the Jews. See Justin Martyr, *Dialogue*, 120; Tertullian, *De Patientia*, 14; *Visio Pauli*, 49; ps.-Hippolytus 705. The last-named author also states that Manasseh restored the city of Baalbek which Solomon had built. Comp. Pesahim 117a, where בכי very likely stands for בעל בכי "Baalbek". It is true Pesahim speaks of the "image fashioned by Micah" פסלו של מיכה as being located at Baalbek, but we find the wicked king mentioned in connection with this image. See Seder 'Olam 24, which reads: Manasseh was exiled to Babylon, and with him the image of Micah. Comp. note 61 and vol. V, p. 13, note 72. The Jewish sources contain nothing about the ascension of Isaiah, and accordingly the Jewish part of the Ascension of Isaiah is very likely limited to Isaiah's martyrdom, the rest being of Christian origin.

104 Aggadat Bereshit 14, 32. Here it is also stated that Isaiah, the greatest of the prophets (or one of the most prominent of the prophets), and Obadiah, the most insignificant of them, did not prophesy before they received permission from the Great Synedrion. They both prophesied in seventy-one tongues; comp. vol. VI, p. 344, note 6. Isaiah was as great a prophet as Moses; PR 4, 14a. Comp. vol. VI, p. 44, note 242, and see also Baraita di-Yeshu'ah 45; Aggadat Bereshit, *loc. cit*; note 242 on vol. III, p. 108. According to a Jewish tradition found in ps.-Jerome, 1 Chron. 33.19, the prophet Hozai mentioned there is none else but Isaiah. The book of Amoz, the father of Isaiah, is referred to in Ascension of Isaiah 4.22. Comp. note 25.

105 On the kinship between Isaiah and Manasseh, see note 94.

106 Seder 'Olam 24. Comp. Ratner, *ad loc.*, and note 103.

107 Yerushalmi Sanhedrin 10, 28c; Babli 103a; PK 25, 162a–162b; MHG I, 113–114; DR 2.20; Ruth R. 2.14; Targum and ps.-Jerome on 2 Chron. 33.13; PRE 43; Abba Gorion 36. The "Prayer of Manasseh" offered while he was a prisoner in Babylon forms part of the Canon of the Greek Bible. On the oven, see the articles by Krauss and Nestle in *Zeitschrift für die alttestamentliche Wissenschaft*, XXII, 309, *seq.*; XXIII 326, *seq.* and 337 as well as Bacher, *R. E. J.*, XLV, 291, *seq.*

108 Sanhedrin Mishnah 10 (11). 1; ARN 35, 108: EZ 9, 189 (it

is said here that Manasseh's repentance was accepted for the sake of the pious destined to be born of him); Aggadat Bereshit 9, 23. The apocryphal works the Prayer of Manasseh and Tobit 14.10 share this view favorable to Manasseh. On the other hand, the prevalent opinion in rabbinic literature is that Manasseh is one of the few Jews who lost their portion in the world to come; comp. Sanhedrin, *loc. cit.*, and the references given in note 100 on vol. IV, p. 75, as well as Tan. B. III, 43; Tan. Mezora' 1; Yerushalmi Sanhedrin 10, 27a and 29b; Babli 102b–103a. Apocalypse of Baruch 64 agrees with this view, and maintains that Manasseh, though he prayed, did not really repent. Aggadat Bereshit, *loc. cit.*, likewise speaks of Manasseh's prayer and words of repentance which were uttered "with lips of deceit". Comp. Sanhedrin 101b.

¹⁰⁹ Sanhedrin 102b, Ahab and Jeroboam (the two other Jewish kings who, like Manasseh, lost their share in the world to come; comp. the references cited in preceding note) excelled Manasseh in learning; the former was able to interpret the Book of Leviticus in eighty-five ways, and the latter in one hundred and three. The "greater the scholar the stronger his evil inclination" is a favorite saying with the Rabbis; see Sukkah 52a (bottom). Comp. also vol. VI, p. 311, note 34.

¹¹⁰ Sanhedrin 102b.

¹¹¹ *Constitutiones Apostolicae*, II, 23, which is very likely based on a Jewish legend; comp. Yoma 8 (end), which reads: He who says: "I shall sin and then repent", no opportunity is given him for repentance. Comp. note 27 on vol. IV, p. 61.

¹¹² Sanhedrih 103a. The statement about the burning of the Torah by Amon is taken from Seder 'Olam 24, but here בָּעַר very likely means "swept away". He committed incest with his mother (not out of passion, but to defy God and the Torah). This is very likely due to a play on the word אָמוֹן with אֵם "mother". Of his father Manasseh it is said that he committed incest with his sister, and of Ahaz that he set aside the Jewish laws of marriage. Manasseh is further accused of having cut out the divine Name from the Scriptures. Comp. notes 40 and 95.

¹¹³ Sanhedrin 104a. Comp. vol. II, p. 314 (below).

¹¹⁴ Shabbat 57b; Seder 'Olam 24. Another view (Shabbat, *loc. cit.*) is that Josiah was pious from his infancy. His repentance mentioned in 2 Kings 23.25 refers to the fact that when he reached the age of majority (at eighteen; comp. Ginzberg, *Unbekannte Sekte,*

64–65) he annulled all the verdicts pronounced by him before that time, and from his own pocket he re-imbursed all those who suffered loss by this annulment.

¹¹⁵ Sanhedrin 103, which is an attempt to exlplain the "finding" of the Torah. Comp. also Kimhi on 2 Kings 22.8, and note 112.

¹¹⁶ Yoma 52b (on the correct reading, comp. Rabbinovicz, *ad loc.*); Yerushalmi Shekalim 6, 59c and Kimhi on 2 Kings 22.11. Many medieval authors (comp. the references cited by Friedmann in *Ha-Goren* VII 10–13, and Shu'aib, 10d; Lekah on Exod. 16.32) quote Shekalim, *loc. cit.*, differently from our text. According to their reading the book "found" was the book of Deuteronomy, and the same statement is made by Jerome in Ezek. 1.1 (comp. Nestle, *Zeitschrift f. alt. Wissenschaft* XXII, 170-171) undoubtedly on the authority of his Jewish teachers. The "finding" of the Torah was of such importance for the life of the Jews, that they began to date a new era from that event, and it is this era which Ezekiel used. The high priest Hilkiah found the Torah under the threshhold (read אלתא instead of אולמא; comp. Targum on Josh. 24.26) of the Temple hall at midnight after the setting of the moon. See Targum on Ezek. 1.1 and Tosefta-Targum in Wertheimer, *Ozar Midrashim* II, 53.

¹¹⁷ Megillah 14b. Here also it is remarked: Eminence is not for women; two eminent women are mentioned in the Bible, Deborah and Huldah, and both proved to be of a proud disposition. Deborah was haughty towards Barak (comp. vol. IV, p. 36, and note 75 pertaining thereto) and the prophetess Huldah spoke of Josiah as the "man" (comp. 2 Kings 22.15), without giving him the title of king. This "unpleasant" feature of their character is indicated by their "ugly" names, the former was called Deborah "bee", and the latter Huldah "weasel". On the kinship between Huldah and Jeremiah, see vol. IV, p. 5, and on her husband, see vol. IV, p. 246. The prophetess had an academy in Jerusalem; Targum on 2 Kings 22.14 and on 2 Chron. 24.22.

¹¹⁸ Yoma 52b; Horayyot 12a; Keritot 5b; Shekalim 6, 59c; Tosefta Yoma 3 (2).7 and Sotah 13.1. In all these sources it is stated that besides the holy ark, the king also hid the following holy objects: the holy oil, the vessel with the manna, the rod of Aaron with its almonds and blossoms, as well as the coffer with the offering of the Philistines. In other sources different holy objects are mentioned as having been hidden; comp. ARN 41, 135; PRK 32a; ER 25, 129. Comp. vol. III. pp. 48, 179, 307; vol. IV, pp. 320, *seq.*, as well as Kimhi on 1 Kings 6.19 and on 2 Chron. 35.3. The last named author quotes a

Midrash not found in the extant midrashic literature, according to which Solomon, at the erection of the Temple, provided a secret place to be used later for "hiding" holy objects. Ps.-Jerome on 2 Chron., *loc. cit.*, quotes the Jewish tradition, according to which Ahaz had removed the holy ark from the Temple, which remained in the house of Shallum, the husband of the prophetess Huldah, until the days of Josiah. Yoma Mishnah 5.3 seems to presuppose that there was a holy ark in the second Temple. This, however, does not contradict the story of the hiding of the ark by Josiah, as it is quite probable that at the erection of the second Temple they fashioned another ark. The Talmud 52b explains the Mishnah differently. On the "hiding" of the altar of Moses by Solomon, see Mekilta Bahodesh 11, 73a, which reads: On the day upon which the one (altar) was built (that of Solomon), the other (that of Moses) was hidden.

119 Ekah 1, 91–92 (comp. also *ibid.*, introduction, 22, where it is stated that at first they worshipped idols secretly, then publicly); Ta'anit 22a–22b; Tosefta 2.10; PK 27, 168a; Yerushalmi Kiddushin 1, 61a; Shemuel 25, 62. Zohar III, 114a; ps.-Jerome on 2 Chron. 35.22–25. In the version of Ekah made use of by R. Solomon ha-Yatom, 119 the reading was הורו במשיח in agreement with Yerushalmi, *loc. cit.* Comp. also Tan. B. IV, 167; Tan. Mass'e 12. On Pharaoh the "lame", see note 123.

120 Megillah 14b.

121 Megillah 3a; Mo'ed Katan 28b; Targum on Zech. 12.11.

122 Seder 'Olam 24; Ta'anit 22b; Ekah 1, 92; Yerushalmi Kiddushin 1, 61a; Josephus *Antiqui.*, X, 5.1. The Rabbis, as well as Josephus, understand 2 Chron. 35.25 to refer to the Book of Lamentations, in which Jeremiah laments the fate of the "anointed of the Lord" (4.20), by which Josiah is meant. Comp. also Targum on 2 Chron., *loc. cit.*, and the references cited in note 119.

123 PK 27, 168a; WR 20.1; Tan. B. V, 7; Abba Gorion 3; Koheleth 9.2. In the last-named source it is said that this Pharaoh seized the throne in behalf of his widowed daughter who claimed her dowry from the estate of Solomon. According to this view, Pharaoh the "lame" is identical with Shishak, Solomon's father-in-law; comp. vol. IV p. 182. The interpretation of Neco, the name of the Egyptian king, as though it were נָכֵה "lame" is often found in Jewish and Christian writings; comp. Megillah 3a; Mo'ed Katan 28b; Targum Zech. 12.11, and 2 Chron. 35.20; Peshitta on 2 Kings 23.29; Aphraates, 471 (top).

¹²⁴ Horayyot 11b; Keritot 5b; Shekalim 7, 49c–49d. On the basis of 1 Chron. 3.15, the Rabbis maintain that Josiah had three sons: Jehoiakim, Johanan, (to whom the name Jehoahaz was given on his accession to the throne), and Zedekiah (also called Shallum and Mattaniah); comp. note 1 on vol. IV, p. 291; Targum on 2 Chron., *loc. cit.*; WR 10.8; Seder 'Olam 24. Ratner, note 26, finds a contradiction between Seder 'Olam and the other sources with regard to the question of who was the first-born son of Josiah. It is very strange that, though quoting Horayyot, he did not notice that the difficulty raised by him was raised and disposed of in the Talmud.

¹²⁵ WR 10.6; Tan. Lek 20; Aggadat Bereshit 48, 99; Sanhedrin 103b (according to one opinion, he tattooed his "membrum" with the Name of God); Baraita di-Yeshua'h 45; ps.-Jerome on 2 Chron. 36.8. Comp. note 112.

¹²⁶ Sanhedrin 103b. To the reply made to him that God said: "Mine is the silver, and Mine is the gold", he rejoined: "Did He not say: The heavens are the heavens of the Lord, but the earth hath He given to the children of men"?

¹²⁷ Sanhedrin 103a; 'Arakin 17a. The reverse was the case in the time of Zedekiah. God would then have reduced the world to its original chaos on account of the sinfulness of that generation, were it not for the piety of the king. On Zedekiah's piety, see note 1 on vol. IV, p. 291. The view that the Jews went into captivity during the reign of a pious king, when the people had no excuse for their sinfulness, is also found in Apocalypse of Baruch. 1.3; vol. IV, p. 256.

¹²⁸ BR 94 (end; is חוץ לפיליה to be read instead of ופיילה?); WR 19.6; Shekalim 6, 50a; Seder 'Olam 25; Josephus, *Antiqui.*, X, 6.3. The Haggadah concerning Jehoiakim's peculiar death is an attempt to reconcile the contradiction between 2 Kings 24.6 and 2 Chron. 36.6. Comp. also Jerome on Jer. 22.12, and Hippolytus, *In Daniele*, 641, where the story of Jehoiakim is confused with that of Zedekiah.

¹²⁹ Sanhedrin 82a and 104a.

¹³⁰ WR 19.6; Shekalim 6, 50a; 2 'Eser Galuyyot 114; Seder 'Olam 25. On the legend concerning the keys, comp. note 24 on vol. IV, pp. 303–304.

¹³¹ Josephus, *Antiqui.*, X, 7.1; comp. the following note.

¹³² Seder 'Olam 25; Sifre D., 321; Tan. Noah 3; Gittin 88a; Sanhedrin 38a, and Yerushalmi 1, 19a (comp. also *ibid.*, 18b–18c, concerning the scholars exiled to Babylon with Zedekiah); Nedarim 7, 40a; WR 11.7; BaR 11.3; Esther R., introduction; Hallel 97; Shir

8.11 and 12; 'Eser Galuyyot 10. With the exception of the first and last-named sources, all the others identify the "exile of the scholars" with the exile of Jehoiachin. The hegemony of Babylonian Jewry over the rest of the Jews is thus explained; comp. Tan. *loc. cit.* The "exile of the scholars" during the reign of Jehoiakim, as given in Seder 'Olam and 'Eser Galuyyot, *loc. cit.*, must not be emended to agree with the other sources (comp. Ratner, note 9), since Josephus, *Antiqui.*, X, 6.3, likewise maintains that the exile of the nobility took place during the reign of Jehoiakim; the nobility of Josephus and the flower of scholarship of the Rabbis are identical. Comp. vol. IV, p. 383.

¹³³ Josephus, *Antiqui.*, X, 6.3; comp. the preceding note.

¹³⁴ WR 19.6 (Nebuchadnezzar's wife is called שמירמה,שמירמית and שמירעם; the last form of the name is explained: "because she was born in thunder") and 10; PK 25, 162b–163b; Shir 8.6; Sanhedrin 37b. See also Josephus, *Antiqui,.* X, 7.1, whose favorable opinion of Jehoiachin flatly contradicts the words of Scripture in 2 Kings 24.9 and 2 Chron. 36.9. It is quite likely that he drew upon the Haggadah which maintains that sorrow and suffering changed the wicked and Godless king into a saint. With Jehoiachin the holy ark came to Babylon (Seder 'Olam 25; Tosefta Shekalim 2.18; Yerushalmi 6, 49c; Yoma 53b; against this view see the references cited in note 118), and it was in this land, in the city of Nehardea, that he erected a synagogue using as building material the stones and bricks brought with him from the Holy Land. The holiness of this synagogue was evidenced by the Shekinah which used it from time to time as its abode, see Megillah 29a; comp. the geonic interpretation of this passage in 'Aruk, s. v. שף 1; Rashi, *ad loc.*; Sha'are Teshubah 71; Iggeret R. Sherira 26; Epstein in *Schwarz-Festschrift*, 326. The life history of this king illustrates the truth of the wise adage, "Never despair". For thirty-seven years he languished in prison, yet at the end of this time he not only gained his liberty but received great honors. When Nebuchadnezzar who had kept him prisoner died (as to the contradiction between the date given in 2 Kings 25.27 and that in Jer. 52.31, see Seder 'Olam 28), the new king Evil-Merodach immediately set him free, and spoke to him comfortingly as follows: "Do not feel grieved at having been a prisoner this long time; forget not that thy captor was a king like thee, and not an ordinary man; to avenge the injustice done by him to thee, I dishonored his dead body" (comp. vol. IV, p. 339). Evil-merodach gave Jehoiachin royal garments, and settled an allowance upon him. See 2 ARN 17, 38.

¹³⁵ PK 25, 163b; WR 10.56; Shir 8.6; Sanhedrin 37b–38a.   In all these sources it is said that Zerubbabel was a son of Jehoiachin, but they differ as to how to harmonize this view with 2 Chron. 3.17, *seq.*, which seems to contradict it.   According to the Talmud, this scriptural passage contains a number of attributes of Zerubbabel, whereas the Midrash maintains that these attributes are assigned to Jehoiachin. The Talmud is also of the opinion that Zerubbabel is identical with Nehemiah.

¹³⁶ Tan. B. I, 140; Tan. Toledot 14; Aggadat Bereshit 44, 89; Targum on 2 Chron. 3.24.   Anani mentioned in 2 Chron. *loc. cit.*, it said in these sources to be the name of the Messiah (= "the one from the clouds"; comp. Sanhedrin 98a in reference to Dan. 7.13: ארו עם ענני שמיא, and 96b בר נפלי "son of the cloud", as a designation of the Messiah), and שבעה following this name describes the Messiah, "the one endowed with seven (שבעה) divine gifts."   Comp. Is. 11.2, and vol. VI, p. 193, note 61.

X. EXILE

Vol. IV, (pp. 291–340).

[1] PR 26, 129b. Shallum (1 Chron. 3.15) is taken to be another name for Zedekiah. This name was given to him either because he was "perfect" (*shalem*) in his conduct (comp. note 119), or because in his days the Davidic dynasty came to an end (*shalem*). See Horayyot 11b; Yerushalmi Shekalim 6, 49b; Jerome on Jer. 22.11. It is curious that this Church Father gives the identification of Shallum with Zedekiah as his own view, and states that Jewish tradition considers Shallum to have been some other son [of Josiah. On the respective ages of Josiah's sons, see Tosefta Sanhedrin 4.11, and references given in note 124 on vol. IV, p. 284.

[2] PR 26, 129b. On the correct reading of the text comp. Ginzberg *Compte Rendu*, 32 = *R.E.J.*, LXVII, 145–146. According to others, he made him take the oath of allegiance by the "horns of the altar", or, as some maintain, by the Abrahamic covenant. See PK 27, 168b; Ekah 2, 15; Koheleth 9.2; Esther R. 1.8. On the taking of an oath by the Torah, see Ginzberg, *Unbekannte Sekte*, 132–133. On the swearing by the Abrahamic covenant, see note 284 on vol. I, p. 294.

[3] Ekah 2, 114–115; Nedarim 56a; Tan. B. II, 33, and V, 8. The first passage maintains that Nebuchadnezzar killed the members of the Synedrion in a very cruel manner. The word חי in the passage cited from Tan. means "raw", and this seems to be the original form of the legend. Nebuchadnezzar lacked refinement, and was in the habit of eating raw meat. Subsequently חי was taken in its ordinary sense, and hence the statement in Ekah that he was caught eating a piece of flesh from a live hare.

[4] Nedarim 65a. On the halakic principle underlying this Haggadah, see *Or Zaru'a Shebu'ot* 6–7.

[5] A quotation from an unknown Midrash by Rashi and Kimhi on 2 Kings 25.4; Jer. 39.4; Ezek. 12.13; *Kad ha-Kemah*, Shebu'ah, II, 75. On the enormous length of this cave, see 'Erubin 61b; Tan. B. IV, 9; PR 26, 131a, and parallel passages cited by Buber on Tan. *loc. cit.* and by Friedmann on PR, *loc. cit.*

[6] PR 26, 131a. Read ונתנו בכלוב "and he put him in a cage" (this the Babylonians actually did with their prisoners) instead of

382

ונתנם בתנור which makes no sense, though the legend records elsewhere that the Babylonians put the captive Manasseh in an oven (comp. vol. IV, p. 279). On the "old" Halakah presupposed here that perjury is punishable with death, comp. Ginzberg, *Unbekannte Sekte*, 136. In Esther R. 1.8 Nebuchadnezzar's words are made to harmonize with the later view of the Halakah which maintains that perjury is not a capital crime.

⁷ Tan. B. V, 8. This is the source of Yalkut II, 257 (end of 2 Kings). Comp. note 23 on vol. I, p. 60. Jeremiah's prophecy that the king would lose his mind (comp. Jer. 4.9; לב is taken to mean "mind" and not "courage", comp. vol. V, p. 57, note 189) was thus fulfilled on this occasion. Had Zedekiah retained his right sense, he would rather have committed suicide than witness the execution of his children. See Ekah 1, 87.

⁸ PR 26, 131a–131b, where יחזקאל should probably be read instead of ירמיה. Comp. Josephus, *Antiqui.*, X, 8.2, which reads: And these things happened to him, as Jeremiah (34.3) and Ezekiel (12.13) had predicted to him that he should be caught and brought before the king of Babylon, and should speak face to face with him, and should see his eyes with his own eyes; and thus far did Jeremiah prophesy, but he was also made blind and brought to Babylon but did not see it, according to the prediction of Ezekiel. As to Zedekiah's fate in captivity, see 2 Targum Esther 1.2 (end) where it is said that Pelatiah the son of Benaiah (comp. Ezek. 11.13, and accordingly either יהוידע of Targum is a faulty reading for בניהו or we must read בן בניהו בן יהוידע; see 1 Kings 2.29) remonstrated with Nebuchadnezzar on account of his cruelty to the Jews. He said to him: "When one delivers his flock to a shepherd, and a bear comes and snatches away a sheep, of whom will it be required?" The king answered: "From the shepherd will it be required." Whereupon Pelatiah rejoined: "Let thine ears hear what thy mouth has uttered." The king then ordered to bring Zedekiah before him, and he removed the iron and brass chains from him, and changed his prison garments for others. The similarity between the words of Pelatiah in Targum and those of Paltiel, "the prince of the people" (comp. Ezek. 11.1), in 4 Ezra 5.16–18 is obvious, though in this pseudepigraphic writing it is Ezra who is the shepherd and not Nebuchadnezzar, as in Targum. On Pelatiah, see also note 21. The imprisonment of Zedekiah and his final release are referred to in Targum on Ps. 107.10, *seq.*, whereas Josephus, *Antiqui.*, X, 8.7, maintains that Nebuchadnezzar kept Zedekiah in prison until he

died, and buried him magnificently (comp. notes 117–118), but he freed the high priest from his bonds. In Tehillim 90, 389 יהויכין is very likely to be read instead of צדקיה. In explanation of Hab. 2.15 it is said that the biblical verse refers to the indignities inflicted by Nebuchadnezzar on Zedekiah whom he gave to eat and drink things causing diarrhoea, thus exposing him to derision. See Tan. B. II, 33; Esther R. 1.8; Jerome on Hab. *loc. cit.* (who quotes as his authority *quemdam de Hebraeis, qui sapiens apud illos* = חכם, *et* δευτερωτής = מִשְׁנָה, *vocabatur*). The coarse form of this legend in Jerome is very likely to be ascribed to his own account, and not to the learned Hebrew. Comp. note 107.

⁹ Sanhedrin 103a. Comp. note 119 and note 127 on vol. IV, p. 284.

¹⁰ Sifre N., 78; Sifre Z., 75; PK 13, 115b, where it is said that the people spoke scornfully of Jeremiah as "that descendant of a proselyte". On Rahab, the ancestress of prophets and priests, see vol. IV, p. 5. On the scornful reference to his descent, comp. vol. III, p. 388, the similar remark about Phinehas. That Hilkiah the father of Jeremiah is identical with the high priest bearing this name in the time of Josiah is maintained by the Church Fathers Clemens Alexandrinus, *Stromata*, 1.21, and Hippolytus on Susannah 1.1, who considers Jeremiah to have been the brother of Susannah (this is how the passage is to be understood), the daughter of the high priest Hilkiah. In Jewish sources, Kimhi on Jer. 1.1 is perhaps the first who explicitly declares that Jeremiah's father was the high priest Hilkiah; but Targum Jer. 1.1 probably presupposes this view.

¹¹ BR 64.4, where מנשה is very likely to be read, instead of איזבל, in accordance with Rashi on Ezek. 20.14. This correct reading is more in harmony with history, for it makes Jeremiah's father flee from the wicked king Manasseh, not from the wicked queen Jezebel. Comp., however, Ascension of Isaiah 2.12, with regard to the false prophet Belchira (living at the time of Manasseh), who is said to have been a nephew of the false prophet Zedekiah, who flourished in the reigns of Ahab and Jezebel. Jeremiah was born on the ninth of Ab (the day on which the Temple was burned), and his birth was announced to his father by the wicked Pashhur. Hence the prophet curses not only the day of his birth, but also the man who brought the "tidings" to his father, saying: "A man-child was born unto thee" (Jer. 20. 14–15). See Kimhi on Jer., *loc. cit.*, and *Seder ha-Dorot*, 3298.

¹² ARN 2, 12; Tehillim 9, 84. Comp. note 318 on vol. I, 306.

While still in his mother's womb, he cried: "I shall not leave it before I receive my name." His father said: "I shall call thee Abraham." But the unborn babe replied: "This is not my name." The father continued to suggest many other names, but the unborn babe insisted that none of the proposed names would fit him. Finally Elijah the prophet appeared and proposed the name Jeremiah, because in the days of this child God will raise up (ירם "raise up" and יה "God") an enemy against Jerusalem, who will lift up his hand against it. "This," assented the unborn babe, "is my name." I shall be called Jeremiahu (the full form of Jeremiah ירמיה is ירמיהו Jeremiahu), adding in this way the last part of thy name (אליהו=) to my own. See 2 Alphabet of Ben Sira 17b. For other etymologies of the name Jeremiah (among which there is one deriving it from the Greek ἐρημία "desert"), see PK 13, 115a; Ekah Z. 76; Koheleth 1.1.

13 PR 26, 129a–129b, and, in a shortened form, Ekah Z., 62 (here it is correctly written כהן and not כ' גדול, since the "water of bitterness" might be administered by an ordinary priest), and 134. Zion the mother of Israel is a favorite metaphor with the pseudepigraphic writers and the New Testament; see Apocalypse of Baruch 3.1, and the parallels cited by Charles. The Haggadah maintains that Jeremiah was meant in the promise made by God to Moses that He will raise up a prophet "like unto thee" (Deut. 18.18), and although there "hath not arisen a prophet in Israel like Moses" (Deut. 34.10), the lives of these two prophets show so many striking resemblances, that the description of Jeremiah as "a prophet like unto Moses" is well justified. Moses prophesied for forty years, so did Jeremiah; Moses prophesied concerning Judah and Israel, so did Jeremiah; Moses was attacked by members of his own tribe (*i. e.*, the Levite Korah), so was Jeremiah (comp. Jer. 20.1); Moses was thrown into the water, and Jeremiah into a pit; Moses was saved from death by a bondwoman (Exod. 2.5), and Jeremiah by a slave (comp. Jer. 38.9; the name Ebedmelech is explained as "slave of the king"; Comp. note 66); Moses addressed words of exhortation to the people, so did Jeremiah. See PK 13, 112a; Ekah Z. 75; Midrash Tannaim 111; a quotation from an unknown Pesikta in Midrash Aggada, 160, on Num. 30.11, where many more parallels are drawn between the life of Moses and that of Jeremiah. Comp. also Kaneh (caption אש תמיד), who seems to have made use of the same source as Midrash Aggadah. Moses was the first in the long row of prophets and Jeremiah the last; the prophets Haggai, Zechariah, and Malachi, who lived after his time,

retained only a trace of the old prophetic power. See PK 13, 116a, where the text is to be corrected in accordance with Midrash Aggada, 160, on Num. 30.11. As to the meaning of פקידה which is rendered by "trace", see Nega'im 5.3. In his modesty and humility Jeremiah declined the honor to be compared with Moses. When God told him to take the place once occupied by Moses and to become the leader and guide of the people, he rejoined: "Who am I to take the place of Moses? May it be granted to me to be like his pupil." See Midrash quoted by Shu'aib, Mattot, 91d. As to Jeremiah's being equal to Moses, see Matth. 16.14, and the Christian tradition concerning the "two witnesses" (Rev. 11.3), according to which the one is Moses and the other Jeremiah; see Bousset, *Antichrist*, 208, and see also vol. VI, p. 340, note 112. Jeremiah, Isaiah, Jacob, and Adam are the four men who are described in the Bible as "the creatures of God". See PR 26, 129a, and comp. also *ibid.* 27, 133b, as well as Mekilta Bo 16, 19a, with regard to the statement that Jeremiah was consecrated to the prophetic calling while still in his mother's womb. Jeremiah, however, was not the only prophet sent to the wicked generation. For ninety years before the exile two prophets admonished Israel twice daily to repent and mend their ways, if they did not want to be banished into captivity. See PK 16, 124b; PR 33, 153; Ekah 2, 117. But the Israelites said to Jeremiah: "After all the sins we have committed we are ashamed to return to God." To this God replied by the mouth of Jeremiah: "If ye come back to Me, ye return to your father, and children are never ashamed to come back to their father." See DR 2.24; PK 25, 165a. Jeremiah's teacher was the prophet Zephaniah, a great-grandson of king Hezekiah (comp. Ibn Ezra and Kimhi on Zeph. 1.1; Maimonides in his introduction to his *Yad*), and when the disciple began to prophesy, he limited his activity to speaking in the streets, whereas Zephaniah preached in the synagogue. See PR 26, 129b. In vol. IV, p. 296, lines 6 and 7, read Zephaniah instead of Zechariah.

14 PK 13, 115b, which reads: As Jeremiah was scornfully spoken of by the people as "that descendant of the harlot Rahab" (comp. the references given in note 10, to which should be added PK 13, 11b–12a; Ekah Z., 74, 75; unknown Pesikta quoted in Midrash Aggada, 160, on Num. 30.11), so was Uriah referred to by the people as the "Gibeonite", because he came from Kiriath-Jearim (Jer. 26.20), a city which originally belonged to the Gibeonites (comp. Josh. 9.17), and therefore the Bible takes pains to emphasize the fact that this

prophet was of noble descent, a priest, comp. Is. 8.2. The identity of Uriah killed by Jehoiakim with the priest Uriah in Is., *loc. cit.*, is presupposed in many old sources; comp. Sifre D., 43; Ekah 5, 159; Makkot (end); Targum on Is., *loc. cit.* These sources, however, understand the passage in Is. to mean: God spoke to Isaiah: the good tidings foretold by the prophet Zechariah will be fulfilled, as the evil predicted by Uriah (his prophecy consisted of Micah 3.12) was fulfilled. According to this view, Isaiah had no personal relations with Zechariah or Uriah. Clemens Alexandrinus, *Stromata*, 1.21, asserts that the prophet Habakkuk was a contemporary of Jeremiah and Ezekiel, but in the same passage it is stated that Jonah and Habakkuk were contemporaries of Daniel. Comp. Index under the respective names of these prophets.

¹⁵ Mo‘ed Katan 26a; Ekah, introduction, 27, and 1, 43. The old rabbinical sources know of no other writings of Jeremiah than the book bearing his name, the Book of Lamentations, which is said to be the "scroll" mentioned in Jer. 36.2, *seq.*, and the Book of Kings. See Baba Batra 15a, and comp. the sources cited at the beginning of this note. The statement of Baba Batra, with regard to the Book of Kings, is to be understood that the prophet was the editor thereof. This becomes evident when we consider the similar statements made there concerning other biblical books, as, *e. g.*, the following ones: Hezekiah and his associates *wrote* the books of Isaiah, Proverbs, Song of Songs, and Ecclesiastes; the men of the Great Assembly *wrote* the books of Ezekiel, the twelve Minor Prophets, Daniel, and the Scroll of Esther. Comp. further details concerning this use of כתב in note 89 on vol. IV, p. 277. The apocryphal and pseudepigraphic literature knows at least of three additional writings by Jeremiah. They are: 1) Epistle of Jeremiah, a letter written by the prophet to the Jews who were about to be led as captives to Babylon, in which he warns them against idolatry It is a Midrash on Jer. 10.11, and is a canonical book in the Greek Bible. 2) The Paralipomena of Jeremiah, also known under the title, the Rest of the Words of Baruch, an originally Jewish work, but with considerable Christian additions and interpolations. Though ascribed to Jeremiah, the chief interest of this work centres around Ebed-melech the Ethiopian, the friend of the prophet; comp. note 58. On a third pseudepigraphic writing ascribed to Jeremiah, see Schürer, *Geschichte* (4th edition), III, 393. Eupolemus (?), 454b–454c, narrates how the wicked king Jehoiakim attempted to burn Jeremiah on account of his prophecies predicting the destruction of

the Temple and the captivity of the people. It is not likely that this writer had made use of an apocryphal writing of Jeremiah. In all probability this statement of Eupolemus is based on a (fanciful) combination of Jer. 36.23 with 26.8, *seq.* The biblical narrative about the burning of Jeremiah's writings was changed to an attempt at burning the author. In the very late compilation known as the Ma'aseh-Buch (comp. No 163,49b) we meet for the first time in rabbinic sources with a reference to non-canonical writings of Jeremiah, which are said to have consisted of lamentations. Zephaniah, the teacher of Jeremiah (comp. note 14), is also credited with an additional work, and fragments of the Apocalypse of Zephaniah are still extant. See Schürer, *op. cit.*, 367–368.

    16 Ekah 1, 71; Tan. Lek 20; Yerushalmi Sanhedrin 10, 29c. Opinions differ as to the nature of the sins which caused the destruction of the Temple and the captivity. See Shabbat 119a, 139a; Yoma 9b; Yerushalmi 1, 38c; Ta'anit 5a–5b; Nedarim 81a; Baba Mezi'a 30b (which reads: Jerusalem was destroyed because the people dispensed justice according to the "strict law"); Yerushalmi Hagigah 1, 76b; 2 ARN 5, 18; ER 14, 71 (comp. Yoma, *loc. cit.*), and 18, 96; EZ 1, 168; Ekah, introduction, 1 and 27 (on the seven cardinal sins which they are said to have committed, see Sifre 26.21 and Mishle 6, 56; comp. also note 60, on vol. IV, p. 269) as well as 1, 41, 56–57, 62, 69–70, 92–93; Ekah Z., 59, 75, 77; PK 13, 112b; 15, 120b–121a; PR 25, 125b; 27, 132b–133a; BaR 9.7; Koheleth 1.13; Baraita di-Yeshua' 45b. It is noteworthy that the Rabbis did not consider idolatry as the sin which caused the severe punishment of Israel. They even maintain that the Israelites were convinced of the vanity of the idols, and the idolatry was merely to give expression to their dissatisfaction with the law, the burden of which was too heavy for them, especially the injunctions regulating sexual life. See Sanhedrin 63b. Neglect of the study of the Torah is most frequently mentioned as the main cause for Israel's severe punishment, and besides this a number of other sins, transgressions as well as moral wrongs, are mentioned as having contributed to make God wroth with His people. In Yerushalmi Rosh ha-Shanah 5, 58d (towards the end), and Ekah, 1, 62, it is stated that because they did not release their Hebrew slaves (comp. Jer. 34.8, *seq.*), they themselves were given over to slavery. The same view is shared by ps.-Tertullian *De Carmine adv. Marcionem*, 3, 235. The view that their evil treatment of Jeremiah caused the exile is found in Ecclus. 49.7 and EZ 9,188. That the destruction of Jerusalem and the exile of Judah were mainly

due to the sins of the "ten tribes" is maintained in Assumption of Moses 3.5; comp. also Baruch 2.26; Apocalypse of Baruch 77.10. See, on the other hand, 1.3 of the last-named work, where it is said that the sins of Judah were greater than those of Israel. Eupolemus (?), 454b, following closely the words of Scripture, asserts that Jeremiah was sent by God, and found the Jews sacrificing to a golden image, the name of which was Baal.

17 Ekah 4, 152; an unknown Midrash quoted in *Sefer ha-Musar* 18, 129b–130a. The text in Ekah is not quite clear, as one fails to see the connection between the friendly relations of the ten tribes with the Egyptians and the assistance of the latter offered to Judah.

18 Sanhedrin 89b; Yerushalmi 11, 30b. This Hananiah was originally a true prophet; see Sifre D., 84; Sanhedrin 90b; Yerushalmi, *loc. cit.*; Midrash Shir 10a; Hallel 103 (towards the bottom). In the last-named source עזור בן חנניה is corrupted to חנניה מישאל ועזריה בן עזול. In Midrash Shir 12a (bottom), the text is not to be emended with the editor to חנניה, it refers to 1 Kings 13.18 and 22.11.

19 Yerushalmi Sanhedrin 11, 30b; Midrash Tannaim 63–64; Tan. Wa-Yera 13. As to the conception that God always fulfils His word if it is a promise to bestow "good" upon man, whereas He sometimes changes His word if it contains a threat to do harm to man, see BR 53.4, and the numerous parallel passages cited by Theodor.

20 PR 26, 129a–129b; Yerushalmi Sanhedrin 11, 30b; Midrash Tannaim 64. On Jonathan, see also Hallel 103 (towards the bottom); on the pious Ebed-melech see vol. IV, pp. 318, *seq.* Jeremiah, on hearing Hananiah's false prophecy, said: "Amen! the Lord do so." His punishment for having "flattered" the wicked was that he almost lost his life at the hands of the grandson of the man whom he had flattered; Sotah 41b–42a with reference to Jerem. 28.6 and 36.13.

21 2 Alphabet of Ben Sira 21b; R. Joseph Kimhi on 1 Kings 10.1 (comp. Dukes, *Rabbinische Blumenlese*, 267), with the addition: And she (the queen of Sheba) descended from Abraham through his children with the concubines. This is based on the identification of שבא in 1 Kings, *loc. cit.*, with שבא in Gen. 25.3; comp. MHG I, 379, and note 311 on vol. I, p. 298. The legend about Solomon's marriage with the queen of Sheba is perhaps of Arabic origin, as it is not found in old Jewish sources antedating the Mohammedan period. The name Bilkis, however, given in Arabic sources to the queen of Sheba seems to be the Hebrew פילגש "concubine", and this would point to the Jewish origin of the legend. Comp. note 41 on vol. IV, p. 145. Later

Kabbalists changed "mother" to "ancestress", maintaining that Nebuchadnezzar was not the son but the descendant of the queen of Sheba.
Nebuchadnezzar's wife was Semiramis; comp. note 106 and note 134
on vol. IV, p. 287.   A son-in-law of Nebuchadnezzar was the viceroy
of Mesene, and at his request Jewish captives were sent to his dominion,
but only slaves, while the freemen among the Jews remained in Babylon.
This was done at the suggestion of Pelatiah (comp. note 8), who remarked to Nebuchadnezzar: "We (freemen) ought to remain near
thee, and the slaves may be sent away."   See Kiddushin 72b.   Nebuchadnezzar, being the king of Babylon, is also described as the "grandson of Nimrod", the first king of that country; see Pesahim 94b.
This, however, is probably not to be taken in a genealogical sense.

²² Sanhedrin 95b (but here nothing is said about Nebuchadnezzar
being related to Sennacherib); Tosefta-Targum on Is. 32; Ekah, introduction, 30, where Sennacherib is said to have been the grandfather
of Nebuchadnezzar.   Comp. also Ekah, introduction, 23; 2 Targum
on Esther 1.2, 11, and 4.1; vol. IV, p. 269 and note 59 pertaining thereto.

²³ Sanhedrin 96a; for another version of this legend, see vol.
IV, p. 275.

²⁴ Ekah, introduction, 23; Tehillim 79, 359–360; Koheleth 12.7;
2 Targum Esther 1.2, 11, and 4.1; PK 5, 50b–51a; PR 15, 74a; Shir
2.13.   The Rabbis seem to have taken קלקל (Ezek. 21.25) to mean
"shooting"; the divination employed by Nebuchadnezzar, accordingly,
did not consist in the "shaking of arrows", but in "throwing"
them.   Comp. Cassel, *Esther*, 287.   The three last-named sources
cited above maintain that the seventy years of the Babylonian exile
are to be counted from the time when the heavenly voice began
to be heard in Nebuchadnezzar's palace, while the actual period of
the exile lasted only fifty-two years.   Comp. however vol. IV, p. 366.
During these fifty-two years the land of Judah was entirely deserted
by "all that lives"; neither man, nor beast, nor fowl, nor fish was to
be found there (comp. Jer. 9.9), and for seven years the soil thereof
was "brimstone and salt, and a burning, that it is not sown", so
that the attempts made by the Samaritans to till the soil were in vain.
Seven hundred species of "clean" fish, eight hundred of "clean" beasts
and numberless species of fowl left the Holy Land at the time of the
exile, and settled in Babylon (the fish travelled through the abyss)
and, with the exception of the turbot, they all returned with the res-
toration of the captivity.   See Seder 'Olam 27; Shabbat 145b; Yoma
54a; Yerushami Ta'anit 4, 69b; Kil'ayim 9, 32c; Ketubot 12, 25b;

PK 13, 113b–114; PR 1, 3a; Ekah, introduction, 34. The cedar-tree likewise came at the time of the exile to Babylon, where it was brought by Nebuchadnezzar, who had spoiled all the cedar groves of Palestine to enrich his own country. It is to this that the prophet refers saying: "Yea, the cypresses rejoice at thee, and the cedars of Lebanon; since thou art laid down, no feller is come up against us" (Is. 14.8); Ekah 1, 64. The palm was brought to Babylon forty years prior to the exile so that Israel, accustomed to the fruit of the palm (sweet fruit is the proper food for the students of the Torah), should not lack it. See PK 13, 114a; Yerushalmi Ta'anit 4, 69b. The Jews were the first to introduce the use of the "mill" in Babylon, their young men having been forced by Nebuchadnezzar to take the handmills with them from Palestine to the land of their captivity. See Ekah 5, 159. Several of the above statements of the Haggadah and many others concerning the exile (comp., *e. g.*, note 16) reflect the views of the Rabbis about the catastrophe in the year 70, C. E., notwithstanding the references made to the biblical passages dealing with the "first exile". Comp. also Yerushalmi Sanhedrin 10, 29c, which reads: Israel was not exiled until he had become divided into twenty-four sects, as it is written: "I send thee to the children of Israel, to the *rebellious nation*" (Ezek. 2.3). It is quite obvious that the sectarianism at the end of the second commonwealth is meant. Another statement (*ibid.*) reads: Israel was not exiled until he had neglected the law of circumcision and other divine commands. It is not impossible, though not very likely, that this wishes to convey the idea that Pauline Christianity is responsible for the destruction of the second Temple. Comp. note 16 (beginning) and note 29 (towards end of page).

²⁵ Ekah Z., 63, 70, 134; comp. note 27. Michael, the guardian angel of Israel, had to be found first before "his" people could be conquered. Comp. the same view with regard to the guardian angels of Egypt, vol. III. p. 25. As to the conception that the "right hand" of God is bound as long as Israel is in exile, see Ekah, 2, 110—111, and note 4 on vol. II, p. 187.

²⁶ Ekah Z., 61; PR 29, 139b–140a. On Abika (not Akiba as in the text, which is a printer's error), see Güdemann, *Monatsschrift*, XXIX, 132, who identifies him with Chagiras of Adiabene, whose heroic exploits during the wars with the Romans in 70 C. E. are described by Josephus, *Bell.*, V, 11.5. That Abika is said to have fought against the Babylonians is not necessarily an anachronism; comp. the end of the note 24. When Gabriel (it is he who is spoken of in Ezek. 10.2 as the "man clothed in linen") received the command "to fill both

his hands with coals of fire from between the Cherubim and dash them against the city" (of Jerusalem), he had to ask one of the Cherubim to be kind enough and fetch the coals for him (the celestials need lovingkindness like the terestrials) for he would have been burned immediately if he had approached the place of the Cherubim. For three years Gabriel kept the almost extinguished coals in his hands, hoping that Israel would repent and Jerusalem would thus be saved. When he realized, however, that his hope was doomed to disappointment, he was ready to dash the coals with fury; but at that moment God called to him: "Gently, gently! There are men in Israel who are kind to their fellow-men. Had Gabriel carried out his intention, Israel would have been annihilated, and thus its survival is due to the lovingkindness shown by some of them, on account of whose merits Gabriel was admonished by God not to act too furiously in his work of destruction. See WR 26.8; Tan. B. III, 41 and 84; Tan. Emor 3; Shemuel 24, 121; Ekah 1, 75–76; Mishhle 1, 47–48; Yoma 77a. On the part played by Gabriel in the destruction of the Temple, see Ekah 2, 97–99, where many haggadic embellishments are found about the narratives (visions?) given in Ezek. 9 and 10. As to the mark set by the angel upon the foreheads of the pious (Ezek. 9.4–6; see note 122 on vol. IV, pp. 416-417), comp. Shabbat 55a; Tan. B. III, 41; Tan. Mishpatim 6. It is stated in these passages that the pious were marked by the angel with ink, the wicked with blood, the ink-mark warded off the angels of destruction, the blood mark incited them. The "justice" of God insisted that the pious be also punished for not having guided the wicked back to the path of righteousness. The demand of justice was granted, and the pious were even the first upon whom the punishment was visited. Comp. Ezek. 9.6.

²⁷ Yalkut II, 1001, without giving its source but very likely quoting Ekah Z. The view that the destruction of the Temple was never achieved by the hand of man, but that the angels (or the heavenly fire) burned it is often met with in the talmudic and midrashic literature. Michael and Gabriel are mentioned as the angels who carried out the work of destruction. Comp. Sanhedrin 96b; Ekah 1, 76; 2, 109–110; DR 1.17; Tehillim 36, 252; Ekah Z, 61; Aggadat Shir 5, 39; Midrash Shir 30b. Comp. note 25. Most of the Midrashim just cited speak of the angels as keeping guard over the Temple, which accordingly was indestructible as long as they watched over it. A somewhat different version of this Haggadah reads: As long as the Shekinah dwelled in it, the Temple could not be destroyed; but the Shekinah gradually with-

drew from its place between the Cherubim to its original abode in heaven, and this left the Temple and the holy city unprotected. Ekah, introduction, 25; Rosh ha-Shanah 31a; PK 13, 114b; ARN 34, 102; Aggadat Shir 5, 39; comp. note 98 on vol. IV, p. 278 with regard to the "ten stations" travelled by the Shekinah. Noteworthy is the statement found in Pesikta and Ekah that for thirteen and a half years the Shekinah, after withdrawing from the Temple, dwelled on the Mount of Olives, from where it proclaimed, three times daily, to the people: "I will go and return to My place, till they acknowledge their guilt and seek My face." Comp. Hosea 5.15. In contrast to the view that finally the Shekinah returned to heaven, there are also authorities who maintain that "the Shekinah, never left the western wall;" Tan. B. II, 5–6; Shir 2.9; Tehillim 11, 98–99; ShR 2.3. The western wall is the only remnant of the former Temple building.

²⁸ Comp. the "sending away" of Samuel from the calamitous battle in note 42 on vol. IV, p 64. See also Apocalypse of Baruch 2, according to which Jeremiah, Baruch, and the other pious men were commanded by God to leave the city one day before the enemy was to enter it, in order that their presence might not render it impregnable. Comp. vol. IV, p. 322.

²⁹ PR 26, 131a; 2 Targum Esther 1.2, 11; PK 13, 115b–116a; Koheleth 3.16 and 10.6; WR 4.10; Sanhedrin 103a. On the view that the angel destroyed the Temple, see, besides the references given in note 27, also Apocalypse of Baruch 7–8 and 80. This apocryphal work is also acquainted with the legend about the keys of the Temple; the rabbinical sources dealing with it are given in note 150 on vol. IV, p 286; comp. also the references at the beginning of this note, as well as Ta'anit 29a; ARN 4, 24; 2 Targum Esther 1.3, 12. The last high priest was Seraiah (comp. 2 Kings 25.18), a brother of Baruch; see Sifre N., 78, and the parallel passages cited by Friedmann, as well as Ekah 2, 113. Comp. also *Shitah Mekubbezet* on 'Arakin 16a. As long as Israel brought the daily offering (besides circumcision, this was the only divine command observed by them; comp., however, note 24 end, and note 16 beginning) Jerusalem was impregnable. The enemy succeeded in entering the city only after the services of the Temple had ceased owing to the lack of sacrifices. For a time the enemy supplied the Jews with the necessary animals but finally they sent them up a swine instead of a sheep. See Apocalypse of Daniel (towards the beginning), which undoubtedly follows Baba Kamma 82b (comp. Josephus, *Antiqui.*, XIV, 2.2), where the episode with the swine is said to have taken place at the time of the

war between Aristobulus and Hyrcanus. Another version of the legend about the swine reads as follows: When the enemy approached the Temple, the gate shut of itself, and would by no means open. It was of no avail to the enemy that he brought three hundred and sixty camels laden with iron axes and tried to force the gate open, as it "swallowed up" all the rams (comp. the statement concerning the "magnetic iron" in vol. IV, p. 276). Finally פרנטוס (according to Perles, *Schwartz-Festschrift*, 305, Haterius Fronto, mentioned by Josephus, *Bell.*, VI, 4.3 and 9.2; but perhaps פטרנוס, Paternus, is to be read; comp. Schürer, *Geschichte*, 4th edition, I, 649) brought a swine, slew it, and sprinkled its blood upon the Temple, defiling it thereby. Whereupon the gate opened, and the enemy entered the Temple. When, however, Nebuchadnezzar wanted to enter the holy of holies, the doors closed and would not open, until a heavenly voice called out: "Open thy doors, O Lebanon, that the fire may devour thy cedars" (Zech 11.1). Whereupon they opened. See 2 Targum 1.2, 11–12, which in the main follows Sanhedrin 96b and Targum Lam. 2.9. On the defilement of the Temple by the enemy and on the blasphemies uttered by them against God, see Ekah 2, 113, and ER 1, 5. The Temple was taken on the seventh of Ab, and the work of destruction began immediately; on the ninth towards evening the enemy set fire to it, and on the tenth it was burned down completely; Seder 'Olam 27; Ta'anit 29a; Yerushalmi 4, 69c (top), and Megillah 1, 70c. It was the first year of the Sabbatical cycle, and on the first day of the week, the ninth of Ab, when the enemy seized the Temple just at the moment when the Levites chanted the song: "And He hath brought upon them their own iniquity and will cut them off in their own evil" (Ps. 94.23). See Seder 'Olam 30; Tosefta Ta'anit 5 (3). 9; Babli 29a; Yerushalmi 4, 68d; 'Arakin 11b–12a; Soferim 18. These sources state that the destruction of the second Temple took place exactly on the same day of the week and of the month and in the same year of the Sabbatical cycle as the first. Comp. also Josephus *Bell.*, VI, 4.5–8, and *Antiqui.*, X, 8.3; Schürer, *Geschichte* (4th edition) I, 631. The statements of the latter are far from being correct. מוצאי שבת is not Sabbath night but Sunday, as the context shows, since there was no service in the Temple at night; ערב is not found in correct texts, and is certainly a scribal error.—God in His mercy ordained that the destruction of the Temple, as a result of which the people went into captivity, should take place in the warm days of the summer, otherwise the exiles would have suffered greatly from the cold on their way to Babylon. See Tan. B. III, 41.—Just as the destruction of the Temple would never have been accomplished by the Babylonians, if they had not been assisted by God in a miraculous way (comp. above), even so was the conquest of Jerusalem brought about directly by God. For three and a half years Nebuchadnezzar besieged the holy city without making the slightest progress. He finally decided to raise the siege and return to Babylon. When he was about to carry out his intention, the thought occurred to him (thus did God ordain) to measure the height of the city walls, and after taking the measurements in two days he found out to his great joy that the walls sank daily two and a half hand-breadths. He remained outside the walls till they had disappeared entirely, and he entered the city. See Ekah, introduction, 30. On the view that the gates of the Temple opened of themselves, see Yoma 39b and Josephus, *Bell.*, VI, 5.3, who reports this miracle to have taken place shortly before the destruction of the second Temple. Comp. note 24 (end). The designation of the Temple as Lebanon (Yoma, *loc. cit.*, Gittin 56b, and 2 Targum Esther 1.2, 12), is also known to Jerome; comp. his commentary on Jerem. 22.20. Azulai, *Midbar Kedemot*, s. v. ירמיה, quotes from a Midrash on Lam. the following legend: Jeremiah and Nebuchadnezzar were intimate friends in their childhood. The future ruler of the world once said to his Jewish friend: "If I become king, I shall burn the Temple of Jerusalem, destroy the city, and drive its people into exile." Jeremiah, who knew by the Holy Spirit that Nebuchadnezzar was destined to do great things, began to plead with him for the Jews, but without much success. The only request he granted him was that he (Jeremiah) should be permitted to save as many as would be able to leave Jerusalem in the few hours from noon until sunset. When the fatal day of the destruction of the Temple arrived, Jeremiah was absent from the city (comp. vol. IV, p. 303), returning to it about sunset, and thus was unable to save a person. Comp. also Horowitz, *Bet 'Eked*, I, 37, whose reference to the source of this legend is misleading, as there can be no doubt that he copied it from Azulai. Bernstein, *König Nebucadnezar*, 27, note 1, gives a somewhat different version of this legend, alleged to be taken from "cabbalistic works"; but the correctness of the statement may be doubted. Bernstein, *ibid.*, quotes from "cabbalistic works" the legend that Nebuchadnezzar, greatly moved by the tears and lamentations of his friend Jeremiah, ordered to have the Temple rebuilt and the people return from the exile. It is quite certain that Jewish sources contain nothing of the kind, and it seems that Bernstein must have confused Jewish with Arabic sources. Comp. Mas'udi, *Muruj al-Dhahab*, I, 100.

395

³⁰ Gittin 57b; Sanhedrin 96b; Ekah 4, 148–149, and introduction, 23; Yerushalmi Ta'anit 4, 69b; PK 15, 122a–122b; Koheleth 3.16 and 10.4; 2 Targum Esther 1.2,12. In the last-named source Nebuchadnezzar and not Nebuzaradan is the avenger of the prophet Zechariah. In Sanhedrin, *loc. cit.* (comp. also ShR 46.4), it is explicitly stated that the king was not present at the conquest of Jerusalem, which was entirely the work of Nebuzaradan. It is true that the Bible speaks of the campaign against Jerusalem as the work of Nebuchadnezzar; but this is due to the fact that the general was so overawed by the king that whatever he did he considered it as the work of his master, whose likeness he had attached to his chariot, so that he might always be reminded of him. Apocalypse of Daniel (beginning) follows in the main Sanhedrin, but has one new point to the effect that it was Gedaliah the son of Ahikam who told Nebuzaradan the real cause of the seething blood. This explains why he was appointed governor over Judah by the Babylonian general. On the virgins who wove the curtains for the sanctuary, see also Apocalypse of Baruch 10. 18–19. Midrash Aggada on Num. 30.15 (158) maintains that the blood of the murdered Zechariah bespattered the walls of the sanctuary, and in consequence thereof the Shekinah left the Temple and did not return until the time of Isaiah. Comp. the references in note 27 on the "stations of the Shekinah". Ratner, note 17 on Seder 'Olam 27, justly suggests that the Zechariah legend was known to this tannaitic work. In the Christian Apocryphon *Protevangelium of James* 24, Zechariah, the father of John the Baptist, is substituted for his namesake Zechariah, the prophet and high priest in the time of King Joash. Comp. vol IV, p. 259. In Matth. 22.35 (but not in the parallel passage Luke 11.51) the father of the murdered prophet is called Berechiah, owing to a confusion of the pre-exilic prophet Zechariah (the son of Jehoiada) with the post-exilic prophet, the author of the biblical book Zechariah, whose father's name was Berechiah. Comp. also Josephus, *Bell.*, IV, 5.4; Moore, *Journal of Oriental Society* XVI, 317 *seq.* Midrash Aggada, *loc. cit.*, counts the following martyred prophets: Hur (comp. Index, s. v.); Shemaiah, who was killed by Basha, king of the ten tribes; Ahiah of Shiloh (comp. note 5 on vol. IV, p. 180); Zechariah, who was killed by king Joash; Isaiah, who was sawn asunder by Manasseh (comp. Index, s. v.); Jeremiah, who was stoned by the Egyptian Jews. Comp. note 42. For the miracle of the never-congealing blood, comp. also the quotation from an unknown Midrash in *J.Q.R.*, N. S. VII 133, with regard to the blood of the goat slaughtered by the brethren of Joseph

(comp. Gen.37.31), which, it is said, will remain uncongealed until the advent of the Messiah. As to the large number of priests killed by Nebuzaradan, see also Ekah 2, 108. As to the latter's conversion to Judaism, comp. vol. IV. p. 311, where it is assumed that he remained in the service of Nebuchadnezzar even after the destruction of the Temple, and accordingly he did not become a proselyte. In Sanhedrin, *loc. cit.*, it is stated that God intended to have Nebuchadnezzar's descendants become proselytes, but the angels objected, for they did not want the wicked king who destroyed God's house to be granted such a distinction. With regard to the army which participated in the destruction of the Temple, the view is expressed that it will not rise on the day of resurrection, but at the same time it will be spared the torments of hell. See Yerushalmi Shebi'it 4, 35c; Ruth R. 1, 17. Comp. also Tosefta Sanhedrin 13.5 and Seder 'Olam 3 (end).

[31] PR 26, 131. Comp. vol. IV, p. 303.

[32] On the weeping of the angels (= Is. 33.8), see also vol. I, p. 281. On this occasion as well as on those of the flood and of the drowning of the Egyptians God silenced the song of the angels; Ekah, introduction 24, 24. Comp. vol. VI, pp. 12, 165. The weeping of the angels at the destruction of the Temple is also found in Apocalypse of Baruch 77.2.

[33] On the designation of Abraham as the "friend" and "beloved" of God, see vol. V, pp. 207–208.

[34] On the rejection of the Torah by the "other nations", see vol. III, pp. 80, *seq.*

[35] In the Midrash the words of Abraham addressed to the first three letters only of the alphabet are given.

[36] On the part of Moses in the Messianic work of redemption, see vol. II, pp. 302, 373; vol. III, pp. 312, 481. For the designation of "faithful shepherd", see vol. II, p. 301.

[37] The plaints of Moses and the people are later insertions in the old legend about the great lament, as may be seen from the language, which is Aramaic, whereas the rest is Hebrew. Similarly the Rachel episode did not originally form part of this legend.

[38] For a similar case where the sun is forced to do his work, see vol. III, pp. 207–209. On the "sixty fiery scourges", see vol. VI, 150, note 896 and p. 332, note 84.

[39] Ekah, introduction, 24, Ekah Z., 63, 66–67, 71–73, 138–140, 142–144. See also Menahot 53b, which reads: In the hour when the Temple was destroyed God found Abraham there praying. God said to him: "What doth My beloved in My house?" "I came on account of

my children," replied Abraham. "Thy children", said God, "have committed sins, and have been banished." "Perhaps", rejoined Abraham, "without intention, through ignorance." "No," said God, "they did it presumptuously." "May be", pleaded Abraham, "only a small portion of them sinned." "No," remonstrated God, "many of them are guilty." "Had it been Thy will, " rejoined Abraham, "they would have repented." "Nay", said God, "their wickedness waxeth when they prosper." Abraham then began to weep and mourn, saying: "God forbid that there should be no salvation for them." A heavenly voice then proclaimed: "The Lord called thy (Israel's) name 'A green olive-tree' (Jer. 11.16); Israel is like an olive tree: its product comes after pressure and crushing; even so will Israel's salvation come after its suffering." This account is a haggadic paraphrase of Jer. 11.15–16. In BHM V, 63–64, it is Jacob who leads in the great lament, and makes the angels, as well as the souls of the pious (in line 2 from below ונשמתן is to be read), weep for Israel. He was consoled only after he had received assurance from God that Israel's sufferings at the hands of his oppressors would save him from the torments of hell. Comp. vol. I, p. 236. For another version of the lament, see 2 Targum Esther 1.2 (towards the end); ARN 4, 24, 165; second version 7, 21; ER 28, 148–150; Ekah 1, 42, 56, and 59; PR 28, 135; PK 22, 148b (פסקא אחרת). In Pesikta the whole of nature mourns for Israel. It is very likely presupposed here that with the destruction of the Temple nature deteriorated, and will not regain its former excellence until the advent of the Messiah. Comp. Sotah Mishnah 9.2; Tosefta 15.1–2; Babli 48b–49a; Yerushalmi 9, 24b. See also Pesahim 42b; Baba Batra 25b; Tan. Tezawweh 13. For further references to the great lament, see Berakot 3a; 7a (top), 59a; Hagigah 5b; an unknown Midrash quoted by Makiri on Is. 52, 195 and 196 (the paragraph כנגדם אמר דוד on p. 196 is quoted as Pesikta in Makiri on Ps. 31, 204); Zohar III, 172a. The Zohar legend about the "tears of God", shed for the suffering of Israel, turning into pearls is probably based on Berakot 59a. On Rachel's intercession for her children, see vol. I, pp. 361, 415; note 202 on vol. I, p. 369; vol. II, p. 135; ER 28, 148; ps.-Rashi on Abot 3.12. Although the destruction of the Temple was a great loss, it was nevertheless fortunate that God poured out His wrath upon "stones and wood" and not upon Israel. The destruction of the Temple saved Israel from annihilation. See Kiddushin 31b (comp. Rashi, caption איסתעייא מילתא); Tehillim 79, 360, and 92, 408 (which reads: Songs and music at the erection of the Temple, and songs and music at the destruction of the Temple); Ekah 4, 148; ER 28, 150–151. In the exile God made Israel swear five oaths: not to attempt to reconquer the Holy Land by force of arms; not to rebel against the nations ruling over them; not to divulge the appointed time of the redemption; not to despair of the final redemption (this, it seems, is the meaning of שלא ירחקו; differently Rashi); not to divulge the "secret" (of the calendar) to the other nations. At the same time God made the nations swear not to oppress Israel too hard. See Ketubot 111a; Shir 2.7. Comp. also Tan. B. I, 38–39, and the parallel passages cited by Buber in note 134. God assured Israel that He would redeem them in the time to come, not as the nations, and even Israel, thought that the destruction of the Temple amounted to the repudiation of Israel. See ShR 31.10; PR 31, 143b, 146b; Berakot 32b.

⁴⁰ Ekah, introduction, 34; PK 13, 113a–113b; PR 29, 137a.

⁴¹ PR 27, 131b. Comp. the references given in the preceding note.

⁴² Ekah, introduction, 34; PK 13, 113b. On the idea that God accompanied Israel in exile, see also PR 31, 144b, and note 4 on vol. II, p. 188. Opinions differ as to the fate of Jeremiah (and Baruch) after he had been carried off to Egypt. According to our text of Seder 'Olam 26, when Nebuchadnezzar conquered Egypt, Jeremiah and Baruch were "exiled by him to Babylon", whereas Rashi, on Jer. 44.14, has Palestine instead of Babylon. Comp. also Yerushalmi Sanhedrin 1, 19a (top), and the parallel passages on margin, where it is stated that Jeremiah, Ezekiel, and Baruch fixed the calendar outside the Holy Land; as the context shows, this can only refer to Babylon. With regard to Baruch, Megillah 16b explicitly states that he lived (and died) in Babylon. This is in agreement with Baruch 1.1. Comp. also Ratner note 50 on Seder 'Olam 26, and *Ha-Misderonah* I, 37. In Apocalypse of Baruch 10 and 33 it is said that Jeremiah was told by God to go to Babylon to console the exiles, whereas Baruch remained in the Holy Land with the rest of the people. According to The Rest of Words 4.5, Jeremiah was carried off captive to Babylon. The different versions about Jeremiah's martyrdom reflect the difference of opinion as to the country in which the prophet finally settled. The legend about the prophet's martyrdom is very likely of Jewish origin, although the rabbinic literature contains only one reference to it. But Heb. 11.37 seems to allude to it. An unknown Midrash quoted in Midrash Aggada, Num. 30.15, reads as follows: The Jews in Egypt stoned Jeremiah, but his body was buried by the Egyptians who loved him, because

through his prayers the crocodiles (on החמנו חיים, see Löw in *Judaica*, 341) disappeared from the Nile, and ceased to ravage the country. Later Alexander disinterred the body, and buried it in Alexandria. On Jeremiah as a helper against the crocodiles, see also the extract from an Armenian pseudepigraphic work in *Apocrypha Anecdota*, II, 164. The legend about the prophet's martyrdom in ps.-Epiphanius, *De Vitis Prophetarum*, s. v. "Jeremiah", agrees in the main with Midrash Aggada. On the other hand, the Rest of Words, 9, maintains that Jeremiah suffered his martyrdom not in Egypt (= Tapheneh in ps.-Epiphanius), but in Jerusalem, and a popular tradition still current points to a spot in the north of the holy city as the prophet's grave. Jeremiah's martyrdom is also mentioned in *Visio Pauli* 49, and by Hippolytus, *Susanna* 1.1. Other Christian writers (comp. Victorinus of Peteau, *Apocalypse of John*, 11.1; ps.-Tertullian, *Carmen Adversus Marcionitas* 3, 245 and 257) count Jeremiah among those who never "tasted death". This view must have been widespread, as it left its traces in Arabic sources (comp. Friedlaender, *Chadhirlegende*, 269–270). Still it is very doubtful whether it is of Jewish origin. It is more likely that Christian legend transferred to Jeremiah certain features which originally belonged to his disciple Baruch (on a similar confusion between master and disciple, see note 66, end), who, according to Jewish tradition was one of those who "entered paradise alive"; comp. vol. IV, p. 323. See also the remarks in notes 13 and 66 on Jeremiah as one of the "two witnesses". In 'Aktan IV (end; Carmoly's edition) it is said that Jeremiah prayed for death, as he could no longer endure to see Israel suffer. Whereupon a heavenly voice was heard saying: "Wait until thou seest the destruction of Babylon, and then I will grant thee peace (אניחך), until I build My house for ever." God then "hid" him. This undoubtedly presupposes that the prophet did not die, but it may be doubted whether this passage is genuine, as it seems to be a fabrication of Carmoly's. Jeremiah is not among the "ten pious men", who, according to 'Aktan 1, "entered paradise alive". The statement in Shalshelet 99b–100a, 101a about the martydom of Jeremiah and about his meeting with Plato in Egypt (who first ridiculed the prophet, but later admired him) is taken from Christian sources. Comp. also Abravanel on Jer. 5.1.—The Ben Sira legend is so closely interwoven with the life of Jeremiah that it may be worth while to give here its main feature in connection with the Jeremiah legends. This prophet surprised once, in a public bath, wicked men of the tribe of Ephraim, and found them committing onanism; he reproached them for their sin. Far from repenting, they forced the prophet to follow their example, threatening that if he refused, they would commit sodomy, using him as the object of their lust. Shortly after the prophet's virgin daughter came to bathe in the same place, and conceived by absorbing the sperm released by her father. Nine months later she gave birth to a son, who, immediatly after he left his mother's womb (comp. note 12), began to speak, saying to her: "Do not be ashamed though the people may accuse thee of having led an immoral life, tell them that I am Ben Sira, that is, 'the son of Jeremiah'" (the numerical value of סירא is 271, the same as that of ירמיהו). After a long conversation with his mother, in which he told her, among other things, that his father Jeremiah likewise spoke immediately after his birth (comp. vol. IV, p. 294), he requested her to provide him with a good meal consisting of bread, meat, and wine, as he was not like other infants who are nourished by the breasts of their mothers. At the age of one year he was sent to school, where his display of wisdom and learning caused masters and pupils to marvel. No sooner did the teacher begin to instruct him in the Hebrew alphabet than Ben Sira composed proverbs in accordance with the order of the letters. The teacher exclaimed: "In truth, nature changed its order." Ben Sira, however, remarked: "This is nothing new, as Baruch did it before me, when he composed the alphabetic lamentations (Book of Lamentations) at the command of Jeremiah, who recited to him the letters of the alphabet, while he immediately formed the verses." Ben Sira spent seven years at school; when he left it, there was nothing "big or small" which he did not know. He could tell, for instance, by looking at it how many grains a measure (= *seah*) of wheat contains. The fame of his wisdom spread all over the world, and hence the wise men of Nebuchadnezzar became envious of him, and by means of slander and all kinds of wild accusations attempted to have Nebuchadnezzar kill him, but all his machinations against him were of no avail. Nebuchad- nezzar was even ready to abdicate his throne in his favor, but Ben Sira refused to become king, as he was not a descendant of David. Nebuchadnezzar then wanted him to marry his daughter, but, of course, he refused to marry a Gentile woman. For this affront the king was about to kill him, but Ben Sira's great wisdom saved him. See 2 Alphabet of Ben Sira. This curious little book, containing fables legends, and tales, in all of which Ben Sira is the central figure, is not of a homogeneous character. The unusual (not miraculous) birth, the marvellous precociousness, and other features of the Ben Sira legend are decidedly anti-Christian in character. Jesus, the son of Sira (= Ben Sira)

performed charitable deeds, the recipients thereof should be unworthy and undeserving. See Baba Kamma 16b.

⁴⁵ PK 17, 132a–133b; PR 31, 145b; WR 16.1; Ekah 4, 150–151; Ekah Z., 71 and 142; Yoma 9b; Tan. B. III, 42; Shabbat 62b–63b. In the last-named passage the statement is found that the wood growing in Jerusalem had the pleasant flavor of cinnamon (and could be used as perfume by the women). But at the time of the destruction this kind of wood was "hidden" (= disappeared), with the exception of a very small piece which was preserved and is to be found in the treasure of queen Zamzamai (= Zenobia, queen of Palmyra). On cinnamon in Palestine see the references given by Löw, *Aramäische Pflanzennamen*, 292. There was so much cinnamon there that it was used as fodder for goats, Comp. Yerushalmi Peah 7, 20a (bottom). When the holy city was conquered, Nebuchadnezzar issued an order to his armies to refrain from any immoral acts with married women, because the "God of the Jews hates unchastity". All the single women in Jerusalem got quickly married, to protect themselves against any attack by the Babylonian soldiers, with the exception of three widows who remained unprovided with husbands, and they were the only women who were ravished. See Ekah 5, 157 and Aggadat Shir 5, 38. Against this view comp. Yebamot 16b, which, explicitly speaks of the licentiousness displayed by the Babylonian troops on this occasion. See further Ekah 1, 46 (bottom); 5, 157 (the explanation of שחן as a euphemism for בעל, "had sexual intercourse", is known also to Jerome on Is. 47,2, who, in agreement with Sotah 10a, takes שחנן in Jud. 16.21 to have this meaning; comp. vol. VI, p. 208, top); Esther R.2.3; Targum on Lam. 5.13. As to the beauty of the inhabitants of Jerusalem, see also Kiddushin 49b (which reads: Of ten measures of beauty Jerusalem has nine and the rest of the world one); ARN 28,85. Comp. further Gittin 58a; Targum on Lam. 4.2; vol. IV, p. 332, with regard to the great charms of the young men of Jerusalem.

⁴⁶ PR 28, 135a, and 31, 144a; Ekah 5, 155–156 (this command Nebuchadnezzar gave to Nebuzaradan who is called Arioch, in Dan. 2.14, who took charge of the transport of the exiles); Tehillim 137, 522; ER 28,150.

⁴⁷ PR 28, 135a–135b; Tehillim 137, 522–523; Targum on Lam. 5.5 (which reads: The holy books were torn in pieces, and the parchment was used for bags which, filled with water from the Euphrates, were carried by the princes of Judah); ER 28, 154; 2 Targum Esther 1.2

(towards the end). In the last passage it is asserted that Jeremiah said to Nebuchadnezzar and his army: "Go not to your idols to praise them; know that ye have taken captive and killed a people which was already captured and slain (*i. e.* it was God who made the victory over Jerusalem possible; comp. vol.IV,p.303, and Sanhedrin 96b, which reads: Thou killest a slain people, thou burnest a burned palace, thou grindest ground flour), and ye have no reason for vainglory." Jeremiah marched along with the captives beyond Bari (comp. the following note), until they reached a certain country, where he bitterly wept and sobbed. Two tears fell from his eyes, and they became two fountains which exist to this day. In the Christian legend (Acts of Andrew and Matthew towards the end) the flesh and hair torn from a martyr changed into trees. In the Midrashim quoted above, and especially in ER 28, 154, God's wrath against Israel changed into love for them, when the people at the banks of the Euphrates experienced in their hearts feelings of remorse and repentance of their sins. It was then that God broke out in a great lament (comp. vol. IV, pp. 304, *seq.*) for the suffering of the people.

⁴⁸ PR 28, 135b–136a; Tehillim 137, 523; 2 Targum Esther 1.2 (towards the end; בית כורו or rather בית בורי is to be emended to בני באר); Aggadat Bereshit 63, 128. On Bari (in Italy?), see Bacher, *Monatsschrift*, XLI, 604 and in *R.E.J.*, XXXIII, 40–44; Lévi, *R.E.J.* XXXIII, 278–282 and XXXV, 224.

⁴⁹ Sanhedrin 96b; Midrash Tannaim 145. As to Nebuchadnezzar's reluctance to undertake the campaign against Jerusalem, see vol. IV, pp. 300–301.

⁵⁰ Yebamot 16b; Ekah 1, 74.

⁵¹ PK 19, 137–138a; Ekah, introduction, 9.

⁵² Yelammedenu in Yalkut on Obadiah; comp. also PK 19, 138a–138b; Midrash Shir 39a. On the Edomites as the destroyers of the Temple, see also PK 3, 25b, 26a–26b. On Edom = Rome, see Index, s. v. "Edom". Comp. vol. III, p. 332. In Esther R. 1.2 it is said that the דיקומני ואנוסטיאני counselled Nebuchadnezzar to undertake the war against Jerusalem and to destroy the Jews. They were punished for their evil counsel, and they themselves were destroyed. The יכולנו וברקוליאני then took their place. As to the meaning and correct reading of the Hebrew words just quoted, see Sachs, *Beiträge*, I, 113; Cassel, *An Explanatory Commentary on Esther*, 17–19. דקוריוני is very likely to be read instead of דיקומני and כלוני ופרטוריאני instead of יכולני וברקוליאני. The Midrash remarks that the *Decuriones* and

Augustiani (comp. Tacitus, *Annales*, XIV, 15.2, which reads: *Equites Romani cognomento Augustianorum aetate ac robore conspicui*) advised the destruction of the people, and as a punishment the power was taken away from them (the Senate) and given to the *Calones* and *Praetoriani*. R. Benjamin of Tudela, in his *Itinerary* 8, likewise reports that Titus undertook the campaign against Jerusalem at the special order of the Senate, the Decuriones and Augustiani of the Midrash. That Nebuchadnezzar stands here for Titus and that the account refers to the destruction of the second Temple is quite obvious. Comp. the following note and note 24 (end).

⁵³ Yerushalmi Ta'anit 4, 69b; Ekah 2, 108; BR 53, 14; ShR 3.2 and 27.1; Tan. Yitro 5; Tehillim 5, 54–55. On the part played by the Palmyrenes in the destruction of the Temple, see also Yebamot 16b, and note 45. The tradition about the Palmyrene archers who took part in the campaign against Jerusalem is historically sound; comp. Cagnat, *L'Armée Romaine au Siège de Jerusalem*, in the supplement to *R.E.J.*, XXII, 39. The legend, however, which is ever fond of drawing parallels, speaks not only of the participation of the Palmyrenes in the war against Jerusalem under Titus, but also of the assistance they rendered Nebuchadnezzar. The parallels are often carried so far that one is not quite sure whether the legend, in speaking of the destruction of the Temple, refers to that of the first or the second. The legend, for instance, about the birth of the Messiah on the day of the destruction of the Temple is often mentioned (Yerushalmi Berakot 2, 5a; Ekah 1, 89–90; Ekah Z., 133; Panim Aherim, 78; Aggadat Bereshit 67, 133; a quotation from an unknown Midrash by Grünhut in his edition of Makiri on Prov., 103b); but there is no way of telling whether the destruction of the first or the second Temple is meant. Comp. also the preceding note and note 24 (end). As to the sufferings of the exiles, see also Ekah, introduction, 6 (which reads: "their bodies burned"; from thirst?); 1, 61; ER 28, 154. In the last-named passage מיתת קרח means "a death like that of Korah", and not a "death by frost". On the death of Korah, see Sanhedrin 52a, and vol. III, p. 299, according to which Korah and his congregation died by heavenly fire which consumed their souls, but left their bodies intact. In the same manner, remarks the Midrash, was the death of many of the exiles, whom God granted a sudden death, which did not distort or disfigure their bodies.—The death of the pious is as great a calamity as the destruction of the Temple, and hence the day on which the pious Gedaliah was killed (on the third of Tishri, fifty-two

days after the destruction of the Temple; comp. Seder 'Olam 26, and note 39 by Ratner) was declared a fast-day for all time. See Rosh ha-Shanah 18b; Sifre D. 31; Tosefta Sotah 6.10. The pious Gedaliah acted in accordance with the law, and refused to be guided by the "evil talk" against Ishmael the son of Nethaniah (comp. Jer. 40.14–41.1, 2), and received him kindly. Yet it was careless on his part not to take precautions against the possibility of Ishmael's attack. The rule of conduct is: Do not believe evil talk, but disregard it not entirely. The murderous act of this Ishmael illustrates the truth of the saying: "Trust not a proselyte even in the twenty-fourth generation." Ishmael was the descendant, twenty-four generations removed, of Jerahmeel by a marriage with the non-Jewish princess Atarah (1 Chron. 2. 26), whom he had married for the sake of glory. See Yerushalmi Sanhedrin 2, 20b, and Horayyot 3, 48 (towards the bottom); Ruth Z., 48; PR 22, 111b.—On the view that the prominent inhabitants of Jerusalem were exiled to Spain, and especially to Toledo, see Shalshelet 101a.

54 PR 31, 144 (as to the "dwarf" Nebuchadnezzar, see note 96), and in a shortened form 28, 136a; ER 28, 149; Tehillim 137, 524; 2 Targum Esther 1.2 (towards the end); Eldad and the sources depending on it (comp. Epstein, 5 and 42–43, as well as BHM VI, 15); Targum on Ps. 137.4; 'Eser Galuyyot 14; second version 115; Aktan 24.

55 PK 31, 144a, and the other sources cited in the preceding note. On the "sons of Moses" who number more than six hundred thousand (this was the number of Israel at the time of the exile), see Berakot 7a; Targum Yerushalmi Exod. 34.10; note 540 on vol. III, p. 279.

56 Pliny *Hist. Nat.*, 31.2, agrees with the Rabbis (Sanhedrin 65a, in an alleged conversation between R. Akiba and the Roman general Tineius Rufus; BR 11.5; Tan. Ki-Tissa 33; PR 23, 119b) that this river rests on the Sabbath, whereas Josephus, *Bell.*, VII, 5.1., maintains just the opposite, that it rests on week-days and flows on the Sabbath. The anonymous author of the *Itinerarium a Burdigala Hierusolem usque* maintains that the pool of Solomon dries up completely on the Sabbath. Josephus and the Rabbis differ also as to the location of this river. The former maintains that it is situated in Syria, between Acrea and Raphanea, whereas the latter implicitly assume that it is somewhere in a country very far from Palestine. Comp. the rabbinical legends concerning the ten tribes referred to below. For the references to the river Sambation in Christian, Mohammedan, and Samaritan writings see Nöldeke, *Beiträge zur Geschichte des Alexanderromans*, 48; Epstein, *Eldad*, 13–16; Grünbaum in *Zeitschrift der Deutschen*

Morgenländischen Gesellschaft, XXII, 627; Kazwini, *Cosmography*, II, 17; Mas'udi, *Muruj al-Dhahab*, I, 161; *Kobez 'al Yad* IV, 13. Comp. also the following note. The view that the ten tribes, or at least some of the tibes, dwell beyond the "river Sambation" is widespread, and is found not only in the talmudic-midrashic literature, but also in many medieval writings. Comp. Yerushalmi Sanhedrin 10, 29c, which reads: One part of Israel (*i. e.*, the northern tribes) was exiled beyond the river Sambation, one part to Daphne near Antiochia, and the third part was carried off (literally, "covered") by a cloud. When the time of redemption will come, all the exiles from the three diasporas will return. See BR 73.6 (which says: The ten tribes are beyond the river Sambation); PR 31, 146a–147a; Tan. B. I, 203, and IV, 79; BaR 16, 25 (here it is said the "mountains of darkness" is the place to which the third part was carried off); comp. also Targum Yerushalmi Exod. 24.10; *Kobez 'al Yad*, IV, 42; Neubauer, *J.Q.R.*, I, 14, *seq.* "Where are the ten tribes"; Lewin, *Wo wären die zehn Stämme zu suchen*, 17–25. Comp. also Ginzberg *Haggadot Ketu'ot* 43–45. This clearly shows that the hope for the return of the ten tribes and the salvation of "all Israel" is not limited to the circles in which the apocalyptic literature originated (comp., *e. g.*, Tobit, Testament of 12 Patriarchs and 4 Ezra), as has been maintained by many modern scholars. As far as can be ascertained, R. Akiba is the only one among the old Rabbis who taught that the "ten tribes were repudiated by God for ever" (Mishnah Sanhedrin 10.3), and he was strongly censured for this view by the Talmud, Sanhedrin 110b. There can be no doubt that R. Akiba, as an active propagandist for the Bar Kokeba revolt, attempted to fire the enthusiasm of Palestinian Jewry by telling them that the future of Judaism depended entirely upon them, the descendants of Judah and Benjamin. That the ten tribes were transported in a miraculous way beyond a river, where they lived undisturbed as pious Jews, is presupposed in 4 Ezra 13.41–50. Comp. also Josephus, *Antiqui.*, XI, 5.3. The holiness of the Sabbath is "attested" by the river Sambation, and also by a certain fish which spends the Sabbath resting on the banks of the river, and by a mountain from which silver is taken every day in the week with the exception of the Sabbath when no silver can be found there. See Sode Raza in Yalkut Reubeni on Gen. 2.2. The Palestinian (Syrian?) place called שבת to which reference is made in an Egyptian inscription (comp. Müller, *J.Q.R.*, N.S., IV, 652) was probably situated on the river of the same name mentioned by Josephus, *Bell.*, VII, 5.1. Kaufmann (*R.E.J.*, XXII, 285) suggests that the legend about Sambation is due to the confusion of חול "sand" with חל "week-day"; the river that throws up sand became the river that "works" on week-days only. This suggestion, though rather ingenious, is for more than one reason quite untenable. For further details concerning the Sambation legend, see *Shebet Musar* 11, 38b; *Kobez 'al Yad*, IV, 40. For the vast literature on this subject, comp. Krauss, *Lehnwörter*, s. v.

⁵⁷ Eldad and the sources that are based on it; comp. Epstein, Eldad 5, 14, 17, 27–29, 40–41, 43–44, 57–58, 64–65, who calls attention to the Arabic versions of this legend about the "Land of the Blessed". It escaped him, as it did many of the other scholars dealing with this legend, that in the Narrative of Zosimos we have this Jewish legend with very slight Christian additions. Instead of the "sons of Moses", we have here the "sons of Rechab" who were carried by a cloud to the "Land of the Blessed", the entrance to which is made inaccessible by an impassable river. On the sons of Rechab, comp. vol. III, p. 380; PR 31, 147a (where it is said that the Land of Sinim is their dwelling-place); Midrash Aggada on Num. 24.22 (which reads: The sons of Jonadab the Rechabite were not exiled, but God sent them to the "mountains of darkness" (comp. the preceding note); 2 Alphabet of Ben Sira 28, which reads: The descendants of Jonadab (=the Rechabite; comp. 29a) live in paradise where they entered alive. In the Narrative of Zosimos the land inhabited by the sons of Rechab is described as the paradise on earth, and the life of its inhabitants as that of angels. The only difference between 2 Alphabet of Beb Sira and the Christian pseudepigraphic work is that the latter explicitly states that the Rechabites, though living many hundred years, die in the end, whereas according to the Jewish source, they do not "taste death". The substitution of the "sons of Rechab" for the "sons of Moses" is very likely not due to a Christian hand, but is a "Jewish variant". See also R. Benjamin of Tudela's *Itinerary*, ed. Asher 70, where the sons of Rechab appear as "free" Jews, not subjected to other nations. *Shibhe Israel*, 218, quotes the following from the Yalkut on Obadiah: In the future the Messiah, accompanied by the sons of Moses, will betake himself to mount Seir to judge the sons of Esau. This passage is not found there, nor, as far as can be ascertained, in any other place of the Yalkut.

⁵⁸ Rest of the Words of Baruch 1–8. For the numerous variants of the legend about the "sleepers" in Christian and Mohammedan sources, see Heller in *R.E.J.*, XLIX, 190, *seq.* Closely related to the Ebed-melech legend is the one given by the Talmudim concerning Honi

(= Onias) ha-Me'aggel, who is said to have slept seventy years, from the destruction of the Temple until the end of the Babylonian exile. Comp. Ta'anit 22b, and Yerushalmi 3, 66d. It seems that the Legend about the stoning of Jeremiah found at the end of the Rest of the Words (comp. note 42) is in some way connected with the stoning of Onias (= Honi) narrated by Josephus, *Antiqui.*, XIV, 2.1. According to Ta'anit 22b, Onias, however, was not stoned, but died shortly after he awoke from his long sleep. For further details concerning Ebedmelech, see note 66.

⁵⁹ Rest of the Words of Baruch 1–3.

⁶⁰ Comp. the similar story about the vain attempt of the Roman government to locate the grave of Moses; Sifre D. 357; Midrash Tannaim 226; 'Aktan 6. In the last-named source it is Hadrian who attempted in vain to find the grave of Moses. In that passage this wicked ruler is said to have travelled throughout the Holy Land to visit the graves of the kings and prophets. His attempt, however, to find the grave of Moses was fruitless.

⁶¹ 2 Maccabees 2.4–8; Josippon 3. The legend about the hiding of the holy vessels, recorded in the Rest of the Words of Baruch 3, is based on 2 Maccabees, whereas in Apocalypse of Baruch 6.7–10, Baruch sees an angel descend into the holy of holies and take from there the veil, the holy ark, the mercy seat, the two tables, the holy raiment of the priests (the high priest?), the altar of incense, the forty-eight precious stones wherewith the priest (= high priest) was adorned (the Hebrew original read: ארבעוה טורי אבן, which was misread as ארבעים ושמנה אבן), and all the holy vessels of the tabernacle. The angel then said to the earth: "Earth hear the word of God, and receive what I commit to thy care to guard until the last times"...And the earth opened its mouth, and swallowed them up. For the similar view of the Rabbis about the fate of the holy vessels, see vol. III, pp. 48, 161; vol. IV, pp. 24, 234, 282, 350, 354. Comp. also the references in notes 62–64, and Friedmann in *Ha-Shiloah*, XIII, 54 *seq*.

⁶² Ekah 2, 114, which reads: The gates were thus rewarded for the honor they paid to the holy ark (comp. vol. IV, p. 156); Tan. IV, 51, which reads: All the holy vessels were brought to Babylon, with the exception of the gates. See also Sotah 9a (here it is said that the enemy had no power over the gates, because they were made by David); BaR 15.13; Tan. Beha'aloteka 9. Comp. also 4 Ezra 10.22; Assumption of Moses 3.2; vol. III, p. 300.

⁶³ Read: Shomer ("the guardian"). Bar Hebraeus, *Tarih Muhr-*

asar, 70, speaks of the priest Simeon (שמעון) as the one who hid the holy vessels. There cannot be any doubt that he is dependent upon Jewish tradition, and it is probable that he confused שמור or rather שומר with שמעון.

⁶⁴ Masseket Kelim 88–91. On Bursif (= Borsippa; according to Shabbat 36a, it is identical with Biblical בבל), see also Sanhedrin 109a and BR 28.11, where it is said that those dwelling in this place suffer from a weak memory.—According to some Kabbalists, the destruction of the Temple was not a reality, but it appeared to the people as though it had actually taken place (docetism); the Temple disappeared from the sight of man, and will become visible again in messianic times. Comp. Zohar II, 240b, and Yalkut Hadash, s. v. חרבן, Nos. 7 and 18.

⁶⁵ The old authorities differ as to whether Baruch was a prophet or not. Mekilta Bo (פתיחתא), end, reads: Baruch was greatly distressed because he did not receive the prophetic spirit, whereas the disciples of the former prophets (Joshua the disciple of Moses, Elisha the disciple of Elijah and many others) succeeded their masters as prophets. To console him, God told Jeremiah to speak to Baruch as follows: "Baruch, there is no need of a fence, if there is no vineyard; of what use is the shepherd, if there is no flock?" Comp. also *ibid.*, 1b, where it is stated that prophecy is a prerogative of the Holy Land, and though it is true that Ezekiel and Jeremiah prophesied in other countries, their career was begun in the Holy Land. On the other hand, Seder 'Olam 20, Sifre Z., 75, Megillah 14b, and Sifre N., 78, count not only Baruch, but also his father and grandfather and uncle (comp. Jer. 51.59) among the prophets. Those sources also state that he was related to Jeremiah, both having been descendants of Rahab the harlot. She was accordingly the ancestress of eight priests, who were prophets at the same time; these are: Jeremiah, his father Hilkiah, his uncle Shallum, and the latter's son Hanamel (comp. Jerem. 32.7), Baruch, his father Neriah, his grandfather Mahseiah, and his uncle Seraiah. According to some, the priest and prophet Ezekiel, as well as his father Buzi, who was also a prophet, likewise belong to Rahab's descendants. Comp. Yalkut II, 1074 (end) on 1 Chron. 4.23; note 12 on vol. IV, p. 5. In the apocalyptic and pseudepigraphic literature Baruch is presupposed to have been a prophet, and is said to have been the author of three prophetical works: 1) Baruch; 2) Apocalypse of Baruch (Syriac); 3) Apocalypse of Baruch (Greek). On the relationship between Jeremiah and Ezekiel, see notes 42 and 93.

⁶⁶ Apocalypse of Baruch 1–77. As for Baruch and the pious men

having been "sent away" by God from Jerusalem before the day of the destruction of the Temple, see vol. IV, p. 303, and note 28. On the hiding of the holy vessels, see notes 60, 61. That Baruch was one of the distinguished and pious men who never "tasted death" is also the view of the Rabbis. Comp. Sifre N., 99; Mo'ed Katan 16b; PRE 53 (comp. Luria *ad loc.* and Tehillim 7, 72); 2 ARN 43, 122; PR 26, 130b, where he is identified with Ebed-melech the Ethiopian (comp. Jer. 38.7; he is called the Ethiopian, *i. e.*, the "black", antiphrastically, because he was the only "white", *i. e.*, pious, man at the court of king Zedekiah), and of this man it is explicitly stated that he entered paradise alive. See Derek Erez Z. 1 (end), and the parallel passages cited by Tawrogi, to which should be added PRK (Grünhut's edition, 83); 'Aktan 12. In the last-named source, however, Ebed-melech is said to have been a proselyte and accordingly he is not identified with the priest Baruch (comp. the preceding note). He is further described there as one of the ten rulers who became proselytes; they are: The king Hiram, Ebed (*i. e.*, Ebed-melech; מלך "king" is taken as the title of Ebed); Antoninus, Talmai (Ptolemy of Egypt, at whose command the Septuagint was prepared), Monobaz (king of Adiabene), Tobai (?), Bolan (king of the Khazars); the queens Bithiah (the foster-mother of Moses), Helena (queen of Adiabene), and Beruria (Valeria; Comp. Gerim 2.4; Mekilta Bo 15, 18a; Yebamot 46a). In the Christian legend it is Jeremiah, and not his disciple Baruch, who is one of the immortals. Comp. notes 13 and 42. Comp. however also II Macc. 2.1 *seq.* and 15.15.

⁶⁷ Apocalypse of Baruch 78–87. Comp. also vol. IV, p. 319.

⁶⁸ As to the view that Baruch and Jeremiah were exiled to Babylon, see note 42, and comp. vol. IV, p. 320.

⁶⁹ Book of Baruch.

⁷⁰ The Greek Apocalypse of Baruch is a description of this ascension.

⁷¹ Megillah 16b; Shir 5.5. On the view that Baruch entered paradise alive, see note 66.

⁷² That Baruch was a disciple of Ezekiel is not mentioned elsewhere. It is very likely that "teacher" is not to be taken literally. Comp. vol. VI, p. 317 (top).

⁷³ Not only Moses' body shows no signs of decay (comp. vol. III, p. 473), but also those of other pious men; comp. Shabbat 152b; Baba Mezi'a 84b. When Hadrian opened the tomb of David (comp. note 60), he was amazed at the high color of the face; he pressed

the flesh with his finger, and the blood began to circulate. Admiringly the wicked king called out: "This man deserved to be the ruler of the entire world, since even after his death he is like the living." See 'Aktan 23.

⁷⁴ *Gelilot Erez Israel* 101a; a somewhat different version of this legend is given by R. Pethahiah of Ratisbon 4b–5a. On gold dust, see also vol. IV, p. 350.

⁷⁵ R. Pethahiah of Ratisbon 5a–5b; comp. also the remarks of R. Benjamin of Tudela (I, 67; II, 141–143) about the tomb of the prophet Ezekiel. A geonic responsum in Schechter's *Saadyana*, 123, mentions the "synagogue of Ezekiel", Daniel, Ezra, Baruch, and the masters of the Talmud. This very likely means the synagogue erected by Ezekiel (in the place where later his mausoleum was built?), and frequented by Daniel, Ezra, Baruch, and other great men. A "Daniel synagogue" in the neighborhood of ברנשא (Birnos, on the road from Bagdad to Hilla?) is mentioned in the Talmud by authorities living in the third century. Comp. 'Erubin 21a, and Berliner, *Beiträge zur Geographie*, 28.

⁷⁶ Megillah 3a and Sanhedrin 94a (top), where in reference to Dan. 10.7 it is remarked that the men who were with him were the prophets Haggai, Zechariah, and Malachi; yet it was he, though not a prophet, who was found worthy to behold the vision. Palestinian sources, however, tannaitic as well as amoraic, count Daniel among the prophets. Comp. Mekilta 1b; PK 4, 36b; PR 14, 61 (where the anthropomorphism of the "prophets" refers to certain anthropomorphic expressions used in Dan.); Seder 'Olam 20; Josephus, *Antiqui.*, X, 11.4 and 7; Matth. 14.25. See also Sanhedrin, where Hananiah, Mishael, and Azariah are designated as prophets, and it would be very strange if their great friend (Daniel) were not of that rank. It seems that the old authorities spoke of the "Book of Daniel" as belonging to the Hagiographa and not to the prophetical part of the Canon. Later, however, the "Book of Daniel" was confused with its author, and hence the statement that he was not a prophet. But the writing of a prophet is not necessarily a prophetic book, as may be seen from the Book of Psalms, which belongs to the Hagiographa, though David was a prophet. Comp. Seder 'Olam 20; Mekilta Bo (פתיחתא), 2a; Yerushalmi Sotah 9, 24b. See also note 108 and note 18 on vol. IV, p. 349. For the views of the later authorities concerning Daniel, see Fischer, *Daniel*, 100–102. For the attribute "man greatly beloved" given to Daniel (Dan. 10.11), see the explanation in Koheleth 9.7 and

Tan. B. I, 88. He is said to have been also called Memuchan and Hathach (comp. vol. IV, pp. 337 and 419), as well as Sheshbazzar (comp. Ezra 1.8). The last name signifies: "He was in distress six times", as Daniel was the eye-witness of three exiles (the first under Jehoiakim, the second under Jehoiachin, and the third under Zedekiah); he was at the point of losing his life with the rest of the wise men of Babylon (Dan. 2.13), of being devoured by the lions, and finally he witnessed the throwing of his three companions, Hananiah, Mishael, and Azariah, into the fiery furnace. See PR 6, 23b. As a reward for the faithfulness with which he served his "earthly king" (Nebuchadnezzar), he was chosen to serve his heavenly King, and thus Daniel (=Sheshbazzar) was the first to lay the "foundation" of the house of God" (Ezra 6.16); PR, *loc. cit.* Combining Dan. 1.3 and 6 with Is. 39.7, the Haggadah maintains that Daniel and his three companions were descendants of the kings of Judah; some authorities, however, are of the opinion that his companions did not belong to the tribe of Judah. See Josephus, *Antiqui.*, X, 10.1; Sanhedrin 93b; PRE 53; "Hebrew tradition" in Jerome on Is., *loc. cit.* Comp. Fischer, *Daniel*, 33–39. That Daniel was the son of Jeconiah (=Jehoiachin) is asserted only by Bar Hebraeus, *Chronicon Syriacum*, 27, and Ma'aseh Daniel (beginning). The latter source also narrates that during the carnage which took place at the conquest of Jerusalem by Nebuchadnezzar (comp. vol. IV, p. 304) a soldier entered the house of study in which Daniel and his three companions were sitting. He first intended to kill them, but God "gave them favor in the sight" of the soldier. He did not kill them, but took them captive to Babylon.

⁷⁷ 'Abodah Zarah 55b; Yerushalmi 2, 41d; Yoma 76b. In Tan. B. I, 110–111 the story of the refusal of Daniel and his three companions to partake of the food is told in a circumstantial manner, whereas Josephus, *Antiqui.*, X, 10.2, rationalizes the biblical narrative of Dan. 1.8, *seq.* Zohar II, 125b, gives the menu of Nebuchadnezzar's table, and adds that Daniel was saved from the lions as a reward for his having refrained from eating the forbidden food offered to him at the table of Nebuchadnezzar. But Daniel's piety did not ʹconsist exclusively in his strict observance of the dietary laws; lovingkindness, charity, and praying were his chief merits. See ARN 4, 21. It is therefore not surprising that according to one view, Daniel is the promised Messiah; comp. Sanhedrin 98b. Nevertheless the miracles wrought for Daniel, as well as God's granting of his request were not due to his own merits, but to those of Abraham. See Tan. B. I, 111; Berakot 7b. Against this view comp. ARN *loc. cit.*

⁷⁸ Midrash Megillah 176. Comp. vol. IV, p. 276, and note 76, with regard to those men as the "eunuchs" (סריסים) of whom Isaiah spoke. On the other hand, it is maintained in Sanhedrin 93b that they were perfect in body and intellect, but that they were called סריסים, "eunuchs", because they "emasculated the worship of idols from among their generation". Comp. vol. IV p. 331 (towards the end). In Yerushalmi Shabbat 4, 8d, it is said that although they were made eunuchs, they regained their former state in the fiery furnace. Comp. also Jerome on Is. 56.4–5, and ER 26, 131. "The eunuchs that keep My sabbaths", of whom the prophet speaks, is said to refer to Daniel's three companions.

⁷⁹ The apocryphal Book of Susannah in its Greek version, as well as in the Hebrew translation thereof in BHM VI, 126–128, and in Yerahmeel 65. A similar motive to the one in the Susanna story is found in the rabbinic legend about the false prophets (=vol. IV, pp. 336–337). Comp. Frankel, *Monatsschrift*, XVII, 447, and Brüll, *Jahrbücher*, II, 8, *seq.* These two scholars also call attention to the story told in Sanhedrin 5.2 about the careful examination of witnesses by a certain Ben Zakkai (according to the Talmud, 40a–40b, it was the famous Rabban Johanan ben Zakkai but this is doubtful), which reminds one of the part played by Daniel in Susanna. Comp. note 108.

⁸⁰ Tan. B. I, 90. For the interpretation of the stone which was "cut out without hands" (Dan. 2.34) as referring to the Messiah, comp. Tan. B. II, 91–92, and Tan. Terumah 7. Josephus, *Antiqui.*, X, 1.4, in affected mysteriousness, wants to convey the same statement as the Midrashim. According to the very late compilation Ma'aseh Daniel 19, Daniel cured Nebuchadnezzar by prayer from the injury he received while attempting to ascend the throne of Solomon. The injury (a broken leg) of Nebuchadnezzar is mentioned also in *Panim Aherim* 57–58; Abba Gorion 4 (he atempted to ascend the throne in Riblah, while he sat in judgment over Zedekiah); 2 Targum Esther 1.2; comp. vol. IV, p. 160 and vol. VI, p. 453.

⁸¹ BR 96.5; Tan. B. I, 213 (here Daniel is contrasted with the heathen rulers who asked for divine honors). Comp. also PK 9, 76a; WR 27.4; Tan. B. III, 91; Midrash Shir 43a; vol. II, p. 129.

⁸² Sanhedrin 93a, in explaining Daniel's absence from Babylon during the incident of the three men in the furnace; comp. the following note. With regard to the export of swine from Alexandria, comp. Menahot 4.4, which reads: No cow or sow is permitted to leave Alex-

andria without having its womb cut out, that it should not be able to conceive.

[83] Ekah, introduction, 23 (comp. 5, end); Koheleth 12.5. As to Daniel's absence, comp. also the preceding note. Against this view, see Shir 7.8. Here it is stated that the three men whose lot it was to represent their nation at the worship of the image (according to some, the entire Jewish representation consisted of twenty-three men, twenty of whom obeyed the command of Nebuchadnezzar; superior courts are composed of twenty-three members; comp. Sanhedrin 1.4) asked Daniel for advice, but he referred them to Ezekiel, saying to them: "There is a prophet (Daniel himself was not a prophet; comp. note 76) before you; go to him." In Ma'aseh Daniel, 119, it is said that Daniel, like his companions, was commanded by Nebuchadnezzar to worship the image, and like them he refused to obey. The king, however, decreed to put the three men to death but not Daniel. Comp. also Hippolytus on Dan. 3.16, who remarks: Daniel, though he stood at a distance and kept silence, encouraged them to be of good cheer, as he smiled at them. Josephus, *Antiqui.*, X, 10.5, speak of the three men as Daniel's kinsmen (comp. note 76), who, like himself, were made rulers by Nebuchadnezzar over his whole kingdom.

[84] WR 33.6; BaR 15.14; Shir 2.14; Tan. B. I, 38–39, and IV, 52; Tan. Noah 10 and Beha'aloteka 9; Yelammedenu in *'Aruk*, s. v. רא 2; Aggadat Bereshit 7, 15–16; Tehillim 18, 229; Yerushalmi Sanhedrin 3, 21b. On the etymology of the name Nebuchadnezzar (נבו=נבח "barked"; כד "a pitcher of water"; נצר "chirped"), see also BR 90.3, where it is said that this wicked king was also called טפסר (comp. Jerem. 51, 27) because he was a fool (טפש=), though old in years (שר בשנים), whereas Joseph was called אברך because he was wise (אב בחכמה), though young (רך בשנים).

[5] Sanhedrin 92b (מלכיות is here the same as אומות in Tan., differently Rashi); Tan. III, 14; Tan. Noah 10 and Zaw 2; Tehillim 22, 188; Shir 7.9, where the names of the offices (?) given in Dan. 3.2 and 27 are explained in detail. The death of those who threw the pious men into the furnace is mentioned in the Bible (Dan. 3.22), and in the Additions to Daniel found in the Septuagint this verse reads: And the king's servants, that put them in, ceased not to make the furnace hot with naphtha, pitch, tow, and small wood; so that the flame streamed forth above the furnace forty-nine cubits. And it spread, and burned those Chaldeans whom it found about the furnace. The "forty-nine cubits" is a haggadic explanation of חד שבעה (Dan. 3.19), and is found

also in Tehillim 28, 229, though in a somewhat different form. In the Midrashim quoted, as well as in Sanhedrin, *loc. cit.* (read הימיקסירום instead of הימק סורו), it is said that Nebuchadnezzar himself was half burned on this occasion, see note 90. Comp. 76 on vol. I, p. 176.

⁸⁶ Tan. B. I, 40–41; Tan. Noah 10; Aggadat Bereshit 7.17. Against this view, comp. the references given in the next note, according to which it was an angel (Gabriel), and not God Himself, who saved the three men from death. Comp. also note 33 on vol. I, p. 201, with regard to the rescue of Abraham from the fiery furnace. For the prayer of the three men, see the following note.

⁸⁷ Pesahim 118a-118b (יורקמי, the name of the angel of hail, is composed of יהו=י"ו "God", and רגם=רקם; comp. Syriac כאפא רגומיתא, "hail stones"; hence Yorkami is the correct transliteration; the various etymologies of this name given by the lexicographers are not to be taken seriously); Abba Gorion 34; Ma'aseh Abraham (Horowitz' edition 45–46; here it is Michael who attempted to get ahead of Gabriel and rescue the three men); ShR 18.5; PRE 33; Tan. Tezawweh 12 (here the competition between Michael and Gabriel relates to the rescuing of Abraham); Tehillim 117, 480; PR 35, 160b; Midrash Esther 66. In the apocryphal Prayer of Azariah 26–27 it is said: But the angel of the Lord came down into the furnace together with Azariah and his fellows, and he drove the flame of the fire out of the furnace, as it had been a moist whistling wind, so that the fire touched them not at all, neither hurt nor troubled them. Comp. alosc 4 Maccabees 6.6, which reads: "Thou, when the three friends in Babylon freely gave their lives to the flames......, didst make as dew the fiery furnace, and deliver them unharmed...turning the flame upon their adversaries." The Midrashim go still further, and state that the furnace turned into a pleasure-ground. Comp. PR, *loc. cit.;* Shir 7.8 (end; the text is obscure; טלנוס must not be emended to פלנוס, as it explains אור and not כבשן; אווקי is still more puzzling); Tan. B. III, 14; Tan. Zaw 2. The Haggadah (Sanhedrin 92b, below, and Shir 7.9, beginning) calls attention to the fact that the three men appeared robed in their best garments to be thrown into the furnace, because "even when one's life is in danger one ought to be mindful of the duties laid upon one by his position." Of a strange nature is the following statement of the Talmud (Ketubot 33b): Hananiah, Mishael, and Azariah would have paid homage to the image if they had been flogged. Comp. Tosafot, *ad loc.* The idea conveyed by this statement is that even martyrs cannot always endure the tortures of a slow death.

[88] The apocryphal Prayer of Azariah and the Song of the Three Children in the Additions to Daniel in the Septuagint and in Theodotion. Reminiscences of this or a similar prayer and song by the three men are found in many passages of rabbinic literature; comp. Pesahim 118a (the Hallel is said here to have been composed by these men); Tan. B. I, 40; Noah 10; ShR 20.1 and 18.5 (here it is said that Gabriel collaborated in the composition of Hallel; on Gabriel see preceding note); Tehillim 117, 480; Aggadat Bereshit 7.17; Aggadat Shir 2.29; Zohar III, 57a. Comp. also Mahzor Vitry 320–322 and 337–338.

[89] PR 35, 160b, with the additional remark: Gabriel attended upon the three men as does a disciple upon his master, because "the righteous are greater than the angels" (comp. Index, s. v. "Angels", and see further Yerushalmi Shabbat 6, end, which reads: The three men made it possible for the angel to withstand the fire of the furnace, and not the reverse); DR 1.12. On Gabriel, see note 87, and note 55 on vol. IV, p. 268.

[90] Sanhedrin 92b–93a (as to the correct text, comp. note 83, according to which, one of the miracles was that Nebuchadnezzar was half consumed by the fire of the furnace and not that the bottom dropped out); Shir 7.9; Tan. B. I, 41, and III, 14; Tan. Noah 10 and Zaw 2; Aggadat Bereshit 7, 14. On the drinking cups made of the skulls of slain enemies, see Herodotus, IV, 65; Frazer, *Golden Bough* III, 372. Comp. further note 345 on vol. II, p. 129. The Karaites (comp., e. g., Hadassi, *Eshkol*, 45b below and 134a) accuse the Rabbis of ascribing this barbarous practice to the prophet Ezekiel. It is difficult to tell whether this accusation is due to ignorance or malice; the text of the Talmud (Sanhedrin, *loc. cit.*) makes it absolutely clear that it is Nebuchadnezzar, not Ezekiel, who is said to have committed this barbarous act. God does not wish to be praised by the wicked, who call on Him in time of distress, but forget Him in time of happiness; that is why the angel prevented Nebuchadnezzar from continuing his prayer of God. See WR 16.4; Tan. B. II, 37; Tan. Wa-Era (end). The words of praise to God uttered by Nebuchadnezzar: "For all His works are truth, and His ways justice" (Dan. 4.34), contain all the praises of God found in the Psalms of David. See WR 13 (end); Tehillim 5, 55–56; comp. also Josephus, *Antiqui.*, X, 10.6. Yet Nebuchadnezzar had a poor conception of God's true essence, as may be seen from his description of the angel as one whose appearance is like a son of God (Dan. 3.25). An angel struck him on his mouth, saying: "Correct thyself! Has God any sons?" Nebuchadnezzar profited by this lesson, and

the next time he spoke of the angel of God (Dan. 3.28), and not of His son. See Yerushalmi Shabbat 6 (end); ShR 20.10 (here it is also stated that Nebuchadnezzar's words, "and none can stay His hand", Dan. 4.32, are blasphemous, conveying the idea that God in His omnipotence does not refrain from doing injustice; comp. Baba Kamma 38a); Shir 7.9; Shemuel 5, 60 (read משולח instead of משלו); Aggadat Bereshit 27, 55. This anti-Christian Haggadah (the last-named source reads: The Babylonians maintain God has a son; on Babylon = Rome, see Index, s. v.) is the Jewish reply to the argument of the Church Fathers that in Dan., *loc. cit.*, the expression "son of God" refers to Jesus. Comp. *e. g.*, Hippolytus, *ad loc.*

⁹¹ Tan. B. I, 41; Tan. Noah 10 (read: למלאך instead of למלך; the angel bade them leave the furnace, but they did not obey until they received permission from the king); Aggadat Bereshit 7, 17; Shir 7.9.

⁹² Sanhedrin 93a (they got married in Palestine, and begot children; comp. note 78); Midrash Shir 32a–32b; PK 11, 99a; Tan. B. V, 25–26; Tan. Ki-Tissa 14 and Re'eh 16; BR 56.19. As to the fate of the three men, two other opinions are mentioned. According to one, they died immediately after they were saved from the fire of the furnace. Their death was caused by the "evil eye" with which people looked at them because of the miracle wrought for them. The other view maintains that they died in a very peculiar manner. Enormously large multitudes of heathens assembled to see them leave the furnace, and these multitudes were so exasperated at the Israelites for having forsaken their God (the three men were the only Israelites steadfast in their religion; see note 83), that they spat at them; the three men fell into the spittle and were drowned. The last view is extremely bizarre, and it is possible that the correct reading is בקר "by cold" instead of ברק "in spittle". Comp. Yerushalmi Shabbat 14, 14c, and Baba Mez'ia 107b, where two views are given as to the most frequent causes of death: 1) Most people die from cold (קר = צנה); 2) the "evil eye" is responsible for most deaths. Accordingly the two views concerning the death of the three men ("evil eye"; cold) only wish to convey the idea that they died in the same way as most people. In Baba Mezi'a the word used for cold is רוח "draft", and רוק is phonetically and graphically similar to it. In the Tanhumas, and PK, *loc. cit.*, the expression נוש של רוק "mass of spittle" is used with reference to the rest of the Israelites (the heathens spat at them, that they became a "mass of spittle"), and not with regard to the three men. At all events, the expression נוש של רוק in

these sources supports the reading of רק in Babli, and the suggested emendations are rather doubtful.

⁹³ Shir 7.8 (according to another opinion, the three pillars are the three patriarchs; comp. vol. VI, p. 104, bottom); Tehillim 1, 5; comp. vol. II, p. 350. As to the conversion of the heathen on this occasion, see also Shir 1.3 and 4.1; 'Aseret ha-Dibrot 70. Delegations of the people waiting on Ezekiel are also mentioned on other occasions. Before the destruction of the Temple people came to argue with him about his prophecies foretelling the imminent captivity of Israel. They said to him: "If Abraham received the Holy Land as a reward for having fulfilled one commandment (circumcision?), how much more can we expect to remain in possession of this land when we fulfil many commandments!" Ezekiel replied: "Ye eat with the blood, cutting off parts from a live animal to consume them; ye lift your eyes unto your idols to worship them; ye shed blood, and stand upon your sword, delaying the execution of justice; ye work abominations, and commit sodomy; ye defile every one his neighbor's wife. Ye do not even fulfil the Noachian commandments (comp. vol. I, pp. 70–71), and yet ye say: The land is given to us for inheritance." See Tosefta Sotah 6.9, which is a paraphrase of Ezek. 33.24–26. The same passage contains the two other paraphrases of these verses. After the destruction of the Temple the elders came to the prophet and said to him: "When the master sells his slave, does he not thereby renounce his claim to him? Now God sold us to the nations of the world, and accordingly we are no longer under His jurisdiction." The prophet replied: "Does the master renounce his claim to his slave if he gave him for a time to another master, with the understanding that he would take the slave back after the expiration of that period?" See Sifre N., 115; Tan. B. V, 50; Tan. Nizzabim 3 (this is the source of Yalkut II, 359, where Wa-Yikra Rabbah is erroneously given as source); 2 ARN 11, 28. When the elders came to Ezekiel to hear from him the word of God, the prophet was told by God that He "would not be inquired of" by them (comp. Ezek. 20.1–3). The prophet pleaded for them with God, saying: "Wouldst Thou forsake them, and not 'be inquired of' by them even for the sake of the Torah?" Thereupon God changed His decision, saying unto Ezekiel: "I will yet for this (the sake of the Torah) be inquired of by the house of Israel." See Yelammedenu in Yalkut II, 358, on Ezek. 20.3. When Ezekiel received from God the revelation concerning the future Temple, he said: "We are in exile in the land of our enemies, and Thou commandest me to reveal to Israel the plan for the Temple!" God, however, informed him that the study of the Temple laws by Israel is as acceptable

to Him as the erection of the Temple. See Tan. Zaw 14; Yelammedenu in 'Aruk, s. v. צר 3; WR 7.3. Comp. also vol. I, 235. The purpose of revealing to Ezekiel the vision of the heavenly throne (Ezek. 1.1, seq.) was to demonstrate to him that God is not in need of the services performed in the Temple, since innumerable hosts of angels minister to Him in heaven; hence it is for Israel's sake that the Temple will be rebuilt. See WR 2.8; ER 6, 34. Ezekiel, like his father Jeremiah (comp. Tosefta-Targum quoted by Kimhi on Ezek. 1.3, and see also the quotation from a MS. given in note 42, where Buzi is said to be the name of Jeremiah, on the strength of the assertion that he is identical with Buzi the father of Ezekiel), lived in a time of terrible depravity and sinfulness, to atone for which God inflicted great suffering upon him. See Sanhedrin 29a with reference to Ezek. 4.4 and similar passages. On the sins of Israel, see the passage cited above from Tosefta. One of the most wicked acts of this generation was the fashioning of the "image of jealousy" (Ezek. 8.5), which was an abomination in the eyes of the Lord. By means of witchcraft they had fashioned out of stone two figures, a male and a female, embracing one another like husband and wife. See Hasidim 46. A similar reminiscence of the Virgil legend is found in the Armilus legend; see Ginzberg, *Jewish Encyclopedia*, II, s. v. "Armilus". A very strange statement occurs in the Jewish Peter legend (second version of Aggadta de-Shimon Kefa 9) that Peter (= Kefa "stone") was so called because he occupied as his seat the stone on the river Kebar, from which Ezekiel used to deliver his prophecies. The sentence והיה יוצא קול לו מהאבן is not quite clear. Does it perhaps mean: And he (Peter) became famous on account of this stone?

⁹⁴ Sanhedrin 92a (this passage also gives the different view that the quickening of the dead is to be understood as an allegory; but in opposition to this opinion, a Tanna remarks: I am a descendant of one of the men quickened by Ezekiel, and here are the phylacteries which came down to me from him); PRE 33; ER 5, 23–24 (Ezekiel was rewarded for his great love for his people, and was found meritorious to perform this great miracle); Targum Yerushalmi on Exod. 13.17 (comp. vol. III, p. 9); Tan. B. II, 84; ShR 31.5. On the view that usurers are excluded from the resurrection, see the references given by Luria, note 130 on PRE loc. cit. On the beauty of the Jewish youths, see the references in note 45. In contrast to the view that Ezekiel, on this occasion, showed lack of trust in God's omnipotence, it is maintained in BR 19.11 (this is the source of Zohar III, 200a), that the prophet was the only one of five (the others are: Adam, Cain, Balaam, and Hezekiah;

comp. note 730 on vol. III, p. 359 and vol. VI, p. 368, note 86) who gave the expected answer to the questions put to them by God. Ezekiel is praised for the strictness with which he observed the law, especially the dietary regulations; comp. Hullin 37 b. But the dietary laws given by Ezekiel in his book, which on the surface seem to contradict the laws of the Torah, nearly caused his work to be excluded from the Canon and be "hidden"; Shabbat 13a, and the parallel passages on the margin. The legend that Ezekiel was the teacher of Pythagoras, mentioned for the first time by Clemens Alexandrinus, *Stromata*, 1.15, is probably of Jewish origin, but the story of his martyrdom (a detailed description of this is found in *Visio Pauli* 49) is certainly Christian, it was nevertheless copied by Yahya, *Shalshelet* 100a top.

⁹⁵ PRE 33. Luria, *ad loc.*, understands the Midrash to say that the people wept because not all the dead came to life again. Comp. also ER 5, 24, and Sanhedrin 92b. This great miracle was wrought by God, that the belief in the resurrection of the dead might become well-established among Israel. It may be stated as a general principle that all the miracles which are to take place in the "time to come" have been performed "in miniature" during the present order of the world. See Tan. B. III, 90–91, and the parallel passages cited by Buber. Comp. also Midrash Shir 43a. Ezekiel is not the only man who made the dead come to life again; in the world to come the righteous will perform the miracle of the resurrection of the dead. See Pesahim 68a; BHM VI, 64. The dead quickened by Ezekiel chanted a song of praise to God as soon as they came to life; Sanhedrin 92b.

⁹⁶ Megillah 11a; PRE 11; 'Aseret Melakim 39; Maamar 'Aseret Melakim 54; Aggadat Esther 8; 'Aktan 12; 2 Targum Esther 1.1 (beginning and end); comp. note 82 on vol. I, p. 178, and Index, s. v. "Cosmocrator". Though he was the ruler of the entire world, Nebuchadnezzar did not enjoy his life for a moment; a glance at his dwarfish figure (on this point, see BR 16.4; ER 31, 158; PK 13, 112a, below; PR 31, 144a) sufficed to mar his pleasure in life. See Tan. B. II, 90; Tan. Terumah 4.

⁹⁷ Shabbat 150a (top; perhaps it means with a snake coiled about *his neck*); PRE 11 (which reads: Not a bird opened its beak without the permission of Nebuchadnezzar); Midrash 'Aseret Melakim 42–43. Comp. also Judith 11.7.

⁹⁸ Tan. B. I, 185. As to Nebuchadnezzar's reluctance to undertake the campaign against Jerusalem, see vol. IV, pp. 301–302.

⁹⁹ Nebuchadnezzar's claim to be a god and his ignominious end are often referred to in the Haggadah. Comp. the references given in

the following three notes and Judith 11.2. The deification of the Roman Caesars was well known to the Jews, and occupied their imagination to a great extent.

¹⁰⁰ Mekilta Shirah 2, 36a; 6, 39b; 8, 41b; Mekilta RS 58 and 66; Tosefta Sotah 3.10. Comp. also Koheleth 5.2 and Hullin 89a. In the last passage Nimrod (vol. I, p. 178), Pharaoh (vol. II, p. 347), Sennacherib, Hiram (vol. IV, p. 335), and Nebuchadnezzar are contrasted with the great men in Israel who were modest and humble, whereas the heathen rulers claimed to be gods. Mekilta, 41b, and Mekilta RS, 66, do not count Nimrod among those that claimed divinity. See Tan. B. II, 23 and 31; ShR 8.2; Tan. Wa-Era 9; Tan. in Makiri on Ps. 9, 59 (not in our Tanḥumas). These sources speak of Pharaoh, Hiram, Nebuchadnezzar, and Joash (comp. vol. IV, 258) as the four kings who pretended to be gods and ended ignominiously by being abused in "modo foeminarum". Comp. note 16 on vol. IV, p. 259. See also BR 11.5, which reads: Adam and his descendants would have enjoyed eternal life, were it not for the fact that God foresaw that Hiram and Nebuchadnezzar would claim to be gods; Hallel 94a-94b (partly based on Baba Batra 75a); BaR 9.24. Comp. further notes 102, 105, and 107.

¹⁰¹ Pesahim 94a–94b; Hagigah 13a. On the distance between the heaven and the earth, see vol. I, p. 11.

¹⁰² Tan. B. II, 23 (while in the state of a beast he was misused by the other beasts, and this was his punishment for considering himself more than human; according to *ibid.*, 33, this was his punishment for his attempted abuse of Zedekiah; comp. notes 100 and 107); Tan. WaEra 9; ShR 8.2; Tan. in Makiri on Ps. 9, 59. Comp. also Mekilta Shirah 6, 39b, which is to be explained in accordance with Tan. B. II, 33.

¹⁰³ Yerahmeel 66, 205–206. The old authorities speak of seven years (=שבעה עדנין in Dan. 4. 22) which he lived as a beast; comp., e. g., Josephus, *Antiqui.*, X, 10 6; WR 182. Comp. the following note.

¹⁰⁴ Yerahmeel 46, 205–206, which in the main agrees with Chronicon Paschale 1, 299. It is very likely that these authors like many others (comp. Gaster, *ad loc.*,) had before them an apocryphal (of Jewish origin?) history of Daniel. Comp. note 18 on Vol. IV, p. 349. With the exception of Yerahmeel, the rabbinic literature knows nothing of this legend. In reference to the advice given by Daniel to Nebuchadnezzar (Dan. 4.22), the Rabbis remark that the king heeded it for one year. As long as he was charitable and kind to the poor, the heavenly decree against him was not carried out. His doom overtook him only after he had ceased

to give alms. See Aggadat Shir 1, 25 and 64. Opinions differ as to whether Daniel acted rightly in attempting to prevent the punishment of the wicked king, According to the Midrash just quoted, he did it in the interest of the needy exiles, whose suffering he hoped to ameliorate thereby, and hence no blame is attached to him. Others, however, maintain that Daniel committed a sin in attempting to save Nebuchadnezzar, and he was punished for it as, shortly after, he lost the high position he had held at court. Some authorities even assert that in consequence of this sin he was thrown into the den of the lions. See Baba Batra 4a; ShR 30.24; Shir 3.4 (end); Tan. Mishpatim 4 (this is the source for the quotation from Midrash Haggadol given by Schechter, Aggadat Shir, 69); Zohar I, 13b. In the last-named source the following statement is quoted from the "Book of King Solomon". As long as one shows compassion to the poor, his face retains "Adam's features", with the result that animals fear him (comp. note 113 on vol. I, p. 94). Hence as long as Nebuchadnezzar was kind to the poor, he retained his human form; but when he ceased to give alms (comp. above), he became a beast. Nebuchadnezzar's guardian angel (his name was Kal; comp. the Babylonian locality called Kalnebo, Sannhedrin 63b) was first "thrown down", before the doom overtook the king. See ShR 21:5; comp. also vol. III, p. 25. According to Esther R. I. 8, Nebuchadnezzar did not change bodily, but only mentally, so that when the two highest officers of the state (= Cyrus and Darius; comp. Shir 3.4) saw him act as an animal, they drove him from the palace, after having taken off all his garments, so that he almost remained naked. As to the sins committed by Nebuchandezzar, which were the cause of his severe punishment, see ER 15, 74, and Index, s. v. "Sins, Eight Cardinal". As late as the second century C. E. the house of Nebuchadnezzar, the den of the lions into which Daniel was thrown, and the furnace where the great miracle was wrought for his three companions were pointed out by the Jews of Babylon. See Berakot 57b and comp. vol. VI, p. 447, note 54.

¹⁰⁵ Midrash in Yalkut II, 367, on Ezek. 28 (read: בדיל "lead" for ברזל "iron" in the description of the third heaven). For other descriptions of the "heavens" fashioned by Hiram, see MHG II. 57–58 (the beginning, "four kings claimed to be gods, etc.", agrees literally with Tan. as quoted in Makiri on Ps. 9, 59; see the quotation in note 100; accordingly Tan. is the source of MHG); *Bet 'Eked*, II, 20—21 and 28–31; Ma'asiyyot (Gaster's edition, 6–7); BHM V, 111–112 (comp. Jellinek, introduction, 33); Tan. Bereshit 7 (which reads: Hiram erected his palace by means of machines "between the Ocean-Atlantic-and the Adri-

atic"). Comp. also vol. I, p. 178, and note 36 on vol. IV, p. 142. As to the seven kinds of metal out of which Hiram fashioned the seven heavens, see Enoch 52.2; Origen, *Con. Cel.* 6.22. Comp. further Jeremias, *Babylonisches im neum Testamente*, 24, *seq.* Tan., *loc. cit.*, as well as *Bet 'Eked*, II, 19, points out that the four kings who claimed to be gods (Pharaoh, Sennacherib, Nebuchadnezzar, and Hiram; comp. note 100) built their palaces "over the water". Herodotus, I, 181, mentions a famous building at Babylon which had eight towers, and it is quite possible that the legend about Hiram's palace contains some reminiscence thereof. As to Hiram's claim to divinity, see Mekilta Shirah 8, 48b = Mekilta RS, 66 (the Mekiltas are the oldest sources which identify the "prince of Tyre" mentioned in Ezek. 28.1 with Hiram); 9.5 and 96.5; Baba Batra 75a; Hullin 89a; Tan. B. I, 213, and II, 23–25, 30; Tan. Wa-Era 9; ShR 8.2; Hallel 91. Comp. further the references in note 100. The Haggadah maintains that this Hiram is identical with Hiram the friend of Judah (Gen. 38.11), who continued to be a friend of the latter's descendants, and assisted Solomon in the building of the Temple. He received his reward for this by being granted a very long life, surviving all the kings of the house of David and those of the ten tribes. See BR 84.8; Tan. B. I, 184. The Church Fathers are likewise acquainted with this Haggadah; comp. Aphraates, 84–85; Ephraem, II, 189 F; Jerome on Ezek. 28.11; Book of Adam 125–126. See Ginzberg, *Haggada bei den Kirchenv.*, II, 126–128. For the Arabic version of the Hiram legend, see Steinschneider, *Arabische Literatur der Juden*, 12. According to 2 Alphabet of Ben Sira, 28b, 29a, 37a, Hiram, as a reward for his assisting Solomon to build the Temple, entered paradise alive, and remained there for a thousand years. But when he became proud and claimed to be a god, he was driven out of paradise and made to enter hell. In many sources where the men who entered paradise alive are enumerated (comp. Derek Erez Z. 1, end, and Index, s.v. "Paradise, Entered Alive"), Hiram king of Tyre is given as one of them. In note 62 on vol. IV, p. 155 it is suggested to accept the emendation חירם מצור "Hiram of Tyre" (the architect of Solomon's Temple) instead of חירם מלך צור; but in view of 2 Alphabet of Ben Sira, this emendation is not tenable. For several etymologies of the name Hiram (also spelt חורם), see *Rimze Haftarot*, Terumah. That Hiram was Nebuchadnezzar's step-father is found only in WR 18.2 (but not in the parallel passage in Tan. B. III, 38), and one is tempted to emend the text and read, in accordance with Yalkut, *loc. cit.*, נבוכדנצר בְּעַל אמו instead of בְּעַל אמו

של נבוכדנצר. But the context clearly shows that the Midrash lays emphasis on tne fact that Hiram was killed by Nebuchadnezzar who was closely related to him. An obscure statement is the one of Yelammedenu in 'Aruk, s. v. מל 6, that Jeremiah's prophecy against "all that have the corners of their hair polled" (Jer. 9.25) is directed against Hiram. See also Bernstein, *König Nebucadnezar* 24, *seq.*

[106] Sanhedrin 93a; Tan. B. III, 7 (here it is stated that it was Semiramis, Nebuchadnezzar's wife, and not his daughter, whom the false prophets tempted to sin); Tan. Wa-Yikra 6; Midrash Aggadah, Lev. 51 (very elaborate) PRE 33; PK 24, 164–165; Mekilta RS, III (comp. also *ibid.* 86, with regard to the orthography אחאב=אחב); Makiri, Prov. 19, 5a-6b; We-Hizhir I, 97; Ma'asiyyot (Gaster's edition 20–21). On the relation of this legend to the story of Susanna, comp. note 79. The Church Fathers Origen (*Epistola ad Africanum*) and Jerome on Jer. 29 give this legend as they heard it from their Jewish teachers. According to their version, the false prophets used to assure the women that they were destined to become the mothers of the Messiah if they yielded to their wishes. This is hardly connected with the legend that the Messiah would be born and brought up in Rome (= Babylonia). Comp. Sanhedrin 98a (the correct reading is אפיתחא דרומא; comp. Rabbinowicz, *ad loc.*) and Tan. Tazri'a 8. In some editions of Tan. this passage is missing undoubtedly on account of the objections raised by the censors. Comp. Buber, note 65 on Tan. B. III, 38.

[107] Shabbat 149b. Comp. also Tan. B. II, 33, where מבזה אותו בקלון means sodomy, as is often the case in the midrashic–talmudic literature, and hence the corresponding punishment of Nebuchadnezzar. See notes 100 and 102. The statement in Tan. dispels all doubt about the meaning of אותו צדיק in Shabbat, *loc. cit.* It refers to Zedekiah, and not to Jehoiachin. As to Zedekiah being described as "that righteous man ", see notes 8, 119.

[108] Sanhedrin 93a; PK 25, 165a; Tan. B. III, 7; Tan. Wa-Yera 6; PRE 33 (which reads: The angel Michael saved Joshua = Jehoshua from death by fire; the garments of the latter were seared because he was very near the false prophets); Mekilta RS, 111; Midrash Aggada on Lev. 5.1. According to Justin Martyr, *Dialogue*, 116, Joshua himself had contracted a marriage unworthy of him. The same author remarks that Joshua was called by the prophet "a brand plucked out of the fire" (Zech. 3.2) διὰ τὸ ἄφεσιν ἁμαρτιῶν εἰληφέναι, which shows that he was not acquainted with, or did not accept, the rabbinic tradition that the high priest was thrown into the fiery furnace by Nebuchadnezzar.

Another legend (comp. Yerushalmi, Ta'anit 4, 69b) has it that at the time of the destruction of the Temple eighty thousand young priests (comp. vol. IV, p. 315) were burned at the stake, Joshua being the only young priest who escaped this frightful death. Hence the designation applied to him by Zechariah. As to Jehoshua's friends mentioned in Zech. 3.8, see Horayyot 13a, where they are said to have been prophets (= Hananiah, Mishael, and Azariah; see Sanhedrin, *loc. cit.*; BR 56, end; note 76); 2 ARN 28. The Church Fathers (comp. e. g., Tertullian, *Adversus Judaeos*, 14; *Lactantius*, IV, 14) explain the story of Joshua allegorically as referring to Jesus (= Joshua). This is perhaps the reason why the Haggadah finds fault with Joshua, for the Rabbis desired to combat the Christian allegory.

¹⁰⁹ BR 96.6; Tan. B. I, 213. Comp. note 81.

¹¹⁰ Sanhedrin 93a. On Daniel's leaving Babylon, see vol. IV, p. 328.

¹¹¹ Shir 7.9; Zohar II, 175a. Comp. vol. IV, p. 245.

¹¹² BR 67. This is closely related to, but not directly dependent on, the apocryphal story of Bel and the Dragon, placed in the Septuagint and Theodotion among the additions to the book of Daniel. This apocryphal work consists of two separate stories. In the first, Daniel by a clever device exposed the trickery of the priests of Bel, who made it appear that the idol consumed the food and drink set before it. In the second, Daniel slays the dragon god, by putting into its mouth cakes made of pitch, fat, and hair, after eating which it burst asunder. Directly based on the Greek Apocrypha is the story of the dragon as given in Yerahmeel (comp. Gaster, *The Unknown Aramaic Original of Theodotion's Additions*, 75–94), in Bereshit Rabba di-Rabba (comp. Neubauer, *Book of Tobit*, 39–43, and Epstein in *Magazin*, XV, 78–79), and in Shalshelet, 99b. Comp. vol. IV, p. 346 and note 8 pertaining thereto.

¹¹³ Yerahmeel 66, 206, and the medieval Christian chronicles. Comp. Gaster, *ad loc.*, and note 104.

¹¹⁴ Seder 'Olam 28 (comp. Ratner, *ad loc.*); PK 27, 168b; WR 20.1; Tan. B. III, 54, and V, 8; Tan. Ahare 1; Megillah 11a (it is said here that he reigned forty-five years); Koheleth 9.2; Josephus, *Antiqui.*, X, 11.1. Comp. vol. IV, p. 344 and note 3 pertaining thereto.

¹¹⁵ Shabbat 149a.

¹¹⁶ Tan. B. III, 38; Tan. Tazri'a 8; WR 18.2; *Bet 'Eked* II, 20. According to the version of this legend in 2 Targum Esther 1.1 (beginning) and Jerome on Is. 14.19 (he describes it as a "fable told by the Hebrews"), it was not Evil-merodach who feared to ascend the throne of his father,

but the magnates of the state, fearing the reappearance of Nebuchadnez-zar, would not let him do it. Yerahmeel 66, 206–207, seems to have been acquainted with the version of the legend as given by Jerome, and hence he states that Evil-merodach was imprisoned together with Jehoiachin. The rabbinical sources do not know of this incident, but it is given by Jerome. The second statement of Yerahmeel, that it was Jehoiachin who advised Evil-merodach to take out his father's corpse from the grave, is not found elsewhere, either in Jewish or in Christian sources. Kimhi on 2 Kings 25.27 quotes the reading of the Midrash (WR *loc. cit.*, is very likely meant), according to which, during the time that Nebuchadnezzar lived among the beasts one of his sons ruled in his stead. This son was killed by his father when he returned. It was the fear of being overtaken by a similar fate that made Evil-merodach cautious before he ascended the throne of the kingdom. An entirely different reason for taking out Nebuchadnezzar's corpse from the grave is given in 2 ARN 17,37. According to this source, after the death of Nebuchadnezzar, his son Evil-merodach wished to set Jehoiachin free, as he was not a rebel and was kept in prison without any valid reason (comp. the similar statement by Josephus, *Antiqui.*, X, 11.2), but the magnates of the state objected to it, saying to him: "A king cannot revoke the edicts of his dead predecessor, unless he drags the corpse of the dead king out of the grave". Evil-merodach did not refrain from acting in conformity with their words in order to be able to set king Jehoiachin free. There can be no doubt that 2 ARN is based on a fuller text of Seder 'Olam 28, where the words as they stand at present (וגררו בשביל לבטל מרותיו) are hardly intelligible. Comp. note 134 on vol. IV, p. 287, and Bernstein, *König Nebucadnezar*, 64–69.

117 Seder 'Olam 18; Mo'ed Katan 28b. According to Josephus, *Antiqui.*, X, 8.7, Zedekiah died during Nebuchadnezzar's life-time, who buried him with great honors. There is also a Haggadah maintaining that Zedekiah was killed by Nebuchadnezzar. Comp. PRE 53, according to the reading in Batte Midrashot, III, 32. See further the quotation from an unknown Midrash in Hasidim 107 concerning the eight kings, descendants of David, who died by the sword. In note 107 on vol. IV, p. 107 an attempt was made to explain this passage by assuming that Athaliah is one of the שמנה מלכים; but this is hardly accept-able, as the text speaks of kings who were descended from David, where-as Athaliah was not of Jewish descent at all. It is therefore more likely that this Midrash is likewise of the opinion that Zedekiah was killed by Nebuchadnezzar. Comp. also note 8.

¹¹⁸ 2 ARN 43, 122.

¹¹⁹ 'Arakin 17a; Sanhedrin 103a. Comp. also Shabbat 149a, where Zedekiah is described as אותו צדיק, "that righteous man" (on this passage see note 107); see also Mo'ed Katan 17b; Tehillim 7, 72. Against this favorable view of Zedekiah, see 2 ARN 43, 122. The kindness shown by Evil-merodach to Jehoiachin (comp. 2 Kings, end) is declared by the Haggadah to have been due to the intercession of Daniel in behalf of the imprisoned Jewish king. Daniel admonished the Babylonian king to be mindful of the punishment which overtook his father Nebuchadnezzar for the cruel treatment he meted out to captive kings, whom he imprisoned for life. Evil-merodach heeded Daniel's counsel, and released not only Jehoiachin but also all the other kings who had been imprisoned by his father. See Targum Esther 1.1. Comp. also 2 ARN 17, 37. As to Nebuchadnezzar's cruelty, who never released a prisoner, see also WR 18.2; Tan. B. III, 38; Tan. Tazri'a 8. As long as Nebuchadnezzar lived, no mouth smiled, so that at his death the entire world burst forth in jubilation. See Shabbat 149b. Comp. note 96.

XI. THE RETURN OF THE CAPTIVITY

Vol. IV, (pp. 343–361).

[1] Sanhedrin 22a and Shir 3.4. These sources give different views as to the way the ominous words were written.

[2] Josippon 6c–7b; it was borrowed and elaborated by Yerahmeel 67, 207–212. The old rabbinic sources did not know of a war of the Chaldeans against the Medo-Persian empire. Josippon is very likely indirectly dependent upon Josephus, *Antiqui.*, X, 11.2. The statement of Koheleth 4.8 that Belshazzar was born on the day upon which Gabina (נביא) the son of Harsum died is very obscure. That Harsum (חרסום) is identical with Croesus is very unlikely, though Gabina and his father are described as having been exceedingly rich. Comp. Perles, *Beiträge*, 18, and the literature on חרסום by Krauss, *Lehnwörter*, s. v. The rabbinic sources consider Nebuchadnezzar as the father of Evil-merodach, and the latter as the father of Belshazzar. See Seder 'Olam 28; BR 44. 15; PK 2, 14a; Shir 3.4; Esther R. 1.8. Comp. also the references in note 116 on vol. IV, p. 339. Merodach the father of Nebuchadnezzar (Jerome on Is. 39.1 quotes this as a Jewish tradition; although this view is not explicitly stated in any part of rabbinic literature, it is presupposed in the last three Midrashim just cited; comp. also vol. IV, p. 275, bottom) was a king, but his three descendants were "cosmocrators". Tan. Ki-Tissa 5; PK, Shir, Esther R., *loc. cit.* The list of Babylonian kings in Midrash 'Aseret Melakim, 43, is confused, and this is partly due to the corrupt state of the text. Yerahmeel, 67, 6, gives the names of Evil-merodach's three sons as Regosar (ריגוסר), Lebuzar Duk (לבחר דוך), and Nabar (נבאר), who was Belshazzar. The names are taken from Josephus, *Antiqui.*, X, 11. 2, but badly mutilated. According to this historian the name of Evil-merodach's son was Niglissar, who was the father of Labosordacus, who in turn was the father of Nabo-andelus = Belshazzar.

[3] Megillah 11b, where the error of Belshazzar's calculations is demonstrated. In the text p. 344 line 6 from below, read forty-five instead of twenty-five, and in the following line, two instead of five. Comp. vol. IV, p. 366, and note 19, as well as note 24 on vol. IV, p. 301.

[4] Shir 3.4. Here it is also stated that Belshazzar did not die of his wounds immediately, but was in death agony for a night (accord-

ing to some authorities, for a night and a day). On the desecration of the holy vessels by Belshazzar, see Nedarim 62a; 'Abodah Zarah 52b. The queen, at whose advice Daniel was called in to read the mysterious writing on the wall, was Belshazzar's mother, according to Ma'aseh Daniel, 120; but according to Josephus, *Antiqui.*,X,11.2, his grandmother. The "fall of Babel" was the work of the angels Michael and Gabriel; BR 63 (end); Tosefta-Targum Is. 21.5. The peculiar way in which Belshazzar met his death proved to him that the precautions taken by him to protect his life were not only in vain but the direct cause of his death; Shir, *loc. cit.* Comp. also Tehillim 75, 338, which contains a reminiscence of the wars preceding the death of Belshazzar; see note 2. According to Panim Aherim, 60, Belshazzar was killed by a candelabrum falling on his head; but according to another reading (comp. Buber, *ad loc.*), the rebels, under the command of Cyrus and Darius, crushed his skull with a candelabrum. This is based on the haggadic interpretation of צפית (Is. 21.5), which is supposed to mean "candelabrum"; comp. Tosefta-Targum, *ad loc.*, and the passages of BR and Shir referred to above. When a successor to Belshazzar had to be elected, the two candidates were Darius and Cyrus, the leaders of the revolt. The former insisted that Cyrus ought to be made king because Daniel, on the authority of Isaiah (comp. Is. 45), used to salute him as the future king while still in the service (אפיקין = *officium*) of Nebuchadnezzar. Cyrus, however, declined the honor, pointing to the writing on the wall, which, according to the interpretation of Daniel, read: Thy kingdom is... given to the Medes and Persians; hence Darius the "Mede" (on his paternal side; his mother was a Persian woman) was to be the immediate successor of Nebuchadnezzar. See Panim Aherim and Shir, *loc. cit.* On the night when Belshazzar was to be killed all Israel came to Daniel and said to him: "All the sufferings predicted by Jeremiah for Israel were fulfilled; but the one prophecy of good tidings, that at the end of seventy years Babylon would be destroyed, has not been fulfilled as yet." Daniel consoled them, assuring them that it entirely depended upon them whether the "kingdoms" should have dominion over them or not; if they obeyed God, no foreign monster would rule over them; Shir, *loc. cit.* Comp. also WR 13.5; ARN 34, 100; Tehillim 70, 363. In the text, vol. IV, p. 345 (top), wheaten is a printer's error for barley.

⁵ Ma'aseh Daniel 120–121; the king of Mosul(= Babylon) is, of course, none other than Belshazzar, against whom Cyrus was engaged in war; comp. notes 2 and 4. The Yemenite Jews tell the following story: Their forefathers had settled in that country forty-two years prior to

the destruction of the first Temple. When Ezra, on the return of the exiles from Babylon, called upon them to do likewise and to return to the Holy Land, they refused because they knew that the second Temple would also be destroyed and that Israel would once against be sent into captivity. Ezra cursed them for their refusal, that they should for ever live in poverty. That is why the Yemenite Jews are poor till this day. They, on their part, cursed Ezra that he should not find his last rest in the Holy Land; this also was fulfilled. See R. Solomon Adeni, in the introduction to his commentary on the Mishnah (beginning); Safir *Eben Sappir*, I, 99a. It is therefore very strange that Mohammed accused the Jews of north Arabia, the neighbors of the Yemenite Jews, of believing that Ezra was the "son of God"; comp. Koran 9.30. Did he confuse the "messenger of God" with the "son of God"? An old Jewish tradition identifies the prophet Malachi ("My messenger" or "messenger of God") with Ezra; comp. Megillah 15a; Targum and Jerome on Mal. 1.1. Megillah, *loc. cit.*, however, also gives the different view that Malachi was identical with Mordecai, who as the "next one to the king" (Comp. Esther, end) was called Malachi, "the kingly one". Comp. Seder 'Olam 20, where Mordecai and Malachi are counted as two prophets. See also notes 33, 38 and 50.

⁶ Bereshit Rabbete of R. Moses ha-Darshan, quoted from a MS. by Epstein, *Magazin*, XV, 78–79, and by Raymond Martinus, *Pugio Fidei*, 956. There can, of course, be no doubt that this legend is based upon the apocryphal writing Bel and the Dragon (but it is not directly taken from it), where the following story is told: The mob was so infuriated against Daniel for having exposed the tricks played by the priests of Bel and for having destroyed the dragon (comp. note 112 on vol. IV, p. 338) that they threatened to destroy the king (Theodotion alone gives his name as Cyrus) if he would not deliver Daniel unto them. The king was compelled to comply with their demand, and cast him into the lions' den, from which, however, he was saved in a miraculous way. In Septuagint this apocryphal work is described as having been taken from the prophecy of Habakkuk the son of Jesus (= Joshua) of the tribe of Levi. This prophet is said to have been sent by God to Daniel while he was in the lions' den; comp. note 13. As to the rabbinical view concerning the father and descent of Habakkuk see Index, s. v. In contrast to the Rabbis, who are unanimous on the point of Daniel's royal descent (comp. note 76 on vol. IV, p. 326), this apocryphal work declares him to have been a priest, and his father's name is given as Abal. Comp. note 56 (middle).

⁷ Rosh ha-Shanah 3b–4a (as to the statement that the name of the king was Darius, whereas Cyrus was an attribute describing him as "the worthy one", כרש being identical with כָּשֵׁר, and that besides these names, he was, like all other Persian kings, also called Artaxerxes, ארתחששתא, see Seder 'Olam 30, and Ratner, note 11); Megillah 12a; which reads: God said to the Messiah: "I must complain against Cyrus (a haggadic interpretation of Is. 45.1). I wanted him to rebuild the Temple and to take the exiles back to the Holy Land; but all he did was to proclaim through his kingdom: Whatsoever there is among you of all His people let him go up" (2 Chron. end). Cyrus disappointed still more the hopes set upon him. When he noticed that the Babylonian cities became desolate because the Jews emigrated from there to the Holy Land, he forbade them to leave the country. See Shir 5.5 and 6.8–10; Koheleth 10.12; Esther R., introduction 8; Midrash 'Aseret Melakim 44. The degeneration of Cyrus is quite amazing. At the destruction of the Temple he wept bitterly, and as a reward for his tears the Medes (= Persians) received the dominion over the world; he became not only a "cosmocrator", but he was also found worthy to sit on the throne of Solomon (with the exception of Nebuchadnezzar, he was the only Gentile ruler who was thus distinguished). See **ER** 20, 114; Esther R. 1.2, 13; PRE 11; Midrash 'Aseret Melakim 44; 1 and 2 Targum Esther 1.2 (end); Aggadat Esther 8. Comp. Index, s. v. "Cosmocrators" and "Solomon, Throne of". On the proclamation of Cyrus to the Jews to return to the Holy Land and to rebuild the Temple, see 3 Ezra 2.1–14. As to the views concerning Cyrus expressed by the Rabbis, it should be noticed that the Palestinian authorities are rather favorable to him, whereas the Babylonians censure him severely. The Roman yoke which weighed heavily upon the Palestinian Jews made them look at the Persians as the friends of the Jews. Their favorable opinion of Cyrus expresses their sympathy for the Persians. The Babylonian Jews, on the other hand, suffered terribly at the hands of the Mazdic priests who were very powerful in the Sassanide empire, and they considered the Romans as "the lesser evil", and the "destroyers of the Temple" were preferred to the "builders of the Temple' (= the Persians under Cyrus), so that Cyrus and the Persians came in for a great deal of blame. See Berakot 8b and 46b; Yoma 10a; Megillah 11a; Ketubot 48a; Gittin 17a (top); Kiddushin 49b and 72a; Baba Kamma 117a; Baba Mezi'a 28b; Sanhedrin 98b (top); BR 74.2; PK 4, 33b–34a and 40a, and parallel passages cited by Buber on the last passage. The dominion

of the Persians over Israel was the consequence of the victory of Dobiel (comp. Dan. 7.5), the guardian angel of the former, over Gabriel, who was punished for having delayed the execution of the punishment decreed by God against Israel (comp. note 26 on vol. IV, p. 302). Gabriel was deposed from the high office, which was given over to Dobiel for twenty one days. During this time Dobiel subjected to the Persians twentyone kingdoms, besides the Island of Pearls (on the Persian Gulf). He also obtained for the Persians the grant to levy taxes upon the Jews. However, not satisfied with this, he demanded for the Persians the privilege to levy taxes also upon the Jewish scholars, and he received a written promise to that effect. At the moment when the heavenly seal was to be put on this writ granted to Dobiel, a voice was heard exclaiming: "O Master of the world, if all the sages of the world were in one scale of the balance and Daniel in the other, would he not outweigh them all?" It was the voice of Gabriel exclaiming these words from "behind the curtain" (on the curtain, see Index, s. v.), as he had been expelled from the presence of the Lord and was not permitted to enter the place occupied by the "heavenly family" within the curtain. Hearing Gabriel's words, God spoke: "Who is it that pleads for My children?" On being informed that it was Gabriel, He permitted him to enter within the curtain. As soon as he was inside, Gabriel noticed the writ in the hands of Dobiel, and attempted to snatch it away from him. Whereupon the latter swallowed it and thus caused it to be blurred. This is the reason why the levy of taxes upon the scholars in the Persian empire is not carried out strictly. However, when the guardian angel of Javan (Greece) received the dominion over Israel, all the pleadings of Gabriel to mitigate the hardships of the Greek yoke over the Jews were of no avail. See Yoma 79a (on the correct text see Rabbinovicz).

⁸ The apocryphal writing Bel and the Dragon in the Greek Additions to Daniel. See notes 6, 13 and 18, as well as note 112, on vol. IV, p. 338. A Hebrew translation of this Greek work is found in Yerahmeel 72, 220–221, and Josippon 3, 4b–5a. In these sources it is the king Darius who urged Daniel to pay homage to Bel.

⁹ Ma'aseh Daniel 121–122. According to Josephus, *Antiqui.*, X, 11. 4, Darius sent for Daniel to come to him to Media, and he conferred great honors upon him.

¹⁰ The old sources (Josephus, *Antiqui.*, X, 11.4; Seder 'Olam 28–29; Shir 3.3), in agreement with the statement of the Bible and the historical facts, make Darius succeed Cyrus (Cambyses, the son and

direct successor of Cyrus, is not mentioned in rabbinic sources), whereas the late compilation Ma'aseh Daniel, 120–121, reverses the order. According to Josippon 3, 3a Darius and Cyrus divided among themselves the empire of Belshazzar, the former taking the city of Babel and its surroundings, and the latter the rest.

¹¹ Josippon 3, 7b–7d, where the edict of Darius appointing Daniel as viceroy is given in full. In this edict the nations are called upon not only to acknowledge Daniel as their master, but also to pay homage to his God.

¹² Tehillim 64, 311, and 24, 208 (here it is stated that an angel assumed the form of a rock to close the den and thus protect Daniel against his enemies); Shir 1.1; PR 6, 25a–25b; BaR 14.3. According to Josippon 3, 2b, a little girl playing in front of Daniel's house betrayed him to his enemies. According to the Halakah, one must sacrifice one's life in God's honor if one is ordered to commit a sinful act, but not for the sake of performing a divine commandment. Hence Daniel did more than was required by the law when he risked his life for the sake of prayer. Comp. note 14. BaR 13.4 remarks: Had Daniel been thrown into the fire by Darius, he would have perished, because divine homage was paid to him by Nebuchadnezzar, and the law reads: The images of their gods shall ye burn with fire. Comp. Sanhedrin 93a, Josippon 3, 3b and vol. IV, pp. 337–338.

¹³ Josippon 3, 8b–8c, which is an adaptation of the story given in the apocryphal writing Bel and the Dragon (comp. note 112 on vol. IV, p. 388; notes 6 and 8) in conformity with the biblical narrative about Daniel in the lions' den. Daniel's life was saved by the prayers of his three companions Hananel, Mishael, and Azariah; Tehillim 55, 292. A Christian adaptation of this story is found in ps.-Matthew 35. On the whole, legends about saints being spared by ferocious beasts are very common in Christian literature, but extremely rare with the Jews. Comp. vol. II, p. 332; Sanhedrin 39a; Ahimaaz, 112, and the legend concerning R. Samuel ben Kalonymos in Ma'aseh-buch, No. 161. On the view that Darius rose in the early morning, see Leket Midrashim, 23a.

¹⁴ Tehillim 64, 311. Comp. vol. II, p. 121. According to the Halakah, Daniel (and Jacob, see vol. II, *loc. cit.*) was permitted to interrupt this recitation to greet the king (comp. Berakot 2.2), but he did not avail himself of the leniency of the law; comp. note 12.

¹⁵ Josippon 3, 8c; comp. Bel and the Dragon in the version of Theodotion, 38.

¹⁶ Tehillim 64, 312, which reads: There were four lions for each person. But Josippon 3, 8c, knows only of ten lions, and in Bel and the Dragon the number is seven. The explanation given by the enemies of Daniel for his not having been devoured by the beasts is also found in Josephus, *Antiqui.*, X, 11.6; comp. Sanhedrin 39a.

¹⁷ Josippon 3, 9b–10a (the edict concerning the Temple is partly based on 3 Ezra 15, *seq.*); Yerahmeel 74, 223–244, where, strangely enough, Shushan is said to have been the birthplace of Daniel. Comp. note 76 on vol. IV, p. 326.

¹⁸ Megillah 3a. As to the question whether Daniel and his three companions were prophets or not, see references given in notes 76 and 108 on vol. IV, pp. 326 and 337 respectively. Comp. also Sanhedrin 93a, where, according to one reading (see Rabbinovicz, note 50), the Talmud maintains that the three companions of Daniel were not prophets. It is true that this statement is put into the mouths of the false prophets Ahab and Zedekiah. Josephus, *Antiqui.*, X, 11.7, not only speaks eloquently of the prophet Daniel, but states also that he wrote "several books...and one is still read by us till this time." The rabbinic literature knows only of one book by Daniel, if we except the very late work Ma'aseh Daniel. Josephus seems to have known, besides the biblical Book of Daniel, several others ascribed to him. Or did he consider the Greek additions to the book of Daniel as separate works by Daniel? On the Apocalypse of Daniel, known still to some writers of the Middle Ages, see note 104 on vol. IV, p. 334. Based on an old Apocalypse of Daniel is perhaps the statement of Johannes Malala, *Chronographia* 97. 257, that Cyrus (comp. note 6) threw Daniel into the lions' den because he refused to reveal to him whether he would be victorious in the war against Croesus or not. After Daniel's marvellous escape from death, Cyrus realized that he had done an injustice to the man of God, and asked his forgiveness. Daniel not only forgave him, but also announced to him that he would gain a complete victory over Croesus. Daniel also showed him the prophecies in the book of Isaiah relating to him. The last statement is also found in Josephus, *Antiqui.*, XI, 1.2, and Shir. 3.4. Comp. also James, *Lost Apocrypha* 20.

¹⁹ BR 98.2; Tehillim 31, 239–240. Comp. also Megillah 12a. Daniel erred in the calculation of the end of time. The curse pronounced against those who "reckoned the end of time" (Sanhedrin 97b) is to be explained accordingly. If Daniel himself failed in fixing the time accurately, it would be futile for any other mortal to attempt this task.

Notwithstanding this anathema, there are many treatises by medieval authors dealing with the "end of time" revealed to Daniel. If we disregard the pseudo-epigraphical writers, Josephus, *Antiqui.*, X, 11.7 (towards the end), is one of the earliest interpreters of the vision of Daniel, but after giving his view thereof (in his opinion, Daniel also wrote concerning the Roman government), he adds: "But if anyone is inclined to another opinion about them, let him enjoy his different sentiments without any blame from me." The "other opinion" very likely saw in Daniel's visions a prophecy bearing upon the contemporary history of the prophet.

²⁰ R. Benjamin of Tudela 74–76; R. Pethahiah 7b. *Chronicon Paschale* 92. 396, also mentions the magnificent mausoleum of Daniel, who is said to have been buried among the kings (of Babylon). All these legends very likely have their origin in the statement of Josephus, *Antiqui.*, X, 11.7, that when "Daniel became famous, an account of the opinion men had that he was beloved of God, he built a tower at Ecbatana in Media." Josephus then adds that it was a most elegant building and wonderfully made, and that it is still remaining and preserved to this day, and to such as see it, it appears to have been lately built, and to have been no older than the very day when any one looks upon it; iti s so fresh, flourishing, and beautiful, and in no way grown old in so long a time... Now they bury the kings of Media, of Persia, and Parthia in this tower to this day; and he who was entrusted with the care of it was a Jewish priest, which thing is also observed to this day. According to old rabbinic sources, Daniel left Babylon for the Holy Land, availing himself of the permission granted by Cyrus to the exiles, and bceame the governor of his native country; Shir 5.5 and Sanhedrin 93b. Josippon 3, 5b agrees in the main with Josephus, and makes Daniel settle in Shushan. There can be no doubt that the old rabbinic sources quoted were of the opinion that Daniel died in the Holy Land, where he spent the remainder of his life. Comp. notes 17 and 23.

²¹ R. Pethahiah 9a.

²² *Gelilot Erez Israel*, 101c.

²³ Josippon 3, 5b. In 3 Ezra, which is the source of Josippon (comp. the following note), Zerubbabel is one of the three body-guards of the king and not a high official. Josephus maintains that Zerubbabel was appointed head of the Jews by Cyrus, and this is very likely based on the identification of Sheshbazzar, the "prince of the Jews" under Cyrus, with Zerubbabel (Ezra 1.8); comp. Ibn Ezra, *ad loc.* PR 6, 23b, and Sanhedrin 93b (here it is supposed that Daniel preceded

Nehemiah in the office of governor, hence his identity with Zerubbabel
is assumed) on the other hand, identify Sheshbazzar with Daniel;
comp. note 76 on vol. IV, p. 326. When the Samaritans, Josephus
continues, attempted to prevent the building of the Temple, Zerubbabel
was sent by the Jews to Media to plead their cause before king Darius,
the son of Hystaspes; *Antiqui.*, XI, 4.9. Comp. note 26.

²⁴ 3 Ezra 1–57; Josephus, *Antiqui.*, XI, 3.3–9 (with slight variants); Josippon 3, 10a–11a. Comp. also Baba Batra 10a, which has
the statement concerning the ten "mighty things existing in the world",
wine being one of them.

²⁵ *Zerubbabel.* As to the part to be played by Zerubbabel in
the Messianic times, see Alphabet R. Akiba, 27–28, where it is said that
he will recite the Kaddish after the lecture to be delivered by God on
the new Torah which He is to reveal through the Messiah. All men,
including the wicked in hell and the Gentiles, hearing the Kaddish,
will respond: Amen. This will cause God to extend His compassion
to all His creatures, even to the sinners, and He will send Michael
and Gabriel to open the gates of hell that its dwellers should be set
free. Together with Elijah (comp. vol. IV, p. 233) Zerubbabel, in the
time to come, will explain all the obscure passages of the Torah, and
reveal all its mysteries; quotation from Midrash in Halakot Gedolot
(Hildesheimer's edition, 223, top). See also Pirke Mashiah, 75, and
BHM VI, 63, as well as Kalir in his lamentation בימים ההם (at the end
of Lamentations, according to Roman rite), where Zerubbabel is described as the "Messianic herald", at whose call Michael and Gabriel
will undertake the war of annihilation against the pagan world.
There is some connection between this legend and the one about Zerubbabel's "superhuman" voice· comp. vol. I, p. 59. Not quite clear is
the part attributed to Zerubbabel in Ma'aseh Daniel, 128, where it
is stated that the Messiah will ascend the Mount of Olives with Elijah
and Zerubbabel, whereupon Elijah, at the bidding of the Messiah, will
blow the trumpet (comp. vol. IV, p. 234). There can be no doubt that
the text is incomplete; there must have been something said about the
part to be played by Zerubbabel on this occasion. It is rather strange
that the Rabbis never thought of declaring Zerubbabel to be the promised Messiah. The only one of biblical times who was considered by
them as the possible candidate for the Messiaic office is Daniel. See
Sanhedrin 98b (towards the end). Is this view connected with the
supposed identity of Daniel with Zerubbabel? Comp. note 23.

²⁶ Sanhedrin 38a (top). Conp. note 76 on vol. IV, p. 326 and

notes 23,25. Nehemiah was also called התרשתא (Neh. 8.9), because the authorities of that time "absolved" him (= התר) from observing the injunction (decreed by Daniel and his three companions; 'Abodah Zarah 36b) against using the wine touched by a heathen, and permitted him to "drink" (= שתא) wine with the king, whose cup-bearer he was. See Yerushalmi Kiddushin 4, 65b; Midrash 'Aseret Melakimt 44. Nehemiah and his "company" are the authors of the strict law that no vessel or utensil is to be handled on the Sabbath. The people at that time were very lax in the observance of the Sabbath, and hence the strictness introduced by Nehemiah. When the observance of the Sabbath became well established, the rigidity of Nehemiah's law was relaxed. See Shabbat 123b, and comp. Josephus, *Bell.* II, 8.9.

⁷ Sanhedrin 93b. The books of Ezra and Nehemiah are spoken of by the Rabbis as the Book of Ezra. Comp. *e. g.*, Baba Batra 15a. In this passage it is stated that Ezra "wrote" (composed or compiled? comp. note 89 on vol. IV, p. 227) also the books of Chronicles up to 2 Chron. 21.1, and the rest of Nehemiah. Comp. the explanation of the talmudic passage in the geonic responsum published by Ginzberg, *Geonica*, II, 16–17. The unpopularity of Nehemiah shows that there is no rule without an exception. There is a maxim which says: He who is disliked by his fellow-men is also disliked by heaven. Nehemiah and David are exceptions to this rule: both were loved by God, but hated by many of their fellow-men. See Sanhedrin 103b, and comp. Blau, *Masoretische Untersuchungen*, 56, and Ginzberg, *Ha-Zofeh*, III, 121–122.

²⁸ Darius was born on the day when Nebuchadnezzar, after his victory over Jehoiachin, entered the Temple; he reigned for one year only, and was succeeded by Cyrus who reigned three, or, according to one reading, four years. See Seder 'Olam 28 and 29; Megillah 11b (bottom). Comp. notes 10 and 30.

²⁹ The legends about the youth of Cyrus in the classical writers is given by Abravanel in his commentary on Is. 45, whence it was borrowed by many later rabbinical authors.

³⁰ Josippon 3, 11d–12a. Rashi on Dan. 6.29 quotes from Josippon the statement that Darius reigned only one year, when he fell in battle and was succeeded by his son-in-law Cyrus. Our text of Josippon (comp. *loc. cit.*) has an entirely different reading. It is worth noticing that, according to Josippon, the main factor in the return of the exiles was Darius, who called upon Cyrus to participate in this undertaking, and while the

return of the exiles under Ezra, Nehemiah, Mordecai, Joshua, and Zerubbabel took place under Cyrus, the credit for it was due to Darius. Comp. also Josephus, *Antiqui.*, XI, 3.1, who remarks concerning Darius: Now, while he was still a private man, he had made a vow to God that if he came to be king, he would send all the vessels of God that were in Babylon to the Temple at Jerusalem. This vow he faithfully fulfilled as king after he was reminded of it by his great favorite Zerubbabel who had come to him from Jerusalem in behalf of the Jews. Comp. notes 7 and 10. The legend about the celestial fire, as given in Josippon, is, of course, closely related to that found in 2 Macc. 1.19–2.12, but is not directly based on it. Notice especially that 2 Macc. ascribes an important part to Nehemiah in discovering the fire, whereas Josippon ignores him entirely. Comp. note 36; note 60 on vol. IV, pp. 320–321; vol. III, p. 184.

³¹ Zebahim 62a. The prophet knew the exact site of the altar, because he saw the angel Michael sacrifice there. The word "there" very likely refers to the place in heaven exactly corresponding to the terrestrial altar; comp. Mekilta Shirah 10, 43b, and Index, s. v. "Sanctuary, Heavenly". A number of Halakot are referred to the authority of these prophets, especially to that of Haggai, and as late as the second century C. E., the "seat" of Haggai (in Jerusalem) was shown; comp. Tosefta Kelim, Baba Batra 2.3; Rosh ha-Shanah 19b; Megillah 3a (Jonathan ben Uziel composed his Targum of the Prophets under the guidance of Haggai, Zechariah, and Malachi); Yebamot 16a; Yerushalmi 1, 3a; Kiddushin 43a; Nazir 53a; Hullin 137a; Bekorot 58a. Comp. the very interesting remarks on this point by R. Sherira Gaon in *Teshubot Geone Mizrah u-Ma'arib*, No., 140. See also Bacher, *Monatsschrift* 52. 708–709. The hypothesis (see Frankel, *Dark. Ham.* 40) that חַגַּי הַנְּבִיא in many places of the Talmud is an erroneous reading for

חוֹנִי הַגּ' (*i. e.* Onia; comp. note 58 on Vol. IV, p. 320), is not tenable. On the change of the Hebrew Alphabet, see note 44.

³² Yerushalmi Sotah 5, 20b; Pesahim 9, 36c (here it is said that the skull of Araunah was found in the time of Hezekiah, who in consequence thereof ordered the purification of the Temple); Yerushalmi Nedarim 6, 39d–40a; Sanhedrin 1, 18d. Comp. also Aggadat Shir 3, 33. On the Halakot involved in the controversy between the priests, see also Pesahim 17a. This passage quotes a view that the priests gave a correct answer to the question of law put to them. In view of the widespread legend that Adam was buried in Jerusalem in the place upon which the altar was subsequently erected, one is inclined to explain

ארגן היבוסי in the Yerushalmi passages as an erroneous reading of the abbreviation (ארונה היבוסי=א׳רה), which in turn was a scribal error for אדם הראשון=אה׳ר. Comp. Vol. V, p. 126. The proselytes known as the "house of Nebalata" (*i. e.*, from Nebalat; comp. Neh. 11.34), who were quite prominent at the end of the second Jewish commonwealth, are said to have been descendants of Araunah; comp. Tosefta Peah 4.11; Yerushalmi 8, 21a; Sifre D., 110. On burial-places in Jerusalem, see Tosefta Nega'im 6.2; Yerushalmi Nazir 9, 57d; Semahot 14; Baba Kamma 82b. According to these sources, the corpses, by a later ordinance, were removed from all the burial places in Jerusalem, only the graves of the kings and that of the prophetess Huldah were left there.

³³ Megillah 15a; Targum Mal. 1.1, and Jerome in his introduction to his commentary on Malachi. Comp. notes 5 and 38.

³⁴ As to the "several returns" of the exiles, see Seder 'Olam 28–30, and the sources referred to by Ratner in his notes. The majority of the returning exiles belonged to the tribes of Judah and Benjamin; yet some refer to those of all the other tribes; Seder 'Olam 29; Josephus, *Antiqui.*, XI, 5.2. Comp. also 'Arakin 32b–33a (see Tosafot on Gittin 36a, caption בזמן), and note 56 on vol. IV, p. 317.

³⁵ Megillah 16b; Shir 5.5; comp. Kaftor wa-Ferah 10. 231. In Shir it is said that God commanded Ezra to remain in Babylon as long as Joshua the son of Jehozadak was alive. This high priest belonged to a family that occupied the office of the high priest for generations. If Ezra had come to the Holy Land during the lifetime of the latter, he would, on account of his superior merit, have had a better claim to that office. But God dislikes to see the "chain of nobility snap" (*i. e.*, to take away honors from the family and give them to another). He therefore told Ezra to remain in Babylon, so that Joshua should continue as high priest like his ancestors. But after the death of Joshua, Ezra returned to the Holy Land, where he occupied the office of high priest. Comp. Maimonides in the introduction to his Code. On Ezra as high priest, see also Parah 3.5, where it is stated that he "burned a red heifer", and this presupposes that he was a high priest. Ezra was the man for his time, and he would have been high priest even if Aaron were then alive; Koheleth 1.4.

³⁶ Yoma 9b–10a; Berakot 4a, which reads: Miracles would have been wrought for Israel on the second entrance to the Holy Land, like those performed at the first entrance, were it not for the sins of the returning exiles. Had all the Israelites returned, the second Temple would

never have been destroyed; but because the greater part of the nation remained in foreign lands, the Temple built by the returning exiles was not only destroyed afterwards, but even during its existence it lacked many things which lent glory to the first Temple. The following five things were in the first Temple only: The heavenly fire (comp. against this view vol. IV, pp. 353–354), the holy oil of anointing, the ark, the Holy Spirit (revealing itself to the prophets in the Temple; comp. Yerushalmi Sukkah 5, 55a), and the Urim and Tummim. See Shir 8.10; Yoma 21b; PRK (Grünhut's edition, 71); 'Aruk, s. v. כבד; comp. also Josephus, *Bell.*, V, 5.5, which reads: The holy of holies contained nothing. See also Index under the five subjects just mentioned. As to the refusal of the Jews of Yemen to return to the Holy Land, see note 5; on a similar legend concerning the Jews of Germany (who paid dearly for this sin during the Middle Ages), see *Ma'aseh Nissim* I and hence *Sheerit Israel* 3; Brüll, *Jahrbücher*, IV, 39–40. Shalshelet, 33a, maintains the same with regard to the Jews of Spain. With the death of the three last prophets (as to the use of the expression נביאים אחרונים see note 24 on vol. IV p. 84), the Holy Spirit departed from Israel. From time to time, however, a "heavenly voice" used to be heard that revealed to Israel things hidden from human knowledge. See Tosefta Sotah 13.2–6; Babli 46b; Yerushalmi 9, 24b (here Jeremiah and Baruch are described as the "former prophets", in contrast to the three "later prophets"); Yoma 9b; Sanhedrin 11a. At the destruction of the Temple (first?) the prophetic gift was taken away from the prophets and given to children and fools; Baba Batra 12b; comp. also Matth. 21.16. Baba Batra 12a reads: Although the gift of prophecy was taken away from the prophets, it remained with the wise; hence it may be inferred that the wise are greater than the prophets.

³⁷ Yebamot 86b. As to the statement made here that Ezra abolished the custom of having only Levites as officers of the court, see Katz in *Hoffmann-Festschrift* 109 seq. and Ginzberg, *Unbekannte Sekte*, 69.

³⁸ Megillah 15a. In was in connection with this activity for the purity of the Jewish race, that Ezra-Malachi (on the identity of the "scribe" with the "prophet", see note 33) addressed his words of reprimand against those who married "foreign women", found in Mal. 2.10. The Jews of his time revolted against the severe marriage laws of the Torah (comp. vol. III, pp. 246–247), and especially against the prohibition to intermarry with the Gentiles. They declared this law as unjust, saying: "Has not the same God who created Israel also create the other nations?" (comp. Mal. 2.10). See Sifra 18.2. The women

who returned to the Holy Land lost their beauty, and aged before their time, because of the suffering to which they were exposed, and many an inconsiderate husband divorced his wife to marry a foreign woman. Ezra-Malachi (see above) opposed not only the mixed marriages but also the evil of divorce, for even "the altar of the Lord sheds tears for the woman who is divorced by a man who married her as his 'first love'" (comp. Mal. 2.13); Yerushalmi Kiddushin 1, 58b; BR 18.5; Gittin 90b.

39 Baba Batra 15a. On the meaning of the words לו עי in this passage, see Rashi and Tosafot, *ad loc.*, as well as the geonic responsum in Ginzberg's *Geonica II*, 16–17. Comp. note 27.

40 Kiddushin 69b–71a and 71b. Ezra excluded the Gibeonites from entering into the "assembly of the Lord"; Yerushalmi Kiddushin 4, 65c; Shemuel 28, 134; BaR 8.4; comp. vol. IV, p. 10. According to Yerushalmi, an attempt was made at the time of R. Eliezer (or Eleazar) ben Azariah (about 100 C. E.), who was a descendant of Ezra in the tenth generation, to change the statute in order to admit the Gibeonites to complete union with Israel; but it failed. On Ezra's descendants, see Berakot 27b; Yerushalmi Yebamot 1, 3d (top).

41 Tosefta Sanhedrin 4.7; Babli 21b; Yerushalmi Megillah 1, 21b; Tertullian *De Cultu Fem.* 3., Jerome, *Adversus Helvidium* 7. Comp. note 50, and the following note.

42 Sifre D., 48; Midrash Tannaim 43; Sukkah 20a. In the last passage it is pointed out that at three different periods in the history of Israel the Torah was nearly forgotten, and in each case the knowledge thereof was revived by a Babylonian: first by Ezra, then by the Babylonian Hillel, and later by the Babylonian R. Hiyya, who was assisted in his work by his two sons Hezekiah and Judah.

43 Megillah 31b. Comp. the first of the ten "regulations of Ezra" in the text below.

44 Tosefta Sanhedrin 4.7–8; Babli 21b–22a; Yerushalmi Megillah 1, 21b–21c. Comp. also Sifre D., 160; Midrash Tannaim 145, as well as vol. IV, pp. 354 and 357. A thorough discussion of these and similar passages of the rabbinical literature, bearing upon the"changing of the script" by Ezra, is given by Blau, *Zur Einleitung in die Heilige Schrift*, 48, *seq.* Besides the view given in the text, there are two others. According to one, the Assyrian characters (*i. e.*, the square characters) were used by Moses in writing the Torah; but in course of time they were discarded by the Jews, and Ezra re-introduced them again; the other view maintains that "just as the Torah was not changed, even so is

the script in which it was written unchanged": the characters used at present came down from Moses, and were in continuous use by the Jews. Owing to the fact that the square writing was introduced in the time of Ezra, none of Belshazzar's wise men was able to read the writing on the wall which was in the new Aramaic (*i. e.*, square) letters. See Tosefta, *loc. cit.*, where אותו היום is very likely not to be taken literally. As Ezra is the author of the script used for writing the Torah, he was the one to introduce the dots over a number of biblical words, the genuineness of which was dubious. Ezra said: When Elijah comes (comp. vol. IV, p. 233) and asks me: "Why didst thou write these spurious words", I will answer: "Did I not place dots over them, to indicate that they are to be cancelled?" Should he, on the other hand, say: "Thou didst well in writing these words", I shall remove the dots. See BaR 3.13; ARN 34, 101 (second version 37, 98). On the dotted words see Blau, *Masoretische Untersuchungen*, 6–40. In the tannaitic literature numerous references are found to ספר עזרא, the Book of Ezra, *i. e.*, the copy of the Torah written by Ezra. The correct reading, however, seems to be ס' עזרה or rather ס' העזרה "the copy of the Bible kept in the sanctuary." But even if the reading עזרא is correct, it might be explained as the Aramaic form of עֲזָרָה, comp. Kelim 15.6; Tosefta Kelim, Baba Mezi'a 5.8; Yerushalmi Shekalim 2, 47a; Mo'ed Katan 3.4. The alleged writing of Maimonides on the "Codex Ezra", given by Di Rossi, *Meor 'Enayim*, 9, 150–151, bears the mark of forgery. On the other legends concerning this codex, see Sambari, 118–119, and *Gelilot Erez Israel*, 99b.

⁴⁵ Baba Batra 21b (bottom). The rabbinical law in other cases is very strict with regard to competition.

⁴⁶ Popular physiology attributes generative power to garlic, and hence the ordinance to partake thereof on Friday, for according to the Rabbis, the night of Sabbath is to be devoted to conjugal pleasures (in opposition to the Samaritans and other sects who prohibit sexual intercourse on this "holy day"); comp. Ketubot 5.6; Babli 62b; Nedarim 3.10; see the references cited in note 59.

⁴⁷ The meaning of the word סינר is not quite certain, but it is very likely a different spelling for זונרא, the Aramaic transliteration of the Greek ζωνάριον, "belt". It was mainly worn by women, and covered most of the lower part of the body; see Krauss, *Archäologie*, I, 174, and note 631.

⁴⁸ This ordinance is said to have had for its purpose the

restraint of conjugal relations. Comp. Berakot 21b–22b, and Yerushalmi 3, 6c. Many attempts have been made in talmudic, as well as in post-talmudic times, to abolish this law, but they were not entirely successful, at least not in the East. Comp. Ginzberg, *Geonica*, II, 24.

49 Baba Kamma 82a–82b; Ketubot 5a; Baba Batra 22a. Somewhat different are the "regulations of Ezra" in Yerushalmi Megillah 4, 75a. There 1 and 2 are counted as one, and to make up the number ten, Ezra is credited with a regulation which is elsewhere ascribed to R. Jose, a Tanna who flourished about the middle of the second century C. E. (comp. Sanhedrin 19a). The sixth ordinance is explained by Yerushalmi to refer to Friday and had for its purpose to provide the poor with new bread for the Sabbath. A third version of the ten regulations is found in PRK (Schönblum's edition, 40b). This is essentially identical with Yerushalmi Megillah, but it omits number 4, and the number ten is made up by the addition of a new ordinance not found in any other source. A full discussion of the ten regulations of Ezra is given by Bloch, *Sha'are Torat ha-Takkanot*, I, 107–138; comp. also the critical study by Zeitlin, *Takkanot Ezra* in *J.Q.R.*, New Series, VIII, 761, *seq*. Bloch, *op. cit.*, 137–138, attributes the liturgical formula given in Berakot 9.5 to Ezra on the authority of Rashi, *ad loc*. It is very likely that by the expression עזרא וסייעתו "Ezra and his company", Rashi means the Men of the Great Synagogue. Comp. Yoma 69b. On the origin of this liturgical formula, see Ginzberg, in Geiger's *Kebuzzat Maamarim* (Poznanski's edition, 402–403). It is also stated that Ezra pronounced the Tetragrammaton "as it is written"; comp. Tosefta Berakot 7.23; Yerushalmi 9, 14a; Tehillim 36, 251; comp. also Yoma 69b and Yerushalmi Berakot 4.11c. See the discussion of these passages in note 53 on vol. IV, p. 33. In the year of Ezra's return to the Holy Land the month of Elul was a "full one", consisting of thirty days, which has never happened since, for this month is always defective. See Bezah 6a.

50 4 Ezra 3–14. The names of the scribes are transmitted in different readings. The correct one is very likely: Seraiah (שריה), Neriah (נריה which was corrupted to Dabriah) the father of Baruch, Shelemiah (שלמיה), Ethan (איתן), and Aziel (עזיאל). On the characters which the scribes could not read, see note 44. In contrast to the view of this apocryphal work, shared also by many of the Church Fathers (comp., *e. g.*, Irenaeus, III, 21.2; Clemens Alexandrinus, *Stromata*, 1.22; Tertullian, *De Cultu Femin.* 1.3; ps.-Tertullian, *Adversus Marcionitas*

280–281; other references are given by Fabricius, *Codex Pseudepig.*,
I, 1156–1160, and Schürer, *Geschichte*, III, 329), that at the destruction
of the Temple the holy Bible was burned, so that Ezra was charged by
God to write it down anew, the Rabbis maintain that even "Ezra the
Scribe" was not permitted to write one letter of the Torah from memory;
he transcribed, word by word, letter by letter, from the copy of the Torah
before him. See Yerushalmi Megillah 4, 74d; BR 36 (end). On the
seventy books which Ezra was commanded to withhold from the populace
see Ginzberg, in *Journal of Jewish Philosophy and Lore*, I, 34–37, where
it is suggested that it refers to the old halakic literature, which consisted
of fifty-eight mishnaic treatises, the nine midrashic books on Leviticus,
and the Midrashim on Exodus, Numbers, and Deuteronomy. Ginzberg, *op. cit.*, 37, calls attention to Maseket Kelim 88, where it is said
that Ezra and five of his companions (they are the three prophets Haggai, Zechariah, and Malachi, as well as the Levite Shimur and Hezekiah;
on Shimur, see note 63 on vol. IV, p. 321, but he is perhaps identical with
Shelemiah in 4 Ezra mentioned above) wrote down the Mishnah. In
rabbinic literature the Mishnah is often described as the great "secret"
(μυστήριον) which God revealed to Israel (and to Israel only), whereas
the Bible was given to all mankind. Comp. *e. g.*, Yerushalmi Peah
2, 17a; PR 5, 14b; Tan. B. I, 88, and II, 116–117; Tan. Wa-Yera 5,
and Ki-Tissa 34; ShR 47.1; BaR 14.10. In rabbinic literature Ezra
is not one of those who "entered paradise alive" (comp. Index, s. v.
"Paradise, Entering Alive"), whereas 4 Ezra (end) states: And then
was Ezra caught away and taken up into the Place (*i. e.*, paradise),
of such as were like him.   The office of "heavenly scribe" is otherwise
given to Enoch or Elijah (comp. Index).   It is perhaps this glorification
of Ezra which gave rise to the accusation made by Mohammed against
the Jews that they consider Ezra as the son of God. Comp. note 5.
The much discussed Ezra-Salathiel problem is easily solved, if we
assume that the Hebrew original of 4 Ezra had at its opening the
words אֲנִי שָׁלַח אֵל עֶזְרָא. A slight curving of the letter ח made of
שלח אל "the messenger of God" שְׁלַתְאֵל Salathiel. The identification
of Ezra with Malachi (comp. notes 5, 33 and 38) may also have its
origin in these opening words of 4 Ezra, as מלאכי and שלח אל mean
both "the messenger of God".

[51] R. Benjamin of Tudela, 73. According to Josephus, *Antiqui.*,
XI, 5.5, Ezra died in old age at Jerusalem; comp. note 5. Ezra and

Nehemiah died on the second of Tebeth, which day was therefore observed as a fast-day; Megillat Ta'anit (addition) 24.

⁵² R. Benjamin of Tudela, 51; comp. also vol. VI, p. 413, note 75. On an Ezra synagogue in the neighborhood of Mount Ararat, and another in Nisibis, see *Gelilot Erez Israel*, 100a.

⁵³ On this miracle, see also vol. IV, p.326.

⁵⁴ *Gelilot Erez Israel*, 101a–101b. On the destruction of the city of Babylon, see also *Shalshelet*, 101b, quoting an alleged old manuscript. According to the medieval Chronicle, published by Neubauer, II, 185, Darius and Cyrus razed the city to the ground. Comp. vol. VI, p. 424, note 104, end.

⁵⁵ Berakot 67b (towards the end); comp. Rashi, *ad loc.*, and vol. VI, p. 411, note 46.

⁵⁶ Abot 1.1, which reads: Moses received the Torah from Sinai, and delivered it to Joshua, and Joshua to the elders (Josh. 24.31), and the elders to the prophets, and the prophets delivered it to the men of the Great Synagogue. The Great Synagogue was so called because it restored the attribute of "greatness" to God in addressing Him, as did Moses, as the "great God, the mighty, and the awful" (Deut. 10.7). Jeremiah spoke of the "great and mighty God" (Jer. 32.18), omitting the attribute "awful", because "God is awful out of the holy place" (Ps. 68.36), and in his days the holy place (the Temple) was destroyed. Daniel (Dan. 9.4) described God as great and awful, but not as mighty, saying: His children are in chains, and where then is His might manifested? The men of the Great Synagogue, on the other hand, restored all the attributes of God (comp. Nehem. 9.32 and the beginning of the 'Amidah), maintaining that the awfulness and might of God are manifested in His permitting the wicked nations to do what they like. See Yerushalmi Berakot 7, 11c; Megillah 3, 74c; Yoma 69b; Tehillim 18, 164. Comp. also Berakot 33b. Thus the men of the Great Synagogue, though not all of them were prophets (opinions differ as to the number of the prophets who were among these one hundred and twenry men; comp. Yerushalmi Megillah 1, 70d; Berakot 2, 4d; Ruth R. 2.4; Megillah 17b; comp. also ARN, both versions 1, 2; Tosefta 'Erubin 11.22), saw much deeper than Jeremiah and Daniel. See the quotation from an unknown Midrash in Midrash Talpiyyot, whence it is also incorporated in Toledot Adam 1, 26b. Among the members of the Great Synagogue were, besides Ezra and Mordecai (the latter lived more than four hundred years; comp. *Seder ha-Dorot*, 3404), Zerubbabel, Nehemiah, the high priest, Joshua, as well as Daniel's three companions, Hananiah, Mishael, and Azariah. Comp. the geonic *Seder Tannaim*

in Mahzor Vitry 481 and 463, as well as Maimonides, in his introduction to *Mishneh Torah*. The latter quite correctly understands the talmudic-midrashic view about the Great Synagogue to be based on the narrative in Neh. 8–10. This passage, combined with Ezra 2.2, lends scriptural authority to the view of the Rabbis. Maimonides undoubtedly identified Mishael (Neh. 8.4), Azariah (10.3), and Hananiah (10.22) with Daniel's three companions. The view that Daniel was a priest (comp. note 6) is likewise based upon the identification of the priest Daniel (Neh. 10.7) with the famous Daniel. Maimonides, *loc. cit.*, gives the "chain of tradition" from Moses to R.Ashi, the compiler of the Babylonian Talmud, extending over forty generations. Ezra and the men of the Great Synagogue form the middle of the chain, since Baruch, the teacher of Ezra (comp. vol. IV, 355, top), is the twentieth from Moses. Later authorities extend the chain of tradition until the last of the Geonim; comp. 2 Seder 'Olam, 163–165; Seder 'Olam Zuta, 176, as well as *Seder ha-Kabbalah* by R. Abraham ibn Daud. As to the activities of the Great Synagogue, the following are the most notable ones. They edited or declared as canonical the books of Ezekiel, Daniel, Esther, and the Minor Prophets. See Baba Batra 15a (as to the word "write", see note 89 on vol. IV, p. 277); comp. also 2 Seder 'Olam, 174, where it is said that Ezra "wrote" the Book of Judges. Very interesting is the statement found in this chronicle, p.162, to the effect that Moses made use, for the Pentateuch, of the writings which came down from former generations. Josephus, *Contra Apionem*, 1.8, and Seder 'Olam R. 30, maintain that at the end of the Persian period the prophetic spirit departed from among Israel, and this necessitated the final canonization of the holy writings. These authorities very likely also have in mind the activity of the Great Synagogue in connection with the Canon; comp. Tan. Beshallah 16. The men of the Great Synagogue introduced the tripartite division of the oral law, classifying it into Midrash, Halakah, and Haggada; Yerushalmi Shekalim 5 (beginning). Hence the Mishnah contains statements going directly back to these great men; comp. Abot 1.1; Sanhedrin 109b, with reference to the Mishnah 10.1 (see, however, Tan. B. III, 43, where חכמי המשנה can hardly mean the men of the Great Synagogue); Megillah 10b, where a haggadic rule is ascribed to them. They introduced the Feast of Purim, and determined the days when it should be celebrated. See Megillah 2a; Yerushalmi 1, 70d; comp. note 193 on vol. IV, p. 448. On the view that they built up the entire ritual, see note 58. They also ordained that the tithes and the Terumah should be given, though according to the biblical law these obligations ceased when the Jews were exiled. They drew up a document to the effect that they had taken anew upon themselves these duties, and left it in the Temple over night. In the morning they found the heavenly seal placed under the names attached to the document. See Ruth R. 2.4. Very remarkable is the statement of ER 27, 138 according to which the Great Synagogue was acting in Babylonia at the time of Ezekiel. Comp. *Jewish Encyclopedia*, s. v. "The Great Synagogue."

⁵⁷ Yoma 69b. In Shir 7.8 two views are given. According to one, the "desire for idolatry" was eradicated from among Israel in the days of Hananiah, Mishael, and Azariah (they belonged to the Great Synagogue; comp. preceding note); but the other view maintains that this happened in the time of Mordecai and Esther; comp. also 'Arakin 32b. In the Babylonian myth about Ishtar's descent into hell it is also said that during her absence from the earth all creatures lost their desire and appetite for any enjoyment. At present Satan is blind, and thus his power is weakened; but in the time to come the evil inclination will entirely disappear from among men, who will be like angels. See BR 48.11.

⁵⁸ Aggadat Tefillat Shemoneh Esreh 54–55, and, in a somewhat different form, *Eshkol*, I, 19. On the legends presupposed in this midrashic writing, see vol. I, pp. 10, 241, 282, 323; vol. II, pp. 24, 36, 72. "The men of the Great Synagogue formulated the benedictions and the prayers, as well as the benedictions for Kiddush and Habdalah." On the other hand, the view is given that the three partriarchs instituted the three daily prayers: Abraham the morning prayer, Isaac the afternoon prayer, and Jacob the evening prayer. Comp. Berakot 26b and 33b; Yerushalmi 4, 6d; Yoma 28b; Tan. B. I, 195–196, and V, 45 (here it is said that Moses established the daily prayers); Tan. Hayye Sarah 5 and Ki-Tissa 23; Tehillim 19, 164 (the text of Yerushalmi Berakot 7, 11c, is here changed, and instead of מטבע תפלה we have סדר תפלה, thus making Moses the author of the 'Amidah), and 55, 291–292; Mishle 22, 93; BR 60.14 and 68.9; BaR 2.1. Besides Moses and the patriarchs, the following prophets and kings are said to have contributed to the prayer-book. Joshua composed *'Alenu* on his entering into the Holy Land, and *'Al Ken Nekawweh Leka* at the time when Achan confessed his theft. See *Seder ha-Yom* עלינו; Mahkim, 125; Sha'are Teshubah 20a–21a (Hazan's edition; R. Hai Gaon's responsum dealing with the authorship of Joshua is certainly a forgery); Zunz, *Synagogale Poesie*, 4. Solomon is the author of *Yishtabbah* (Orehot Hayyim, 1, 6d; Zunz, *loc. cit.*), while another king, Hezekiah, composed *Adonai*

Elohe Israel; *Seder ha-Yom, ad loc.*, and Zunz, *loc. cit.* *Shoken 'Ad* is
a composition of Isaac's, and is an acrostic containing not only his own
name, but also that of his wife Rebekah; Mahzor Vitry 152. On
Hashkibenu, see vol. II, p. 366. On the view that grace after meals
was composed by Moses, see vol. III, p. 50. Joshua added one benediction to the grace after meals, and later on David and Solomon added another. See Berakot 48b.

XII. ESTHER

Vol. IV, (pp. 365–448).

¹ Yoma 29a; Megillah 13a (here several other etymologies of the name Esther are given; comp. also note 67); Tehillim 22, 185. On the meaning of the name Esther, comp. also 1 and 2 Targum Esther 2.7; Hullin 139b; vol. IV, p. 384. The description of Mordecai in 2 Targum Esther (end) as "Venus that glitters among the stars and is like the dawn of the morning" is taken from the old piyyut מראה כהן (comp. note 42 on vol. IV, p. 145), and has nothing to do with the etymology of his name. He who dreams of the Book of Esther will live to see miracles performed for him. See Berakot 57b.

² 2 Panim Aherim 55; 2 Targum Esther 1.1 (towards the end).

³ Esther R. 1, 9.9; Abba Gorion 12; Midrash Tannaim 37.

⁴ Megillah 11a, which gives also the different view that Ahasuerus owed his throne to his valor and other merits. In contrast to these views, which assume that Ahasuerus did not inherit the throne from his father, 2 Targum Esther 1. 1, 2, describes him as the son of Cyrus the Persian, who was the son of Darius the Mede. Alkabez, 20b, quotes from a Targum on Esther the statement that Ahasuerus was the son of "Cyrus from the empire of Asia". Josephus, *Antiqui.*, XI, 6.1, in agreement with the Septuagint, calls the king Artaxerxes, and adds that he was known by this name "to the Greeks, whereas his real name was Cyrus." On the view that Artaxerxes was the name of all Persian kings, see Seder 'Olam 30, and note 7 on vol. IV, p. 346. Abba Gorion 4 states that Darius was the father of Ahasuerus. The Rabbis give several etymologies of the name Ahasuerus, which is said to contain a hint as to the sad plight of Israel in the days of the bearer of this name. Comp. Megillah 11a; Esther R. 1, 1.1 and 3. On the vast wealth of Ahasuerus see vol. IV, p. 367, end of the last paragraph.

⁵ Megillah 11a–11b; Seder 'Olam 28. The Talmud points out that even Daniel erred in computing the seventy years of the exile fixed by Jeremiah; comp. Vol. IV, 349 (end). See also Letter of Jeremiah 7, and the full discussion of this chronological problem in Lekah on Esther (beginning), as well as *Kad ha-Kemah*, *Purim* II. 43b and comp. further note 24 on Vol. IV p. 301. According to Esther R. 1, 3.15, Ahasuerus gave his feast after the work of the Temple had been stopped

for three years. On Darius ("the last"), the son of Ahasuerus and
Esther, see WR 13.3; Kallah 1, 6a; Esther R. 1.1.   Comp. vol. IV, p. 344
in connection with the cause of Belshazzar's feast.

⁶ Abba Gorion 8, which gives also the different view that the personal reason for the feast was the king's birthday; 2 Panim Aherim 58;
1 and 2 Targum Esther 1.3; Esther R. 1, 3.15, which reads: Ahasuerus
prepared a feast to celebrate the completion of his magnificent throne;
comp. note 13.   The statement found in Septuagint Esther 1.4 that
Ahasuerus celebrated with a feast his marriage to Vashti was also
known to the Rabbis; see Abba Gorion 12–13 (read מְזָּנֵת לְהדִין שׁחור

and comp. Yalkut quoted by Buber; נשׁאת is a more common word than
מזונת); Panim Aherim 59; 2 Targum Esther 1.9, where the text is corrupt,
but MS. K with its לְהון נברא suggests the correct reading לְהדִין נברא.
As to the wars of Ahasuerus, who at first was a small potentate ruling
over seven provinces, and finally, by wars of conquest, became the ruler
of one hundred and twenty-seven provinces, see Megillah 11a; Esther
R. 1, 1.7.

⁷ Megillah 12a; Esther R. 1, 3.18.   Opinions differ as to the guests
described in Esther 1.3 as princes; according to one, they were the
"crowned heads" of the hundred and twenty-seven provinces subject
to Ahasuerus; but another view maintains that they were the sons of
the "crowned heads".   Comp. 2 Targum Esther 1.3; Abba Gorion 8;
Panim Aherim 58.   By the "nobles" (פרתמים) are meant the *Decumani*
and *Augustiani*, who were the guests of honor; Esther R. 1, 3.19.   Comp.
note 52 on vol. IV, p. 315.   As to Ahasuerus' lack of common sense, see
note 49.

⁸ Aggadat Esther 10–11.

⁹ Abba Gorion 8–9; Panim Aherim 58; Esther R. 1.4; ShR 9.7;
1 and 2 Targum Esther 1.4 (in 1 Targum שׁית is to be struck out, as
the hundred and eighty kings correspond to the number of days mentioned in Esther 1.4).   Comp. also PRE 49.

¹⁰ Panim Aherim 58; 2 Targum Esther 1.4.

¹¹ Abba Gorion 9; Panim Aherim 58; 2 Targum Esther 1.4.   Comp.
also Esther R. 1, 4.2, according to the reading given in *Mattenot Kehun-
nah, ad loc.* Septuagint on Esther 1.7 speaks of the precious cup used
by the king at the feast; comp. 2 Targum Esther 1.11.

¹² Megillah 12a; ShR 9.7; Esther R. 1.4; Panim Aherim 58.

¹³ Abba Gorion 2–8; Targum Esther 1.2, Comp. also 2 Targum
1.2, 4, and 7–8; Aggadat Esther 8–9; Esther R. 1.2, 12 and 1.3, 15

As to the fate of Solomon's throne, see vol. IV, p. 160, and the vast literature on the subject given by Salzberger, *Salomos Tempelbau*, 60–74. The sources differ greatly as to the history of the throne. The strangest form of this legend is found in 2 Targum Esther, *loc. cit.*, which reads: When Nebuchadnezzar attempted to ascend and to sit upon Solomon's throne, in possession of which he came at the conquest of Jerusalem, he did not know its mechanism. When he put his foot on the first steps, a golden lion stretched out its right paw, and struck him on his left foot, so that he became lame for the rest of his life. After the conquest of Babylon by Alexander the Macedonian, Solomon's throne was brought by him to Egypt. Shishak the king of Egypt attempted to ascend the throne, as did Nebuchadnezzar before him, and the result of his presumptuousness was the same: his leg was broken by the golden lion, and he was therefore called the "lame Pharaoh" unto the day of his death. When Epiphanes the son of Antiochus (or perhaps Alofernes; the texts have אני׳פורנים and אני׳פונים) destroyed Egypt, he took the throne with him, and put it on a ship (to be sent to Greece). While being moved about, a leg of the throne was loosened from the golden chain holding it (read משישלתא instead of כשישלתא). All the artists and goldsmiths of the world were brought to repair the damage, but none until this day succeeded. When Cyrus arose after Epiphanes, he was found worthy to be permitted to ascend and sit on Solomon's throne, because he assisted in the building of the Temple. Leaving the question of chronology out of consideration (it is hardly conceivable that Targum believed that Shishak lived after Nebuchadnezzar, and Cyrus after Epiphanes), one does not understand why the "pious" Cyrus is made to sit on a broken throne. It seems therefore certain that the text is corrupt, and that the order of the kings was: Shishak (comp. vol. IV, pp. 159-160 and 184), Nebuchadnezzar, Cyrus (the only one who was found worthy to sit on it), Alexander the Macedonian, who in his great wisdom did not make any attempt to ascend the throne, and Epiphanes, in whose time the throne was damaged, so that no further attempts were made to ascend it. The statement in Esther R. 1.2, 12, that the "fragments" of the throne "could still be seen at Rome" as late as the second century C. E., is very likely connected with the above legend about its having been damaged in the time of Epiphanes. That it was finally brought to Rome is the natural inference from the preceding statement given in Esther R., to the effect that it came from Jerusalem to Babylon, from there to Media, from there to Greece, and finally from Greece to Rome. The "four kingdoms" were each in its time in possession of Solomon's throne, the symbol of "Cosmocratia." Comp. *ibid.*, which reads: Nebuchadnezzar sat on this throne; Cyrus sat on it; and when Ahasuerus became king, he too wished to ascend it, but was prevented (by the grandees of his realm) from doing so, as he was not a "Cosmocrator", like the other two. Comp. vol. VI, p. 415, note 80 and pp. 297–298.

14 2 Panim Aherim 56–57; 2 Targum Esther 1.2, 3; comp. Rashi on Micah 1.15. On Elam, comp. also Sanhedrin 24a.

15 Abba Gorion 32; Esther R. 3.9, 19. According to the first source, Ahasuerus did not force the Jews to take part in the festivities arranged by him. On God's hatred of unchastity, see vol. I, p. 153; vol. III, p. 381; note 45 on vol. IV, p. 313.

16 Abba Gorion 9; Esther R. 1.5.

17 Abba Gorion 32–33; Esther R. 3.9, 19; Shir 7.8; Megillah 12a; Aggadat Esther 11 (an alleged quotation from the Talmud). Comp. vol. IV, pp. 382 and 415. Opinions in these sources differ as to whether Israel, because of their participation in the festivities, deserved punishment or not. According to Megillah and Shir, the trouble which overwhelmed Israel shortly after the feast was the punishment for their worshipping the idol erected by Nebuchadnezzar, a sin committed by the entire nation, with the exception of the three men who were thrown into the fiery furnace for refusing to obey the king's command. Comp. note 83 on vol. IV, p. 328.

18 Megillah 12a; PRE 49. As to the desire of Ahasuerus not to offend the religious feelings of his guests, see also Abba Gorion 13, and Esther R. 1.8, which has a statement with regard to the Samaritans, who consider it unlawful to keep wine in leather casks. Comp. Geiger, *Kebuzzat Maamarim* 73–74 and Ginzberg, Notes 389.

19 Abba Gorion 12; Esther R. 1.8.

20 1 and 2 Targum Esther 1.5–6; Megillah 12a; Abba Gorion 12; Panim Aherim 58–59; PRE 49; Esther R. 1.5–6. In the last source the sumptuous use of expensive marble is pointed out.

21 Abba Gorion 10; Panim Aherim 59; 2 Targum Esther 1.7. According to one view given in Esther R. 1.7, the cups were of glass that glittered like gold.

22 Abba Gorion 10–11; Panim Aherim 59; PRE 39; Esther R. 1.7; Megillah 12a, 1 and 2 Targum Esther 1.7.

23 Abba Gorion 11; Panim Aherim 59; 2 Targum Esther 1.8; comp. also Esther R. 1.7, 13, where בפתקא is to be read instead of בפתקא. Josephus, *Antiqui.*, XI, 6.1, also points out that Ahasuerus abolished the Persian custom of compulsory drinking at this feast. The words

of Septuagint on Esther 1.8 οὐ κατὰ προκείμενον νόμον express the same view.

²⁴ Abba Gorion 10; Panim Aherim 59.

²⁵ Esther R. 1.7, 13.

²⁶ Megillah 12a. According to Josephus, *Antiqui.*, XI, 6.1, Ahasuerus commanded all his subjects to stop their work for some time and to attend his feast.

²⁷ Abba Gorion 10; Esther R. 1.5; comp. also 1.4.

²⁸ Abba Gorion 13; Panim Aherim 59–60 (here it is stated that the women refused to participate in the desecration of the holy vessels in which the wine was served to the men; they had therefore to be entertained separately); Esther R. 1.9, 9–10. On the reading יין "שחור "black wine", comp. note 6, where it is shown that הדין שחור "this noble man" is to be read instead. Comp. also Buber's note 45 on Panim Aherim 59.

²⁹ Panim Aherim 60:1 and 2 Targum Esther 1.9.

³⁰ Esther R. 1.9, 10.

³¹ Abba Gorion 13, 14–15; Panim Aherim 60–61; Esther R. introduction (end) and 1.9, 9, as well as 1.11–12; Tehillim 10, 96, and 17, 133; Megillah 12b; 1 and 2 Targum Esther 1.10 and 12 (in 1 Targum Esther Vashti is said to have been the daughter of Evil-merodach). As to the father of Ahasuerus, see note 4. The legend about Vashti's refusal to appear naked reminds one of the story told by Herodotus, I, 8, about Candaules and Gyges.

³² 1 Targum Esther 1.10. On the descration of the holy vessels, see vol. IV, p. 368, and note 28.

³³ Abba Gorion 14; Esther R., Targum, and Lekah on 1.10.

³⁴ Megillah 12b; Targum and Esther R. on 1.10; Aggadat Esther 13 (bottom). Comp., on the other hand, 2 Targum Esther 2.2, which reads: She did not deserve capital punishment, but it was so decreed against her in heaven, in order that the offspring of Nebuchadnezzar should perish. A similar view is found in Panim Aherim 61; comp. also vol. IV, p. 379. Comp. vol. VI, p. 11, note 55.

³⁵ Megillah 12b (בירושלמי, in Rashi and Tosafot, *ad loc.*, is an erroneous reading of the abbreviation בג"ש, *i. e.*, בגזרה שוה; comp. ראב"ן, No. 451, and Ginzberg's remarks on it in the Additions to Raschkes' edition of ראב"ן; see also Rabbinovicz on Megillah, *loc. cit.*; Astruc, 215, and Buber, *Yerushalayim ha-Benuyah* No. 51); Midrash Tannaim 174; quotation from an unknown Midrash by Alkabez, 37a, and 42 (bottom). According to PRE 49, Ahasuerus followed the custom of the kings of Media, who had dancers appear before them at their carousals to en-

tertain them.   According to Josephus, *Antiqui.*, XI, 6.1, Vashti refused to obey the king because the Persian law prohibited married women showing their faces to any man but their husband.   On the favorable comments by the Rabbis on Vashti's refusal, see vol. IV, pp. 376 and 428.   The statement: "*Venit Gabriel et fecit ei membrum virile*", is missing in many editions of Megillah, *loc. cit.*

³⁶ Abba Gorion 15–16 (read, as in Panim Aherim, מומסים "mimus", an allusion to משחק); Panim Aherim 60–61; Esther R., 1 and 2 Targum on 1.12; Megillah 12b.   Comp. PRE 49.   The statement that Nebuchad-nezzar did not strip the convicts naked before their execution is based on Dan. 3.21.

³⁷ 2 Targum Esther 1.12.   Comp. note 35.

³⁸ Megillah 12b; Esther R. 1.13.   The Jewish sages before whom Ahasuerus put the case of Vashti belonged to the tribe of Issachar; Esther R., *loc. cit.*, as well as Abba Gorion 15 and Targum Esther 1.13. Comp. also Megillah, *loc. cit.* (שיודעין לעבר שנים), and Index, s. v. "Issachar, Tribe of".

³⁹ Abba Gorion 16–17; 2 Panim Aherim 61; 2 Targum Esther 1.14. The text of none of these sources is quite correct; but it is certain that this Haggadah considers the seven men as representing the seven countries enumerated there.   The names, however, of the fifth and sixth countries are corrupt.

⁴⁰ Esther R. 1.14.   Here as well as in Megillah 12b and Targum 1.14 the seven names of the king's counsellors are explained allegori-cally.   Comp. the allegorical interpretations of the names mentioned in Esther 1.10 as given in vol. IV, pp. 374–375.

⁴¹ PRE 49; 2 Panim Aherim 61; 2 Targum Esther 1.16.   Against the identification of Memucan with Daniel, see vol. IV, pp. 379, 380, and 394, where the former is identified with Haman.

⁴² Yerushalmi Sanhedrin 4, 22b; Esther R. 1.16.   These two sources also give another view, according to which, "among the nations" the taking of the vote begins with the most prominent member of the court.   On the text of Esther R., see commentaries, *ad loc.*, and Alkabez, 49b (bottom).   The seven princes who sentenced Vashti to death were prominent in the affairs of state as early as the time of Belshazzar. They escaped the doom which overtook this king because they refused to participate in the desecration of the holy vessels; Esther R. 1.14. It is the unanimous opinion of the Haggadah that Vashti was killed; comp. Megillah 12b according to the correct reading in Aggadat Esther 13 (bottom); PRE 49; 2 Panim Aherim 61; Esther R., introduction

(towards the end), and 1.21; Targum Esther 1.1 and 19; 2 Targum 2.1–2. Josephus, *Antiqui.*, XI, 6.2, maintains that she did not lose her life.

⁴³ 2 Targum Esther 1.16.

⁴⁴ Midrash Teman 174.

⁴⁵ Aggadat Esther 15 (bottom). Abba Gorion 17 and Esther R. 1.16 give other reasons for Memucan's hatred of Vashti. Comp. vol. IV, p. 394, and note 97 appertaining thereto.

⁴⁶ 2 Targum Esther 1.18–21.

⁴⁷ Tehillim 22, 194. Comp. vol. IV, p. 445. Ahasuerus is regarded as a "cosmocrator" not only in the Talmud (Megillah 11a, which says that the one hundred and twenty-seven provinces represent the entire world) and several Midrashim (as, *e.g.*, Panim Aherim 56; 2 Targum Esther 1.1, 3; Aggadat Esther 8), but also in Septuagint Esther 3.13. Other Midrashim, however, maintain that he ruled only over half of the world. Comp. PRE 11; ShR 9.7; Esther R. 1.1, 5, and 2.13. In all these Midrashim it is stated that the diminution of Ahasuerus' power was his punishment for stopping the work of the Temple. According to 2 Targum Esther 4.1 (beginning; the text is obscure and very likely corrupt; read דאיתבניאו instead of דאיתבניאו), the work of the Temple was stopped after its seventy-two towers had been completed. On the "cosmocrators", see note 13 (end); vol. I, pp. 177–178, and Index, s. v. The Haggadah draws attention to the correspondence between the number of the provinces over which Ahasuerus ruled and that of the years of Sarah, who lived one hundred and twenty-seven years. The reward for Sarah's pious deeds performed during these years was that her pious descendant Esther ruled over this number of provinces. See BR 58.3; Esther R. 1.1 (end); Tehillim and Panim Aherim, *loc. cit.*

⁴⁸ Abba Gorion 17; 2 Panim Aherim 60; Esther R. 2.1; Targum Esther 1.1. Comp. note 34.

⁴⁹ Abba Gorion 1; Esther R., introduction, 9. The identification of Memucan with Haman is also found in Megillah 12b and Targum Esther 1.16. Against this identification, comp. note 41. As to the characterization of Ahasuerus as a "fool", see also Esther R. 1.22; vol. IV, p. 424; notes 7 and 52.

⁵⁰ Megillah 12a. This passage also gives another view to the effect that Ahasuerus thereby displayed political wisdom.

⁵¹ Megillah 12b.

⁵² Abba Gorion 17–18 (this was their punishment for having advised the king to stop the building of the Temple; comp. note 47); 2

Panim Aherim 61; Targum Esther 2.1. In these sources Memucan is identified neither with Daniel (vol. IV, pp. 377–378), nor with Haman (379). Septuagint has "Man" instead of Memucan.

⁵³ Megillah 12b. The Persians despised the Jewish women, who had lost their beauty on account of their great sufferings (comp. note 38 on vol. IV, p. 355), and God therefore brought it about that among the multitudes of the Persian women not one was found worthy to become queen, and a despised Jewess was chosen by the king as his wife.

⁵⁴ Panim Aherim 65. Comp. also Megillah 13a (towards the end).

⁵⁵ 2 Panim Aherim 63–64; Aggadat Esther 20–21; 2 Targum Esther 2.8. As to the question why Esther did not suffer martyrdom rather than transgress the law that prohibits marriage with a Gentile, comp. Sanhedrin 74a; Aggadat Esther 11.9; 2 Targum Esther 2.8; note 80.

⁵⁶ The genealogy of Mordecai up to Jacob is found in 2 Panim Aherim 62–63; Aggadat Esther 19; Targum Esther 7.1 and 2 Targum 2.5.

⁵⁷ Megillah 13a (top); ʹ2 Panim Aherim 62 and 63; Tosefta-Targum 1 Kings 2.36; 2 Targum Esther 2.5.

⁵⁸ 2 Panim Aherim 82; Shemuel (end).

⁵⁹ Megillah 12b (below).

⁶⁰ PRE 50; Panim Aherim 62. Comp. vol. IV, pp. 370 and 415. On the other hand Shir 7.8 is of the opinion that "most of the men of this generation" were pious. With regard to the designation of Mordecai as "Jew" (יהודי literally the "Judean") in Esther 2.5, though he was a Benjamite, 2 Panim Aherim 82 and Esther R. 2.5 remark that this word characterizes one "as confessing one God" (יחודי=יהודי from יָחַד "confessed the unity of God"); a similar explanation of the name "Jew" is also found in Constitutiones Apostolicae, 2.60. The Midrashim just cited say that Mordecai was like Abraham and Moses; like the former he was willing to suffer martyrdom for God, and like the latter he was ready to "stand before God in the breach" (Ps. 106.23) to save Israel.

⁶¹ Megillah 12b; 2 Panim Aherim 62; PRE 50; 1 and 2 Targum Esther 2.5.

⁶² 2 Panim Aherim 62; Menahot 65a. In Ezra 2.2, Bilshan is taken as an adjective ("master of tongues", a contraction of בעל "master" and לשון "tongue" or "language") of the preceding name Mordecai;

another name of his was Pethahiah. As to Mordecai's mastery of languages, see vol IV, p. 391.

⁶³ Menahot 64b.

⁶⁴ PRE 50. As a descendant of King Saul (comp. the sources cited in note 56) he is said to have been of royal blood. On the view that the aristocracy was exiled together with king Jeconiah, see vol. IV, p. 286.

⁶⁵ Megillah 13a; 2 Panim Aherim 63; 2 Targum Esther 2, 6 and 7; 1 Targum 1.6. According to Josephus, *Antiqui.*, XI, 6.2, Mordecai moved to Shushan after Esther's marriage to king Ahasuerus. The first passage of 2 Targum referred to above seems to be corrupt. It reads; Mordecai and Esther were deported into exile with Jeconiah. Mordecai returned with those who volunteered to go up and build the Temple anew, and Nebuchadnezzar deported him again. The source for this statement is 2 Panim Aherim, *loc. cit.* But there nothing is said about Mordecai's going up to Jerusalem for the building of the Temple, as it had not been destroyed yet. The "two exiles" of Mordecai refer to his exile with Jeconiah and his second with Zedekiah. It seems fairly certain that the sentence ···וחזר תיניגות. is to be read after תרתין.

⁶⁶ Tehillim 22, 192–193; Megillah 13a; Targum Esther and Esther R. 2.7. A miracle was performed for him, and his breasts supplied milk for the babe Esther. On the milk found in the breast of men, see Preuss, *Biblisch-talmudische Medizin*, 476.

⁶⁷ Megillah 13a; Panim Aherim 63; Esther R., 1 and 2 Targum on 2.7; Tehillim 22, 181. Opinions differ as to whether Esther was her real name and Hadassah her attribute, or *vice versa*; comp. note 1.

⁶⁸ Megillah 13a; BR 39.13 (here also two other views are given concerning her age; forty years, as well as eighty, are mentioned); Abba Gorion 18; Panim Aherim 63; Ekah 5, 155; Esther R. 2.7. As a punishment because Saul took away Michal from David by violence, his descendant Esther was taken by force to Ahasuerus and as a reward for his pious act toward his father Noah, Japheth's descendant, Ahasuerus (the Persians are descended from Japheth) was found worthy to marry the virtuous Esther, the descendant of Shem. See Hasidim 397.

⁶⁹ Abba Gorion 18; Esther R. 2.9 and 15; Aggadat Esther 23.

⁷⁰ Megillah 13a; Abba Gorion 18; 2 Panim Aherim 64. The last passage adds: All the ladies of the court vied with one another in offering their services to Esther, as they knew that she would be queen. Comp. also Esther R. 2.15, which reads: The celestials as well the terrestrials loved her.

⁷¹ Megillah 7a and 13a; Aggadat Esther 23.

⁷² Aggadat Esther 21. Comp. vol. IV, pp. 380–381.

⁷³ Abba Gorion 19; Panim Aherim 65; Esther R. 2.17.

⁷⁴ Megillah 13a; comp. also Yoma 29a, which reads: Ahasuerus continued to love Esther all her life as much as on the day he married her.

⁷⁵ 2 Panim Aherim 63 and 64; 2 Targum Esther 2.7. That Esther did not partake of forbidden food is stated also in the Additions to Esther (Prayer of Esther); Megillah 13a and PRE 50.

⁷⁶ 2 Targum Esther 2.9. Some authorities, however, are of the opinion that the maidens waiting upon Esther were Jewesses. Comp. the quotation from an unknown Midrash by Alkabez, 72a, and the following note.

⁷⁷ Targum Esther 2.9. Genunita, "garden", is perhaps an allusion to paradise, which was fashioned on the third day of creation; comp. vol. I, p. 19. According to Alkabez, 71b, Hurfita is to be translated by "haste" (from חרך "he sped"), and is an allusion to Friday, because on that day the people hasten to prepare for the Sabbath; comp. Baba Kamma 32a. See also Megillah 13a.

⁷⁸ Esther R. 2.11; PRE 51. Comp. also Septuagint 2.20. According to some authorities the purpose of Mordecai's daily visits was to prevent witchcraft from being used against her; Esther R., *loc. cit.*, and comp. Tehillim 22, 194, which reads: By means of witchcraft her enemies caused her to become ugly, but a miracle happened and she regained her former beauty. This is said to have happened when Esther sought to see the king in behalf of the Jews. Comp. vol. IV, p. 428.

⁷⁹ Megillah 13a; Septuagint Esther 2.7.

⁸⁰ Zohar III, 275b–276b; Tikkune Zohar 20. The old sources do not know of this docetism, and maintain that the last Darius was the offspring of Ahasuerus' marriage with Esther. Comp. Sanhedrin 74a (Zohar, *loc. cit.*, obviously polemizes against this statement of the Talmud); WR 5.13. Comp. notes 5 and 55.

⁸¹ 2 Panim Aherim 64; 2 Targum Esther 2.10.

⁸² Esther R. 2.11.

⁸³ 2 Panim Aherim 64.

⁸⁴ 2 Targum Esther 2.18. Comp. also Megillah 13a and Josephus, *Antiqui.*, XI, 6.2.

⁸⁵ 2 Panim Aherim 65; 2 Targum Esther 2.19. Against this, see Megillah 13 a (towards the end), where it is said that it was Mordecai

who advised the king to "gather virgins together for a second time," so that Esther might be provoked to jealousy.

⁸⁶ Megillah 13a-13b; Esther R. 2.20. Comp. vol. I, p. 361, and vol. IV, p. 310.

⁸⁷ Abba Gorion 19; Panim Aherim 65. On the descent of Mordecai and Esther from Saul, comp. notes 56 and 64. See also the following note.

⁸⁸ 2 Panim Aherim 65-66; Abba Gorion 20; PRE 50; 1 and 2 Targum Esther 2.21; Megillah 13b (the duties of the chamberlains became more burdensome since the king married Esther; for sexual intercourse causes thirst, and the king's demand for drinks disturbed the chamberlains in their night's rest. That is why they attempted to get rid of the king. Comp. Rashi *ad. loc.*, and Alkabez, 83a); Esther R. 2.21. See also Septuagint 2.21, which reads: And...the chiefs of the body-guard were grieved because Mordecai was promoted, and they sought to kill the king. On the miraculous "opening of locked doors" (which enabled Mordecai to surprise the conspirators), see Acts 5.19, 23. This kind of miracle is very often found in Christian legends. Comp. Günter, *Christliche Legende*, index, s. v. "Türe öffnet sich". It is also known to Jewish sources; comp. Kallah 1, 6a; Ginzberg, *Geonica*, I, 28; vol. II, p. 331. According to Josephus, XI, 6.4, a Jewish servant of the conspirators, by the name of Barnabazuas, betrayed his masters to Mordecai. Josippon 4 and later sources (as, *e. g.*, Yerahmeel 79, 236) assume that the conspirators were relatives of Haman's (thus explaining the latter's hatred for Mordecai), and that the motive of the conspiracy was a political one. At that time Ahasuerus was engaged in a war with the king of Macedonia (or Greece), and the two conspirators attempted to come to the aid of the Greeks by assassinating the king of the Persians. Comp. the Additions to Esther, Addition A (end), which reads: And Haman sought to bring evil upon Mordecai... because of the two eunuchs of the king. In Addition E (Decree of Ahasuerus) Haman is described as a Macedonian, and hence the statement in Josippon that his kinsmen attempted to aid the Macedonians. The statement about the war between Greece and Persia is perhaps based upon an erroneous interpretation of the "two dragons" in the Dream of Mordecai. As to Mordecai's reasons for preventing the assassination of Ahasuerus, see also BR 39.12.

⁸⁹ PRE 50. Sammael removed the poison from the cup, so that Mordecai's accusation should prove false, but Gabriel put it back where it was, and the conspiracy was exposed. See Alkabez, 88a, quoting

from the Commentary on Esther (in MS.) by R. Eleazar of Worms. Comp. a similar legend about Sammael and Gabriel in Sotah 10b, and note 89 on vol. II, p. 36. The midrashic basis in Sotah is מוצאת (Gen. 28.28), and in Alkabez וימצא (Esther 2.23).

⁹⁰ Megillah 13b. Rashi, ad loc., takes משמר to mean "office", and accordingly the two conspirators are said to have held different offices.

⁹¹ 2 Panim Aherim 66, where להחנק is to be read instead of לחנקו, as it is the unanimous opinion of the Haggadah that they attempted to poison Ahasuerus, and not to strangle him; comp. the references given in note 88.

⁹² Aggadat Esther 26. The proverb found there, "Cursed are the wicked who never do a good deed completely", is taken from BR 89.7. Comp. vol. II, pp. 67–68.

⁹³ PRE 50; Panim Aherim 46; Esther R. 3.1. An unknown Midrash quoted by Alkabez, 153b, maintains that Haman found one of the treasures buried by Joseph; comp. vol. III, p. 415. There are different versions of Haman's genealogy, showing his descent from Amalek the son of Eliphaz by his concubine; comp. Targum Esther 5.1; 2 Targum 3.1; Aggadat Esther 26–27; Soferim 13.23. Only few of the names in Haman's genealogy are found in the Bible, the majority are the names of the oppressors and enemies of the Jews in the Roman period. Pilatus (אפליטוס), Herod, Nero (נירן), are easily recognized, but it is difficult to restore all the names, as some of them are badly corrupted. With regard to Haman's descendants it is stated that "some of them taught the Torah in Bene Berak;" comp. Gittin 57b; Sanhedrin 96b. It is well known that R. Akiba had his academy in Bene Berak (comp. e. g., Sanhedrin 32b), and as the legend which makes him a descendant of proselytes might perhaps have been known to the Talmud (comp. Ginzberg, Jewish Encyclopedia, I, 304), it is quite possible that Haman's descendant teaching at Bene Berak is none other than this great Tanna. As the name Haman remained in use among the Persians as late as the third century (comp. 'Erubin 63b; see Variae Lectiones, ad loc.), there is no reason to doubt the statement that one of R. Akiba's ancestors was called Haman, though not necessarily identical with the bearer of this name in the Bible. Comp. vol. VI, p. 195, note 72 (end). The description of Haman as the son of Hammedatha (Esther 3.1) is not to be taken literally, as Hammedatha is only used to describe him as the arch-enemy of the Jews. Seen Yerushalmi Yebamot 2, 4a; Aggadat Esther 26. It is, however, difficult to tell by what principle

of exegesis the Rabbis make המדתא to convey this meaning. Did they think of הם "confounded" and דתא "religion"? The name of Haman's mother was Emtelai, the same as that of Abraham's (comp. vol. I, p. 185), and his maternal grandfather was called Urbeti (עורבתי), *i. e.* "of the ravens". On the view that Haman was a Macedonian, see note 88.

⁹⁴ Abba Gorion 21. This passage also gives several reasons why "Haman was elevated before his fall", one of which is that God made him very rich so that Mordecai might later make use of Haman's treasures for the building of the Temple. Comp. the following note.

⁹⁵ Aggadat Esther 55. Of Haman's sons, his assistants in his Jew-baiting, special mention is made of Shimshai, who occurs also in Ezra 4.8 as denouncing the Jews before the king; 2 Panim Aherim 55 and 66. On Shimshai, see also Megillah 16a and Esther R., introduction, 3. Comp. also note 168. On Haman as an opponent to the building of the Temple, see Abba Gorion 20; Esther R. 3.1; note 105. In the last-named passage it is said that God elevated Haman before his fall in order that people should know thereby how severe is the punishment of those who attempt to obstruct the building of the Temple. Comp. Ratner's note 20 on Seder 'Olam 29.

⁹⁶ Megillah 12b; Targum Esther 1.16. Comp. vol. IV, p. 379.

⁹⁷ Abba Gorion 17; Esther R. 1.16. These sources do not state explicitly the identity of Memucan with Haman, but they seem to presuppose it. Comp. however, note 52

⁹⁸ Lekah 2.32 (very likely quoting an old source).

⁹⁹ Abba Gorion 21; Esther R. 3.1.

¹⁰⁰ PRE 50; Abba Gorion 22; Panim Aherim 46; Esther R. 2.5 and 3.1–2; Targum 3.2; Sanhedrin 61b (the king's command was to pay divine honors to Haman); Josephus *Antiqui.*, XI, 6.5 and 8; Additions to Esther (Prayer of Mordecai 7); comp. note 102.

¹⁰¹ 2 Panim Aherim 66

¹⁰² 2 Targum 3.4. This source obviously does not think that Haman asked for divine honors (comp. the references in the preceding note), and had not Mordecai been a Benjamite he might have paid homage to Haman. Comp., however, Abba Gorion 22; Panim Aherim 66; Esther R. 3.5 (where it is said that Mordecai cited the example of his ancestor Benjamin, though according to these sources Haman demanded divine honors, and the reference to Benjamin is therefore out of place, if we should not assume that it belonged to another source = Targum). On the reason why the Temple was built in the territory

allotted to the tribe of Benjamin, see note 926 on vol. III, p. 458.

¹⁰³ 2 Panim Aherim 66–67; Abba Gorion 23; Aggadat Esther 29.

¹⁰⁴ Josephus, *Antiqui.*, XI, 6.5; Panim Aherim 46. In Targum Esther 3.6, the hereditary enmity is traced further back to that between Jacob the ancestor of Mordecai and Esau the ancestor of the Amalekite Haman. Comp. PRE 50.

¹⁰⁵ Targum Esther as quoted by Alkabez, 155a–155b, and in abridged form in the MSS. of the Talmud, Megillah 15a–15b, where the printed texts are very abrupt. A somewhat different version of this legend is found in Aggadat Esther 55. According to this text, the incident of Haman's selling himself as a slave to Mordecai took place when they both journeyed from Jerusalem to Shushan to appear before the king in connection with the rebuilding of the Temple (comp. vol. IV, p. 393). The bill of sale was written on Mordecai's sandal and not on his knee-cap. Comp. vol. IV, p. 430.

¹⁰⁶ Megillah 13b.

¹⁰⁷ Abba Gorion 24–25; Panim Aherim 46, and 2 Panim Aherim 67; Esther R. and 2 Targum 3.7 (but not in all manuscripts of Targum). An essentially different version of this Haggadah is found in Aggadat Esther 27–29. On the view that the existence of the entire world depends on the existence of Israel, see vol. I, p. 3, and Index, s. v. "Israel". On the days of the week and Israel, see vol. I, pp. 51–52.

¹⁰⁸ Aggadat Esther 29, where it is also stated that Joshua made the sun stand still in the month of Tammuz; comp. Seder 'Olam 11. That Moses was born and died in Adar is an old tradition; comp. Megillah 13b, and the references given in note 44 on vol. II, p. 264. For other versions of this Haggadah concerning the selection of Adar, see Abba Gorion 25–26; 2 Panim Aherim 67–68; 2 Targum (but not in MSS. made use of by David), Lekah and Esther R. 3.7. The following memorable dates of the different months, as given in these sources, should be noticed: The death of Sarah in Heshwan, the organization of the Great Synagogue in Shebat, and the wars against the (worshippers of the) image of Micah in the same month. Comp. Megillat Ta'anit (Addition). The source made use of by Ibn Yahya, quoted by Alkabez, 99a–99b, is very likely related to, if not identical with, Aggadat Esther, *loc. cit.* Haman was a great astrologer (comp. PRE 50) like his forebear Amalek, who hoped to conquer Israel by attacking them at the time when they were under the influence of unlucky stars, but he was defeated by Joshua, who surpassed him in the knowledge of astrology and magic. Joshua

selected as his warriors against Amalek men who were born in the second
Adar, against whom witchcraft has no power. See R. Bahya on Exod.
17.9; R. Eleazar of Worms quoted by Alkabez, 100a. Comp. vol. III,
p. 60 (top).

¹⁰⁹ Aggadat Esther 30. Another version found in Abba Gorion
25–26; 2 Panim Aherim 67–68; Esther R. 3.7. According to PRE 50,
the day chosen by Haman for the annihilation of Israel was Tuesday,
because its constellation is the Lion; comp. Luria, *ad loc.*

¹¹⁰ Abba Gorion 26; Panim Aherim 46 (here it is said: As fish are
swelled, even so shall Haman and his sons be swelled up by the fire
of hell "every year"); Esther R. 1.7. Yalkut II, 1054, on Esther 3.8,
seems to have read a similar statement in Megillah 13b.

¹¹¹ Esther R. 3.7 (beginning); comp. also 2 Targum Esther 3.7,
which reads: When Haman cast lots in order to destroy the holy nation,
a heavenly voice was heard saying: "Fear not, congregation of Israel.
If thou turnest with repentance to God, the lot will fall upon Haman
instead of upon thee." This passage is not found in the MSS. of this
Targum made use of by David.

¹¹² 2 Targum 3.8, which partly follows old sources; comp.
Megilah 13b; Abba Gorion 26; 2 Panim Aherim 68; Aggadat Esther
30–31; Esther R. and Targum Esther 3.8. See also references in notes
114 and 115. It is noteworthy that 2 Targun made use of Palestinian,
as well as non-Palestinian (very likely Babylonian) sources. Haman
speaks of eight days of Passover and the two days of the Feast of
Weeks, and this reflects Jewish life in the diaspora, since in Palestine
the first festival consists of seven days and the second of one day. On
the other hand, the reference to the Sabbatical and Jubilee year
points to the Holy Land, for it is only in that country that the Jews
abstain from tilling the soil in these years. The very late date of the
final redaction of the 2 Targum is betrayed also by the reference to
the reading of the Torah and the translating (into Aramaic) from the
books of the Prophets. In pre-Arabic times the custom was to trans-
late the weekly sections of the Torah into the vernacular, that is, into
Aramaic. Only after Arabic supplanted Aramaic as the language of
the Jews, was the use of Targum limited to the Haftarot. On the throwing down of apples, see Munk, *ad loc.* The explanation given of the
custom of the procession with Hosha'anot is old; comp. PK 28, 180a–180b,
and the parallel passages cited by Buber, *ad loc.* The statement that
on the "Great Fast" (this designates the Day of Atonement only in
Palestinian sources; comp., *e. g.,* Yerushalmi Rosh ha-Shanah 1, 57b,

and 'Abodah Zarah 1, 39b) little children are made to fast is not to be taken literally. Comp. Mishnah and Talmud Yoma 82a.

¹¹³ Abba Gorion 26–29 (in the last line of 26 read מנית instead of זנית); Panim Aherim 68–69; Esther R. 3.8–9; Aggadat Esther 33–34. On Pharaoh as a "cosmocrator", see vol. I, p. 178. As to the vast number of his hosts drowned in the Red Sea, comp. note 43 on vol. III, p. 25. On Amalek, see vol. III, p. 56. On Sisera, see vol. IV, p. 36. On the idea that the existence of the universe is dependent on Israel, see vol. I, p. 3; vol. IV p. 399; Index, s. v. "Israel".

¹¹⁴ Panim Aherim 47; all the other sources (comp. the following note) state that Ahasuerus issued the decree of annihilation. The designation of Haman as "next unto the king" in Panim Aherim is no proof of its dependence on Septuagint (comp. the following note); both sources very likely gave Haman this title which, according to Esther 10.2, was borne by Mordecai.

¹¹⁵ Midrash Esther 68–69; Abba Gorion 29–32 (in Hebrew and Aramaic; the latter seems to be the original form, as the opening line of the Hebrew version is in Aramaic); Esther R. 3.8; Lekah 3.12; Aggadat Esther 36; Yerahmeel 81, 241–244 (the decree of Haman and the edict of Ahasuerus are here combined into one, to which are added many sentences, found in old sources, of the conversation between Haman and the king about the Jews); 2 Targum Esther 3.8 (towards the end) and 4.1. The text of the first passage of Targum contains several corruptions. The sentence ולית אנחנא ידעין (p. 25, line 5, in David's edition) is a gloss to p. 24, line 22, as a variant to ולא ידעין; p. 25, line 10, reads: כל דובנין בשויא זבנין. The accusation made against the Jews is that they buy at low prices and sell at great profits. In contrast to the Midrashim, Targum maintains that Haman's denunciation of the Jews was made in oral conversation with the king. Comp. Megillah 13b, and Yerahmeel, *loc. cit.* As to the statement in Targum that "some of them are dealers in wax", see vol. VI, pp. 264 (top) and 268, note 110 (end). The Greek Additions to Esther (Addition B) contain a letter of the king to the princes of the provinces and the subordinate governors, in which, after calling attention to his "moderation and mildness", he informs them that at the advice of the wise Haman, who is exalted to "the second place in the kingdom" (comp. the preceding note), he decreed the annihilation of the Jewish people, the "nation that stands alone in opposition to all men continually." Josephus, *Antiqui.*, XI, 6.6, used the apocryphal letter of the king, but allowed himself a great deal of liberty in reproducing its text. The rabbinical versions of the letter are, on the

other hand, entirely independent of the Greek Additions. It is, however, to be noted that besides the letter of the king, Addition B knows also of the letters of Haman, just as the Midrashim have a decree by Haman and an edict by Ahasuerus. The Arabic version of Haman's decree (comp. Hirschfeld in *Semitic Studies in memory of Kohut*, 248, seq.) s an almost literal translation of 2 Targum Esther 4.1, and it is strange that this fact escaped Hirschfeld. Perreau published from a Parma MS. another letter of Haman which agrees with Aggadat Esther and Yerahmeel, in *Hebräische Bibliographie*, VII, 46, seq.

116 Abba Gorion 27–29; 2 Panim Aherim 69; Esther R. and 2 Targum 3.9; comp. Tosafot on Megillah 16a (caption ירדי). According to ShR 33.5, Haman offered all his silver and gold as a price for the Jews. See Abba Gorion 29 and Esther R. 3.11. When Ahasuerus said to Haman: "The silver is given thee" (Esther 3.11), the Holy Spirit called out: "The gallows is given thee." This is a play on כסף "silver" and עץ "gallows", both of which words have the same numerical value. On the half-shekel as the basis for Haman's computing the price for the Jews, see Yerushalmi Megillah 1, 70d, and 3, 74a; *Kad ha-Kemah*, Purim, II, 47a.

117 Aggadat Esther 35.

118 Panim Aherim 51 and 2 Panim Aherim 69; Esther R. and 2 Targum 3.14–15. The last-named passage reads: Because Joseph's brethren sold him unto a foreign land, their descendants were sold unto a foreign land (= to a foreigner); but as Benjamin did not take part in this transaction, his descendants Mordecai and Esther became the redeemers of Israel. Comp. vol. II, p. 16–17; Tehillim 10, 93.

119 Megillah 14a (top), and 11a; (here it is said that Ahasuerus hated the Jews more than Haman); Abba Gorion 29; Esther R. 23.10. Comp. vol. IV, p. 406. The attacks of Ahasuerus and Haman on Israel are taken to have been aimed at God; comp. vol. IV, p. 406; 2 Panim Aherim 69.

120 2 Panim Aherim 69.

121 Esther R. 3.15; 2 Targum 4.2. Comp. Esther R., introduction,3.

122 Abba Gorion 32–35; BHM V, 55–56; Esther R. 3.4 (towards the end); Aggadat Esther 38–40. Panim Aherim 47 reads as follows: God sent for the patriarchs and said unto them: "Your children deserve to be destroyed." "Why?" they asked. God replied: "Because they did not sanctify My name in the days of Nebuchadnezzar the wicked, and made it appear as though I had no power to save them." The

patriarchs rejoined: "Do Thou with them as Thou pleasest." When God saw that the attribute of justice was about to prevail, He rose from the throne of justice, and seated Himself on the throne of mercy. The entire "heavenly family" pleaded for Israel, saying: "Didst Thou not create the universe for the sake of the Torah given to Israel, so that its existence depends upon the existence of Israel? If Thou destroyest this nation, what will become of us?" God replied: "Israel did not act as they should." The "heavenly family" continued to plead: "It is known and revealed before Thee that what they did (in obeying Nebuchadnezzar's command to worship the image erected by him) was out of fear." On hearing this pleading God was filled with mercy for Israel. As to the question whether Israel in Mordecai's days deserved to be destroyed on account of their sins, and on the nature of these sins, see PK 19, 140a; PR 33, 151ᵇ (their lack of trust in God nearly brought about their destruction, were it not for the fact that even Jacob, when in distress, despaired of God's help, and they followed the example of their ancestor; comp. note 240 on vol. I, p. 381); comp. further Ekah 3, 134, and the references cited in notes 16, 17. On the idea that the universe depended on the preservation of Israel, comp. vol. I, p. 3; vol. IV, pp. 399, 407; Index, s. v. "Israel". Divination by passages from books (stichomancy), especially by passages from the Bible (Biblomancy) is found in the Talmud (comp. e. g., Hagigah 15a–15b; Hullin 95b), and hence it is quite natural for the legend to make Mordecai ask the children the scriptural verses they had studied. The three verses recited by the children were later inserted in the daily prayer; comp. Baer, 'Abodat Israel (end of 'Alenu). On the wandering of the scholars from town to town, see Baba Batra 8a; on the intercession of the saints among the dead, see vol. IV, 39. The designation of Moses as the faithful shepherd is of frequent occurrence; comp. vol. II, p. 300; vol. IV, p. 308. As to the sealing of the heavenly decree, see vol. III, p. 417, and note 26 on vol. IV, p. 302. According to 2 Targum Esther 4.1 (beginning; part of the text is very obscure), the Holy Spirit revealed to Mordecai the danger threatening Israel (comp. Alkabez, 125a), whereas Targum Esther 4.1 agrees with the Midrashim cited at the beginning of this note, that it was Elijah who gave him this information.

¹²³ 2 Targum Esther 4.1. The passage from וכד אתחייבו to הוא בלחודוי (p. 28. lines 4–9, in David's edition) does not belong to the end, but is a variant of line 1 (p.11, line 12). On the covering of the ark with sackcloth, see Ta'anit 2.1; on the inhabitants of Nineveh, see ibid., and vol. IV, pp. 250–251. The verses of the Bible read by Mordecai (Deut. 4.30–31) are taken from the section read on the Fast of Ab (Tosefta Megillah 4.9 and Babli 31b), but it would seem from this passage

of the Targum that it was read on all fast-days. The custom prevailing now to read Exod. 32.11–14 and 34.1–10 dates from the time of the Geonim; the Mishnah, Megillah (end), has Lev. 26 and Deut. 28 as the sections for fast-days. Comp. also vol. IV, p. 280. The prayer of Mordecai in the Greek Addenda reads like an insertion in the first benediction of the 'Amidah, and accordingly it begins with the description of God in whose power is the entire world, and closes with the supplication to the God of Abraham to redeem His inheritance. This corresponds to קונה הכל...מלך עוזר ומושיע... יי מגן אברהם in the first benediction of the 'Amidah. Josephus, *Antiqui.*, XI, 6.8, follows Septuagint, though not verbatim.

¹²⁴ PRE 50. This short prayer reminds one of the Prayer of Mordecai in the Septuagint. Comp. the preceding note. A Hebrew translation of the Prayer of Mordecai is found in Josippon 4 and hence in numerous later rabbinic works, as, *e. g.*, in Esther R. 4.10, and Yerahmeel 89, 237. Comp. Schürer, *Geschichte*, III, 450–451.

¹²⁵ 2 Panim Aherim 70, in explanation of Esther 4.1. A different explanation of this passage is given in Panim Aherim 51, which reads: He cried: Wrong will be done to the king who does wrong to the innocent. See also Septuagint, which reads: He cried with a loud voice: A nation which has done no wrong is going to be destroyed. On the correct reading of Panim Aherim, see Alkabez, 125a. Comp. also Megillah 15a with regard to the words used by Mordecai in his loud crying.

¹²⁶ BR 67.4; Esther R. 4.1; Panim Aherim 51; comp. vol. I, pp. 321 and 339.

¹²⁷ Abba Gorion 35; Panim Aherim 51 (this passage contains also another opinion to the effect that Esther took precautions to prevent pregnancy; comp., however, note 80); 2 Panim Aherim 70; Esther R. 4.9. Comp. also the different views about the effects of the queen's fright as stated in Megillah 15a and PRE 50.

¹²⁸ 2 Panim Aherim 70; Aggadat Esther 42; Esther R. 4.1. Comp. also BR 84.20; Tehillim 10, 93; Panim Aherim 51; Aggadat Esther 40; vol. II, p. 100.

¹²⁹ Megillah 15b; Baba Batra 4a (according to some authorities, Daniel was called so, because he "decided" the most important affairs of state; according to others, because he was "cut off by Ahasuerus" from the important position he held under the former king; Hathach is derived from חתך "he cut off", "he decided"); Esther R. and Targum 4.5.

¹³⁰ Aggadat Esther 43; comp. vol. I, p. 371.

[131] Abba Gorion 36; 2 Panim Aherim 70 (read ברמז instead of ברוח הקודש, which crept into the text from the next paragraph); Esther R. 4.7.

[132] Esther R. 4.7; Midrash Esther 67; Aggadat Esther 43. The source upon which these Midrashim drew is very likely Josippon 4, where the Dream of Mordecai found in the Greek Additions to Esther is translated into Hebrew. BHM V, 1.16, contains a Hebrew as well as an Aramaic translation of this apocryphal piece. See Schürer, *Geschichte*, III, 450–451. Mekilta Amalek 2, 55a and 56a (= Esther R. 2.7), remarks: Mordecai took notice of the "hint" given him from above. This refers perhaps to the dream in which the future history of Esther was revealed to him. Comp. however vol. IV, p. 421 and note 136.

[133] Aggadat Esther 43; 2 Panim Aherim 70.

[134] 2 Targum Esther 4.1. Comp. vol. IV, pp. 387–388 and 427.

[135] Targum Esther 4.11 Against this view, comp. Josephus, *Antiqui.*, XI, 6.3.

[136] Targum Esther 4.10; Mekilta Amalek 2, 56a; Esther R. 2.7. Comp. note 132.

[137] Abba Gorion 36; 2 Panim Aherim 70; PRE 50; 1 and 2 Targum 4.11. According to Megillah 15a, Hathach did not want to be the harbinger of a painful message, and accordingly Esther was forced to find somebody else to act as an intermediary. Josephus, *Antiqui.*, XI, 6.7, on the other hand, emphasizes the fact that the same person (Hathach) carried on the negotiations between Mordecai and Esther.

[138] Targum Esther 4.12; according to 2 Targum, after the death of Hathach written messages were sent by the queen to Mordecai. A third view is that the Holy Spirit was the intermediary between the two. Comp. Abba Gorion 36 and 2 Panim Aherim 70. PRE 50 maintains that Esther communicated with Mordecai by word of mouth.

[139] Esther R. 4.14. A somewhat different account is found in Josephus, *Antiqui.*, XI, 6.7, which reads: There would certainly arise help from God some other way, but she and her father's house would be destroyed by those whom she now neglected. It seems that Josephus was acquainted with the haggadic interpretation according to which מקום (Esther 4.14) stand for God; comp. Tehillim 22, 182; Targum, Lekah, and Esther R., *ad loc.* See also Buber, note 50 on Aggadat Esther 44. The designation of God as מקום "Place" is found in as early an author as Philo; comp. *De Somniis* 1.11 and Index, s. v. "Place".

[140] 2 Targum Esther 4.13–14. As to the view that Saul was responsible for the suffering of the Jews at the hands of Haman, comp.

Esther R., introduction, 7, and vol. IV, p. 68. On the view that Joshua
slew Amalek by the word of God (this is meant by במילת דשמיא), comp.
vol. IV, pp. 3–4. The passage beginning with וכד קם (not found in
all MSS.) at the end of verse 13 is certainly a later addition. It is
also possible that the sentence אלא אידכרי...לתקלא, if genuine, should
be put at the beginning of this verse where Saul's guilt is pointed out.
The exhortation to prayer is also found in Septuagint 4.8, where המלך
is referred to God; comp. Esther R. 1.9 and Megillah 15a with reference
to the use of מלך "King" in the book of Esther in the sense of the
"Heavenly King". Comp. notes 161, 171, 177.

    141 2 Panim Aherim 70–71. The reason for this fast was to atone
for the sin of the Jews who had partaken of forbidden food at the banquet
of Ahasuerus; Tehillim 22, 182; vol. IV, p. 370. Megillah 15a, Esther R. and 2 Targum 4.16 (the MSS. show that the sentence in Targum beginning with דעד השתא is a later addition, based on the Talmud)
maintain that the queen pointed out to Mordecai the great sacrifice
she is bringing. By going voluntarily to Ahasuerus she was for ever
cutting herself off from her legitimate husband (i. e. Mordecai; comp.
vol. IV, p. 387), as the law does not permit the reunion of husband and
wife if the latter of her own free will, had relations with another man.
Opinions differ as to how the three days' fast is to be understood. Yebamot 121a and PRE 50 are of the opinion that the fast lasted for seventy-
two consecutive hours. On the other hand, Tehillim 22, 183, maintains
that this would have been a physical impossibility; accordingly the fast
lasted really only a little more than twenty-four hours. They began
the fast shortly before night, and finished it shortly after the beginning
of the following night. The Bible calls it a three days' fast because
it began on one day and ended on the third. Comp. Yoma 81b;
Torat ha-Adam 29–81b; Alkabez, 136.

    142 Megillah 15a (comp. Rabbinovicz, *ad loc.*) and Aggadat Esther
45; this is an explanation of ויעבר in 4.17, literally "and he passed over".
Targum, *ad loc.*, interprets the word to mean "and he transgressed the
law", which forbids fasting on festivals; comp. references cited in the
preceding note. According to Seder 'Olam 39, PRE 50, and Esther R.
3.17, the three fast-days were the thirteenth, the fourteenth, and fifteenth
of Nisan, whereas according to Panim Aherim 71 (is this the source of
Rashi on Megillah, *loc. cit.?*), they were the fourteenth, fifteenth, and
sixteenth of that month. The latter view seems to have been shared by
Koheleth 8.5, which reads: *Whoso keepeth the commandment shall
know no evil thing* (Eccles. 8.5); this refers to Esther who was busy

471

in carrying out the commandment of "searching for leaven" (this ceremony takes place at night from the thirteenth to the fourteenth of Nisan), and knew not of the evil decreed by Haman against the Jews. The statement, however, that Mordecai went on the first day of Passover to Shushan to arrange for the fast (one of the main features of the fast was the gathering of the people for public prayer) could only be explained if the fast-days were on the fifteenth, sixteenth, and seventeenth of Nisan. Comp. note 146, and Luria on PRE, *loc. cit.*

143 2 Targum 4.16–5.1. The prayer '*Anenu* taken from the ritual for fast-days is given in Hebrew. The second part of the prayer, beginning with a new alphabet (in the first alphabet read אזה הא אנחנא instead of וזה), is perhaps the oldest specimen of an 'Akedah. On the view that Israel and the Torah are necessary for the existence of the world, see vol. I, p. 3, and Index, s. v. "Israel" and "Torah". Ahasuerus is called in Targum Esther "a foolish king"; see vol. IV, p. 374, and notes 7, 49. In the days of this king the curse was fulfilled: "and there ye shall sell yourselves, etc." (Deut. 28.68); see Megillah 11a; Esther R., introduction, 3. The suffering of innocent children does not fail to arouse God's compassion; see vol. IV, p. 251. God created the world with His left hand; see note 3 on vol. I, p. 3. The angels wept when Abraham was about to sacrifice his son Isaac; vol I, p. 281. The prayer of Esther as found in the Greek Additions to Esther occurs in Josippon 4, whence it is borrowed by many other writers (comp. *e. g.*, BHM V, 5–8 and 12–16, where the Hebrew and Aramaic translations from the Greek [Latin?] text are found), but Targum did not make use of it.

144 Additions to Esther, Addition D; a Hebrew translation thereof is found in Josippon 4. Comp. also Yerahmeel 80, 240.

145 Megillah 15a–15b; 2 Panim Aherim 71. The Talmud further remarks that Esther thought she had committed a sin in describing Ahasuerus, in her prayer, as a dog. To make amends for her disrespect, she later, in her prayer, refered to him as a lion. This remark of the Talmud, as well as the other, that she cried out: "Eli Eli, Lammah 'azabtani,'' is based on the assumption that in Ps. 22 we have the prayer of Esther before she appeared before the king. Tehillim 22, 180–197, contains a paraphrase of this chapter, giving details of Esther's life alluded to therein. See also Yoma 29a. That in the apocryphal prayer of Esther Ahasuerus is called a lion by Esther, has very likely nothing to do with the rabbinical interpretation of this psalm as containing Esther's prayer. Simonsen, *R.E.J.*, XXII, 283–285, explains

the typological interpretation of this psalm by the authors of the New Testament (comp., *e. g.*, Matth. 27.46; Mark 15.34), who refer it to the passion of Jesus, to be due to the fact that this Esther psalm was recited in the Temple and in the synagogue on the fourteenth of Nisan, the original fast of Esther, and it was quite natural for the early Christians to substitute, for the suffering of Esther, the passion of Jesus, which took place on the very same day. This hypothesis, however, cannot be accepted for two valid reasons. In the first place, it may be stated with certainty that the day on which the paschal lamb was sacrificed, far from being a fast-day, was a festival day (comp. Pesahim 4.1 and 5; Yerushalmi , beginning; Megillah Ta'anit 1; Judith 8.6). Then the old sources are of the opinion that Esther fasted not on the fourteenth of Nisan, but on the fifteenth; comp. note 142. It is true the Karaites observe the Fast of Esther on the three days preceding passover (comp. Bashyazi, *Aderet Eliyahu*, end of חג המצות) but this obviously does not prove anything. A short prayer of Esther is found in Targum Esther 5.1.

¹⁴⁶ Tehillim 22, 188, 193, 194; Comp. also 183 (where the words addressed by Esther to God read differently) and 184. On the twenty-second psalm, see the preceding note. On the comparison between Esther and Vashti, comp. note 35. The words used by Ahasuerus, "O for the departed, etc.", are a favorite phrase with the Rabbis; comp. *e. g.*, vol. III, p. 339, with regard to the superiority of the patriarchs to Moses. The Addenda to Esther (Addition D) contain a description of Esther's appearance before the king, which in many points reminds one of that of the Midrash. Note especially the statement in Septuagint that the king beholding Esther looked upon her with fierce wrath, so that she swooned; God then changed the spirit of the king into mildness and the king sprang up from his throne, and raised her in his arms until she came to herself again. Josippon 4 contains a Hebrew translation of this Addition to Esther. Comp. also Esther R. 5.1; BHM V, 13–14. Tehillim, *loc. cit.*, is the source for Aggadat Esther 52–53, as well as for 2 Targum 5.1, where ובני דהמן is to be read instead of המן, in accordance with Tehillim 22, 193.

¹⁴⁷ Megillah 15b; the three angels remind one of the attendants of Esther in the Addition to Esther; comp. vol. IV, p. 427.

¹⁴⁸ 2 Panim Aherim 71. Comp. also Tehillim 22, 194, which reads: An angel struck a blow upon the king's mouth (the text is incomplete, and hence obscure; something was very likely said about a remark made by Ahasuerus derogatory to Esther; comp. *ibid.*, 193), and said

to him: "Thy spouse stands waiting, and thou sittest on thy throne." The queen's charm captivated him against his will, and he arose to meet her.

149 2 Panim Aherim 71. Here it is also stated that Ahasuerus was blind, but his eyes became bright as soon as he directed them towards Esther; whereupon he held out the golden sceptre to her. A miracle happened, and the sceptre extended to the place where Esther stood (the distance is variously described as twelve, sixteen, twenty-four, sixty, and two hundred cubits), so that she was able to touch it. Yea, a still greater miracle happened. Whenever Esther visited the king, the sceptre of its own accord would move towards her; Megillah 15b; Tehillim 22, 194–195.

150 Targum Esther 5.3; Megillah 15b; comp. vol. IV, p. 393.

151 Megillah 15b, where several other reasons are given for this peculiar conduct; comp. also 2 Targum 5.8, and 2 Panim Aherim 71.

152 Panim Aherim 71. The somewhat obscure sentence שלא היתה שומעת וגו׳ means that up to this time Esther did not consent to gratify the king's desire; but now she promised that she would no longer withhold her conjugal duties. On the only wish of the queen that the king would not grant, see the references in the preceding note.

153 PRE 50; Esther R. 5.11 (end). The statement made in the latter source that God would not permit the pious to suffer more than three days, and that accordingly Haman's fall took place on the fifteenth of Nisan, three days after the issue of the decree of annihilation (on the date, see note 142) is based on an old Haggadah; comp. BR 91.7 and 56.1; Tehillim 22, 183.

154 Aggadat Esther 55. Comp. vol. IV, pp. 398–399.

155 Abba Gorion 36,2; Panim Aherim 72 (read with Aggadat Esther 55: יצא בעלך לקרוי פוק לשוק "if thy husband left for the country, it is time for thee to visit the market-place"); Esther R. 5.11.

156 Megillah 15b (top).

157 2 Panim Aherim 72.

158 Abba Gorion 36–37 (on the מולא "furnace" from which Manasseh was saved, see vol. IV, p. 279); 2 Panim Aherim 72; Esther R.5.11; 2 Targum 5.11, where read תנורא "furnace" instead of תורא "ox". On the number of Haman's children, concerning which opinions vary greatly (it is given as thirty, one hundred, two hundred and eight), comp. Megillah 15b; Targum Esther 5.11; Tehillim 22, 181; vol. IV, p. 445. On the view that the pious are saved from all kinds of death, see also vol. II, p. 256.

159 2 Targum 5.14; Abba Gorion 37; Panim Aherim 48 (here Gabriel takes the place of the heavenly voice); Esther R. 5.11; BHM VI, 56; Aggadat Esther 61; an unknown Midrash in Yalkut II, 1059, on Esther 7. In the last two sources the carpenter and smith employed by Haman to make the cross are mentioned by name. According to 2 Panim Aherim 72, Zeresh advised her hubsand not to engage in any evil designs against Mordecai, because the Jews are like a stone: if any one falls on it, he gets hurt; and if it falls on any one, he gets bruised. Haman, however, did not follow her counsel, but that given him by his friends. On the comparison between Israel and a stone, see also Abba Gorion 24 and Esther R. 3.6.

160 2 Targum Esther 6.1; Panim Aherim 73–74; comp. PK 5, 55b; PR 15, 78, as well as the references given in note 76 on vol. I, p. 224, and vol. II, p. 373, with regard to the first night of Passover as the night of miracles. According to some, however, the "disturbed night" was the second night of Passover. Comp. Note 142.

161 Megillah 15b (on the interpretation of מלך "king", Esther 6.12, as referring to the "King of the world", *i. e.* God, see note 140); PRE 50; Panim Aherim 48; 2 Panim Aherim 73; Esther R. and Targumim 6.1.

162 Abba Gorion 37–38 (on the last sentence about the innocent babes, see Makiri on Ps. 8, 50); Esther R. 5.12; BHM VI, 56; 2 Targum Esther 6.1 (Munk's edition). Comp. also Ekah 1, 69–70.

163 2 Targum 6.1. According to another reading, it was the "angel of insomnia" who kept the king awake. Comp. also the following note, and note 167.

164 Abba Gorion 38–39; Panim Aherim 48 (this passage has Michael instead of Gabriel); 2 Panim Aherim 74. The number of times Ahasuerus was thrown out of bed corresponds to the days of the solar year. This correspondence to the solar year is to be noticed also in the number of Haman's counsellors (comp. vol. IV, p. 430). In Aggadat Esther "sixty-one" is to be corrected accordingly. Some maintain that Ahasuerus saw, in a dream, Haman assuming a threatening attitude, and this disturbed his sleep greatly. When shortly after that Haman in the presence of the king expressed his wish to be attired in the royal insignia, Ahasuerus saw in it the fulfilment of his dream; comp. PRE 50; Koheleth 5.2; Esther R. 6.1; BHM VI, 57; Yalkut II, 1057, on Esther 7 (derived from an unknown source); Panim Aherim 75; Targum 5.1.

165 Megillah 15b; Panim Aherim 48; 2 Panim Aherim 74.

166 Megillah 15b; Panim Aherim 48; 2 Panim Aherim 74; comp. Josephus, *Antiqui.*, XI, 6. 10.

167 2 Targum Esther 6.1 (David's edition). Elsewhere it is Satan, the great adversary of man, who appears in the disguise of a beggar. Comp. note 226 on vol. I, p. 272.

168 PRE 50; BHM VI, 57; Abba Gorion 39; 2 Panim Aherim 74–75; Yalkut II, 1057 (towards the end); 2 Targum Esther 6.1 and 9. Comp. also Alkabez, 159b; Midrash Eliyyahu II, 161b; the references in note 164. Shimshai the son of Haman (comp. note 95) was secretary to the king, and in order not to be made to read the passage about Mordecai, he struck it out; but Gabriel (or according to 2 Panim Aherim 75 and Yalkut, *loc. cit.*, Elijah) wrote it down again as soon as it was struck out. See Megillah 15b; 2 Targum, *loc. cit.*; comp. also *Kad ha-Kemah*, Purim, 2, 47–48. In 2 Targum 6.1 read שמשי ספרא instead of עם שופרא, which gives no sense.

169 2 Targum Esther 56.10 (the horse שיפרמ is very likely identical with the famous horse Shabdaz of the Persian king Khorsau II; comp. Yakut III, 250 *seq.*, and accordingly the correct reading is שיפרז); Megillah 16a; PRE 50; BH VI, 57; 2 Panim Aherim 75; Aggadat Esther 62–63. In the last-named source, as well as in Abba Gorion 39, a badly corrupted passage is given about the royal raiment. Comp. Ginzberg's remarks in *Orientalistische Litteraturzeitung* XVIII, 180, top, where it is shown that the Midrash speaks here of Labrat-Lilat as having woven those garments. Comp. also Targum Esther 6.10.

170 Megillah 16a; PK 8, 71b–72b (on the village קרינוס where Haman or, according to others, his father, was a barber, comp. Schlatter, *Verkanntes Griechisch* 65–66 and vol. V, pp. 385-386); PR 18, 93a–93b; WR 28.6; Abba Gorion 40–41; 2 Panim Aherim 75–76; BHM VI, 57; Esther R. 6.10; 2 Targum 6.11; Aggadat Esther 63–64. That Mordecai first thought Haman was mocking him is also stated by Josephus, *Antiqui.*, XI, 6.10. On the view that Haman's fall took place on the day of the 'Omer, that is, on the sixteenth day of Nisan, see note 142.

171 2 Targum 6.11; 2 Panim Aherim 76. According to the latter source and Abba Gorion 41, Mordecai was led in a torch procession; comp. the procession in honor of Joseph, vol. II, p. 74. On the interpretation of "king" in 6.11 as God, the King of the universe, see notes 140 and 161.

172 PK 8, 72b; PR 18, 93b; WR 28. 6; Abba Gorion 41; BHM VI 57; Esther R. and 2 Targum 6.11. The four first-named Midrashim give also the different view according to which Mordecai

Esther [173-176]

did not pay any attention to the honors shown to him. The reason was because the procession started early in the morning when he was reciting the Shema' (comp. Abba Gorion 39, which reads: Haman intended to hang Mordecai at the time of the reading of the Shema'), and he would not permit himself to interrupt his prayer. Comp. similar legends in vol. II, p. 121, with regard to Jacob and in vol. IV, p. 349 (top), with regard to Daniel. According to 2 Panim Aherim 76, Mordecai expressed his thanks to God by reciting the *Hodu* psalm (*i. e.*, Ps. 136), the so-called Great Hallel; comp. Pesahim 117a, where it is stated that Mordecai and Esther composed the Hallel at the time when Haman arose against them.

173 Megillah 16a, and somewhat differently in 2 Panim Aherim 76 and Esther R. 6.11, where it is said that Haman's daughter threw herself out of the window when she realized her father's disgrace. Comp. also Buber's note 38 on Abba Gorion 41. According to Targum Esther 5.1, this daughter of Haman was one of the maidens gathered together in Shushan from among whom a queen was to be selected in the place of Vashti. Her own hopes and her father's expectation were sorely disappointed when a repulsive disease attacked her. Comp. also 2 Targum (Munk's edition), note 291.

174 Megillah 16a; Abba Gorion 41; 2 Panim Aherim 76; Esther R. 6.12. The last-named three sources as well as 2 Targum Esther 6.12 point out that on this day Haman had to perform four kinds of menial services: he acted as barber, masseur, groom, and herald to Mordecai. Comp. vol. IV, pp. 438–439. Alkabez, 167b, quotes from the commentary of R. Eleazar of Worms on Esther that Haman became a leper on that day. Comp. also *ibid.*, 172b.

175 Targum Esther 6.13. According to Megillah 16a, Panim Aherim 48, 2 Panim Aherim 76, and Aggadat Esther 65–66, Zeresh told her husband that he might prevail against any other Israelite, but not against a descendant of the tribe of Judah (יהודים in Esther 6.13 is taken in its original meaning) or the Rachel tribes, who, especially the latter, are always chosen by God to gain victory for Israel. Comp. vol. I, p. 369; vol. III, pp. 57–58 and 223. 2 Targum 6.6 makes Zeresh say to her husband that if his adversary is a descendant or a relative (read קרובי instead of עבדי) of Hananiah, Mishael, and Azariah he would certainly not prevail against him.

176 Abba Gorion 41 (read כתובין "secretaries", instead of כדובין, corresponding to סופרי המלך in PRE 50; in Yalkut II, 1057, סקריטורין is very likely to be read instead of סקנדרין); 2 Panim Aherim 76; Megil-

477

lah 16a. As to the positions held by the sons of Haman, see references cited in note 168 and Ratner's note 20 on Seder 'Olam 29.

¹⁷⁷ Targum Esther 7.3. The first מלך in this verse is taken to refer to God, the second to Ahasuerus; comp. notes 140, 161 and 171. Ahasuerus was wroth with Esther because she continued to withhold from him the secret of her descent. See Panim Aherim 76; comp. the following note.

¹⁷⁸ Megillah 16a; WR 26.8, which reads: The king hinted to her that she should appear as Haman's accuser even if he were not her enemy and that of her people. See Tan. B. III, 84; Tan. Emor 3; Ekah 1.13 (not in ed. Buber); 2 Targum Esther 7.5; Shemuel 24.121– 122. Targum maintains that at that moment the king did not yet know of Esther's noble descent, and accordingly conversed with her through an interpreter. This is perhaps the view of the Midrashim cited above, but Megillah, *loc. cit.*, explicitly states that on this occasion Esther told the king "who she was".

¹⁷⁹ Megillah 16a; on the correct text of this passage, see Rabbinovicz *ad loc.* and Aggadat Esther 66. On Haman as the one who was responsible for Vashti's death, see vol. IV, p. 379.

¹⁸⁰ Targum Esther 7.6; 2 Panim Aherim 76, which reads: He is the adversary of the celestial, the oppressor of the terrestrial, the enemy of the fathers (read לאבות instead of לאומות) and the oppressor of their children. Comp. also 2 Targum Esther 7.6, which reads: This is the one (הא מן=המן) who wished to stretch his hand against the Jewish people, the children of the "Lord of All".

¹⁸¹ Megillah 16a; PRE 50 (where it is said Michael, assuming the form of one of Haman's sons, felled down the trees); 2 Panim Aherim, 76–77; Targum Esther 7.7; an unknown Midrash quoted in the commentary on Esther by R. Judah ibn Shoshan, as cited by Alkabez, 172a. Comp. note 178. According to 2 Targum 77, Ahasuerus commanded to fell trees in the park, so that his anger should find an outlet, but he failed of his object.

¹⁸² Panim Aherim 77. The proverb about the ox reads here: Once the ox has been cast to the ground, many slaughterers are found. Comp., however, Ekah 1, 71; Shabbat 32a. See also Yalkut II, 1059, where הרבה is very likely to be read instead of הבא As to the "wicked" Harbonah being originally a party to the plot against Mordecai, see also Megillah 16a, and 2 Targum Esther 7.9. On the identification of Harbonah with Elijah, see vol. IV, p. 202.

¹⁸³ 2 Targum Esther 7.10, where Haman's entreaties are given in full.

¹⁸⁴ Abba Gorion 41–42; Panim Aherim 47–48; Yalkut II, 1054; Aggadat Esther 60–61; Esther R. 5.11, where the description of the competition of the trees is given in a more elaborate form than in the other Midrashim. An entirely different version of this legend about the cross of Haman is found in 2 Panim Aherim 77 (here it is the cedar-tree which furnishes the cross) and Aggadat Esther 51–58, with which account 2 Targun 7.10 partly agrees. In these sources none of the trees was willing to furnish the cross, because it did not wish to be defiled by the "impure body" of Haman. There can be no doubt that originally those were two different legends: one about the refusal of the trees to furnish the cross for Mordecai, and another about the competition of the trees for the distinction to be used as the cross for Haman. The present form of the legends is rather confused owing to the fact that the cross used for Haman had originally been intended for Mordecai, and accordingly the different motives of the legends could no longer be kept apart. It is difficult to establish the relation of this legend to the Christian legend about the cross of Jesus, but there can be no doubt that there exists some connection between the two cross legends. In 2 Targum, *loc. cit.*, read למסיק לאאכסניא דבר פנדירא, Haman is said to have taken the same "lodging" as the son of Pandora, *i. e.*, Jesus. As to the provenance of the cedar of which the cross was made for Haman, comp. the two views given in Abba Gorion 37. According to one, it was taken from the royal park (comp. Esther 7.8), while the other maintains that it was one of the cedar-trees used by Noah for the ark and was brought to Shushan by Haman's son Parshandatha, who was governor of קרדוניא, where the ark "rested" (comp. note 48 on vol. I, p. 165). He gave it to his father to be used for the cross upon which to hang Mordecai. Comp. also Yalkut I, 256 (end), and II, 1059, as well as 2 Panim Aherim 72–73. According to PRE 50, the cross was made of a beam taken from the holy of holies.

¹⁸⁵ 2 Targum Esther 9.14; Aggadat Esther 73 and Lekah on 9.14, and somewhat differently 1 Targun, which contains also the additional remark that one hundred and eight children of Haman were killed in Shushan. Shimshai was decapitated, and seventy others, as well as Zeresh, fled and were reduced to beggary. That the cross was fifty cubits high and twelve wide is also stated by Abba Gorion 37, and Aggadat Esther 51. On the number of Haman's sons, see notes 158, and 187.

¹⁸⁶ 2 Targum Esther 9.24. Comp. vol. IV, p. 111.

¹⁸⁷ Megillah 15b, which gives also the different view that seventy of Haman's sons became beggars; comp. notes 158 and 185, as well the following note.

¹⁸⁸ Tehillim 21, 181. Comp. Megillah 10b (bottom). Esther received Haman's house with all its treasures, and she appointed Mordecai as superintendent; Targum Esther 8.1–2; Aggadat Esther 70. Comp. also Sabba', Ha'azinu, 162b, who quotes from the Targum of Jonathan ben Uzziel that those killed by the Jews in Shushan were the children of Haman, and those killed in other cities were all Amalekites. Our Targum of Esther 9.14–17 reads somewhat differently.

¹⁸⁹ BR 39.11; PRE 50 (in Luria's edition the text is abridged); Esther R. 8.15; 2 Targum 6.10 (towards the end). The sudden change in Mordecai's life is dwelt upon in Tehillim 22, 184 and Tan. Mikkez 3, and a parallel is drawn between his history and that of his ancestor Joseph. Comp. BR 87.6; Abba Gorion 22; 2 Panim Aherim 66; Esther R. 3.4. A fantastic description of the five presents received by Mordecai from the king (Esther 8.15–16) is found in 2 Targum Esther (David's edition, *ad loc.*); comp. also vol. II, p. 114. On the phylacteries (טוטפן=), comp. Megillah 16a, which contains also the haggadic interpretation of Esther 3.16 found in Targum *ad loc.* Another interpretation of this verse occurs in Haserot 35 and 31, whence in Aggadat Esther 71.

¹⁹⁰ Megillah 16b. On the Jews as masters of the other nations, comp. 2 Targum Esther 10.1.

¹⁹¹ Tehillim 22, 194. Comp. vol. IV, p. 379, and 2 Targum Esther (end). Those among the Gentiles who became converted and were circumcized (this is how Septuagint and Josephus, *Antiqui.*, XI, 6.13, render מתיהדים, Esther 8.17; in Judeo-German *jüdischen* means "circumcise") were not considered as perfect Jews, because their motive for circumcision was not above suspicion; Yebamot 24b. The Amalekites were not admitted at all as proselytes, but were killed; comp. note 188 and vol III, p. 62.

¹⁹² 2 Targum 8.13. The dependence of this edict in favor of the Jews upon the "decree of Artaxerxes concerning the Jews" in the Additions to Esther (Addition E) cannot be doubted, though the divergence between the two edicts is very great. In accordance with Septuagint מהנדריא of Targum is to be emended to מקדוניא. The introductory sentences of the edict in Targum are copied from the "Letter of Artaxerxes" (Addition B), commanding the annihilation of the Jews. There is no trace in rabbinic literature of the last Addition in Septua-

gint, the Interpretation of the Dream of Mordecai.   On the dream in rabbinic sources, see vol. IV, p. 420 and note 132 pertaining thereto.

¹⁹³ Megillah 71a (this passage contains also the controversy whether the book of Esther "defiles the hands", that is, whether it is considered canonical); Makkot 23b; Yerushalmi Berakot 9, 14c; Megillah 1, 70d; Tan. B. I, 217; Tan. Wa-Yehi 8; Tehillim 57; 296; Ruth R. 2, 4; Shitah Hadashah (beginning); Aggadat Esther 77–78.   The last-named source (76) has the following statement: The Megillah (book of Esther) was composed in Shushan, and was forwarded (by Mordecai and Esther) to the Holy Land, that it should be copied into the Assyrian script. The Talmud is given as source for this statement, but neither the printed texts nor the MSS. of the Talmud, with the exeption of one late MS. (comp. Price, Yemenite MS. of Megillah), contain this statement. On the regulations concerning the writing of the Megillah, see Megillah 16b, which reads: The scroll of Esther must be written in lines as though it were the Torah (Pentateuch) itself.   For an explanation of this talmudic passage, see *Sha'are Teshubah*, No. 204, and Meiri *ad loc.* That the name of God is not found in the book of Esther (yet it is hinted at; comp. notes 140, 161, 171) is due to the fact that God did not care to testify to the mixed marriage between Ahasuerus and Esther (comp. Malachi 2.13, and vol. I, p. 69).   The only other book of the Bible which does not contain the name of God (though it is hinted at; comp. note 2 on vol. IV, p. 125) is Song of Songs. This book is devoted to the description of the beauty of man and woman; yet it is not beauty, but the propagation of the human race which is the ideal of marriage. See Hasidim 183, and comp. note 3 of the editor.

¹⁹⁴ Yerushalmi Megillah 1, 70d, which reads: In the time to come all the other parts of the Hagiographa, nay, even the prophetical books, will lose their value, and only the Pentateuch and the book of Esther will retain their worth; Aggadat Esther 81; Lekah 9.28 and 31 (refers it to the time of the Messiah); Mishle 9, 61.   In the last source a view is quoted to the effect that of all the festivals only Purim and the Day of Atonement will be celebrated in the time to come.   Comp. Al Kabez, 208b–209b and vol. VI, p. 58, end.   Esther risked her life for her people, and as her reward a book of the Bible bears her name, and Scripture speaks of Israel as the people of Esther; ShR. 30.3; Makiri, Prov. end.   The source of the latter is a version of Midrash Mishle different from ours, see MHG. I, 339 and Aggadat Esther 23.

LIST OF ABBREVIATIONS OF TITLES OF BOOKS

Abkat Rokel אבקת רוכל...רבי מכיר, Warsaw 1876, quoted by book and chapter.

Abudrahim אבודרהם, Warsaw 1877, quoted by section and page.

Aggadat Bereshit אגדת בראשית, ed. Buber, Cracow 1902, quoted by chapter and page.

Aggadat 'Olam Katan אגדת עולם קטן, ed. Jellinek, Bet ha-Midrasch, V, 57–59.

Aggadat Shir אגדת שיר השירים, ed. Schechter, Cambridge, 1896.

Aggadat Tefillat Shemoneh 'Esreh אגדת תפלת שמונה עשרה, ed. Jellinek, Bet Ha-Midrasch, V, 53–56.

Aggadta de Shimon Kefa אגדתא דשמעון כיפא, ed. Jellinek in Bet Ha-Midrasch V, 60–62.

Aguddat Aggadot אגדת אגדות...חיים מאיר....הורוויץ, Frankfort o. M., 1881.

Al-Barceloni פירוש ספר יצירה להרב...ברצלוני, ed. Halberstam, Berlin 1885.

'Aliyyot Eliyyahu עליות אליהו תולדות...אליהו גאון וחסיד מוילנא...מאת...יהושע העשיל, Stettin, 1861.

Alkabez. See Menot ha-Levi.

Aphraates. The Homilies of Aphraates ed. by Wright, London 1869.

Alphabet of R. Akiba 1 and 2 מדרש אלפא ביתא דרבי עקיבא, ed. Jellinek, Bet ha-Midrasch III, 12–64.

Alphabet of Ben Sira 1 and 2 אלפא ביתא דבן סירא ראשונה ושניה, ed. Steinschneider, Berlin 1858.

Alphabetot אלפא ביתות מדרש, ed. Wertheimer, מדרש אותיות דרבי עקיבא השלם 81–121, Jerusalem 1914.

ARN 1 and 2. מסכת אבות דרבי נתן בשתי נוסחאות, ed. Schechter, Vienna 1887, quoted by chapter and page.

Artapanus περὶ 'Ιουδαίων in Eusebius, Praep. Evang.

'Asarah Haruge Malkut מעשה עשרה הרוגי מלכות, ed. Jellinek, Bet ha-Midrasch VI, 19–35.

'Aseret ha-Dibrot מדרש עשרת הדברות, ed. Jellinek, Bet ha-Midrasch I, 62–90 (quoted by page) and in חבור מעשיות מהמדרשות והאגדות, Venice, 1605, quoted by Commandment.

'Aseret Melakim מדרש עשרת מלכים, ed. Horowitz, Bibliotheca Haggadica I, 38–55, Frankfort o. M. 1881.

R. Asher. Glosses on the Pentateuch by R. Asher b. Jechiel; comp. Hadar.

Astruc. R. Solomon Astruc מדרשי התורה, ed. Eppenstein, Berlin 1889.

ATAO. A. Jeremias, Das alte Testament im Lichte des alten Orients, Leipsic 1907.

Ayyumah Ka-Nidgalot אימה כנדגלות by R. Isaac Onkeneira, Berlin 1701.

Baer, Siddur סדר עבודת ישראל, Roedelheim 1868.

R. Bahya. Commentary on the Pentateuch by R. Bahya b. Asher, Warsaw 1853, quoted by chapter and verse.

BaR מדרש במדבר רבה, ed. Wilna 1887, quoted by chapter and paragraph.

Baraita di-Ma'aseh Bereshit, ed. Chones in Buber, יריעות שלמה 47–50, Warsaw 1896.

Baraita di Mazzalot ברייתא דמזלות, ed. Wertheimer, אוצר מדרשים כתבי יד I, 1–28, Jerusalem, 1913.

Baraita di-Shemuel ברייתא דשמואל הקטן, ed. Frankfort o. M. 1863.

Barceloni; See Al-Barceloni.

Baruch, Greek. The Greek Apocalypse of Baruch, ed. James, Texts and Studies vol. V, Cambridge, 1897.

3 Baruch. See Baruch, Greek.

Batte Midrashot בתי מדרשות Vols. I–IV ed. Wertheimer, Jerusalem 1893–1897.

483

List of Abbreviations

Ben ha-Melek בן המלך והנזיר, ed. Mantua 1557, quoted by chapter.

Benjamin R., Itinerary of ר׳ ספר מסעות בנימין, ed.Grünhut and Adler, Jerusalem (Frankfort o. M.) 1904.

Benjamin R. of Tudela. See Benjamin R. Itinerary of.

Bertinoro. Glosses on the Pentateuch in בעלי התוספות על חמשה חומשי תורה Warsaw 1876.

BHM Vols. I–VI: בית המדרש, ed. Jellinek, Leipsic 1853–1877, quoted by volume and page.

BR בראשית רבה מדרש, ed. Wilna 1887, quoted by chapter and paragraph. Comp. also Theodor.

Caro, Isaac תולדות יצחק, Constantinople 1518, quoted by chapter and verse.

Codex Naz. Codex Nazareus, ed. Norberg, Copenhagen s. a.

Da'at ספר דעת זקנים והוא חבור כולל על התורה הראשון מרבותינו בעלי התוספות.. והשני ספר מנחת יהודה מרבינו יהודה בר אליעזר, Leghorn 1783.

Dhamari. See Manzur.

Debir דביר מאסף עתי לחכמת ישראל, Berlin 1923.

Demetrius περὶ τῶν ἐν τῇ Ἰουδαίᾳ βασιλέων in Eusebius, Praep. Evang.

Derek Erez Z. דרך ארץ זוטא, ed. Tawrogi, Königsberg 1885.

Dibre ha-Yamim or Hayyamim דברי הימים של משה רבינו ע״ה, ed. Jellinek, Bet ha-Midrasch. II, 1–11.

DR דברים רבה מדרש, ed. Wilna 1887, quoted by chapter and paragraph.

DZ לקוטים ממדרש אלה הדברים [זוטא], ed. Buber, Vienna 1885.

Ekah מדרש איכה רבה, ed. Buber, Wilna 1899, quoted by chapter and page, or ed. Wilna 1887, quoted by chapter and verse.

Eldad אלדד הדני, ed. Epstein, Presburg 1891.

Eleh Ezkerah מדרש אלה אזכרה, ed. Jellinek, Leipsic 1853.

'Emek ha-Melek עמק המלך by R. Naphtali b. Elchanan, Amsterdam 1648.

Emunot we-Deot ספר האמונות והדעות חברו...רבינו סעדיה, Cracow 1880.

2 Enoch. The Book of the Secrets of Enoch translated from the Slavonic by W. R. Morfill and edited ...by R. H. Charles, Oxford 1896.

Enoch Hebrew; See Sefer Hanok.

Ephraem. Ephraemi Syri Opera Omnia ed. P. Benedictus and Assemanus, Rome 1737–1743.

ER and EZ סדר אליהו רבה וסדר אליהו זוטא, ed. Friedmann, Vienna 1900, quoted by chapter (old numbering) and page.

'Eser Galuyyot מדרש עשר גליות, ed. Grünhut in Likkutim III, 2–22.

Eshkol אשכל הכפר להרב רבנו יהודה הדסי Goslow 1836, quoted by No., folio and column.

Eshkol ספר האשכול יסדו רבנו אברהם ב״ר יצחק, ed. Auerbach, Halberstadt 1867–1869, quoted by volume and page.

ha-Eshkol האשכול מאסף ספרותי ומדעי, ed. Fuchs and Günzig, Cracow 1898–1909.

Eupolemus περὶ τῶν ἐν τῇ Ἰουδαίᾳ βασιλέων, in Eusebius, Praep. Evang

Eusebius, Praeparatio Evangelica, ed Gifford, Oxford 1903.

EZ. See ER.

Ezekiel, the tragedian. Ἐξαγωγή in Eusebius, Praep. Evang.

4 Ezra, Liber Esdrae Quartus, ed. G. H. Box, Ezra Apocalypse, London 1912.

Gadol u-Gedolah מדרש גדול וגדולה, ed. Jellinek, Bet ha-Midrasch III, 121–130.

Gedulat Mosheh גדולת משה, ed. Amsterdam 1754.

Geonica. Geonica by Louis Ginzberg, I and II, New York 1909.

Ginzberg, Compte Rendu. Compte Rendu des Mélanges Israël Lewy, Paris 1914 = Rev. d. Etud. Juiv. LXVI, 297-315 and LXVII, 133-151.

List of Abbreviations

Ginzberg, Haggada bei den Kirchenv. Die Haggada bei den Kirchenvätern, Amsterdam 1899. Haggada bei den Kirchenvätern II. Die Haggada bei den Kirchenvätern und in der apocryphischen Litteratur, Berlin 1900.
Gorion ספרי דאגדתא in מדרש אבא גוריון, ed. Buber, Wilna 1886.
Güdemann, Religionsgeschichte. Religionsgeschichtliche Studien, Leipsic 1876.

ספר הדר זקנים...תורתן של ראשונים Hadar רבותינו בעלי התוספות זלה"ה על התורה...דבר חדש...הוא הרא"ש, Leghorn 1840.
Hadassi. See Eshkol (1).
Haggadat Teman. The Haggadah according to the Rite of Yemen . . . by William H. Greenburg, London 1896.
Haggoren or ha-Goren. הגרן...נערך vols. I–IX, ע"י שמואל אבא הורודצקי Berditschew-Berlin 1899–1922.
Hallel מדרש הלל הנקרא ספר המעשים, ed. Jellinek, Bet ha-Midrasch V, 87–110.
Haserot מדרש חסרות ויתרות, ed. Wertheimer, Jerusalem 1900.
Hashkem מדרש השכם in Grünhut ספר הלקוטים I, 2–20; comp. Likkutim.
Hasidim ספר חסידים, ed. Wistinetzki, Berlin 1891.
Hazofeh הצופה מארץ הגר vols. I–IV, V, VII הצופה לחכמת ישראל, ed. Blau, Budapest 1911-1923.
Hekalot or 1 Hekalot היכלות רבתי in Jellinek, Bet ha-Midrasch III, 83–108.
3 Hekalot פרק מפרקי היכלות in Jellinek, Bet ha-Midrasch III, 161–163.
5 Hekalot or Hekalot V מסכת היכלות in Jellinek, Bet ha-Midrasch II. 40–47.
6 Hekalot or Hekalot VI ספר היכלות ונקרא גם כן ספר חנוך in Jellinek, Bet ha-Midrasch V, 170–190.
Hemdat ha-Hemdah לקוטים מס' חמדת החמדה, ed. Wertheimer, גנזי ירושלים III, 13b-15a, Jerusalem, 1902.
Hemdah Genuzah ספר חמדה גנוזה והוא תשובות הגאונים, Jerusalem 1863.
Hesed Le-Abraham. Azulai, חסד לאברהם, ed. Lemberg 1860.

Hibbur ha-Ma'asiyyot; See 'Aseret ha-Dibrot.
Hibbur Yafeh. See Rabbenu Nissim.
Hippolytus, Philosophumena, ed. Migne P. Gr. 16.3.
Ps.-Hippolytus. Sermo in Sancta Theophania, Migne Pat. Gr. 10.
ha-Hoker החוקר מכתב עתי מקדש לחכמת ישראל, ed. Fuchs, Cracow 1891–94.
Huppat Eliyyahu חופת אליהו, ed. Horowitz כבוד חופה 45–56, Frankfort o. M. 1888.

Imre No'am ספר אמרי נועם והוא חדושים על התורה Cremona 1560.
Irenaeus. Adversus Haereses, ed. Migne, P. Gr. 7.
R. Isaac ha-Kohen ספר איוב עם פירוש שחבר יצחק כהן, Constantinople 1545.

Jerome. Hieronymi Quaestiones Hebraicae in libro Geneseos e. recog. P. de Lagarde, Leipsic 1868.
Ps. Jerome. Quaestiones hebraicae in II Regum et in II Paralip., in Migne, Patrologia Lat. 23. 1329–1402.
Joel, Chronography. Chronographia, ed. Bekker, Bonn 1837.
Joel, Blicke. Blicke in die Religionsgeschichte . . . I–II, Breslau and Leipsic 1880–1883.
JQR. NS. The Jewish Quarterly Review, New Series, ed. Adler and Schechter, Philadelphia, 1910 seq.
Jub. The Book of Jubilees by Charles, London 1902.
Judah b. Barzilai. See Al-Barceloni.

Kad ha-Kemah כד הקמח, ed. Breit, Lemberg 1880–1892.
Kaftor wa-Ferah. Estori Parhi, כפתור ופרח, ed. Luncz, Jerusalem 1897–1898.
Kaftor wa-Ferah. כפתור ופרח...יעקב ב'ר יצחק לוצאטו, Basel 1581.
Kallah מסכת כלה והברייתא, ed. Coronel, Vienna 1869, also reprinted in Talmud ed. Romm, Wilna 1895.
Kaneh or Kanah ספר הקנה והוא ספר הפליאה, ed. Koretz 1784.

485

List of Abbreviations

KAT. E. Schrader, Die Keilinschriften und d. alte Testament; third edition by Winkler and Zimmern, Berlin 1902–1903.

Kebod Huppah; See Huppat Eliyyahu,

Kebuzzat Maamarim קבוצת מאמרים מאת אברהם גייגר...על ידי שמואל פאזזאנסקי, Warsaw, 1910. with notes by Louis Ginzberg).

Kelale ha-Talmud כללי התלמוד. A. Marx: לר׳ בצלאל אשכנזי in Hoffmann-Festschrift 179–218.

Keli-Yakar. Solomon Ephraim b. Aaron, כלי יקר, Lublin 1602 and frequently reprinted.

Ketoret ha-Sammim קטרת הסמים...על תרגום יונתן וירושלמי, Amsterdam 1671.

Kimha Dabishuna חלק ראשון וחלק שני מהמחזור כפי מנהג ק״ק רומא עם פירוש קמחא דאבישונא Bologna s. a. (1546).

Kinyan-Torah קנין תורה. The so called sixth chapter of Abot found in most editions of this Treatise.

Kisse we-Ipodromin. כסא ואיפודרומין של שלמה המלך, ed. Jellinek in Bet ha-Midrasch V, 34–39.

Koheleth קהלת רבה מדרש, ed.Wilna 1887, quoted by chapter and verse.

Koheleth Z. מדרש קהלת זוטא, ed. Buber, מדרש זוטא 83–130, Berlin 1894.

Konen מדרש כונן, ed. Jellinek, Bet ha-Midrasch II, 23–29.

Lekah מדרש לקח טוב המכונה פסיקתא Gen. and Exod. ed. Buber, Wilna 1880, Lev. Num. and Deut. ed. Padua, Wilna 1884, quoted by chapter and verse or Book and page.

Leket Midrashim ספר לקט מדרשים, ed. Wertheimer, Jerusalem 1904.

Likkute ha-Pardes לקוטי הפרדס, Venice 1519.

לקוטי ש״ס להארי ז״ל. The edition used is that of Leghorn 1785.

Likkutim I–VI ספר הלקוטים,ed. Grünhut, Jerusalem 1898–1902.

Maamar 'Aseret Melakim מאמר עשרת מלכים,ed. Horowitz, אנדת אנדות 54–55, Berlin, 1881.

Ma'areket מערכת האלהות, Mantua 1558.

Ma'aseh Abraham, ed. Horowitz מעשה אברהם אגדת in אברהם אגדות 43–46, Berlin, 1881.

2 Ma'aseh Abraham מעשה אברהם, ed. Jellinek, Bet ha-Midrasch II, 118–119.

3 Ma'aseh Abraham מעשה אברהם אבינו ע״ה ממה שאירע לו עם נמרוד, ed.Jellinek Bet ha-Midrasch I, 25–34.

Ma'aseh Daniel. מעשה דניאל ע״ה, ed. Jellinek in Bet ha-Midrasch V, 117–130.

Ma'aseh R. Joshua b. Levi. מעשה דר׳ יהושע בן לוי, ed. Jellinek, Bet ha-Midrasch II, 48–51.

Ma'aseh ha-Nemalah. מעשה הנמלה, ed. Jellinek, Bet ha-Midrasch V, 22–26.

Ma'aseh Nissim. מעשה ה׳ ומעשי נסים Amsterdam 1723.

Ma'aseh Rokeah ספר מעשה רוקח..חברו.. אליעזר..בן...יהודה קלונימוס ממגציא Sanok 1912.

Ma'aseh Torah מדרש מעשה תורה, ed. Jellinek, Bet ha-Midrasch II, 92–109.

Maasehbuch מעשה בוך, Amsterdam 1723, quoted by No. and page.

Ma'asiyyot or Ma'as. ed. G. Gaster, The Sefer ha-Ma'asiyoth, in "Judith Montefiore" College, Report for the year 1894–1895, Cambridge, 1896.

Ma'ayan Hokmah מעין חכמה, ed. Jellinek, Bet ha-Midrasch I, 58–61.

Magen-Abot. Duran, מגן אבות, Leghorn 1762.

Maggid. R. Joseph Caro, מגיד משרים,Amsterdam 1708.

Malala. John. Chronographia, ed. Dindorf, Bonn 1831.

Manzur. Notes on...commentary... by Aboo Manzur al-Dhamari....by A. Kohut, New York s. a. (1894).

Masnut; See Ma'ayan Gannim.

Masseket Gan 'Eden מסכת גן עדן in ברייתא דשמואל הקטן, ed. Frankfort o. M. 1863. Comp. also Seder Gan Eden.

Masseket Kelim מסכת כלים, ed. Jellinek, Bet ha-Midrasch II, 88–91.

Mattenot Kehunah. R. Issachar Baer b. Naphtali מתנות כהונה on Midrash Rabbah in ed. Wilna, 1887.

List of Abbreviations

Ma'ayan Gannim. Masnut, ...מעין גנים.
עַל סֵפֶר אִיוב, ed. Buber, Berlin 1889.
Mekilta ספר מכילתא דרבי ישמעאל, ed.
Friedmann, Vienna 1870, quoted by
massekta and folio.
Mekilta D. מכלתא לדברים...מאת ש' ז'
שעכטער, reprinted from Lewy-Fest-
schrift, Breslau 1911.
Mekilta RS מכילתא דרבי שמעון בן יוחאי,
ed. Hoffmann, Frankfort o. M. 1905,
quoted by page.
Meleket ha-Mishkan. ברייתא דמלאכת
המשכן...מאיר איש שלום, Vienna 1908.
Melchizedek Fragment in Charles, 2
Enoch 85–93.
Menot ha-Levi ספר מנות הלוי...שחבר...
שלמה הלוי בן אלקבץ, Venice 1585.
Meshalim Shel Shelomoh. משלים של
שלמה המלך, ed. Jellinek, Bet ha-
Midrasch IV, 145; 152.
MHG I and II מדרש הגדול...ספר בראשית
ed. Schechter, Cambridge 1902; מדרש
הגדול...ספר שמות, ed. Hoffmann,
Berlin 1913–1921.
Midrash Abraham מדרש דאברהם אבינו,
ed. Jellinek, Bet ha-Midrasch V, 40-41.
Midrash R. Akiba מדרש ר' עקיבא בן יוסף,
ed. Jellinek, Bet ha-Midrasch V, 31-33;
ed. Wertheimer, Leket Midrashim 18a-
23b.
Midrash Esther. מדרש מגלת אסתר, ed.
Horowitz in Aguddat Aggadot 56–75.
Midrash le-Hanukkah מדרש לחנוכה, ed.
Jellinek, Bet ha-Midrasch I, 132–136.
Midrash Jonah מדרש יונה, ed. Jellinek,
Bet ha-Midrasch I, 96–105.
Midrash ha-Ne'elam; See Zohar Hadash.
Midrash Shir מדרש שיר השירים, ed. Grün-
hut, Jerusalem 1897.
Midrash Temurah מדרש תמורה, ed. Jel-
linek, Bet ha-Midrasch I, 106–114.
Milhamot Melek ha-Mashiah, ed. Jellinek
in מלחמות מלך המשיח Bet ha-Midrasch
VI, 117–120.
Minhat Yehudah, see Da'at.
Mishle מדרש משלי, ed. Buber, Wilna 1893,
quoted by chapter and page.
Monatsschrift. Monatsschrift für Ge-
schichte und Wissenschaft des Juden-

thums, Dresden (later Breslau) 1852
seq.
Moses bar Cepha. De Paradiso, ed. And.
Masius, Antwerp 1569.
Mota Muse. Faitlovitch, Mota Muse,
Paris 1906.

Nahmanides, Derasha תורת ה' תמימה
דרשה שדרש הרמב"ן, ed. Jellinek, Leipsic 1853.
Neweh Shalom. Taussig, נוה שלום, Munich 1872.
Nispahim, Friedmann, נספחים לסדר
אליהו זוטא, Vienna 1904.
Nur al-Zulm, Light of Shade and Lamp
of Wisdom, by Nathanel Ibn Yeshaya,
ed. Kohut, New York 1894.
Nistarot R. Simon; See Pirke Mashiah.

Or ha-Hayyim אור החיים...ר' חיים בר'
בצלאל, Mezirow 1801.
Or Zaru'a אור זרוע חברו...רבינו יצחק ב"ר
משה Vols. I–II, Zhitomir 1862; vol. III–
IV, Jerusalem 1887–1890, quoted by
folio and No.
Ha-Orah ספר האורה...לרבינו שלמה בר'
יצחק, ed. Buber, Lemberg 1905.
Orehot Hayyim ספר ארחות חיים אשר
חבר...אהרן הכהן מלוניל, Florence 1750.
Orient. Ltz. Orientalistische Literatur-
Zeitung, ed. Peiser, Königsberg 1898
seq.
Otot ha-Mashiah אותות המשיח, ed. Jel-
linek, Bet ha-Midrasch II, 58–63.
Ozar Midrashim אוצר מדרשים כתבי יד
I–II, ed. Wertheimer, Jerusalem 1913–
1914.

Pa'aneah Raza פענח רזא והוא פירוש יפה על
חמשה חומשי תורה...היברו...רבינו יצחק
ב"ר יהודה, Prague 1607.
Panim Aherim מדרש פנים אחרים, ed.
Buber דאנדתא ספרי 45–82, Wilna 1886.
Pardes ספר הפרדס...להגאון רש"י זלה"ה
Constantinople 1802.
Perek Gan 'Eden; Comp. Note 90 on
vol. I, p. 31.
Pesikta Hadta פסיקתא חדתא, ed. Jellinek,
Bet ha-Midrasch VI, 36–70.

487

List of Abbreviations

Petahiah R., Itinerary of. See Pethahiah, R. of Ratisbon.

Pethahiah, R. of Ratisbon. סבוב...פתחיה מרעננשפורג, ed. Grünhut, Jerusalem (Frankfort o. M.) 1905.

Petirat Aharon. מדרש פטירת אהרן, ed. Jellinek in Bet ha-Midrasch I, 91–95.

Petirat Mosheh or 1 Petirat Mosheh. מדרש פטירת משה רבינו ע'ה, ed. Jellinek in Bet ha-Midrasch I, 115–129.

2 Petirat Mosheh. מדרש פטירת משה רבינו ע'ה, ed. Jellinek in Bet ha-Midrasch VI, 74–78.

3 Petirat Mosheh דרש לפטירת משה רבינו, ed. Gaulmyn in דברי הימים של משה, ed. Paris 1629, f. 34–59.

Ps.-Philo. Philonis Judaei Alexandrini Libri Antiquitatum, Basel 1527; sometimes the reference is added to James, the Biblical Antiquities of Philo, London and New York 1917.

Philosophumena; see Hippolytus.

Pirke Mashiah ספר אליהו ופרקי משיח ונסתרות ר' שמעון בן יוחאי, ed. Jellinek Bet ha-Midrasch III, 65–82.

Pirke R. Yoshiyyahu. פרקי ר' יאשיהו, ed. Jellinek in Bet ha-Midrasch VI,112–116.

PK פסיקתא...מיוחסת לרב כהנא, ed. Buber, Lyck 1860, quoted by Piska and folio.

Poznanski, Einleitung or Mebo פירוש על יחזקאל ותרי עשר לרבי אליעזר מבלגנצי...וסתפח לו מבוא על חכמי צרפת מפרשי המקרא Warsaw 1913–1914.

PR מדרש פסיקתא רבתי ed. Friedmann, Vienna 1880, quoted by Pesikta and folio.

PRE פרקי רבי אליעזר, Amsterdan 1709 or Warsaw 1852.

PRK פרקי רבינו הקדוש, ed. Grünhut, Likkutim III,or פרקא דרבינו הקדוש, ed. Schönblum שלשה ספרים נפתחים, Lemberg 1877.

Pugio Fidei. Pugio Fidei Raymundi Martini . . . . . Adversus Mauros et Judaeos, Leipsic 1667.

Rabbinovicz; See Variae Lectiones.

ספר ראבי"ה...חברו רבינו אליעזר ברבי ראבי"ה יואל, ed. Aptowitzer, Berlin 1913.

Rabbenu Nissim. ספר מעשיות והוא חבור יפה מהישועה להחכם רבינו נסים ב"ר יעקב, Warsaw 1881.

RAsh: See R. Asher.

Raziel ספר רזיאל המלאך, ed. Wilna 1881, quoted by caption and page.

REBN ראה זה ספר...הנקרא אב"ן העזר שחיבר...אליעזר בר נתן הנקרא ראב"ן Prague 1610, quoted by folio and No.; ed. Raschkes, Jerusalem 1913 (Vol. כ) and 1915 (vol. II).

REJ. Revue des Etudes Juives, Paris 1880 seq.

Reshit Hokmah. ראשית חכמה אשר חבר...אליהו...די וידאש Josefow 1868, quoted by chapter and folio.

Responsen der Geonim ברון לראשונים: עם לאחרונים...מחברת רביעית... מאת אברהם אליהו הרכבי, Berlin 1887,

RITBA ספר חדושי הריטב"א, Amsterdam 1729.

RSBM. פירוש התורה אשר כתב רשב"ם, ed. Rosin, Breslau 1881.

Ruth R. מדרש רות רבה, ed. Wilna 1887, quoted by chapter and verse.

Ibn Sabba' פירוש על התורה שחיבר...רבי אברהם סב"ע ז'ל וקרא שמו צרור המור, Venice 1523, quoted by Parasha ant. folio.

Ps. Sa'adya. פירוש על דברי הימים, ed R. Kirchheim, Frankfort o. M. 1874

Sa'arat Eliyyahu. ...על מות...סערת אליהו אליהו זצוק'ל מווילנא...כתובים ע'י בנו...אברהם, Wilna 1894.

Seder R. Amram. סדור תפלה כמנהג אשכנז...עם סדר רב עמרם השלם, ed. Frumkin Jerusalem 1912.

Seder Gan 'Eden עדן גן סדר, ed. Jellinek Bet ha-Midrasch II, 52–53.

Seder Rabba di Bereshit סדר רבה דבראשית דמרכבה דר' ישמעאל כהן גדול, ed. Wertheimer, Batte Midrasho I, 1–31.

Seder Ruhot סדר רוחות, ed. Jellinek, Be ha-Midrasch V, 176–180.

Sefer Eliyyahu. See Pirke Mashiah.

Sefer ha-Hayyim ספר החיים...ר' חיים בר' בצלאל, Cracow 1593.

List of Abbreviations

Sefer Hanok ספר חנוך, ed. Jellinek, Bet ha-Midrasch II, 114–117.

Sefer Noah ספר נח, ed. Jellinek, Bet ha-Midrasch III, 155–160.

Sefer ha-Yashar ספר הישר לרבנו תם, ed. Rosenthal, Berlin 1898.

Sekel or Sekel Tob מדרש שכל טוב על ספר בראשית ושמות חברו רבינו מנחם ב"ר שלמה, ed. Buber, Berlin 1900–1901.

Sha'are Gan 'Eden גן עדן וניהנם, ed. Jellinek, Bet ha-Midrasch V, 42–51.

Sha'are Simhah. R. Isaac b. Judah ibn Gayyat, שערי שמחה, Fürth 1862.

Sha'are Yerushalaim שערי ירושלים...לר' משה ב"ר מנחם מענדיל רישר, Warsaw 1865.

Sha'are Zedek ספר שערי צדק...תשובות הגאונים, Saloniki 1792.

Shalshelet ספר שלשלת הקבלה לחכם... גדליה'ן יחייא, Venice 1587.

Shem Tob b. Shem Tob ...דרשות התורה הר' שם טוב בר' יוסף, Venice 1547.

Shemuel מדרש שמואל, ed. Buber, Lemberg 1893, quoted by chapter and page.

Shibbale ha-Leket. שבלי הלקט...חברו רבינו צדקיה ב"ר אברהם הרופא, ed. Buber, Wilna 1886, quoted by paragraph and page.

Shir מדרש שיר השירים רבה, ed. Wilna 1887, quoted by chapter and verse.

Shitah. See Shitah Hadashah.

Shitah Hadashah שיטה חדשה לברכת יעקב in מדרש בראשית רבה, Wilna 1887 pp. 376–377.

ShR מדרש שמות רבה, ed. Wilna 1887, quoted by chapter and paragraph.

Shu'aib. Joshua ibn Shu'aib על דרשות התורה, Constantinople 1523, quoted by Parasha and folio.

Sibyll. The Sibylline Oracles, ed. Geffken, Leipsic 1902.

Sifra ספרא דבי רב הוא ספר תורת כהנים, ed. Weiss, Vienna 1862, quoted by chapter and verse.

Sifre D. and N. ספרי דבי רב, ed. Friedmann Vienna, 1864, quoted by paragraph (D = Deuteronomy, N = Numbers) and sometimes the page is added.

Sifre Z. Der Sifre Sutta ... von Dr. S. Horovitz, Breslau 1910.

Sifte Kohen ספר שפתי כהן...חברו, מרדכי הכהן, Wansbeck 1690.

Sikli, Talmud Torah. Poznanski, על דבר הילקוט תלמוד תורה לר' יעקב בר' חנגאל סקילי (= Hazofeh III, 1–22) and in Festschrift-Maybaum, Leipsic 1915, ראשיתו של הילקוט תלמוד תורה לר' יעקב ב"ר חננאל סקילי.

SMG. ספר מצות גדול...רבינו משה ב"ר יעקב מקוצי, quoted by Commandment.

Solomon ben ha-Yatom. פירוש מסכת משקין לר' שלמה בן היתום...על ידי צבי פרץ חיות, Berlin 1909.

Spicilegium Syriacum. Spicilegium Syriacum, ed. by W. Cureton, London 1855.

Syncellus. Chronographia, ed. Dindorf, Bonn 1829.

Tadshe מדרש תדשא או ברייתא דר' פנחס בן יאיר ed.,Epstein in מקדמוניות היהודים, Vienna 1887 pp. I–XLVI.

Talpiot ספר מדרש תלפיות אשר כננו מעשי ידי...אליהו הכהן, Lemberg 1870.

Tan. מדרש תנחומא עם פירוש ענף יוסף ועץ יוסף...לה"ר חנוך זונדיל ב"ר יוסף, Wilna 1833, quoted by Parasha and paragraph.

Tan. B. מדרש תנחומא הקדום והישן, ed. Buber, Wilna, 1885, quoted by Book and page.

Tan., Introduction. Buber, מבוא גדול המפיץ אור על מדרש תנחומא, Wilna 1885.

Targum Jerushalmi, (1) Pseudo-Jonathan ed. Ginsburger, Berlin 1903.

Targum Yerushalmi (2) Das Fragmententhargum ed. Ginsburger, Berlin 1899.

Tefillat R. Simeon. תפלתר' שמעון בן יוחאי, ed. Jellinek in Bet ha-Midrasch IV, 117–126.

Tehillim מדרש תהלים המכונה שחר טוב, ed. Buber, Wilna 1891, quoted by chapter and page.

Ps.-Tertullian—
1) De Jona et Ninive.
2) Sodoma.
3) Genesis.
5) De Execrandis Gentilium Diis.

6) Adversus Marcionitas or Adv. Marcionem.

7) Libellus Adversus Omnes Haereses.

Testament of Job. Greek text in James, Apocrypha Anecdota, pp. 104–137; English translation by Kohler in Kohut Memorial Volume, pp. 264–338.

Theodor מדרש בראשית רבה...על פי כתבי יד...עם מראה מקומות...ופירוש...מאתי יהודה טהעאדאר, Berlin 1912–1916.

Theodoretus. Quaestiones in Genes., ed. Migne, P. Gr. 80.

Theophilus or Theophil. Theophilus of Antiochia, πρὸς Αυτόλυκον, ed. Otto in Corpus Apol. 8.

Tola'at Ya'akob. Gabbai, תולעת יעקב, ed. Constantinople 1560.

Toledot Yizhak. See Caro.

Tosafot. See Da'at.

Tosefta תוספתא על פי כתבי יד ערפורט וויען, ed. Zuckermandel, Pasewalk 1881.

Tosefta Targum. Additions to the Targum on the Prophets found in ed. Leiria 1494 and in Lagarde, Prophetae Chaldaice, Leipsic, 1872.

TShBZ. ספר תשב"ץ מן רבינו שמשון בר צדוק, Warsaw, 1875.

Variae Lectiones. Rabbinovicz, Variae Lectiones in Mischnam et in Talmud Babylonicum, Munich 1867–1897.

Wa-Yekullu מדרש ויכלו, ed. Grünhut in Likkutim II, 16b—19b.

Wa-Yosha' מדרש ויושע, ed. Jellinek, Bet ha-Midrasch I, 35–57.

Wa-Yissa'u מדרש ויסעו, ed. Jellinek, Bet ha-Midrasch III, 1–5.

WR מדרש ויקרא רבה, ed. Wilna 1887, quoted by chapter and paragraph.

We-Hishir or Wehizhir. ספר והזהיר לסדר שמות...ישראל מאיר פריימאן Leipsic 1873.

Yad Yosef. Joseph b. Hayyim Zarfati יד יוסף דרשות, Venice 1616.

Yalkut David ילקוט דוד...מאת...דוד... פויזנער, Warsaw 1879.

Yalkut Reubeni ספר ילקוט ראובני על התורה, Amsterdam 1700, quoted by chapter and verse, sometimes the folio is also given.

Yashar ספר הישר, Venice 1624, quoted by Parashah and folio.

Yelammedenu קונדריס אחרון ממדרש ילמדנו, ed. Jellinek, Bet ha-Midrasch VI, 79–90, quoted by No.

ZATW. Zeitschrift für die alttestamentliche Wissenschaft, Giessen 1881 seq.

Zawaat Naphtali צוואת נפתלי בן יעקב לבניו, ed. Wertheimer in his edition of פירקי היכלות, Jerusalem 1890.

ZDMG. Zeitschrift der deutschen morgenländischen Gesellschaft. Leipsic, 1847 seq.

Zerubbabel or Zerubabel ספר זרובבל, ed. Jellinek, Bet ha-Midrasch II, 54–57, ed. Wertheimer, Leket Midrashim, 9b-13b.

Zohar Hadash ספר זוהר חדש, Leghorn 1866, quoted by Parashah and caption, sometimes the folio of this edition is added.

Zohar Ruth. See Zohar Hadash.

Vol. 5

GINZBERG, LOUIS

AUTHOR

THE LEGENDS of the

TITLE

JEWS

DATE	ISSUED TO
2/2	Efroncik